THE ROUGH GUIDE TO

Trinidad
and Tobago

There are more than two hundred Rough Guide titles
covering destinations from Alaska to Zimbabwe
and subjects from Personal Computers to Pregnancy & Birth

Forthcoming travel guides include

The Algarve • The Bahamas • Cambodia • Caribbean Islands
Costa Brava • New York Restaurants • Rocky Mountains • Zanzibar

Forthcoming reference guides include

Children's Books • Chronicle: China (pocket history)
Online Travel • Weather

Rough Guides Online

www.roughguides.com

Rough Guide Credits

Text Editor:	Yuki Takagaki
Managing Editor	Andrew Rosenburg
Series Editor:	Mark Ellingham
Production:	Julia Bovis
Typesetting	Link Hall
Cartography:	Maxine Repath

Acknowledgements

The authors would like to thank all those at TIDCO, especially Terrence Rojas, and those at the Tobago House of Assembly, especially Amryl Arthurs, who answered endless queries. Thanks also to those at Rough Guides: Yuki Takagaki for her editing, Julia Bovis and Link Hall for smooth production, Michael Monaghan for proofreading, Mandy Muggridge for mapmaking, Sharon Martins for photo research, Helena Smith and Kate Davis for Basics research and Andrew Rosenberg for overall guidance.

Dominique: Thanks to all those who put me up during my research trip, including the *Kariwak*, *Arnos Vale*, *Cuffie River*, *Blue Haven*, *Blue Waters Inn*, *Blue Mango*, *The Naturalist*, *Mt Pelier Cottage*, *Mt Plaisir*, *McEachnie's* and *Pax Guesthouse*. Thanks to Sherman's Auto Rentals and Kalloo's for allowing me to learn how to drive in T&T. Special thanks to Mark and Zena Puddy for their unbeatable hospitality and useful tips and information, all those at *Blue Mango* for a fabulous Christmas, a big respect to the Castara crew, Woody, Brenton, Brenda & Tony, Rebecca and Colin, plus Simon, Nicholas, Christine and others for enjoyable Christmas company. Thanks to the Natural Mystics crew for a fantastic BBQ and sea cruise, plus unforgettable snorkelling. To all those in Grande Riviere for making my new year so special with waterfall trips, moonlight limes, cook outs and memorable pirogue rides: thanks to Pierro, Tepie, Tutan, Nigel, Carlos and Coconut. Thanks to Ingrid and Eric McEachnie for great hospitality, helpful information and fabulous food. Much gratitude for the kindness and warmth of Gerald and Oda Ramsawak at the *Pax Guesthouse* and the fun times with Lousie, Laura and Louie, the London posse in Scarborough. Big, big love and respect for dearest friends Lisa Kewley, her parents and Gaby Hosein and house mates Renee and Kendra for putting up with me during research madness, as well as Michael Cherie for helping me reclaim my car after it was impounded. Back in the UK, big thanks to all UEA fellow creative writers, Elliot and my family who kept me going through emails and phone calls. And finally, last but certainly not least, thanks to the two that maintained my sanity, Joelle and Jah. Big respect.

Polly: Many, many thanks to everyone who gave their invaluable time and insight, particularly Gunda, Jamal, Tano, Nandi and Naomi Busch-Harewood for dinners, TLC, nights out and advice; to Courtenay Rooks for turtles and appreciating my sarcasm; to Stephen Broadbridge for hugely enthusiastic guiding and for sharing contacts; to Max Baden-Semper for putting up with us; to Lawrence "Snakeman" Pierre for introducing me to the wilder side of life; to Dawn Allum at Convenient and John Greenidge at Singh's for transport; and at TIDCO, to Tony Poyer for positive energy and help beyond the call of duty, and to Dianne Parker for checking out the loose ends. Also big up to those who kept me smiling: Andrea Carrington; Phillip Lee Wah; Nick Dagnino and Adela; Larry Bridglal; Peter and Daphne Henry at Pearl's; Claudia and Nigel; and the Tobago crew: Teatray, Anthony, Chance, Barry, Davy and Michelle. Finally, thanks for the support to Celia and Matt (mum and dad), Imogen and Isabella Spencer; Amanda Rolandini-Jensen; and Sasha and Mary Leslie.

At Rough Guides, I'd like to thank Yuki Takagaki for her patience and suggestions.

This second edition published November 2001 by Rough Guides Ltd, 62–70 Shorts Gardens, London WC2H 9AH.

Distributed by the Penguin Group:
Penguin Books Ltd, 80 The Strand, London WC2R ORL.
Penguin Books USA Inc, 345 Hudson Street, New York 10014, USA.
Penguin Books Australia Ltd, 487 Maroondah Highway, PO Box 257, Ringwood, Victoria 3134, Australia.
Penguin Books Canada Ltd, 10 Alcorn Avenue, Toronto, Ontario, Canada M4V 1E4.
Penguin Books (NZ) Ltd, 182–190 Wairau Road, Auckland 10, New Zealand.

Printed in England by Clays Ltd, St Ives PLC
Typography and original design by Jonathan Dear and The Crowd Roars.
Illustrations throughout by Edward Briant.

© Dominique De-Light and Polly Thomas 2001.

400pp. Includes index.

A catalogue record for this book is available from the British Library.

ISBN 1-85828-747-2

THE ROUGH GUIDE TO

Trinidad
and Tobago

Written and researched by
Dominique De-Light and Polly Thomas

**ROUGH
GUIDES**

THE ROUGH GUIDES

Help us update

We've gone to a lot of trouble to ensure that this second edition of the *Rough Guide to Trinidad and Tobago* is as up-to-date and accurate as possible. However, things inevitably change, and if you feel we've got it wrong or left something out, we'd like to know. All suggestions, comments and corrections are much appreciated, and we'll send a copy of the next edition (or any other *Rough Guide* if you prefer) for the best letters.

Please mark all letters "Rough Guide to Trinidad and Tobago Update" and send to:
Rough Guides, 62–70 Shorts Gardens, London WC2H 9AH or
Rough Guides, 345 Hudson St, 4th floor, New York, NY 10014, USA.

Email should be sent to:
mail@roughguides.co.uk

Online updates about *Rough Guide* titles can be found on our Web site at *www.roughguides.com*

The authors

Dominique De-Light is a freelance writer with work published in *Women Travel: A Rough Guide Special*, *Caribbean Beat* and *Firsthand: An Anthology of New Writing*. She lived in Trinidad for three years working as a carnival artist.

Polly Thomas began her travels in the Caribbean as a teenager; since then, as well as co-producing the *Rough Guide to Jamaica*, she has written numerous articles on the region. She now lives in London, works as a full-time editor and freelance writer, and has dreams about pholourie and sada roti.

Readers' letters

We'd like to thank all the readers who wrote in with comments and updates: Adrian Coulling, John Forster, Vashti Harrinarine, John and Anne Lowan, Harriet and Mike Kendrick, Jonathan Sheridan-Jones, Michael Taylor, Ruediger Wentzell and any who forgot to sign their emails.

Rough Guides

Travel Guides • Phrasebooks • Music and Reference Guides

We set out to do something different when the first Rough Guide was published in 1982. Mark Ellingham, just out of University, was travelling in Greece. He brought along the popular guides of the day, but found they were all lacking in some way. They were either strong on ruins and museums but went on for pages without mentioning a beach or taverna. Or they were so conscious of the need to save money that they lost sight of Greece's cultural and historical significance. Also, none of the books told him anything about Greece's contemporary life – its politics, its culture, its people, and how they lived.

So with no job in prospect, Mark decided to write his own guidebook, one which aimed to provide practical information that was second to none, detailing the best beaches and the hottest clubs and restaurants, while also giving hard-hitting accounts of every sight, both famous and obscure, and providing up-to-the-minute information on contemporary culture. It was a guide that encouraged independent travellers to find the best of Greece, and was a great success, getting shortlisted for the Thomas Cook travel guide award, and encouraging Mark, along with three friends, to expand the series.

The Rough Guide list grew rapidly and the letters flooded in, indicating a much broader readership than had been anticipated, but one which uniformly appreciated the Rough Guides' mix of practical detail and humour, irreverence and enthusiasm. Things haven't changed. The same four friends who began the series are still the caretakers of the Rough Guide mission today: to provide the most reliable, up-to-date and entertaining information to independent-minded travellers of all ages, on all budgets.

We now publish 200 titles and have offices in London and New York. The travel guides are written and researched by a dedicated team of more than 200 authors, based in Britain, Europe, the USA and Australia. We have also created a unique series of phrasebooks to accompany the travel series, along with the acclaimed series of music guides, and a best-selling pocket guide to the Internet and World Wide Web. We also publish comprehensive travel information on our Web site: *www.roughguides.com*

Contents

List of Maps

MAP SYMBOLS

═══ Road	▣ Restaurant/bar	⛳ Golf course
═ ═ ═ 4WD road	⌂ Cave	🐢 Turtle nesting site
···· Priority bus route	⌖ Mountains	🏊 Swimming area
- - - Path	▲ Peak	Ⓑ Beach with facilities
- – - Ferry route	⚲ Viewpoint	Ⓑ Beach without facilities
─── Waterway	⚲ Swamp	🗼 Lighthouse
─·─ Chapter division boundary	🎋 Waterfall	ⓘ Information office
◆ Place of Interest	✈ Airport	☒ Post office
‡ Church	Ⓟ Parking	▰ Building
⛤ Mosque	🅟 Petrol station	⁺⁺⁺ Cemetery
▲ Hindu temple	Ⓢ Bank	Park
⚑ Fortress	⚖ Market	Beach
◉ Accommodation	✚ Hospital	

Introduction

Just off the coast of the South American mainland they were once part of, **Trinidad and Tobago** (usually shortened to T&T) form the southernmost islands of the Lesser Antilles chain and the most influential republic in the Eastern Caribbean. They are the most exciting, underexplored and uncontrived of Caribbean islands, rich in indigenous culture. A cultural pacemaker best known as the home and heart of West Indian **Carnival**, the nation can also boast having the most diverse and absorbing society in the region.

Trinidad and Tobago remain relatively inexpensive, and are well geared to independent travellers without being fully fledged tourist resorts. Natural reserves of gas and oil combined with a strong manufacturing industry have ensured economic independence, and you'll find the islands refreshingly unfettered by the pretensions of the tourist trade. Visitors are not corralled in all-inclusives or holed up on private beaches, and – though you could easily spend two weeks exploring seashores, which range from palm-lined white sand fringed by limpid waters to secluded, wave-whipped outcrops – you'll find there's far more to T&T than sun-tans and snorkelling.

These are among the richest destinations in the Caribbean for **eco-tourism**, combining the characteristic flora and fauna of the region with the wilder aspect of the South American mainland. You'd be hard pressed to come up with anywhere that offers such a variety of habitats in such a compact area (Trinidad covers no more than 4830 square kilometres, Tobago just 300). In **Trinidad**, you can hike through undisturbed tropical **rainforest** where towering canopies of mahogany and teak bedecked with lianas and epiphytic plants shelter red howler monkeys and ocelots. The wetlands and **mangrove swamps** harbour all manner of exotic wildlife, while leatherback turtles lay eggs on remote beaches. Huge blue emperor butterflies flit around the cool waters of innumerable inland rivers and waterfalls, and the **birdwatching** – with more than 430 brilliantly hued species – is among the world's best.

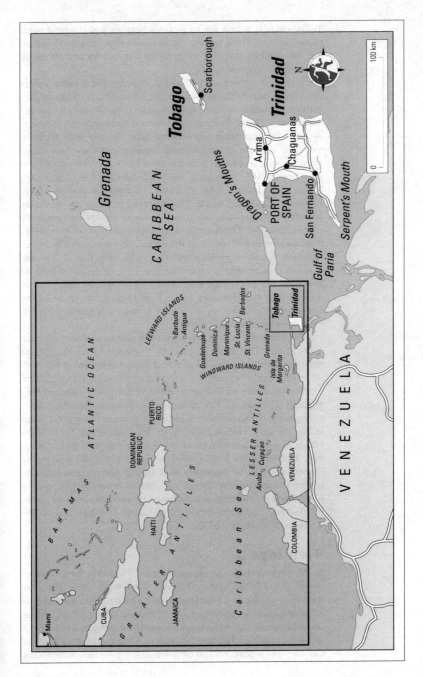

Tobago is best known for its glorious beaches and stunning **coral reefs**, declared third best in the Caribbean by Jacques Cousteau and favoured by graceful seven-metre manta rays and shoals of technicolour tropical fish.

Equally absorbing are T&T's vital, crowded and dynamic **towns and cities**, unique showcases for the architectural, religious and cultural traditions of their cosmopolitan populations. Fretworked townhouses, Georgian-style mansions and barrack-house complexes built for plantation workers sit side by side with temples, mosques, Catholic cathedrals and Anglican churches. The varied ethnic groups brought to labour in the islands after the slaves there were freed in 1834 have given rise to a remarkably varied populace, hailing from India, China, Portugal and Syria as well as Africa, England, France and Spain. Though racial tensions are inevitably present, Trinbagonians (as they're collectively known) generally coexist with good humour, and are proud of the multiculturalism that has so enriched the life of the nation. Nowhere is this more visible than in a lively **music scene** that rivals even that of Jamaica. The steel drum was invented in the Port of Spain suburb of Laventille, while calypso, first developed in African communities, evolved into contemporary soca. That in turn has spawned the Indian-influenced chutney soca and the danceable beats and politically conscious lyrics of rapso.

Trinbagonians have a less harrowing past to contend with than many of their Caribbean neighbours. Neglected by the Spanish for most of their three centuries of rule, Trinidad experienced full-scale slavery for only fifty years, while the Dutch, French and English were too busy fighting over Tobago to dedicate it to the demands of King Sugar. Consequently, the national psyche is characterized by a strong sense of identity and a laid-back enjoyment of the good things in life, the latter best displayed in the local propensity for **liming** – taking time out to meet friends, talk and sink a Carib beer or some rum. Thirteen public holidays and numerous local festivals are mere limbering up for the republic's most famous party, the annual pre-Lenten **Carnival**, where the no-holds-barred debauchery of opening night Jouvert celebrations is followed by two days of pure joy as 5000-strong bands of intricately costumed revellers take to the streets in a celebration of life.

Where to go

As different as chalk and cheese but bound together for the convenience of the British empire, Trinidad and Tobago share little more than their status as a republic. Known chiefly as an island of oil refineries and metropolitan verve, **Trinidad** offers culture, ethnic diversity, music, great food and a wealth of gorgeous beaches. A more conventional holiday destination, **Tobago** boasts archetypal Caribbean beaches thronged by hotels of every budget, watersports, restaurants and a rapidly developing resort ethic. It's impossible to get a full picture of all the republic has to offer without visiting both Trinidad and Tobago, but a regular plane and ferry service make it possible to see the best of both even during a short stay.

A visit to Trinidad will inevitably begin in **Port of Spain**, the brash, bustling capital and centre of Carnival. With its museums, art galleries and restaurants, the best of local music and art, and most of the island's accommodation, this urbane metropolis is a natural base from which to explore the rest of the country. **Chaguaramas** to the west is the capital's playground, a national park with a string of open-air clubs providing lively, sophisticated nightlife. For the ultimate escape, however, it's not far to the rocky, wooded islands of the Bocas.

A sweeping curve of powdery sand and powerful waves, **Maracas Bay** is the first of many lovely beaches along the north coast. Between **Blanchisseuse** and **Matelot** runs a long stretch of completely undeveloped coastline – thirty kilometres of footprint-free sand and total seclusion – while the coastline further east is spectacularly rugged. Dominated by the densely forested peaks of the Northern Range, the northern **interior** offers excellent hiking along hunters' trails, and the birdwatching is superb – even the lazy can see up to forty unusual species in a morning from the verandah of the **Asa Wright Nature Centre**. South of the hills, the traffic-choked Eastern Main Road links the capital with the sizeable town of **Arima** – home to the island's last remaining Caribs – and provides access to swimmable rivers, caves, and the oldest Benedictine monastery in the Caribbean, from which you get an awesome view of the unravelling plains below.

Dominated by flat agricultural plains with a population of primarily Indian descent, **central Trinidad** provides a fascinating contrast to the north. From the ethereal **Waterloo Temple** to the busy market town of **Chaguanas**, Indian culture predominates. Just forty minutes from Port of Spain lies one of the island's richest natural attractions, the mangrove labyrinth of **Caroni Swamp**, home of the striking national bird, the scarlet ibis. On the east coast, the protected wetlands at **Nariva** are the habitat of endangered West Indian manatees and giant anacondas, while four kilometres of fine brown sand lined by groves of coconut palms make **Manzanilla** a favourite spot to recover from the rigours of Carnival.

The burgeoning commercial city of San Fernando is a friendly base from which to explore Trinidad's "deep south", an area largely unvisited by tourists. Modern oil towns such as Fyzabad contrast with the picturesque fishing villages and calm, deserted beaches of Cedros and Erin, and Mayaro Bay on the southeast coast – a stunning, palm-fringed stretch of powdery sand.

Most people travelling to Tobago head for the translucent waters, coral reefs and excellent facilities of the island's low-lying western tip, staying in one of the hundreds of hotels slung along the coastline and playing golf on the island's palm-studded greens. The vibrant capital, Scarborough offers a more genuine picture of local life with its market and historic fort, while the rugged windward or Atlantic coast is best known for the waterfall at Argyll and the island's best scuba diving at Speyside. Heavily visited by day-trippers, the leeward or Caribbean coast is lined by a precipitous snake of tarmac that passes superb beaches at Castara and Englishman's Bay, while Charlotteville in the northwest is the perfect retreat, a picturesque fishing village that tumbles down a hillside to a couple of pretty horseshoe beaches.

When to go

Most people visit T&T between January and March, when Carnival explodes into life, the trees are in bloom and the climate is at its most forgiving: the sun shines, rain is rare and the nights are cool. By May, however, the lack of rain has parched the formerly lush landscape: greens turn to yellow, dust clouds put the views into soft focus and bush fires rage through the hills. The only relief from the aridity takes the form of brief, sudden tropical rainstorms. At the end of May, the rainy season sets in, and the skies open up with dramatic deluges. The rainy season often continues into December, but there's usually a respite from the downpours in September, a period of hot sunshine and blue skies known as the petit carem. It's an excellent time to visit, with flights at low season rates, though you'll find the resorts a little quiet. Officially, the high season (Dec 15–April 15) should mean hiked hotel rates on both islands, but in reality, only Tobago hoteliers bother with two rates, and many smaller hotels charge the same all year round in both islands. Many hotels in and around Port of Spain, however, put up their rates during Carnival week.

	Average daily temperature (°C)		Average daily temperature (°F)		Average monthly rainfall	
	max	min	max	min	mm	in
January	31	21	87	69	69	2.7
February	31	20	88	68	41	1.6
March	32	20	89	68	46	1.8
April	32	21	90	69	53	2.1
May	32	22	90	71	94	3.7
June	32	22	89	71	193	7.6
July	31	22	88	71	218	8.6
August	31	22	88	71	246	9.7
September	32	22	89	71	193	7.6
October	32	22	89	71	170	6.7
November	32	22	89	71	183	7.2
December	31	21	88	69	125	4.9

The Basics

The Basics

Getting there

The price of your plane ticket depends very much on when you go. Tobago's high season is during the summer holidays, at Christmas and at Carnival time. The situation in Trinidad is more complicated, however, as every school holiday and local festival pushes up the price – BWIA has at least six different price categories. Basically it is less expensive to go during the wet season (August to December). It is worth remembering that both Trinidad and Tobago experience an Indian summer known as the "petite careme" in September. This break in the rainy season offers two weeks to a month of hot, dry weather at a time when air fares are usually a steal.

You can often cut costs by going through a **specialist flight agent** – either a consolidator, who buys up blocks of tickets from the airlines and sells them at a discount, or a **discount agent**, who in addition to dealing with discounted flights may also offer special student and youth fares and a range of other travel-related services such as travel insurance, rail passes, car rentals, tours and the like. Some agents specialize in **charter flights**, which may be cheaper than anything available on a scheduled flight, but again departure dates are fixed and withdrawal penalties are high.

If you're planning to spend your whole holiday in Tobago basing yourself in one place, booking a **package holiday** might be your best option. There are legions of specialist companies who can arrange flights, airport transfers and accommodation, often at a significantly lower rate than you'd get independently. You can book all grades of villas and hotels, as well as meal plans, all-inclusive deals (where all meals are included in the room rate) or self-catering apartments. As Trinidad is less geared toward tourists, packages are thin on the ground beyond the birdwatching trips or Carnival packages; Tobago-oriented companies often offer a few days in Trinidad in conjunction with a Tobago trip. Alternatively, the companies listed in this section, as well as Accommodation and Adventures Unlimited, 33 Luis St, Woodbrook, Port of Spain (☎ 628 3731, fax 627 3737, owl@opus.co.tt), can arrange meet-and-greet services, airport transfers, car rental and accommodation booking.

A further possibility is to see if you can arrange a **courier flight**, although you'll need a flexible schedule, and preferably be travelling alone with very little luggage. In return for shepherding a parcel through customs, you can expect to get a deeply discounted ticket. You'll probably also be restricted in the duration of your stay.

If the Caribbean is only one stop on a longer journey, you might want to consider buying a **Round-the-World** (RTW) ticket. Some travel agents can sell you an "off-the-shelf" RTW ticket that will have you touching down in about half a dozen cities; others will have to assemble one for you, which can be tailored to your needs but is apt to be more expensive. RTW tickets that take in **New York** or **Miami** are worth considering, especially if you have the time to make the most of a few stopovers. A sample itinerary might start from either **Melbourne**, **Sydney** or **Brisbane**, continue to Bangkok, then on to Paris, New York, and Los Angeles before returning to the city of origin (from around US$1700).

If you plan to do some **island-hopping** around the Caribbean, BWIA **air passes** can be worthwhile; available for purchase in conjunction with any international carrier, these allow unlimited stopovers within a thirty-day period, and prices start from £281/US$399/A$555/NZ$600. Passes are valid only within the Caribbean region.

Online booking agents and general travel sites

www.etn.nl/discount.htm A hub of consolidator and discount agent web links.

www.princeton.edu/Main/air800.html Has an extensive list of airline toll-free numbers and websites.

www.flyaow.com Online air travel info and reservations site.

www.smilinjack.com/airlines.htm Lists an up-to-date compilation of airline website addresses.

http://travel.yahoo.com Incorporates a lot of Rough Guide material in its coverage of destination countries and cities across the world, with information about places to eat and sleep etc.

www.cheaptickets.com Discount flight specialists.

www.cheapflights.com Flight deals, travel agents, plus links to other travel sites.

www.lastminute.com Offers good last-minute holiday package and flight-only deals.

www.deckchair.com Bob Geldof's online venture, drawing on a wide range of airlines.

www.expedia.com Discount airfares, all-airline search engine and daily deals.

www.travelocity.com Destination guides, web fares and best deals for car hire, accommodation & lodging as well as fares. Provides access to the travel agent system SABRE, the most comprehensive central reservations system in the US.

www.hotwire.com Bookings from the US only. Last-minute savings of up to 40 percent on regular published fares. Travellers must be at least 18 and there are no refunds, transfers or changes allowed. Log-in required.

www.priceline.com Bookings from the US only. Name-your-own-price website that has deals at around 40 percent off standard fares. You cannot specify flight times (although you do specify dates) and the tickets are nonrefundable, nontransferable and nonchangeable.

www.skyauction.com Bookings from the US only. Auctions tickets and travel packages using a "second bid" scheme. The best strategy is to bid the maximum you're willing to pay, since if you win you'll pay just enough to beat the runner-up regardless of your maximum bid.

www.travelshop.com.au Australian website offering discounted flights, packages, insurance and online bookings.

www.uniquetravel.com.au Australian site with a good range of packages and good value flights.

www.gaytravel.com Online travel agent for gay travellers, concentrating mostly on accommodation.

Booking flights online

Many airlines and discount travel websites offer you the opportunity to book your tickets online, cutting out the costs of agents and middlemen. Good deals can often be found through discount or auction sites, as well as through the airlines' own websites.

Flights from the USA and Canada

Cheap flights to Trinidad and Tobago are scarce, although flights from the East Coast are considerably less expensive than from the West Coast. With little competition, the few airlines that service the islands don't have much incentive to offer special youth rates or air passes and the Caribbean doesn't fit neatly into a round-the-world itinerary.

Barring special offers, the cheapest of the airlines' published fares is usually an advance purchase excursion, or **APEX** ticket, although this will carry certain restrictions: you have to book – and pay – at least 21 days before departure, spend at least seven days abroad (maximum stay three months), and you tend to get penalized if you change your schedule.

Round-trip APEX **fares** during low season from New York and Boston start from US$500, US$400 from Miami, US$650 from Chicago and CAN$850 from Toronto. Fares from San Francisco and Los Angeles start from US$760, Vancouver from CAN$1150. **High season** can add $50–$100 to US fares, CAN$100–$200 to Canadian fares. Flights to Crown Point Airport in Tobago cost roughly the same amount, although direct flights are not available; you will most likely have to change planes in San Juan, Barbados or Trinidad.

American Airlines flies most frequently to the islands from North America, with daily flights from

Airlines

Air ALM, US ☎1-800/327-7230, Canada ☎1-800/325-1705, *www.airalm.com*

Air Canada ☎1-888/247-2262, *www.aircanada.ca*

American Airlines ☎1-800/433-7300, *www.aa.com*

BWIA International ☎1-800/538-2942, *www.bwee.com*

Courier flights

Air Courier Association ☎1-800/282-1202, *www.aircourier.org*. Courier flight broker. Membership (1 year $49, 3 years $98) also entitles you to 20-percent discount on travel insurance and name-your-own-price noncourier flights.

Now Voyager ☎212/431-1616, *www.nowvoyagertravel.com*. Courier flight broker and consolidator.

International Association of Air Travel Couriers ☎561/582-8320, *www.courier.org*. Courier flight broker with membership fee of $45 a year.

Discount travel companies

Air Brokers International ☎1-800/883-3273 or 415/397-1383, *www.airbrokers.com*. Consolidator and specialist in RTW and Circle Pacific tickets.

Airhitch ☎1-800/326-2009 or 212/864-2000, *www.airhitch.org*. Standby-seat broker: for a set price, they guarantee to get you on a flight as close to your preferred destination as possible, within a week. Costs are currently $165 (plus taxes and a $29 processing fee) from or to the east coast region of the US; $233 (plus tax & $29 reg. fee) from/to the west coast or (when available) the Pacific northwest; $199 (plus tax & $29 reg. fee) from/to the midwest; and $177 (plus tax & $29 reg. fee) from/to the southeast. (Taxes for all Europe itineraries are $16 eastbound and $46 westbound.)

Airtech ☎212/219-7000, *www.airtech.com*. Standby seat broker; also deals in consolidator fares and courier flights.

Council Travel ☎1-800/226 8624 or 617/528 2091; *www.counciltravel.com*. Nationwide organization that mostly, but by no means exclusively, specializes in student/budget travel.

Educational Travel Center ☎1-800/747-5551 or 608/256 5551, *www.edtrav.com*. Student/youth discount agent.

High Adventure Travel ☎1-800/350-0612 or 415/912-5600, *www.airtreks.com*. Round-the-world and Circle Pacific tickets. The

website features an interactive database that lets you build and price your own RTW itinerary.

Skylink US ☎1-800/AIR-ONLY or 212/573-8980, Canada ☎1-800/SKY-LINK. Consolidator.

STA Travel ☎1-800/777-0112 or 1-800/781-4040, *www.sta-travel.com*. Worldwide specialists in independent travel; also student IDs, travel insurance, car rental, rail passes, etc.

TFI Tours International ☎1-800/745-8000 or 212/736-1140. Consolidator.

Travac ☎1-800/872-8800, *www.thetravelsite.com*. Consolidator and charter broker, with an office in Orlando.

Travelers Advantage Cendant Membership Services, Inc ☎1-877/259-2691, *www.travelersadvantage.com*. Discount travel club; annual membership fee required (currently $1 for 3 months trial).

Travel Avenue ☎1-800/333-3335, *www.travelavenue.com*. Full-service travel agent that offers discounts in the form of rebates.

Travel Cuts in Canada, Canada ☎1-800/667 2887, US ☎416/979 2406. Canadian student-travel organization.

Worldtek Travel ☎1-800/243-1723, *www.worldtek.com*. Discount travel agency for worldwide travel.

Worldwide Discount Travel Club ☎305/534-2642. Discount travel club.

Tour operators

Although phone numbers are given here, you're better off making **tour reservations** through your local travel agent. An agent will make all the phone calls, sort out the snafus and arrange flights, insurance and the like – all at no extra cost to you.

Alken Tours ☎ 1-800/221-6686 or 718/856-7711, *www.alkentours.com*. Tailor-made air and accommodation packages.

American Airlines Vacations ☎ 1-800/321-2121, *www.aavacations.com*. 3-day all-inclusive packages in Tobago starting at $344, plus airfare.

BWIA Vacations ☎ 1-800/780-5501 or 718/520-8100, *www.bwee.com*. Discounted accommodation with airline bookings.

Island Resort Tours ☎ 1-800/251-1755, *www.Islandresorttours.com*. Accommodation bookings and discounted airfares.

Tour Host International ☎ 1-866/729-4678 or 212/953-7910, *www.tourhost.com*. Air, cruise and accommodation services in all price ranges.

TourScan Inc ☎ 1-800/962 2080 or 203/655 8091, *www.tourscan.com*. Tailor-made and all-inclusive packages. 7-nights all-inclusive in Tobago starting at $1469, with airfare from New York included.

Travel Impressions ☎ 1-800/284-0044, *www.travelimpressions.com*. Flights, accommodation bookings and packages in Trinidad and Tobago. 8-nights all-inclusive package in Trinidad starting at $1038.

most US and Canadian cities connecting through Miami and San Juan to Tobago and Trinidad. **Air Canada** flies direct to Trinidad from Toronto three times a week. You can also buy an Air Canada ticket from Toronto to Tobago, but you'll have to switch to LIAT Airlines in Barbados (weekends only).

The Trinidadian airline **BWIA International** offers daily flights at competitive prices from New York and Miami in addition to a 30-day air pass, valid for travel around the Caribbean and available in the US. See p.5 for contact details.

Flights from the UK and Ireland

The vast majority of British and Irish residents visiting Trinidad and Tobago are on some form of package tour which includes a **charter flight** direct to Tobago. This is certainly the simplest way of going about things, and even if you plan to travel independently, a seat on a charter is normally the cheapest way to get there. But charters do have their drawbacks, especially if your plans don't exactly fit into their usual two-week straitjacket.

A Caribbean cruise

The archetypal luxury vacation – a **Caribbean cruise** – is relatively accessible in North America. Prices on a luxury liner can scale the heights of silliness, although if you're willing to bunk in the "lower-class" rooms you can usually cut the price somewhat. Of the scores of shipping companies that peddle all-inclusive cruises, however, only a few include Trinidad and Tobago on their itineraries, and each line routes only a couple of ships per year through Trinidad and Tobago, so be prepared for inflexible travel dates. Another downside of choosing a cruise is that you only get to see the tourist ports, and for just a few hours at that; the ocean liners listed below stop only in Port of Spain.

Cruise operators

The fares quoted are for single person/double occupancy "inside" (no ocean views) cabins, and are exclusive of port charges, which add an extra US$100–150.

Cunard Lines ☎ 1-800/528-6273, *www.cunardline.com*. 7-day luxury cruises leave from Barbados and stop in Charlotteville at highly variable prices, starting around $2500.

Holland America ☎ 1-800/426-0327 or 206/281-3535, *www.hollandamerica.com*. 11-day cruises from Fort Lauderdale, Florida, from $1500.

WindJammer ☎ 1-800/327-2601, *www.windjammer.com*. 13-day cruises leaving from Freeport, Bahamas, for $1375.

Airlines

British Airways ☎ 0845/773 3377, in Republic of Ireland ☎ 0141/2222345, *www.britishairways.com*

BWIA ☎ 020/7745 1100, *www.bwee.com*

Courier flights

Ben's Travel ☎ 020/7462 0022, *www.benstravel.co.uk*
International Association of Air Travel

Couriers ☎ 0800 0746 481 or 01305/216 920, *www.aircourier.co.uk*. Agent for lots of companies.

Flight and travel agents

As well as the agents listed below, check the Sunday papers and free weeklies, *Time Out* and the *Evening Standard* in London. Look for last-minute deals on the internet, Teletext or in Caribbean-oriented newspapers such as the *Voice*, the *Gleaner* and the *Caribbean Times*.

Flightbookers, 177–178 Tottenham Court Rd, London W1P 0LX ☎ 020/7757 2000, *www.ebookers.com*; Gatwick Airport, South Terminal inside the British Rail Station ☎ 01293/568 300; daily 8am–10pm. Low fares on an extensive selection of scheduled flights.

Flynow.com, 125a Gloucester Rd, London SW7 4SF ☎ 020/7835 2000; 597 Cheetham Hill Rd, Manchester M8 5EJ ☎ 0161/721 4000; *www.flynow.com*. Large range of discounted tickets.

London Flight Centre, 131 Earl's Court Rd, London SW5 9RH ☎ 020/7244 6411, *www.topdecktravel.co.uk*; branches citywide. Long-established agent dealing in discount flights.

North South Travel, Moulsham Mill Centre, Parkway, Chelmsford, Essex CM2 7PX ☎ & fax 01245/608 291, *www.northsouthtravel.co.uk*. Friendly, competitive travel agency, offering discounted fares worldwide – profits are used to support projects in the developing world, especially the promotion of sustainable tourism.

STA Travel, London call centre for Europe ☎ 020/7361 6145, worldwide ☎ 020/7361 6144,

other enquiries ☎ 020/7361 6150; Northern Britain call centre ☎ 0161/830 4713; plus branches nationwide; *www.statravel.co.uk*. Worldwide specialists in low-cost flights and tours for students and under-26s, though other customers welcome.

Trailfinders, 1 Threadneedle St, London EC2R 8JX ☎ 020/7628 7628; 4–5 Dawson St, Dublin 2 ☎ 01/677 7888; plus branches nationwide; *www.trailfinders.com*. One of the best-informed and most efficient agents for independent travellers; produce a very useful quarterly magazine worth scrutinizing for round-the-world routes.

Usit Campus, 52 Grosvenor Gardens, London SW1W 0AG ☎ 020/7730 2101, national call centre ☎ 0870/240 1010; branches nationwide. Also in Fountain Centre, College St, Belfast BT1 6ET ☎ 028/9032 4073; Aston Quay, Dublin 2 ☎ 01/602 1600; branches throughout the Republic; *www.usitcampus.co.uk*

USIT Now Belfast ☎ 028/9032 7111, Dublin ☎ 01/602 1777 or 677 8117, Cork ☎ 021/270 900, Derry ☎ 028/7137 1888, *www.usitnow.ie*. Student and youth specialists for flights and trains.

When it comes to **direct flights**, you have a very limited choice. Only British Airways flies direct to Tobago from the UK, departing from London, Gatwick, and only BWIA flies to Trinidad (from Heathrow). While there are no direct flights **from Ireland**, there are good connections via London or, on Aer Lingus or Delta, via New York or Miami.

Direct flights to Tobago from the UK may soon cease altogether as British Airways has announced plans to discontinue service, citing high fuel prices and taxes, unless the T&T government pay a TT$5 million subsidy. At press time, this situation had not been resolved, so it's worth checking with travel agents for the latest options.

Tour operators

Classic Connection, Concorde House, Canal St, Chester CH1 4EJ ☎020/7344 3000, *lindafrance@itc-uk.com*. Flights and hotel packages and discounted Carnival trips.

Caribbean Journeys, 22 Stephenson Way, London NW1 2HD ☎020/7388 9292, *caribbean@wwj.uk.com*, *www.wwj.uk.com*. Tailor-made hotel and villa holidays in Tobago only, concentrating on more upmarket properties with a few guesthouses on the books.

Caribtours, Kiln House, 210 New Kings Rd, London SW6 4NZ ☎020/7751 0660, fax 7751 9030, *www.caribtours.co.uk*. Reliable group offering luxurious packages to Tobago.

The Destination Group, 14 Greville St, London EC1N 8SB ☎020/7400 7037. All types of package or tailor-made holidays to Tobago, including eco-tours and all-inclusives.

Hayes & Jarvis, Hayes House, 152 King St, London W6 0QU, reservations ☎0870/898 9890, other inquiries ☎0870/907 7737, *www.hayes-jarvis.com*. Specialists in holidays to diving destinations. Exotic weddings also organized.

JMC Holidays, 2–4 Godwin Street, Bradford BD7 2ST ☎0870 607 5085, *www.jmc.com*. Specializes in inexpensive package tours to Tobago.

Kuoni Worldwide, Kuoni House, Dorking, Surrey RH5 4AZ ☎01306/742 222; 2a Barton Square (off St Ann's Square), Manchester M2 7LW ☎0161/832 0667; plus branches elsewhere in London, Manchester and Surrey; *www.kuoni.co.uk*. Flexible package holidays and good family deals.

Owner's Syndicate, 6 Port House, Plantation Wharf, Battersea, London SW11 3TY ☎020/7801 9801, *caribbean@owner-syndicate.com*. Good value for villa holidays in Tobago, as well as a few small properties.

Peregor Travel, 2nd Flr, Jubilee House, 7–9 The Oaks, Ruislip, Middlesex HA4 7LF ☎01895/630871, fax 621026, *www.peregor-travel.co.uk*. Competitive packages – both all-inclusives or room only – with the four largest hotels in Tobago.

Regal Holidays, 22 High St, Sutton, Ely, Cambridgeshire CB6 2RB ☎0870/2201777, fax 01353/777897, *www.regal-diving.co.uk*. Specializes in diving packages including eco-dive safaris. Prices start at £919 for five days B&B with two dives a day.

Thomas Cook, 45 Berkeley Square, London W1X 5AE and branches throughout the UK and Ireland ☎0990/666222, *www.thomas-cook.co.uk*. Package holidays, charter and schedule flights.

Trips Worldwide, 9 Byron Place, Clifton, Bristol BS8 1JT ☎0117/987 2626, fax 0117/3311 4401, *www.tripsworldwide.co.uk*. Eco-tours and tailor-made holidays to T&T, in collaboration with Trinidad's Wildways tour company. Knowledgeable staff organize flights, accommodation, transport and tour guides for holidays starting from £800.

Villa Connections, 27 Park Lane, Poynton, Cheshire SK12 1RD ☎01625/858158, *info@villa-connect.com*, *www.villaconnnections.co.uk*. Tailor-made villa and small hotel holidays in Tobago, excursions to Trinidad, Carnival packages and flights and car rental arrangements.

Wildlife Worldwide, 170 Selsdon Rd, South Croydon, Surrey CR2 6PJ☎020/8667 9158, fax 020/8667 1960, *www.wildlifeworldwide.com*. Tailor-made nature-oriented holidays based at Trinidad's Asa Wright Nature Centre and birdwatching or diving tours in Tobago.

Wildwings, 577–579 Fishponds Rd, Bristol BS16 3AF ☎0117/965 8333, fax 0111/9375681, *www.wildwings.co.uk*. Birdwatching and eco-tours packages staying at *Pax* and *Esterel* guesthouses in Trinidad and *Blue Waters*, *Arnos Vale* and *Speyside Inn* in Tobago.

Worldwide Fishing Safaris, 21 Station Rd, Thorney, Peterborough PE6 0QE, ☎01733/271123, fax 01733 271125, *www.worldwidefishingsafaris.co.uk*. Deep-sea and fly-fishing holidays to Tobago including flights and accommodation.

British Airways flies to Tobago once a week on Saturday. Its official prices range from £500 to £2242. Once again, shop around – it's possible to reduce these figures through last-minute deals and by buying advance purchase tickets.

BWIA is Trinidad's own airline. Although its pricing classification is very complicated, the general price range is similar to BA's. There are daily flights from London Heathrow to Piarco, Trinidad; transfers to Tobago on frequent daily BWIA flights can be arranged, and are included in the fare. Prices start at £468 for the end of April or end of September, but soar to £1000 for the twelve days before Christmas. Carnival prices are around £700. These tickets are for scheduled flights though, and are valid for one to six months.

Flights from Australia and New Zealand

The Caribbean is no bargain destination from Australasia. There are no direct flights from Australia or New Zealand to Trinidad and Tobago, so you'll have to take a flight to one of the main US/Canada gateway airports, and pick up onward connections from there.

The best option is Air Canada who offer a through fare to Port of Spain via **Honolulu** and **Toronto**. Fares from the east coast cities of Melbourne/Sydney/Brisbane during low season start from AS$2149 and Perth from AS$2515. A flight from Port of Spain to Tobago on BWIA will cost less than AS$100 return and can be purchased in Australia before departure.

Other options are to go via **New York**, from where there are regular flights to Port of Spain and Scarborough, or **Miami**, which has frequent flights to Port of Spain (see pp.4–6 for full details of routes from North America).

Air New Zealand, United and Qantas has regular services to Los Angeles, with connecting flights to New York or Miami on American Airlines or United: return fares to Miami cost around A$2300 from the eastern states, rising to A$2750 from Western Australia. From Miami to Port of Spain, return flights with American Airlines cost A$370, giving a total return fare in the region of A$3000. **From New Zealand**, Air New Zealand, Qantas and United fly to Los Angeles, with connections on to Miami or New York. Through fares to New York start at NZ$2700, and the return to

---

Airlines

Air Canada, Australia ☎ 1300/656 232 or 02/9232 5222, New Zealand ☎ 09/377 8833, *www.aircanada.ca*

Air New Zealand, Australia ☎ 13 2476, New Zealand ☎ 0800/737 000 or 09/357 3000, *www.airnz.com*

American Airlines, Australia ☎ 1300/650 747, New Zealand ☎ 09/309 0735 or 0800/887 997, *www.aa.com*

BWIA International Airways, Australia ☎ 02/9285 6811, no NZ office *www.bwiacaribbean.com*

Qantas, Australia ☎ 13/13 13, New Zealand ☎ 09/357 8900 or 0800/808 767, *www.qantas.com.au*

United Airlines, Australia ☎ 13/1777, New Zealand ☎ 09/379 3800, *www.ual.com*

Travel agents

Anywhere Travel, Australia ☎ 02/9663 0411 or 018 401 014, *anywhere@ozemail.com.au*

Budget Travel, New Zealand ☎ 09/366 0061 or 0800/808 040.

Destinations Unlimited, New Zealand ☎ 09/373 4033.

Flight Centres, Australia ☎ 02/9235 3522 or for nearest branch ☎ 13 1600, New Zealand ☎ 09/358 4310, *www.flightcentre.com.au*

Northern Gateway, Australia ☎ 08/8941 1394, *oztravel@norgate.com.au*

STA Travel, Australia ☎ 13 1776 or 1300/360 960, New Zealand ☎ 09/309 0458 or 09/366 6673, *www.statravel.com.au*

Student Uni Travel, Australia ☎ 02/9232 8444, *Australia@backpackers.net*

Thomas Cook, Australia ☎ 13 1771 or 1800/801 002, New Zealand ☎ 09/379 3920, *www.thomascook.com.au*

Trailfinders, Australia ☎ 02/9247 7666.

Usit Beyond, New Zealand ☎ 09/379 4224 or 0800/788 336, *www.usitbeyond.co.nz*

Port of Spain or Crown Point will add another NZ$460 or so.

Package holidays from Australia and New Zealand to Trinidad and Tobago are few and far between, and many specialists simply act as **agents** for US-based operators, tagging a return flight from Australasia onto the total cost. **Cruises** (see p.6), most of which depart from Miami, account for the largest sector.

The luxury end of the market is also catered for by Caribbean Destinations and Contours, both of which offer **resort**- and **villa-based** holidays as well as cruises, with a choice of accommodation on Trinidad and a limited range on Tobago. Prices start at around A$3500 for 14 days (based on twin-share accommodation and low-season airfares from Australia), but really the sky's the limit.

None of the adventure-tour operators venture to Trinidad and Tobago; for **independent travellers**, the cheapest way to visit the Caribbean is as part of a round-the-world or American holiday, making creative use of airpasses – see p.3.

Red tape and visas

Citizens from most western European countries do not require a visa for stays of less than three months, and US citizens may stay up to two months without a visa. Nationals of Australia, New Zealand and South Africa all require visas before entering the country. You can apply for visas through the offices listed below or else have your travel agent obtain one on your behalf. On arrival, you will have to provide an address where you will be staying, proof that you have adequate finances for the length of your stay and a return or ongoing ticket. Your passport must be valid for the duration of your trip.

Visa extensions, from an extra three months to one year, cost TT$100, but if you want one you must be prepared for some tortuously slow bureaucracy. Despite Trinidad and Tobago's relaxed lifestyle, the country's immigration department is as strict as those of Britain or the US. Prepare yourself thoroughly and take an unlimited stock of patience; you will be asked for endless proof of income, reasons for your visa extension and letters from Trinbagonian individuals and organizations. It is best to speak on the phone to someone at the **Immigration Office** first

(67 Frederick St, Port of Spain; ☎868/625-3571) about what you'll need. The policy regarding visa extension is not clear cut – your success may depend on the individual officer you get to see on the day.

Applications for **work permits**, which are required for certain types of paid and unpaid employment, are available at the **Ministry of National Security**, Abercromby St, Port of Spain, ☎868/623 2441.

Trinidad and Tobago embassies, high commissions and honorary consuls abroad

UK
High Commission, 42 Belgrave Square, London SW1X 8TNT ☎ 020/7245 9351, fax 823 1065, *trintogov@tthc.demon.co.uk*

US
Embassy, 1708 Massachusetts Ave, NW Washington, DC 20036-1975 ☎202/467 6490 or 6491 or 6492 or 6493, fax 785 3130, *embttoba-go@erols.com*

Canada
High Commission, 200 First Ave, Ottawa, Ontario K1S 2G6 ☎613/232 2418 or 2419, fax 232 4349, *www.ttmissions.com*

Consulate General, 2005 Sheppard Ave East, Suite 303, Willowdale, Toronto, Ontario M2J 5B4 ☎416/495-9442, fax 495-6934.

Australia
Honorary Consul, PO Box 109, Rose Bay, New South Wales 2029 ☎612/9337 4391, fax 9437 4564.

New Zealand
Honorary Consul, Level 2525, 151 Queen Street, Auckland ☎09/302 1860, fax 302 0923.

Money, banks and costs

Trinidad and Tobago is undoubtedly one of the cheapest Caribbean destinations due to its low profile on the tourist market. If you live like a local, it is possible to survive on £20/$US28 a day – if you're prepared to take the least expensive accommodation, eat at low-cost cafés and street stalls and limit your travel to public transport. If, however, you stay at tourist accommodation and eat at restaurants, you will need at least £60/$US85 a day. Obviously if you rent a car this will be an added expense – around £30–40/$US45–60 per day.

During **Carnival season** all accommodation rates in Port of Spain are increased – a rise of 10 to 100 percent depending on the hotel. Carnival season often sees other price rises, such as entrance fees to clubs, drinks and taxi fares. Therefore if you intend to enjoy yourself during Carnival season, budget on £100/US$140 a day and up.

Costs vary around T&T – food and drink is less expensive in the countryside than the cities. Tobago is more costly than Trinidad as a result of its greater tourist trade. **Accommodation** is cheaper outside Port of Spain and the Crown

Point area. **Restaurants** vary greatly in price: fine dining establishments, recognizable by their plush decor, charge TT$150 plus per meal; the more basic restaurants, with plastic tables and buffet-style service, offer huge meals for less than TT$30.

Some independent travellers tend to be penny-pinching, especially when it comes to **taxi fares**. But although bargaining is sometimes expected when negotiating fares to off-route destinations, most prices are fixed. Many Trinbagonians assume that all foreigners are rich, considering many get paid the minimum wage – currently TT$7 an hour – and since the average wage is between TT$250–500 per week, a dollar is certainly worth more to them than it is to you. Under the circumstances, a few extra dollars on a taxi fare should not be begrudged.

Currency

The local currency is the **Trinidad and Tobago dollar**. This is usually abbreviated to **TT$**, and is divided into one hundred cents. Coins start at 1 cent and range up through 5, 10 and 25 cents. Notes start at 1 dollar and are in denominations of 5, 10, 20, 100. It is best to keep some of your cash in small denominations. Supermarkets and bars can usually exchange TT$100 but taxis and street vendors often can't and should be paid with TT$20 or less.

Travellers' cheques and credit cards

Take along a mixture of **cash**, **credit cards** and **travellers' cheques** to cover all eventualities. Travellers' cheques and credit cards are accepted in most restaurants, malls, high-class shops and hotels. In smaller establishments and rural areas they are unlikely to take anything but local currency. **Personal cheques** are not usually accepted in hotels, and if you stay in a host home you may find they do not have the facilities for payment by credit card.

Changing money

It is best to buy only a small amount of TT$ abroad, as the exchange rate is much more favourable in the country – you may gain as much as 5–10 percent on the transaction. The exchange rate at the time of publication was around TT$6 to US$1 and TT$9 to £1. **Piarco Airport Exchange Bureau** (6am–10pm) has a

reasonable rate of exchange, although it is not as competitive as those of the banks in Port of Spain. Travellers flying into Tobago can change money at the Republic Bank (Mon–Thurs 8–11am & noon–2pm, Fri 8am–noon & 3–5pm) in **Crown Point Airport**.

T&T **banks** will exchange most major currencies and travellers' cheques. Commission varies; some banks charge nothing for Amex cheques, while others impose a mandatory charge of around TT$5. You'll always receive a lower rate for cash than for travellers' cheques. There is usually no separate exchange counter, so avoid going during lunch hour (noon–2pm) or be prepared for a long wait – early morning is the best time to catch the queues at their shortest. In **Trinidad** there are banks in most towns and all cities, as well as at the airport. In **Tobago** there is only one bank outside Scarborough, in Crown Point Airport, so bear this in mind when you head off to remoter regions. Both Piarco and Crown Point airports have 24-hour cash machines, which will provide cash advances on credit cards. Cash machines on both islands are marked on the TIDCO (T&T tourist board) maps.

Banking hours vary slightly depending on the bank, but usually they are open between Monday and Thursday from 8am to 2pm. Opening hours on Fridays are 8am to noon, and 3pm to 5pm. Most banks in Trinidad's larger malls open and close later (9am–6pm) with no break. It is also possible to get local currency by using international ATM cards at cash machines, which can be found at the airports and in larger towns.

Outside banking hours money can be exchanged in the larger hotels and in some shops in Port of Spain, though at a less advantageous rate. Most shops and vendors will accept **American dollars** for purchases – pay in small denominations and be prepared to receive your change in local currency.

Wiring money is a fast but expensive way to send and receive money abroad, and should be considered only as a last resort. The money wired is available for collection, in local dollars, from a variety of outlets, including the local Hi-Lo supermarket chain, within a few minutes of being sent via Western Union (☎0800/833 833) or Moneygram (☎0800/018 0104); both charge on a sliding scale, so sending larger amounts of cash is better value. Thomas Cook (☎01733/318922) have a much cheaper flat rate but it takes one to two days for the money to arrive and they can only send drafts which must be paid into a local bank account. They charge a minumum of £25 for this service and the money takes the same time as a cheque to clear.

Check with your bank before travelling to see if they have reciprocal arrangements with any banks in the countries you are visiting.

Visa TravelMoney (*www.visa.com*) This is a disposable debit card pre-paid with dedicated travel funds that you can access from over 457,000 Visa ATMs in 120 countries with a personal identification number (PIN). When your funds are depleted, you simply throw the card away, (it's recommended you buy at least a second card in case your first is lost or stolen; up to nine cards can be bought to access the same funds – useful for couples or families travelling together). Visa offer a 24-hr emergency assistance toll-free number; from Trinidad and Tobago call ☎ 1-800-847-2911. Cards are available worldwide though Thomas Cook and Citicorp (*www.visa.com/pd/trav/main.html*).

Information and maps

Local and foreign offices and representatives of the T&T tourist board, TIDCO (Tourism and Industrial Development Company of Trinidad and Tobago), send out standard information packs on request, which include useful accommodation and Calendar of Events booklets, as well as some glossy promotional pamphlets and sometimes a road map.

Though they're few and far between, it's worth visiting the **local tourist board offices** (see p.16) once you've arrived; they dole out advice on hotels, transport and activities as well as free attraction/road maps and flyers. The main office is in Port of Spain, but the information booths at Crown Point and Piarco airports are more accessible and better equipped to deal with the public.

Other sources of local information are the **radio** and **national press** (see pp.33–34), which carry advertisements for upcoming events, and three free tourist-oriented publications, *Discover Trinidad and Tobago* (www.discovertrinidad.com), *Tobago Today*, *Inns and Outs of Trinidad and Tobago* and *Time Out Trinidad and Tobago*. Written by local people and updated annually, glossy, fact-filled *Discover* includes features on subjects such as Carnival and eco-tourism, suggested touring schedules, and hotel, restaurant and tour operator listings, while the monthly *Tobago Today* newspaper (available in Tobago only) carries Tobago listings and topical features such as goat racing for the Easter issue as well as Tobagonian recipes and hints on etiquette. First published in 2000, *Inns and Outs* is a glossy annual publication which deals with Trinidad and Tobago separately, and has sections on Carnival as well as shopping, art and craft, eco-tourism and business as well as accommodation, eating and nightlife listings on both islands. *Time Out* (not linked to the UK-based magazine) is a quarterly mini-listings title with sections on music, tours, shopping, dining and yachting. All are available at hotels and tourist offices.

Trinidad and Tobago on the internet

There are hundreds of T&T-oriented **websites**, which differ hugely in style and content – and the number of sites grows all the time. Hotels are lining up to market properties online (we list websites in the Guide accommodations sections), and it's a convenient, hassle-free way to book your holiday. The listings below are for sites with high-quality general content, and lots of links to get you started, as well as a few more specific sites.

www.visittnt.com
Maintained by TIDCO, this is the best all-rounder with country details, attraction listings, flight information and feature pages on Carnival, soca and calypso, with links to lots of other pertinent sites.

www.search.co.tt
Exhaustive directory of T&T-related sites. Essential stuff.

www.carnaval.com
The best T&T Carnival site, with features on everything from mas camps and pan-yards to music, accommodation and restaurants. Pretty good for visits to Port of Spain, too.

www.lanic.utexas.edu/la/cb/tt
Huge directory of T&T-related links, organized by category, from academic research and arts and culture to business and economy, and the environment.

www.homeviewtnt.com
Slick site with extensive content, from live feeds to WE FM and other stations, sports, news, music, Carnival, history, listings and loads of Trini titbits. A good place to start.

www.seetobago.com/trinidad/pan/bands _tt.htm
Everything you ever wanted to know (and probably some stuff you didn't) about steel pan in T&T.

www.steelpansttil.com
All things pan related, from pan news, events and links to online sales of new pan instruments.

www.pantrinbago.com
Official website of Pan Trinbago, T&T's steel pan governing body, with lots of background on the genre as well as info on pan competitions.

www.trinbagocarnival.com
Carnival site with a huge amount of info,

from lists of previous road march, king and queen or mas band winners to background on the event in general.

www.trinidad-online.org
Stark-looking but useful site with chat-rooms, links, travel, personals, features on books and CDs and links to relevant sites.

www.triniradio.com
Internet radio station, allowing you to listen to Trini music for free while you browse other pages. Also on offer are a Trini dictionary, recipes, a chatroom and a calendar of events in T&T.

www.stoutweb.com/triniwww.tiewww.ang elfire.com/ma/maxforte
Website of Arima's Carib community, with articles pertaining to Carib history and current affairs.

www.triniweb.com
Buy Trini products online, listen to YES FM live, or browse the articles on news, business, music, politics, carnival, among others. There's a lot to get through, and its mostly quality stuff.

www.hotep.bigstep.com
Interesting, African-oriented homepage, with a link to the "Trinicenter" page of thoughtful T&T-related articles and book reviews.

www.intr.net/goyewole/calytent.html
Virtual calypso tent, with plenty of soca- and kaiso-related info and lots of links.

www.trinibase.com
Fact-heavy site with local statistics and links to all things Carnival and Trinbagonian.

www.carnival.ncc.com
Home page of the National Carnival Commission; plenty of useful Carnival information including summaries of previous years winners.

Map and travel book suppliers

UK and Ireland

Blackwell's Map and Travel Shop, 53 Broad St, Oxford OX1 3BQ ☎01865/792792, *www.bookshop.blackwell.co.uk*

Easons Bookshop, 40 O'Connell St, Dublin 1 ☎01/873 3811, *www.eason.ie*

Heffers Map and Travel, 20 Trinity St, Cambridge, CB2 1TJ ☎01223/568 568, *www.heffers.co.uk*

Hodges Figgis Bookshop, 56–58 Dawson St, Dublin 2 ☎01/677 4754, *www.hodgesfiggis.com*

James Thin Melven's Bookshop, 29 Union St, Inverness, IV1 1QA ☎01463/233500, *www.jthin.co.uk*

John Smith and Sons, 26 Colquhoun Ave, Glasgow, G52 4PJ ☎ 0141/552 3377, *www.johnsmith.co.uk*

The Map Shop, 30a Belvoir St, Leicester, LE1 6QH ☎0116/2471400.

National Map Centre, 22–24 Caxton St, London SW1 0QU ☎020/7222 2466, *www.mapsnmc.co.uk*

Newcastle Map Centre, 55 Grey St, Newcastle upon Tyne, NE1 6EF ☎0191/261 5622, *www.traveller.ltd.uk*

Ordnance Survey of Northern Ireland, Colby House, Stranmillis Ct, Belfast BT9 5BJ ☎028/9066 1244, *www.osni.gov.uk*

Ordnance Survey Service, Phoenix Park, Dublin 8 ☎01/820 6100, *www.irlgov.ie/osi/*

Stanfords, 12–14 Long Acre, London WC2E 9LP ☎020/7836 1321, *www.stanfords.co.uk*; maps by mail or phone order are available on this number and via *sales@stanfords.co.uk*. Other branches within British Airways offices at 156 Regent St, W1R 5TA ☎020/7434 4744, and 29 Corn St, Bristol BS1 1HT ☎0117/929 9966.

The Travel Bookshop, 13–15 Blenheim Crescent, London W11 2EE ☎020/7229 5260, *www.thetravelbookshop.co.uk*

USA and Canada

Adventurous Traveler Bookstore, PO Box 64769, Burlington, VT 05406 ☎1-800/282-3963, *www.AdventurousTraveler.com*

Book Passage, 51 Tamal Vista Blvd, Corte Madera, CA 94925, ☎415/927-0960, *www.bookpassage.com*

Elliot Bay Book Company, 101 S Main St, Seattle, WA 98104 ☎206/624-6600 or 1-800/962-5311, *www.elliotbaybook.com*

Forsyth Travel Library, 226 Westchester Ave, White Plains, NY 10604 ☎1-800/367-7984, *www.forsyth.com*

Globe Corner Bookstore, 28 Church St, Cambridge, MA 02138 ☎1-800/358-6013, *www.globercorner.com*

Map Link Inc., 30 S La Patera Lane, Unit 5, Santa Barbara, CA 93117 ☎805/692-6777, *www.maplink.com*

Phileas Fogg's Travel Center, #87 Stanford Shopping Center, Palo Alto, CA 94304 ☎1-800/533-3644, *www.foggs.com*

Rand McNally, 444 N Michigan Ave, Chicago, IL 60611 ☎312/321-1751, *www.randmcnally.com*; 150 E 52nd St, New York, NY 10022 ☎212/758-7488); 595 Market St, San Francisco, CA 94105 ☎415/777-3131; around thirty stores across the US – call ☎1-800/333-0136 ext 2111 or check the website for the nearest store.

Travel Books & Language Center, 4437 Wisconsin Ave, Washington, DC 20016 ☎1-800/220-2665, *www.bookweb.org/bookstore/travellers*

The Travel Bug Bookstore, 2667 West Broadway, Vancouver V6K 2G2 ☎604/737-1122, *www.swifty.com/tbug*

World of Maps, 118 Holland Ave, Ottawa, Ontario K1Y 0X6 ☎613/724-6776, *www.itmb.com*

World Wide Books and Maps, 1247 Granville St, Vancouver V6Z 1G3 ☎604/687-3320, *www.worldofmaps.com*

Australia and New Zealand

The Map Shop, 6 Peel St, Adelaide ☎08/8231 2033, *www.mapshop.net.au*

Mapland, 372 Little Bourke St, Melbourne ☎03/9670 4383, *www.mapland.com.au*

Mapworld, 173 Gloucester St, Christchurch ☎03/374 5399, fax 03/374 5633, *www.mapworld.co.nz*

Perth Map Centre, 1/884 Hay St, Perth ☎08/9322 5733, *www.perthmap.com.au*

Specialty Maps, 46 Albert St, Auckland ☎09/307 2217, *www.ubd-online.co.nz/maps*

Tourist offices in Trinidad and Tobago

Trinidad

Information Office, Piarco Airport ☎ 664 5196.

TIDCO, PO Box 222, 10–14 Philipps St, Port of Spain ☎ 623 6022 or 1932, fax 623 3848, *www.visittnt.com*

Tobago

Information Office, Crown Point Airport ☎ 639 0509.

TIDCO, Unit 26, TIDCO Mall, Sangster's Hill, Scarborough ☎ 639 4333, fax 639 4514.

Tobago House of Assembly Division of Tourism, Level 3, NIB Mall, Carrington St, Scarborough, Tobago ☎ 639 2125 or 4636, fax 639 3566, *tourbago@tstt.net.tt*

TIDCO offices and representatives abroad

Canada

The RMR Group Inc, Taurus House, 512 Duplex Ave, Toronto MR4 2E3 ☎ 416/485-7827 or 1-888/535-5617, fax 485 8256, *assoc@thermrgroup.ca*

UK

Morris Kevan International Ltd, Mitre House, 66 Abbey Rd, Bush Hill Park, Enfield, Middlesex EN1 2QE ☎ 020/8350 1015, fax 020/8350 1011, *mki@ttg.co.uk*

USA

Cheryl Andrews Marketing Inc, 311 Almeria Ave, Coral Gables, Florida 33144 ☎ 305/444-7827 or 1-888/595-4868, fax 305/447-0415, *CAMktg@aol.com*

There are no TIDCO offices in Australia or New Zealand.

Maps

The tourist board hand out free **maps** of both Trinidad and Tobago, showing main roads, beaches and tourist attractions, and these are adequate for mainstream exploration. The best alternative for those who want to get off the beaten track and drive the minor roads is the 1:150,000 **road map** issued by the Land and Survey Department; though the print quality of the photos on the reverse is appalling and the last update was in 1990, it's the most detailed and useful source available and not too huge that it's impossible to use (though it's increasingly hard to find outside T&T). The *Historic Tobago* map, sold on the island by gift shops and the tourist board, has a comprehensive listing of local attractions and their historical background on the reverse.

Insurance

Trinidad and Tobago has only the most basic public health system; consequently if you fall ill while visiting the country it is advisable to go to a private doctor or hospital (see overleaf). Medical treatment is expensive; it is therefore essential that you take out travel insurance before entering the country.

Before paying for a new policy, however, it's worth checking whether you are already covered: some all-risks home insurance policies may cover your possessions when overseas, and many private medical schemes include cover when abroad.

In Canada, provincial health plans usually provide partial cover for medical mishaps overseas, while holders of official student/teacher/youth cards in Canada and the US are entitled to meagre accident coverage and hospital in-patient benefits. Students will often find that their student health coverage extends during the vacations and for one term beyond the date of last enrollment.

After exhausting the possibilities above, you might want to contact a specialist travel insurance company, or consider the travel insurance deal we offer (see box). A typical travel insurance policy usually provides cover for the loss of baggage, tickets and – up to a certain limit – cash or cheques, as well as cancellation or curtailment of your journey. Most of them exclude so-called dangerous sports unless an extra premium is paid: in Trinidad and Tobago this can mean scuba-diving, windsurfing and trekking, though probably not kayaking. Read the small print and benefits tables of prospective policies carefully; coverage can vary wildly for roughly similar premiums. Many policies can be chopped and changed to exclude coverage you don't need – for example, sickness and accident benefits can often be excluded or included at will. Flights paid for with a major credit or charge card offer some automatic cover, but usually only while travelling

---

Rough Guides travel insurance

Rough Guides now offers its own **travel insurance**, customized for our readers by a leading UK broker and backed by a Lloyds underwriter. It's available for anyone, of any nationality, travelling anywhere in the world.

There are two main Rough Guide insurance plans: **Essential**, for basic, no-frills cover; and **Premier** – with more generous and extensive benefits. Alternatively, you can take out annual **multi-trip insurance**, which covers you for any number of trips throughout the year (with a maximum of sixty days for any one trip). Unlike many policies, the Rough Guides schemes are calculated by the day, so if you're travelling for 27 days rather than a month, that's all you pay for. If you intend to be away for the whole year, the **Adventurer** policy will cover you for 365 days. Each plan can be supplemented with a "Hazardous Activities Premium" if you plan to indulge in sports considered dangerous, such as scuba-diving or trekking. Rough Guides also does good deals for older travellers, and will insure you up to any age, at prices comparable to SAGA's.

For a **policy quote**, call the Rough Guides Insurance Line on UK freefone ☎ 0800/015 0906, US toll-free 1-866/220 5588, or, if you're calling from outside elsewhere on ☎ 44 1243/621 046. Alternatively, get an online quote or buy your cover at *www.roughguides.com/insurance*

to and from your destination. If you do take medical coverage, ascertain whether benefits will be paid as treatment proceeds or only after return home, and whether there is a **24-hour medical emergency number**. When securing baggage cover, make sure that the per-article limit – typically under £500 – will cover your most valuable possession. If you need to make a claim, you should keep receipts for medicines and medical treatment, and in the event you have anything stolen, you must obtain an official statement from the police. Keep photocopies of everything you send to the insurer and don't allow months to elapse before informing them – most insurance policies require that you inform them of a loss within a specific time.

Health

Travelling around Trinidad and Tobago carries little risk to your health: the islands are non-malarial, there are no mandatory immunizations (though some are recommended; see below) and the chlorinated tap water is safe to drink. The most likely hazards are overexposure to the sun, too much rum and the inevitable minor stomach upsets that come with unfamiliar food and water. If you do find yourself in need of minor medical attention, remember that most insurance policies require you to pay up initially and retain the receipts for the claim you'll submit once you get home.

The main **hospitals** in **Trinidad** are Port of Spain General and the Mount Hope complex in St Augustine; there are also small, poorly equipped regional hospitals in all the main towns, as well as the more efficient private establishments such as St Clair Medical Centre in Port of Spain. **Tobago's** sole public hospital is in Scarborough, next to the Fort complex. You won't have to pay for treatment at public hospitals, but will be charged a fee at Mount Hope and all others listed; however, the long waits and severely stretched facilities make it more sensible to plump for a private option straight away, particularly as your insurance should eventually cover costs in any case.

Though we have recommended reliable doctors and medical centres throughout the guide, it's also wise to enquire at your hotel if you need attention. Many have a resident nurse or can recommend someone who'll be there quickly. In Trinidad, you can call a Red Cross **ambulance** on ☎ 627 8215 during office hours, 627 8214 in the evening. In Tobago, call ☎ 639 2222 or 639 2781. For an ambulance from a public hospital, call ☎ 990.

If you prefer **alternative medicine**, Trinidad's best **homeopath** is Harry Ramnarine, an ex-sur-

---

Regional hospitals

Trinidad

Arima District Hospital, Queen Mary Ave, Arima ☎ 667 4714.

Community Hospital, Western Main Rd, Cocorite, Port of Spain ☎ 622 1191 or 628 8330.

Mount Hope Hospital (Eric Williams Medical Sciences Complex), Eastern Main Rd, St Augustine ☎ 646 4673, 662 3552 or 645 2640.

Port of Spain General Hospital, 169 Charlotte St, Port of Spain ☎ 623 2951 or 2952.

San Fernando General Hospital, Independence Ave, San Fernando ☎ 652 3581 or 3580.

St Clair Medical Centre, 18 Elizabeth St, St Clair, Port of Spain ☎ 628 1451 or 8615.

Tobago

Tobago County Hospital, Calder Hall Rd, Scarborough, ☎ 639 2551 or 2552.

---

geon turned alternative practitioner. His practice is at 403 Rodney Rd, Chaguanas (☎ 665 8041), but as his waiting lists are extremely long, it's best to make appointments as early as possible. In Tobago, you can get advice on herbal treatments, and buy medicinal herbs and alternative health products, from E&F Health Foods, Scarborough Mall, Carrington Street, Scarborough (☎ 639 3992).

Before you go

Though you should ensure that you're up to date with polio and tetanus vaccines, no **jabs** are needed to enter Trinidad and Tobago unless you're travelling from a country where smallpox vaccinations are required. However, typhoid, yellow fever and hepatitis A immunizations are worth considering if you think you'll be spending a lot of time off the beaten track. Take precautions to ensure that you're as healthy as possible before you travel; have a **dental check-up** and bring supplies of any **prescription medicines** that you use regularly, as well as the generic name of the product in case you need more after you've arrived.

Staying healthy in the heat

Heat and **humidity** make cuts and grazes slower to heal and more vulnerable to infection than in temperate climates; clean all wounds scrupulously, apply iodine or antiseptic spray or powder (cream just keeps a cut wet and slows down healing) and try to keep the wound dry. You can use rum to clean wounds if nothing else is to hand. Sea water is said to help a cut heal fast, but as most of the ocean carries plenty of bacteria alongside the salt, you may be risking infection.

The benign but unsightly fungal skin disease **pityriasis** – known locally as *lota* – is common; it appears on white skin as circular crispy patches and as lighter patches of discoloration on black skin. It's passed on through contact, and can be hard to avoid if you're susceptible. Though there are a thousand "bush remedies", the best treatment is to apply an anti-fungal cream, sulphur-based lotions or anti-dandruff shampoo. Failing to dry your feet properly and constantly wearing trainers or boots provide the perfect conditions for the **athlete's foot** fungus to flourish – treat it with anti-fungal cream, stick to open sandals as much as possible and wear flip-flops in communal showers and around the pool.

Be stringent about personal hygiene. If you live in a cool climate, your skin will need to adjust to the heat; sweat ducts take a little while to open sufficiently, and blocked ducts can cause an itchy **prickly heat** rash. To treat or avoid it, wear loose cotton clothes, take frequent cold showers without soap and dust with medicated talcum powder afterwards. Avoid sunscreen or moisturizer on affected areas and try to spend some time in an air-conditioned room if it gets really bad.

With sweet fizzy drinks often the only available refreshment, **dehydration**, heat exhaustion and sunstroke can also be a problem – symptoms are light-headedness, headache, tiredness and nausea. If affected, rest in a cool place, drink lots of water (especially nutritious, easy-to-find coconut water) and take regular doses of a rehydration solution (see "stomach problems", below). Avoid **sunburn** by basking for no more than half an hour per day to begin with, getting some shade between 11am and 2pm, and always using a good quality, high-factor cream – remember that sunscreen loses its effectiveness over time, so make sure your supply is less than a year old. Bear in mind that you will be especially vulnerable to sunburn on boat trips, and that UV rays can penetrate even on cloudy days. If you do get burnt, liberally apply fresh aloe vera, after-sun cream or a weak vinegar solution. Sunscreen and after-sun are widely available in T&T.

Travel medical kit

Listed below are items that always come in handy; though you can purchase most of them while in T&T, it's cheaper to buy at home and much more convenient to have them with you when you need them.

Band-Aids
Scissors
Bandages and sterile gauze
Antiseptic spray or iodine liquid
Antiseptic wipes
Painkillers/aspirin
Diarrhoea remedy
Calamine lotion or any bite-soothing remedy
Medicated talcum powder
Thrush and cystitis remedies
Anti-fungal cream

Aloe vera

The thick, spiky stems of **aloe vera** grow profusely throughout T&T, and in Tobago it's common for hustlers to sell them on the beaches. A staple of local healing and skin care, the plant is a veritable cure-all, drunk as a purgative, used as a conditioning rinse and applied to cuts, grazes and burns to draw out infection. It's an excellent remedy for sunburn, heat rash and insect bites, and is even distilled into aloes wine.

To extract fresh aloe gel from the stem, cut off a section and pare away the spiky edges. Slice in half and wipe the vaguely mauve gel onto the affected areas, scratching the surface to release more jelly as needed and being careful not to get it on clothing – it leaves a stubborn purple stain.

Stomach problems

Though serious dysentery-type **stomach bugs** are very rare, taking common-sense precautions lessens the chances of a bout of "travellers tummy". If you buy fresh fruit and vegetables, wash and peel them yourself. Stick to obviously popular food vendors and restaurants (all licensed, government-inspected vendors display a badge), and wash your hands well before you eat. If you do fall victim to **diarrhoea**, try to rest and drink plenty of fluid: water, herb tea, fruit juice, clear soup and especially nutritious, vitamin-packed coconut water, rather than fizzy drinks or beer. After every bowel movement and once an hour, drink a glass of water mixed with a teaspoon of sugar and half a teaspoon of salt to make up for lost minerals, and eat small quantities of bland foods like rice or bread; avoid fruit, fatty foods and dairy products. See a doctor (we've listed these in the Guide) if symptoms persist for more than three days. Though you may be tempted to take a commercial anti-diarrhoea remedy, this will merely prevent the body from flushing out whatever is troubling the system; use these only if you cannot get to a toilet, or before a long journey. Though it's generally heavily chlorinated and safe (if a bit unpalatable) **tap water** can sometimes become slightly contaminated after heavy rain, particularly in rural areas. It's probably best to stick to cheap and widely available mineral water during short stays unless you've got the constitution of an ox.

Animal and plant hazards

Though there are no harmful **snakes** in Tobago, Trinidad's forests harbour four venomous varieties; the fer-de-lance and the bushmaster or pit viper (both known as mapepire, pronounced "mah-pee-pee"), and two species of brightly coloured coral snake (for more detailed information on T&T's snakes, see "Fauna and flora", p.349). As snakes shy away from contact with humans, bites are very rare, but it's best to wear long trousers, shoes or boots and socks when walking in the bush, and to refrain from investigating rock crevices with your bare hands. If you do encounter a snake – blocking a hiking trail etc – simply move it gently out of the way with as long a stick as you can find, and if you're unlucky enough to be bitten, keep calm; death from a snake bite is almost unheard of in these parts, and your worst enemy is panic since violent activity causes the venom to spread more rapidly through the system. If someone else is bitten, reassure the victim and keep them immobilized. Bandage the affected area tightly (if the bite is on a limb, tie a tourniquet above it), note down all that you can about what the snake looks like (but on no account try to capture it), and seek medical help immediately; all local hospitals have stocks of the relevant antidote.

In recent years, a rise in the incidence of **rabies** among cattle, cats and dogs, spread by the feeding activities of **vampire bats**, has meant that it's best not to disturb sleeping bats and avoid petting stray animals; many have mange in any case. If you see a cat or dog behaving strangely, report it to the police. If you are bitten, seek medical attention immediately.

Insect and arachnid bites

Insect bites can be a real nuisance, particularly if you visit during the wet season (Dec–May). **Mosquitoes** and **sand flies** (the latter deliver a small but incredibly itchy and long-lasting bite) are usually at their most aggressive at sundown, especially around standing water such as swamps or ponds. Cover your arms and legs at dusk and use plenty of strong insect repellent: a spray, roll-on and a cream are useful, and repellents are widely available in local supermarkets. If you dislike using chemicals, try citronella or lavender oils, or the Avon moisturizing cream Skin So Soft, which mosquitoes seem to hate. Once you've been bitten (and no matter how thorough your precautions, you will be), do not scratch the bites at any cost. Even touching them will make the itching last a lot longer, and breaking the skin almost always results in infection and scars. Applying soothing creams or sprays may help – homeopathic pyrethrum is particularly good – but one of the best remedies is a coating of fresh aloe vera gel (see box, opposite).

Though there is no malaria in Trinidad and Tobago, the *Aedes aegypti* mosquito can transmit **dengue fever**, a flu-like disease distinguished by headaches, dizziness, rashes on the torso, severe muscle pain and aching limbs, nausea and vomiting. It is only life-threatening if you are very young, old or infirm and succumb to the more serious **dengue haemorragic fever**, and as the periodic outbreaks are dealt with by the government through aerial spraying and warnings to get rid of collected water on private land, this isn't something to panic about. As there is no vaccination, the best way to avoid dengue is to avoid mosquitoes – if you arrive during an outbreak, choose a hotel room with anti-insect gauze on the windows.

Large, hornet-like **wasps** (known as jackspaniards) are common throughout both islands and deliver a nasty sting; keep well away, especially if they seem to be building a nest. **African bees** – distinguishable by their brown-black head and thorax and black-tipped orange abdomen – made the journey from Venezuela in the late 1970s and are now common throughout Trinidad. They are extremely aggressive if disturbed, so keep out of their way; do not wear strong perfume in the bush and avoid brushing leaves and branches, where hives are often hidden, particularly during the dry season when the majority of honey is produced. If you disturb a nest and the bees swarm, stand still, and don't try the old trick of plunging into water – the bees will simply wait for you to surface. Never kill a bee if you've been stung, as this will cause it to emit a pheromone which attracts even more bees. And don't panic – remember that despite the "killer bee" scare stories, it would take more than 300 of these painful stings to lead to the demise of a healthy adult.

There are a number of creepy-crawlies to watch out for in forested areas. **Scorpions**, found on both islands, are particularly fond of dead wood. Though their sting is painful, it is not usually serious; the severity of the effect varies with individual susceptibility, but you should consult a doctor if worried; you might want to avoid the local remedy of eating the offender. Some **centipedes** can also deliver a painful bite. To minimize chances of a nip or sting from either, step over rotting wood while walking in the bush rather than treading on it, and if your surroundings are rustic, shake shoes before putting them on, and check under toilet seats before using them. The bite of **tarantulas** is about as severe as a wasp sting, and though it will inevitably be unsettling, you need only seek medical attention if you feel seriously unwell. The large black or red-brown **leaf-cutting ants** (*bachac*) that you'll see everywhere also deliver an extremely painful nip – they are easy to spot, so avoid them.

Marine animals

Given the local predilection for consuming **shark**, you could be forgiven for believing that the waters of Trinidad and Tobago are swarming with voracious great whites; however, this is far from the truth. Death-by-jaws is unheard of on the beaches and you are only likely to encounter a shark (usually of the rather benign nurse variety) if you go snorkelling or scuba diving around their reef feeding-grounds or dive into very deep offshore water; as many species rest in the day and hunt at night, they're unlikely to be aggressive. Endowed with sharp teeth and a bit of an attitude if cornered, **barracuda** are best admired from a distance, as are moray eels. Don't stick your hand into rock crevices when diving or snorkelling, and never touch **coral**; quite apart from killing the organism with a caress, you'll probably come away with an unattractive, slow healing rash, particularly if you touch fire coral. A far more likely encounter is with one of the many spiny black **sea urchins** that inhabit reefs and bays; if you tread on one, remove as much of the spine as possible, douse the area in vinegar (or even urine) and see a doctor; washing with vinegar is also the best way to treat **jellyfish** stings. Most common are the globular, 4–5cm "wasp" variety which occasionally swarm onto beaches – their sting is no worse than a bee's, but take care to avoid the long trailing tendrils of the purple Portuguese man-of-war, fairly common in the waters around Trinidad; seek medical help if you think you've been stung by one of these, and don't touch specimens that have washed up on the beach, as they remain harmful for weeks.

Take care to avoid the poisonous **manchineel trees**. They are easy to identify; they grow to around 12 metres, with a wide, spreading crown of small, dark green leaves on long stalks and innocuous-looking green flowers. The milky sap, however, causes severe skin blisters. Do not touch any part of the tree, and don't even shelter under the boughs when it's raining. Although manchineels have been removed from many popular beaches and warning signs put up where they've been allowed to remain, some still grow unnoticed in wilder coastal areas, and the round, green and incredibly poisonous fruit occasionally wash up on other stretches of sand, so take care if you're beachcombing.

Sexual health

As cases of **sexually transmitted diseases** such as gonorrhoea and even syphilis – not to mention HIV – are on the increase, casual sex is a pretty reckless pastime. Though the government reports 17,000 cases of HIV infection in Trinidad and Tobago, the popularly quoted layman's figure is that one in ten people carry the virus. Bringing **condoms** – and using them – makes sense. Following strenuous government health campaigns, safe sex awareness is fairly good, and condoms are widely available – the most popular local brands are Rough Riders (ribbed) and Panther – but you might feel more secure if you use a familiar brand name from your home country. If you use the **contraceptive pill**, take more supplies than necessary, as vomiting or diarrhoea may lessen its effectiveness.

Women's health

Sadly, it's inevitable that time in the tropics creates the perfect conditions for a bout of **thrush** – bring bifidum acidophilus capsules with you, and take them daily to balance yeasts. Bring plenty of Canesten cream or pessaries, keep heavily perfumed products and soap away from the vagina and always wear cotton underwear if you know you're susceptible. Dehydration and the stress of travel can encourage **cystitis**; to avoid it, drink copious amounts of water and be rigorous about vaginal hygiene. If you suffer regularly, bring sachets of acidifying remedies which contain potassium citrate. You should bring more than enough sanitary protection, as your favourite brand will be more expensive, and bear in mind that flushing towels or tampons down the toilet is will often send them straight to the sea.

For advice on HIV/AIDS, call the **National Aids Hotline;** ☎ 625 2437. For **Alcoholics Anonymous** call ☎ 665 1251, and advice on drug related issues is available on ☎ 627 0337.

Accommodation

Though Trinidad and Tobago are not the most tourist-oriented islands in the Caribbean, this doesn't mean that there's any shortage of places to stay. In Trinidad, due mostly to the annual Carnival invasion and the flow of business travellers and visitors from other Caribbean islands, there is plenty of accommodation in Port of Spain and the larger towns, as well as guesthouses and hotels on or near most of the better beaches. Tourist-oriented Tobago has every category of room in the Crown Point area, and plenty of options throughout the island.

Though it's always reassuring to have pre-arranged somewhere to stay for the first couple of nights, you should have no problem finding suitable accommodation once you've arrived. The staff at the tourist board desks at Piarco and Crown Point airports can direct you to a place that suits your plans and budget. Many hotels, particularly in Tobago, also offer airport pick-ups as an extra incentive.

Though accommodation in T&T is cheaper than you might expect for a Caribbean destination – ranging from as little as US$20 per night for a basic room in Port of Spain to US$50–70 for a standard air-conditioned, balconied unit throughout the islands – it's still likely to be your major **expense**. Most hotels and guesthouses in Trinidad use year-round rates which change only at Carnival time, but in tourist-oriented Tobago, properties tend to have two rates; one for the summer **low season** (mid April–mid Dec) and another for the winter **high season** (mid Dec–mid April). However, many local hoteliers are perfectly open to a bit of **haggling**, particularly in summer. You may also get a discount if you arrange to stay for more than a couple of weeks. Don't be surprised if the Trini in front of you gets the same room at a lower rate; this is normal practice, and ensures that local people get as much from their resorts as the tourists.

There are a couple of hidden extras to watch out for: **room tax** (10–15 percent) and **service charge** (10 percent) are added to quoted room rates. Throughout the Guide, we have taken the tax and service charge into account when giving price codes, but it's worth checking whether these charges have been included each time you rent a room.

■ ACCOMMODATION

Accommodation price codes

All accommodation listed in this guide has been graded according to the following **price categories**:

① under US$10	④ US$35–50	⑦ US$100–150
② US$10–20	⑤ US$50–70	⑧ US$150–200
③ US$20–35	⑥ US$70–100	⑨ US$200 and above

Rates are for the cheapest double or twin rooms, including 10 percent tax and 10 percent service charge where applicable. In Tobago, rates quoted are those used during the high season, normally mid December–mid April. During low season (mid April–mid December) rates are liable to fall by up to 25 percent. There are no high and low seasons in Trinidad, but rates may rise by up to 70 percent during Carnival. Many hotels give rates in US dollars – we have followed suit. Payment can be made in either US or TT currency.

There is one time of year when you simply cannot count on getting a room in Trinidad: three weeks or so before and after **Carnival**. This is the biggest event in the local calendar, and rooms must be booked months in advance – even the grottiest of box-cupboards are in demand, and Carnival regulars don't leave Trinidad without reserving a room for the following year. Most hotels, bed and breakfasts and host homes (see below) offer special Carnival packages for the Friday before Carnival to Ash Wednesday; expect to pay between US$70–90 per night for a basic room, and anything up to US$200 in the smarter hotels. It's worth checking the local newspaper classified columns (the *Express*, *Newsday* and *Guardian* classifieds are available online; see p.33) or, if you have any contacts in Trinidad, asking around to see if any locals have a spare room to rent – many people open up their homes to make a little cash at this time of year and you'll probably pay less than at an established hotel or guesthouse.

Whatever level of accommodation you choose, you can pretty much guarantee that it will be clean; West Indian hygiene standards tend to be high, and even the most basic of rooms will usually be spotless.

Hotels, guesthouses and camping

Most of T&T's **resort-type hotels** cluster around the better beaches of Tobago; here you'll find everything from expansive, landscaped enclaves with hundreds of rooms, high walls and private beaches to "eco-hotels" and holistic havens. In between these are no-nonsense concrete monoliths dedicated to the needs of the package tourist, and legions of 8- to-12-room properties with pastel decor, loud bedspreads and a pool. Thankfully, the **all-inclusive** trend that's swept through the rest of the Caribbean has not yet caught on here. At many resorts, however, you may be offered the option of a "meal plan" – the most common are CP (Continental; room and breakfast), MAP (Modified American; room, breakfast and dinner) or FAP (Full American; room and all meals including snacks and tea etc).

In Trinidad, large-scale hotels meet international standards; air-conditioning, TV (usually satellite or cable), telephone, jacks for internet access, private bathroom with hot water and maybe a balcony as well as restaurants, bar and a pool on site. However, most of the smartest hotels cater largely to business travellers, so you won't find much in the way of organized entertainment or a holiday atmosphere.

It's difficult to define local interpretations of exactly what a **guesthouse** is; it can be a couple of rooms tacked on to a private home or a smoothly run 9-room establishment. Whatever form it takes, you won't necessarily pay any less than you would at a hotel. Generally, though, a guesthouse is a small-scale property with less in the way of facilities than you would expect at a hotel; a pool is not guaranteed and you're more likely to get a fan than an a/c system. You may also be offered cold water or a shared bathroom.

Budget-minded travellers should note that a disproportionately high number of T&T hotel and guesthouse rooms have a **kitchen** or kitchenette (the latter usually consists of a hot plate and fridge), which doesn't necessarily mean a hugely hiked rate. Most provide utensils; make sure that an inventory is taken in your presence to ensure that you are not held liable for breakages that occurred before you arrived.

Lastly, though **camping** is a popular activity for Trinidadian families during holiday weekends – many of whom construct their own makeshift dwellings from tarpaulins rather than using regular tents – it's not recommended in either island unless you are with a local group or can be sure that someone will stay awake to provide security. Hike Seekers (see p.48) lead regular group camps in some of Trinidad's most beautiful unspoiled parts.

Host homes and bed and breakfasts

Private **host homes** and **bed and breakfasts** are excellent and inexpensive accommodation options; neither attract room tax or VAT, and you may get a little more insight into local lifestyles and attitudes than you'd experience in a regular hotel or guesthouse. Monitored and inspected by the tourist board, host homes consist of little more than a spare room in someone's house. They normally rent at around US$35 per person, though owners are often open to a bit of bargaining, especially if you plan an extended stay. Bed and breakfast – basically the same deal as a host home but with your morning meal included in the room rate – is best arranged through the **Bed and Breakfast Associations** that oversee this kind of accommodation. In Trinidad, write to the Trinidad and Tobago Bed and Breakfast Co-Operative, PO Box 532b, Port of Spain, ☎ & fax 663 4413, *la-belle@trinidad.net*, or contact Accommodations Unlimited, corner of Ariapita Avenue and Luis Street, Woodbrook ☎629 3731, fax 628 3737, *owl@opus-net-worx.com*. In Tobago contact Ms Miriam Edwards, c/o Federal Villa, 1–3 Crooks River, Scarborough, ☎639 3926.

What you get for your money varies enormously in both host homes and B&Bs; from a/c and a private bathroom with hot water to a bed, a fan and a shower at the end of the corridor. Whatever the facilities, most hosts tend to be extremely hospitable and great sources of local information. TIDCO's Accommodation booklet (available from their offices worldwide) has extensive listings of host homes and B&Bs on both islands.

Villas, beach houses and long-term rentals

Most **holiday villas** rented to tourists are in Tobago; most have full staff and ample facilities such as a kitchen and pool. Though you might expect a villa to break the bank, they can actually be quite cost effective if you're travelling in a group; plan on paying US$150 per week for the most basic villa to as much as US$4000 for something in the lap of luxury. Most are privately owned, but represented by **agencies**; in Tobago, contact the Tobago Villas Agency on Shirvan Road, PO Box 301, Scarborough, ☎ & fax

639 8737, or Island Investments, 30 Shirvan Rd, ☎639 0929, fax 639 9050, *islreal@tstt.net.tt*. In the UK, try The Owners' Syndicate, 6 Port House, Plantation Wharf, Battersea, London SW11 3TY, ☎020/7801 9801, fax 801 9800, *ownerssyndicate@compuserve.com*

In Trinidad, there are **beach houses** in many "resort" areas; Manzanilla, Mayaro and the Toco coast are particularly well served. Beach houses are generally geared for locals on a break (you'll often have to bring your own towels, linen and kitchen utensils), and you can get some real bargains by scanning the local papers. Bear in mind though, that there are often two rates; one for Trinidadians and another (more expensive) for foreigners; rental periods start from a weekend.

If you are planning to stay in Trinidad for a month or more, it's well worth considering a **furnished apartment**. The best place to start looking is the newspaper classified pages, particularly in the *Trinidad Guardian* (this, the *Express* and *Newsday* include classifieds in their online editions; see p.33). One-bedroom apartments in and around Port of Spain rent at around TT$800–1500 per month, though good deals can be hard to find and you'll probably see loads of rooms before you find one to suit you. Ads for "tourist" or "vacation" accommodation often mean higher rates, though you might get a more palatial apartment for the extra money and you'll probably pay less than in a hotel.

Getting around

Travelling around Trinidad and Tobago takes ingenuity and patience. Public transport is minimal and erratic, and an unofficial, private system of route taxis and maxi taxis has developed to fill the gaps.

There are four types of transport available: **buses, maxi taxis, route taxis** and **private taxis**. If you wish to see more than the urban areas, however, it is advisable to **rent a car**. It is also useful if you're planning to go out late at night; public transport runs all night – albeit infrequently – in Port of Spain and San Fernando, but elsewhere it peters out after midnight. Whatever form of transport you are using, avoid travelling at **peak hours** (6–8am, 3–6pm), when the roads are clogged and maxis and taxis heave with people.

Buses

There is a small network of **public buses**; in Trinidad they travel between towns, cities and villages and in Tobago between Scarborough and outlying villages. The introduction of a rural bus service in Trinidad and an expansion of services in Tobago in recent years have greatly improved bus travel, making it a viable option for the independent traveller. Previously it was an exercise in frustration, and outlying villages were impossible to reach. Now, though the service is still erratic, you will eventually reach your destination. **Bus** stops are often small concrete shelters on the side of the road; sometimes just a sign on a telephone pole. **Tickets** must be bought in advance, either from the main terminus in Port of Spain, the Scarborough bus terminal or from small general stores around the country. Weekly and monthly tickets are available from the main bus stations.

Along **Trinidad**'s east-west corridor, the former course of the railway – running parallel to Eastern Main Road – has been designated a **Priority Bus Route**, reserved for buses and maxis. The service is somewhat flexible in its interpretation of the timetables, so patience is essential. Despite its drawbacks, this is the least expensive and quickest form of transport.

There are two types of buses in Trinidad, the **blue transit** – known as "Super Express" – and the red, white and black **ECS bus**. Despite its name, the blue transit is the slower option, and has no air conditioning or music. You can sit or stand on these – during rush hour they become very sweaty and crowded. ECS buses (weekdays 5am–9pm, weekends 6am–8pm) are quicker and run every ten to fifteen minutes during peak time (7–8am, 4–6pm), at off-peak, every twenty minutes. They are also air-conditioned, play music and allow only seated passengers.

All buses in Trinidad leave and terminate at **City Gate** in Port of Spain. This is the main transport hub of Trinidad, sometimes referred to as **South Quay** in official literature. (It is also the main terminus for maxi taxis that travel across the country.) ECS **fares** from Port of Spain work out at around TT$3 for Tunapuna, TT$4 to Arima, Chaguanas or Piarco airport and TT$6 for a longer haul – to San Fernando or Sangre Grande, for example. Super Express transit costs around 50 cents less and runs from 4am–10pm every half hour. A rural bus service, also leaving from City Gate, now runs from Port of Spain to the following destinations: Blanchisseuse (TT$8), Lopinot (TT$4), Sangre Grande via Toco (TT$4) and Matelot (TT$8) – though the latter was suspended at press time due to road works. The service also connects Arima with Blanchisseuse (TT$8). The rural buses run from 3.30am to 7pm, usually every two hours, though there are more frequent buses at peak hours bringing commuters to and from the commercial centres.

In **Tobago**, all buses leave from the terminal on Greenside Street in Scarborough. The buses are blue-striped minibuses that travel both windward and leeward sides of the island with more frequent services operating at peak hours. The timetable varies and though some information has been included in the appropriate sections, it is always wise to check before setting out. Officially the buses run from Scarborough to Crown Point (TT$2), Charlotteville via the windward coast (TT$8), Mount Thomas via Golden Lane (TT$6), L'Anse Fourmi via the leeward coast (TT$10) and Black Rock (TT$2).

Information on bus services in Trinidad can be obtained from the security office next to the ticket booth in City Gate, or by ringing ☎623 2262 ext 291, or 234. For information on buses in Tobago call ☎639 2293.

Maxi taxis

Maxi taxis are minibuses containing ten to twenty people – privately owned but formed into associations with set routes and standardized fares. In the past they were famed for their loud music, which made the maxi a travelling disco, but a law – passed to assuage worries that children were grooving aboard their favourite "party maxi" after school – now requires drivers to pay for a license if they wish to play music in their vehicles.

A ride in a maxi can be an entertaining experience, however. The interior often reflects the tastes of the owner, and may declare anything from religious faith to a devotion to love, money and good times. More ornate maxis have padded ceilings, photographs of favourite personalities and hand-painted interiors. Many have a recognizable slogan across their front windshield: the nickname of the driver, perhaps ("Mister Painter", "Young Adult" or "Black Man Redemption"), or their personal motto.

The maxis are organized by region and have **colour-coded** stripes relating to the area in which they work. Each area has a main meeting point for maxis in the nearest large town. In Trinidad, **yellow-striped** vehicles work from Port of Spain to the Western Tip; **red stripes** in the east; **green stripes** in the centre and south of the island; **black stripes** in and around Princes Town; and

brown stripes from San Fernando to the southwest peninsula. **Blue-striped** maxis operate in Tobago; there is only one set route, from Scarborough to Charlotteville, and the rest are used mainly to ferry schoolchildren or as private charters for tourists.

As the vehicles are privately owned they are a law unto themselves, with **no set timetable**. There are more of them around during busy periods (every five minutes between 6–10am and 3–8pm). The later it gets, the fewer there are; after 8pm you can expect a 10- to 20-minute wait. During the night, maxis run intermittently, serving areas with fetes and concerts, and commuting between the major towns.

Maxi **routes** radiate out from the main centres, which means that to get from one small town to another you may have to travel twice the distance. They can be hailed anywhere along their route – just stick out your hand and if they have space they will pick you up – but it is often quicker to go to the main stand; since maxis wait until they are full before leaving, they may not have free seats until they reach their destination. Once you are aboard, the maxis will let you off at any point; press the buzzers by the windows, just above head height, to stop the bus.

Fares are fixed, and go up only when the price of petrol does. The rates are not displayed as it is presumed that everyone knows their fare. Where possible these prices have been listed in the guide. Usually these range between TT$2 and TT$5; from Port of Spain, for example, it costs TT$3 to Chaguanas, TT$4 to Arima and TT$5 to San Fernando. Long distances to out-of-the-way places work out to be more expensive as you will probably have to take more than one maxi. If you're unsure of the fare, it is best to give TT$10 and wait for the change (you're not likely to be short-changed, and besides it's a very small sum).

It takes a while to get used to the maxi system in T&T as there are many variables: drivers sometimes make detours to pick up more passengers, or take a faster route if the vehicle is full. **Off-route drops** may also be made, though this depends on the driver's good will and the destination requested.

Route taxis and private taxis

Route taxis follow similar rules to maxis, but they rarely have a main meeting point; the stands for their various destinations are scattered around the towns and cities. They can take a maximum of **five passengers** and are usually slightly more expensive than maxis. Taxis will not leave their stand until they are full, which means you may have to wait while the driver cries out, "one to go". They are usually quicker than maxis as they have fewer passengers and therefore stop less, but they are more cramped as everyone squeezes in with shopping bags and personal belongings. They are every bit as entertaining as maxis, as passengers will often strike up conversations about current affairs and controversial topics.

To stop a taxi en route, hail it with your hand. There is a widely accepted code of **hand signals**; point left or right to indicate which direction you want to take at the next major turn-off. When entering the car it is normal to greet the other passengers with a "good morning" or a "good afternoon". To stop the taxi tell your driver you want to get off as you approach your destination – in Trini speak, "nex corner drive".

Private taxis take you directly to your destination, with you as the only passenger. They are **unmetered**, so a price must be agreed beforehand, and they can work out to be just as expensive as a cab in Britain or the US. If you want to be taken door to door, they are the only official option, although it is often possible – and more economical – to bargain with a route taxi driver to drop you where you want.

The only way to distinguish between private cars and vehicles for hire is the **number plate**: private cars have **P** at the front, route taxis (and maxis, though these are easily recognizable by their stripes; see above) have **H** for hire. Some P licensed cars also operate as taxis. These are actually illegal, but have become an accepted part of the transport system. They usually operate late at night or on small distances restricted to a few roads, and their main raison d'etre seems to be to transport people with large bags of shopping up steep hills – although many look as though they wouldn't be able to drive five metres.

Driving

Driving in T&T requires **patience** and constant **alertness**; you simply cannot take your eyes off the road for one moment, and the packed streets of Port of Spain with their complicated one-way systems can be a nightmare at first. Throughout the islands, drivers will habitually stop at short notice, turn without indicating and happily block the traffic to stop and chat with a friend. The best thing to do is accept it; beeping your horn out of irritation will just get you withering stares, though horns are widely used as a thank-you gesture and as an indication of an intention to overtake.

Often you will feel that Trinbago drivers must have a sixth sense that enables them to judge when taxis and maxis will brake sharply in front of them or when cars might overtake (often on corners) despite oncoming traffic; you probably don't, so stay aware of the position of taxis and maxis, expecting them to brake at any moment, and always drive **defensively**. Trinbago drivers are generally courteous, especially when confronted with a rental car, often stopping to allow you to pull out or shouting advice whether you need it or not. Some, however, take to the road at night with only one headlight or taillight, and being dazzled by full-beam headlights soon becomes the norm. Flash once to alert the other driver; if they don't dip, reduce speed and keep your eyes to the left verge of the road. Another puzzling practice is the use of **hand signals**, an art which route taxi drivers have perfected and one which is often appropriated by those gesturing in the middle of a heated in-car debate. In general, an up-and-down movement indicates that the driver in front is about to stop, though it can be an instruction to stop due to a hazard ahead. Whatever the motivation, slow down if faced with a hand signal.

Though the wide lanes and fast flow are actually less of a problem than traffic and pedestrian-choked city streets, driving on **highways** can feel initially hair-raising – a favourite Trinbago habit is a high-speed weaving technique which looks as though it ought to cause a multiple pile-up, but rarely does. In such cases, take extra care, especially behind taxis and in the **tropical rains**. Storms often seem to come out of nowhere, catching drivers unawares and causing plenty of accidents as visibility is reduced and the wet and oily road surfaces turn into the equivalent of black ice; slow down and put on your headlights if necessary.

Local **traffic lights** can be confusing. There are usually three, each relating to the relevant lanes; left for left-hand turn-offs, middle for straight on, right for right-hand turns. In Tobago, you'll see drivers breaking red lights to make a left-hand turn; this is entirely legal so long as you come to a full stop at the line and check that the coast is clear before moving off. In Trinidad, you'll see flashing red or yellow lights at major road junctions; both mean "proceed with caution"; yellow means it's primarily your right of way, red that it's someone else's.

A widespread disrespect for authority, and the idea that "we don't drive fast enough to have an accident", mean that many traffic regulations are cheerfully ignored. The wearing of **seat belts**, is compulsory, but is seldom practised or enforced. **Drinking and driving** is also illegal, though the attitude toward it is more laid back in T&T than in some other countries; many people will go to the beach at the weekend, have a few drinks and drive home. The law also demands that drivers be properly attired; it's possible to be charged for "driving bareback", so always keep a T-shirt handy.

You'll find **Tobago's** roads much quieter than those in Trinidad; the main hazards are blind corners on tiny roads (sound your horn if you can't see), the occasional monumental pothole, and cows put out to graze by the road. Both Tobagonians and their animals tend to take their time when moving out of the way or crossing the road; drive slowly, particularly if you have to cross an animal's tethering rope. The **roads** in T&T are much better than those on many other Caribbean islands due to the country's relative prosperity and natural access to the finest asphalt in the world from the Pitch Lake (see p.221). Despite these advantages, and the government's best

efforts, you will still find bumpy roads; the country straddles geological fault lines which break up the surface with annoying frequency. In some areas, such as southwest Trinidad, the roads have to be repaired every few months.

Road signs are based on the **English system** (although distances and speed limits are in kilometres), and you must drive on the left. The speed limit is **80kph** on highways and **55kph** on main roads in built-up areas. Tobago's speed limit is **50kph**.

Petrol stations are scarce outside urban areas – in Tobago, those in Scarborough stay open until 11pm–midnight, but others shut up shop by 9pm (see p.319 for details). It is therefore wise to keep the tank full, especially if you're planning to make long journeys. Though there have been improvements in their hours, opening earlier and later, most are only open for a few hours on Sunday.

Car rental

Of the major **international chains**, only Thrifty has locations on Trinidad and Tobago, though both Holiday Autos and Suncars work through local suppliers; there are however many local firms (see box below). All companies require you to be **25 or over** and have held a driving licence for a minimum of two years; and most firms request a deposit, usually a credit card imprint. All request that you carefully check the car before you take it away. You may be offered a **collision damage waiver** at extra cost (usually US$3–5

Car Rental Firms Abroad

UK

Holiday Autos ☎ 0870/400 0000, *www.holidayautos.com*

Suncars ☎ 0870/500 5566, *www.suncars.com*

Thrifty ☎ 01494/751600, *www.thrifty.co.uk*

North America

Budget ☎ 1-800/527-0700, *www.budgetrentacar.com*

Dollar ☎ 1-800/421-6868 or 1-800/800-6000, *www.dollarcar.com*

Kemwel Holiday Autos ☎ 1-800/422-7737, *www.kemwel.com*

Thrifty ☎ 1-800/367-2277, *www.thrifty.com*

Australia

Avis ☎ 13 6333; *www.avis.com*

Hertz ☎ 13 3039, 1800/654 313, *www.hertz.com*

Thrifty ☎ 1300/367 227, *www.thrifty.com.au*

New Zealand

Avis ☎ 09/526 2847 or 0800 655 111 *www.avis.com*

Hertz ☎ 0800 654 321, *www.hertz.com*

Thrifty ☎ 0800 737070, *www.thrifty.co.nz*

Car, Motorbike and Bike Rental Firms in Trinidad and Tobago

Trinidad

Cars

Auto Rentals, Piaro Airport ☎ 669 2277. One of Trinidad's largest car rental firms with eight branches around the islands.

Econo Cars (*econocar@trinidad.net*), 191–193 Western Main Rd, Cocorite ☎ 622 8072; Piarco Airport ☎ 669 1119. One of the cheapest firms around.

Kalloo's Car Rental, 32 Ariapita Ave, Port of Spain ☎ 669 4868, ext 6320. Friendly and efficient, with branches throughout Trinidad and Tobago, including the airport.

Singh's, 7–9 Wrightson Rd, Port of Spain ☎ 623 0150, fax 627 8746, *singhs1@tstt.net.tt*. Huge, spanking-new fleet, reasonable rates, 24hr call-out service and several branches islandwide, including Piarco.

Motorcycles

Greene's General Cycle Ltd, cnr Skinner St and Eastern Main Rd, Arouca, ☎ 646 2453 or 646 7433, *greenes@tstt.net.tt*. Trinidad's only motorcycle and scooter rental service.

Tobago

Cars

Auto Rentals, Crown Point ☎ 639 0644. Located next to the airport building this firm has branches on both islands.

Baird's, Crown Point ☎ 639 2528. Rents jeeps, buses, motorbikes and scooters at reasonable rates.

Convenient, Tropical Marine, Western Main Rd, Chaguaramas ☎ & fax 634 4017, *crl@carib-link.net*. Reasonable rates and excellent personalized service; with a branch in central Trinidad.

Rattan's, Crown Point ☎ 639 8271. Has an branch close to the airport. Friendly service.

Rollocks, Crown Point ☎ 639 0328. Small local firm renting jeeps and cars based near the airport.

Sherman's, Lambeau ☎ 639 2292 or 639 3084. *shermans@trinidad.net*. Extremely efficient and helpful service; will deliver car to your hotel or meet you at the airport. Free day of car rental with every seven days rented.

Signal, Chaguaramas Hotel and Convention Centre, Western Main Rd, Chaguaramas ☎ 800 2277 (toll-free). Excellent rates, with airport pickups/dropoffs.

Singh's, Crown Point ☎ 639 0624, *singhs1@tstt.net.tt*. Large fleet, reasonable rates and a 24hr call-out service; with a branch in Trinidad.

Thrifty, Crown Point and *Turtle Beach* hotel ☎ 639 8507 or 8062. Friendly, reliable service based at the airport.

Motorcycles

Baird's, Crown Point ☎ 639 2528. Reliable local firm with reasonable rates.

Bicycles

First Class, Crown Point, pager ☎ 662 3377, ID1973. Bicycles are displayed on the roadside by the entrance to Store Bay beach.

Fun Rides, Shirvan Rd ☎ 639 8889. Convenient to Mount Irivine and Buccoo.

Glorious Rides, Pigeon Point junction ☎ 639 7124. Cheap and cheerful service.

Marco Polo Tourism, Mount Irvine Beach car park ☎ 639 7420. Offers bike rentals, as well as tours and sports activities.

---

per day); without one, you may be liable for damage. If your car is stolen and you don't have the keys, you will have to pay the car's replacement costs, so never leave keys in a parked car. **Prices** vary according to the time of year and the availability of promotional rates or frequent-flyer discounts, so shop around; they tend to start at around US$35 per day in Trinidad and US$50 in Tobago for the smallest vehicle, inclusive of third-party insurance and unlimited kilometres. Larger companies can usually rent you **baby car-seats** on request.

A valid international **driving license** or one issued in the US, Canada or the UK is required for driving both cars and motorcycles for up to ninety days. Apply to the Licensing Division on Wrightson Road, Port of Spain (☎ 625 1031) if you intend to stay longer.

Travelling between Trinidad and Tobago

There are two options available if you wish to travel between the islands – the **ferry**, slow but inexpensive, and the **plane**, quick but pricier. It is far easier to go by air, though if you have spare time the boat crossing can be a romantic starlit experience.

Travelling from Trinidad to Tobago, boats leave Monday to Friday at 2pm, and Saturday and Sunday at 11am, from the Government Shipping Passenger Service opposite Twin Towers on Wrightson Road, Port of Spain, usually at 2pm. This journey takes five to six hours and can be rough – take **sea-sickness tablets**, as strong currents in the Bocas make even the staunchest stomach queasy. The crossing from Tobago to Trinidad is usually calmer; the boat leaves at 11pm Monday to Sunday from the Scarborough docks on Carrington Street.

Tickets cost TT$50–60 return for a seat, a cabin for two is TT$160. These should be bought in advance, unless you're prepared to join the queue at least three hours before the boat leaves. The ticket office at the Government Shipping Service in Port of Spain is open Mon–Fri, 7am–3pm. In Scarborough, you can buy tickets at the ferry terminal on Carrington Street. For further information call ☎625 4906 or 3055 ext160 or 161, or 623 2901, or look up *www.patnt.com/ferry.htm*

Since Air Caribbean closed down in October 2000 the main inter-island operator is BWIA – though LIAT (☎627 6274) also makes a daily flight between the islands (TT$300 return). Currently, BWIA offer a daily service of seven to ten flights a day

---

Travelling between the Caribbean islands

Three **airlines** fly between Trinidad and Tobago and other Caribbean islands and nearby destinations. BIWA (☎627 2942,*www.bwee.com*) flies from Trinidad to Barbados (1–3 flights daily), Antigua (1 daily), Jamaica (1–2 daily), Grenada (3 daily), St Maarten (3 times a week), St Vincent (1 daily), St Lucia (2 daily), Guyana (3 daily) and Caracas (2 daily). LIAT (☎627 6274) flies from Trinidad (5 flights daily) and Tobago (1 daily) to all islands in the eastern Caribbean, linking up with various connecting flights. Caribbean Star, (☎268/480 2561, *www.flycaribbeanstar.com*) flies to Antigua (2 flights daily), Dominica (2 daily), Grenada (2 daily), St Kitts (1 daily), St Vincent (2 daily) and Tortola (1 daily) from Trinidad.

BWIA and LIAT both sell Caribbean air passes that allow for multiple trips around the Caribbean on their airline only. LIAT charges US$85 plus taxes for each island visited, three to six islands allowed within one month. Possible islands include Puerto Rico, St Thomas, St Croix, Tortola, St Kitts, Anguilla, Nevis, Saint Martin, Antigua, Guadeloupe, Dominica, Martinique, St Lucia, Barbados, St Vincent, Grenada and T&T. The pass can only be bought outside the Caribbean in conjunction with a long-distance air ticket. BWIA's thirty-day air pass costs US$468 and covers fewer islands. You must book your full itinerary in advance (changes cost US$20), fly BWIA from the US, and you may not visit any island more than once unless it's a stopover en route to another island.

As with everything in the Caribbean, airlines are more informal than their European and American counterparts. Flights are cancelled at the last minute and planes do not necessarily leave on time. Always ring ahead to check your departure time, and be prepared to alter your plans.

For those who prefer a slower pace of travel, traveling by **boat** is an inexpensive alternative to high airline prices. *M/V Windward* (☎624 2279, fax 627 5091) is a reasonably priced 600-metre passenger and cargo boat that connects Trinidad with St Lucia, Barbados, St Vincent and Venezuela. Predominantly a cargo boat, transporting mainly bananas, it unloads for several hours at each port allowing passengers to do a little sightseeing. The itinerary changes according to cargo pickups and holidays so it's wise to call ahead before making any plans. Cabins are available, though it's wise to book them ahead of boarding, as they're popular, and there's a restaurant and duty-free shop on board. Ticket prices start from US$50 for a one-way trip, depending on the destination. Another option frequently used by backpackers is offering to serve as crew for yachts cruising around the Caribbean. In exchange for cooking, cleaning and other menial tasks free transport may be given. Hang around the marinas and get friendly with yacht owners if you want to pursue this option.

(TT$150 one way and TT$300 return); check with the airline for flight details (in Trinidad ☎627 2942, in Tobago ☎660 2942). For general enquiries on flight arrivals and departures ring Piarco Airport ☎669 8048 ext 247 or 204 during office hours) or Crown Point International Airport ☎639 8547.

Communications, post and phones

passport or a driving license. If items are valuable it is better to have them sent by registered mail.

Most towns and villages have a **post office**; these are open from Monday to Friday from 8am to 4.15pm. **Post boxes** on the street are small, red, rare and easily missed; many still bear the insignia of the British postal service, a survival of the colonial era. **Stamps** are sold at post offices. Letters and postcards to anywhere in the world cost TT$3.25. Beautiful aerogrammes, decorated with scarlet ibises, can be sent worldwide for TT$1 from any post office.

There is no need to be out of touch when you are in Trinidad and Tobago. There are public payphones – most of which can be used to make international calls – all over the country, while the postal service is trustworthy.

Mail

Since the running of the postal service – now snappily known as TT Post – was taken over by a New Zealand-based firm, services have become a lot more reliable. Outgoing and incoming **post** travels reasonably quickly (one to two weeks to Europe and the US, three to Australia). The closer you are to the capital, the sooner you will get your letters.

If your post is a matter of urgency, it is best to arrange a **private box** at the general post office in the capital; you can then have your letters sent poste restante to any post office in T&T. They will keep your mail for up to two weeks – to collect you must bring ID such as a

---

Useful numbers

Area code for Trinidad and Tobago 868
Local and international operator 0
Directory enquiries 6411

Phoning abroad from Trinidad and Tobago
International calls from private phones (not with a Companion card), are cheaper between 5pm and 8am.

To the UK dial 011, then 44 then the area code (without the first zero) and number. Cost TT$4.50 per min.

To the US and Canada dial 1, then the area code and number. Cost TT$4.50 per min.

To Australia dial 011, then 61, then area code and number. Cost TT$6.85 per min.

To New Zealand dial 011, then 64. Cost TT$6.85 per minute.

Phones

Using the **telephone** in T&T is simple. Following incidences of fraudulent use of phonecards, public phones that take phonecards only are being phased out, replaced with units that take twenty-five cent coins for local calls; you'll need to put in a dollars' worth minimum if you're calling a cellular phone.

The easiest and cheapest way to make **international calls** is to use the **Companion phonecards** issued by Telecommunication Service of T&T (TSTT) and available in newsagents, pharmacies, supermarkets and TSTT offices. These come in denominations of TT$10, TT$30, TT$60 and TT$100 (exclusive of VAT). Each has a security number (you scratch off the security strip to find it), which you punch in after dialling ☎888 2273 from any public or private phone. You then dial the international number, and are advised of your credit balance before being put through. Hotels and guesthouses offer a telephone service but the rates are usually a lot higher than using a Companion card. Numbers that are toll-free in the US can be called from T&T

by dialling 880 rather than 800 – you will be charged TT$6 per minute.

You can **rent a cellular phone** from Caribel (☎652 4982, *www.caribel.com*) for around US$35 per week plus call charges; rentals can be arranged online and phones can be delivered anywhere in Trinidad. Bear in mind that you'll pay for both incoming and outgoing calls. If you're planning on bringing your own cellphone to T&T, note that only tri-band units will work

As TSTT has a monopoly your **mobile** phone will not work on the islands unless you register with them on the number below. Phones must be TDMA and digital compatible. The company offers two options. The prepaid card service requires TT$215 to activate and cards worth TT$30, TT$75, TT$100 or TT$200 (excluding VAT); calls are charged at TT$1.99 off-peak, TT$2.99 peak. The "roamer" service will activate your phone every time you come to T&T and costs TT$115 to activate, TT$100 to license, with a TT$1000 deposit billed to a credit card for international calls and a TT$15 per day activation charge. Call **Mobile Phone Enquiries** ☎800 2355 for details..

The media

Dipping into the local media is an excellent way to acclimatize yourself to the nation's cultural and political life. From the outspoken columnists and scurrilous headlines of the daily papers to the many locally produced slots on TV, the media offer a fascinating picture of Trini society – especially during Carnival, when TV shows preview costumes, road march songs and fetes, and the papers hotly debate the merits of the year's calypsos.

Newspapers

Trinidad's main **daily newspaper** is the *Trinidad Guardian* (*www.guardian.co.tt*), a stately broadsheet with a somewhat conservative attitude. The other well-established dailies are the tabloid *Express* (*www.trinidadexpress.com*) and *Newsday* (*www.newsday.co.tt*); picture-dominat-

ed with plenty of space for their sometimes outspoken **columnists** – look out for Kevin Baldeosingh and Keith Smith. All the dailies have fat weekend editions with extended music, lifestyle and kiddies' features, but the selection of salacious weekend scandal rags – *Bomb, Blast, Heat, The Mirror* and particularly *Sunday Punch* – are incredibly popular; *Blast* claims to be the most widely read title in T&T. All carry hysterical headlines and plenty of bikini-clad women, as well as some wicked political satire and thinly disguised attacks on public figures. **Tobago** boasts only one paper, *Tobago News*, which is published on Fridays and concentrates on local events. Sold at Piarco and Crown Point airports, supermarkets and book stores, **foreign** magazines – *Time, Newsweek, Cosmopolitan* etc – are easy to get, but newspapers – bar *USA Today* –

Radio stations and frequencies

Radio 90.5, 90.5 FM. Indian music.

Swar Milan, 91.1 FM. Indian music and religious programming.

Hott 93, 93.1 & 93.5. Comedy, local music and chat.

Love FM, 94.1 FM. Gospel music and religious programming.

The Rock, 95.1 FM. Nonstop "alternative" music (mostly soft rock) for the more mature listener.

WEFM, 96.1 FM. Pumping local music, good breakfast show with Nikki Crosby (5–9am) and reggae, hip-hop and R&B from Matsimela sound system and Rodney "Fireball" King.

Radio 97, 97 FM. Dated hits from the 1970s, 80s, and 90s, interrupted only by news and sports reports.

YES FM, 98.9 FM. Lively and firmly music-based, with soca, reggae and hip-hop.

100 FM. News and easy-listening music.

Masala, 101.1 FM. Indian music, chutney and chat.

Power 102, 102 FM. Soca and reggae, interspersed with lighthearted chat; humorist Sprangalang dons the headphones Mon–Fri 2–6pm.

103 FM. Music and talk with an Indian flavour.

104 FM, News, business and sports reports, comedy and talk shows.

The Vibe (Comedy Tempo), 105 FM. Comedy, news and music, with the excellent Errol Fabian and Rachel Price breakfast show (5–9am).

Sangeet Radio, 106.1 FM. Indian film music and chutney.

Radio Trinidad, 730 AM. Magazine programmes, government info slots and music.

are practically nonexistent; try the airports. Of the local glossies, lifestyle and culture magazine *Ibis* and women's magazine *Esse* are worth a look, and Carnival souvenir magazines from previous years provide a good insight into T&T's biggest festival; all magazines are sold in pharmacies and supermarkets. Local newspapers are sold at petrol stations, supermarkets, pharmacies and by vendors who trade at busy corners.

TV and radio

Trinidad and Tobago have two **terrestrial TV** stations. TV6 broadcasts on channels six and eighteen, and government-owned TTT on channels two and thirteen. All show American soaps and game shows – *The Bold and the Beautiful* and *The Young and the Restless* maintain as strong a grip on the local imagination as they do in most other Caribbean islands – alongside some more locally focused programming. Local news (plus the main international stories) is shown on TV6 at 8am, 5pm, 6pm and a main slot at 7pm, while TTT has news headlines at 6am, 6pm and 9pm. **Cable TV** is universally available in Trinidad and Tobago; many hotels also have **satellite TV**.

Radio is hugely popular in Trinidad and Tobago. As well as keeping the nation tapping its collective toes, the radio is a good source of information on upcoming events and parties. Talk shows give insight into local culture and attitudes, while music programming reflects Trinidad's kaleidoscopic musical styles (see pp.341–347). From November until Ash Wednesday, most stations are entirely devoted to soca and calypso, but after Carnival, the mood switches abruptly and you'll hear reggae, R&B, hip-hop, rock and the inevitable "slow jams". The best stations to hear contemporary local music are **Yes FM, POWER 102, The Vibe** (Comedy Tempo) and **WE FM** (With Energy For Music). Daily newspapers carry listings of radio programmes.

Trouble, harassment and drugs

Visiting Trinidad and Tobago poses few security risks. Most islanders are generally more interested in going about their business than in harassing you or one another, and though downtown Port of Spain can feel a bit hairy at night, it's hardly a den of iniquity with a criminal on every corner.

If you use your common sense and take the **precautions** you would in any strange environment, you should find the prospect of trouble is minimal. Avoid walking alone or in small groups late at night or on deserted beaches and forest trails, keep flashy jewellery to a minimum, think twice before accepting lifts from strangers and don't go telling everyone where you're staying – or letting new acquaintances into your hotel room. Carry only as much cash as you need, get small bills when changing money so that you don't have to pull out wads of hundreds and never leave belongings unattended on a beach or in a car. Have your valuables locked in a hotel safe or use the security deposit box if you have one. In **rural areas** of both islands, you have lit-

> To call the police in an emergency, dial
> ☎ 999; for emergency services (fire and
> ambulance), it's ☎ 990.

tle to fear – many Tobagonian doors are still sometimes left unlocked – but as a foreigner you may be a target. If you're unlucky enough to be the victim of theft or other offences, report the incident immediately, as you'll need a police report to make any insurance claim. Local officers are generally pleasant and happy to help, though things may take a little longer than you're used to.

Trinidadians are far more likely to avoid tourists than hassle them; even in the more heavily tourist-oriented Tobago, **harassment** hasn't reached anything like the proportions you'd encounter in more established destinations. Many locals make their living from foreign visitors; you will be approached on the beach by vendors selling crafts or aloe vera, but most are extremely polite and rarely pushy. If you do feel that someone is hassling you, letting other people know will probably embarrass the offender into checking his or her behaviour. Remember, though, that you are in someone else's country and that personal space may not be as important here as it is at home, so try not to get worked up over trivialities.

Drugs

It's common for visitors to the Caribbean to assume that all West Indians move around in a permanent haze of marijuana smoke. Though many people do of course indulge, this is hardly the reality. **Cannabis** (also weed, herb, ganja) is illegal to grow, sell or possess in Trinidad and Tobago, and penalties are severe. Tourists caught in possession are highly likely to be deported without a moment's notice, and jail sentences and fines are frequently imposed; the excuse that "it's OK at home to carry a little marijuana for personal use" is not acceptable. Local people who choose to smoke do so with extreme caution, shutting windows and doors and lighting plenty of incense. You probably will be offered weed (sometimes sold ready-rolled), particularly in Tobago. If you don't want it, refuse politely and firmly; if you do, be extremely careful about who you buy from, and equally cautious when smoking. Don't light up in the street, bars, nightclubs and popular beaches, and never leave the associated paraphernalia lying around your hotel room.

Marijuana is not the only illegal drug with a local following; powder and, particularly, **crack cocaine** are becoming increasingly common in T&T. Geographically well-placed as a convenient transshipment point from South America, both Trinidad and Tobago have been badly affected; narcotics police regularly patrol stretches of the coastline, and there are "crack blocks" in every large town.

However, you are more likely to be offered the drug in Tobago, where some visitors' taste for cocaine has provided a lucrative market. The same rules apply as with marijuana; if you are offered it, refuse calmly and politely. Also remember that where there is crack, there is also **crack-related crime**, including robberies and muggings; be wary walking late at night, check the security of your hotel room and beware of putting too much trust in new-found friends. Finally, do not consider taking drugs out of the country under any circumstances; customs officers have seen all the methods of concealment before and it is highly likely that you will be caught.

Women travellers

Like other Caribbean countries, T&T has a predominantly macho culture. Trinbago women usually go out in groups or with their partners, so be prepared to meet surprised reactions if you're a woman travelling on your own.

As independent travellers are still a novelty in the country, women travelling solo will experience a greater degree of **harassment** than they would in Europe, the US or Australia. However, this usually consists of verbal comments and is rarely threatening. It's customary in T&T to be friendly to strangers, acknowledge people passing in the street and even make small talk with them. As a woman you will be expected to be flattered by the attention, and the comments are often very humorous – though also very direct and sometimes very lewd. It is important that you follow all the normal safety precautions, but you are more likely to find people warning you to be careful than actually to experience any trouble.

Foreign women, of all ethnicities, will usually get more of this attention. The idea of women visiting the Caribbean to find romance is so entrenched that as an independent woman traveller expect to be approached by men with this in mind. In Tobago, the situation is so common that some men will openly introduce themselves as "beach bums," and the terms "rent-a-dread" and "rastitute" are often heard. If sex is not on your agenda, say no and mean it; giggling, blushing or presenting the boyfriend-back-home excuse will be read as a come-on. If you feel that someone has a sexual interest in you, trust your instincts; they probably do. Even women in couples will be approached – so don't think because your partner is on hand you'll escape the "sweet talk".

On the whole it is best to watch the Trinbago women and learn. They are confident and assertive and will respond to comments politely but firmly, often with a joke. T&T is still a traditional society; in

Women's organizations

There are lots of international organizations based in T&T with sections dedicated to women, often with both local and foreign women members. **Network** (☎ 628 9655) is a subsidiary of an NGO relating to women that can put you in touch with the relevant group. The **Women's Affairs Division** (☎ 625 7425 ext 265) is a government department that oversees NGOs focusing on women's issues activities, and includes the **Domestic Violence** (☎ 800 7283) and **Rape Crisis** (☎ 622 7273 or 622 1079).

towns and cities women will be smartly dressed in shirts and skirts, leaving the more revealing outfits to fetes and parties. If you want to reduce unwant-

ed attention it is best to follow their example. Swimsuits and bikinis should be restricted to the beach or the river – many local women bathe with a t-shirt and shorts over their swimwear, and nude or topless sunbathing is definitely not acceptable on T&T's beaches – it's also illegal.

Feminism has made few inroads here, though women make up nearly 40 percent of the workforce. **Sexism** remains an accepted part of Trini life. Women are a favourite topic for Trinbagonian men, who usually refer to them as "tings". Trini men are known for their smooth "lyrics", as chat-up lines are known locally. These are often imaginative but usually very crude. An unending source of debate in male Trinbago culture is women's bottoms. Highly popular calypsos on this subject include "Wine up to the Big Truck" by Machel Montano and the controversial hit by Iwer George, "Bottom in the Road".

Disabled travellers

There is little infrastructure in place for those with disabilities in Trinidad and Tobago. A small but growing number of hotels and guesthouses do have disabled facilities; these are mentioned in the text where they are available.

If you want to make local contacts, try **Disabled Peoples' International** or **Disabled Woman Network**, both based at 13a Wrightson Rd, Port of Spain (☎ 625 6658 or 627 0203).

Planning a holiday

Organised tours and holidays are available specifically for people with disabilities – Tripscope will put you touch with specialists for trips to a certain country. If you want to be more independent in your travels, it's important to become an authority on when you must be self-reliant and when you may expect help, especially regarding transport and accommodation. It is also vital to be honest – with travel agencies, insurance companies and travel companions. Know your limitations and make sure others know them. If you do not use a wheelchair all

the time but your walking capabilities are limited, remember that you are likely to need to cover greater distances while travelling (often over rougher terrain and in hotter temperatures) than you are used to. If you use a wheelchair, have it serviced before you go and carry a repair kit.

Read your travel insurance small print carefully to make sure that people with a pre-existing medical condition are not excluded. And use your travel agent to make your journey simpler: airline or bus companies can cope better if they are expecting you, with a wheelchair provided at airports and staff primed to help. A medical certificate of your fitness to travel, provided by your doctor, is also extremely useful; some airlines or insurance companies may insist on it. Make sure that you have extra supplies of drugs – carried with you if you fly – and a prescription including the generic name in case of emergency. Carry spares of any clothing or equipment that might be hard to find; if there's an association representing people with your disability, contact them early in the planning process.

Contacts for travellers with disabilities

UK
Tripscope, The Vassall Centre, Guild Ave, Fishponds, Bristol BS16 2QQ (☎ 08457/585641, fax 0117 9397736, *www.justmobility.co.uk/tripscope*). A UK-registered charity which provides a national telephone information service offering free advice on international transport for those with mobility problems.

North America
Directions Unlimited, 123 Green Lane, Bedford Hills, NY 10507 ☎ 1-800/533 5343 or 914/241 1700. Tour operator specializing in custom tours for people with disabilities.
Travel Information Service ☎ 215/456 9600. Telephone-only information and referral service.

Wheels Up! ☎ 1-888/389-4335, *www.wheelsup.com*. Offers discounts on airfare, tours and cruises for disabled travellers. Also publishes a free monthly newsletter.

Australia
ACROD (Australian Council for Rehabilitation of the Disabled), PO Box 60, Curtin ACT 2605, (☎ 02 6282 4333); 24 Cabarita Road, Cabarita NSW 2137 (☎ 02 9743 2699). Provides lists of travel agencies and tour operators for people with disabilities.

New Zealand
Disabled Persons Assembly, 4/173-175 Victoria St, Wellington, New Zealand (☎ 04/801 9100). Resource centre with lists of travel agencies and tour operators for people with disabilities.

Food and drink

One of the highlights of time spent in Trinidad and Tobago is the chance to sample the fantastic cuisine, a unique and addictive blend of African, Indian, Chinese, European and Latin American influences. It's hard to overemphasize the centrality of food to Trinbagonian culture; a true Trini would never lime without a full stomach, and many leisure activities – river or beach limes – revolve around the preparation of food. It's rare to visit a private home without being offered something to eat, and you may be regarded as rude if you refuse, but as the local cuisine is so good, you'll find yourself hungry more often than not.

Trinbagonian cuisine

Although you may be offered insipid tourist-oriented fare in T&T's larger hotels, **local cooking** still reigns supreme for the most part. "Local" can mean anything from **Indian curry** and **roti** to Creole coocoo and oil down (see below), or Spanish and **South American**-style **pastelles** and **arepas** (Christmas cornflour patties filled with ground meat, olives and raisins and cooked wrapped in a banana leaf).

Local cooks have a far lighter hand with the **hot pepper** than you might expect, preferring to allow the delicate flavours of fresh herbs such as the ubiquitous coriander-like **chadon beni** to come through. Heat is added later at the table, in liberal dashes of fiery **hot pepper sauce**. This can be shop-bought, but is home-made by serious cooks, most of whom also add a dash of marinade – their own secret recipe – to everything they cook. If you don't like things too hot, remember to say so when eating out, or your meal may be automatically smothered with pepper sauce and a gloopy conglomerate of tomato ketchup and mustard; if you like things a bit spicy, ask for "slight pepper".

Creole cooking

In culinary terms, **Creole** refers to African-style cooking which has picked up many other influences along the way. Usually served with a slice of **zaboca** (avocado), **pelau** is classically Creole, utilizing the "browning down" tradition of caramelizing meat in nearly burnt brown sugar. The layer of semi-burnt food at the bottom of the pan is regarded by some as the best part of the dish. Pelau centres on chicken, to which rice, pigeon peas, garlic, onions and vegetables are added and cooked in coconut milk; its poor cousin is well-seasoned **vegetable rice**.

Caramelizing is also used to make the traditional Sunday **baked chicken**, accompanied by cheesy macaroni pie and potato or green fig salad. Another Creole staple is **callaloo**; chopped dasheen leaves cooked with okra coconut milk and occasionally crab meat into a glutinous, pleasantly slimy mixture that's sometimes pureed into a soup. It's often served with **coocoo**, a kind of cornmeal polenta flavoured with okra. Almost always backed up by a hearty rearguard of ground provisions (see "Fruit and vegetables", p.40), other Creole main meals include spicy **oxtail** (cow's tails stewed with vegetables and butter beans or split peas), and **curry goat**: tender goat (and sometimes mutton) cooked in a curry sauce. Two dishes not for the squeamish are **black pudding**, a highly spiced pigs' blood sausage, and **souse**; pigs' or chickens' feet marinated in lime juice and peppers, served cold. A classic accompaniment to main meals is **oil-down**; vegetables (particularly breadfruit or cassava) stewed in coconut milk.

Though increasingly rare these days, "**wild meat**" such as agouti, lappe, manicou, tattoo,

quenk and even iguana end up in the pot where available; these days, the best place to taste wild meat is in rural communities; it's also a staple of Tobago's harvest festivals.

Creole **soups** include **san coche**, a lentil soup cooked with pig's tail for flavouring, and **cowheel soup**, thick with split peas and slowly cooked meat which should fall off the bone. Many feature seafood; **fish broth** is a watery and delicious fortifying soup padded out with boiled green bananas and dumplings, while **pacro water** is similar but substitutes pacro (a small mollusc known as **chip-chip** in Trinidad) for fish. Reputed to be a strong aphrodisiac, it's sometimes called "Man Water". You'll also see Cajun-style seafood chowder on many restaurant menus

Seafood in general is extremely popular; you'll be offered thick steaks of dense and delicious kingfish, shark, grouper, tuna, cavalli, carite, barracuda and dolphin (the fish, not the mammal), as well as smaller fillets of "red fish", moonshine, snapper, parrotfish, flying fish and fresh-water tilapia. Creole-style fish is usually fried or stewed in a peppery tomato-based marinade of onion, sweet and hot peppers and garlic, while **curry crab and dumplin'** (crab cooked in its shell with a coconut curry and sauce served with bland boiled dumplings) is a marvellous Tobago speciality. Though you'll mostly see it on the menus of smarter restaurants, local **lobster** is doused in the classic butter of lemon, garlic or herbs and sometimes curried, while the slightly chewy and extremely nutritious **conch** (lambie) is made into chowder, curried or steamed, or, occasionally, marinated in lime and served raw in a ceviche salad.

Indian cooking

Though the obvious staple of Trinidadian Indian cooking is **curry**, the T&T version is somewhat different to that served in India, using fresh hot peppers rather than chilli paste and a blend of curry powder that's peculiar to the islands. One of the most popular curry dishes is **duck**, which forms the centrepiece of a "curry duck lime". The unofficial national dish, **roti**, is made by everyone and eaten as a convenient lunch or evening snack. A stretchy flat bread (called a skin) is used to wrap curried meat, vegetables or fish, a style of preparation that originated in Trinidad. There are several variations of roti skin including **dhalpourri** (with seasoned, ground split peas layered into the dough), **sada** (cooked on a hot griddle and usually cooked in the early morning only, and served with delicious fresh tomato "choka") and **buss-up-shut**, a thin, tasty shredded skin that resembles a torn cloth shirt and is usually used to spoon up mouthfuls of curry. Paratha is a plain roti skin. **Fillings** range from curried chicken and beef to conch, goat and shrimp. Common vegetarian fillings (also used to complement the meats) are **channa** (curried chickpeas), **aloo** (curried potato), **pumpkin** (usually very sweet), **bodi** (green beans) and **bhaji** (spinach-like greens); in a restaurant, you may be offered a bowl of thin and peppery lentil **dahl** as an accompaniment. Many vendors include meat on the bone in their roti – if you don't fancy following locals in sucking out the marrow, ask for no bones, and if you have problems consuming a roti without dribbling channa down your front, try keeping the greaseproof paper wrapping on and peeling it down as you eat.

The other mainstay of Trinidadian Indian cookery is the vast array of **chutneys** and **relishes**, ranging from super-sweet to tart or pepper hot. The recipes are too numerous to list, but look out for sweetly curried mango on the seed, peppery **anchar** and **kucheela**, a hot mango pickle that's universally plopped into rotis, doubles (see p.42) and aloo pies.

Fruit and vegetables

Local **fruit and vegetables** are plentiful and relatively cheap, particularly if you buy from large markets rather than supermarkets, which charge quite a lot more for their wilting specimens. You'll see some unfamiliar fruits alongside the more recognizable items; super-sweet and extremely popular, the **sapodilla** is grey and globular with gritty, sweet pulp, while **chenets** are cherry-sized with smooth green skin and a large seed surrounded by a thin covering of sweet, slightly acidic flesh. The knobbly green and brown skin of the **soursop** surrounds a delectable milky white pulp that is often made into ice cream or drinks; its smaller cousin the **sweetsop** is less common. The round **pomme cythere** (called pomsitae) is sweet and yellow when ripe, but is often eaten green with salt and pepper as "chow", as is the star-shaped **carambola** (five finger) and unripe mango. Round with a purple or green skin, **kymets** are quite rare and completely delicious with a gloopy, off-white pulp inside; equally sought-after, **balata** fruit are

similar to chenets, with a stone in the middle surrounded by glutinous, perfumed goo; take care when eating both, though, as they leave a sticky chewing-gum-like substance on the lips. **Mamee apples** are the same size as an orange, but with smooth grey-green skin, and have several seeds and dense apricot flesh that tastes faintly of peach. If you arrive during the June-to-August season, don't miss out on the perfumed white flesh of the crimson-skinned, pear-shaped **pommerac**.

Green-skinned with a soft, aromatic, orange flesh, **pawpaw** (papaya) is a staple of hotel fruit plates, as are bananas (often called **figs** – look out for the exceptionally tasty, tiny finger variety or young green bananas boiled and eaten as a savoury), **watermelon** and **pineapples**; the local fruits are powerfully perfumed and very sweet. **Passion fruit** (granadilla) and **guava** are often blended into drinks. **Citrus fruit** is ever-popular; you'll see lemons, limes, oranges and grapefruit (the latter two sweeter than in cooler climates), while **portugals** are easy-peel, thick-skinned mandarins with lots of pips and juice.

The king of the island fruits, though, are the many varieties of **mango** which grow so profusely in rural areas that whole communities are perfumed with the distinctive aroma of rotting fruit during the season (roughly April to August). The most popular (and most expensive) type is the rosy, medium-sized julie, while the long stringy mango is best avoided unless you have dental floss handy. Bright orange West Indian **cherries** are too sour to eat raw, but are juiced and sugared to make a refreshing drink.

The most frequent **vegetables** seen on the Creole dinner plate are the Caribbean staples known locally as **blue food** or **ground provisions**; boiled root vegetables such as the many varieties of **yam**, which range from the delectable powdery yellow type to the more dense white tubers, as well as chewy, purple-tinted **dasheen** and **tannia**, softer, white-coloured **eddoe**, **cassava**, **sweet potato** and regular potatoes. Dasheen leaves are also hugely popular, cooked up with **okra** (ladies' fingers) to make callaloo (see p.39). You'll also see aubergine (locally called **melongene**), **christophenes** – pear-shaped and light green with a bland, watery taste similar to marrow – as well as pumpkin, green **bodi** string beans and **breadfruit** (pembois), green and thick-skinned with clothy white flesh that can be baked, boiled or fried. Definitely an acquired taste, **caraili** is long and thin with knobbly green skin and tastes bitter enough for its acclaimed properties as a blood cleanser to seem plausible, while **pak choy** arrived with Chinese immigrants and is widely used. Popular accompaniments to most meals are slices of avocado (**zaboca**) and fried, pounded or boiled **plantain**, a larger, denser but still sweet member of the banana family.

Thanks to the Indian influence, **pulses** (referred to as peas) are widely used; you'll see red lentils cooked into dahl, green lentils cooked with vegetables in a coconut oil-down sauce, chickpeas curried into channa, and pigeon or gungo peas and black-eye peas cooked with rice, seasoning and coconut milk to make the Caribbean classic of rice and peas.

Eating out

In **Trinidad**, where the tourism industry is just beginning to develop and most people prefer to eat at home, a serious **restaurant culture** is only just beginning to develop. There are some splendid and stylish places to eat Indian, Creole, Chinese and international cuisine in and around Port of Spain, where you'll also find a huge lunchtime variety in the shopping mall food courts, but the majority of eateries are no-nonsense places where decor and ambience come second to the food, which is invariably inexpensive and delicious; curries, roti, Chinese staples, macaroni pie and lentils, potato or green fig salad, Creole-style fish and chicken or the ubiquitous pelau.

When Trinidadians do eat out, it's often to fill up on the marvellous array of **street food.** Almost every city corner is an impromptu trading post for some kind of food, particularly brown paper bags of salted (or "ital") freshly roasted peanuts. Western Main Road in the St James district of Port of Spain offers particularly rich pickings, with food available throughout the night. All vendors are subject to stringent regular hygiene checks; a clean bill provides an official badge, so eating on the hop rarely constitutes a health risk.

In **Tobago**, you'll see more variety in the restaurants, many of which are decidedly upscale and aimed at the tourist market, with prices to match. Local seafood, curries, Creole sauces and roti do feature, but you'll encounter plenty of imported US steak or fish and chips as well. With fewer office workers and late-night revellers to

fuel the trade, street food is far less widely available, and the best place to sample typical Tobagonian dishes such as **crab and dumplin** is probably the *Blue Crab* restaurant (see p.295) in Scarborough or the tiny cookshops in the market serving up for the traders.

On both islands, **breakfast** is traditionally a hearty meal, ideally taken with a steaming mug of **chocolate tea**; hot chocolate made with fresh cocoa rolled into an oily ball with nutmeg, cinnamon and sugar, which is grated and mixed with condensed milk and water. Designed to stand you in good stead for a hard day's work, a local breakfast may consist of smoked mackerel or herring cooked up with onions and hot peppers, fried fish or the classic semi-salad **buljol**, an extremely successful blend of soaked, boiled and flaked saltfish, fresh onions, tomatoes, lime juice and hot peppers, usually eaten with avocado and a couple of light, airy rolls called **hops**. Other popular breakfast breads include banana bread or fried **bakes**, non-yeast rolls of variable shape that are sometimes sweetened or flavoured with grated coconut to make the classic **coconut bake**. If you don't fancy eating heavily in the morning, most hotels offer a "continental" option of toast, juice, fruit and coffee or tea.

One important point to note is the addition of a **tax** (up to 15 percent) and a **service charge** (usually 10 percent) to your bill; these extras are not usually included in prices given for individual dishes, and can make what seems a moderately priced meal considerably more expensive. If the service charge is included, you don't need to leave a tip.

Fast food and street food

Though the international **fast-food** chains – *Pizza Hut, Kentucky Fried Chicken* and *McDonald's* – are now a part of the scenery, local outlets still manage to draw the crowds; best for chicken is *Royal Castle*); which uses a tasty blend of spices and herbs in the batter and serves flying-fish sandwiches and veggie burgers; there's a delicious chadon beni-laced, not-too-hot pepper sauce to dollop on everything as well. *Mario's* or *Pizza Boys* are other good options for pizza, and all branches deliver, while the chain of *Donut Boys* do a nice line in fancy cakes, filled croissants and doughnuts.

However, Trinidad's **street food** is by far the best option if you're after a bite to eat on the go, with everything from halal meat or fish sandwiches to fried chicken and, of course, **roti**. Everybody has their favourite roti shop or stall, and you're guaranteed to find something tasty if you head for the vendors along Western Main Road in St James, Port of Spain. Other good shops include *Patraj* in Tragarete Road, *The Hott Shoppe* on Mucurapo or Maraval roads, the *Home Restaurant* in St James and Arima and *Ali's* on Back Chain Street, San Juan.

The other popular Indian snack is **doubles**, two pieces of soft, fried **bara** bread sandwiching a runny channa curry and spiced up with cucumber pepper sauce and kucheela mango chutney. Curried potato wrapped in *bara* bread and fried **aloo pies** are another popular snack, as are cheese, beef or fish pies sold from large wicker baskets in the streets or hole-in-the-wall shops; there's usually more pastry than filling, though. A little less substantial are the selection of seasoned breads such as the incredibly addictive **pholouri** (split-pea balls served with tart and tasty tamarind sauce) or **sahina**, a ground channa and dasheen leaf fritter.

Port of Spain's Savannah and most junctions along the Eastern Main Road are flanked by the flaming flambeaux of vendors selling small local **oysters** harvested from mangrove swamps. Said to revive flagging libidos, they're served with a peppery, vinegary tomato sauce and slurped from a cup. However, fears of contamination by industrial pollution and the threat of cholera have led to periodic government bans; buy only from vendors who have a queue.

Creole street delicacies include the staple **corn soup**, a thick and satisfying split-pea broth with vegetables, chunks of young sweet corn on the cob and mini dumplings – a favourite hangover cure; pick a vendor with a queue as quality can vary. Boiled in a thin, flavoured broth or roasted on coals, **corn on the cob** itself is also popular, though it can be a little tougher than you may be used to. **Accra**, a peppery salt fish fritter, hails from the African population, while the ubiquitous

bake and shark is best consumed on the sand at Maracas beach, where vendors compete to produce the tastiest version of this sandwich of fried bread and a slab of shark meat. At Maracas, you'll also be offered a choice of chadon beni, garlic and tamarind sauces as well as avocado, salad and coleslaw as an accompaniment. Elsewhere, you may be unlucky enough to encounter stale bake and cold fish; check when it was cooked before buying. Jamaican **jerk chicken** and pork spiced up in a tasty pimento-based marinade and cooked over a wood fire, is increasingly popular in Trinidad, with stalls dotted all over the city; it's often served with **festival**, a sweetish fried dumpling.

In recent years, Trinidadian Rastafarians have popularized **ital** cooking, which strictly speaking refers to fresh vegetables, fruits and pulses prepared with no salt or additives. However, though Trini ital food stalls haven't managed to relinquish salt, the cooking remains some of the most wholesome you'll find, with beautifully seasoned soya mince, black-eye peas, split-peas, rice, macaroni pie and mixed vegetables served in a carton as "food" or in a roti skin; check the truck near to *KFC* in Independence Square, Port of Spain (Wed–Sat), or *Chinkies Night Beat* (Tues–Sun), opposite *Smokey and Bunty* in St James or at the croisee in San Juan.

Desserts and sweets

With so much locally grown cane sugar and raw cocoa, it's not surprising that there's plenty on both islands for the sweet tooth. **Desserts** like the moist and delectable **paimie**, a coconut, cornmeal and pumpkin pudding boiled in a banana leaf (or plastic wrap these days) and **pone**, a wet cake made with cassava and sometimes sweet potato spiced with nutmeg, or the classic **black cake** – a ridiculously rich, rum-soaked Christmas speciality – are sublime, and there are a thousand variations of chocolate cake. Sold everywhere from street stalls, homemade fruit **ice cream** is particularly good, as is the Guinness-flavoured variety. Pastries include stodgy and delicious **currant rolls**, **rock cakes**, **bread pudding** and **sweetbread**, a spicy, fruity loaf.

Sweets come in numerous varieties. In Tobago, look out for **benet**, a tooth-crunching ball of sesame seeds and sugar, and **coconut cake**, a slab of shredded coconut boiled in sugar syrup and pink food colouring. **Tamarind balls**

take a little getting used to, combining the tart taste of tamarind with sugar and salt, as do **salt prunes** (seasoned, sweet-and-sour prunes rolled in a dusty red colouring, often dropped into white rum for flavour) and **red mango**, which is green mango, well-seasoned with spices and sugar and doused in bright red colouring. Other candies include **toolum**, a sticky ball of grated coconut, molasses and ginger, **pawpaw** balls, shredded green papaya boiled in sweet syrup and rolled in sugar, guava cheese, stewed guavas reduced into a jelly similar to a pungent Turkish delight, and an amazingly sugary **fudge**, while the often sickly sugared and fried **Indian sweets** come in hundreds of varieties. Among them, **kurma** (sweet fried dough balls) is probably the most popular, sold everywhere in plastic bags, but **sawain** (noodles, raisins and nuts simmered in condensed milk and spiced with cardamom and cinnamon) is less common. The best time to buy them is during Hosay (see p.46), when vendors line up along the Western Main Road in St James.

Drinking

Given the local capacity for consuming huge amounts of **beer**, it's hardly surprising that the national brews go down extremely smoothly. The market leader, **Carib**, is a light, golden lager while its close competitor, **Stag**, is a little sweeter and marketed as "a man's beer". Both taste better drunk out of the bottle, though they're increasingly available on tap. Newer locally brewed lagers such as **Samba**, or the Guyanese **Polar**, have yet to make an impact on local drinkers. **Guinness** is brewed in Trinidad but, though bitter and refreshing, it bears little similarity to the draught or bottled versions produced elsewhere. The sweeter **Royal Extra** or **Mackeson** stouts are excellent local alternatives.

Both dark (called "red") and white **rum** are downed with equal enthusiasm, the white rum tending to be less abrasively strong than the overproof brands of other islands; T&T regular rums stick to 43 percent volume. **Angostura/Fernandes** produce the most popular brands, **Old Oak** and **Vat 19** white and gold rums, and **Black Label** red rum. **Royal Oak** and **Angostura Premium White** are a little higher in quality, and the paint-stripping **puncheon** should be consumed with caution. Though it's illegal to produce and possess, home-produced cane spirit – called **bush rum**, **babash** or **mountain**

dew – is eternally popular, with a distinctive engine-oil aroma, a strangely pleasant taste and a wicked kick (it's rumoured to be strong enough to make ice sink to the bottom of the glass), but take care to ensure that it's been distilled cleanly. Many drink their rum straight or with water, but Coke, tonic and coconut water are all excellent mixers, often with a splash of **Angostura bitters** (see box on p.44). Trinidadian **rum punch** is delicious, using blended fruits, syrup, bitters and a generous topping of ground nutmeg. Sweet and strong homemade **wines** – cashew, banana, aloes, hibiscus etc – are also excellent if you can get your hands on them; imported wine is widely available, though it's usually fairly expensive. Brand-name **spirits** are expensive and much sought after, but various local alternatives (**Angos Dry** gin, **Molotoff** vodka) are more than acceptable. Imported Jamaican coconut rum is a favourite tipple, and locally produced **Mokatika** coffee liqueur is a worthy after-dinner drink, often mixed with milk.

Of the available **soft drinks** beyond Coca-Cola and Sprite, energy-boosting **Ginseng-Up** is best in lemon-and-lime or apple flavours but comes in pineapple and bitter "original" as well, while **Bentley** is a refreshing bitter lemon soda. **Carib Shandy**, in sorrel and ginger varieties, is a delicious thirst-quencher, but the best thing to drink in the heat is vitamin and mineral-packed fresh **coconut water**, sold in water or jelly varieties; the contents of one nut will keep you going for ages. Grouped around Port of Spain's Savannah and busy junctions, vendors will expertly chop off the outer husk with a machete to expose a drinking hole (ask for a straw as the juice and husk stains clothing), and then chop the nut in two so you can scoop out the jelly using a portion of the husk as a spoon.

Made from boiled tree bark, cloves and aniseed, reddish-brown (and sometimes yellow) **mauby** is deliciously bitter and refreshing, but a bit of an acquired taste; it is said to be a tonic as well as a great way to cool off; Mauby Fizz is a commercially produced soda variation. Other unusual drinks include tart, bright pink **sorrel**, made from the petals of a member of the hibiscus family and usually enjoyed at Christmas with a dash of rum, as is the strong **poncha crema**, an eggnog boosted with plenty of rum. **Sea moss**, a white and glutinous preparation made from sea moss and milk, is widely believed to enhance sexual performance; other stamina-

The Angostura saga

Being producer of T&T's favourite rum is honour enough, but having cricket supremo Brian Lara as figurehead and years as a main sponsor for the steelpan competition Panorama ensures that **Angostura** enjoys the highest profile of any Trinbago company. Trinbagonians stick by Angostura with nationalistic zeal, declaring its rum the best in the world and adding a dash of its **aromatic bitters** to everything from drinks to marinades, soups and puddings, as well as swearing by the mixture as a cure for almost any ailment.

The company was founded by **J.G.B. Siegert**, a German surgeon who left his homeland to join Simon Bolivar in the fight for Venezuelan independence from Spain. Alarmed at the debilitating stomach ailments which plagued Bolivar's troops, Siegert began experimenting with South American herbs and spices to concoct a remedy. In 1824, he succeeded, creating the secret blend of botanicals that still make up the bitters today. He named his tonic after the Venezuelan town where Bolivar's movement was based.

Popularized by sailors who brought wind of its curative powers to England, the mixture was first exported six years later, and demand increased rapidly. Production was shifted to the more economically and politically stable Trinidad, and the George Street plant dominated the small town of Port of Spain. Siegert died in 1870, his company's affairs taken over by his sons. The founder's great grandson Robert Siegert, who took the helm in 1928, steered Angostura to ever-greater heights, establishing the Caribbean's most modern distillery in 1949 and exporting Trinidad's beloved product all over the world.

As the company became more valuable, so foreign investors began to make increasingly generous takeover bids. By now, however, Angostura had become so entrenched in the psyche (and the economy) of Trinidad that the government stepped in, taking control of the company in the mid-1950s, and returning it to Siegert Holdings, who offered cut-price shares to employees and affirmed Angostura as the "people's distiller".

Despite its bitters being voted the world's worst displayed product by the British Advertising Council in 1995 (the packaging has changed little since 1824), Angostura has gone from strength to strength, buying out other local distillers, establishing a shiny new factory on the outskirts of Laventille and winning scores of awards; no less than seven monarchs, including Britain's Queen Elizabeth, have given bitters the royal stamp.

The company continues to take its traditions seriously, and the **secret recipe** for bitters remains cloaked in mystery. None of the five people who have memorized a section of the recipe are allowed to enter the blending room (or even travel) together. After mixing the ingredients, each sends their part of the blend down a chute to the same percolating container that's been used since the company began trading in Trinidad, where the herbs and spices are "shampooed" in alcohol for twenty hours before fermentation and bottling.

Tours of the Laventille factory take place on Wednesdays (US$5.75; $12 with lunch) and are well worth taking in – they cover the history of the company as well as a look around the distilling areas and a chance to sample some of the products; call ☎ 623 1841 ext 170.

inducing potions are the **bomb**, a blended concoction of Guinness, nutmeg and condensed milk or a carton of Supligen energy drink. Cinnamon- and nutmeg-infused **carrot juice** and **peanut punch**, blended with condensed and fresh milk, are a meal in themselves, sold from stalls all over the island; vendors will add glucose or granola for an extra energy burst. The best place for delicious blended juice drinks are *Hardline Vegetarian* and *Mother Nature* in Port of Spain (see p.99); aside from wonderful fig, pineapple or beetroot and cane juice blends, they also sell channa, okra and male or female "sex" punches.

Festivals and public holidays

Trinbagonians have a well-deserved reputation for partying. With thirteen public holidays there are plenty of occasions to celebrate, and no religious event passes without some festivity. Banks and workplaces close and many take the opportunity to enjoy the country's beaches. Concerts are organized, shops have holiday sales and the newspapers are full of events and articles relating to the celebrations.

Public holidays embody T&T's cultural and ethnic diversity: there are holidays acknowledging Hindus, Muslims, Baptists, Roman Catholics, trade unions, and those of African and Indian descent. Every year there is a debate whether the Chinese should be given a day for Chinese New Year. There is frequent debate, too, as to whether the country has too many days off, but each festival is avidly defended by its own lobbying group, and no politician is likely to risk offending a sector of the community.

There are other celebrations that, for all intents and purposes, are public holidays though they are not officially recognized as such. The most famous is **Carnival**, held on the Monday and Tuesday before Easter. In Trinidad, especially in Port of Spain, everything shuts down for these two days, and often for Ash Wednesday as well, while people recover from the festivities.

Most celebrations are local events based on African and Indian traditions, which entail audi-ence participation, such as dancing, singing along to songs and eating. **Street festivals** feature local artists, good street-stall food and lots of music. Makeshift bands, with instruments ranging from a bottle and spoon to steel drums, drive around in the back of pick-up trucks entertaining spectators.

Many **religious days** are also celebrated in small ways, even by those who are not followers of the religion – many Trinbagonians will light a *deya* for the Hindu festival **Diwali**, then the next week light a candle for the Roman Catholic cele-bration of **All Soul's** day (Nov 2).

For the latest information on festival events, Contact TIDCO at ☎ 868/623 6022; see also p.16.

Festival Calendar

January

New Year's Day A quiet day, usually spent recov-ering from the festivities of "Old Year's Night" as New Year's Eve is known in T&T. This public hol-iday signals the opening of Port of Spain's calyp-so tents, where calypsonians compete with each other in a battle of wit and satire in the run-up to February's **Calypso Monarch Competition** (for more on this competition, see p.105).

February

Carnival Monday and Tuesday The country's most famous festival, celebrated nationwide with costumed street processions and lots of music. Carnival will fall on February 11–12, 2002; and March 3–4, 2003; March 23–24, 2004; March 7–8, 2005 (for a detailed description of Carnival events, see p.104). Ash Wednesday is known as "Carnival cool-down", with revellers heading to Maracas and Manzanilla for huge beach parties.

The **Crate Race** used to take place in August in central Trinidad, but due to its popularity it has now been moved to Chaguaramas in Trinidad's Northwest Tip, and takes place three to four times a year, in February, March, August and October. The participants build makeshift sailing craft – no motors or real boats are allowed. Many spectators, however, come to see the all-women teams decked out in bikinis rather than the inge-nuity of the craft.

March

The **Phagwah** festival, celebrated nationwide, is best seen in central Trinidad. It's not a public holiday, but many Trinis of all backgrounds participate. Based on the Indian tradition – known as Holi – that celebrates the arrival of spring, it has grown in popularity over the years to become the Hindu equivalent of Carnival. (See p.187 for more on this festival.)

Good Friday and **Easter Monday** are public holidays in T&T. People make enormous meals, visit relatives and head to the beach. On the Tuesday after Easter in Buccoo on Tobago, **crab and goat races** are held. These bizarre spectacles are entertaining to watch – though for those betting on their favourite they're no laughing matter. (for more on these races, see the box on p.279) Tobago also hosts the **Carib International Fishing Tournament** at Pigeon Point at this time of year.

Shouter Baptist Liberation Day, held on March 30, is a new public holiday in recognition of the African-based religion that suffered persecution in colonial Trinidad (for more information on Shouter (or Spiritual) Baptists see p.337). The day has not yet become an established tradition and therefore the celebrations are somewhat subdued.

Crate Race (see February).

April

The festival of **La Divina Pastora** is held on the third Sunday after Easter in Siparia in southern Trinidad. The Black Virgin statue is carried in a procession through the streets of the town, while locals, decked out in new clothes, celebrate the event with general feasting and merrymaking (see p.219). **Rapso Month** is a recent addition to the musical calendar and has a tendency to get shifted back and forth but usually starts after Easter. It features lots of concerts by new and old Rapso artists (for more on Rapso see p.347). As well as large concerts, there are workshops for aspiring Rapso singers which culminate in the "Breaking New Ground" concert in Port of Spain. Featuring up-and-coming young artists it's an excellent place to spot new talent and hear the concerns of local youth.

May

Pan Ramajay is a month-long steel-band festival held all over T&T. Small-pan ensembles play a wide range of music including classical and jazz, with a large dose of improvisation.

Indian Arrival Day on May 30 commemorates the arrival in 1845 of the first indentured Indian labourers in Trinidad (for more on the background to this holiday, see p.329).

Yachties from all over the Caribbean come to compete in the **Angostura Yachting Week Regatta**. Most of the events are held around Pigeon Point, Mount Irvine and Stone Haven bays in Tobago. **Ganga Dashara** on May 17 is a Hindu river festival held in Blanchisseuse.

June

The Islamic festival of **Hosay** changes date every year, moving between May and June. Originally a procession of mourning commemorating the martyrdom of Hussein and his brother Hassan, grandsons of the prophet Mohammed, in Trinidad the event has become carnivalesque, with a spectacular procession of handmade tombs and excellent tassa drumming. The biggest display of tombs and drumming takes place in St James, a suburb of Port of Spain, though it is also celebrated in Curepe, Tunapuna, Couva and Cedros. (For more on this festival see p.92).

Corpus Christi is a Roman Catholic public holiday on June 14. Some small villages celebrate it with processions but in urban areas it tends to be a quiet day.

Labour Day on June 19 is a public holiday in recognition of the trade unions and workers in T&T. It is most publicly celebrated in Fyzabad in southern Trinidad, the town at the centre of the establishment of the powerful Oil Workers' Union (see p.220 for more information).

St Peter's Day on June 29 (or the nearest weekend) is celebrated in fishing communities throughout T&T with huge fishermen's fetes on the beaches, where pots of fish broth sustain dancing to the strains of pumping sound systems.

July

The **Charlotteville Fisherman's Fete**, held on Man O' War Bay beach, Tobago, in the middle of the month, is one of the largest fetes in Tobago – a wild beach party that goes on all night, allowing the hardworking fishermen to celebrate the impact of the income they bring into the village.

The **Tobago Heritage Festival** is held in the last two weeks of July all over the island. Festivities include a traditional calypso competition, an "old-time" Tobago wedding ceremony and sports events. Local delicacies and art and crafts are specially made and sold to highlight the island's culture.

In Trinidad the Horticultural Society holds its **Annual Flower Show** a fabulous opportunity to see the beautiful exotic flowers of the islands.

August

Emancipation Day on August 1 commemorates the abolition of slavery in 1834 with a procession through Port of Spain. During the week leading up to it you will see many people dressed in traditional African clothes in affirmation of their heritage. Talks, workshops and performances are held in the grandstands at the Queen's Park Savannah, where an "Emancipation village" showcases local arts and crafts and African goods.

Tobago celebrates Emancipation Day with the **Great Race**. Speedboats navigate the dangerous currents of the Dragon's Mouth in a race from Trinidad to Tobago. It starts from Chaguaramas in the morning, but the festivities take place at the finishing line at Store Bay in Tobago in the afternoon.

Columbus' Discovery Day was replaced by Emancipation Day in 1985, but diehards of the older festival still celebrate it in Moruga in southern Trinidad (see p.230).

Independence Day on August 31 celebrates T&T's independence from Britain in 1962. Flags and bunting decorate all public buildings, banks and large institutions, while fetes and street parties feature performances by local soca and dub artists.

The last week in August also sees the **Santa Rosa Festival** in Arima in the north part of central Trinidad. Celebrating the culture and tradition of the first Trinbago people, the Amerindians, it has musical and acrobatic performances as well as the obligatory feasting and street parties.

Crate Race (see February).

September

A quiet month, September sees the **Royal Oak Derby** for horse race enthusiasts and the **Caribbean Latin Jazz Festival**, which brings musicians from all over the world to T&T.

October

Mid-October sees the start of the **Best Village Competition**, also known as the **National Folk Festival**, a nationwide event where villages send their best dancing troupes, musicians, actors, playwrights, handicrafts and cooks to contests in Port of Spain. The competition lasts until November when the Prime Minister announces the winner. The **T&T Awards**, prizes for local popular musicians, are also held in this month. The island's equivilant of the Grammys, this event sees the Trinibagonian elite come out in glitzy outfits to congratulate successful musicians from all aspects of the country's music scene.

Towards the end of the month is the **World Steel Band Festival**, also known as "Pan is Beautiful". Concerts hosted in venues around Trinidad feature the best steel bands displaying their skills by playing everything from classical music to the latest calypso tunes plus a specially composed piece for the competition.

During Tobago's annual **Cycling Classic Festival**, cars make way for the hordes of cyclists that take up the roads in a furious race under the tropical sun.

At the end of October, the festival of **Diwali** honours Mother Lakshmi, the Hindu goddess of light and spiritual wealth. Many households light up their yards with *deyas* (tiny flickering oil lamps in clay bowls), irrespective of their religion, while Hindus prepare large amounts of food and invite their friends for a Diwali meal. The **National Council of Indian Culture** celebrates Diwali with nine days of shows, stalls and events (for more information see p.189).

Crate Race (see February).

November

Trinidad's **Pan Jazz Festival** is an international event celebrating the diversity of the steel drum with open-air concerts given by pan ensembles from around the world. These events can be expensive, but there is usually a free night of entertainment down on Brian Lara Promenade in Port of Spain. The festival usually occurs every year, though lack of finances has led to cancellations in recent years.

December

December is the season of the **parang** – a tradition of nativity songs sung in Spanish with a mix of French patois dating from colonial days. Parang groups perform in many bars and nightclubs during this time; local groups go from door to door, filling the streets with the rich, haunting music. Hearing these songs you could be forgiven for thinking you were in South America – until you detect the deep Trinbago accents of the singers. (For more on parang, see p.34).

Eid-ul-Fitr has no fixed date as it signals the beginning of the Islamic New Year and is determined by the position of the moon. A relatively private and subdued affair, the festival marks the end of Ramadan and a month of fasting for Muslims with ritual songs sung in mosques around the country. Donations are given to the poor and gifts exchanged.

Christmas Day, December 25, is celebrated in typical Trinbago fashion with large social gatherings and plenty of food and drink. People visit friends and relatives during the day and eat the obligatory Christmas fare; ham, pastelles (see p.38) and the rich and fruity black cake. In the evening the festivities continue in bars, clubs, fetes and parties.

Boxing Day on December 26 is the public holiday that marks the start of the Carnival season. Radio stations start to play continuous soca and calypso music, and fetes and parties are advertised with increasing frequency.

Outdoor activities and adventure tours

Tour operators in Trinidad and Tobago

Local tour companies' offerings range enormously from eco-oriented **hiking** excursions, **bird-watching** trips and **kayaking** to more conventional **driving tours** of the islands' "highlights": Caroni Swamp, markets in Chaguanas, Ajoupa pottery, the Pitch Lake, the islands off the Chaguaramas coast and Gasparee caves, the Northern Range with birdwatching at Asa Wright and the north coast beaches. There are hundreds of tour companies in T&T, and the list below represents the very best of the bunch. Note that you'll often get a reduced rate if you book in groups of four or more; some operators will not set out with less than four in any case.

"Eco", birding, cultural and adventure tours

Avifauna, c/o Roger Neckles, 17 Morne Haven Condominiums, Gilkes St, Morne Coco Rd, Diego Martin, ☎633 5614, fax 633 2580, *www.trinidad.net/avifauna*. Trini-English Neckles is one of the island's most respected bird photographers, and his tours – ranging from Asa Wright to Aripo Savannah – are excellent for serious ornithologists and amateur birdwatchers alike, and there are some Tobago options too. Tours cost US$60 per person.

Caribbean Discovery Tours, c/o Stephen Broadbridge, 9b Fondes Amandes Rd, St Ann's, Port of Spain, ☎624 7281, fax 624 8596, *www.caribbeandiscoverytours.com*. Entertaining, informative hikes and safaris aboard a rugged Land Rover, all with a birdwatching and animal-spotting slant. One of the best for Nariva, with kayaking (water levels permitting), a walk in Bush Bush and a slap up lunch at Kernaham Village, as well as Northern Range waterfalls, a central Trinidad day tour which includes Caroni swamp, and trips to Petit Tacarib including accommodation, food, hikes and boat transfers (US$75 per day). Tours cost US$50–100 per person.

Chaguaramas Development Authority, Airways Rd, Chaguaramas, PO Box 3162, Carenage, ☎634 4364 or 4349, fax 625 2465, *www.chagdev.com*. Waterfall and walking tours around the Chaguaramas peninsula as well as trips "down de islands", including Gasparee Caves and hiking on Chacachacare from US$25 per person (see p.119).

Hike Seekers, Pierre Felix Drive, Diego Martin, Trinidad, ☎632 9476,

A far cry from your average sun-sand-and-sea Caribbean destination, T&T offers plenty to do beyond the beach, and the hugely rich natural environment affords plenty of opportunity for outdoor activities such as birdwatching and hiking, while offshore pursuits include a wide range of watersports.

Birdwatching

Birdwatching is a popular pastime among tourists and locals alike; Trinidad and Tobago rank among the world's top ten countries in terms of bird species per square kilometre, boasting a species diversity unmatched in the Caribbean; more than **430 recorded species** and around 250 known to breed. Migrant species from South America are most common between May and September, while birds from North America visit between October and March. The dry months (January to March or April) are traditionally the most popular time for birders to visit;

during the wet season, however, birds tend to grab whatever chance they can to feed between the showers, so you'll still see a lot of activity.

The best place to start in Trinidad is the acclaimed **Asa Wright Nature Centre** (☎667 4655; see p.151) in the middle of the Northern Range; workers assert that you can see as many as 150 species even on a relatively short visit, and it is certainly the only place where you can see the nocturnal, cave-dwelling **oilbird** without having to take a strenuous hike. Other essential stops include the **Caroni Bird Sanctuary** (see p.184), south of Port of Spain, where you can take an afternoon boat tour to see the startling flocks of **scarlet ibis**, the national bird and most arresting of the 156 species that live in this swampland. The **Point-a-Pierre Wild Fowl Trust** (☎637 5145 or 662 4040; see p.192) is an important conservation centre for endangered species of waterfowl nestling amid an industrial wasteland, and following a successful breeding

---

jdelamore@hotmail.com. Excellent for adventurous types, the programme of hikes is led by ex-soldier Lawrence "Snakeman" Pierre, whose exhaustive knowledge of bush trails ensures trips to the less accessible parts of Trinidad, as well as Paria, Rincon, Madamas and Sobo waterfalls, Guanapo Gorge, and Tamana and Cumaca caves; bush camping is also available. Full-day hikes US$40, overnights US$50.

Island Experiences, 11 East Hill, Cascade, Port of Spain ☎625 2410, fax 627 6688, *gunda@wow.net*. Lively, knowledgeable tailor-made eco-cultural tours that provide an excellent insight into Trinidadian life. Great for mas camps and panyards around carnival time, and evening and daytime city tours, including bars and live calypso and steel pan, throughout the year. Daytime excursions are wonderfully offbeat, combining stock stop-offs such as Asa Wright or Caroni with more unusual places such as Arima market or St James for roti. Island tours are extremely varied, ranging from Pitch Lake and San Fernando to Chaguanas bazaar and pottery. German- and English-speaking guides available for 1–4 persons. Half-day tours from US$25, full-day from $60, evening tours $25.

Rooks Tours, 44 La Seiva Rd, Maraval, Trinidad, ☎622 8826, fax 628 1525, *www.pariasprings*

.com. Excellent, informed birdwatching and eco-tours with an experienced naturalist and a team of specialized guides. Tours include birdwatching trips all over Trinidad, Northern Range waterfall hikes, Tamana bat caves, adventurous and soft mountain bike excursions as well as horticulture tours to turtle watches and a couple of Tobago options. Trips range from US$40–60.

South East Eco Tours, Fuentes St, Rio Claro, ☎644 1072, *secotour@tstt.net.tt*. Walks and hikes with community-based guides in Trinidad's south east; destinations include Nariva, Ortoire River and Trinity Hills Reserve. US$35–80.

Wildways, 10 Idlewild Rd, Knightsbridge, Cascade, Port of Spain, ☎ and fax 623 7332, *www.wildways.com*. One of the best-organized tour operators, which ploughs most of its profits back into eco-educational programmes for local schools. Hikes, kayaking trips and mountain bike rides to Trinidad's Arena forest, Tamana bat caves, Marianne, Paria and Salybia waterfalls, Mount El Tucuche and the rainforest around Grande Riviere; Tobago excursions include the Buccoo ponds, Charlotteville hikes and the forest reserve. Overnight tours, trips to Guyana and customized packages are also available. US$70–110 per person, with reductions for groups of four or more.

programme it now offers the opportunity to see ibis up close.

The best **book** to bring is Richard Ffrench's encyclopedic *Guide to the Birds of Trinidad and Tobago*, which describes calls as well as plumage, habitats and behaviour. For **online birding information**, visit Russell Barrow's Birds of T&T site (*www.interlog.com/~barrow*), or Trinidad Birding (*www.inct.net/~billmurphy/ index.htm*). There are plenty of tour companies and individual guides that specialize in **birding tours** of the island (see p.48 for details). Good places to go birdwatching include the **Arena Dam**, just south of Arima, and Reservior (see p.195), **Hollis Reservoir**, **Mount St Benedict** (p.159), the Northern Range along the **Arima–Blanchisseuse Road** (pp.149–153), the **Piarco Water Treatment Plant** near the airport, **Nariva Swamp** on the east coat (p.202) and **Oropuche Lagoon** in the southwest (p.218).

In Tobago, head for **Little Tobago** (or Bird of Paradise Island) on the windward coast (see p.315) to see seabirds in their natural environment; the **Bon Accord Lagoon**, **Arnos Vale Estate**, **Hillsborough Dam** and the **Grafton Caledonia Bird Sanctuary** (see p.266, p.285, p.307 and p.281 respectively) are also fine bird-watching sites. At the protected **Tobago Forest Reserve** (see pp.302), there are plenty of well-trained guides to accompany you.

All of the above sites are particularly rich in bird life, but you need a permit from WASA to enter Arena dam, Hollis and Hillsborough reservoirs,

and the Wildlife Division to go to Nariva (see p.196 and p.203).

Hiking

Trinidad and Tobago are ideal for **hiking**, though you'll have to be pretty hardy if you plan to attempt long walks in the searing sun – the best plan is to start early and cover plenty of distance before the midday heat sets in, or choose a hike that goes through forest; most of the best trips do. You don't have to be supremely fit to go hiking if you stick to easy trails, nor do you need any special equipment. There is excellent hiking to be had in the forests of the Northern Range and the Chaguaramas hills; other areas offer less public land and are poorly geared up for walkers.

It's a terrible idea to hike alone as there is no one to provide assistance or raise the alarm if you run into problems; experienced local hikers never set out with less than two people. There are plenty of tour companies that provide private hiking trips (see box p.48), but another, less expensive option is to join one of the excellent local groups on their regular jaunts into rural areas; best of these is **Hike Seekers** (see p.48). Hikes take place most weekends: you assemble at 7am at an allotted meeting point, pay your TT$20–30 and set off. You must provide your own transport, food and water, though the group can usually get you there if you call ahead. Call for details of upcoming walks. Established for more than one hundred years, the **Trinidad and Tobago Field Naturalists'**

Things to bring on a hike

Shoes

A pair of stout shoes with good grip suffice if you don't have hiking boots – trainers are inadvisable as they have less hold and don't allow feet to breathe. Clip your toenails short before a long or steep walk to prevent rubbing, and always wear socks to protect against blisters and ticks – it's a good idea to tuck your trousers into socks if walking through land grazed by animals, which will give you a barrier against the little mites.

Clothes

Wear cotton trousers or leggings to protect against nettles, razor grass and insects, with a long-sleeved shirt over a vest in case you need to cool off; a hat is good protection against sun

and rain and you should carry a light waterproof raincoat in rainy season. Bring a swimsuit if a dip might be on the agenda.

Food

Bring a sandwich lunch as well as concentrated high-energy food such as chocolate, dried fruit or nuts; a bag of cut sugar cane is great for maintaining energy and quenching thirst. A good-quality water bottle is a necessity and you'll appreciate the worth of one that keeps your liquids cool.

Sundries

Map, insect repellent, sunscreen, a good torch and spare batteries, toilet paper, rope, matches and plasters.

Club (PO Box 642, Port of Spain ☎687 0514, www.wow.net/ttfnc) is another, slightly less visitor-friendly group that hike on the last Sunday of each month; trips leave from St Mary's College in Port of Spain at 6.15am, and most cost TT$10. Their definitive *Trail Guide* (see "Books", p.364) makes essential reading if you can get hold of it, describing nearly fifty walks in minute detail.

Abiding by **hiking etiquette** will ensure that the trails you walk stay beautiful. Starting a bushfire is to be avoided at all costs; do not discard matches or cigarettes and make sure that cooking fires are completely extinguished. Stick to paths and trails wherever possible; carelessly placed feet destroy plants and crops and may lead to soil erosion, as well as drastically increasing your chances of getting lost. Leaving **litter** is a criminal offence; bring rubbish – including cigarette butts – home with you, and bury or burn used toilet paper. Finally, don't collect plant or wildlife specimens, and try to keep noise to a minimum so as not to disturb wildlife.

Watersports

Snorkelling and **scuba diving** are extremely popular; both are far better in **Tobago**, where the water is clearer due to the island's relative distance from sediment-heavy currents from the South American mainland. The best dive spots are centred around Speyside on the windward coast, where you can see pristine reef and a host of fish, including deep-water manta rays and the odd shark. Other top spots are offshore Charlotteville and the Sister's Rocks on the leeward side, as well as the Shallows or Flying Reef at Crown Point; Buccoo Reef remains the most popular, as the disintegrating coral sadly reveals. Everywhere, you'll see a dazzling variety of fish, from sizeable barracuda and grouper to angel, parrot, damsel and butterfly fish as well as spiny sea urchins and lobster nestled among the coral. Throughout the Guide, we have listed reputable dive operators (most of whom also rent snorkelling gear for around US$10 per day) in relevant sections; for more details on prices, see p.246.

If you prefer to stick to **swimming**, bear in mind that undertows and strong currents make many of Trinidad's (and some of Tobago's) beaches downright risky. However, most of these are marked with red flags, with yellow and red flags marking safe areas; in their absence, don't swim until you've checked with somebody local. The regular Sunday crowds, hordes of food vendors,

excellent facilities and a swathe of fine yellow sand and cool, clear green water make Maracas Trinidad's most popular beach; a few miles down the road at Las Cuevas and Blanchisseuse lie several more stunning places to swim, though all are sometimes subject to rough seas and undertows. At the other end of the North Coast the Toco surrounds offer sublime swimming, as does Mayaro in the east, the longest (and probably the widest) stretch of sand on the island. Away from the oil refineries, many parts of the south coast offer fabulous swimming as well.

Most agree, though, that T&T's best beaches are in Tobago, where the water is cleaner and calmer and the tourist infrastructure more developed. The epitome of a Caribbean seashore, Pigeon Point with its crystal-clear water, white sand and pretty palm-thatched gazebos is the queen of them all, though its overt commerciality rather mars the spot. Nearby Store Bay and Mount Irvine are also lovely, but the undeveloped allure of Castara, Parlatuvier, Englishman's Bay and Pirate's Bay on the leeward side are far more stunning. Beyond the ocean, both islands offer marvellous possibilities for **freshwater swimming**. Some of the most stunning waterfalls are Argyll in Tobago and Blue Basin, Paria, Maracas and La Laja in Trinidad; though these are just a few of the many beautiful cascades.

Most of the larger Tobago hotels have all you need in the way of non-motorized **watersports** – kayaks, small sailboats, windsurfing etc. In Trinidad, Chaguaramas is the main watersports area, where you can take a guided kayak tour (see p.138). Thankfully, jet-skis have yet to make an impact in T&T, and environmentalists are already pushing for a total ban. If you're serious about **windsurfing** or want to watch one of the many local competitions, contact the **Windsurfing Association of Trinidad and Tobago** (c/o Wayne Graham ☎628 8908).

During the winter, big breakers – especially around Mount Irvine in Tobago and Toco in Trinidad – make ideal conditions for **surfing**. You can rent boards in Tobago, but in Trinidad you'll probably need to bring your own; check with the **Surfing Association of Trinidad and Tobago** (c/o Allan Davies ☎623 0920) for details of events and further contacts.

T&T also boasts excellent sport **fishing**, though at around US$250 for a half day and $400 for a full day, it doesn't come cheaply. However, as many boats accommodate up to six, and rods, tackle and bait are included, it makes sense to share the cost. For your money, you're pretty much guaranteed some excitement; main catches include marlin, sailfish, tuna and dolphin. Boats for charter are listed throughout the Guide wherever available, and if you want more information about sport fishing, contact the **Trinidad and Tobago Game Fishing Association**, 91 Cascade Rd, Port of Spain (☎624 5304).

The main **yachting** centre is Chaguaramas. A calm natural harbour outside the hurricane belt, this strip of marinas is a haven for yachties sheltering from rough weather in other parts of the Caribbean and taking advantage of the insurance benefits, namely lower premiums, such

protection affords. Chaguaramas is also the base for boat trips "down de islands", normally rumsoaked party cruises to the series of islands off the north west coast (see p.127). For more information on yachting services, contact the **Trinidad and Tobago Yachting Association** at the Sailing Centre in Chaguaramas (☎634 4519), the **Yacht Services Association** at Crews Inn marina in Chaguaramas (☎634 4938), or the **Trinidad and Tobago Yacht Club** at Bayshore, Point Cumana (☎637 7945). You can also consult the **Boaters' Directory**, available from marinas in Chaguaramas and the tourist board's Marine Industry Section (☎623 1932).

Competitive sports

Trinidad and Tobago offer a wide variety of competitive sports for both spectators and participants. Sport is as much a national pastime as liming, and local people are justifiably proud of their country's sporting prowess; Trini-born cricket supremo Brian Lara is exalted as a hero and Ato Bolden's gold medal at the 1997 Olympics electrified Trinidad and, particularly, Tobago, where he was born.

Cricket and other team sports

A Caribbean obsession, **cricket** remains a national passion in T&T, and is the source of much debate. As long as you're not foolish enough to criticize Brian Lara, the "Prince of Port of Spain" and holder of the highest Test score in the world (375) – and the highest first-class total (501), mentioning cricket to any Trinbagonian is pretty much guaranteed to break the ice, and if the Windies are playing, you'll hear radios tuned into the match everywhere you go, from banks to Royal Castle. Main matches take place during March and April at the Queen's Park Oval in Port of Spain and on the central Queen's Park Savannah itself, and are great fun even if you're not a cricket fan; soca blares in the intervals, plenty of cold Carib gets downed, and fans are vocal in their support

or derision, blowing whistles, beating drums, shouting raucous comments and dancing to the soca that blares out between each over. Tickets for Test matches cost TT$40–TT$200 for an all-inclusive pass to the "Trini Posse" stand, where flowing drinks and a party atmosphere make it a day's lime rather than an afternoon watching a spectator sport; tickets are available from the **Queen's Park Cricket Club** (94 Tragarete Rd, Port of Spain; ☎622 2295 or 6050). Other major games take place in the south at Guaracara Park, Point-a-Pierre. Details of forthcoming play schedules are available from the club and are also heavily advertised in the media; for further information on the local game, contact the **Trinidad and Tobago Cricket Board of Control** at Isaac Junction, Couva (☎636 1577). Alternatively, check out any of the thousands of informal amateur games that take place on Port of Spain's Savannah and any spare scrap of land every weekend; most towns and villages have their own thriving team. For online information about the West Indies team, visit their homepage at *www.cricinfo.com/link_to_database/NATIONAL/WI*. The Trini Posse supporters' website has details on match tickets and statistics from past Test matches at Queen's Park Oval.

The rules of cricket

The **rules of cricket** are so complex that the official rule book runs to twenty pages. The basics, however, are by no means as Byzantine as the game's detractors make out. There are two teams of eleven players. A team wins by scoring more **runs** than the other team and dismissing the opposition – in other words, a team could score many runs more than the opposition, but still not win if the last enemy **batsman** doggedly stays "in" (hence ensuring a draw). The match is divided into innings, when one team **bats** and the other team **fields**. The number of innings varies depending on the type of competition; one-day matches have one per team, Test matches have two.

The aim of the fielding side is to limit the runs scored and get the batsman "out". Two players from the batting side are on the pitch at any one time. The bowling side has a **bowler**, a **wicket-keeper** and nine **fielders**. Two umpires, one standing behind the stumps at the bowler's end and one square on to the play, are responsible for adjudicating whether a batsman is out. Each innings is divided into overs, consisting of six deliveries, after which the wicketkeeper changes ends, the bowler is changed and the fielders move positions. The batsmen score runs either by running up and down from wicket to wicket (one length = one run), or by hitting the ball over the boundary rope, scoring four runs if it crosses the boundary having touched the ground, and six runs if it flies over. The main ways a batsman can be dismissed are: by being "clean bowled", where the bowler dislodges the bails of the **wicket** (the horizontal pieces of wood resting on the stumps); by being "run out", which is when one of the fielding side dislodges the bails with the ball while the batsman is running between the wickets; by being caught, which is when any of the fielding side catches the ball after the batsman has hit it and before it touches the ground; or "LBW" (leg before wicket), where the batsman blocks with his leg a delivery that would otherwise have hit the stumps.

These are the bare rudiments of a game whose beauty lies in the subtlety of its skills and tactics. The captain, for example, chooses which bowler to play and where to position his fielders to counter the strengths of the batsman, the condition of the pitch and a dozen other variables. Cricket also has a poetry in its esoteric language, used to describe such things as fielding positions ("silly mid-off", "cover point", etc) and the various types of bowling delivery ("googly", "yorker", etc).

Football

Football (soccer) is also extremely popular, with support for the T&T national team, known as the "Soca Warriors" (*www.socawarriors.homestead.com*) nothing short of fanatical. Major matches take place at the National Stadium on Wrightson Road, Port of Spain (☎623 0304 or 0305); for more information, contact the Trinidad and Tobago Football Association, 15 Warner St, Port of Spain (☎652 1172), or the Trinidad and Tobago Football Federation at the same address (☎622 4427, *www.virtualcaribbean.com/ttff*. Trinidad and Tobago Football Online (*http://welcome.to/ttfootball*) has everything you need to know about T&T's beautiful game.

Golf

While it's not the greatest **golfing** destination in the Caribbean, T&T does boast some lovely courses, most of which have clubs and carts for rent as well as in-house caddies. In Trinidad, the best is probably St Andrew's in Moka, Maraval (☎629 2314). The only public course is the nine-hole Chaguaramas Golf Course, Bellerand Rd, Chaguaramas (☎634 4227 or 4364). There's only one course in Tobago, eighteen palm-dotted holes attached to the *Mount Irvine Hotel* (☎639 8871); St Andrews and Mount Irvine also host various professional and amateur tournaments (for details see "Festival Calendar", pp.45–48). For more information on the local golfing scene, contact the Trinidad and Tobago Golf Association (☎625 2115).

Other sports

Basketball is also catching on fast; some games are held at the National Stadium – for more details, contact the stadium (see above). Other popular sports include **hashing**, a kind of cross-country race with lots of beer and rum drinking. The *Pelican Inn* in Port of Spain is a good place to make contacts if you want to have a go, and it's worth visiting the website of the Port of Spain Hash Harriers: *www.geocities.com/poshashhouse*. **Cycling** is also popular; for details call the Trinidad and Tobago Cycling

Federation; ☎624 0384. Though Port of Spain's Savannah is no longer a venue for galloping gee-gees, **horse racing** remains a popular sport. Major meets take place at the Santa Rosa Race Track, Arima, ☎646 7223 or 2450. A recent addition to the local sporting scene is **drag racing**; regular, well-attended meets take place at the Wallerfield Race Track on the Arima outskirts; for more information contact Autosport Promotions at ☎671 6112.

Fitness freaks will find Trinidad well-equipped with **gyms**, which tend to get packed in the run-up to Carnival, when everyone wants to look their best in their skimpy costumes. For a reliable establishment, contact the **Trinidad and Tobago Aerobic and Fitness Association**, 48a Pembroke St, Port of Spain (☎627 0370). If you want to keep up your game, you'll find **tennis** courts at the *Hilton*, *Cascadia* and *Crowne Plaza* hotels in Port of Spain and the *Mount Irvine*, *Turtle Beach*, *Crown Point Beach* and *Grafton* hotels in Tobago; the latter also has air-conditioned **squash** courts, as does the *Pelican Inn* in Port of Spain and *Cascadia* hotel in St Ann's, Port of Spain

Shopping

Trinidad and Tobago offers a wide variety of souvenirs and products to suit every budget. You can buy everything from woven palm hats on the beach to the most expensive jewellery in Frederick Street in Port of Spain. Local artists produce fine woodcarvings, shell and bead jewellery, paintings and beaten copper pieces. T&T also has an excellent reputation for producing good music and talented writers – purchasing a few books and CDs will enable you to carry a little of the country's culture back home.

The widest variety of shops is in Port of Spain in Trinidad and Scarborough in Tobago. **Opening hours** are Monday to Friday from 8am to 5.30pm, and on Saturdays from 8am to 2pm. Malls are open for longer, Monday to Saturday from 9am to 8 or 9pm. As with everything in T&T, these times are changeable – opening hours depend on the shop and the mood of the individual shopkeeper.

T&T's rich **musical culture** (see pp.341–347) has spawned an astonishing variety of styles – steel drum, calypso, soca, rapso, chutney, dub and parang – and produced many marvellous songs with strong lyrics and powerful rhythms. Local labels to look out for are Rituals, Mad Bull, Jo-Go, Engine Room and Kiskedee Records. The best places to buy music are Crosby's, 54 Western Main Rd, St James, and Rhyner's, 54 Prince St, both in Port of Spain, but you'll find music shops in most malls and along main streets. For those on a limited budget roadside vendors sell inexpensive pirate copies of popular reggae and soca tracks.

Local **bookshops** are usually full of US titles and schoolbooks. The chain Trinidad Book World and the Metropolitan Book Suppliers in Port of Spain sell the widest range of books by local authors. Many Trinbagonian authors are published by British and American publishers however, so – if you want to get a taste of T&T's culture – it may be best to buy their work before you come (see p.361).

A wide selection of inexpensive **fabric** can be found in shops in Port of Spain on and around Queen Street. Imported from all over the world, the cloth on offer far exceeds any choice provided by shops in New York or London. Locally designed **clothes** range from the most elegant evening-wear to beautiful batiks to model on the beach. Well-executed, colourfully attractive hand-painted T-shirts, featuring everything from Bob Marley to the T&T wildlife, are sold in malls and shops, on the street and from beach stalls. Good quality souvenir T-shirts can be bought from Zoom, which has outlets nationwide.

Local crafts such as carved calabashes, woven palm grasshoppers, shell jewellery and carved driftwood are usually sold on or near the more popular beaches and in souvenir shops. Ornate carvings are also sold in art galleries and at individual stalls that occasionally appear on country roads. You'll often see Rastafarians selling handmade leather sandals from market stalls or on the street.

T&T has some of the highest quality **coffee** and **cocoa** in the world, unavailable outside the country, where the high grades are mixed with lower grades by multinational coffee suppliers such as Nescafe and Cadburys. Local coffee in a variety of delicious flavours, such as coconut and rum, can be bought in souvenir shops. The rich, creamy cocoa can be bought in small shops and from street vendors – ask for cocoa sticks. These are solid blocks of cocoa that have to be melted, and then mixed with milk and sugar.

They say the reason the island's White Oak **rum** is not well-known worldwide is because the locals keep it to themselves and consume the total production. Trinidad's famous **Angostura Brewery** produces a wide range of excellent rum as well as their ever-popular bitters. These are readily available in many local shops. Starting at TT$40 for a litre of white rum, they are excellent value and make a popular souvenir.

Prices

Prices are generally higher in Tobago than in Trinidad, and prices of most purpose-made souvenirs are hiked up as a result of the tourist trade. Paintings and woodcarvings may seem expensive in comparison with other local produce, but these works of art are unique and the prices are far lower than can be found in an art gallery back home.

If you are looking for **bargains**, check out the streetside vendors and small backstreet shops. Souvenir shops, boutiques and the malls have higher prices, though they usually have a wider variety of products on offer. Bargaining is conducted to a certain extent with street and beach vendors but not in shops. Vendors may lower the price a little but do not push for too much; this is their livelihood, after all.

Directory

Addresses and directions Street signs and house numbers can be confusing in T&T, as some roads have none and most houses are unlabelled. Consequently addresses often include "Corner of" (abbreviated to "cor.") followed by the names of two cross streets. When someone is giving directions, they will often describe the route by landmarks, and the colour and shape of the building; people often know a street but not its name, so be aware of such visual clues.

Children As most local people are fond of children and used to accommodating their needs, you'll find that travelling with youngsters is rarely a problem, and can often help to break the ice. Almost all local hotels are happy to accept families, and many provide baby-sitting services; alternatively, you can usually find someone reputable by asking around. As many of the beaches in Trinidad (and some in Tobago) can be risky for swimming, it's best to keep a close eye on small children when in the sea; even Maracas has a strong undertow; Tobago's Store Bay and Pigeon Point are the calmest you'll find, but Macqueripe in Trinidad can be quite benign too. Check with locals; if there's a chance of risk, stick to paddling.

Cigarettes The most widely available international brand of cigarettes is T&T's locally made Benson and Hedges, which also come in the lights and menthol varieties. There are also several local brands – du Maurier (strong, also available in lights and menthol), Mt D'or (strong) and Broadway (similar to B&H). Other foreign brands can be found in large supermarket chains and malls. **Bidis** (Indian cigarettes) are also available. Known locally as hemp, they are actually made from low-grade tobacco wrapped in a eucalyptus leaf tied with cotton – no filter, plenty of tar. They can be bought from street vendors and some local shops in Trinidad's northwest corridor.

Departure tax On leaving the country by air or boat you must pay TT$100 in local currency after you have checked in and before you pass through security. Ensure you have the right amount as changing TT$ outside the country is difficult and uneconomical. It is possible to avoid the queues at the departure tax desk by paying the tax through a cash machine in the airport's Bureau de Change; the machine takes the amount off your card and gives you a departure tax form.

Electricity Currents run on 110 or 220 volts, 60 cycles. The current is often sluggish around peak times, particularly in Tobago, making everything run a little less efficiently than at home.

Embassies and consulates Foreign diplomatic missions and honorary consuls are all based in Trinidad, most of them in or near Port of Spain, and are listed on p.108.

Etiquette T&T is a conservative and friendly society. As a foreigner you will be treated politely and the same will be expected of you. Outside the cities, it is polite to acknowledge people passing on the street with a nod of the head (upwards), "good day" or just "alright". Before starting any conversation, whether buying something in a shop or asking for directions, the local custom is to say "good morning" or "good afternoon".

Everything is slowed down in T&T; people take a little longer to interact, converse and to serve you. If you arrange to meet someone, be prepared to wait – being on time in T&T means being 30–45 minutes after the time originally arranged, and no apologies will be given. Don't

get frustrated; be flexible and tolerant and you will save yourself a lot of stress.

Gay and lesbian Officially it is still illegal to be gay in Trinidad and Tobago but there is a creeping acceptance of the gay community and the government is under pressure to change the law. The legislation is rarely enforced but it does mean that there are no openly advertised gay clubs or bars – the scene is very underground and all events are publicized by word of mouth. Gay and lesbian travellers are unlikely to suffer any direct prejudice – the typical attitude you'll meet is "I don't agree but it's not my business". Even so, be aware of your surroundings and be discreet in your behaviour if you do not want to attract any negative attention. There are a few bars and clubs in urban areas that are gay friendly, such as the *Pelican Inn, Smokey and Bunty's* and *Just Friends* in Port of Spain. For more on the local gay scene, visit *www.gaytrinidad.f2s.com*

Laundry There are plenty of laundries in T&T that do dry-cleaning; those that also do "wet" cleaning are listed in the Guide. Hotels and guesthouses usually have facilities to do washing, whether it is a laundry service or a concrete sink out back. Some people earn a living from hand-washing; ask your host for the local washer.

Photography Print film is less expensive in T&T than in Europe, but getting it developed can cost 25 percent more. In Port of Spain many shops develop within the hour; there are no budget rates for a longer waiting time. Slide film is very expensive and difficult to get outside the capital; there are no development facilities apart from those offered by a few professional photographers. As a result of these high prices, photography is not as common as it is in Europe or the US. People are therefore less used to having their photograph taken, and you will be conspicuous if you walk the streets with a camera round your neck. Be discreet and ask for permission when taking pictures of locals.

Religion Religious faith still holds strong in T&T, especially in Tobago. Though you may see overtly sexual dancing and hear lewd lyrics, the people are still morally quite conservative. Couples in T&T tend to be very undemonstrative in public, although at fetes and parties you may see highly erotic dancing between friends and lovers. If you dance this way with a stranger you may well be considered immoral. Beachwear should be restricted to the beach; nude and topless bathing is not allowed. Obscene language is illegal and though the law is not often enforced, it is important to be aware of it.

Time Trinidad and Tobago is four hours behind Greenwich Mean Time (five during the summer months), and one hour ahead of Eastern Standard Time.

Tipping Most taxi drivers in Trinidad don't expect a tip, but in Tobago, where many make their living from foreign visitors, a 10 percent tip is usual if you are the only passenger. Never tip in a route taxi or a maxi. Restaurants often add a service charge into the bill; if this is the case, a tip is not necessary – if it's not included, 10–15 percent is the norm. If you're staying in a hotel, you might consider leaving some dollars for your hotel chambermaid.

Working It is illegal to take paid employment while staying in T&T on a tourist visa. Some cultural exchanges can be arranged to teach languages and specific skills, but these should be worked out before you arrive.

The Guide

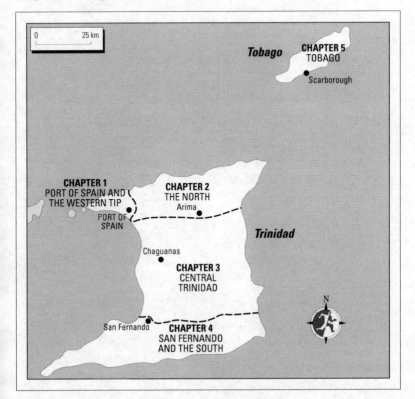

Chapter 1

Port of Spain and the Western Tip

rinidad's **Western Tip** – a peninsula extending between the Gulf of Paria and the Caribbean towards Venezuela – encompasses both the most urbanized and the least developed parts of the island. Along its southern curve, between the rainforested mountains of the Northern Range and the gulf, sprawls **Port of Spain**, the country's capital and the commercial and cultural centre of the island. Nearly a third of Trinidad's population lives within its boundaries. For years it has enticed people from the rural areas with its employment prospects, metropolitan verve and late-night entertainment; no matter where you go in Trinidad, locals will speak of visiting the capital as "goin' to town". Port of Spain's thriving economy has also attracted many immigrants from other islands, making it the hub of the southern Caribbean.

Beyond the western residential districts of Port of Spain, the landscape becomes increasingly rural. The **Chaguaramas** area, much of which is still covered by ancient rainforest, has been sensitively developed, with open-air clubs and restaurants unobtrusively incorporated into the landscape. Large areas of national park are etched with a network of forest trails, while the area's largely undeveloped sandy beaches and sheltered coves offer opportunities for swimming and watersports.

The further west you go, the more wild and undeveloped the terrain becomes. Beyond Chaguaramas, the Western Tip crumbles into a series of rocky islands separated by rough, swirling channels known as the **Bocas del Dragon** – the Dragon's Mouths. Though the islands – the largest of which are **Gaspar Grande** and **Chacachacare** – lie just a short distance offshore, they are completely free of motorized traffic. In the eighteenth century, they were a refuge for whalers, smugglers and pirates; today, they are the preserve of yachting enthusiasts, fishermen and anyone in search of tranquillity.

Port of Spain and its suburbs have a wide range of **accommodation** to suit all budgets. Whether you are visiting the city for Carnival or plan

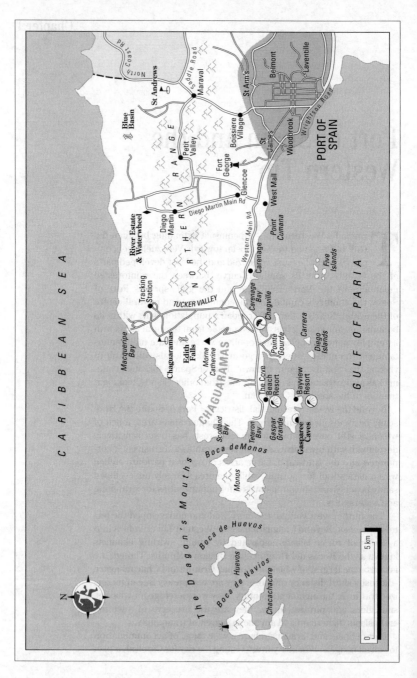

to explore other parts of Trinidad, you will almost certainly end up staying here at some point. Beyond the city, there are several accommodation options in the Western Tip, most of which are the preserve of the yachties who moor at the peninsula's marinas. The whole of the area – and the rest of Trinidad, can be reached within a day's travel, whether by the excellent public transport network or rented **car**.

Port of Spain

PORT OF SPAIN occupies a crucial place in Trinidad's national psyche. The government and media are concentrated here, keeping the city in the public eye. It is the hub of Trinidad's booming economy, and the main port of arrival for many immigrants from other Caribbean islands. It's also the crucible of Trinidad's rich **cultural life**, with countless mas camps, art galleries, panyards and theatres; it was here that Carnival was first established in Trinidad, and – in the suburb of Laventille – the steel pan was invented.

Port of Spain is a bustling city, proud of its cosmopolitanism and style. Some 51,000 inhabitants jostle for space in and around its compact centre; the latest soca tunes blare from shops, cars and pavement stalls, while locals lime on street corners. Yet beneath the hectic urban rhythms, you can still feel the quieter pulse of rural Trinidad. The green, crumpled folds of the Northern Range provide a constant backdrop, hand-painted advertisements co-exist with sleek new shopping malls, and street traders sell tree bark flavourings alongside disposable lighters. Despite its capital city status, Port of Spain is a friendly place where everyone seems to know everyone else, and at times its atmosphere can seem almost village-like.

The mish-mash of architectural styles can seem rather ugly at first sight, especially **downtown**, with its traffic-choked streets, grimy docks and frenzied commercial activity. On exploring the city, however, you'll come across many fine nineteenth-century buildings: dignified churches and state offices, the grandiose mansions of colonial planters, and quaint "gingerbread" houses, so named because of their intricate fretted woodwork. Many of these older buildings are located **uptown**, a gracious district arranged around the large open space of the **Queen's Park Savannah**, which was created by enlightened town planning in the early nineteenth century.

The city's suburbs – **Woodbrook**, **Belmont**, **St Ann's**, **St James** and **Laventille**, previously old plantation estates, stretch along the flat coastal plains and creep up the hills of the Northern Range. These districts pulsate with multicultural vitality: Muslim processions and African drumming can be heard on their streets, Hindu temples rub shoulders with panyards. It is here that many **mas camps** are located and, in the months preceding Carnival, the costumes are made.

And **Carnival** – the Monday and Tuesday before Ash Wednesday – is of course the very best time to be in Port of Spain. The city's

volatile mix of style, hedonism, creativity and joie de vivre explodes
onto the streets, and bands of fantastically arrayed revellers wind
their way through the city to be judged in the grandstands on
Queen's Park Savannah.

Some history

Port of Spain became Trinidad's capital almost by accident. In 1757,
the new Spanish governor, Don Pedro de la Moneda, discovered the
governor's residence in the then capital St Joseph to be uninhabit-
able following a series of attacks by pirates, and established his base
in Port of Spain instead, a more convenient location in any case. At
that time, the town consisted of no more than two streets with a few
hundred residents. Though built on swampy ground that was prone
to flooding, it did have the great advantage of a fine natural harbour,
and quickly became established as the permanent capital.

As French Catholics flooded into Trinidad in the 1780s, the capital's
economy boomed and the city spread. Land was reclaimed from the
sea, and streets were built over the surrounding mangrove swamps
and woods. The last Spanish governor, Don Maria José Chacon, greatly facilitated this expansion when, in 1787, he diverted the Rio Santa
Ana (now St Ann's River) to the outskirts of the town, along the foot of
Laventille Hill, alleviating the floods that had often troubled the city.

Chacon was less effective, however, when it came to defending the
city against the **British**, who in 1797 invaded and took over the
island. A devastating fire in 1808 led the British governor, Sir Ralph
Woodford, to make a number of improvements to the city, establishing the Queen's Park Savannah and developing Woodford Square.
Learning from Spanish mistakes, the British also improved the city's
defences by building Fort George and Fort Picton.

After **emancipation** in 1834, freed slaves left plantations to find
work in the capital, squatting the hills to the east of the city, where
they established the suburbs of Laventille and Belmont. With a growing population of workers, traders and entrepreneurs, the city
sprawled outwards into the old plantations of Maraval and St Ann's.
Indian immigrants, brought to Trinidad under indentured labour
schemes, settled in St James. In addition, settlers from China,
Portugal, Venezuela and Syria all came to Trinidad to try their luck
on the island. Descendants of these groups, and those of the French,
Spanish, African and Indian communities, ensure that Port of Spain
retains its cosmopolitan mix of peoples and cultures.

As the nation's capital, Port of Spain has naturally been the focus
for both the **political turmoil** and the **growing prosperity** of the
twentieth century. From the water riots of 1903, through the independence movement of the 1950s down to the bloody coup attempt
of 1990, **Woodford Square** has been an arena of political strife. The
dredging of the city's **deepwater harbour** in the 1930s made Port of
Spain the leading port of the southern Caribbean, while the discov-

ery of offshore oil in the 1970s left the city with a sleek **financial district**, dominated by the imposing twin towers of the Central Bank. And although a slump in oil prices in the 1980s put a dent in the nation's newfound economic confidence, the last decade or so has seen a wave of buoyant consumerism, with the city getting a facelift via dozens of new malls and offices. A government-sponsored beautification programme has brightened up many of the city's public spaces, and a new National Library is under construction, while the currently ugly and semi-abandoned foreshore area is slated for major redevelopment.

Arrival

Port of Spain is about 20km northwest of **Piarco International Airport**, where a small **tourist information office** (daily 8am–midnight; ☎669 5196) can provide you with **maps** and **information** on the capital and the island as a whole. Official **airport taxis**, which wait outside the main entrance, will take you into the town centre for US$20 (30min, 1hr during rush hour, 6–8am and 4–6pm). Prices to all destinations, quoted in US$, are listed in the domestic arrival hall. Taxi drivers will also accept local currency.

Alternatively, you can walk out of the airport onto the main Golden Grove Road (behind the wire fencing), and take a shared **route taxi** to Arouca Junction on the Eastern Main Road (TT$2). From there, you can catch an eastbound **red-band maxi taxi** to **City Gate**, the main transport terminus downtown (TT$3.50). **Route taxis** to Arouca Junction from the airport are also open to negotiation to take you direct to Port of Spain, and at TT$60–80 are a cheaper option than the official airport taxis.

For a route taxi map, see pp.68–69.

A **bus** runs into town twice a day from the main exit (Mon–Fri 8am & 4pm; TT$6). You pay at the end of the journey, when you reach the main bus terminus.

By sea

All ships arriving in Port of Spain dock at one part or another of **King's Wharf**: boats from **Tobago** at the **Government Shipping Service Passenger Service** opposite Twin Towers on Wrightson Road, and ships from **Venezuela** (though the service is currently suspended) at the **Cruise Ship Complex**, next door on Wrightson Road. Private taxis tout for passengers at both places; the route and maxi taxis that run along Wrightson Road are much cheaper, but since the Tobago boat docks at around 5am, you may opt for convenience over economy.

Orientation and information

Port of Spain has a compact city centre based on a grid system. The **downtown area** is bordered by the **docks** on the Gulf of Paria and Wrightson Road. **Brian Lara Promenade/Independence Square**

For a map of
Port of Spain,
see p.75.

runs parallel with the docks and spans the width of the city centre.
City Gate, the main transport terminal, and many route taxi ranks
are located in this area. Most of the sights are within walking distance of each other, but bear in mind that the hot sun drains your
energy. The **uptown** area is ranged around the large expanse of the
Queen's Park Savannah.

As many of the inner suburban districts become increasingly commercialized, it is getting hard to tell where the **suburbs** begin and the
city centre ends. There are four main roads out of the central downtown area. **Wrightson Road** from downtown joins the Audrey Jeffers
Highway, which takes you to Diego Martin, West Mall and the west.
Tragarete Road runs from uptown Park Street through Woodbrook
before joining the Western Main Road into St James. **Saddle Road**
leads from the northwest corner of the Queen's Park Savannah to
Maraval and eventually Maracas Beach. From the northeast corner of
the Savannah, **St Ann's Road** takes you to St Ann's and Cascade.

TIDCO, 12–14 Philipps St (Mon–Fri 8am–4.30pm; ☎623-6022)
can provide **tourist information** including details on accommodation and tour operators, and maps of Trinidad and the major towns.
They also produce monthly and yearly calendars of festivals, sports
and Carnival events.

City transport

There are four types of **transport** to get around Port of Spain and its
environs: **buses**, **yellow-band maxi taxis**, **route taxis** and **private
taxis**. Buses run to Diego Martin and down to the Western Tip, but it is
usually easier to catch a **route taxi**. There are plenty of these around
during the day, especially at peak hours. After midnight, however, especially from Monday to Wednesday, it is difficult to find transport except
on the most popular routes – when setting out at night, check with the
taxi driver about how easy it will be to return to your accommodation,
and if necessary ask them to collect you at an appointed time.

Buses

As taxi and
maxi taxi
fares are
subject to
change (and
sometimes go
up in an
instant for
those who look
like they don't
know the fare),
you're best off
make a habit
of paying with
a TT$10 note
and waiting
for change.

While PTSC buses provide a fast, cool means of travelling longer
distances between towns, they are not the best means of getting
around the capital; they are irregular and infrequent, and tickets for
most routes must be purchased in advance. It is usually easier, therefore, to catch a route taxi or maxi taxi. All buses start from **City
Gate**; for bus information contact ☎623 2341. The three routes
serving Port of Spain and its environs are:

To Central Port of Spain (City Gate special): City Gate, Abercromby St, New
St, Frederick St. TT$1.50, every 30min (5.30am–5.30pm).

To Chaguaramas: same as Diego Martin route, but once on Audrey Jeffers
Highway the bus continues onto the Western Main Rd; passing West Mall, West
Moorings, Glencoe, Carenage and Chaguaramas, ending at The Cove beach.
TT$2, Mon–Fri, every 30min (5am–9pm), Sat & Sun hourly (5am–7pm).

To Diego Martin: Wrightson Rd, Ariapita Ave, Mucurapo Rd, Audrey Jeffers Highway, Diego Martin. TT$3, hourly (6am–8pm).

Maxi taxis

Maxi taxis operating in Port of Spain and the west have yellow stripes painted on them. Routes are set (see map overleaf) although some drivers may be willing to make off-route drops, and if the maxi is empty, the driver may vary the route in the hope of picking up some passengers.

There are three main places to catch maxi taxis for travelling around Port of Spain. For **Diego Martin/Petit Valley**, the maxi rank is at the junction of South Quay and St Vincent Street. Maxis bound for **Maraval** (and sometimes **Diego Martin**) via **St James** start at the corner of Charlotte and Oxford streets. Maxis for **Carenage** and **Chaguaramas** via **Ariapita Avenue**, **Woodbrook**, start at Green Corner (corner of St Vincent and Park streets). For further information ring ☎623 2341 and ask for the maxi taxi facility.

To Diego Martin: TT$3; short drops on route, eg, St James, TT$2; off-route drops add TT$3 to the fare. Route ends at Diego Martin waterwheel.

To Maraval: TT$2; off-route drops add TT$2 to the fare. Route ends at Maraval village/Paramin.

To Petit Valley: TT$3; short drops on route, TT$2; off-route drops add TT$3 to the fare. Route ends at Mount Coco Rd.

To Woodbrook: TT$2; no off-route drops. Route continues to The Cove or Carenage.

Route taxis

Route taxis hold four to five people in addition to the driver, and apart from the H numberplate they are indistinguishable from private cars (which have P numberplates). They come in various states of repair: though some are brand new and air-conditioned, the majority are old but functional cars. If you're unlucky you may get a wreck with no windows, rusty paintwork and rattling doors. The same rules apply to route taxis as to maxi taxis; all off-route drops depend on the driver's goodwill. Starting points for the routes are dotted around Port of Spain (see map pp.68–69). From 7pm until 5am, many taxi stands relocate to Brian Lara Promenade/Independence Square.

To Belmont: cor. of Charlotte and Queen streets. TT$2 flat fee; off-route drops add TT$1 to the fare.

To Diego Martin: cor. of Abercromby St and Brian Lara Promenade/ Independence Square South. TT$3.50 to the route end at Diego Martin waterwheel; short drops within Diego Martin TT$2, except from West Mall to Diego Martin, TT$3.50; off-route drops add TT$3.50 to the fare. The route goes through Four Roads and down Diego Martin Main Rd. After 6pm Diego Martin taxis can be found near the Arthur Cipriani statue on Brian Lara Promenade.

To Laventille: cor. of Nelson and Prince streets. TT$2.50 to route end at Red Hill; TT$2 to Our Lady of Laventille Shrine; off-route drops add TT$1 to the fare.

Port of Spain

To Maraval/Paramin: cor. of Charlotte and Duke streets. TT$2 flat fee; off-route drops add TT$2 to the fare. Route ends at Maraval village/beginning of Paramin. Jeeps at end of route charge TT$2.50 into Paramin.

To Petit Valley: cor. of Abercromby St and Brian Lara Promenade South; after 6pm near the Arthur Cipriani statue on the promenade. TT$3.50 to Petit Valley; short drops TT$2; off-route drops add TT$3.50 to the fare. Route ends at Mount Coco Rd at the Capaldeo Flats.

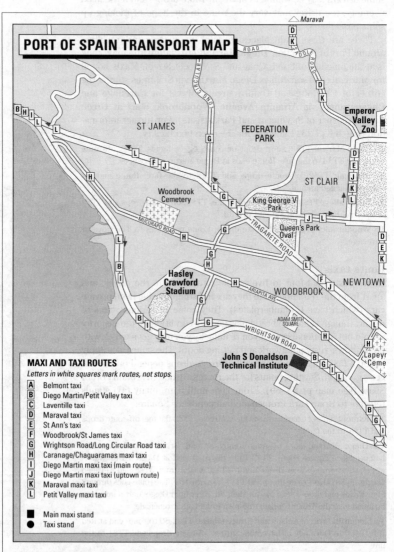

To St Ann's: Hart St, same side as the Trinity Anglican Cathedral. TT$2 to St Ann's hospital; TT$3.50 to *Cascadia Hotel*; TT$4.50 to end of Ariapita Rd; off-route drops add TT$2 to the fare, except those to the *Hilton Trinidad* (usually around TT$10). Route ends at Ariapita Rd.

To St James/Tragarete Rd: Hart St, on the side adjacent to Woodford Square, from 7pm–5am cor. of Independence Square and Henry St. TT$2 flat fee; off-route drops add TT$2 to the fare; no off-route drops into Woodbrook.

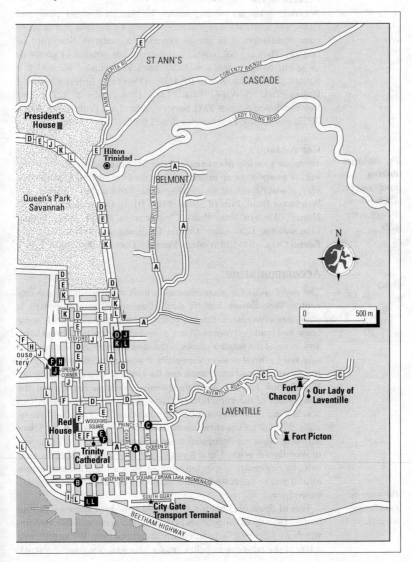

To **Wrightson Rd/Long Circular Rd**: cor. of Chacon St and Brian Lara Promenade/Independence Square South (next to *McDonald's*); after 6pm near the Arthur Cipriani statue. TT$2 up to Jean Pierre Complex, TT$2.50 for rest of route; off-route drops add TT$3 to the fare. Route ends at *Ambassador Hotel* on Long Circular Rd.

Private taxis

Nonroute taxis are distinguishable by their H number plate and clean, well-maintained appearance. While they will take you direct to your destination, they are as expensive as cabs in New York or London. They are not hailed on the street, but ordered by phone or by going to their ranks at Brian Lara Promenade/Independence Square, the *Holiday Inn* or the *Hilton*. Reputable firms include: **Ice House Taxi Service**, Brian Lara Promenade ☎627 6984; **Independence Square Taxi Service**, Brian Lara Promenade ☎625 3032; and **Kapok Taxi Service** ☎622 6995 (*Kapok Hotel*).

Car rental

For advice on driving conditions in Trinidad and Tobago, see p.28.

There are a variety of **car rental firms** in Port of Spain. Most usually ask for a deposit or an imprint of your credit card, and as prices can vary, it's worth calling around. Reputable firms include **Singh's**, 7–9 Wrightson Road, Port of Spain ☎623 0150; **Convenient**, Tropical Marine, Western Main Road, Chaguaramas ☎634 4017; **Signal**, Chaguaramas Convention Centre, Chaguaramas ☎634 2277; and **Econo Cars**, 191–193 Western Main Rd, Cocorite ☎622 8072.

Accommodation

The main areas for accommodation in Port of Spain are the city centre, **Woodbrook** and **St Ann's-Cascade**. The **city centre** is obviously convenient, though you may have to put up with some noise and cramped rooms. There's one big international hotel here, and some of the smaller places in the area offer excellent rates outside the Carnival season, especially if you are prepared to accept rooms with shared bathrooms and fans instead of air conditioning. **Woodbrook** has the most inexpensive accommodation and the lion's share of the **guesthouses**. These are usually more basic than hotels – with less likelihood of air conditioning – but it is increasingly difficult to tell them apart. Guesthouses usually offer fewer services, homelier decor and more of a personal touch. Transport to Woodbrook is good, and if you stay at the eastern end of the suburb, the city centre is only ten minutes' walk away. This area is also ideal if you're interested in mas camps, as the majority of them are based here.

For more on guesthouses see p.24.

Port of Spain also holds a large number of **host homes** – private houses (mostly in Woodbrook) converted to accommodate visitors, which are a good option particularly at carnival time. We've reviewed a few of the larger ones below (many have just one room for rent),

---

Accommodation price codes

All accommodation listed in this guide has been graded according to the
following **price categories**:

① under US$10	② US$10–20	③ US$20–35
④ US$35–50	⑤ US$50–70	⑥ US$70–100
⑦ US$100–150	⑧ US$150–200	⑨ US$200 and above

Rates are for the cheapest double or twin rooms, including 10 percent tax and
10 percent service charge where applicable. In Tobago, rates quoted are
those used during the high season, normally mid December–mid April.
During low season (mid April–mid December) rates are liable to fall by up to
25 percent. There are no high and low seasons in Trinidad, but rates may rise
by up to 70 percent during Carnival. Many hotels give rates in US dollars – we
have followed suit. Payment can be made in either US or TT currency.

---

but a full listing of host homes is contained in the tourist board
accommodation booklet (see p.16).

The **St Ann's-Cascade** area at the base of the Northern Range is
greener, breezier and less urbanized than Woodbrook or the city centre, and, now that transport links have improved, makes an excellent
base, extremely convenient for the Queen's Park Savannah at
Carnival. **Newtown**, which shares many of the advantages of
Woodbrook, also has a few slightly more expensive guesthouses.
Though it lies outside the city limits to the north, **Maraval** feels more
like a Port of Spain suburb these days; it's easily accessible and also
has a good range of accommodation (see pp.23–25).

The busiest time of year for accommodation is **Carnival**, and if you
intend to stay during this time it's essential to book well in advance.
Regular carnivalgoers book their accommodation on Ash Wednesday
for the following year, and most hotels require as much as six
months' notice. It is still possible to find rooms nearer the time, provided you don't expect to get your first choice. If booking within a
month of Carnival, settle for anything you can get.

Carnival prices, which can be up to 50 percent higher than normal high season rates, usually apply from the Friday preceding
Carnival through to Carnival Tuesday. The majority of hotels and
guesthouses insist on a 5- or 7-night minimum stay, which you'll
have to pay for even if you don't stay for the whole period. Where
Carnival rates apply, we've listed the normal rate first, followed by
the Carnival rate.

Hotels

Abercromby Inn, 101 Abercromby St ☎623 5259, fax 627 3858,
aberinn@carib-link.net. Rooms are on the small side, but clean and well
equipped with cable TV, telephone and a/c; most have en-suite bathrooms but
a few rooms share, and deluxe units have microwave and fridge. Communal
sun deck, good central location and breakfast included. ④/⑤.

Alicia's House, 7 Coblentz Gardens, St Ann's ☎623 2802, fax 623 8560, www.aliciashousetrinidad.com. Located on a quiet road close to the Queen's Park Savannah, all rooms have wicker furniture, a/c, phone and cable TV; most are en suite, but a few share bathrooms, and there's a swimming pool and sundeck. Meals are available, and breakfast is included in Carnival rate. ④/⑧.

Ambassador, 99A Long Circular Rd, St James ☎628 9000, fax 628 7411, www.ambassadortt.com. Fairly plush hotel opposite the US ambassador's residence, with a restaurant, cocktail lounge, swimming pool, ballroom and nightclub. Large, luxurious rooms with a/c, cable TV and en-suite bathrooms; those facing front have excellent views over Port of Spain, so ask for one specifically. Rates include breakfast. ⑦/⑨.

Cascadia, Ariapita Rd, St Ann's ☎623 3511, fax 627 8046, www.cascadiahotel.com. Well-maintained if rather sterile, with excellent facilities: squash and tennis courts, gym, pool, popular nightclub, water park and restaurant and bar. Rooms are modern and bright with patio, a/c, phone, cable TV and bath. All rates include breakfast. ⑦/⑨.

Chancellor, 5 St Ann's Ave, St Ann ☎623 0883, www.thechancellorhotel .com. Upmarket, newish place tucked down a side road near the *Normandie*. The spacious, modern rooms all have a/c, cable TV, phone, dataport and en -suite bathroom; suites are also on offer, as are fridges on request. There's a lovely pool with a waterfall, a bar and an air-conditioned restaurant. Breakfast included in Carnival rate. ⑦/⑧.

Pleasantly detached from the city heat and noise, Maraval (just north of the Savannah) has several excellent accommodation options. Listings start on p.110.

Crowne Plaza, Wrightson Rd ☎625 3366, fax 625 4166, www.crowneplaza .com. Glitzy corporate hotel with all mod cons: pool, three restaurants, bar, gym, business centre. Equipped with hairdryer, iron and board, coffeemaker and a/c, cable TV and phone, all rooms have excellent views over the Gulf of Paria or Port of Spain, and the downtown location is convenient. Breakfast is included in the rates. ⑨/⑨.

Hilton Trinidad, Lady Young Rd, St Ann's ☎624 3211, fax 624 4485, www.trinidadhilton.com. "Upside down" hotel built down the side of a hill, with the reception at the top and the floors numbered downwards from 1 to 11. Each room has a balcony with excellent views over Port of Spain and the hotel's landscaped garden, plus all the usual *Hilton* luxuries. Breakfast included. ⑦/⑨.

Kapok, 16–18 Cotton Hill, St Clair ☎622 5765, fax 622 9677, www.kapok.co.tt. Elegant, stylish place decorated with rattan furniture and batik. All rooms are spacious with a/c, satellite TV, radio, clock, phone, dataport and en-suite bathroom; front-facing rooms on the upper floors have fabulous view of the city, and studios and suites with kitchen facilities are also available. There's a renowned restaurant (see p.100), wine and coffee bar, swimming pool, gym and sundeck on site, and breakfast is included in Carnival rate. ⑦/⑧.

Normandie, 10 Nook Ave, St Ann's ☎624 1811, *normandie@wow.net*. On a quiet cul de sac five minutes' drive from the Queen's Park Savannah, this is one of the city's more atmospheric hotels, with a lively feel provided by the annual Carnival concerts, and by the on-site theatre, art gallery and 21 excellent shops as well as a popular restaurant and café. All rooms have polished floorboards, a/c, cable TV, phone with voice mail and en-suite bathroom, and there's a lovely pool. Breakfast included in the room rate. ⑥/⑧.

Guesthouses and host homes

Copper Kettle, 66–68 Edward St ☎625 4381. Basic rooms, some with a/c, some with fans; all have en-suite bathrooms. Slightly run-down, but inexpensive for its central location. There also a good bar and Creole restaurant on site. ③/⑤.

Fabienne's, 15 Belle Smythe St, Woodbrook ☎622 2773. Friendly atmosphere and comfortable, if rather sparse, rooms with en-suite bathrooms and standing fans; some have a/c. There's also a swimming pool and laundry facilities. ④/⑥.

Fondes Amandes, 9b Fondes Amandes Rd, St Ann's ☎624 7281, fax 624 8596, *caribdis@wow.net*. Charming family home set in the St Ann Hills with a pool and flower-filled garden that attracts local birdlife. The rooms are eclectic; some have a private bathroom, and one large unit accommodates groups. Breakfast is included in all rates. ④/⑥.

Gunda's Apartments, 11 East Hill, Cascade ☎625 2410, fax 627 6688, *gunda@wow.net*. Lovely, homely studio apartment overlooking the city, with spacious main room and separate kitchen and bathroom. Genial, generous host is a great source of information on Port of Spain and Trinidad in general. ④/⑥.

Halyconia Inn, 7 First Ave, Cascade ☎623 0008, fax 627 8623, *http:/community.wow.net/halyconia*. Sprawling colonial mansion converted into a basic, functional dormitory-style hostel; most rooms have bunk beds and sleep four or more (b; extremely good value if travelling in a group), and there are a couple of agreeable doubles with a/c, phone and cable TV. Inn includes a large pool, kitchen facilities and a canteen dining room. ④/⑥.

Johnson's, 16 Buller St, Woodbrook ☎628 7553. Friendly, helpful hosts and spotless, well-maintained rooms with fans, cable TV and a/c. Guests have use of a shared kitchen and lounge. Excellent value, and just ten minutes from the town centre. ④/⑥.

Katsura, 17a Hillside Ave, Cascade ☎625 6637, fax 622 9968, www .katsuratrinidad.com. Radiating zen-like calm, this Japanese-style guesthouse has carp in the pond and gorgeous views over town. Modern, attractively decorated rooms have a/c and en-suite bathroom, and TVs and fridges are available for a little extra. Carnival rates include breakfast. ④/⑦.

La Calypso, 46 French St, Woodbrook ☎622 4077, fax 628 6895, *lacalypso@tstt.net.tt*. Functional but lacking atmosphere, with spartan decor Facilities vary from room to room – some have a/c, cable TV, kitchenette and bathroom, others are just a simple room with shared bathroom. There's also a jacuzzi, sundeck and use of the pool at *Alicia's*. ④/⑥.

La Maison Rustique, 16 Rust St, St Clair ☎ & fax 622 1512. Rooms at the front of this converted colonial house are airy and spacious; those at the back dark, cramped and overpriced. Some are en suite, but only one has a/c (most have a fan). A small self-catering cottage in the back yard, with separate doorbell, is also available to rent. ⑥/⑦.

Mauge's, 15 Gordon St ☎ & fax 625 2335, www.chrisbern.com/mauge's. Pleasant, modern and central, but rooms are on the small side. All have fans, a/c, TV and VCR, but only half have en-suite bathrooms. Carnival rates include breakfast, and there's occasional live entertainment at the restaurant/bar. ③/⑦.

Melbourne Inn, 7 French St, Woodbrook ☎623 4006, www.geocites.com /melbournebds, melbourn@caribsurf.com. Homely guesthouse with large rooms, ceiling and standing fans, and private or shared bathrooms. There's a sundeck and a large communal verandah. ③/④.

Par-May-La's Inn, 53 Picton St, Newtown ☎628 2008, fax 628-4707, www.parmaylas.com. On a quiet street (though very convenient for downtown), with helpful hosts and a communal verandah where breakfast – included in the rates – is served. Very spacious a/c rooms with phone, TV and en-suite bathroom. ⑤/⑦.

Pavilion Inn, 149 Tragarete Rd ☎633 8167 or 628 2547, www.pavilioninn .com. Opposite the Queen's Park Oval and above the *Cricket Wicket* bar, the rooms here – named after cricket grounds in the Caribbean – are convenient for matches and for Carnival. All are clean and appealing, with a/c, cable TV and private bathrooms, and rates include breakfast. ⑤/⑦.

Pearl's, 3–4 Victoria Square East ☎625 2158. A large old colonial mansion with a verandah overlooking picturesque Victoria Square, this is one of the best-value places in Port of Spain. The basic rooms have fans, sinks and 1960s furniture. Friendly, helpful hosts, and perfectly situated for carnival and downtown sightseeing. ②.

Pelican Inn, 2–4 Coblentz Ave, Cascade ☎625 6271, fax 624 7486, *theinn@pelicaninn.co.tt*. Old colonial house with verandah overlooking busy Coblentz Ave next to a popular pub/disco; expect some night-time noise. Functional, neat rooms with tiled floors, ceiling fans, a/c and en-suite bathrooms. Breakfast is included in Carnival rate. ④/⑦.

Schultzi's, 35 Fitt St, Woodbrook ☎622 7521. Lovely old colonial house presided over by an effervescent host. Rooms are eclectic: some have a/c, cable TV, fridge and private bathroom, others a fan and shared facilities. There's a kitchen for guests to use, a fancy wood-panelled bar and a lovely mosaic-tiled jacuzzi out back. Breakfast included in Carnival rate. ③/⑥.

Sundeck Suites, 42–44 Picton St, Newtown, ☎622 9560, fax 628 4707. Bright, modern self-catering apartments with kitchenette, ceiling fans, a/c, en-suite bathroom and TV; half of them also have a small balcony. There's a sundeck on the roof, and facilities for the disabled. ⑤/⑦.

Trinbago, 37 Ariapita Ave, Woodbrook ☎ & fax 627 7114, *tourist@tstt.net.tt*. Inexpensive and central with a tiny pool and a balcony overlooking Ariapita Avenue – perfect for watching Carnival pass by. Rooms vary; some have a/c, some just a fan, while a few share bathrooms; sister property *Tourist Villa* at 7 Methuen St (☎ & fax 627 5423) offers more of the same if this is full. ③/⑤.

Ville de French, 5 French St Woodbrook ☎625 4776. Large rooms in an old, well-located colonial house, all with fans and sinks, some en suite; there are a couple of self-contained units with kitchen as well. Excellent value, and breakfast is included in the Carnival rate. ③/⑥.

Williams Villa, 69 Luis St, Woodbrook ☎628 0824, fax 622 7782, www.williamvilla.com. Comfortable and homely but efficient place in a great location. The spacious rooms have a/c, phone, cable TV, fridge and en-suite bathroom; one has a kitchenette. Breakfast is included in all rates. ⑤.

Downtown Port of Spain

Dating back to the 1780s, Port of Spain's **downtown** area is the oldest part of the city. Despite its run-down appearance, this is the **shopping** and **finance centre** of the capital, constantly reinventing itself in a frenzy of modernization. Within the compact grid of streets surrounding broad **Brian Lara Promenade/Independence Square** and bustling **Frederick Street**, internationally known shops jostle for

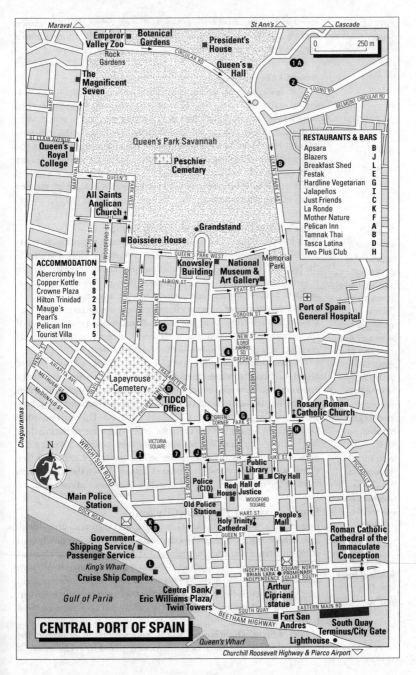

CENTRAL PORT OF SPAIN

Emperor
Valley Zoo
Botanical
Gardens
Rock
Gardens
President's
House
Queen's
Hall

The
Magnificent
Seven

0   250 m

❶A
❷

BELMONT CIRCULAR RD

CIRCULAR RD

LADY YOUNG RD

BELMONT CIRCULAR RD

ST CLAIR AVENUE

Queen's
Royal
College

Queen's Park Savannah

Peschier
Cemetery

QUEEN'S
PARK WEST

RESTAURANTS & BARS

Apsara	**B**
Blazers	**J**
Breakfast Shed	**L**
Festak	**E**
Hardline Vegetarian	**G**
Jalapeños	**I**
Just Friends	**C**
La Ronde	**K**
Mother Nature	**F**
Pelican Inn	**A**
Tamnak Thai	**B**
Tasca Latina	**D**
Two Plus Club	**H**

All Saints
Anglican
Church

Boissiere House

Grandstand

ACCOMMODATION

Abercromby Inn	**4**
Copper Kettle	**6**
Crowne Plaza	**8**
Hilton Trinidad	**2**
Mauge's	**3**
Pearl's	**7**
Pelican Inn	**1**
Tourist Villa	**5**

QUEEN'S PARK WEST

Knowsley
Building

National
Museum &
Art Gallery

Memorial
Park

ALBION ST

KEATE ST

GORDON ST

⊕
Port of Spain
General Hospital

❸

NEW ST
LORD
HARRIS
SQ
OXFORD ST

Lapeyrouse
Cemetery

Ⓒ

❹

Ⓓ
**TIDCO
Office**

❻ GREEN
CORNER
Ⓕ PARK ST **Ⓖ**

Ⓔ

Rosary Roman
✝ Catholic Church

Ⓗ

VICTORIA
SQUARE

Ⓣ
❼
Ⓙ

EDWARD ST

ST VINCENT ST

ABERCROMBY ST

FREDERICK ST

HENRY ST

CHARLOTTE ST

PICCADILLY ST

DUKE ST

Public
Library

City Hall

Main Police
Station

Police
(CID)

Red
House

Hall of
Justice

WOODFORD
SQUARE

People's
Mall

Roman Catholic
Cathedral of the
Immaculate
Conception

Old Police
Station

Holy Trinity
Cathedral

HART ST

QUEEN ST

DOCK ROAD

Ⓚ
❽

Government
Shipping Service/
Passenger Service

King's Wharf

Ⓛ

Cruise Ship Complex

WRIGHTSON ROAD

INDEPENDENCE SQUARE NORTH
BRIAN LARA PROMENADE
INDEPENDENCE SQUARE SOUTH

Arthur
Cipriani
statue

EASTERN MAIN RD

Gulf of Paria

Central Bank/
Eric Williams Plaza/
Twin Towers

SOUTH QUAY

Fort San
Andres

South Quay
Terminus/City Gate

BEETHAM HIGHWAY

Queen's Wharf

Lighthouse ●

Port of Spain

space with old Spanish warehouses, coffee exporters' offices, finance houses and the paraphernalia of the docks, while the thoroughfares are jammed with traffic, pedestrians and pavement vendors.

Around the docks

Port of Spain scarcely presents its most picturesque face to the visitor on arrival; whether you've come from the airport, disembarked from a boat or travelled by bus from another part of the island, your first sight of the capital will probably be the gritty industrial area **around the docks** at the southernmost edge of the city. This is the nexus of the city's transport system, the location of the **King's Wharf** docks and the **City Gate** bus station. Within its tangle of congested roads and transport terminals, however, are a couple of curious relics of the colonial era.

King's Wharf and the Cruise Ship Complex

Though services were suspended at the time of writing, Global Steam Ship Company usually offer a passenger boat from Port of Spain to Guiria in Venezuela; to find out if services have resumed, call ☎ 625 2547. Otherwise take the boat from Pier One in Chaguaramas (see p.126).

With its busy docks, vast warehouses and jagged, industrialized skyline of cranes, gantries and mounds of containers, **King's Wharf** is the hub of Trinidad's booming import–export trade. Everything from imported cars to green bananas passes through this hectic port, as dockers heave cargoes onto pick-up trucks, administrators scuttle about with sheaves of paperwork, and entrepreneurs fume while customs clearance grinds along its slow and painstaking course. Most of the action takes place in the early hours, when it's still relatively cool; activity gradually slows as the temperature rises.

The deep-water harbour, dredged in the 1930s, allowed Port of Spain to accommodate deep-draught ships, boosting Trinidad's economy and consolidating the city's position as the most important port in the southern Caribbean. It is also the **arrival** and **departure point** for boats to other Caribbean islands. The **Cruise Ship Complex** on King's Wharf caters for cruise passengers during their few hours on dry land. When a ship is docked it comes alive in a frenetic burst of activity, with shops selling souvenirs and duty free goods, and an overpriced craft market outside. When the ship leaves, most of the shops close and the complex becomes a ghost town.

South Quay Bus Terminus/City Gate

See p.66 for details of buses from City Gate.

Commonly referred to as **City Gate**, the grand Victorian stone building on South Quay, just to the east of the docks, was originally Port of Spain's **train station**. The railway, established in 1876 with a line to Arima, was shut down in the 1960s and is now remembered with nostalgia as Trinidad's roads become increasingly traffic-clogged. City Gate remains the hub of Trinidad's transport system, however, and is now the terminus for PTSC buses and maxi taxis running to all parts of the country.

Port of Spain's **lighthouse**, built to warn fishermen away from the rocky coastline, has since been marooned inland by reclamation. It now stands looking somewhat out of place in the middle of a traffic island on Wrightson Road behind City Gate. The heavy traffic that thunders past has turned the lighthouse into a Trinidadian leaning tower of Pisa, skewing it 5° from the vertical. It is not open to the public, and its only function today is to serve as an advertisement hoarding for a local paint company.

Fort San Andres
The unassuming terracotta-painted building that stands between City Gate and the maxi taxi terminus on Broadway is **Fort San Andres**, the best example of a wooden Spanish fort in Trinidad. Built in 1787, it was Port of Spain's main defence when the British invaded ten years later. Though it stayed as the site for a city museum, the few dusty portraits on display at present are hardly worth a look. When the fort was built, the sea lapped against its southern stone rampart; now, the nearest shoreline is occupied by the busy docks.

Brian Lara Promenade/Independence Square
The wide boulevard that runs the width of the city centre just north of the docks is **Brian Lara Promenade/Independence Square**. It consists of two parallel streets, divided by a paved area, that have been furnished with benches and chess tables, making it a popular after-work hang-out where locals lime on the benches; stalls are set up against closed offices and street food vendors do a brisk trade. During the festival season, the promenade hosts **free concerts** and performances, advertised in the local press and radio.

The cumbersome moniker is a result of frequent name changes in recent decades. Until independence in 1962, the thoroughfare was called Marine Square (the land had been reclaimed from the sea in 1816); there's still a sign bearing this name at the centre of the promenade. Rechristened Independence Square in 1962, it was later renamed in honour of Trinidad's most famous cricketer. Most locals still call it Independence Square, while media and tourist publications use both names. This has resulted in an official compromise: the two parallel streets are named Independence Square north and south, while the paved area between them is known as the promenade.

The western end of the promenade is dominated by the twin towers of the **Central Bank of Trinidad and Tobago**. Opened in 1985, the two 22-storey buildings are the highest in Trinidad. The heart of Port of Spain's **financial district**, the complex houses the Central Bank, the Prime Minister's offices and the Central Bank Auditorium. Halfway down, at the junction with Frederick Street, is the **Arthur Cipriani statue**. A white French Creole who had served in the British West Indian Regiment during World War I, Cipriani campaigned energetically for compulsory education and self-government for the island. As president of the Trinidad Workingman's Association (later the Trinidad Labour Party) and mayor of the city in the 1920s, he

The Drag Mall
is open
10am–5pm.

was the only legislator of his day to defend workers' rights, though by the following decade his increasingly reformist stance had disillusioned many former supporters. He died in 1945 and is buried in the Lapeyrouse Cemetery in Woodbrook (see p.89).

Just east of the statue, opposite the *Royal Castle* fast-food outlet, is the **UCW Drag Brothers Mall**. Locally known as the "**Drag Mall**", the ten small shops specialize in handmade leather sandals, local arts and crafts and Rastafarian souvenirs. If none of the sandals take your fancy, you can have a pair made to your own design.

As you continue east down the promenade, you come to the imposing **Roman Catholic Cathedral of the Immaculate Conception**, another legacy of Governor Woodford's post-fire reconstruction. Catholicism, the religion of the Spanish–French Creole establishment, had come to play a major role in the political and cultural life of Trinidad, and Woodford, though himself an Anglican, realized a building appropriate for state occasions was required. The twin-towered Gothic cathedral took sixteen years to build, and was finally completed in 1836. The ironwork frame was shipped from England, while the blue metal stone came from the local Laventille quarries; for the high altar, **Florentine** marble was imported from Italy. Period drawings on display in the National Museum show that when the church was completed, on newly reclaimed land, the sea lapped against its eastern wall. In 1984, the cathedral underwent extensive renovations, including the addition of sixteen new **stained-glass windows**, made to order in Ireland, which depict the many ethnic groups which have contributed to the population of Trinidad and Tobago. The church is open to all, and has services every evening and on Sundays. All Catholic holidays are celebrated; special masses are held at Christmas, Easter and on Ash Wednesday.

The Chee
Mooke Bakery
on the north
side of
Columbus
Square sells
the most
delicious bread
in town. Open
Mon–Sat
6am–6pm.

The promenade comes to an end just east of the cathedral at diminutive **Columbus Square**. Despite its brightly painted statue of the explorer, the square is very run-down, with beggars hanging out on the street corner.

Frederick Street and around

Frederick Street is Port of Spain's main shopping drag, a narrow street crammed with shops and malls selling clothes, shoes, materials and souvenirs; its pavements are thronged with street vendors selling home-made jewellery, belts, cassettes and arts and crafts. Like much of the downtown area, it's in the throes of modernization, with new malls and expensive shops opening every month. At the **People's Mall** on the corner of Frederick and Queen streets, small stalls and tiny shops sell clothes and shoes imported straight from New York, alongside hand-painted T-shirts, incense and Rasta craft.

Woodford Square

Halfway up Frederick Street, the pretty, tree-shaded **Woodford Square** is named after the British governor who had it built in the early nineteenth century. Its western side is dominated by the grand Edwardian facade of the **Red House**, seat of Trinidad and Tobago's parliament. On the south side stands the city's **Anglican Cathedral**, while in the square itself are a picturesque colonial bandstand and an elegant, if not always functional, cast-iron fountain supported by mermaids and mermen, which dates back to 1866.

Woodford Square is best known, however, as a centre of **political activism**. As early as 1903 it was the scene of a protest meeting against the introduction of new water rates; the demonstration quickly got out of hand, and in the ensuing riots the original Red House was burned to the ground. It was in 1956, however, that the square's reputation as a political cockpit really got going with the establishment of the "**University of Woodford Square**". This was the brainchild of **Eric Williams**, historian, father of the national independence movement and first prime minister of the country, who would deliver weekly public lectures in the square on the issues of the day. In the 1970s, the square became a focal point for the Black Power movement, who renamed it the "people's parliament". It held the largest funeral ever seen in Port of Spain, that of Basil Davis, a young activist shot by the police during Black Power protests in the 1970s.

Woodford Square remains a lively political forum where issues are fiercely debated; in the southeast corner, a blackboard lists the topic for discussion each day. Predominantly middle-aged men argue passionately about about local affairs to international events. Anyone can join in, if they can get a word in edgeways; it's not a platform for the faint-hearted or soft-spoken.

The Red House

Beneath its massive green copper cupola, the imposing neo-Renaissance **Red House** is actually more a faded, peeling terracotta. The seat of Trinidad and Tobago's parliament inherited its popular name from an earlier building on the site, which was painted bright red to celebrate Queen Victoria's diamond jubilee in 1897. The present structure, completed four years after its predecessor was burnt down in the 1903 water riots, was itself attacked in the coup (see box on p.80), and bullet holes still scar the stonework. Outside the front entrance, facing Woodfood Square, an eternal flame commemorates government and security personnel who died in the 1990 coup.

Members of the public can view the parliament in session on Fridays at 1.30pm; use the entrance on Knox Street.

The Public Library, Hall of Justice and City Hall

On the northwest side of Woodford Square stands the **Trinidad Public Library**, built in 1901. Newspapers are pasted up daily outside the main entrance of this large cream stone building, incongruously sandwiched between two brutally functional modern slabs of glass and concrete. A new high-rise library building, making a prominent addition to the Port of Spain skyline, is under construction near the *Crowne Plaza* hotel. To the current library's left is the plain,

The 1990 coup

At 6.30pm on July 27, 1990, **Yasin Abu Bakr**, leader of the fundamental-
ist revolutionary group **Jamaat-al-Muslimeen**, announced on television
that he had overthrown the government of Trinidad and Tobago. Thirty
minutes earlier, members of the group had stormed the Red House and
taken several government ministers hostage, including Prime Minister
Arthur Robinson. The police headquarters around the corner on Sackville
Street was firebombed and all but destroyed (see opposite). **Looting** took
the capital by storm, and a **state of emergency** was called, requiring all
citizens to remain indoors after dark.

The Jamaat-al-Muslimeen had already had many run-ins with the
authorities over a land dispute and the killing of one of its members by the
police. Relying on the army to support the revolt, they also hoped to capitalize on public discontent with the government's harsh fiscal policies, satirized by the calypsonian Sparrow in his song *Capitalism Gone Mad*. Yet
however little love they may have had for the government, few
Trinidadians were willing to support its violent overthrow by an armed
group of religious extremists. With little public support, and surrounded
by loyal government troops, the rebels surrendered after a six-day siege,
only after negotiating an amnesty agreement with the police which guaranteed that perpetrators of the coup would not be arrested for their activities. Nonetheless, Bakr and 113 other Jamaat members were taken into
custody as soon as they surrendered, and remained in jail for two years
whilst the courts debated the validity of the amnesty, which, they said, had
been granted only as a means of preventing the hostages from being killed.
The Jamaat members were eventually set free after a ruling by the UK
Privy Council that the amnesty was invalid, but that it would be against due
process to have the suspects rearrested and tried for the offences com-
mited during the coup. The leaders remain at liberty today, and Jamaat-al-
Muslimeen membership continues to rise.

Many Trinidadians found it hard to believe that such events could take
place in stable, democratic, fun-loving Trinidad. With characteristic
humour, the crisis was soon turned into a fund of amusing stories. Ask any
Trinidadian about the coup and you will hear tales of wild **"curfew parties"**
and imaginative explanations given to the police of the five TVs found in a
neighbour's house.

modern-looking **Hall of Justice**; built in 1979, it houses the Supreme
Court of Trinidad and Tobago. To the right of the library is another
concrete pile, the 1961 **City Hall**, home to Port of Spain's council
and the mayor's office.

Holy Trinity Cathedral

The Anglican **Holy Trinity Cathedral** on the south side of Woodford
Square was another of the governor's many initiatives to improve the
public spaces of Port of Spain. The original idea was to build it in the
middle of the square itself, and work was already under way when
Woodford bowed to popular protest and moved it to its present site.
This elegant stone church was built in 1818 along traditional Gothic

lines, with a large clock tower. The cool, shady interior is relatively unadorned, its outstanding feature the mahogany hammer-beam roof, made in England and modelled on a medieval original in London's Westminster Hall. A life-size **effigy of Governor Woodford** lies on his tomb by the south wall; the plaques nearby commemorate various other colonial dignitaries.

Trinidad Theatre Workshop

The dilapidated stone building opposite the Holy Trinity Cathedral, on the corner of Hart and Abercromby streets, was the original home of the **Trinidad Theatre Workshop** (TTW), now moved to Rust Street in Woodbrook. Founded in 1959 by poet and playwright Derek Walcott, it established a theatrical tradition in Trinidad, made acting a recognized profession and launched the careers of many of the Caribbean's most famous actors. Errol Jones, Stanley Marshal and Albert Labeau were all influential in the development of the TTW, and among the many actors to cut their teeth here was Helen Camp, who went on to establish the internationally successful Trinidad Tent Theatre.

Although the TTW enjoyed its heyday in the 1960s and 1970s, Walcott's 1992 Nobel Prize for literature inspired a regeneration of the centre, giving rise to a new generation of talented Trinidadian actors. Many who were influenced by the TTW – including Roger Roberts, Wendell Manwarren and Cecilia Salazar – were in turn instrumental in the establishment of prestigious local theatre groups such as the Bagasse Company. At the new base, 17 Rust St in Woodbrook (☎622 2217 or 628 0356), the TTW holds acting workshops, as well as staging the excellent "Friday Night Limelight" talent shows at the Little Carib Theatre (8pm onwards; small cover charge).

The Old Police Station

Contrary to appearances, the ruined building just west of Woodford Square at the corner of Sackville and St Vincent streets is not an old monument, but wreckage of the **Old Police Station** that was fire-bombed in the 1990 coup. While some maintain that it's an eyesore that ought to be demolished, others would prefer it to remain as a warning to any who might think of following in the Jamaat-al-Muslimeen's footsteps. Although a new headquarters has been built on the other side of the road, the old building is currently being refurbished for police use – much to the consternation of local conservationists, who wanted it opened up to the public as a museum.

On the wall of the new police station is the emblem of Trinidad and Tobago's police force, consisting of a hummingbird and a police badge inside a Star of David. The hummingbird is the national symbol which replaced the crown after independence, while the star is a colonial leftover that has given rise to much confusion. Contrary to popular belief, it is not the Jewish Star of David but the symbol of Governor Picton's patron saint, St David.

Rosary Church

At the corner of Henry and Park streets stands the **Rosary Roman Catholic Church**. Built between 1892 and 1910, this dignified Gothic Revival church is the most impressive of the city's three cathedrals, though its imposing towers and ornate stonework are hemmed in by buildings on all sides. You're in luck if you find it open, for the spacious interior is an oasis of peace in the hectic city, and the old **stained glass**, with its finely detailed Biblical scenes, is the most beautiful in Port of Spain. Unfortunately the effect is somewhat spoilt by the fluorescent lighting, peeling paint and general dilapidation; the church is currently raising funds for repair work.

Uptown

Ranged around the broad, grassy expanse of the **Queen's Park Savannah** and framed by the foothills of the Northern Range, Port of Spain's **uptown** district oozes prosperity. Along the wide boulevards that ring the Savannah, the palatial mansions of the colonial plantocracy compete with the *Hilton* hotel, the residences of the republic's president and prime minister, and the glitzy modern headquarters of insurance companies. Away from this circuit of roads, which forms Port of Spain's busiest one-way system, the streets exude the sober opulence of embassy quarters the world over, untouched by the urban razzmatazz of downtown Port of Spain.

Queen's Park Savannah

The **Queen's Park Savannah** is Port of Spain's largest open space. Within the 3.7-kilometre circuit of its perimeter roads, its grassy expanse is crisscrossed by paths and shaded by the spreading branches of old samaan trees. Originally part of the St Ann's sugarcane estate, the Savannah was bought by Governor Woodford in 1817 and developed into a city park. Subsequent attempts to build on parts of it were seen off by vigorous public protest, and the park has remained its original size.

See the Carnival calendar of events on p.104 for detailed descriptions of the various Carnival competitions.

Often deserted during the hot daylight hours, the Savannah comes to life after 4pm, with football games, joggers, and couples and families taking an early evening stroll. It is particularly busy between 4pm and 8pm, when temporary food stalls, serving tasty local snacks such as roasted corn, bake and shark, pholouri and rotis are set up. People take their daily constitutional, sit and chat on the benches lining the circumference of the park, or play football and cricket; and in the windy months of March and April, the Savannah is full of children flying kites.

The **Trinidad Turf Club** at the southern end of the park was once Trinidad's premier horse racing track. The races have now moved to Arima (see p.162), but all the Carnival competitions, including

Panorama, Dimanche Gras, Parade of the Bands and Champs in Concert, are held in the grandstands. Many other events take place here, including performances by visiting international artists. Though the seats are numbingly hard, the setting is incomparably atmospheric, with performances taking place against a backdrop of the mountains and the starry Caribbean sky.

Right in the middle of the Savannah, in total contrast to the public conviviality taking place all round, is an eerie enclave of silence. From behind its high stone wall, the **Peschier family cemetery** – burial ground of the owners of the St Ann's estate – exudes an air of mystery. The graveyard is closed to the public, and all that can be seen over the wall is an ancient and towering palm tree.

Queen's Park West

Travelling clockwise around the Savannah on **Queen's Park West**, you'll come across numerous examples of gingerbread architecture built by the Glaswegian architect George Brown, who had the distinctive fretted woodwork mass-produced and used it extensively on all his buildings. Dating from 1904, the ornately decorated **Knowsley Building** on the corner of Chancery Lane resembles a child's fantasy doll's house; it's odd to think that it now houses government offices. The **George Brown House** at the corner of Stanmore Avenue is somewhat plainer, though still graced by a great deal of refined fretwork. **Boissiere House** on the corner of Cipriani Boulevard is fondly called the "**Gingerbread House**" by locals, and you'd be hard pushed to find a better example of the style. It's a splendidly whimsical concoction of fretted wooden finials and bargeboards, with stained glass depicting meandering strawberry vines and a small pagoda-like roof over one room. None of these buildings is open to the public, which is a pity, since their interiors are reputed to be just as graceful and imaginative.

National Museum and Art Gallery

The imposing, gabled building at the corner of Frederick and Keate streets is an appropriately grand setting for the **National Museum and Art Gallery**. Built in 1892 as part of the preparations for Queen Victoria's jubilee, it still has the legend **Royal Victoria Institute** inscribed over its door. The museum's collection is extensive, covering everything from early **Amerindian history** to the technology of the **oil industry**. Despite recent improvements, however, some of the artefacts remain unlabelled or poorly displayed; nonetheless, the museum provides an essential overview of the history and culture of Port of Spain and of Trinidad and Tobago, as well as housing an excellent collection of works by local artists; it's well worth a couple of hours of your time.

On the ground floor, in front of the entrance is a wall of photographs from past Carnivals which provide a glimpse of the skill of Trinidad's mas makers and designers; the selection includes Peter Minshall's seminal *Man Crab* and *Washer Woman* King and Queen designs, from the 1983 presentation *The River*. However, the terrible labelling makes it difficult to know what's what. In the room to the left, there's an interesting chronology of the development of the **steel pan** as a musical instrument (for more on pan, see p.345), while a dusty collection of old **Carnival costumes** does scant justice to the art form, though it does give some idea of the detailed work involved. Otherwise, the ground floor is taken up with racks of locally found **geological specimens**, including some enormous quartz crystals, as well as a re-creation of a 1940s **barracks yard**, and displays on local history up to independence (look out for the yellowing photos of Port of Spain through the ages), and on **industry**, from coconuts and cocoa to sugar and rum.

The National Museum and Art Gallery is open Tues–Sat 10am–6pm, Sun 2–6pm; free.

The fabulous permanent exhibit of **Trinidadian art** starts on the stairs leading to the upper level, where there are family scenes by **Peter Minshall** and delicate nudes in watercolours and ink by **Stephen Gumbrell**. The upper level is taken up almost entirely by a brightly lit room, the wooden ceiling restored to its original glory. Rich with colour and intricate detail, **Leroy Clarke**'s huge *Queen of the Bands* and *Weavers of the Dust* make a stunning start to the collection, while **Shasti Mahraj**'s *Check Valve* is a marvellous depiction of the madness of Carnival; **Bruce Holley**'s *Bacchanalia* is a similarly visceral portrayal of Jouvert morning. Interspersed between ambitious sculpture and other installations are lithographs of the old Port of Spain by **Michel Cazabon** and works by internationally known contemporary painters such as **Carlisle Chang, Boscoe Holder, John Newel Lewis, Nina Squires** and **Dermot Lousion**. Many of the works draw on Trinidadian folklore, such as **William Chen**'s uncharacteristically spooky *Papa Bois* (a friendly spirit who serves as protector of the forest); Alfredo Codallo's rendition of local folklore characters includes most of the well-known suspects, from the Soucouyant (a woman who turns into a ball of fire to travel the countryside searching for human blood to drink), to Douens (faceless children who died without being christened) and La Diablesse, a beautiful woman with one cloven hoof who leads drunken men to their deaths.

The Magnificent Seven

North of Queen's Park West on Maraval Road stands a bizarre group of mansions affectionately known as the **Magnificent Seven**. A magical-realist parade of European architectural styles with a tropical slant, these remarkable buildings are the result of the competing egos of rival plantation owners, each of whom tried to outdo his neighbours in grandeur. All the mansions were constructed in 1904, except for Hayes Court, which was built in 1910. Although none of the buildings is open to the public, their exteriors are easily seen from the road, most of them in dire need of repair.

The first of the seven is **Queen's Royal College**, Trinidad's most prestigious school, whose former pupils include the authors VS and Shiva Naipaul, and the country's first prime minister, Eric Williams. It's built in Germanic Renaissance style, with arcaded balconies and cream-and-ochre stucco offsetting the blue limestone cornerstones; the tall clock tower can be seen from all over Port of Spain.

Hayes Court, home to the Anglican bishop of Trinidad, is next, a grand mansion displaying a mix of French and British architectural influences. **Mille Fleurs** is an elaborate gingerbread house, with intricate wooden fretwork. Now the office of the National Security Council, it was originally built for Dr Henrique Prada, a successful doctor who went on to become the city's most distinguished mayor between 1914 and 1917.

Roomor, a florid exercise in the French Baroque style, was commissioned by the estate owner Lucien Ambard. The building is composed of Italian marble and tiles from France, while its columns, galleries, towers and pinnacles are decorated with elaborate ironwork. The **Archbishop's House**, official residence of the Roman Catholic archbishop of Port of Spain, is a weighty neo-Romanesque pile of Irish marble and red granite, capped by a copper roof.

The next house along is **Whitehall**, a Venetian-style palazzo whose gleaming white paintwork gives it the air of a freshly iced birthday cake. Originally the home of a cocoa estate owner named Agostini, the building has had a somewhat chequered history. During World War II it was commandeered by the US military, after which it became a cultural centre, a library and then a broadcasting unit. In 1954 it was sold to the Trinidadian government and now houses some of its departments.

The most outlandish structure of the seven, **Killarney**, stands at the northern end of Maraval Road just before it turns east into Circular Road. A fairy-tale castle of brick and limestone, bristling with turrets and spires, it was built for a German plantation owner named Stollmeyer by the Scottish architect Robert Giles, who modelled it on Queen Victoria's residence at Balmoral. The architectural historian John Newel Lewis perfectly captured the delicious absurdity of Killarney when he wrote: "A German built a bit of an untypical Scottish castle in Trinidad and called it by an Irish name. He must have been by that time a Trinidadian, because only Trinidadians do these things." The Stollmeyer family sold the castle to the Trinidadian government in 1979, and it now houses government offices.

Emperor Valley Zoo and Botanical Gardens

On the northern side of the Savannah is the **Emperor Valley Zoo**, a magnet for local kids, with balloon and novelty-sellers aplenty round

*The Emperor
Valley Zoo is
open daily
9.30am–6pm,
with last
tickets sold at
5.30pm. Adults
TT$4, children
(3–12 years)
TT$2.*

the entrance, but also worth a wander to get a close-up look at Trinidadian species that you're unlikely to see in the wild. The animals are well kept, if housed in rather compact cages, and the zoo makes a nice place to while away an hour or two. Opened in 1952, its collection of local and foreign animals – though small by international standards – is reputedly the most extensive in the Caribbean, and includes **brocket deer**, **quenk**, **otters**, a large selection of **monkeys**, aquarium fish and **snakes** (note the markings of the venomous fer-de-lance and bushmaster if you intend to hike in the bush), as well as **ocelots**, **spectacled caiman** and numerous **birds**, including parrots, toucans and pink "scarlet" ibis, whose carotene-supplemented diet doesn't appear to have been successful in sustaining their usual crimson plumage. For more on the flora and fauna of Trinidad and Tobago, see p.348–354.

*The Botanical
Gardens are
open daily
6am–6pm;
free.*

Next door to the zoo, and spreading back from the Savannah toward the President's House, is the exquisite **Botanical Gardens**, established in 1820 by Governor Woodford and the botanist David Lockhart and home to the one of the oldest collections of exotic plants and trees in the western hemisphere. There are no official guides, though some knowledgeable Trinidadians frequent the gardens, and someone will usually offer to show you round for a small fee. It's a good idea to take up one of the offers, as most of the labelling has disappeared, and the tours usually come with a few anecdotes – Anthony Brown is particularly good. Though guides know all the botanical names, they'll also give you the local terms: "Hat Stand", "Raw Beef" and "Napoleon's Hat" are some of the more unusual, and colourfully named, specimens. A small **cemetery**, partly fenced off from the rest of the gardens, contains the crumbling gravestones of Lockhart and many of the island's governors, including Solomon Hochoy. Beneath the Palmiste palms, a plaque marks another burial, that of an Australian wallaby, a pet of the Prince of Wales which died during his visit to the island. At the weekends, the gardens are busy with school groups, parties of strollers and groups of regulars who congregate on their favourite benches for a spot of ol' talk. Otherwise, you'll often have the place more or less to yourself.

Behind the Botanical Gardens, in well-manicured gardens, stands the **President's House**. This austere, stately villa was built in 1876 as the residence of the island's British governors, and continued to fulfill this function until independence in 1962. The grounds are not open to the public, but you can get a good view of the building from the Botanical Gardens. The **Prime Minister's Residence** is hidden from view behind the President's House, and likewise is closed to the public.

St Ann's

From the northeast corner of the Savannah, next to the *Hilton*, St Ann's Road heads past the Queen's Hall (a favourite venue for Carnival) into the leafy suburb of **ST ANN'S**. Primarily a residential area that melts almost seamlessly into the equally chi-chi Cascade district to the east, St Ann's offers little in the way of sightseeing, but there are a couple of attractions worth checking out. Follow St Ann's Road for about five minutes until the road divides; take the right fork and you'll get to the *Cascadia* hotel, home of the *Coconuts* nightclub and a popular **waterpark** with a couple of looping slides (Sat, Sun and public holidays 10am–5.30pm; TT$20). The left fork, Ariapita Road, threads into the hills that divide St Ann's from Cascade and Diego Martin. Follow the road to its end and you'll meet the banks of the St Ann's River, where there are several popular spots from which to "take in the springs". Otherwise, turn off the main St Ann's Road onto Upper Ariapita Road, and negotiate the steep incline to get to **Belle Vue Estate** (☎624 7717), a former cocoa plantation 900 feet up in the hills. Now a private home and equestrian centre, Belle Vue also has a small **museum** in the original cocoa house (where pods were dried) with displays on the processing of this delectable pod, and there's also a small collection of **animals**, including peacocks, toucans, parrots, turtles and agoutis. You can hike a series of **trails** of varying length and difficulty around the estate and cool off afterwards in a lovely natural-style **pool** fed by spring water. If you want to exert your muscles even further, walk ten minutes uphill to **"The Pines"**, a plateau surrounded by a forest of Caribbean pine that affords marvellous views down to Port of Spain and inland over the hills that surround Port of Spain. Horse riding lessons and hacks are also available; to arrange these or a visit to Belle Vue, you must first call ahead.

The western suburbs

Crammed between the Gulf of Paria to the south and the uphill incline of the Northern Range, the **western suburbs** of Port of Spain are the cultural centre of the capital. For most of the year, the area looks purely residential, but as **Carnival** draws near, many of the houses are converted into mas camps, where the bands who organize the parades have their bases (see p.90). The creative energy of **Carnival production** is concentrated in **Woodbrook**, while the streets of **St James** come alive with revellers at night throughout the year. The prosperous residential area of **St Clair** is far more sedate and aloof, while the thriving commercial centre of **Newtown** also holds the offices of many of Trinidad's radio stations.

Woodbrook

The elegant old district of **WOODBROOK** stretches for about a kilometre across the flat expanse between **Tragarete Road**, **Philipp Street** and the **Maraval River**. The area was originally a sugar cane estate owned by the Siegert family, creators of Trinidad's famous Angostura Bitters (see p.44), and many local streets – such as Carlos, Luis and Siegert streets – bear their names. The suburb, first settled in 1911, was traditionally a middle-class residential area, and its streets are still graced by old houses with wonderful fretwork barge-

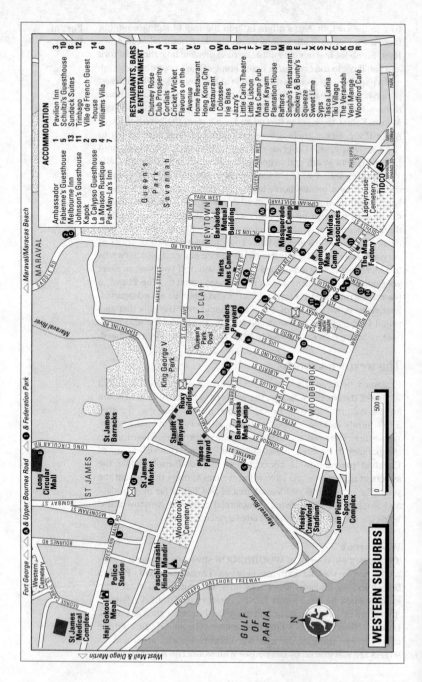

WESTERN SUBURBS

ACCOMMODATION

Ambassador	3
Fabienne's Guesthouse	5
Melbourne Inn	13
Johnson's Guesthouse	1
Kapok	2
La Calypso Guesthouse	9
La Maison Rustique	4
Par-May-La's Inn	7
Pavilion Inn	3
Schultzi's Guesthouse	10
Sundeck Suites	8
Trinbago	11
Ville de French Guest -house	12
Williams Villa	14
	6

RESTAURANTS, BARS & ENTERTAINMENT

Chutney Rose	T
Club Prosperity	A
Cordials	J
Cricket Wicket	H
Flavours on the Avenue	V
Home Restaurant	G
Hong Kong City Restaurant	O
Il Colosseo	W
Irie Bites	P
Jazzy's	D
Little Carib Theatre	I
Little Lisbon	F
Mas Camp Pub	Y
Omar Kayam	N
Plantation House	U
Rafters	M
Singho's Restaurant	B
Smokey & Bunty's	E
Squeeze	L
Sweet Lime	X
Syps	S
Tasca Latina	Z
Tiki Village	C
The Verandah	K
Veni Mange	Q
Woodford Café	R

Maraval/Maracas Beach △

Maraval △

Fort George △   △ & Upper Bournes Road   ◁ & Federation Park

Western Cemetery

GEORGE CABRAL ST

Haji Gokool Meah

St James Medical Complex

Police Station

BOURNES RD

MOONERHAM ST

BOMBAY ST

Paschimtaashi Hindu Mandir

Long Circular Mall B

St James Barracks

LONG CIRCULAR RD

ST JAMES

St James Market G

Woodbrook Cemetery

WESTERN MAIN RD

King George V Park

Queen's Park Oval

SERPENTINE RD

Maraval River

SADDLE RD

MARAVAL RD

HAYES STREET

ST CLAIR

Queen's Park Savannah

NEWTOWN

Barbados Mutual Building

PARK WEST

QUEEN'S PARK WEST

Harts Mas Camp

ALCAZAR ST

RUST ST

FICTION ST

Invaders Panyard

Roxy Building

Stadiff Panyard

Phase II Panyard

Barbarossa Mas Camp

WARREN ST

CARLOS ST

LUIS ST

ROSAINO ST

ALFREDO ST

ALBERTO ST

GALLUS ST

ANA ST

PETRA ST

DE VERTEUIL ST

O'CONNOR ST

SMYTHE ST

BELLE SMYTHE ST

WOODBROOK

ARIAPITA AVE

MUCURAPO RD

Hasley Crawford Stadium

Jean Pierre Sports Complex

Masquerade Mas Camp

CIPRIANI BOULEVARD

Legends Mas Camp

D'Midas Associates

The Mas Factory

FITT ST

CORNELIO ST

MURRAY ST

FRENCH ST

Adam Smith Square

Lapeyrouse Cemetery

PHILLIPS ST

PARK ST

GREEN CORNER

TIDCO Z

DE LUCIA ST

MAHAIMA GRAND SPA

MARACAS ROYAL RD

MUCURAPO FORESHORE FREEWAY

GULF OF PARIA

N

500 m

0

West Mall & Diego Martin ◁

boards, delicate balustrades and finials. Though it has become increasingly commercialized in recent decades, it is a safe and pleasant area to stay, with several good restaurants and a handful of lively nightspots.

At the edge of Woodbrook, on Philipps Street, is the entrance to the **Lapeyrouse Cemetery** (daily 6am–6pm), a walled burial ground dating back to 1813. Victorian tombs adorned with Gothic spires, angels and ornate fretwork are eerily framed against the lush, tropical backdrop; long strands of ivy trail over the unkempt graves, while gravediggers, shaded by makeshift tents, dig spaces for new residents. The Siegert family is buried here, as are the Trinidadian labour leader Arthur Cipriani, the calypsonian Melody, and Charlie King, the policeman killed in the Butler Riots in the 1930s (see p.330). The names on the gravestones provide clues to the diverse origins – Chinese, Spanish, African, Indian and European – of Port of Spain's inhabitants, and the inscriptions reflect its varied religious affiliations: Catholics, Anglicans, Baptists and many other faiths are represented here. The cemetery's newest residents, the vagrants who sleep in the more dilapidated tombs, have become a talking point in recent years, provoking press articles about the problem of homelessness.

At the western end of **Tragarete Road** – a mix of shops, restaurants and offices – stands the **Queen's Park Oval**. Originally built in 1896, this is Trinidad's premier **cricket ground**, hosting national and international matches in season (Feb–April), as well as doubling as a concert venue – the annual Soca Monarch competition is held here at Carnival time. Even if you're not a cricket fan, it's well worth making the effort to attend a Test or One-Day match here: a unique and hugely enjoyable experience. The game is a national obsession in Trinidad, and matches are followed with a passion, especially if local hero Brian Lara – the "Prince of Port of Spain" – is playing. The atmosphere is rowdy but good-natured, with fans draped in the national flag, music blaring from sound systems after every over and wicket, and vendors selling cold beer and nuts around the stands.

Woodbrook is home to numerous **mas camps**, which burst into life during Carnival season, from November to February. Now famous for its calypso nights, the **Mas Camp Pub** (see p.103) on the corner of Ariapita Avenue and French Street was once the workshop and headquarters of Peter Minshall's Callaloo mas camp, which subsequently relocated to Chaguaramas (see p.120).

The long-established **Mas Factory**, run by Albert Bailey one block away on Buller Street, is famous for its portrayal of traditional characters and skilful wire bending. They'll let you watch the Carnival costumes being made if you ring in advance (☎628 7600). Round the corner at 15–17 Kitchener St, **D'Midas Associates** also provide good examples of traditional Carnival design with lots of feathers, sequins and beading – all the painstaking, handmade work which is

The Queen's Park Oval is open 8am–4pm; ask the security guard on the gate to let you in. Seats in the stands cost TT$35–80, or you can pay TT$150–180 for an all-inclusive ticket to the Trini Posse stand (food and drink included). For information call ☎628 4177.

The Callaloo registration office, which changes venues most years, is always open Nov–Feb; ☎634 4491 for current information.

gradually being cut out by more modern, profit-oriented bands. Again, you can see the costumes being made if you ring in advance (☎622 8233). As with all mas camps the opening hours are variable; usually from 9am until at least 10pm.

Mas camps

Mas camps – the headquarters of the Carnival bands – are established throughout Port of Spain in old gingerbread family homes or converted shops. During the Carnival months furniture is stored away and the largest room turns into a workshop full of feathers, sequins and sewing machines. Some of the long-established camps have now become year-round mas factories. The camps provide a focus for the whole Trinidadian art community; many a famous Trinidadian artist, actor, dancer or writer will be found at a mas camp during the Carnival season.

All the bands display some ten to twenty designs, divided into the different **sections** of the band, at their camp in the run-up to Carnival. Anyone can choose a costume from the designs, and watch as it is made; prices start at about US$100. In recent years costumes have increasingly catered to the masqueraders' desire to wear as little as possible in the tropical heat, though Minshall and a few others still make more elaborate, artistic creations. If you're arriving in town just before carnival, you might want to book your costume online; bands' sites are listed below.

The list below represents a selection of the best-known mas camps in Port of Spain: for a full list of bands, contact the National Carnival Bands Association, Queen's Park Savannah ☎627 1422, or TIDCO ☎627 5912. Near Carnival time, the bands are often listed in newspapers. The National Carnival Commission's website (www.carnivalncc.com) has more on Mas, as does *www.carnaval.com*.

Barbarossa
26 Taylor St, Woodbrook
☎628 6008, *www.barbarossaintl.com*
(Richard Affong)

Callaloo Company
Building C, Western Main Road,
Chaguaramas
☎634 4491, *www.callaloo.co.tt*
(Peter Minshall)

D'Midas Associates
15–17 Kitchener St, Woodbrook
☎622 8233
(Stephen Derek)

Funtasia
36a Maraval Rd
☎622 4326, *www.funtasiainc.com*

Harts Ltd
5 Alcazar St, St Clair
☎622 8038, *www.hartscarnival.com*
(Thais & Gerald Hart)

Legends
88 Roberts St, Woodbrook
☎622 7466, *www.legendscarnival.com*
(Mike Antoine and Ian McKenzie)

Mas Factory
15 Buller St, Woodbrook
☎628 7600
(Albert Bailey)

Masquerade
49–51 Cipriani Blvd, Newtown
☎625 7257, *www.masquerade.co.tt*
(Wayne Berkley)

Old Fashioned Sailors
51 Pelham St, Belmont
☎624 3692
(Jason Griffith)

Poison
1 Harroden Place, Petit Valley
632 3986, *www.poison.co.tt*
(Michael Headley)

Trini Revellers
35 Gallus St, Woodbrook
☎625 1881, *www.revellers.com*
(Richard Bartholomew)

At the eastern end of Woodbrook, at 26 Taylor St, is the **Barbarossa mas camp**. This popular band attracts the young and beautiful of Port of Spain, and during Carnival season its bikini mas designs are displayed on the porch. Visitors are welcome to view production.

St James

It was in **ST JAMES** that the British landed in 1797. Legend has it that they fortified themselves with rum punch that they found here, giving themselves the courage to capture Port of Spain. Once the Peru sugar cane estate, the area was settled by **Indian** indentured labourers after emancipation (see p.329). The names they gave to their streets – Calcutta, Delhi and Madras – bear witness to their homesickness.

Today, St James is one of the capital's most cosmopolitan districts, with residents from all the country's ethnic groups. The streets are lined with modern houses with Indianesque capitals on concrete columns and colourful clusters of puja flags in the gardens; the upper storeys often remain unfinished, an empty frame of reinforced concrete stilts waiting for the next generation to provide the cash to build upwards. It's a bustling place, especially at night when it becomes the prime liming spot in Port of Spain. Music blasts from cars, bars and clubs; locals dressed in clubbing gear lime alongside old men in jeans and T-shirts; and street stalls sell roti, oysters, corn soup, halal sandwiches and jerk chicken.

The approach to St James from Woodbrook at the start of the Western Main Road is dominated by the imposing **Roxy Building**. It was built as a cinema, but its ritzy classical-moderne colonnade now houses a branch of *Pizza Hut*. On the other side of the road is a statue in tribute to the grandmaster of calypso, the late **Lord Kitchener** (see p.343). The entrance to St James itself is marked by the bridge over the Maraval River, on which an ornate green and pink oriental-style iron **archway** was built in 1997 to draw tourists and heighten local pride.

Western Main Road, which runs through the centre of St James is a broad thoroughfare lined with shops, bars and takeaways. Street vendors sell vegetables, incense and crochet work on corners during the day, while at night there is a food stall every couple of metres along the street. Halfway down the road, **St James Market** fills the air with the smell of fresh fish and meat in the early mornings. There are some old gingerbread houses, mostly turned over to commercial use – look out for the lottery outlet with the eye-catching red, gold and green surrounding wall. Towards the western end of the road, the **Haji Gokool Meah Mosque** is one of the oldest in Trinidad. Built in 1927, this tiny white-and-green minareted building is typical of the Muslim places of worship found throughout the island; it is not open to the public, however.

Western Main Road is most notable, however, as the scene of the annual Muslim **Hosay** processions, which take place over four days in May or June (see box on p.92). In the weeks running up to Hosay,

Port of Spain

The Barbarossa mas camp is open 24 hours during Carnival season.

it is possible to watch the craftsmen building the ornate minareted tombs made from bamboo and coloured paper (**tadjahs**) that are carried in procession; the houses where they work have large flags planted in their yards.

There are only five families who build the structures each year, four based in St James and one in Cocorite. Families have to be approved by a local committee, and strict rules apply – they must be the direct descendants of Indian immigrants with an ancestral tradition of *tadjah* building. The task involves great financial, physical and spiritual sacrifice; the materials can cost up to TT$30,000, and the builders have to fast during daylight hours and refrain from alcohol and sexual activity for the duration. Understandably, perhaps, not many of the younger generation find the prospect appealing, and as the years pass fewer and fewer *tadjahs* are being built.

The *tadjah* families also resent the fact that the bars of St James make a mint on Hosay night – many local people watch the proceedings with a beer or rum in hand, despite the fact that the festival is a fairly solemn event in essence, and supposed to be non-alcoholic. There is talk of reducing the onlookers' alcohol consumption by moving the pro-

---

Hosay

The Islamic festival of **Hosay**, commemorating the martyrdom of Mohammed's grandsons Hussein and Hassan during the *jihad* (Holy War) in Persia, has been celebrated in Trinidad ever since the first Indian Muslims arrived in 1845. Its exposure to the island's other cultures has turned it into something carnivalesque, with lewd dancing and loud music, but local Shi'a Muslims have recently taken great pains to restore the occasion's solemnity.

Hosay is celebrated in Curepe, Tunapuna, Couva and Cedros (see p.158, 160, 000 and 000 respectively), but the best place to see it is undoubtedly in St James. Trinis of all religions come here to view the festivities, which are held over four days in either May or June. All the parades start at 11pm at night and continue into the early hours of the morning.

The first procession is **flag night**, when hundreds of devotees walk through the streets with multicoloured flags representing the beginning of the battle of Kerbela, in which the brothers lost their lives.

On the **second night**, two small *tadjahs* are carried slowly through the streets to the throbbing beat of tassa drums; the shredded paper fires at the side of the road are there to warm up the drums, which tightens the skins and produces a better sound.

The **third night** is the most spectacular. Large *tadjahs* more than two metres high are paraded through the streets, while dancers carry two large sickle moons representing the two brothers. At midnight there is the ritual "kissing of the moons", as the dancers symbolically enact a brotherly embrace.

On the **fourth night** the exquisite *tadjahs* are thrown into the sea, a sacrifice to ensure that prayers for recovery from sickness and adversity will be answered.

---

cession away from the bar-lined Western Main Road to Mucurapo Road and the coastal highway; this would also bring the event closer to the sea where the *tadjahs* are finally disposed of. Watch the press for future developments, and the exact date of the festivities.

The southern edge of St James is bounded by Mucurapo Road and the **Woodbrook Cemetery**, also known as Mucurapo Cemetery. The tombs are nowhere near as ornate or picturesque as those of Lapeyrouse Cemetery (see p.89), although the grounds are much better tended. The Trinidadian sportsman and aviator Mikey Cipriani is buried here, as are calypsonian Natty Myers and the musician Sel Duncan.

Off Mucurapo Road at 2b Ethel St is the spectacular **Paschimtaashi Hindu Mandir**. A gleaming white modern interpretation of traditional Hindu religious architecture, the temple has tall round towers and latticed windows that let you view the ornate statues of Hindu gods inside. These **murtis** (religious images worshipped by Hindus), brought from India, represent the ten major incarnations of **Lord Vishnu**; at the back of the temple is a shrine to the goddess **Kali**. The temple's pundit, Mr Persaud, is an approachable man who will happily explain the significance of the temple and its sculptures; his approach, informed by comparative religion, is very accessible, and he will refer to the philosophers of all the major religions in his explanation of Hindu beliefs.

To see one of the most spectacular views of Port of Spain, it is well worth taking a taxi up to **Fort George**, a popular family picnic spot at weekends, just ten minutes' drive from the Western Main Road. If you're feeling energetic, it's a one-hour walk; after a steep climb on St James Terrace, the incline becomes gentler and it's a relaxing stroll to the top. Built in 1804, the fort defended the island against the French Caribbean fleet during the Napoleonic Wars; you can see the original cannons and cannonballs, and a replica of the dungeon. Stone defensive walls, surviving to a height of one to two metres, surround the wooden signal station designed by the exiled West African Ashanti Prince Kofi Nti. During the nineteenth century, Fort George housed the largest contingent of British troops in the Caribbean. At some point, these soldiers mutinied, although the details, suppressed at the time, are still buried in the depths of British military records.

To the northeast of St James is the residential area of **Federation Park**. Its name, and those of the streets in the area – St Lucia Street, Antigua Drive, St Vincent Avenue and so on – commemorate the idealism of the short-lived West Indies Federation, which lasted from just 1958 to 1962 and collapsed when its two largest members, Jamaica and Trinidad, withdrew (see p.331). During the two world wars this area, along with King George V Park in St James, housed internment facilities for Germans residing on the island. Federation Park is now the home of well-to-do Trinidadians and government officials.

The best time to visit the Paschimtaashi Hindu Mandir (☎ 622 4949) is after 2pm, when the pundit is free to show you around; call first to make an appointment.

Fort George is open 10am–6pm, admission free. Private taxis leave from the corner of Bourne's Road and Western Main Road; the fare is around TT$10.

Port of Spain

The Wayne Berkley Camp, 49–51 Cipriani Blvd ☎ 625 7257, is open daily 9am–5pm.

The Harts Mas Camp, 5 Alcazar St ☎ 622 8038, is open daily Sept–Jan 8am–4pm.

Newtown and St Clair

Amid the unlikely surroundings of **NEWTOWN**, a quiet, predominantly residential suburb, is the mas camp of the band **Masquerade**, run by **Wayne Berkley**. Winner of the prestigious band of the year award eight times in the last 25 years, Berkley designs for Port of Spain, St Vincent, St Martin and Notting Hill carnivals every year. He is famous for his use of strong colours, his professional construction and some of the best "bikini mas" designs (see p.335). Visitors are welcome to view production, which takes place from August to mid-January.

Berkley's only serious rival is Peter Minshall, leader of the band Callaloo. An example of his work can be seen up the road at the **Barbados Mutual Building at** 16 Queen Park West, where the lobby is dominated by his 15-metre **mural** made of thousands of sequins tagged to plastic netting, colourfully depicting the flowers and hummingbirds of Trinidad.

ST CLAIR is more upmarket, an enclave of well-to-do Trinidadians whose lavish houses are protected by high walls, ferocious dogs and sophisticated security systems. It is also home to the long-established **Harts Mas Camp**, run by the same family since 1959. Famous for their designs of abstract colours and revealing, erotic costumes, the Harts are at the forefront of the development of "bikini mas".

The eastern suburbs

Port of Spain's **eastern suburbs**, which nestle on the lower slopes of the **Northern Range**, are its oldest. In **Belmont**, original wooden houses survive from the days of the area's first settlers, while the ramshackle wooden houses of **Laventille** – the city's poorest area, and the birthplace of the steel pan – seem to tumble over one another down Laventille Hill. The many panyards located in its winding lanes make it an essential stop for the pan enthusiast.

Belmont

BELMONT's maze of narrow winding lanes is one of the most densely populated areas of Port of Spain. The city's first suburb, it was settled in the first half of the nineteenth century by Africans who had escaped slavery on other Caribbean islands. The names of these early residents are commemorated in streets such as Zampty Lane. After emancipation, they were joined by freed slaves from Trinidad and a number of peoples from West Africa. In 1868, the tribal chieftain of the **Rada community** – a religious group from the French protectorate of Dahomey – bought land in the area to establish a settlement. Representatives from the Mandingo, Ibo, Yoruba and Krumen tribes also came to live here, and Belmont became an established African settlement. The community was well-organized and close-knit, ensuring the survival of African traditions such as the Orisha religion (see p.338), whose feasts and festivities are still practised in the area.

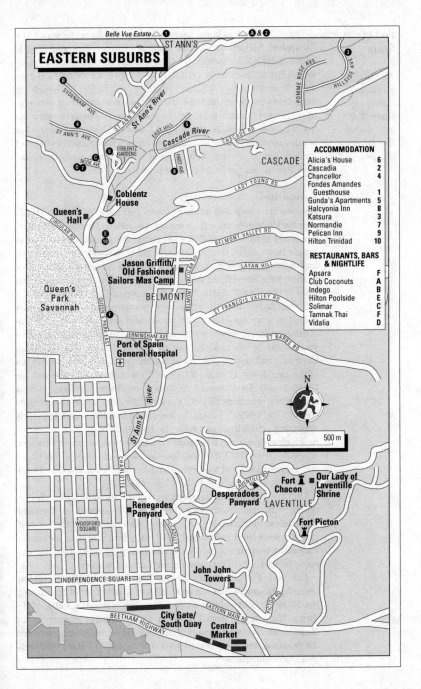

EASTERN SUBURBS

ACCOMMODATION

Alicia's House	6
Cascadia	2
Chancellor	4
Fondes Amandes Guesthouse	1
Gunda's Apartments	5
Halcyonia Inn	8
Katsura	3
Normandie	7
Pelican Inn	9
Hilton Trinidad	10

RESTAURANTS, BARS & NIGHTLIFE

Apsara	F
Club Coconuts	A
Indego	B
Hilton Poolside	E
Solimar	C
Tamnak Thai	F
Vidalia	D

*The Old
Fashioned
Sailors Mas
Camp ☎ 624
3692 is open
Dec–Feb daily
2–10pm.*

Today, Belmont is home to the mas camp of Jason Griffith's **Old Fashioned Sailors** band. The nautical costume has appeared in Carnival since the nineteenth century, when revellers would impersonate British sailors – a tradition that took on a new satirical edge with the arrival of the US Navy on the island in 1941. Though the band dress as sailors during Carnival, they decorate their own costumes, so every outfit is unique. Griffith, who has been bringing out his band since 1968, retains a loyal following; his is one of the few bands to remain faithful to traditional themes such as sailors or fancy Indians and production techniques at a time when many bands are abandoning them in the pursuit of profit.

Laventille

Between the steep and winding streets and alleys of **LAVENTILLE**, ramshackle houses made from salvaged boards and galvanized roofing perch on the hillside in defiance of gravity. The place hums with life as people bustle about their business, washing at standpipes in the road and exchanging gossip on street corners. The suburb was established in the 1840s when freed slaves squatted the area, right "on the eyebrow of the enemy", as the Trinidadian novelist Earl Lovelace put it.

Laventille has often been dismissed as a slum, and many visitors are put off by scare stories involving bandits and street crime. Much of this is exaggerated, however, and provided you take the usual precautions you should be no more at risk than in downtown Port of Spain. Exploring with a local resident will certainly help you to get more out of the area; Elwyn Francis (☎ 627 3377), a trained tour guide with the Chaguaramas Development Authority, conducts excellent walking tours of the area from TT$50. Despite all the rumours of what goes on "behind the bridge", Laventille has an undeniable – and extremely appealing – confidence and verve, perhaps born of the fact that within its winding streets **the steel pan**, Trinidad's most famous instrument, was born (see p.345). The area has spawned many a great pan player and calypsonian, and was celebrated by the Nobel laureate **Derek Walcott** in his poem "The Hills of Laventille".

On Laventille Road a large cultural centre, its walls strikingly decorated with pan illustrations, houses the **Desperadoes Panyard**. Established by Rudolph Charles, the Desperadoes are the longest-running steel band in Trinidad, with many first places at the annual Panorama tournament to their credit (see p.345). Visitors are welcome to watch them rehearse during Carnival season.

Laventille Hill is crowned by **Our Lady of Laventille Shrine**, an imposing landmark that can be seen from all over Port of Spain. Atop the 16-metre belfry of this white stone church stands a statue of the Virgin Mary, a gift from France in 1876. Pilgrims journey to the shrine from all over the country on the feast of the Assumption, and the devotions are popular with several of the island's many other religious denominations.

Just opposite the shrine, the crumbling remains of **Fort Chacon**
takes its name from the last Spanish governor of the island, who built
it in 1770 to deter British attacks. His choice of location proved a
poor one, however, as the fort did little to prevent the British from
overrunning the island in 1797. Its current ruinous state seems to
reflect its sad past, and there's little to be seen apart from a dilapidated stone wall. The fenced-off remains, currently used as a police
wireless station, are closed to the public.

To the west of the shrine is **Observatory Street**, on the site where
the Spanish navigator and astronomer **Don Cosmos Damien
Churruca** made history in 1792 by establishing the first accurate
meridian of longitude in the New World.

Downhill from the shrine on Picton Road is **Fort Picton**, built by
the notorious British governor of that name (see p.328) in the late
1790s. The circular stone building, with thick walls and small key-

---

Panyards

The best way to hear pan is live, in the open air. There is nothing as romantic as hearing the rich chiming harmonies drifting on the wind on a warm
starry night. Throughout the year Port of Spain hosts events in which pan
figures prominently, but for free entertainment you can go to the open-air
panyards and listen while the musicians practice. If you're lucky, you may
hear the band's full repertoire, including excellent renditions of jazz and
classical numbers, as well as the usual calypso, or even get a quick lesson
after the rehearsal. The most accessible panyards to visit in Port of Spain
are Desperadoes, Amoco Renegades and the BWIA Invaders and Phase II;
frequent Panorama champions Exodus are based in St Augustine on the
Eastern Main Road (see p.153).

Amoco Renegades
www.renegades.co.tt.
138 Charlotte St, Port of Spain

Blue Diamonds
George St, Port of Spain.

BWIA Invaders
Tragarete Rd,
opposite the Queen's Park Oval,
Woodbrook.

Carib Tokyo
2a Plaisance Rd, John John,
Laventille.

Desperadoes
Laventille Community Centre,
Laventille.

Humming Birds Pan Groove
Fort George Rd, St James.

Kool
25–27 Baneres Rd, St James.

Laventille Sound Specialists
Eastern Quarry, Laventille.

**Neal and Massy Trinidad All
Stars**
46 Duke St, Port of Spain.

North Stars
63 Bombay St, St James.

Pan Vibes
St Francois Valley Rd,
Port of Spain.

Pandemonium
3 Norfolk St, Belmont.

Phase II Pan Grove
13 Hamilton St, Woodbrook.

Starlift
Starlift Drive, St James.

T&Tec Power Stars
14 Western Main Rd, St James.

---

hole windows, was intended to protect Port of Spain from counterattack by the recently defeated Spanish. A tunnel is said to have linked the fort to King's Wharf. The construction of this bolthole – known as "**Picton's Folly**" – would suggest that the British were still far from confident about their ability to retain the island.

In recent years, Laventille has become something of a political football, with successive governments outlining new plans to improve the area. The postmodern apartment blocks at the base of the hills are the **John John Towers**, the controversial result of an initiative to create much-needed housing. Unfortunately, wrangles over who had rights to move into the apartments left them empty for many years.

Eating

Though Trinidadians traditionally prefer a meal at home to eating out, citizens of the capital are a sophisticated lot, and in the last few years, Port of Spain's **restaurant** scene has burgeoned. Along Ariapita Avenue in particular, some twenty upscale establishments have opened up, serving fancy – and often delicious – nouvelle Caribbean cuisine in beautifully lit surroundings. You should dress smartly, though not necessarily formally, and you'll usually need to reserve a table. If you're after something more casual, there are scores of **cafés** and small fast-food outlets in the downtown area, with a few plastic tables for diners. Among the ubiquitous **roti shops**, the *Hot Shoppe* and *Patraj* chains are reliable; elsewhere **Creole** and **Chinese** food dominate the menus. Additionally, the shopping malls have food courts serving huge, satisfying meals for less than TT$20, and if you're really in a hurry, you'll find branches of *Royal Castle*, *Mario's*, *Pizza Boys* and *KFC* all over the city.

Port of Spain's huge range of **street food** is best eaten in St James or, to a lesser extent, Independence Square. At the latter, look for a truck that parks just to the right of *Mario's* pizza joint, and sells some of the best vegetarian food you'll find in town (Mon–Sat 7–10pm); you can fill a roti with channa, pumpkin, bhajee, potatoes and stewed soya chunks, or have the fillings with peas-and-rice and macaroni pie.

Some **bars** – such as *Martin's* – also serve lunch and dinner, and all the big **hotels** have smart restaurants serving international food at expensive prices – open to anyone who can afford them; we've listed those that are particularly good.

We've listed phone numbers only for restaurants where you might need to book a table.

Dining prices

Each restaurant listed in this guide has been categorized according to the following grades: **budget** (under TT$25); **inexpensive** (TT$25–70); **moderate** (TT$70–150); **expensive** (TT$150+). These ratings relate to the price for a starter and main course.

Downtown Port of Spain

Blazers, cor. of Duke and Edward streets. Cheerful, bright and spotless air-conditioned cafe serving reliable Creole staples – red peas, callaloo, vegetable rice, coocoo, macaroni pie, salads – as well as barbecue fish and chicken, pitta and submarine sandwiches and burgers. Mon–Fri 7am–4pm. Budget.

Breakfast Shed, Wrightson Rd, next to the Cruise Ship Complex. Established in 1936 to provide workers' meals, and still churning out hearty, inexpensive fare, this large shed is lined with outlets selling excellent local food, served at long communal trestle tables; look around before you buy, some cooks are better than others. Delicious traditional breakfast of bake and shark and cocoa for TT$15. Daily 6.30am–3pm. Budget.

Festak, 106 Frederick St. Intimate West African restaurant decorated with Ghanaian artefacts. Tasty, filling food cooked by the knowledgeable and informative Mr and Mrs Senah, who have spent many years in Ghana. Extremely good value. Mon–Sat 11am–11pm. Moderate.

Hardline Vegetarian, 44 Park St. Adorned with piles of fresh fruit and vegetables, this tiny lunch or early dinner stop, with limited space for eating in, serves up delicious, healthy vegetarian meals – vegetable rice, steamed vegetables, soya stew, marinated dumplings – as well as fruit salads and delicious fresh juices. Mon–Fri 6am–6pm. Budget.

Jalapenos, Victoria Square, cor. of Duke and Shine streets ☎625 1766. Mexican restaurant set in a lovely old fretworked house. The brightly lit, lime-and-orange painted interior is a bit unsettling, but the food is good, with all the usual suspects; ceviche (a chilled, marinated seafood salad cooked in lime juice), and red chilli shrimps are excellent starters, and mains range from fajitas, tostadas, enchiladas and tacos to pasta, steaks, paella and Mexican pizza. The margaritas are excellent. Mon 10am–4pm, Tues–Fri 10am–10pm, Sat 5–10pm. Moderate/Expensive.

La Ronde, *Crowne Plaza*, Wrightson Rd ☎625 3366. Revolving restaurant that gives a fantasic 360° view of Port of Spain; the location is more of a draw than the unremarkable international cuisine, but the Thursday night seafood menu is sumptuous, as is the Sunday brunch (12.30–2.30pm). Daily noon–2.30pm & 7–11.30pm. Expensive.

Mother Nature Vegetarian Restaurant, St Vincent St. Excellent, creative vegetarian meals and fruit salads in a buffet-style café. Wonderfully filling fruit punches made from everything from beetroot to papaya are blended on the spot. Mon–Fri 5am–5pm. Budget.

Newtown and St Clair

Hong Kong City Restaurant, 86A Tragarete Rd, Newtown ☎622 3949. Large portions of standard Chinese fare in a very plush upstairs restaurant. Daily 11am–11pm. Inexpensive.

Omar Kayam, 9 Warner St, Newtown. Small and intimate restaurant, serving spicy Indian food in a soothing atmosphere. Mon–Sat 11am–10pm. Moderate.

Rafters, 6a Warner St, Newtown ☎628 9258. Colonial stone building with an American-style bar for buffet lunches and Friday night limes, and an elegant dining room serving à la carte international cuisine for dinner. Good food, with something for everyone. Mon–Sat 11.30am–3.30pm & 7–11pm. Moderate/Expensive.

Syps, 3a Cipriani Blvd, Newtown. Small, intimate coffee bar and restaurant, lovingly decorated and serving light lunches and dinners of crepes, quiche, crab backs, burritos and tacos. Coffees – from espresso to mocha – are delicious, and wine and beer are also on offer. A great spot for an afternoon lime. Mon–Thurs 10am–10pm, Fri & Sat 10am–midnight, Sun 10am–2pm & 6–10pm. Moderate.

Tiki Village, *Kapok Hotel*, 16–18 Cotton Hill, St Clair ☎622 6441. One of Port of Spain's better hotel restaurants, with lovely views over the savannah and city, and elegant decor; a bubbling spring and rattan furniture provide a relaxing ambience. The Chinese/Polynesian cuisine is excellent; go for the dim sum or the weekday buffet lunches. Daily 6.30am–10.15pm. Expensive.

The Verandah, 10 Rust St, St Clair ☎622 6287. Exclusive, classy restaurant in a coolly converted gingerbread house decorated with plants and local art, with a pretty open-air patio for evening dining. Fabulous "freestyle Caribbean" cooking: lots of fresh herbs and attention to the details that matter. The salmon with onions and peppers, and cheesecake with stewed guavas are especially good. Mon–Fri 11.30am–2pm, Thurs & Sat also 7–10.45pm. Moderate/Expensive.

St Ann's and the Savannah

Apsara, 13 Queen's Park East ☎623 7659. Top-end traditional Northern Indian dishes, from tandooris to rogan jhosh, served in very plush surroundings (shares the same building as *Tamnak Thai*, below). Lots of vegetarian choices, and delicious desserts. Daily 11am–11pm. Expensive.

Indego, 1 Carib Way, off Sydenham Ave, St Ann's ☎624 6954. One of the best locations in Port of Spain, on a verandah high in the St Ann's hills that affords wonderful city views. Food is delicious, from unusual salads, bruschetta and ceviche as starters, to chicken and beef brochettes, imaginative seafood (try fish sautéed with capers, olive oil, garlic and white wine) for mains. Lovely desserts, and a programme of live music (see p.103). Tues–Sat 6–11pm. Expensive.

Solimar, 6 Nook Ave, St Ann's ☎624 6267. Creole, European, Latin American, Oriental and African dishes served in rustic taverna decor. Holds food festivals celebrating everything from the Scottish Burns Night to curries of India, with a highly qualified and experienced chef. March–Nov Tues–Sat, Dec–Feb Mon–Sat 6.30pm–2am. Expensive.

Tamnak Thai, 13 Queen's Park East ☎625 0647. Elegantly decorated in rich Thai style, this upmarket place has indoor and outdoor sections, the latter ringed by a carp-filled pond and lush foliage. Cooked by a native Thai chef, the food is excellent, with all the regulars represented: green curry, stir-fries and rice dishes. Good wine list, and excellent service. Daily 11am–11pm. Expensive.

Vidalia, *Normandie*, 10 Nook Ave, St Ann's ☎624 1181. Wide spread of tastefully cooked Creole staples and international favourites, from breakfasts to sandwiches, salads, steak and pasta, served in an airy, plant-filled dining room decorated with works by local artists. Daily 7am–10pm; closed for lunch on Sat. Expensive.

St James

Chinkies Night Beat, Western Main Road, opposite *Smokey and Bunty's*. Rasta-run Italian-style food stall serving a loyal clientele with delicious veggie concoctions as well as fried fish, bake and shark and fresh juices. A great pre- or post-clubbing option. Tues–Sun 7am–late. Budget.

Home Restaurant, 67 Western Main Rd. Solid, no-nonsense and reliably delicious local food: fried or coconut bakes, sada rotis, buljol and pies for breakfast, and a lovely array for dinner. Roti fillings – with buss-up-shut or dhalpuri, paratha or sada skins – run the full range from bodi and melongene to all the meats, and you can get pelau, stewed chicken and macaroni or shepherd's pie as well. Mon–Sat 6am–6pm, Sun 6am–4pm. Budget.

Little Lisbon, 7 Long Circular Rd ☎622 6113. Pleasant Portuguese restaurant with outdoor and air-conditioned indoor seating. Strong on seafood, the menu makes a nice change from local fare: garlic pork, marinated for three days, is a great starter, as is fish soup. Mains of fish and lobster cooked Portuguese style dominate, but there's also kebabs, steak and lovely, unusual veggie choices. Lunchtime set specials are great value, as are the seafood nights (Fri & Sat) – three courses for TT$99. Mon–Sat 11.30am–2pm & 6.30–10.30pm, Sat 6.30–10.30pm. Moderate.

Singho's Restaurant, Level 3, Long Circular Mall. Large restaurant serving excellent Chinese food amid typical red and gold decor. Daily 11am–11pm. Moderate.

Woodbrook

Chutney Rose, 30 Fitt St, cor. of Ariapita Ave ☎628 8541. Elaborately decorated Indian restaurant serving Trini-style dishes for lunch – lamb koftas, fish with rice, peas, dhal and salad, or shrimp and fish in herbs with curried cauliflower – and traditional Northern Indian cuisine in the evening, from samosas to biryanis and plenty of tasty vegetarian options. There's also a takeaway on site serving good rotis. Mon–Sat 11am–3pm & 6–11pm. Moderate/Expensive.

Flavours on the Avenue, 40 Ariapita Ave, cor. of Cornelio St ☎628 8687. Genteel, colonial-style decor and piped-in world music accompany the sophisticated, small but flavoursome portions of "contemporary Caribbean" cuisine; maui maui in tomato salsa with potato croquettes, melongene and plantain, is particularly good, and all the usual seafood and meats are represented too. Good cocktails, and toothsome desserts. Mon–Sat 11am–3pm & 6–11pm. Expensive.

Il Colosseo, 47 Ariapita Ave ☎623 3654. Fancy Italian restaurant serving authentic food, cooked by a genuine Italian chef, in grand Renaissance-style surroundings with plaster cherubs and engraved glass. Good bread, excellent pasta, tasty seafood choices and some decent wines. Mon–Fri 11am–2.30pm & 6–10.30pm, Sat 6–10.30pm. Expensive.

Irie Bites, 68 Ariapita Ave. Jamaican jerk shack painted red, gold and green that's the best of the cluster on this stretch of Ariapita Avenue. Properly seasoned with Jamaican spices and cooked over pimento wood, the jerk chicken, pork and fish are served with festival (a sweetish fried dumpling), and there's also curry goat with white rice and green banana. Mon–Thurs 11am–8pm, Fri & Sat 11am–9pm. Budget.

Plantation House, 38 Ariapita Ave, cor. of Cornelio St ☎628 5551. Upmarket dining in an exquisitely maintained, elegantly decorated gingerbread house. Service is attentive and friendly, and the delicious "nouvelle Creole" cuisine ranges from chicken crepes, mussels and crab cakes to Cajun specialities – blackened shrimp and fish, jambalaya – to Caribbean-style fish and rabbit casserole. Mon–Fri 11.30am–2.30pm & 6.30–10.30pm, Sat 6.30–10.30pm. Expensive.

Sweet Lime, cor. of Ariapita Ave and French St. With outdoor tables positioned next to *Mas Camp Pub*, this is a great spot for people-watching over a drink, or

Port of Spain

There are several excellent restaurants and cafés in Maraval, which makes a nice getaway from the city. Listings start on p.111.

a meal from a solid, predictable menu: satay chicken, crab backs, mussels and shrimp for starters, and plenty of seafood for mains, as well as ribs and steaks. Good kids' meals, and daily specials such as rotisserie (Thurs) and kebabs (Fri) on offer. Sun–Thurs 4pm–midnight, Fri & Sat 5pm–1am. Moderate.

Veni Mange, 67 Ariapita Ave ☎622 7533. Delicious Caribbean cuisine with an international flavour and tasty vegetarian options in a stylish, bistro-type setting. It's a favourite spot for Trinidadian celebrities, with a friendly atmosphere and lively party scene on Fridays. Mon–Thurs 11.30am–3pm, Wed also 7.30pm–midnight, Fri 11.30am–11.30pm. Moderate/Expensive.

Woodford Café, 62 Tragarete Rd. Tasty and filling traditional Creole cuisine – oxtail, stewed chicken, curried conch, barbecue ribs – in a pleasant, airy café; very popular at lunchtime with office workers. The menus change daily, and vegetarian options are always available. Mon & Tues 11am–3.30pm, Weds & Thurs 11am–10pm, Fri & Sat 11am–10.30pm. Inexpensive/Moderate.

Drinking, nightlife and entertainment

Trinidadians seem to live to party, celebrating anything from a public holiday to the end of a workday, and Port of Spain has a wide variety of places to let your hair down. There are a few excellent **nightclubs**, though most are outside the downtown area, and if you want to dance it's also worth keeping an eye out for flyers and posters advertising large parties known as **fetes**, usually held out of doors in community centres and sports complexes. Usually featuring DJs and live bands, these lively events draw large, enthusiastic crowds. Fetes are also advertised in local newspapers and on the radio (see p.34).

Most bars (many of which have dancefloors) and nightclubs come alive after 10pm and are busiest from Thursday to Sunday. Many state that they are open "till", which means that they close when the last customers leave, usually around 2–3am, though some, such as *Smokey and Bunty's*, keep going all night. If a place advertises its opening hours as "anytime, anyday", it means that the owners have a 24-hour license and open and close when they feel like it.

In recent years, a number of **casinos** (tacitly known as "members clubs" to contend with local gambling laws) have sprung up around town, most with roulette, baccarat, black jack and stud poker on offer. If you fancy a flutter, try Ma Pau, corner of French Street and Ariapita Avenue (daily 6pm–4am; ☎624 3331).

The capital also boasts a number of good **theatre** companies, including the **Trinidad Theatre Workshop** (TTW), the **Bagasse Company**, **Ragoo Productions** and **Raymond Choo Kong Productions**. The TTW (see p.81) puts on world-class drama, specializing in the work of Derek Walcott, while most of the other companies focus on lighthearted comedies. All productions have a Trinidadian flavour, since even foreign comedies are given a local twist.

Bars

There are **rum shops** on practically every corner in Port of Spain. These tend to be small, basic shacks frequented by middle-aged men.

Bars (especially "sports bars") are usually a little more upmarket, with pumping music. It is often difficult to differentiate between **bars** and nightclubs, as many bars have dancing areas.

Cricket Wicket, 149 Tragarete Rd, Woodbrook ☎628 6766. Opposite the Queen's Park Oval and next door to Invaders panyard, this small, mostly open-air bar overlooks busy Tragarete Road. Packed when cricket matches are on, it's a laid-back spot for an evening drink, and snacks are available. Mon–Sat 11am–2.30am.

Indego, 1 Carib Way, off Sydenham Ave, St Ann's ☎624 6954. The fabulous location high in the St Ann's hills makes this a great spot for an quiet drink, with the black pool of the Savannah and the light of the city twinkling below. The bar area is small, but there's live music (don't miss jazz on Wednesdays), and lovely cocktails concocted by the effervescent host – try the mango daiquiri. Tues–Sat 6pm–late.

Martin's, 13 Cipriani Blvd, Newtown ☎623 7632. Friendly and intimate bar with plant-bedecked, shady patio seating area out back. Also serves lunch and dinner – international food with a Creole flavour. Mon–Sat 11.30am–midnight, Sun 6pm–midnight.

Mas Camp Pub. cor. Ariapita Ave and French St, Woodbrook ☎627 4042. Newly refurbished, with pool tables in a back room, and an air-conditioned main area that's popular with an older, local crowd, who come to dance to oldies on Fridays. There's usually a calypso show on Wednesday evenings, and other themed nights, from Latin to karaoke, throughout the week. Mon–Fri 11am–1/2am Sat–Sun 11am–4am. Entrance varies depending on the night; calypso shows cost TT$40–50.

Pelican Inn, 2–4 Coblentz Ave ☎624 7486. A Caribbean version of an English pub. Popular with local regulars and tourists, the enduring *"Pello's"* is quiet during the day, but comes to life at the weekend (Fridays and Sundays are particularly busy) with a mixed crowd, packed dance floor and resident DJ. Daily 11am–2am. Small cover charge at weekends.

Smokey and Bunty's, cor. of Dengue St at 97 Western Main Rd, St James; no phone. Named after the owners' nicknames, this local institution is a popular late liming spot, drawing a very mixed crowd – young, old, arty, gay and straight. The clientele spills onto the pavement, loud music dominates and a funky atmosphere prevails. Open Mon–Thurs 10pm–3am, Fri–Sun 10pm–7am.

Squeeze, 61 Tragarete Rd. Appropriately named for its minute dimensions, this friendly bar draws a sociable drinking crowd at the weekends, when there are regular drinks promotions. Open Mon–Thurs 5pm–2am, Fri & Sat 6pm–2am.

Tasca Latina, 16 Philipps St ☎625 3497. Spanish taverna-style bar and restaurant with a dance floor and friendly atmosphere. Live entertainment, popular and lively at weekends, attracts a mature crowd. Entrance TT$30. Mon–Fri 11am–2am, Sat 4pm–2am, Sun 11am–midnight.

Nightclubs

Club Coconuts, *Cascadia Hotel*, Ariapita Rd, St Ann's ☎628 9696, *www.clubcoconuts.com*. Draws a fairly young, fashionable and mostly local crowd. Thursday is reggae night; other nights have calypso, dancehall and soca music, and cover charge varies depending upon the night and whether you have a flyer guaranteeing cheap entry. Wed–Sat 9.30pm–4.30am. Wed TT$60, free drinks all night; Thurs student ID gets you free entry; Fri TT$50; Sat TT$20/25.

Club Prosperity, Upper Bournes Rd, St James. Brightly painted with African flags, this is the regular venue for Friday night Nyabinghi reggae jams, and other special Rasta or reggae-oriented events. Best for those acquainted with the scene.

Cordials, 72 Tragarete Rd, Woodbrook ☎628 8627. Dimly lit, social place popular with a mature crowd, with excellent music from DJs on Friday nights, and drinking at tables at other times. Mon–Sat 11am–late. No cover charge.

Carnival calendar

Bear in mind that dates and schedules for Carnival change from year to year; check www.carnivalondenet.com, www.carnaval.com, www.trinbagocarnival.com and www.guardian.co.tt for updated calendars of events.

January

Opening of Calypso Tents: calypsonians battle it out in the "tents" – these days regular buildings – for a place in the finals. The best known venues are: Spektakula Forum, 111–117 Henry St ☎623 2870; Kaiso House, Deluxe Cinema, Keate St (c/o TIDCO ☎627 5912); Calypso Revue, SWWTU Hall, 1d Wrightson Rd ☎625 1351; Yangatang, NUGFW Hall, Frederick St (c/o TIDCO ☎623-6022); Maljo Kaiso, Stalk Hill Theatre, Richmond St ☎623 0074; and Kaiso Karavan Naipaul Building, cor. of Queen and Sanchez streets, Arima ☎667 2262.

Stickplay Competition: an exciting and skilful traditional sport based on the stick fighting of the 1880s, an art thought to have originated in the practice of using bamboo sticks to fight fires in the cane field.

Panorama Competition: steel pan bands display their skill in all types of music as they compete for the prestigious first prize. The finals are held in February.

Junior Calypso Competition: children compose and sing hard-hitting calypsos, full of satire, humour and social commentary.

National Chutney Soca Monarch Competition: hear the best of Trinidad's popular music played by local artists. The finals are held in February.

International Soca Monarch Competition: international soca stars sing for the prestigious Trinidad Soca Monarch title. The finals are held in February.

Talk Tent: Similar to the calypso tent, but featuring cabaret and comedy artists. Performances occur throughout the Carnival season.

February

Calypso Fiesta: calypsonians engage in a battle of wit and satire – go with a Trinidadian who can explain the political references.

Kiddies' Carnival: the children's costumes and characters rival those of the adults. There are three **parades**: at the **Red Cross Children's Carnival** ten

---

Jazzy's, 48 Western Main Rd, St James ☎ 628 6355. A true Trini clubbing dive – dark, hot and seedy, always full and pumping at the weekends. Mon–Thurs 11am–1/2am, Fri–Sun 11am–3/4am. Entrance (weekends only) TT$10.

Liquid, ground floor, Maritime Plaza, Barataria ☎ 675 9958. One of the newest clubs in Trinidad, and with a mission to attract a rather upmarket but party-hard crowd. Nights vary; expect some rock, pop and Latin amongst the soca and reggae. The main room and dancefloor are lavishly decorated – check out the water features – and there's an excellent lights and sound system as well as a VIP area and black leather sofa-studded Champagne Lounge. Entrance fee varies.

Poolside Fiesta, *Hilton Trinidad*, Lady Young Rd, St Ann's ☎ 624 3211. Depending on your point of view, this is either an essential part of your holi-

---

days before Carnival; at **St James Kiddies' Carnival** the week before Carnival; and at the **Junior Parade of the Bands** in the Savannah on the Saturday before Ash Wednesday.

Panorama Finals: a day-long marathon pan competition, fuelled by adrenaline and free-flowing rum. Queen's Park Savannah's rowdy North Stand is the place to be if you want to party, while the grandstand is for those who want a more sedate view of the proceedings. Though seats in the stands are inexpensive (TT$30–50), those on a budget or wishing to move around should go on "the tracks", the road leading towards the stage where the bands practice. Panorama takes place on Saturday before Ash Wednesday.

Dimanche Gras (Carnival Sunday): the finals for the King and Queen of Carnival and the Calypso Monarch Finals: after weeks of build-up in calypso tent competitions, the best calypsonians sing their hearts out for the prize of Calypso Monarch. The sheer size of the King and Queen costumes, and the skill, sequins and special effects expended, are amazing, though with each year the entrants are look more and more like sculptures on wheels. At the Queen's Park Savannah grandstands.

Jouvert (pronounced *Joovay*, from "**Jour Ouvert**", the break of day): marking the beginning of the festivities, Jouvert is "dirty mas", raw, earthy and energetic. Wear as little as possible and no jewellery. Starts 2am Monday before Ash Wednesday and continues till dawn.

Carnival Monday Parade of the Bands: bands parade their costumes through the streets of Port of Spain; individual bands follow set routes, but there is no set route for the whole parade. From 1pm.

Carnival Tuesday Parade of the Bands: the full display of all the costumes. The route is the same as Carnival Monday; the best place to view the costumes in their full effect is from the stands at the Queen's Park Savannah or at the bleachers set up at the various judging points around the town. Starts 8am.

Ash Wednesday: International soca artists, calypsonians and DJs entertain a huge post-Carnival crowd on Maracas (see pp.137–140) and Manzanilla (see p.201) beaches. The parties are getting busier each year; if you're driving, leave early or be prepared for a slow journey home; a quieter alternative is Blanchisseuse (see p.142).

Champs in Concert: A parade of the winning bands, held in the Queen's Park Savannah grandstands the weekend after Carnival.

day experience, or a somewhat tacky, trite trot through Trinidadian culture. Featuring steel band, calypso, limbo, fire eating and irreverent commentary from local actor Glenn Davis, the show is surpassed by the extensive buffet that ranges from Chinese and Indian dishes to Creole staples, with delicious puddings including seldom-found guava cheese. Mon; dinner from 7pm, show 8pm. TT$169.

Spektakula Forum, 111–117 Henry St ☎623 2870 or 0125. Large building next to the Ministry of Planning department. Home of one of the great pre-Carnival calypso tents (many of the past and present grandmasters of the art form and calypso monarchs have performed here), this also serves as a concert venue out of Carnival season. Events are advertised in the press. Entrance TT$40–60.

Two Plus Cultural and Recreation Club, 94–96 Henry St ☎627 8224. Near the junction with Park Street, this club hidden upstairs is a popular venue for ballroom dancing fanatics. From Monday to Thursday a teacher holds lessons from 7–9pm, then the music – ranging from old calypsos to reggae and soca – continues to the early hours. No entrance fee except for special events.

Upper Level, West Mall ☎637 1753. Pumping, friendly place playing soca, reggae and R&B to a sociable crowd of mostly local dancers. One of the most laid-back options in town, this is an essential part of your Port of Spain nightlife experience. Cover charge varies.

Theatres

The Trinidad **theatre season** is from March to the end of November. After this Trinidadians become preoccupied with Christmas events, such as Parang concerts (see p.341) and the continuous live entertainment of the Carnival season. Tickets cost from TT$20 for smaller amateur productions to TT$60+ for the well-known companies.

Central Bank Auditorium, Twin Towers financial complex, Brian Lara Promenade ☎623 0845. Entrance through Eric Williams Plaza. The most comfortable and high-tech theatre in Port of Spain features productions by well-known Trinidad theatre companies – usually comedies. Wear long sleeves to counteract the overenthusiastic a/c.

Little Carib, cor. of White & Roberts streets, Woodbrook ☎622 4644. Opened in 1948, this intimate and historic theatre concentrates on plays and shows highlighting local talent and culture.

The Queen's Hall, 1–3 St Ann's Rd, St Ann's ☎624 1284. Opposite the *Hilton Trinidad*, this is the largest arts venue in Trinidad, featuring drama, dance, music and fashion shows. Tickets from TT$25–60.

Under the Trees, *The Normandie*, 10 Nook Ave, St Ann's ☎624 1181. Atmospheric evening performances featuring local artists – doing everything from solo comedy performances to local plays – under the stars, in the grounds of the *Normandie* hotel.

Shopping

Port of Spain's **main shopping area** is based around **Frederick Street** and the few outlying malls such as **West Mall**, **West Moorings**, **Ellerslie Plaza**, **Maraval** and **Long Circular Mall**, St

James. Foreign **imported goods** can be bought all over town, especially in the large malls.

Since most Trinidadians have their clothes made to measure, there is an abundance of **textile** shops. Concentrated on Queen Street, these offer a greater variety of materials than you'd find in New York or London at very reasonable prices. Between 1984 and 1991, Trinidad banned the import of **clothes**, spurring the country's fashion industry to great heights and bringing forward a wave of first-rate designers. Look out for **Radical Designs** (Excellent City Centre Mall, Frederick St; and *Normandie* hotel, 100 Nook Ave, St Ann's), featuring elegant, funky clothes by Diane Hunt; the **Z Meiling** store (*Kapok* hotel), selling classic cuts and stylish underwear by Meiling, Trinidad's top designer; **The Cloth** (*Normandie* hotel), for Robert Young's brightly coloured abstract designs on loose cotton. **Zoom** (Excellent City Centre Mall, Frederick St ☎624 7873) sells the best-quality T-shirts in the city, while **Ontic Designs** (corner of Ariapita Ave and French St ☎627 7549) have a beautiful range of batiks. **Mode Alive** (34 Frederick St) is good for fabrics.

Local music is sold by street vendors touting the latest soca cassettes, though these are poor-quality pirate copies, and none of the money goes to the original artists. For retail CDs and cassettes, try any of the music stores on Frederick Street, such as **Cleve's One Stop Music Shop**, at the back of a small mall at no. 58, and **D Trini Shop** (City Gate; ☎623 6510); **Crosby's** (54 Western Main Rd, St James ☎622 7622) also has a wide selection. These record shops also sell tickets for all the big fetes and concerts. If you're inspired to become a pan player or a Parang singer, head for **Music and Equipment Ltd** (36 Duke St), **Music House** (116 Oxford St), or **Lincoln Enterprises** (68 Ariapita Ave ☎628 7267) to buy a cuatro or a **steel pan**.

Crafts can be found at street stalls and, at higher prices, in the malls. **Poui Designs** at 60 Ellerslie Plaza in Boissiere Village, Maraval, has a wonderful selection of locally made crafts, from miniature wooden rumshops to hand-painted postcard-sized watercolours and classy ceramics from the Ajoupa pottery. For the best selection of handmade leather sandals and Rastafarian goods, visit the shops at the **United Craft Workers Drag Brothers Mall**, (southern end of Piccadilly Street and Brian Lara Promenade). There's a large selection of wickerwork on sale at the **T&T Blind Welfare League** (118 Duke St ☎624 1613). **Susan Dayal**'s beautiful handcrafted wire decorations can be found in the Normandie Market (10 Nook Ave, St Ann's ☎625 3197). **African Trophies** (39 Tragarete Rd, with a branch at 12 Roberts St ☎622 9476) specializes in fine African carvings, furniture, clothes and jewellery. If you're looking for **Indian crafts** and **ornate filigree jewellery**, however, the best place to shop is in Chaguanas (pp.185–188).

Port of Spain

African Trophies functions as a cultural centre as well as a shop, with a library and space to view videos on African culture.

Bookshops in Port of Spain don't carry a huge range, concentrating mostly on school textbooks and imported cook books, and stocking little work by local authors. There are a few exceptions, though: downtown, head for **Trinidad Book World** (87 Queen St ☎623 4316), which has a large selection, and is particularly strong on Trinidadian writers. **Metropolitan Book Suppliers** (upstairs at Colsort Mall, Frederick St ☎623 3462) is good for books on the history and culture of the island. The biggest selection, though, belongs to **Classic Book Services** at 7 Royal Palm Plaza in Maraval, where you'll find a compact but thoughtful selection ranging from novels by writers from Trinidad and Tobago and the Caribbean to tomes on history, politics, religion, culture and cookery.

Listings

Airlines American, 63–65 Independence Square ☎627 7013, fax 669 0261; BWIA, 30 Edward St ☎627 2942; LIAT, 9–11 Edward St ☎627 6274; Air Canada, Piarco Airport ☎669 4065.

Airport 24hr information line: ☎669 8047 or 8048 or 8049 ext 204 or 247.

Art Galleries 101 Art Gallery, 101 Tragarete Rd, Woodbrook ☎628 4081; Art Creators, Flat 402, Aldegonda Park, 7 St Ann's Rd, St Ann's (Mon–Fri 10am–5.30pm, Sat 10am–2.30pm; ☎624 4369) exhibits prominent Trinbagonian artists such as Leroy Clarke and Neal Massy; Gallery 1,2,3,4, *The Normandie*, 10 Nook Ave, St Ann's (daily 9.30am–5pm; ☎625 5502) is a small four-room gallery featuring local well-known artists in all media; and On Location, Long Circular Mall, St James ☎628 3404.

Banks Bank of Commerce, 72 Independence Square ☎627 9325; Citibank, 12 Queen's Park East ☎625 1040; First Citizen, 50 St Vincent St ☎623 2576; Republic Bank, 11–17 Park St ☎625 4411; Royal Bank, 19–21 Park St ☎623 1322; Scotiabank, 1 Frederick St ☎623 1253.

Cinemas Excellent value for money and entertaining as much for the audience participation as the films. A double bill costs TT$15–20 and usually features American action movies and international blockbusters. You are still allowed to smoke in Trinidad's cinemas, and alcohol and other refreshments are on sale. Deluxe, 9–11 Keate St ☎623 6532; Globe, cor. of St Vincent and Park streets ☎623 1063. See press for details.

Embassies and high commissions British High Commission, 19 St Clair Ave, St Clair (Mon–Thurs 7.30am–noon & 1–4pm, Fri 7.30am–12.30pm; ☎622 2748, fax 622 4555); Canadian High Commission, 3–3a Sweet Briar Rd, St Clair (Mon–Thurs 7.30am–4pm, Fri 7.30am–1pm; ☎622 6232, fax 628 2619); US Embassy, 15 Queen's Park West (Mon–Fri 7.30–11am; ☎622 6371, fax 628 5462).

Hospital Port of Spain General is at 169 Charlotte St ☎623 2951 or 2955, 625 3622, 623 7715, though you may have to wait a few hours to be seen if you turn up at casualty. Two efficient options if you're in a hurry and have good medical insurance are the private Community Hospital, Western Main Rd, Cocorite ☎622 1191 or 628 8330 and St Clair Medical Centre, 18 Elizabeth St, St Clair ☎628 1451 or 1452 or 8615.

Internet In downtown Port of Spain, head for Multi Marketing Computers, upstairs at Town Centre Mall (Mon–Thurs 9am–5pm, Fri 9am–6pm, Sat

9am–3pm). In Woodbrook, *The Web Cafe*, 59 Carlos St (Mon–Sat 8am–7pm), has delicious food as well as computer terminals. In Maraval, try Jus' Click in Royal Palm Plaza (Mon–Fri 9am–5pm, Sat 10am–3pm). Access at all cafés starts at TT$10–15 for half an hour.

Laundry Lewis John Coin Laundries, 44 Diego Martin Main Rd, Diego Martin ☎622 9026; Simply Clean Laundromat, 135 Long Circular Rd, Maraval ☎628 1060. Most people do their own washing or have someone who does it for them, so laundries can be hard to find. Ask around for the local clothes-washer.

Money transfers Moneygram, at Hi-Lo stores all over town ☎627 2000; Western Union, 44–58 Edward St ☎623 6000.

Pharmacies Bhaggan's, Independence Square (Mon–Thur 8am–11pm; ☎627 5541); Alchemists, 57 Duke St (Mon–Sat 8am–1am; ☎623 2718); Kappa Drugs, cor. of La Seiva and Saddle roads, Maraval (Mon–Fri 7.30am–10.30pm, Sat & Sun 8am–10.30pm; ☎622 2728); Express Drugs, 102 Western Main Rd, St James (Mon–Fri 7.30am–11pm, Sat & Sun 7.30am–10pm; ☎628 1527).

Police Main Police Station, Wrightson Rd ☎625 2684; general crime can also be reported to the CID, in the white building on the cor. of St Vincent and Knox streets ☎627 4145. In emergency dial 999, or the rapid response lines ☎622 5412, 623 8975 or 623 1786.

Post office TT Post, Tragarete Rd, opposite Roxy roundabout.

Sport facilities The Hasley Crawford Stadium, cor. of Ariapita Ave and Wrightson Rd ☎623 0304, contains an athletics track and football field, and hosts both local and international events. The Jean Pierre Sports Complex next door has facilities for lawn tennis, netball, basketball, table tennis, gymnastics, badminton and a gym. Events are advertised in the local media.

Swimming pool YMCA, Benbow Rd, off Wrightson Rd (daily noon–3.45pm; ☎625 9622). TT$6 for a 45min session. You can swim at the *Hilton* (see p.72) for TT$30 and at the *Cascadia* hotel (see p.72) for TT$20.

Tour operators Island Experiences, 11 East Hill, Cascade ☎6252410, fax 627 6688, *gunda@wow.net* are best for city and panyard/mas camp tours. For excellent eco-based tours in the city and surrounds, call Caribbean Discovery Tours, Fondes Amandes Rd, St Ann's ☎624 7281, fax 627 3526, *www.activecaribbean.com/caribbeandiscoverytours*; and Paria Springs, 44 La Seiva Rd, Maraval ☎622 8826, fax 628 1525, *www.pariasprings.com*.

Travel agents Alstons Travel, 67 Independence Square ☎625 2201, fax 625 3682; Courtesy, 43 Tragarete Rd ☎628 9271, fax 627 6412; and Haygem, 55 Edward St ☎625 5328, fax 624 4889.

Visa extensions Immigration Division, 67 Frederick St ☎625 3571. Ring before you go to get advice as to exactly what you need for your extension, and be prepared for a long wait and for more than one visit.

Maraval and Paramin

Some five kilometres north of central Port of Spain, **MARAVAL** lies at the base of the Northern Range, surrounded by lush green hills. Originally a small village on the outskirts of the capital, it is rapidly becoming an upmarket residential suburb, with a concentration of hotels and guesthouses aimed at middle- and upper-income visitors.

Maraval and Paramin

Getting to Maraval

Though it is officially outside the boundaries of the capital, **Maraval** is increasingly thought of as a suburb of the city, and many people stay here because of its proximity to central Port of Spain; regular **maxi** and **route taxis** do the ten-minute run up the Saddle Road from the northwest corner of the Queen's Park Savannah. After 8pm during the week, it gets harder to find taxis into the area, and if you intend to be in town after 10pm, be sure to prearrange your return journey. To negotiate the steep hill up to Paramin, you need to catch a **jeep** from Maraval village junction (TT$10). Driving yourself isn't advisable given the twisting, narrow road and sheer drops.

Dominating the hillside at the centre of Maraval is the cream and maroon neo-Romanesque **Maraval-Paramin Roman Catholic Church**, originally built in 1879, enlarged in 1934 and now somewhat overshadowed by an adjacent, rather ugly, school building.

Beyond Maraval and the expansive, well-kept St Andrew's golf course, the road takes a scenic route over the Northern Range, providing good views of the forested slopes of the Maraval valley and eventually arriving – after many steep inclines and hairpin bends – at Maracas Beach on the north coast (see pp.137–140).

See pp.68–69 for details on where in Port of Spain to catch taxis to Maraval.

Immediately west of Maraval, up the slopes of the Northern Range, is the quiet neighbourhood of **PARAMIN**, the "herb basket of Trinidad". The local cottage industry produces "Paramin seasoning", whose ingredients include French and Spanish thyme, peppermint and onions. The local population is of Spanish ancestry, the descendants not of colonial Spaniards but of Venezuelans who came here in the nineteenth century to plant cocoa. This close-knit community maintains many of its Venezuelan traditions, most famously its **Parang** singers, who travel from house to house during the Christmas season, singing nativity songs in a mix of French and Spanish. The Monday before Christmas, Paramin hosts a **Parang festival** at the soccer field at the lower end of town. On Carnival Monday, the town is overtaken with blue devils – traditional Carnival characters that enable people to express their wilder side – feting in the streets. Harvest Sunday, the second Sunday in November, is celebrated with games, music and traditional feasts of wild meat.

Accommodation

Most of the **hotels** and **guesthouses** are located on Saddle Road, which runs through the centre of Maraval. Many of them are new and fairly upmarket; their high standards and wide range of facilities – restaurants, swimming pools and jacuzzis – are, unsurprisingly, reflected in the prices (see p.23 for details of the accommodation price codes used in these listings).

Hotels

Royal Palm Suite Hotel, 7 Saddle Rd ☎ 628 5086, *royalpalm@trinidad.net*. Impersonal and rather shabby yet functional place with a variety of rooms; all have a/c, en-suite bathroom and cable TV, and some have kitchenette. Facilities include a swimming pool, 24-hour taxi service, on-site shops, restaurants, bars and laundry service. Breakfast included in Carnival rate. ⑥/⑧.

Suites Elysees, 123A Long Circular Rd ☎ 622 4111. These spacious two-bedroom self-catering apartments are excellent value. The cream-and-grey building has no sign or number, so it can be difficult to find. Carnival rates last from January to April. ④/⑥.

Villa Maria, 48A Perseverance Rd, Haleland Park ☎ 629 8023, fax 629 8641, *vilmar@tstt.net.tt*. Quiet, well-kept hotel opposite St Andrew's golf course at the north end of Maraval, with a restaurant and cocktail bar overlooking the swimming pool. All rooms have cable TV, a/c and en-suite bathrooms, and breakfast is included. ⑤/⑦.

Guesthouses

Carnetta's Inn, 99 Saddle Rd, Maraval ☎ 628 2732, fax 628 7717, *www.carnettas.com*. Well-laid out rooms in two Maraval sites, one with a restaurant and bar. All come with a/c, phone, cable TV – some have kitchenette. The owners are extremely hospitable and great for local information. Breakfast included in Carnival rate. ⑤/⑦.

Jireh's Guesthouse, 109 Long Circular Rd ☎ 628 2337. Neat colonial house with a homely atmosphere, where the cool rooms all have a/c, cable TV and bathrooms; some have a kitchenette, others just a fridge. Laundry facilities and meals are available. ④/⑦.

Monique's Guesthouse, 114–116 Saddle Rd ☎ 628 2351, fax 622 3232, *www.moniquestrinidad.com*. Long-established and friendly, with a variety of plush rooms; all have a/c, phone, and cable TV – some have kitchenette and balcony, and one is fully equipped for people with disabilities. Decent restaurant and bar. ⑤/⑦.

Zollna House, 12 Ramlogan Terrace ☎ 628 3731, fax 628 3737. Comfortable guesthouse with friendly and knowledgeable hosts, if a little overpriced considering the location (difficult to get to without a car). Rooms with fans. Breezy communal balcony overlooks the Maraval Valley. Breakfast included. Off La Seiva Rd off Saddle Rd. ④/⑦.

Eating and entertainment

Maraval's **restaurants** tend to be upmarket, and serve food geared to international tastes; though good, it can be bland in comparison with the local Creole food and expensive compared with equally tasty meals offered at downtown restaurants or street stalls. After dark, most people go into Port of Spain for amusement, and Maraval stays quiet. There are the usual small rum shops, while *Flags* restaurant has a bar-cum-disco that plays American-English easy listening.

Restaurants

Adam's Bagels, 15a Saddle Road, Maraval ☎ 642 2973. Busy and fabulous lunch or early dinner spot, with a bakery (selling great bread, fresh hummus and snacks) at the front and tables in the air-conditioned rear section. The bagels, ranging from cinnamon to onion, are excellent and generously filled, and soups, salads, baked potatoes and rolls filled with Middle Eastern spiced chicken are delicious. Delivery available. Mon–Sat 7am–6pm. Inexpensive.

Bamboo Terrace, *Carnetta's Inn*, 99 Saddle Rd ☎628 2732. This intimate, softly lit dining room with its fish tanks and position overlooking the Maraval River is perfect for a romantic dinner. Local specials change daily, and the regular menu has all the local staples, from seafood chowder to fish and chicken, served with tasty side dishes. Creole breakfasts, and burger or jerk chicken lunches, are also good. Daily 7–10am, noon–2pm & 7.30–11pm. Moderate.

Brothers Steakhouse, 100 Saddle Rd ☎625 5108. Appealing, understated decor and wooden floors add a touch of class, and there's seafood as well as the main draw: the excellent imported steaks, cooked in all styles. Good wine list, too. Mon–Sat 7–11pm. Moderate/Expensive.

Gourmet Club, upstairs at Ellerslie Plaza ☎628 5115. Exclusive fine dining establishment serving very good quality Italian and Greek fare. Mon–Fri 11am–3pm & 6–11pm; Sat dinner only. Expensive.

Vie de France, Long Circular Rd. Bakery and café with the air of a chain-restaurant. The air-conditioned dining room is pleasant, though, and the food is reliable if unexciting: omelettes, fry-ups or cinnamon and apple pancakes for breakfast, and bagels, sandwiches (pastrami and roast beef alongside the tuna and cheese), pasta, steaks and burgers for lunch and dinner. Delicious pastries and cakes, and good espresso and cappuccino. Daily 7am–10pm. Inexpensive.

Nightlife

The Attic, Shoppes of Maraval ☎622 6922 or 8123. Latin nightclub that attracts a mature crowd; the liveliest nights are Fri and Sat. Daily 4pm–4am. Cover varies.

Outer Limits, Royal Palm Plaza, 7 Saddle Road ☎622 0100. Sports bar with pool tables, one reserved for women only, and regular free drinks promotions. Daily 11am–2am.

West to Chaguaramas

From Port of Spain, the Western Main Road winds its way along the coast, past the turn-off to the residential suburbs of **Diego Martin** and **Petit Valley**. The WMR is lined with development: high-rise apartments, the ever-expanding **West Mall**, and exclusive suburbs such as **West Moorings** and **Goodwood Park**. After upmarket **Glencoe**, the landscape becomes less obviously urban, and the communities smaller. Lining the road are rickety wooden stalls selling fruit and vegetables or fresh fish weighed out on old-fashioned scales, and the rum shops – some faded, some decked out in the colours of Fernandes distillers or Pepsi – carry advertisements for "Stag – the man's beer" or hand-painted signs requesting "no urine here". The drinking holes add a touch of life, with people dressed in everything from suits to boxer shorts conducting their business and liming by the roadside. The sea comes in and out of view, providing breathtaking glimpses of calm blue waters and the rocky, forested protrusions of the islands in the Bocas (see pp.126–130).

West to Chaguaramas

The **Chaguaramas** area is distinguished by wide expanses of grassland and miles of untouched forested hills, much of which have been set aside to form the Chaguaramas National Park. Beyond the cluster of former military buildings left over from World War II, when the US Army had a huge military base on the peninsula, a plethora of **yachting** facilities draw some three thousand vessels each month, which come to be serviced or to wait out the hurricane season. Perma-tanned American and European yachties, typically dressed in sun-bleached cutoffs and crumpled T-shirts, and sporting ponytails, are frequently the butt of the witty Trinidadian *picong*, but bring enough business to the area to keep the sniping at bay.

Diego Martin and Petit Valley

The residential districts of **DIEGO MARTIN** and **PETIT VALLEY** are built on land once owned by the River Estate cocoa plantation. Bought by the government in 1897, the area has undergone massive development in the last hundred years. There are few specific sights, apart from the odd historic building and a scenic waterfall. Amid the suburban development of the Diego Martin Main Road, watch out for "Rainorama", a large modern corner house that is the home of the calypsonian Lord Kitchener, and was named after his 1973 calypso about that year's washed-out Carnival.

River Estate

At the top end of Diego Martin Main Road (at the end of the Diego Martin maxi route) is the Diego Martin Estate, better known as **River Estate** these days, an enclave of lush greenery that forms a surprising contrast with the sprawling, suburban environment just a couple of minutes away. The old estate house – a wooden building of elegant simplicity – has benefited from a sensitive restoration, and the small **museum** (daily 10am–6pm; free, but donations are appreciated) inside has a rather bizarre but engaging diorama called "The River", depicting a random history of the estate with the help of floor-pad triggered sound effects. In the basement, black-and-white photos and a slide show centre on cocoa production at the estate, which was owned by Cadbury's from the mid-nineteenth to the mid-twentieth century. Across the road, the large, nonfunctioning **water wheel** dates back to 1845, when the estate produced sugar. An aqueduct once ran from the Diego Martin River to power the wheel, which in turn drove the rollers that crushed sugar cane for the production of molasses.

Opposite the museum, the estate's original **coach shed** is now used as storage space for the local panyard. Behind this are some original **barrack houses**, among the few surviving examples of the galvanized-roofed wooden shacks where the indentured plantation workers had to live. Each building consisted of four rooms, each of which was occupied by a family. The appalling conditions have been described by Trinidadian writers such as Alfred Mendes (see p.361). Few barrack houses are left, thanks to government efforts to improve living conditions.

Blue Basin Waterfall

One of the most accessible falls in Trinidad, **Blue Basin** is also one of the smallest. Like so many others in on the island, the six-metre cascade has been affected by the general reduction in water levels, and no longer gushes with its full force. The setting, with rainforest on all sides, is still beautiful, however, and blue emperor butterflies and exotic birds flutter through the undergrowth. The small circular pool at the base of the fall is good for bathing, and while it gets busy at weekends and after school, you will often find it deserted on weekdays.

To get to the Blue Basin Waterfall from Port of Spain, take a Diego Martin maxi to the end of its route (TT$3), then a route taxi to the base of the waterfall (TT$2–3).

The waterfall is considered sacred by some religious groups, and you may come across Baptists or Rastafarians conducting their rituals by the waters. Baptist flags fly from tall bamboo poles along the track, and offerings – candles, fruit and rice – are scattered by the waters' edge. The area around the waterfall is rumoured to be a favourite haunt of "bandits" out to relieve you of your wallet, and tourism officials are loath to recommend the place to visitors. If you do fancy a dip, it's best to go early in the morning with a group, or visit with a local guide such as Lawrence "Snakeman" Pierre (☎632 9746). Downriver from the waterfall are various good bathing pools; at weekends they are filled with children "takin' in the springs". To reach the waterfall, keep on the main road past the water wheel, then turn right onto Blue Basin Road. Go up the steep hill till you reach a sign pointing to a track for the waterfall, and follow this on foot for five minutes.

The Trinidad and Tobago Yacht Club provides yachting facilities and offers deep-sea fishing trips. US$275 for four hours, US$350 for six hours, US$425 for 8 hours; contact Mr Sagomes ☎637 8771 or Mr Da la Rosa ☎637 7389.

West Mall, West Moorings and Glencoe

The area stretching from Diego Martin to Carenage, now known as **West Mall**, **West Moorings** and **Glencoe**, was a swamp until it was reclaimed in the 1940s. These days, it's characterized by luxury houses defended by high walls and fierce-looking dogs. Postmodernist apartment blocks by Stephen Mendez (one of Trinidad's foremost architects) dominate the skyline, while West Mall provides the latest in upmarket American-style shopping. **Glencoe** is the home of the Trinidad and Tobago Yacht Club.

Carenage

The first clearly recognizable settlement on the WMR, **CARENAGE** sprawls far into the hills, its winding lanes flanked by modern concrete homes, dilapidated huts and general stores covered in posters and hand-painted adverts. There is little to see in Carenage, apart from the crumbling wooden **St Peter's Chapel** at the water's edge,

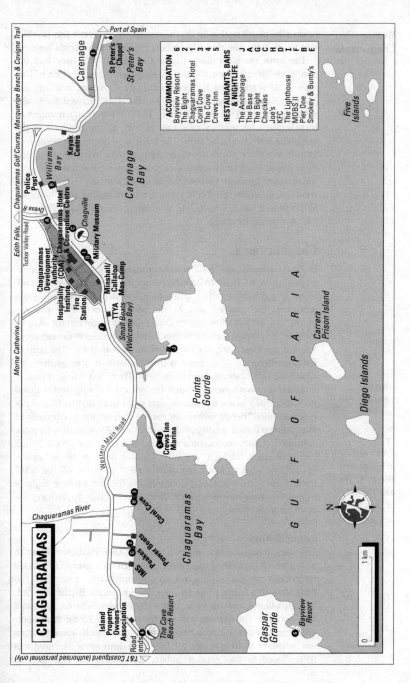

ACCOMMODATION
Bayview Resort   6
The Bight   2
Chaguaramas Hotel   1
Coral Cove   3
The Cove   4
Crews Inn   5

RESTAURANTS, BARS
& NIGHTLIFE
The Anchorage   J
The Base   A
The Bight   G
Checkies   C
Joe's   H
KFC   D
The Lighthouse   I
MOBS II   F
Pier One   B
Smokey & Bunty's   E

CHAGUARAMAS

next to the petrol station on the main road. On St Peter's Day (the last Sunday in June), the clergy bless fleets of fishermen's boats here.

The town owes its name to the fact that it was here that the Spaniards brought their ships to be careened (scraped clean of barnacles). After the Spanish departed in 1797, Carenage sank into torpor as a sleepy fishing village, but its character changed drastically with the arrival of the Americans in 1941. When Chaguaramas was turned into a US military base (see below), all the residents of the peninsula were relocated here. The town soon acquired a seedy reputation as a place where American soldiers went to have fun and find local women, but these days, a maritime flavour has returned, with the masts of pleasure yachts moored at the marinas visible over the rooftops. Opposite the Yacht Club, a mini **shopping mall** houses a Hi-Lo supermarket, a branch of Republic bank and *Pizza Boys* and *Vie de France* food outlets.

Chaguaramas

Beyond Carenage, the WMR winds through the mountainous, forested peninsula of **CHAGUARAMAS** (pronounced Shag-ger-*rarm*-ms). Home to red howler and capuchin monkeys, armadillos, ocelots and anteaters, the greater part of the area has remained virtually untouched, with shallow beaches and miles of virgin rainforest in its interior, and is now a protected **national park**. Leisure development has, for the most part, been sensitive and unobtrusive. The strip of flatlands along the south coast is the only built-up area, shelter to a scattering of restaurants and nightclubs. There is a string of **beaches** along the south coast, though the sea can be dirty and polluted here, especially in the wet season, and signs warn that bathing is not recommended. Better swimming can be had on the north coast at **Macqueripe Beach**, a delightful cove that's easily accessible by road.

Come to Chaguaramas on a weekend and you'll see people liming on the beaches, taking a "seabath", fighting the currents in kayaks, cycling and jogging along the quiet roads that strike off the WMR toward the north coast, and hiking in the forests; while at night, a more glamorous crowd comes in from Port of Spain to frequent the open-air nightclubs.

Maxis for Chaguaramas leave from Green Corner in Port of Spain and run to Chagville Beach (TT$4) and The Cove (TT$6). See also pp.68–69.

Some history

The name Chaguaramas, derived from the Amerindian word for the palms which once lined this coast, is the only remnant of the area's indigenous population. The region's natural harbour provided the **Spanish** with a hiding place for their ships when the **British** invaded, though when it became clear that defeat was inevitable, the ships were scuttled. The harbour was also the reason the **US military** wanted the area as its Caribbean base during World War II, leasing it from the British in 1940 in return for fifty used destroyers. The area was then closed to the general public, the population relocated to

Carenage (see p.114) and the military base which now forms Chaguaramas town constructed.

The American soldiers, initially greeted with a warm welcome, quickly became unpopular. Many Trinidadians resented the US occupation of the best beaches and countryside within easy reach of the capital, as well as the social effect of having so many young American men living in the region. The GIs outnumbered the local men, who could not compete with GIs' ostentatious wealth, and the resentment this generated was immortalized by Lord Invader in his famous calypso *Working for the Yankee Dollar*:

> *"Rum and Coca-Cola, Go down to Point Cumana,*
> *Both mother and daughter, Working for the Yankee*
> *Dollar."*

The situation was not improved by the Americans' attitude towards **race**. A 1945 edition of *Life* magazine reported that "US soldiers confused by the mix of colour lines would keep a brown paper bag at the doorway to their parties. Anyone whose skin was lighter than the bag was considered 'white' (and allowed entry)." Some would argue that this persists today in the admission policies of the peninsula's glitzy nightclubs, where cover charges have been known to vary according to the skin colour of prospective patrons.

With the growth of the **independence movement**, Chaguaramas became a focus of conflict between the British colonial government and the local population. In April 1960 thousands of local residents marched through the rain to campaign for the return of Chaguaramas. Their goal was achieved the following February, when the area was returned to Trinidad and the Americans departed.

Chaguaramas has long been a recreational area for Trinidadians, and with this in mind the government declared the region a **national park** in 1961, also granting protected status to the area's wildlife and rainforest. The developed area, which contains many buildings abandoned by the Americans, was promoted as the seat of the future Caribbean parliament, but these plans were thwarted by the collapse of the West Indian Federation in 1962. Subsequently the **Chaguaramas Development Authority** was established, to maintain the nature reserve and encourage leisure-oriented businesses into the area. In 1999, the peninsula served as the venue for the **Miss Universe** competition, and subsequent beautification has seen an upgrade in the CDA's hotel and cavernous conference facilities.

For details of the accommodation price codes used in these listings, see p.23.

Accommodation

Despite all the leisure facilities in Chaguaramas, there is relatively little accommodation in the area; most visitors stay in the capital, just twenty minutes' drive away.

The Bight, Peakes Marina, Western Main Rd, Chaguaramas ☎634 4839, fax 634 4387, *pys@cablenett.net*. Ten smart rooms in Peakes boatyard, used mainly by visiting yachties. Overlooking the marina right by the sea's edge, rooms are tastefully furnished and have a/c, cable TV and en-suite bathrooms. ⑤/⑦.

Chaguaramas Hotel and Convention Centre, Western Main Rd, Chaguaramas ☎634 2379, fax 634 2377. Refurbished to house the 1999 Miss Universe Pageant entrants, this is a somewhat soulless but functional place where the modern, tiled rooms all have cable TV, phone and a/c. There's a restaurant and bar on site, and a pool is planned. ⑦.

Coral Cove, Western Main Rd, Chaguaramas ☎634 2040, fax 634 2248, *www.coralcovemarina.com*. Newish, rather uninspired but efficient and friendly hotel. Rooms are clean and modern, with a/c, cable TV, phone and kitchenette. ⑤.

The Cove, Western Main Rd, Chaguaramas ☎634 4319, fax 634 4278. Spacious, peaceful and well-maintained self-catering apartments sleeping two to six. Most have TV and fridge, and daily maid service is provided. Use of *The Cove* beach resort is free for occupants, and meals are available. ④/⑥.

Crews Inn, Point Gourde, Chaguaramas Bay ☎634 4384, fax 643 4175, *www.crewsinnltd.com*. Overlooking the busy marina and patronized mostly by a well-to-do yachtie crowd, this is the smartest place to stay in Chaguaramas. The tiled, sparkling rooms have all mod cons, kitchenette and balconies overlooking the sea, and there's a good restaurant, bar, gym and a lovely pool. ⑦.

Williams Bay

Past Carenage, the WMR trundles along the south coast parallel to the sea, its twists and turns revealing lovely vistas out to the Bocas and back to Port of Spain. Beyond the red-dusted towers and chutes of the prominent bauxite loading plant, the road makes one final monumental twist before descending towards **Williams Bay**, where signs indicate that you're now in the Chaguaramas National Park. The beach here is nothing to shout about, as it's slim and lapped by brownish waves tinted with petrol rainbows from the boats moored at *Pier One* nightclub at the far side of the bay. It does get busy at weekends with local bathers, who bring coolers packed with food and drink and make a day of it, but as with the rest of the coast here, swimming isn't recommended. There are a couple of reasons to linger here – you can rent a kayak from the **Kayak Centre** (daily 6am–6pm ☎633 7871), in a signposted building in the concreted lot to the east side of the bay. Paddling about in the waters off Chaguaramas costs TT$25 for a single kayak and TT$35 for a double; both rates are per hour. Another energetic option is to rent a **mountain bike** from Bay Sports next door (☎637 7281); a straight rental costs TT$20 per hour, but you're better off paying an additional TT$10 for a **guided ride** along the paved roads in the interior of the National Park – one of the nicest (as long as it's not too hot) and least intrusive ways to see the area's wildlife and natural beauty. Bay Sports is open on Saturdays, Sundays and public holidays from 6am to 6pm (daily 10am–6pm during Carnival season), but will accommodate groups of five or more during the week. Tours should

Pier One
☎*634 4472*
*operate a boat
to Guiria in
Venezuela each
Wednesday
(4hr; TT$370
one way, $780
return).*

be booked a day in advance, though turning up on spec is usually fine at the weekend.

West to
Chaguaramas

West to Small Boats

Beyond Williams Bay, the WMR's winding curves give way to a long, straight stretch flanked by the rather ugly structures that together comprise the closest thing Chaguaramas has to a town. The place was constructed in three months in 1940 by the US military and local labour, and turned over to civilian use in 1961. Today it consists mostly of aircraft hangars, warehouses and official buildings that have been converted for use by businesses or government departments, as well as the hulking presence of the **Chaguaramas Hotel and Convention Centre**, its curving, incongruously grand flagpole-lined driveway looking out of place amongst its no-nonsense neighbours. Several minor roads strike off the WMR here toward a gently inclining parallel road that's simply known as "the back road", home to training camps for firemen and soldiers with the Trinidad Defence Force. Penned in by the high hills that spread back from the coast, the heat can get oppressive here, but it's worth braving the sun to check out the surprisingly interesting **military museum**, and, in Carnival season, Peter Minshall's **Callaloo mas camp**. If you plan on exploring the fantastic rainforest of the Chaguaramas interior, you'll also have to pay a visit to the offices of the **Chaguaramas Development Authority**, from where you can book tours and arrange access to more remote parts of the peninsula.

The Same
S@me Internet
Café, *in the*
Chaguaramas
Hotel and
Convention
Centre
*(Mon–Fri
8am–7pm, Sat
9am–5pm) has
several
extremely fast
terminals;
access costs
TT$8 for
15min.*

Chaguaramas Development Authority

On the back road on Chaguaramas town, behind the *Chaguaramas Hotel and Convention Centre*, is the orange-painted facade of the **Chaguaramas Development Authority (CDA)** (Mon–Fri 8am–4pm; ☎634 4227 or 4364, fax 634 4311, *www.chagdev.com*), set up to promote and maintain the region, and doing an excellent job of opening up this pristine countryside for recreation. They offer excellent **tours**, led by experienced and knowledgeable guides, to the **Bocas** (see p.126) and educational excursions into the **Chaguaramas National Park**, most of which pass through the lush vegetation, rivers and cultivated forest of the **Tucker Valley** (see p.122), the first citrus plantation on the island. Perhaps the best hike is to **Covigne River**, a fairly strenuous 1.8-mile, one-hour hike along a river bed, which includes a beautiful section of twisting gorge, and a rope-aided climb up a waterfall to an emerald bathing pool surrounded by rainforest. On the way back, you can pick your own nutmeg at an abandoned plantation and splash around in a swimmable spring. The CDA also provides guides for the **Edith Falls** trail and **Morne Catherine** (see pp.123 and 124). Much of the CDA's work is with local school groups, and if you're lucky, you'll be able to join one of these hikes at a fraction of the normal rate – it's well worth calling ahead to check the schedule of tours. Otherwise, you'll pay the regular rates, between US$8 and $25, which cover transport from the CDA office to the start of the hike and back. You should bring water and snacks with you on all trips as there's nowhere to buy them, and unlike many tour companies CDA do not provide refreshments.

It's possible to rent a tent from the CDA (TT$40–80 per day) and **camp** at two designated sites in the forest. There are no facilities, save the drinkable water from the nearby stream, but the environment is awe-inspiring as you pitch your tent in virgin rainforest, surrounded by parrots, monkeys and bubbling brooks.

Chaguaramas Military History and Aviation Museum

The Military History and Aviation Museum ☎ 634 4391 is open daily 9am–5pm; TT$10. Free guided tours are available on request

Located on the Western Main Road next to the coastguard training ground and heliport, the **Chaguaramas Military History and Aviation Museum** is hard to miss – there's a large sign out front and a collection of military hardware on the forecourt, including a monumental ex-US Army **LARC** ("lighter amphibious resupply cargo") vessel. An 88-ton hulk once used to transport ships, it's an undeniably impressive machine. Inside the main building, wedged between more hardware, the exhibits chronicle the military history of Trinidad and Tobago from 1498 to the present, and though the presentation can be somewhat haphazard, it's an absorbing, and occasionally touching, array, worth a glimpse if only because it so sharply counteracts the usual beaches-and-palms image of the Caribbean. First items are a recreation of a World War II **trench** and a German **machine-gun bunker**, complete with flashing lights simulating explosions and battle sounds, followed by a series of photos and explanatory panels highlighting the extensive (and often overlooked) role of local soldiers in international warfare; while paintings and text deal with famous pirates, the history of the Trinidadian police, and local battles, with detailed drawings of the battle of Scarborough Bay in Tobago and the British takeover of Trinidad. Newspaper photographs from the **1990 coup** give a glimpse of the turmoil in Trinidad during the six-day siege (see p.80). The collection ends at a small shop that sells military prints, pamphlets and a lovely selection of greeting cards.

Callaloo mas camp

The Minshall mas camp is open Mon–Sat 10am–6pm. For more information, or to arrange a visit, call ☎ 634 4491.

The **Callaloo mas camp**, opposite the old heliport in a large warehouse-type building surrounded by a wire fence, is the workshop of Trinidad's most famous mas band, led by designer **Peter Minshall**. Known for innovative techniques, high quality and immensely detailed mas presentations, Minshall and his crew use everything from leaves to bottle tops to lengths of fibreglass to manufacture the amazing costumes that have often won them the title of **Band of the Year**. While most mas camps are based in Port of Spain, Callaloo has been leased this building as a reward for its contribution to Trinidad Carnival. Open year-round, the camp is busiest in the run-up to Carnival, when the crew work 24 hours a day in a whirl of fabric, sequins and natural materials. Outside Carnival season, the camp

West to Chaguaramas

Peter Minshall and the Callaloo Company

If you ask any Trinidadian their opinion of **Peter Minshall**, be prepared for a long reply. In a country where Carnival is of the utmost importance, the theatrical Minshall is the most talked about, most controversial and most admired of all the Carnival designers, and his unique combination of traditional Carnival characters and innovative techniques is presented with a strong sense of theatre.

Born in Guyana and raised in Trinidad, Minshall studied theatre design at the Central School of Art and Design in London, becoming a mas designer almost by accident after his mother asked him to make a costume for his sister. The design, called **"Flight of the Hummingbird"**, won Junior Carnival Queen and Individual of the Year, and made such an impression on Trinidad that it was even featured on postage stamps.

Minshall returned to England, where he designed his first Carnival band for the **Notting Hill Carnival** in 1975, and embarked on a career as a theatre designer. Returning to Trinidad soon afterwards, he designed Paradise Lost, the first of many nationally acclaimed bands that he has contributed to the nation's Carnival. His **Callaloo Company**, formed in 1991, includes many of Trinidad's top actors, dancers and artists, and functions as a production company, mas factory and performance group. This close-knit and loyal crew takes its name from Trinidad's national dish, whose various ingredients reflect the country's ethnic mix; "all ah we is one" is the company's philosophy.

Unlike many Carnival costumes, which are thrown away on Ash Wednesday, Minshall's creations decorate houses throughout Trinidad. While most contemporary mas presentations tend to concentrate on escapist, fantasy themes with minimal costumes, Minshall's lavish and detailed works deal with spiritual and political issues – the environment, the interconnectedness of humanity and the transience of life. Many of his pieces are more like kinetic sculptures than costumes in the traditional sense – huge puppets with moving limbs, and butterflies with enormous fluttering wings. In emphasizing the aspect of Carnival that allows people to escape their own identity by playing a role, Minshall is continuing the tradition of Carnival as theatre for all: "In most countries," he has often remarked, "people pay to see others perform, however in Trinidad people pay *to* perform."

Sadly, though, while Minshall still brings out a band each Carnival, it's been several years since he produced **King and Queen** designs. While the creations produced by other bands are undeniably impressive constructions, Callaloo Company's absence from the Dimanche Gras show has left a rather yawning creative gap in the art form. One of Minshall's greatest talents – his ability to produce enormous designs that are so skilfully crafted that even the tip of a far-off wing or tail moves and dances along with the wearer – hasn't been equalled by his rivals, and these days the kings and queens look more like human-powered, highly decorated and rather lifeless floats.

---

*For more on
Trinidad's
Carnival, see
pp.104 and
334.*

makes costumes and puppets for international events such as the **Olympic Games** and **World Cup** ceremonies, and **Jean Michel Jarre** concerts. It also makes and restores furniture. Visitors are welcome, though bear in mind that during Carnival season production is at its most hectic; look around as quickly and quietly as possible, to avoid disrupting production.

Chagville Beach and Small Boats

Immediately beyond the police post at the start of the WMR's straight stretch, **Chagville Beach** is an unremarkable pebbly strip, fringed by grass and almond trees and separated from the road by a car park and a garish drive-in *KFC* outlet. The sea can sometimes get quite rough, though it is less so in the mornings. Although swimming is not recommended during the wet season due to downstream pollution, the water still gets packed with bathers at weekends and public holidays. Facilities are limited – basically toilets that are sometimes open, a car park, a bar and, (as well as the *KFC*), a snack parlour-cum-rum bar, *Checkies* – but there are plenty of restaurants within five minutes' drive in either direction of the beach.

A calmer– though not necessarily any cleaner – spot for bathing is a couple of minutes' drive down the road at Williams Bay, adjacent to the Trinidad and Tobago Yachting Association. Known locally as **Small Boats**, this is a popular place for Trinis to take a dip, but it's not recommended for those unused to the waters because they are polluted – in any case, you'll probably be put off by the refuse washed up by the sea. There are no facilities, but refreshments can be bought at the fashionable *Anchorage* restaurant and bar nearby.

Tucker Valley

Back on the WMR opposite the police post, the **Tucker Valley** Road strikes into the interior toward the north coast. It's a truly beautiful drive, with pastures and fields dotted with enormous, bromeliad-smothered samaan trees to each side, gently rising to meet forested peaks.

After a couple of minutes' drive, you'll pass the unmarked right-hand turnoff to the Covigne trail (see p.119) and, a few minutes' further, a haphazard group of gravestones and the dilapidated St Chad's church to your right. This is pretty much all that's left of **Mount St Pleasant** village, a thriving settlement that was home to workers during the colonial era, when this fertile valley was planted with citrus, cocoa and coffee as part of the Tucker Estate. Among the plain gravestones you can pick out the rather grand tomb of Amelia Tripp, daughter of the estate's former English owner, William Sanger Tucker. The CDA plan to restore the church and build a museum here, but so far, the only construction has been carried out by builders on the set of the **Merchant Ivory** movie *The Mystic Masseur*, based on the book by Trinidadian novelist of V.S. Naipaul; several scenes were filmed here in January 2001. Set back from the road, some of the buildings are new (though given a suitably weathered treatment), while others were committed to the big screen in all their ramshackle glory.

Edith Falls and Chaguaramas Golf Course

Back on Tucker Valley Road, you'll soon pass the well-signposted left turn to the **Edith Falls**. This will take you onto Bellerazand Road, from where the beginning of the trail to the falls – on the left of the road just before the practice range of the Chaguaramas Golf Course – is clearly marked. It's an easy 30-minute walk (1.5km) through the rainforest, which is rich in **exotic flora**: fluffy stands of enormous bamboo, halyconia flowers, fishtail palms, and rubber trees seeping their black squidgy sap. **Red howler monkeys** roar like sea lions; yellowtails and bluejays glide around, and large **blue emperor butterflies** brush past, unperturbed by your presence. At the end of the trail, you must scramble up a few boulders to reach the waterfall. Water seeps through the steep craggy rockface, sending showers tumbling 180 metres into the shallow pool below. Bear in mind, though, that the falls slow to a trickle in dry season (Nov–June).

The Chaguaramas Golf Course is open daily 7am–6pm; you'll pay TT$45 for nine holes, $5–50 to use the driving range and $30 to rent clubs. There's a small café on site.

Beyond the falls trail, Bellerazand Road cuts straight through the nine-hole **Chaguaramas Golf Course**, built by American servicemen during World War II on a former tonka bean plantation. From the golf course, you can follow a **hiking trail** up through the forest to Macqueripe Beach, with gorgeous views of the north coast at several points. To find it, you'll need to enlist the services of a CDA tour guide (see p.119).

Macqueripe Beach and the Tracking Station

Tucker Valley Road ends at the small, picturesque cove of **Macqueripe Beach** (daily 7am–6pm), on Trinidad's north coast. Entry to Maqueripe is free, but you'll be charged TT$10 to drive down to the car park overlooking the beach, from where a fairly steep steps lead down to the water. A curve of coarse brown sand sheltering beneath a steep, wooded hillside, it's an idyllic spot with stunning sunsets and a distant view of Venezuela's Paria Peninsula, marred only by a concrete platform built when the beach was the favoured swimming spot of US servicemen. The sea on this side of the peninsula is unpolluted and good for swimming, if a little chilly, and though the beach can get crowded at weekends, you'll often find it deserted the rest of the time. Strong currents make it unwise to swim out too far. There are no facilities on the beach (bring your own food and drink), but there's a changing room in the car park (TT$1).

In the 1930s and 1940s, Macqueripe was a fashionable resort, the haunt of movie stars such as Errol Flynn, but no real facilities remain. There are changing rooms and toilets in the car park (TT$1), and you will need to bring your own refreshments – the nearest food outlets are *KFC* or *Checkies* (see p.122).

West to Chaguaramas

As the road to the tracking station is blocked by a locked barrier, you'll need to contact the CDA (see p.119) if you want to drive up; walkers and cyclists can go round the gate.

Almost opposite the security station where you pay to use the Maqueripe car park, a signposted right turn leads to the Bamboo Cathedral, a rather whimsical but apt name for the tunnel of bamboo that encloses a section of the tarmac, the thick foliage allowing shafts of green-tinged sunlight to filter through. It was a pretty enough spot to inspire renowned Trinidadian artist and national hero **Michel Cazabon**, who included the Cathedral in the many paintings he made of the Tucker Valley in the nineteenth century. Once through the bamboo, the road snakes upward toward the rusting bulk of the **tracking station** at the top of the ridge. This huge dish was erected by the US military in the 1950s to track nuclear missiles; however, its main claim to fame is less sinister. The dish's technology soon became redundant, and the radar scanner was converted into a radio transmitter in 1960; on August 12 of the same year it was used to transmit the first radio signal to be bounced off a **satellite** – the signal was received at Floyd Air Force Base in New York. The station was used to develop the technique until 1972, when it was abandoned.

The tracking station stands on a nine-acre plateau which affords gorgeous **views** of Tucker Valley, the north coast and of Venezuela, and if you trust the rusting structure, you can climb up the dish for an even better 360° panorama. On the way down, keep an eye (or an ear) out for the wide variety of **birds** and troops of **howler monkeys** that inhabit the area.

Morne Catherine

Opposite the Military Museum, the Cano Ventura Road snakes northwards into the hills toward the forested peak of **Morne Catherine**, the Chaguaramas National Park's highest. As with the route to the Tracking Station, the Cano Ventura Road is barred by a gate, so you'll need to contact the CDA (see p.119) if you want to drive up; again, walkers and cyclists have free access. It's a gorgeous, if steep, drive, the road overhung with trees and bamboo; gaps in the foliage reveal lovely views of the virgin forest on the opposite ridge. A fork off to the right leads to a radar ball, but there's nothing much to see there; instead, you can stop anywhere along the road to appreciate the abundant birdlife, from toucans to oropendolas and hummingbirds. Very few cars drive up to this spot, and the only noise is the rustling, creaking forest and its inhabitants. For birdwatching tours of Morne Catherine, contact the CDA or Caribbean Discovery Tours ☎624 7281.

The marinas: Peakes, Crews Inn, Coral Cove and Industrial Marine Services (IMS)

The **marinas** along Western Main Road have been developed in recent years to serve the rapidly growing yachting fraternity, which docks in Trinidad to avoid the hurricane season in the rest of the Caribbean.

Even if you're not a yachtie, you'll find the marinas useful for their extensive facilities. **Peakes** has a supermarket, ATM, a fast-food outlet and a well-stocked boat shop. Deluxe **Crews Inn Marina** has a doctor's service, an attractive restaurant, a branch of Hi-Lo supermarket, a bank and a series of smart shops selling everything from marine equipment to books. There's also a branch of Republic Bank at the roadside just before the Inn. **Coral Cove Marina** has several maritime-oriented shops as well as the *Cyber Sea Internet café*; they charge TT$15 per half hour of internet access, sell foreign newspapers and magazines, and books (including Chris Doyle's indispensable *Cruising Guide of Trinidad and Tobago*), and have a book exchange service. The **Industrial Marine Services** provides technical and maintenance support for yachties and their craft. **Executive Marine** (Unit 2, Shipwright Building, Crews Inn marina ☎625 0850 or 634 2219) offer deep-sea fishing trips at night or during the day (from US$450 per half day) as well as "Party" and the more sedate "Cocktail" limes (from US$350 per half day).

The Cove

The Cove (daily 7.30am–6.30pm), at the end of the Western Main Road, is a narrow beach of imported yellow sand with the most developed and well-maintained facilities along this stretch of coast. The sea is calm and regular pollution checks have cleared the water for swimming. The TT$6 entrance charge means that the beach is usually quiet. A lifeguard is on duty during the day, and facilities include changing cubicles, showers, toilets and a swimming pool. There is also a bar serving refreshments and light meals (6.30am–2am).

Beyond The Cove, the land due west belongs to the Trinidad and Tobago coastguard, and is closed to the public.

Eating and entertainment

Chaguaramas has several excellent **restaurants**, **bars** and **nightclubs**. The only problem is the lack of public transport after dusk – if you don't have a car, it's best to arrange a return taxi in advance. Most of the clubs run **"free drinks"** nights, for which you'll pay cover charge; around TT$40 with a flyer, TT$80 without. Pick up flyers from the venues, and from shops in the larger Port of Spain malls.

Anchorage, Point Gourde Rd, Chaguaramas ☎634 4334. Expensive European-style food with a local flavour served in an open-air restaurant overlooking the water – one of the most romantic views in Trinidad during the day, though you can't see much at night. Elegant casual dress is required. Also operates as a nightclub at weekends, mostly attracting an older crowd. Dance to a variety of music (Thursday's Latin night is usually very busy) and watch the catfish swirl about the pier. Opening hours and entrance fee vary, starting at TT$50.

The Base, cor. of Airways and Macqueripe Rd, Chaguaramas ☎634 4004. Huge hangar of a place that opens only for live shows, carnival fetes and one-off parties, most of which attract a young, well-to-do crowd; all events are pub-

West to Chaguaramas

If you're into yachting, look out for The Bocas, *a free monthly magazine written by and for the yachtie community; the classifieds include ads from boat owners in need of crew members.*

licized in the press and on radio. The club has, however, been the subject of press allegations that it operates a racist door policy. Car park parties here tend to be looser affairs. Entrance fee varies.

The Bight, Peakes Marina, Western Main Rd, Chaguaramas ☎634 4839. This neon-bedecked air-conditioned bar, with its few tables, huge TV for showing sports fixtures, plus breezy verandah restaurant overlooking the marina, is a popular yachtie hangout. The international menu is hugely varied, from good local and continental breakfasts, to salads, sandwiches and burgers for lunch, and seafood, steaks and chops for dinner. Daily 7.30am–midnight. Moderate.

Buccoo Rouge, Upper Level, West Mall, West Moorings ☎632 4601. Upmarket French seafood restaurant, whose specialites include exquisite lobster bisque and delicious desserts from the chef, who previously cooked for Francois Mitterand and the QE2. The oyster bar is open all day. Open Mon–Sat 11am–11pm. Expensive.

Joe's, Coral Cove Marina. Simple Italian café chain serving unremarkable but reliable salads, steak sandwiches, burgers, hoagies, pasta and pizza. Takeaway is available, and it's a useful stopgap if you need to eat in a hurry. Mon–Sat 11am–10pm. Inexpensive.

The Lighthouse, Crews Inn Marina, Point Gourde, Chaguaramas ☎634 4384. Attractive open-air restaurant and bar overlooking the yacht marina, underneath a red-and-white striped lighthouse. Serves tasty international food with Creole specialities aimed at mainly yachtie clientele. Daily 7.30am–10pm. Bar open till 11pm. Moderate/Expensive.

MOBS II, Welcome Bay, Chaguaramas ☎634 2255, *www.mobs2.net*. Expansive open-air venue that opens carnival fetes and concerts only – these are advertised in the press and on radio. The location overlooking Small Boats beach is extremely picturesque at night, and the amphitheatre terrace design ensures good views of the stage. Entrance fee varies.

Pier One, Western Main Rd, Chagville ☎634 4472 or 4426. Pretty open-air nightclub overlooking the sea that attracts yuppyish crowd. Best for the steaming Latin night (Thurs; dance classes available); Friday is a free-drinks free-for-all, with all types of music. Live acts are publicized in the press and on radio. Entrance fee varies.

Smokey and Bunty's, Western Main Rd, Carenage. Sister-branch of the St James drinkers' institution, this new effort is rarely as busy, but an indoor section with pool tables and an outdoor courtyard with seating make it a nice spot to sink a few Caribs or fill your belly with Creole specials or burgers. Daily 11am–2am. Budget.

The Bocas

When you hear Trinidadians refer to the **BOCAS**, they talk of "down de islands" in tones of wistful longing. These rocky islets are separated from the mainland, and from one another, by the **Bocas del Dragon (Dragon's Mouths)**, a series of channels connecting the Gulf of Paria with the Caribbean. The name is appropriate, for the coastlines here are jagged and rocky, and the sea hides treacherous currents and undertows that can make even the short journey to the nearest island, **Gaspar Grande**, a rough ride. Dolphins frequent the waters hereabout, so keep your eyes peeled; if you're lucky, you may even see a leatherback turtle or a pilot whale.

The islands had a thriving **whaling industry** in the eighteenth century, with whaling stations on Gaspar Grande, **Monos** and **Chacachacare**. Today they are sparsely inhabited, their interiors covered with dense forest, and lacking any roads. Scattered around the coasts are a few holiday homes, accessible only by boat. The islands have always been the Trinidadians' escape from the mainland, but apart from the *Bayview* resort on Gaspar Grande, there are no hotels, guesthouses, restaurants or bars; visitors must bring their own food. Once there, for the most part, you will be alone with the birdsong and the sound of the sea. The atmosphere is so still it can verge on the uncanny, especially on deserted Chacachacare, with its abandoned leper colony and tales of ghosts.

Getting to the islands

The **Island Property Owners' Association** marina (on Western Main Road, just before The Cove) is home to boats, known locally as **pirogues**, that make regular trips to the islands. Prices are for up to six people, so it's cheapest to go in a group or else share a boat with mainlanders who commute to and from their jobs at holiday homes. One-way fares are TT$50 to Gaspar Grande (unless you're staying at the resort; see p.128, Bayview Resort), TT$60 to Monos and TT$400 to Chacachacare; for more information, call ☎634 4331. Members of the **Trinidad and Tobago Yacht Club** (☎637 4260) can also arrange transport to and from the islands. If you want to **tour the Bocas** for the day, you can also rent a boat (and driver) for about TT$600. Before disembarking, arrange a pick-up time to ensure that you're not stranded on the islands.

Both the CDA (see p.119) and **Caribbean Discovery Tours** (☎624 7281; see p.48) run a variety of day-trips to the Gasparee Caves, Chacachacare and other islands. They also offer diving trips around the area as well as **fishing** tours. The islands are renowned for their **fishing**, and it is possible to go out with local fishermen in Gasparee Bay; ask at the Island Property Owners' Association marina.

Gaspar Grande

Just fifteen minutes by boat from the mainland, **GASPAR GRANDE** (also known as **Gasparee** and **Fantasy Island**) is the most accessible of the islands. The eerie **Gasparee Caves** at Point Baliene – "Whale Point", named for its former role as a whaling station – were once used by pirates to hide their booty; these days, the only thing that glitters are the walls and the huge, green-tinged stalactites and stalagmites. It's also an excellent place to observe the **fruit bats** which live in the caves and the many local species of bird which congregate outside them. If you want to **visit**, you'll first need to contact the Chaguaramas Development Authority (see p.119); turn up on spec, and you're likely to find the entrance locked up. CDA tours, including the boat from the mainland, cost US$20; alternatively, you can arrange your own vessel and pay the TT$20 fee, though you'll still need to let the CDA know when you'll be visiting.

Of the eight caves on the island, the one that's open to the public is the largest; to get there, follow the signposted concrete path from the jetty through the forest; look out for unusual peeling, shiny-tan coloured trees, whose rather un-PC nickname, "naked Indian", derives from the colour of the bark. If you've prearranged your trip, you'll meet your **CDA tour guide** by the white-and-mustard painted wooden house just before the mouth of the cave. An impressive, cathedral-like cavern of some 35 metres deep, it's a mysterious and weirdly beautiful place that hasn't been ruined by the electric lights and 72 steps that take you to the bottom. Reflected sunlight causes calcium crystals in the rocks to sparkle, and a deep, clear, marvellously turquoise tidal pool, the **Blue Grotto**, reflects the extravagant colours and strange shapes of the stalactites and stalagmites; swimming is officially prohibited, but you may be able to take a dip if touring with a small group. Past the pool, there's a short path to the back of the cave, where you can gaze up at roosting bats and pick out the rock formations that have been given apt nicknames such as "the Lovers", "Buddha" and the "Virgin Mary". Apart from the chirping fruit bats and dripping water, the cave is totally silent.

Incidentally, the small rocky island you'll see to the east on your way to Gaspar Grande is **Carrera**, Trinidad's equivalent of Alcatraz. Its only building is the prison, established in 1876, where convicts still do hard labour. It's said that a few individuals have braved the strong currents and shark-infested waters to swim to the mainland, but officially, there's never been a successful escape.

Bayview Resort

To get to the resort, take the Bayview *resort boat from the* Island Property Owners' Association *at* The Cove *(see opposite). Shuttle service every hour on the half hour, 8am–6.30pm. TT$2.*

On the other side of Gaspar Grande from the caves, the **Bayview** resort (☎678 9001 or 9002; ④) consists of a restaurant, café, beach with facilities, swimming pool, hotel and self-catering apartments. The small beach, with shaded palm huts, a sun deck, and a **water-slide** into the sea, is popular with locals at the weekend. The resort provides pleasant rooms with ①/③, phone, en-suite bathroom and fridge; some have a sea view. Fully furnished **apartments** can be rented for the same price per person. The *Lobster House* restaurant (7.30am–late daily), built to resemble a steamboat, has a lovely view over the sea to the mainland. It serves excellent fresh fish; the average meal costs around TT$70.

Scotland Bay, Monos and Huevos

Though actually part of the mainland, **Scotland Bay** is always considered as being "down de islands", since it can only be reached by boat. A favourite with Trinidadian weekenders, this idyllic small cove right at the end of the Western Tip is blessed with soft sand and calm waters that are good for snorkelling. Yachts are often moored in its shelter, although the beach has no facilities. Spreading back from the shore is some gorgeous primary rainforest inhabited by multiple exotic creatures; red howler monkeys, their eerie roars echoing around the bay, are perhaps the most vocal residents. It was from nearby **Staubles Bay** that the government shelled the Northern Range during the Black Power uprising in the 1970s (see p.331).

Scotland Bay looks out across the swirling waters of the Boca de Monos to the island of **Monos**, uninhabited except for a few holiday homes belonging to rich Trinidadians. The densely wooded interior once supported a large colony of red howler monkeys – the island's name is Spanish for apes – but these are now confined to the mainland. Beyond the sheer western ramparts of Monos and another fierce *boca* lies the privately owned and seldom-visited island of **Huevos**.

Chacachacare

Chacachacare (*shak*-a-chak-ar-ee) is the largest island of the Bocas and, an hour's boat ride from the mainland, also the farthest-flung. It is utterly peaceful, and its idyllic coves, with their excellent **fishing** and **swimming**, are ideal for those who want to get away from it all. There are none of the well-to-do holiday homes found on the other islands, and the mountainous interior is covered in dense forest. There is just one useable road, leading from the jetty to the lighthouse; the others, which once serviced the **abandoned leper colony**, have long been overgrown, and only tracks remain.

The island's name may derive from *chac-chac*, the Amerindian word for cotton, which grows profusely on the island, or might have something to do with the chattering of the monkeys once found here. Amerindian remains, dating from around 100–400 AD, have been discovered on the island. Under Spanish rule it became a cotton plantation, and subsequently a whaling station was established. It developed into a popular health and holiday resort with Trinis from the mainland until, to their consternation, a leper colony was established in 1887. The Dominican nuns ran the colony like a prison, and conditions provoked strikes among the patients to gain such rights as male-female fraternization. The last 30 patients left in 1984, and all that remains are the decaying wooden houses, the infirmary (with bottle and papers still on the shelves), the nuns' quarters and the chapel, all visible on the right as you approach the island from the mainland. You're free to explore the structures, but as they're all derelict, you should watch your step. Also on this stretch are a string of lovely **beaches**, with pale sand and shallow, calm, crystal-clear water; these see some traffic at weekends, but are often deserted during the week.

Chacachacare is now uninhabited except for its wildlife (look out for unfeasibly large iguanas), and the two men who work the small,

If you're interested in birdwatching or nature walks, contact Caribbean Discovery Tours ☎ 624 7281 or Paria Springs ☎ 622 8826.

The Bocas

The CDA
☎ *634 4227*
offer guided
walks to the
lighthouse or
the salt pond
for around
US$25
including
transport.

white **lighthouse,** built in 1885, although the leper colony is said to be haunted by the ghost of a nun who committed suicide after becoming pregnant by a local fisherman. On the southeast of the island is **La Tinta Bay**; the name, meaning ink in Spanish, alludes to the black sand of its beaches. Once a favourite place for smugglers, today this coarse-grained beach is deserted save for the refuse washed up by the tide, and the odd iguana and scavenging hawk. Nearby is the **Salt Pond**, a marsh-fringed sulphurous lake that provides the perfect habitat for unusual trees such as the campecho, known locally as the **bread and cheese tree** on account of its textured fruit and cheesy taste. The odd **manchineel** tree also grows on the island's beaches. Its beautiful yellow flowers hide the fact that it produces a sinister fruit, used by the Amerindians to make poisoned arrows. Avoid contact with any part of this tree: its sap causes painful blisters (see p.22).

Blue Devils, Carnival

Pan player

Making Carnival costumes

Carnival masqueraders

Central Port of Spain

Boissiere House, Port of Spain

Football on the beach at Las Cuevas, Trinidad

Baptist prayer flags at Toco, Trinidad

Waterloo Temple, Trinidad

Caroni Swamp, Trinidad

Grande Riviere beach, Trinidad

Ice cream stall at Maracas Bay, Trinidad

Hand-painted sign in central Trinidad

Coconut grove on Manzanilla beach, Trinidad

Chapter 2

The North

The north of Trinidad is an eighty-odd kilometre stretch dominated by the rainforested mountains of the Northern Range, which form a rugged spine through the centre of the region, and boast the island's highest peaks, El Cerro del Aripo and El Tucuche. Trinidad's most splendid beaches line the coast to the north of the range, with the enduringly popular Maracas Bay and Las Cuevas playing host to what often seems like the entire population of Port of Spain come the weekends. Beyond Las Cuevas lies the glorious seashore of Blanchisseuse, where the North Coast Road dissolves into kilometres of undeveloped coastline. The Arima–Blanchisseuse Road then swings inland through the forest, providing an opportunity to see most of the island's prolific bird life at the Asa Wright Nature Centre.

Away from the uninhabited, jungle-smothered hills are some of Trinidad's most **densely populated** areas outside of Port of Spain and home to the majority of the island's **African** population. Though you'll see the odd temple, mosque and prayer flag, Indian culture is far less visible here than in the south; Creole cooking reigns supreme and the soundtrack that blares from shops, bars

---

Accommodation price codes

All accommodation listed in this guide has been graded according to the following **price categories**:

① under US$10	② US$10–20	③ US$20–35
④ US$35–50	⑤ US$50–70	⑥ US$70–100
⑦ US$100–150	⑧ US$150–200	⑨ US$200 and above

Rates are for the cheapest double or twin rooms, including 10 percent tax and 10 percent service charge where applicable. In Tobago, rates quoted are those used during the high season, normally mid December–mid April. During low season (mid April–mid December) rates are liable to fall by up to 25 percent. There are no high and low seasons in Trinidad, but rates may rise by up to 70 percent during Carnival. Many hotels give rates in US dollars – we have followed suit. Payment can be made in either US or TT currency.

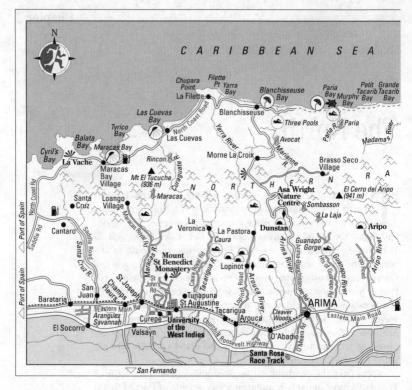

TIDCO's road map has all the major attractions marked.

and maxis is **soca** and Jamaican **dancehall** rather than chutney (see p.345). To the south of the mountains, a string of busy communities crowd along the traffic-choked **Eastern Main Road** (EMR) and the faster flowing **Churchill Roosevelt Highway** which runs parallel to it; both end abruptly just east of Arima, replaced by the winding minor roads that span the weatherbeaten northeast coast. Inland of the EMR, river valleys cut into the Northern Range, providing access (and public transportation) to the naturally abundant interior.

The main transport artery of the **East–West Corridor**, the EMR is the route to a host of interior attractions; there are **waterfalls** and **river swimming** at **Maracas Valley**, **Caura** and the **Hollis Reservoir**. The **Heights of Guanapo Road** boasts two of the island's most spectacular cascades, **La Laja** and **Sombasson**, as well as the challenging **Guanapo Gorge**, a spectacular water channel that's not for the fainthearted. Many of the towns along the EMR are equally absorbing, particularly **St Joseph**, the island's first Spanish capital, with its historic church and barracks. The largest town in the region, **Arima**, is great for window

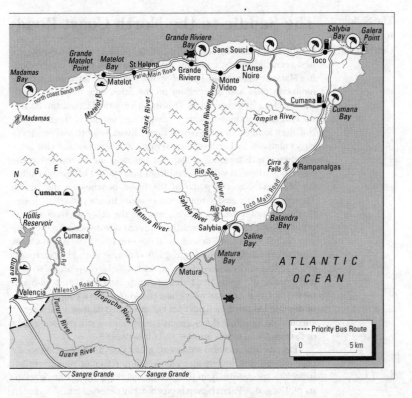

shopping and for the town's **Carib** parade in late August at the **Feast of Santa Rosa**.

Past Arima, the road continues to the **Northeast Tip**. This wild and rugged peninsula, jutting some 20km into the Atlantic Ocean, is Trinidad's best-kept secret. The populace is overwhelmingly friendly, and along the **Toco coast** on its northern side, **leatherback turtles** clamber up the wave-battered sandy beaches to lay their eggs.

Though parts of the north are well served by **public transport** – buses, taxis and maxis serve every village and town along the East–West Corridor – a **car** is useful to visit the more remote north coast, where you're likely to encounter long waits for intermittent public transport if you don't have your own vehicle. Surprisingly, there is not a huge amount of **accommodation** in the region; though there are lovely guesthouses at Blanchisseuse and Grande Riviere, it's often easier to explore from Port of Spain as you can see all the sights during day trips. However, the remote northeast, reached after a minimum of three hour's driving from town, is the only place where you might be better off renting a room.

The Saddle to the North Coast Road

Saddle Road (usually called "the Saddle") makes one of the region's best scenic journeys, climbing the western flank of the range dividing Maraval valley from Port of Spain, squeezing through a narrow mountain pass and descending on the other side into lush **Santa Cruz** valley. However, most visitors drive straight past the Saddle turn-off and continue upwards, navigating the coastal fringes of the Northern Range along the **North Coast Road**, smooth and spectacularly enhanced by borders of glittering Caribbean sea and cliff sides smothered with tangled jungle, that becomes quite crowded at the weekends when crowds descend from nearby Port of Spain heading for **Maracas Bay** and some of the finest **beaches** on the island. Though it's Trinidad's major concession to sun, sand and sea, Maracas is not a "tourist beach", and like the other seashores in the region, you'll find more local than foreign devotees soaking up the sun. Nonetheless, the Maracas coast does represent the island's most **tourist-oriented** region, a ravishing coastline sprinkled with rest stops selling crafts and cold drinks, designated "scenic areas" to stop and admire the view and miles of sandy beaches with well-maintained facilities. You can whisk past the whole lot in a couple of hours of driving, but the area hasn't yet compromised its local character or succumbed to leisure development; most villages still rely on **fishing** or **farming**, and hotels are few and far between.

Beyond Maracas and shimmering **Las Cuevas**, a beautiful sandy cove riddled with underwater **caves**, the north coast remains quiet, maintaining equanimity in the face of seemingly inevitable development. Gorgeous **Yarra beach** is customarily deserted and slow-paced village life at hamlets such as **La Filette** make for a pleasant distraction from the sea. At **Blanchisseuse**, you can choose between a host of small-scale **guesthouses** and countless rugged beaches; beyond here, the coast road ends, replaced by miles of **undeveloped coastline**. Perfect coconut-littered beaches and a series of **waterfalls** – **Paria** is particularly beautiful – make this prime **hiking** territory, and you can even stay in the area; **Petit Tacarib Bay** houses the island's most remote guesthouse.

North Coast Road transport

Maxis from Port of Spain City Gate run to Maracas (TT$8), Las Cuevas (TT$9), La Filette (TT$9) and Blanchisseuse (TT$15) fairly frequently, especially during peak hours. **Route taxis** are more limited in number but can be picked up from Port of Spain. The excellent new rural bus service, with its small red-and-yellow shuttles, runs from Port of Spain City Gate to Blanchisseuse (to Almond Brook guesthouse). Shuttles leave Blanchisseuse at 5.30am, 6.30am, 10.30am, 3.30pm and 7.30pm, and cost TT$8; a short drop is TT$2. The shuttles also go from Blanchisseuse to Arima (TT$8).

The Saddle to Santa Cruz

Gliding by St Andrew's Golf Course and the last of Maraval's grand residences, Saddle Road begins its serpentine ascent into the Northern Range. The roadside buildings gradually give way to abundant rainforest, and after a succession of hairpin bends, two four-metre high stone pillars mark a **junction**. To the left is the **North Coast Road**; to the right, **Saddle Road** squeezes through a narrow gorge of solid rock (if driving, beep your horn and approach with caution) before meandering downhill through pastoral **Santa Cruz valley**, a half-hour scenic jaunt along a single main road through cattle pastures and farmland to the urban bedlam of San Juan (see p.154). Neat cocoa groves, crumbling **tapia** houses and dilapidated gingerbread mansions are punctuated by towering samaan trees and impressive clumps of bamboo, mango, sapodilla and banana, while a thriving **quarrying** concern has gouged messy yellow scars into the hillsides. Cricket supremo **Brian Lara** spent his childhood in **Cantaro Village**, the valley's largest community. The place has a friendly, suburban feel, its main focus the lively main street, lined with shops and rum bars, which swings off from Saddle Road. Past the village, the Saddle cuts through the countryside for several beautiful kilometres before the roadside houses of the San Juan suburbs block the views.

A serene Port of Spain satellite cut off from the city and the coast by mountains rather than distance, the valley is the starting point for a hilly but popular **hike** to Maracas Bay along the **La Sagesse trail** – less often attempted are treks to Las Cuevas or the Maracas–St Joseph valley, for which experienced guides are essential to prevent you from getting lost. As the La Sagesse–Maracas Bay route is so heavily travelled, it's pretty easy to follow on your own; however, reports of robberies make it sensible to travel with a group, and preferably with a local guide; see "Basics" (p.48) for a list of options. It's a pleasant eight-kilometre, two- to three-hour up-and-down hill walk through secondary forest with good views of the northern coastline on the descent; to get to the start, turn off the Saddle at Gasparillo Road (marked by a signpost for a quarry) and carry straight on, passing the quarry on the right. The hike begins where the houses end; ask for directions to the first stretch of path.

The North Coast Road to Maracas

Taking the left turn at the Saddle-North Coast Road pillars sets you off on one of Trinidad's most dramatic drives, teetering along three-300-metre cliffs and tunnelling past precipices of teeming rainforest with the occasional view of faraway peaks swinging into sight. Bois cano trees drop claw-like leaves onto the tarmac and mineral springs pour

The Saddle to the North Coast Road

If you're hungry, try the roti shop-cum-general store on the main road near the petrol station on the outskirts of Cantaro; alternatively, there are plenty of small local restaurants in the village.

The North's best beaches	
Blanchisseuse	p.144
Las Cuevas	p.140
Maracas	p.137
Paria	p.148
Toco	p.172

down into roadside gullies; the water is chilled, delicious and safe to drink, and in places has been channelled through bamboo pipes at which people stop to fill bottles. Despite its spiralling course, this is also one of the smoothest roads on the island, built by US Army engineers in 1944 as a recompense for the American occupation of the Chaguaramas peninsula (see p.116), which deprived Port of Spain residents of sea bathing at Macqueripe and other western bays. This route to Maracas Bay was offered as the alternative, and it's still sometimes called the "American Road".

The first of many panoramas stretches over the Maraval valley and across the hills to the tiny spice and parang centre Paramin (see p.110) and down into the outskirts of Port of Spain, with the sea just visible over the National Stadium and compacted buildings of Woodbrook and Mucurapo. Cliffs and jungle close in beyond here (though you get a few glimpses of Santa Cruz to the right), but a few kilometres further on, the vegetation dissolves to reveal a marvellous coastal prospect, the ocean far below dotted with rocky islets. The largest is 100,000-square-metre **Saut D'eau**, a breeding colony for brown pelicans and home to the chestnut-collared swift and the rufous-necked wood rail. Getting down to the sea isn't easy from here, though; the cliffs are steep and most bays are only reachable by boat. However, a secluded dip is the reward for a stiff 20-minute walk down to **Cyril's Bay**, a pebble beach just before the La Vache lookout point; to make the descent, look for a cream painted board house. Just past the house, a road sign says "slow, sharp bend"; beyond this and a couple more hairpin bends is the overgrown mouth of the path, next to a grassy lay-by where you can park. The agreeably strenuous walk weaves down through balata-dominated evergreen forest humming with bird and animal life. As the path nears the sea, you pass a stone house; if at home, owner Frank welcomes visitors to his menagerie of ducks, geese, dogs and squirrels. You must also pass through his land to get to a three-metre **waterfall** which he has harnessed and dammed – as it's his drinking water, swimming is discouraged. He also guides trips to nearby islands and caves aboard his pirogue; one nearby cavern supports a colony of **oilbirds** (see p.351). Swimming is pretty safe – the murkiness of the water is the result of sediment from the River Orinoco rather than pollution, and there are a couple of offshore rocks that you can dive from.

Taxis from Port of Spain to Maracas (TT$8) leave from the corner of George and Prince streets, Port of Spain.

La Vache Scenic Area

Past Cyril's Bay, the road continues its stomach-lurching circumnavigation of the cliffs. The brightly painted *Hot Bamboo Hut* is a friendly roadside stop for soft drinks and coconut candies, though it's usually only open on weekends; cool breezes and sea views add to its allure. Tourist trinkets and coconut shell or crystal jewellery are on sale, as are chess pieces fashioned from shark bones. If you

The magnetic road to Maracas Bay

A small stretch of apparently ordinary tarmac between La Vache and Maracas Bay has a unique claim to fame; according to local folklore, this is the "**magnetic road**", where vehicles roll up the incline in defiance of gravity. Though it cannot be rationally explained, it's easily experienced. Stop just before the North Coast Road begins its descent to Maracas Bay. As the cliffs to the right recede, revealing the Northern Range, the road ahead appears to have a definite upward incline. On stopping your vehicle, putting the gears in neutral and releasing the handbrake, you'd assume that the car would obey the rules of gravity and roll backwards; however, you move in what you would imagine to be completely the wrong direction. Although the more level-headed conclude that this apparent marvel is nothing more than an optical illusion, more romantic locals insist that the contrary movement is the work of God, Obeah or a bizarre magnetic field.

stop by between 4 and 6pm, ask the owner to call the flock of **toucans** that inhabit the forest above, and watch them swoop impressively down to their cliff-side roosts. The air cools noticeably as you climb to **La Vache Scenic Area**, a viewpoint overlooking the sea laid at the highest point on the North Coast Road; the coastal views are marvellous. At weekends, vendors sell fruits and cold drinks to the hordes on their way to Maracas beach, and likely-looking targets are serenaded by the resident **busker**, who improvises calypsos; he'll expect a few dollars if he makes you laugh.

Below La Vache, a precipitous tarmac road leads 280m down the cliff to a former cocoa estate house on a secluded bluff – now a hotel and restaurant but closed for refurbishing at the time of publication. With magnificent views of Balata Bay to the right and Cyril's to the left, occasional glimpses of Venezuela, and a **beach** so seldom used it might as well be private, this will be the only accommodation option between Maraval and Maracas.

The hotel is also the point from which to explore **Balata Bay**, a pretty shingle and coarse sand beach with two small rivers running into the ocean; take the concrete path that leads off to the right just before the guesthouse, and ask permission from the caretaker who lives on the estate surrounding the bay. There's also a bench trail, or a wide footpath, which runs westward along the coast to Cyril's Bay.

Maracas Bay

The smell of burning brake linings fills the air as the road plunges toward **MARACAS BAY**, three-quarters of an hour's drive from Port of Spain. The most popular stretch of shore on the island, this is more than a beach – it's an institution. Hundreds make the traditional Sunday pilgrimage from Port of Spain, lining up to cross the temporary metal bridge well before noon to show off their newest swimwear, frolic in the water and promenade around *the* place to

*As the long
queues and
filled tables
hint, Richard's
and Natalie's
serve the best
bake and
shark in
Maracas; both
are in the car
park.*

*Joining
fishermen
aboard their
pirogues for a
day or night
can be
arranged at
any local
fishing beach
for a couple of
hundred TT
dollars, but
make sure
you've got
your sea legs
before setting
out.*

swim, sunbathe, network – and be seen by everyone else to be doing it in style. Deck chairs, umbrellas, coolers packed with beer or rum and hampers of cooked food are de rigueur, while boogie boards flash through the surf, muscle-men play beach tennis and local lads put on the occasional acrobatics display – if they can find space between the beach accoutrements. It's also the island's main Ash Wednesday chill-out spot, where revellers come to relax after the mayhem of Carnival, and sound systems keep the prostrated bodies twitching to the beat.

At the eastern end of the bay, *Uncle Sam and Son's* bar pumps reggae and soca over the sand, while the bake and shark vendors do a roaring trade. Unusually for a Caribbean beach, Maracas is whole-heartedly dedicated to local people rather than tourists, and you'll find yourself sharing the sand with everyone from Port of Spain's fashionable elite to extended families enjoying a day in the sun. On weekdays it's a much quieter place – the sand is almost empty and the extensive facilities built by the tourist board look a bit out of place.

Maracas deserves all this attention; it's a gorgeous beach, a gen-erous 1850-metre curve of fine off-white sand bordered by groves of skinny-stemmed palm trees. To the west of the bay, a river divides the bathing area from **Maracas Bay Village**, a fishing hamlet whose catch is in demand throughout the north; super-fresh carite, cavalli, shark and "small fry" are sold here once the boats return in the after-noon. Here you'll find a couple of snack parlour-cum-rum bars, a loose arrangement of houses, lots of beached pirogues and drying nets, a profusion of scavenging dogs and fewer people bathing; most stick to the main beach and avoid the odd fishy entrail. Wherever you swim out to sea, you'll get a sublime view of the beach and its back-drop; cloud-tipped peaks rise up in a majestic swell of deep green, while the forested bluffs funnel breezes on even the hottest of days. Licked into a fury by passing currents and the wind tunnel effect of the surrounding headlands, the waves often reach a metre high and make for an exhilarating swim; the water is usually clear and emer-ald green. It's never a good idea to go out too far, however, as the tides and undercurrents are often dangerously strong; stick to the areas between red and yellow flags. Lifeguards stand by (daily 10am–6pm), whistling furiously if anyone goes too far.

Practicalities

Built by the tourist board in the mid-1990s, Maracas' **facilities** have transformed the beach and somewhat obscured its beauty; concrete huts interspersed with palm-thatched shade covers are scattered all over the main stretch of sand. The huge car park (TT$10 per entry; you'll get a ticket if you park elsewhere at weekends) has a block of showers, changing rooms and toilets (daily 10am–6pm; TT$1). The sole supplier of **watersports** is Blackbeard's, based outside *The Seaside* restaurant and bar and in a little hut on the beach. They rent windsurfers (TT$100 per day), boogie boards (TT$20 per hour), surf kayaks (TT$30 per hour), banana rides – inflatable bananas holding up to four people (TT$25 for 10min), and also **beach chairs**, **umbrellas** and **hammocks** (TT$20 per day).

For **accommodation** there is the imaginatively named *Maracas Bay Hotel* (☎669 1914, fax 623 1643; ⑦), a bland if serviceable dollop of concrete at the west end of the bay. Rooms are plain but well equipped, with tile floors, en-suite bathroom, a/c, balcony and restaurant on site. For those on a more limited budget *Ayhe's Guesthouse* (☎676 8406; ③) has run-down rooms with bed, fan, en-suite bathroom and plastic furniture, but at the western edge of the beach you're right in the fishing village, and the fishing cooperative – where fish is bought and sold – is on your doorstep. Next door is *Bab's Guesthouse* (☎669 4064; ⑤), a bright blue building with a charming elderly owner who rents out a large apartment downstairs consisting of two bedrooms, a lounge, kitchen and bathroom. Sparsely furnished, dark and a bit shabby, it's in a great location nonetheless. You may also be able to rent a room in the village (ask for Uncle Sonny in the village), though if you fancy camping contact *ABC Camping* in the fishing village – look out for their sign. Five minutes drive east of Maracas Bay between Tyrico and Las Cuevas beaches is the delightful *Oropendola Cottage* (☎669 1772; ⑤). Perched above Diamier Bay, this spacious, rustic wooden two-storey house has two bedrooms, fans, a lounge, a well-equipped kitchen and a lovely sundeck with views of neighbouring Maracas Bay. Set in tropical gardens with mango trees and antherium lilies, and a bath outside serving as a makeshift pond, the cottage is fantastic value for the space and setting – though you'll need a car if you're not to feel cut off. There's also a small bar on the property decorated with oropendola's nests which gets busy on Sundays.

When it comes to **eating**, bake and shark is the obvious choice; if you don't fancy shark, some shacks serve kingfish instead. Alternatively, you can also find aloo and fish pies or roti. The expensive *Maracas Bay Hotel* (see above) is a good option for a sit-down meal of fish or local fare. For one that comes with a view of the beach *The Seaside* (10am–6pm daily; inexpensive/moderate) opposite the main car park serves large local meals at reasonable prices. On Sundays its yellow and blue concrete bar is packed and pumping to the latest soca tunes. The *Bay View* restaurant (Mon–Sun 10am–10pm), on the headland west of the bay, has great views and serves inexpensive, tasty seafood for lunch and dinner if it's ordered in advance – pop in with your order on the way to the beach, then eat before returning home. On the beach, alcohol is sold at *Uncle Sam*'s bar and from a couple of shacks on the sand; all of the bake and shark vendors sell soft drinks or freshly squeezed orange juice.

Transport from Port of Spain to Maracas is erratic. Maxis cost TT$8 but are unreliable on the weekends. Most people travel by pri-

The petrol station on the eastern edge of Maracas Bay is the last on this section of coast, so it's wise to fill up if you haven't already done so. Open Mon–Sun 7am–7pm.

vate car, and it's not uncommon for people to hitch a ride home with friends they've made during the day.

Tyrico Bay

Hidden from Maracas Bay by a steep headland, **TYRICO BAY** is about one kilometre east. Inexplicably popular with the Indian community, who flock here for weekend picnics, family beach cricket tournaments and camp-outs, the bay is roughly half the size of Maracas with slightly less in the way of wave action, making it a better choice if you are travelling with children. Luxuriant, fine yellow sand and a gentle shelf add to the feeling of calm, and as there are no food and drink vendors, Tyrico is quieter and more unspoiled than its neighbour. The only buildings are the lifeguard towers (guards are on duty daily 10am–6pm) and portable toilets, and you can drive right down to the sand.

Las Cuevas Bay and around

After an inland curve that provides impressive views of the jagged double apex of Mount El Tucuche, Trinidad's second highest mountain (see p.157), the North Coast Road turns back to the sea at **Las Cuevas Bay**, the north coast's second most popular strip of sand, with a fishing village spreading uphill to the east of the beach. That much further from Port of Spain, Las Cuevas is less of a fashion parade at the weekends than Maracas, and during the week, it's often deserted – a situation that might change now that permission has been granted for construction of a £110-million five-star hotel, with golf course, private villas and apartments taking up two-thirds of Las Cuevas Bay. Understandably the locals are fighting to protect what they have: a wide and clean, unadorned swathe of whitish sand, fringed by coconut palms and inviting green sea. Headlands enclose the bay in a tight horseshoe, affording protection from the wind and a relatively gentle surf. Named by the Spanish after the caves that riddle the rocks to the west end of the bay as well as the seabed, Las Cuevas is a great place for beachcombing, especially along the seldom-visited western reaches, littered with shells and stones. The only drawback is the legendary **sandfly** population, a particular problem in the late afternoon or after rain – take repellent and try to cover up as the day wears on.

North Coast Road maxis and taxis from Port of Spain (see p.136) usually stop at Las Cuevas (TT$9); unless you're lucky enough to meet one for Blanchisseuse, you'll have to thumb a lift to go any further.

Though there's no development on the beach itself, there is a car park above the bay (free), as well as changing rooms, showers and toilets (10am–6pm; TT$1). Lifeguards patrol and put out yellow and red flags to mark safe bathing spots. Vendors sell water coconuts, and if you're **hungry**, try *McLean's* bar at the western edge of the car park, a favourite with local fishermen, serving budget-priced Creole breakfast and lunch alongside the Carib and rum; even wild meat – manicou, iguana or agouti – is on offer if you ask in advance. The *Las Cuevas Rec Club*, right on the road before the bay, is a low-key **drinking** spot; they also sell pholouri and aloo pies. Currently there's

.nowhere to **stay** in Las Cuevas unless you want to camp out on the beach, but that is soon to change. Planning permission has been granted for a large hotel on the beach – including a golf course – so catch the sleepy village while you can.

One Thousand Steps Beach

On the eastern outskirts of Las Cuevas, secluded **One Thousand Steps Beach** is so called because of the seemingly endless concrete steps which wind down the cliffs to the sand. Easily missed and ideal for a secluded swim, this curve of soft greyish sand is backed by almond trees – one growing horizontally over the sand – and a few **manchineels**, which should be treated with caution (see p.22). At the eastern end, the sea has pounded a lookout hole through the rocks, and you can climb over boulders at the western corner to another deserted bay. Though the water is often glassily smooth, you should be careful when swimming here, keeping to a depth you can stand in – the tides can be strong even on apparently calm days, and there's no one to help if you encounter problems. To find the beach, turn down Mitchell's Trace, a dirt track opposite the larger Rincon Trace, which strikes inland from the North Coast Road a kilometre or so east of Las Cuevas. The latter is also the route to spectacular **Rincon Waterfall** and pools, a two-and-a-half-hour uphill walk through the bush. You'll need a guide to find this and nearby **Angel Falls**, though the latter is often dry or filled in by small landslides. Laurence Pierre (☎634 4284) makes a good guide as he knows the area intimately. East of the Las Cuevas is **Fort Abercromby**; there's little to see here apart from the cannons marking the headland, but the small beach is good for snorkelling.

La Filette and Yarra

The wide, clear road surrounding Las Cuevas narrows as it enters the fishing village of **LA FILETTE**, an improbably pretty cluster of neat houses and blooming front gardens straddled over two hillocks. A parlour in the centre of town (opposite a phonecard booth) sells groceries and snacks, while a rum bar on the western outskirts is good for watching the world go by with a "beastly" cold beer or for gossiping with the fishermen about the rumoured **contraband** landing spots on this part of coast.

Beyond the village, after a long, straight stretch of road, all vehicles must slow down to cross a rickety plank bridge over one of the **Yarra River's** many strands. There are four smaller plank bridges to cross before the road passes a young teak plantation and enters **YARRA**, a rather deserted hamlet made up of grand beach houses. Look out for a grassy turn-off towards the sea, the only one not leading to a house; this goes to **Yarra Beach**, another perfect, deserted seashore. Wide and sweeping, with white sand fine enough to remain on the limbs long after a shower, Yarra has two main bays which shift in size and shape according to the season. Offshore is a rock painted with the legend "Yaradise Bay", and as you're likely to have the whole place to yourself, it's not difficult to imagine that you really are in Eden. Another Yarra River tributary runs down to the sea, sometimes deep enough for a white-water body surf right into the ocean, where the water is pleasantly active and clear. As always on this coast, take care while swimming and be sensible if you feel strong tides. About 30m past the entrance to the beach, look out for another offshore rock on which the word "**hollyweed**" has been painted in foot-high letters – an allusion to the bales of marijuana which are said to be imported and exported from these beaches.

Blanchisseuse

Five minutes' drive along the narrow, jungle-lined road from Yarra brings you back to the coast and into **BLANCHISSEUSE** (pronounced "blaan-she-shers"), the last village before the road tails off into the bush. With a population of around three thousand, Blanchisseuse isn't exactly a hamlet, and the clutch of ever-growing flashy holiday homes on the western outskirts – some garish, some tasteful – are testament to its growing popularity as a retreat. The incongruous, yellow "taj mahal" dominating the hill below *Surf's Country Inn* and the private home taking over the sand at surfer's beach have incurred the wrath of the locals. At present, though, things are still pretty quiet; the atmosphere is relaxed and supremely friendly, and there are as many local holidaymakers as there are foreign. Tourists divide their time between the succession of marvellous sandy **beaches**, or hiring a local guide and hiking through the rainforest for river swimming in the unpolluted waters of nearby **Three Pools**, **Paria Beach** and **waterfall**, or the **Avocat Waterfall** on the Arima–Blanchisseuse Road (see pp.145 and 148).

*Taxis for
Blanchisseuse
($TT16) from
Port of Spain
leave from the
corner of
George and
Prince streets.
Maxis (TT$15)
leave from
City Gate as
does the rural
bus service,
clustered
around peak
hours.*

Accommodation

Blanchisseuse has the greatest number of **rooms** along this part of the coast. It's wise to book ahead if visiting on weekends or national holidays when Trinidadians come down for a bit of rest and relaxation. All the guesthouses are small scale; tucked away at the very end of the road, *Laguna Mar* is the largest and most professional, with twelve rooms. The rest of the guesthouses are strung along the North Coast Road, with the majority in the more lively surrounds of the upper village. If you've got a tent – or a piece of tarpaulin, the local material of choice – you can **camp** on the beach at the *Marianne Beach Resort* for TT$30 per tent; this includes the use of toilets, showers and rather lax security protection.

Almond Brook, North Coast Rd ✆678 0822. By far the most atmospheric place in the upper village, with wood-panelled rooms decorated with shells and plants; all have mosquito nets, private bathroom and queen-size bed; one has a full kitchen, the others fridges. Breakfast is included in the rates, and the extremely genial owner also rents a two-bedroom beach house in its own garden with a verandah and full amenities. ⑤.

Laguna Mar ☎669 2963 or c/o Zollna House, 12 Ramlogan Development, La Seiva, Maraval; reservations also taken on ☎628 3731, fax 628 3737, *www.lagunamar.com*. The most established hotel in Blanchisseuse, *Laguna Mar* takes pride of place at the end of the road with its own access to Marianne beach. Rooms are on the inland side of the road, housed in blocks of six with a lovely communal balcony; each has two double beds, fans and private bathroom. The German/Trinidadian owners are well-known local figures and great hosts. They also have a 3-bedroom villa to rent. ⑤.

Northern Sea View Villa, North Coast Rd and Wilson Trace ☎669 3995, *elope@tstt.net.tt*. The least expensive option in town, these two basic apartments offer little in the way of luxury, but the location opposite Marianne beach is great and the owners are extremely friendly. Both have two bedrooms with a fan, a kitchen, verandah and living room. Excellent if in a group or on a budget. ④.

North Star View, North Coast Rd ☎637 7619 or 4619. Owned by the same family as *Northern Sea View*, this spacious yellow villa, on the hill before the road descends to Marianne beach, has clean, basic rooms with a shared bathroom or a self-contained studio apartment with wooden floors, double bed, kitchenette with microwave and a constant sea breeze from the balcony. ⑦.

Second Spring on the Sea, LP191, Paria Main Rd ☎669 3909, fax 638 7393, *secondspring@trinidad.net*. Small bed and breakfast with friendly owners and close to the beach. The nicely decorated rooms have fan and kitchenette. ⑤.

Surf's Country Inn, North Coast Rd ☎669 2475, fax 669 3016. Precipitously placed above the surfers' beach, the four rooms in this soon-to-be-expanding inn are great value, attractive and fully mosquito-screened, with terracotta floor tiles, fridge, fan, nice bathroom and verandah or terrace. The on-site restaurant is excellent; rates include breakfast. ⑤.

Vista Del Mar, North Coast Rd ☎662 7534, fax 663 1454. A coolly attractive blue and white building overlooking the surfer's beach; two self-contained apartments with rattan furnishings, a/c, full kitchen, living room and a verandah with great sea views, while bedrooms and bathrooms are suitably luxurious. There's a sundeck, hammock-dotted gazebo and barbecue pit on the lawn below – meals are available on request. ⑤.

Windrush, Paradise Hill Rd ☎669 5111, fax 623 1634, *delisle@cariblink.net*. A well-maintained private home tucked away on the corner of Paradise Hill Road in the upper village, offering bed and breakfast. You're living pretty much with the family, but the double room is pleasant, spotless and comfortable with a private bathroom. Also available is a cottage opposite Marianne beach with two bedrooms – one single and one double – full kitchen, living room, patio and private garden. ④.

The village

Lower Blanchisseuse to the west is the older portion of the village, an attractive assortment of weather-beaten board houses and crumbling tapias wreathed by rambling bougainvillea and neat croton hedges. Steep cliffs plunge down to the ocean and breaks in the palms or almond trees reveal the white-tipped waves of the intensely blue sea below. The villagey atmosphere is sealed by a couple of rum bars, a fishermen's co-operative building, a post office and a boxy,

Another accommodation option is the secluded nature resort at Petit Tacarib, a half-hour boat journey (or four-hour walk) from Blanchisseuse. Stephen Broadbridge (see p.148), organizes all transport and accommodation.

single-spired Catholic **church** overlooking the sea, complete with three bells housed in an outdoor tower. Young men stare as a vehicle passes by, octogenarians while away the hours in front of the bars and chickens pick for scraps in the middle of the tarmac.

Upper Blanchisseuse begins after Paria Main Road descends the hill and loops inland to meet the Arima–Blanchisseuse Road. This is the main residential section of Blanchisseuse, dominated by the attractive arched windows and blue porticoes of the Georgian-style **police station**. General stores (including the wonderfully named *Fattah Foods*) and pastel-painted homes cluster by the roadside, while residential streets trail uphill into the bush. Behind the police station is the community centre and a playing field which sees some serious football in the late afternoon. A small roadside restaurant, *Wayside Hut*, has a nice gazebo to sit in and watch the world go by. Further up opposite *Almond Brook* guesthouse is Bob's Artistic Creations (Mon–Sun 8am–5pm), which sells beautifully carved walking-sticks, masks, mirror frames and wall hangings made from calabashes and poui, cedar and mahogany.

Past the shop, buildings start to thin out, and another downhill stretch brings the coast road to sea level, running parallel to Marianne beach, the town's largest (see opposite). The last building is the *Cocos Hut* restaurant (see p.146); beyond here, the road runs parallel to the Marianne River lagoon, ending at the **Silver Suspension Bridge** which straddles the water and is a popular swimming spot with bridge diving possibilities. Over the bridge, the tarmac ends, replaced by a rutted dirt road. You can drive on for a kilometre or two (not recommended in the rainy season), but otherwise, the only means of progressing east to Paria and beyond is on foot (see pp.147–149).

Blanchisseuse beaches

Like most beaches in this section of coastline, those of **Blanchisseuse** are ruggedly beautiful. However, while it's unlikely that you'll be swept away during your first dip, they do have a reputation for rough and **treacherous waters**, particularly between November and February when mighty breakers crash onto the sand and the surfers come into their element. Whatever the time of year, it's wise to ask local advice before taking the plunge, and keep to a depth you can stand in.

The first of the three main beaches can be reached via a concrete walkway opposite the huge yellow villa before you enter the lower village. Popular with crowds of sun-bronzed surfers, the beach has been locally renamed in their honour as **surfer's beach**; its true name – **L'Anse Martin** – is seldom used, though it is marked as such on the sign. The seashore here is wide and open with an almost imperceptible shelf that makes for excellent waves. Craggy rocks border each end and the forest drips down from the cliffs onto the sand. It's also popular for a spot of late afternoon **fishing**, with anglers casting lines from the water's edge.

The second beach is accessible by an easy path next to the fishermen's co-operative in the lower village. This fishermen's beach is a place to lime and admire the view rather than to swim, since the measly pebble shore is littered with dead boats and straddled by a half-built wooden jetty; the concrete foundations of the unbuilt portion are gradually being eroded by the surf. Just 50m further down the road, though, down some steps marked by a broken sign atop a green pole, is a marvellous **bathing beach**, with around 200m of soft grey sand and giving a feeling of complete seclusion. Headlands provide protection and gentle waves, while almonds and sea grapes tangle down the cliffs. Watch out for a few offshore rocks while swimming.

Marianne is the main – and the longest – beach in Blanchisseuse, stretching around 2km from the busiest portion of the upper village, where concrete steps lead down to the sand, right to the *Cocos Hut* restaurant (see p.146) and the river lagoon at the end of the North Coast Road. It's a completely breathtaking seashore, wide and straight with both coarse and fine yellow sand battered by crashing waves and awe-inspiring views of the uninhabited coast beyond – the perfect place to watch the moon rising over the headlands from the east. At the eastern end is a huge, vegetation-smothered boulder; past this, the clear Marianne river water is partially dammed by the sand into a **lagoon** – an inviting place to swim, particularly if the sea looks rough. Locals tend to congregate here for an after-work bathe, and fishermen paddle rough canoes in search of freshwater salmon.

If you want to travel to Paria Bay by boat, local fishermen will be willing to take you for the right price.

Following a track over the forested headland at the eastern corner of Marianne takes you to another seldom-used and unnamed beach, but most choose to swim right opposite the lagoon. The owners of *Laguna Mar* resort (see p.143) have cut a path through the swampland which divides the eastern portion of the beach from the road, and put in a couple of picnic tables and benches. You can use the showers and toilets at a sandy car park grandly named the *Marianne Beach Resort* (TT$5), 100m or so west of the *Laguna Mar* entrance. You can also rent a tent here for TT$40 and park your car for TT$10.

Marianne River and Three Pools

Spanned by the **Silver Suspension Bridge** – graceful and still solid despite its hundred years – the **Marianne River** is the source of much local recreation, as well as the village's name: dating from French Creole times, "Blanchisseuse" refers to the laundresses who washed clothing in the river. Regular buses of **bird-watchers** park up at a lay-by to the side of the bridge to see the green woodpeckers, yellow orioles and silvered antbird.

The Marianne itself is a typical Northern Range watercourse, originating at Brasso Seco (see p.150) and tumbling downhill, carving deep swimming pools and waterfalls along the way. You can take a watery trek along the riverbed to **Three Pools**, an hour or so from the mouth of the Marianne. Most people hire a guide in the village to lead the way and draw attention to the abundant plant, bird and animal life, but it's a fairly straightforward route that you can follow independently. Following the riverbed is the fastest way to get there, a combination of splashing through calf- (and sometimes waist-) deep water and swimming (sticking to the banks takes a lot longer), so don't carry anything that can't get wet. To reach the pools, take the path into the woods to the right of the road just before the bridge (the "No Entry" sign is universally ignored); you meet the water after five minutes. Overhung by vines, ferns and huge buttress-rooted trees, it's a gorgeous and easy wade, bar the odd overhanging bank. Though the water deepens to form several enticing swimming pools along the way, the stunning Three Pools easily surpass any of the other swimming spots. At around 12m across, the first is the least impressive, though it does have a **water-slide** of sorts, formed by the current coursing through a narrow rock channel. Over this, the smooth grey rock which forms the pools begins; huge boulders rise up from water so deep it's hard to touch the bottom, and a second gushing channel creates a **natural jacuzzi**. Though it's the smallest, the last pool is the most impressive, overhung by tall cliffs. The water here has worn a deep channel, carving the rock into bizarre folds and small caves; you can swim right in and climb a little to see the waterfall above. To go beyond this point to Avocat Falls, you'll need a guide; almost everyone in the village knows the way, or you can go with jovial Eric Blackman, owner of *Northern Sea View Villa* (see p.143). He leads a two-hour trip to Three Pools that takes in kayaking, hiking and swimming (TT$80 per person), an all-day tour of the Avocat Waterfall (TT$50) and a four-hour walk to Paria (TT$50). Eric also rents kayaks on the beach by the river mouth ($TT20 for 30min), and for TT$10 he'll take an instant photograph of you on the beach.

Eating and drinking

Blanchisseuse has a good but limited selection of low-key **restaurants**, most of which offer a choice of meat, fish or vegetarian dishes. You should however give advance notice (at breakfast time) for dinner as many kitchens cook to order or close early. Prices are moderate – expect to pay around TT$100 for dinner. Grandest are the hotel restaurants; by far the most popular is *Cocos Hut* (☎628 3731), a converted cocoa drying house across the road from *Laguna Mar*. The Germanic decor and music policy may be more evocative of the Rhine than the Caribbean, but once soca replaces the marching bands and owner Frank Zollna turns on the charm, this intimate eatery with indoor and outdoor seating is great for a sit-down meal. Moderately priced dinners consist of tasty, local-style fish, chicken, beef or pork, though vegetarians are catered for – ask in advance. Breakfast (eggs, bacon, toast and fruit etc) and lunch (hot meals or salads and sandwiches) are served daily. The bar is nice for an evening drink, its end-of-the-road location and regular clientele providing a sense of cosy isolation. Another option for semi-upmarket dining is the open-air restaurant at *Surf's Country Inn* (☎669 2554), beautifully located on a boardwalk overlooking the sea and shaded by silk cotton boughs. The seafood-based menu stretches to innovative preparation of vegetables; they also do break-fast and lunch. All are moderately priced. In the upper village, try *Gilbert's*, perched on the cliff by a bend in the road with a couple of tables overlooking the sea. Breakfasts of bake and scrambled egg, bacon or cheese sandwiches, and lunch or dinner of stew or jerk chicken, peas, vegetables and potatoes with onions are tasty and inexpensive.

Blanchisseuse tends to quiet down early, but as the locals still need to lime and unwind at the end of a day's work, the **rum shops** are fairly lively after dark, particularly on a weekend. In the lower vil-lage, *Casbah* is a classic Trinidadian drinking hole with a pool table, dim lights, a verandah for catching the breeze and "no bareback, spitting on the floor or obscene language" notices painted on to the walls. The *Butterfly Rec Club*, behind the playing field in the upper village, is more or less the same, bedecked with coloured fairy lights. Another large bar-cum-parlour in the lower village tends to close early.

The north coast bench trail

Beyond Blanchisseuse, the North Coast Road gives way to the only remaining piece of **undeveloped coastline** in Trinidad. The next piece of tarmac is some 30km away in Matelot (see p.177); in between, you'll find some of Trinidad's most impressive **hiking** along a **bench trail**; the local name for the old donkey tracks cut in the late nineteenth century for transporting goods and produce between the villages and servicing the then-thriving cocoa estates. Well-trodden, the trail dips and climbs through the remnants of abandoned estates and secondary forest, with the sea swinging spectacularly in and out of view.

There are periodic government suggestions for the construction of a **road** along this stretch of the coast; environmental groups and landowners (most of the coast is in private hands) have successfully lobbied against the idea, though most agree that it's only a matter of time before tarmac is laid through the forest. At present, though, the area remains a sanctuary for bird and animal life, and many of the beaches are prime laying spots for the **leatherback turtle** (see p.345).

Though few attempt it, you can hike the bench trail all the way from Blanchisseuse to Matelot, but only the fittest could hope to complete the journey in a day. Most make the trip in two stages, camping in the bush along the way. Though the trail is easy to follow, it is not a good idea to walk in this area alone; it's remote enough to make getting help difficult if you run into trouble, and reports of

The Saddle to the North Coast Road

drug landings at deserted bays suggest that you may feel safer if accompanied by a guide (and his/her cutlass). If you prefer a solitary hike, walk during the week; Saturdays, Sundays and public holidays are prime times for local hiking groups or individual ramblers to take to the bush.

Blanchisseuse to Paria Bay

Though you should start the Paria hike with a full bottle, don't worry about conserving water; the trail passes streams from which it is safe to drink.

From Blanchisseuse, the most often-attempted hike is the moderately challenging round-trip trek to **Paria Bay** and its inland **waterfall**, which you can do in a couple of hours at a good pace, though most stop to admire the scenery and make a day of it. Past the suspension bridge, the track passes beach houses for the first couple of kilometres; an uphill fork makes an attractive if unnecessary detour, bringing you back to the main trail after a few minutes. Logging vehicles have widened the bench trail in some parts, and as a result it can get muddy in the rainy season, but little can detract from the marvellous forest around; look out for massive bachac nests and a splendid specimen of the weird **cannonball tree**, with its heavily perfumed, rotund pink flowers and dangling, twisted branches which sprout five-centimetre-wide brown "cannonballs" from the base of the trunk to the main boughs. Birdsong is a constant accompaniment, the soothing calls often shattered by the raucous shriek of passing parrots.

There's an alternative route to Paria Bay and waterfall from Brasso Seco (see p.150), but you'll need a guide; try Carl Fitz-James Jnr (☎ 667 5968), who lives in Brasso Seco.

Depending upon your pace, you'll reach Paria Bay in two to three hours. The **beach** is an idyllic 1km of fine, coconut-littered golden sand backed in true treasure island-style by jungle and groves of palms. Other than a fisherman's shelter, it's completely undisturbed, with craggy grey rocks out to sea and a river at the eastern end; the high headland above is **Paria Point**. A cliff at the western corner has been eroded at the base to form an arch. Swimming is safe and the waves are usually moderate. If you want to press on to the **waterfall**, walk two-thirds of the way up the beach and head inland at the track. The path, through anthurium lilies and forest, meets the Paria River, which brings you to the waterfall in about fifteen minutes. Crystal clear and freezing cold spring water crashes down the 5-metre cascade into a deep swimming pool around 10m across.

Paria Bay to Matelot

Past Paria Bay, the bench trail is less well-travelled and a little more overgrown. After ten minutes' walk, you come to another attractive beach, **Murphy Bay**. You can carry on up the coast from here to **Petit** and **Grande Tacarib bays**; the walk to Petit Tacarib will take around an hour and a half. Both have marvellous sandy beaches, separated by half an hour's walk and the inexplicably named **Trou Bouilli-Riz Point**; from here, it's a six-hour walk to civilization at Matelot.

Another hour and a half from Grande Tacarib along the bench trail through jungle, you come to **Madamas Bay**, a curve of deserted off-white sand which rivals Paria in beauty. Half an hour inland from the beach is another gorgeous cataract, **Madamas waterfall**, though you'll need a guide to find it. However, if you want to see the area without straining your muscles, you can arrange to **stay** at **Petit Tacaribe**, but as preparing for guests is time-consuming, the resort only takes groups of four or more, preferably for stays longer than four days. Still, if you have the chance, it's well-worth the stay. *Petit Tacaribe* is undoubtedly the most unusual resort in Trinidad, a magical place completely secluded and drenched in natural beauty. Almost single-handedly, local landowner Gordon Dalla Costa has built three cedar-framed bamboo cabanas and a cooking shed right above the bay; the whole ensemble is simply called *Petit Tacaribe* (c/o 5 Moore Ave, St Ann's, Port of Spain; ☎624 1774, *www.active-caribbean.com/caribbeandiscoverytours*; Stephen Broadbridge handles reservations at *caribdis@wow.net*; ⑤). Rates cover all meals and transport, including boats and excursions into the forest. Most people get there via boat from Blanchisseuse (organized by the *Tacaribe* owners), which costs TT$200 each way and takes about half an hour; six people and their baggage can cram in, but you can always hike if you're feeling hardy. Rates cover food and drinks, though you should buy any extras – beer, rum, chocolate etc – yourself. Leatherbacks lay eggs on the sand during the March–June season, and as the surrounding bush is well-stocked with agouti, armadillo, manicou and quenk, you may get wild meat for dinner as well as freshly caught fish or chicken brought up from Blanchisseuse. Days are spent lazing on the beach or in the hammocks, hiking to Madamas, hunting in the bush or bird-watching, and if you like the natural life, this is a chance in a million.

The Arima–Blanchisseuse Road

Inland from Blanchisseuse, the **Arima–Blanchisseuse Road** cuts south through the middle of the steamy Northern Range forest, climbing high into misty, breeze-cooled peaks and descending to the **Asa Wright Nature Centre**, one of the Caribbean's finest bird-watching sites. Small villages like **Morne La Croix** and **Brasso Seco** seem contentedly stuck in a time warp, and make excellent starting points for exploring the **waterfalls** that course through the mountains. Light filtering through the overhanging canopies of mahogany, teak, poui, cedar and immortelle colours the tunnel-like road green, and every available surface is smothered in plant life; mosses, ferns and lichens cover rocks and tree trunks already laden with massive wild pine bromeliads; vines and monkey's ladder lianas trail down to the tarmac, and the manic calls of crested oropendolas and bearded bellbirds echo across the peaks.

Wet and humid, the first portion of road from Blanchisseuse is carpeted by composting leaves. A succession of hairpin bends sets a slow pace as the road begins a gentle climb, each quarter mile

marked by a post at the roadside put in during English control of the
island. Just before the twenty-and-a-quarter mile marker, look out
for a neat grove of pommerac trees to the left; here, a track leads
past a few modest dwellings and provision grounds to the **Avocat
Falls**. After a ten-minute walk, you reach a river (a tributary of the
Marianne); turn left and walk along the banks or the shallow riverbed
for twenty minutes until you reach a watery junction. Wade across
the river and grab hold of one of the roots that wreathe the steep
bank. Haul yourself up, and straight in front of you is a pretty 12-
metre cascade with a deep pool below; there are even some vines for
swinging on.

Morne La Croix

Past Avocat, the Arima–Blanchisseuse Road climbs a steep hill
before entering the tiny hamlet of **MORNE LA CROIX**, a pretty village where most of the inhabitants still speak French Creole as well
as Trini English. Development comes slow in the middle of the
Northern Range; when government planned to install electricity
poles in 1996, there was much debate over whether the villagers

*For a glossary
of Trini
English terms,
see pp.356–
358.*

wanted a current at all – to date, only a few houses and the general
store are hooked up. Just beyond the town, look for a hedge of pur-
ple-flowered vervain, a favourite haunt of yellow-breasted ruby-topaz
hummingbirds and the red-crested tufted coquette. There are some
impressive views of the mountains below here, too, and you're more
or less guaranteed to see **bird life** wherever you stop; the spectacular metre-long, teardrop-shaped nests of the crested oropendola are
commonplace. As the road climbs ever higher, you pass a lookout
point adjacent to a dirt road called Andrew's Trace. A break in the
forest and an elevation of just over 600m provides chilly breezes and
sweeping views across the valleys, with the sea just visible if the
mists haven't set in; ornate hawk-eagles and black or grey hawks
coast on the thermal updraughts as they scan the bush for food.

Brasso Seco

The only sizeable village past La Croix, **BRASSO SECO** is tucked
away at the end of a signposted turn-off from the Arima–
Blanchisseuse road. A ten-minute drive past converted cocoa houses
and still-occupied tapia houses brings you into the village's main
street, where there's a rum shop-parlour, a church, a school and an
overwhelmingly languorous atmosphere; kids play cricket in the
middle of the road, young men lime outside the rec club and everyone has time to greet each other with an exchange or a wave.

There are some lovely walks in the area; naturalist Courtenay
Rooks (☎622 8826, fax 628 1525, *www.pariasprings.com*)
guides **nature hikes** and **birdwatching trips** from his base at Paria
Springs, a ten-minute drive from the centre of the village. These

include a difficult hike up Morne Bleu to see virgin rainforest and
blue-capped tanagers (1 day, US$45), a birdwatching tour along the
Paria/Arima/Blanchiesseuse Road (1 day, US$55) and a leisurely
stroll to the Madamas Waterfalls whilst butterfly- and birdwatching
(1 day, US$45; he also does the latter on mountain bikes for US$50).
For more details on his island-wide tours, see p.49. Rooks also acts
as agent for a number of host homes in the Brasso Seco area, all of
which offer a fabulously tranquil setting in which to while away a few
days. All cost US$25 per person per night, plus US$5 for breakfast,
and US$10 for lunch or for dinner – you're best off taking the meal
options, as there's nowhere to buy food hereabouts. As most of the
host homes have been converted from private homes, facilities vary
enormously. *Peña Blanca*, an old cocoa house high in the hills with
wonderful views over the valleys and an outside porch for barbecues,
is one of the most attractive. The four bedrooms all have double
beds, and there are two bathrooms, a kitchen and living room.
Tucked into the hillside, *Paria Heights Mountain View* is an equally good choice, with a spring water-fed swimming pool under construction at the time of writing, basic but serviceable bedrooms with
mosquito nets, and a kitchen, bathroom and living room. Brasso
Seco resident Carl Fitz-James Jnr (☎667 5968) is another good
guide for exploring the many local waterfalls; he lives in the village –
ask anyone to direct you to his home.

Asa Wright Nature Centre and around

A bird-watcher's paradise contained in the 800,000 square metre
Spring Hill estate, the **Asa Wright Nature Centre** (PO Box 4710,
Arima, Trinidad; ☎667 4655, fax 667 4540; in US via Caligo
Ventures ☎1-800/426 7781, fax 914/273 6370; ⑨) was originally a
coffee, citrus and cocoa plantation. In 1947 it was bought by one Dr
Newcome Wright and his Icelandic wife, Asa. Both were keen amateur naturalists and bird-watchers, so when the New York Zoological
Society set up the Simla Tropical Research Station on neighbouring
land, the couple began to accommodate visiting researchers. After
her husband died, Mrs Wright sold the land on condition it remained
a **conservation area**; a nonprofit-making trust was set up in 1967,
which established a nature centre to accommodate naturalists and
birdwatchers, a first in the Caribbean. Simla closed in 1970, but
donated its land and the research station to the centre – botanists
and ornithologists still study here. Today Asa Wright is Trinidad's
most popular birdwatching retreat, and commitment to conservation
remains; a further square kilometre of land recently acquired from
the government will be left in a natural state, and an interpretative
centre is under construction to raise environmental awareness
among local kids.

The centre revolves around the **great house**, a ninety-year-old
maze of polished mahogany floors and stately heirlooms with a

verandah overlooking the spectacular Arima valley. At 360m above sea level, the views of the rainforest are incredible, and since Mrs Wright began feeding them in the 1950s, the verandah has attracted a huge variety of **birds**; you can see up to forty species per day. If you're not staying at the centre it's a good idea to get there before 10am to avoid the rush. Face-level feeders attract dazzlingly colourful, thumb-sized hummingbirds, and trays of fruit below are gorged by green and red-legged honeycreepers, blue-grey tanagers and white-bearded or golden-headed manakins as well the ever-present and precocious bananaquits and a host of more sporadic visitors. Matte lizards and agoutis clear up the scraps, and the surrounding trees glitter with the brightly coloured feathers of nesting and roosting birds; rufous-tailed jacamars, toucans, mot-mots, woodpeckers, trogons, yellow orioles and the yellow-tailed crested oropendola, which nests in a bois cano tree to the left of the verandah. This multitude of bird-life attracts daily crowds, the low murmur of voices broken by the excited squeals of an unusual sighting, or by the whirr and click of paparazzi-standard zoom lenses. A network of well-marked **trails** for walks ranging from ten minutes to two hours threads through the grounds; you can walk them alone or join the expertly conducted **guided tours** (daily 10.30am & 1.30pm; free). Residents of more than three nights get a tour of **Dunston Cave**, which houses the world's most accessible colony of **oilbirds**.

*For more on
oilbirds, see
p.351.*

The centre is open to the public (daily 9am–5pm; US$10); the entrance fee includes an hour-and-a-half tour and access to the verandah and you can have an excellent buffet lunch for TT$50; sandwiches and drinks are available on the verandah if you don't want a cooked meal. Resident guests tend to be middle-aged American bird fanatics toting state-of-the-art binoculars or camera equipment, and checklists of a day's sightings are enthusiastically compiled over sunset rum punches. **Accommodation** is quite luxurious, with large screened verandahs, en-suite bathroom and two double beds; rates include three meals a day and afternoon tea. Informed field trips to Trinidad's premier birdwatching sites are also on offer to resident guests.

For those who want an even closer brush with nature the *Alta Vista Rainforest Resort* (☎629 8030, fax 629 3262, *altavista@tstt.net.tt, www.come.to/alta-vista*; ③), a couple of bends up from *Asa Wright*, offers the total natural rainforest experience at bargain prices. Six rudimentary log cabins with bed and curtained-off toilet and sink are surrounded by lush rainforest, gardens and a verandah for bird-watching. Steps descending under christophene plants lead to a freshwater pool fed by a mountain spring. If you're the only guests, you can use the communal kitchen, otherwise a cook is brought onto site.

Heading towards Arima the road dips downhill, rounding spectacular corners and passing hillsides cleared for christophene culti-

vation, the vines supported by a rough trellis network. As you near
Arima (see p.162), the jungle thins out and a few sporadic buildings
– including a bar – appear at the roadside. Look out for the tiny do-
it-yourself Hindu temples to the left of the road just before the right
turn to Calvary Hill; locals refer to the area as "**temple village**".

The East–West Corridor

Running along the southern flank of the Northern Range, the
East–West Corridor is the main route between the east and west
coasts of the island. It is traversed by the **Eastern Main Road**, a driver's nightmare for the unfamiliar, ruled as it is by capricious local
driving practices. If they're not avoiding the rush by taking the
Priority Bus Route, a fast-track commuter thoroughfare built where
the now-obsolete **train tracks** were in service, the back-to-back
maxis and route taxis that shuttle between each community seem to
delight in stopping abruptly with insouciant abandon that's terrifying
if you're behind the wheel but extremely convenient if you're relying
on **public transport**. Hot and dusty as it is, the slow pace does at
least allow you to absorb the commercial chaos; lined by a constant
parade of shops, stalls, restaurants, bars and offices, the EMR buzzes
with life – dodging delivery trucks, shoppers throng the pavements
and vendors fill the air with the sweet aromas of street food. The mer-
cantile aspect doesn't let up until you've passed **Arima**, the corridor's largest town and home to what's left of Trinidad's **Carib** community. In between, some interesting towns are slung along the road;
bustling **San Juan** with its frenetic crossroads and the old Spanish
capital of **St Joseph**, where elegant colonial edifices sit incongruously with this century's rash of concrete, are both worth exploring
for their historical connections and varied architecture, but most of
the communities are so close together, it's hard to tell where one district tails off and another begins.

However, as the EMR skirts the foothills of the Northern Range
and a host of attractions, there's good reason to navigate this often
fraught route; all of the sights can be seen in day-trips from Port of
Spain. Inland of St Joseph, the **Maracas Valley waterfall** crashes
magnificently down 90m of sheer rock to a decent bathing pool; the
area is a holy spot for followers of the Hindu, Orisa and Spiritual
Baptist faiths. East of the falls, **Caura** and **Lopinot** have plenty of
possibilities for **picnicking**, **hiking** and **river swimming**; the latter
also has a network of **caves** to explore. At 240m above sea level, the
Mount St Benedict Monastery dominates the hillside, providing a
panoramic view of the Caroni plains and a restive spot for **afternoon
tea**. Beyond Arima, the buildings let up and almost-impenetrable
rainforest rises sharply from the road, but a few country lanes lead to
some marvellous natural attractions; **La Laja** and **Sombasson waterfalls** are two of the most impressive on the island, while **Guanapo**

Gorge, a 400m water channel overhung by towering grey rock, is completely breathtaking. At **Aripo**, you can hike through undisturbed forest to the island's largest cave network and see a colony of squawking **oilbirds**; the forests are also richly populated by the full quota of Trinidad's **mammals**, and hunters make regular forays after agouti, armadillo, wild pig and manicou; if you're really lucky, you might catch sight of an ocelot on the flanks of **El Cerro del Aripo**, the island's highest mountain. Inland of quiescent **Valencia**, the **Hollis Reservoir** rises like a sea in the middle of the forest, a host of birdlife twittering in the trees.

The EMR is paralleled by the snaking **Churchill Roosevelt Highway**, which doubles up as an impromptu market place; fruit and vegetable stalls, and trucks marked "fresh Maracas fish", line the hard shoulder while itinerant vendors hawking everything from Portugal oranges to Congo peppers, steering wheel covers, toys and newspapers lie in wait at the traffic lights, and road signs tacked to the bridges – locally called "walkovers" – exhort you to "relax and enjoy the drive". The highway comes to an abrupt **end** after Arima, replaced by a smaller dual carriageway which takes you on to the Eastern Main Road and Valencia.

San Juan

The westernmost of a succession of communities that sprawl along the length of the Eastern Main Road, brash, commercial **SAN JUAN** (pronounced sah-wah) avoids being a Port of Spain satellite by the skin of its teeth. The town's focal point is the "**croisee**" (pronounced *kwaysay*), a bustling junction marked by the Scotiabank clock tower, which was named when French Creole was the main local vernacular – "croisee" translates as "crossroads". It's a scene of agreeable, organized pandemonium; doubles vendors, fruit and vegetable stalls and racks of sportswear line the streets while gangs of limers compete for the pavement with perusing buyers, and fleets of taxis honk endlessly. The croisee is equally lively after dark, when the flambeaux of oyster salesmen throw up whiffs of pitch oil and "power punch" milkshake vendors provide party-goers with sustenance.

South of the croisee, between the EMR and the highway, is **El Socorro** district, a community dominated by the **Aranguez Savannah**, a main venue for the annual **Phagwa** celebrations in March (see p.46). If you're **hungry**, forgo the host of eateries on the EMR and head for Back Chain Street, adjacent to the Savannah, where *Ali's* serve up particularly delicious roti.

St Joseph

Past the vast West Indian Tobacco Company and Carib beer factories at **Champs Fleurs** on the outskirts of San Juan, a major junction of the EMR leads to the Uriah Butler Highway, the route to the "deep south" (see p.204); left of the highway is the smart Eric Williams Medical Science Complex at Mount Hope, Trinidad's best-equipped hospital. After the junction, the EMR's commercial trappings temporarily thin out; once you pass the Water and Sewerage Authority (WASA) offices, a venue for one of the larger **carnival fetes**, you're in **ST JOSEPH**, Trinidad's oldest European town and first official **capital**. The streets of St Joseph are lined with genteel colonial French and Spanish architecture jostling with newer concrete structures, market stalls and swarms of children attending one of the many schools, and it's one of the better places along the EMR to get a flavour of the East–West Corridor.

Permits to visit dams and reservoirs can be obtained from the St Joseph's WASA offices, Farm Rd (☎ 662 2302)

Some history

In 1592, acting on behalf of Spanish Governor Don Antonio de Berrio y Oruna, Lieutenant Domingo de Vera founded a town on the site of an Amerindian settlement. Christening it **San José de Oruna**, de Vera built a church, a prison-cum-police barracks, Governor's residence and a *cabildo* (town hall). In 1595, **Sir Walter Raleigh** attacked San José, burning down the church and the barracks in an attempt to seize control of the island; by 1606, both were rebuilt, only to be destroyed by the **Dutch** in 1637 and ransacked by **Caribs** in 1640. In 1687, Capuchin missionaries arrived from Spain, settling in a monastery adjacent to the church, and San José struggled along for the next eighty years. Neglected by Spain, which dismissed Trinidad as little more than a convenient stop-off during journeys to South America, the five-hundred-odd residents scratched a living through small-scale farming.

During the eighteenth century, San José began to prosper as a **plantation town**, but in 1766 it was hit by a devastating **earthquake**. It never really recovered from this blow, and eighteen years later Don José Maria Chacon, the last Spanish governor, relocated the capital to Port of Spain. San José's troubles weren't over yet, however; in 1837, a detachment of the West Indian Regiment stationed at the police station **mutinied**. Led by a Yoruba ex-slave known as Daaga, they were protesting against the apprenticeship system that kept freed Africans in a state of semi-slavery for four to six years after so-called emancipation. They set fire to the barracks, seized ammunition and fought for several days before being overwhelmed. In the aftermath, forty Africans lay dead; a firing squad **executed** Daaga and two of his comrades in front of the police station. Since then, the population has grown and turned the town into a bustling commercial centre, with residential districts expanding to the north into what has become Maracas–St Joseph Valley.

The town

Old meets new as you cross the bridge into town; on the left is the old **police station** and **barracks**, the graceful curves and porticoes smothered by a coating of blue paint. Directly opposite is the imposing and elaborate **Mohammed Al Jinnah Memorial Mosque**, resplendent with a crescent and star-topped main dome flanked by two minarets; there's not much to see inside, but if you want to take a look, check at the caretaker's house, left of the Moslem school behind the mosque.

Opposite Al Jinnah, **Abercromby Street** strikes uphill into the mountains. A couple of hundred metres up, **St Joseph's Catholic Church** has undergone many changes since it was first consecrated in 1593. Its three previous incarnations were sacked along with the rest of the town, and today's Gothic-style stone and red-brick structure dates back to 1815. Impressed by the religious devotion of the townspeople who clubbed together to fund the first stages of construction, British Governor Sir Ralph Woodford, though a Protestant himself, donated £2000 towards construction and laid the foundation stone. Inside, beautiful **stained-glass** windows depict the Holy Family, St John and St Andrew; the ornate Italian marble **high altar** was imported from Dublin in 1912. The graveyard behind contains headstones with inscriptions in French, English and Spanish; the oldest tombstone in the island, a weathered slab known as the **tombstone of the pirate**, is marked with a skull and crossbones and the date 1682, but no one knows the identity of the buccaneer below. Further up Abercromby Street and framed by elegantly fretworked colonial houses, **George Earl Park** was the old Spanish town square, used for evening promenades, military parades and as a burial ground; the single remaining stone, dated 1802, commemorates one Mr Thomas.

Accommodation

There's no **accommodation** in St Joseph itself, but there are two good options nearby. Tucked away on the upper reaches of Upper Quarry Drive in Champs Fleurs (follow the signs), the excellent-value *Mountain View Guesthouse* (☎645 0700; ④; ⑤ at Carnival time) has apartments with sitting room, full kitchen, TV, a/c; they can accommodate four people. Route taxis, which run all day from the junction of Quarry Drive and the EMR, can take you to your door for about TT$3. Slightly further away at 108 Valley View Drive in the Maracas–St Joseph Valley (see below), *La Belle Maison* (☎ & fax 663 4413, *la-belle@tstt.net.tt*; ⑤), is a beautifully designed private home with a verandah that's good for birdwatching. Owner Merle Lynch is also a booking agent for the Bed and Breakfast Co-Operative and a mine of local information, and *La Belle* is an excellent, friendly base for exploring the area. The three rooms have lovely valley views and private or shared bathrooms; breakfast is included and tours of the island are available.

The Maracas–St Joseph Valley

Turning inland opposite the mosque, Abercromby Street becomes **Maracas Royal Road** less than a kilometre from the EMR, crossing the grand First River Bridge and winding north into the lush **Maracas–St Joseph Valley**, overlooked all the way by the peaks of **El Tucuche**, the island's second highest mountain. **Maracas** itself is a tiny place, all but swallowed by the suburbs of St Joseph; once you've passed its postal agency and steepled church of St Michael, the houses thin out, separated by clumps of fluffy bamboo and neat provision grounds. Some 10km from the EMR, the road ends at **Loango Village**, where there's a bar and a parlour. The bumpy tarmac of San Pedro Road, which makes a T-junction with the end of the Maracas Royal Road, provides easy access to the **bathing pools** along this section of the Maracas River, the deepest usually being filled with swimmers from the village. The riverbed is scattered with the sparkling bronze sedimentary rocks which fed rumours of local gold deposits in the first years of the twentieth century.

From here, you can **hike** over the mountains to Maracas Bay, a stiff two-hour trek along an old fisherman's trail that's been more or less unused since the construction of the North Coast Road. Another possibility – if you've got stamina and don't mind heights – is to climb the 936-metre **El Tucuche** (variously pronounced *tuh-cutchee* or *too-koosh*). It's an 8-hour round trip, and some of the trail is bordered by a terrifying 300-metre cliff, but you'll be rewarded by spectacular epiphyte-laden **montane** forest as well as high-altitude, mist-drenched **elfin** forest. If you're lucky, you'll see **red howler monkeys** and the **golden tree frog**, Trinidad's only endemic animal, which lives in the waterlogged leaves of wild pine bromeliads. If you want to tackle Tucuche, a **guide** is essential – see p.48 for a list of options, but Laurence Pierre and Courtenay Rooks are particularly recommended.

Route taxis run from Curepe junction to Maracas Valley between 7am and 6pm; the fare is around TT$4; you'll pay more if you go off-route along Waterfall Road.

Maracas Waterfall

Most people head to the valley for **Maracas Waterfall**, one of Trinidad's highest; to get there, turn right from the Maracas Royal Road onto the signposted Waterfall Road; the turn is about 8km from the EMR. After five minutes, the road starts to climb; here, you'll probably be met by Trevor Raymond, a local hunter and unofficial guide to the falls who rushes out of his house at each passing car. He's pleasant, knowledgeable and used to the bush, and reports of robberies suggest it might be wise to hire him if he's not already taking someone else up; you negotiate the fee, anything between $TT20–50. It's safest to park at the bottom of the hill, where there are people around, but you can drive up for another five minutes and park by an abandoned building. After fifteen minutes of uphill walking along a wide rocky track lined by groves of tall balata trees, a path strikes off to the right. This leads to the **first cascade**, three tiers of mini-waterfalls with two swimmable, ice-cold **pools**; the main waterfall is another twenty minutes' walk. Signs warning "no candles" posted on tree trunks are puzzling until you near the falls; here you'll see clusters of black and red candles or pools of wax on the rocks, left by followers of the Hindu, Spiritual Baptist and Orisha religions, who regard the waterfall as a sacred place, marking it with tall coloured flags among the trees. Rumours that some of the rituals performed here are not altogether wholesome give the place a somewhat eerie feel, but little can detract from the awesome beauty of the waterfall. Falling some 90m down a sheer rock face, the water splashes on to a rocky basin, the sunlight shimmering rainbow prisms through the droplets of spray. Water levels are low during the dry season, but you can almost always take a shower. Trevor Raymond can also guide you to **Three Steps**, a series of pools at the top of the falls where he's constructed a cooking hut and a place to camp.

Curepe and St Augustine campus

Loosely arranged around the Eastern Main Road, **CUREPE** is another of the EMR's busy transport hubs. The Priority Bus Route runs parallel to the road here, and maxis and taxis trickle off to park up outside the bus terminus – a converted train station – and hawk for trade. Cars heading for the Southern Main Road or Churchill Roosevelt Highway create a constant traffic jam, and there's little to stimulate the imagination.

Just past the junction, the Priority Bus Route mounts an attractive cut-stone flyover, and a tunnel cuts underneath it to the island's academic powerhouse, the **University of the West Indies St Augustine Campus**. Usually referred to by its acronym, UWI (yoowee) also has branches in Jamaica and Barbados. The spacious campus was formerly a sugar plantation, and the great house now serves as the principal's home. The students are a cosmopolitan Caribbean mix who descend on Port of Spain en masse for special club nights, and the campus is the annual venue for Trinidad's priciest **all-inclusive Carnival fete**, a massive party which usually boasts every single soca performer of note.

Practicalities

If you want to explore the Northern Range from here, route taxis and maxis run east and west along the EMR and inland along all the major roads, though the more remote your destination (Lopinot, for example), the longer you'll wait. Most inland taxis leave from the EMR and the appropriate junction; ask locals where to catch one. Out of the few **accommodation** options *The Caribbean Lodge*, 32 St Augustine Circular Rd (☎645 2937, fax 645 2358; ②), is by far the best choice, a supremely friendly, attractive place adjacent to UWI campus. Rooms are not fancy, catering mainly for visiting students, but they are functional and very clean with shared or private shower; some have a/c and kitchenette. There's an area for washing clothes and meals are available. Those who don't mind a few restrictions can try the rather overpriced *Hosanna Hotel*, Santa Margarita Circular Road, St Augustine (☎662 5449, fax 662 5451, *hosanna@caribe-link.net*, *www.hosannahotel.com*; ⑤); signs warning "no smoking, no unmarried couples, no arms and ammunition, no alcohol" are pasted up in reception. Rooms are quite nice, with a/c and TV, and there's a restaurant and intermittently-filled pool.

For **food** and **drink**, you'll find the usual selection of local restaurants and darkened rum shops along the EMR; there are late night roti and doubles vendors at Curepe junction, while *KFC* and *Pizza Hut* share a building on the highway. If you're in the mood to **party** on the EMR between St Augustine and Tunapuna is the excellent Sunday School dance (10pm–4am; TT\$10) run by Rastafarian sect Twelve Tribes. It's held right on the road; look for red, gold and green Rasta flags draped over the entrance. Kay Donna drive-in **cinema** is on the corner of Churchill Roosevelt Highway and the Southern Main Road; turn right at Curepe junction, and check daily newspapers for programme details.

Mount St Benedict

Just past the main body of Curepe, the **Exodus panyard** occupies the corner of the EMR and St John's Road, its pans stacked neatly in the practice space. Until 1998, when Arima's Nutones steelband scoooped the coveted **National Panorama** title, Exodus – guided by long-time arranger Pelham Goddard – were one of only two bands from the East Zone to clinch the annual pan tournament – they won in 2001 with "A Happy Song" – and they regularly take the regional title.

See p.345 for more on steel pan music.

Crucifix-lined St John's Road climbs uphill through St John's village to the **Mount St Benedict Monastery**, still a place of pilgrimage. A network of eye-catching white-walled, red-roofed buildings dominating the hillside, the monastery was established in 1912 by Benedictine monks fleeing religious persecution in Brazil. The first of its kind in the Caribbean, it initially consisted of nothing more than a mud-walled, thatch-roofed ajoupa at the peak of Mount Tabor, which was eventually abandoned in favour of this more accessible site. Additional buildings were added over the years, including a gorgeous burnt orange central tapia house in 1918, now crumbling slowly. With a boxy steeple tower forming the tallest portion of the complex, the imposing **church** was consecrated as an **abbey** in 1947. In keeping with the their motto *ora et labora* (prayers and work), the 25-odd resident monks are a vibrant, active community, maintaining an apiary and producing delicious yoghurt and honey for commercial sale. Mount St Benedict houses the Caribbean's main regional training college for priests, the **St John Vianney and the Uganda Martyrs Seminary**, which is also UWI's theology faculty. The nearby **St Bede's Vocational School** is run by the monks, who teach local youngsters practical skills such as machining, welding, plumbing and carpentry.

Taxis for Mount St Benedict leave from the corner of St John's road and the EMR. The fare is TT\$3 to the monastery.

At 243m above sea level, even the monastery's car park commands spectacular views across the Caroni plains to the Trinity Hills and Mount Tamana. Adjacent to the monastery, the *Pax Guesthouse* (☎ and fax 662 4084, *stay@paxguesthouse.com, www.paxguest-house.com*; ⑤) is the traditional spot for **afternoon tea** (daily 3–6pm; moderate), a feast of homemade breads, cakes and pastries taken at the tea garden or a terrace facing the hills. Catering mainly for birders and nature lovers – you can hand-feed the hummingbirds from their terrace – *Pax* has varnished wood floors, antique furniture (including an ancient phonograph) and an atmosphere of complete peace. Recently modernized rooms lead from an impeccably clean, dormitory-like corridor and are fitted with solid furniture made by the monks or taken from plantation homes. Some have private bathroom, and numbers 1–7 have clear views over the central plains. Rates include breakfast and an excellent three-course evening meal; the dinner gong echoes through the corridors at 7.30pm. Non-guests can eat at the guest house restaurant if they ring ahead.

Recommended local ornithologist Ishmael Angelo (☎ 628 1753, tacaribe@tstt. net.tt) is the main tour guide at Pax, and is an excellent choice for trips to other birdwatching sites in the area; see p.48 for prices.

Pax's manager Gerard Ramsawak organizes **birdwatching tours** through the two square kilometres of surrounding land, home to a huge array of birds; the elevation means that raptors – hawks, vultures, kites and falcons – are particularly common, as are woodpeckers, parrots and hummingbirds. Five **trails**, ranging from half an hour to two hour's walking wreathe through jungle and secondary forest of Caribbean pine; a beautifully illustrated trail guide is available from the guesthouse. For a panoramic view of Trinidad that surpasses even the vistas at the monastery, take the Alben Ride trail and climb the **fire tower**, built to give warning of blazes in the cane fields below; the views are completely awe-inspiring, particularly at dusk when the sun disappears behind faraway Port of Spain and the lights twinkle in the distance.

Caura Valley

Curepe merges imperceptibly into **Tunapuna**, yet another nondescript collection of shopfronts and residential roads which uses the EMR as its main street – of the many food shops here, *Loveys* is a particularly good for roti. Just to the east, the Caura Royal Road turns off into the **Caura Valley** to the north – one of the most popular **picnic spots** in the East–West Corridor. Carved by the multi-tributaried, serpentine Tacarigua River, the valley was nearly turned into a reservoir in the 1940s, but though the inhabitants were relocated to Lopinot (see opposite), the proposed **dam** was never built, thwarted by the sandy soil.

The Royal Road passes Caura waterworks about a kilometre from the EMR; 5km further north is a right turn to the first popular swimming spot; a graffiti-smothered abandoned building here is the last vestige of the abandoned dam project. Picnic tables line the bamboo-fringed riverbanks, and at the weekends, cooking fires smoulder and the water is crowded with families enjoying a dip. From here, there are several walkable dirt tracks of varying lengths into the **Tacarigua Forest Reserve**, an attractive patchwork of abandoned plantations and lower montane woodlands. Hikes range from ten-minute jaunts to whole-day treks to the peak of El Tucuche. There's another equally popular swimming site a little further up the Royal Road, with a larger, rutted car park that usually accommodates enormous buses. Both places offer passable **river swimming**, but as the surrounding countryside is predominantly farmed, rumours of pesticide pollution are common, and the shallow water often looks murky in the dry season.

Past the picnic spots, high walls of bamboo form an intermittent tunnel over the road, opening up occasionally to reveal the small-scale farmlands and homes of **La Veronica** hamlet. As the Royal Road emerges onto the riverbanks again, the water deepens a little and picnicking is more secluded. The road is eventually terminated by a tributary of the Tacarigua. The drive back to the EMR affords some spectacular views of the central plains that are easily missed on the way up.

If you need extra snacks or cold drinks for your picnic, there's a bar and a parlour on the road before the Caura picnic spots.

Lopinot

Uninspiring and easily missed if you're not scanning a map, **Arouca** is notable only as the point where you turn off the EMR for snaking Lopinot Road, which shoots north through gorgeous, undulating countryside of richly fruited vales and hillsides of jungle and Caribbean pine. Eight kilometres from the EMR, **LOPINOT** is a pretty hamlet clustered around a sports field and the neat flower beds of the **Lopinot complex**, a former cocoa estate that has been transformed into a beautiful, secluded picnic spot (daily 6am–6pm; free).

The valley was first settled by one Charles Josef, **Compte de Lopinot**, a planter who fled Haiti following Toussaint L'Ouverture's 1791 revolution. After a spell in Jamaica, he arrived in 1800 with his wife and 100 "faithful" (so the on-site board assures us) slaves. It's not difficult to see why he chose to settle in this absurdly abundant alluvial valley surrounded by high, protective mountains, and the cocoa thrived. He built a *tapia* estate house, a prison and slave quarters and amassed a small fortune before his death in 1819. The Compte is buried alongside his wife by the Arouca River, which runs through the valley, and local legend has it that on stormy full moon nights his ghost rides through the estate on a white horse.

The modest **great house** has been carefully restored, with a glassed-over section showing the original mud walls behind the newly rendered exterior. Meticulously maintained, the surrounding gardens are linked to the road by a quaint wooden bridge, its roof smothered with ferns and wild pine bromeliads, while picnic tables are shaded by several enormous samaan trees with branches laden down by epiphytic plants. On the grounds are a restored cocoa dry-

Lopinot's annual harvest – a festival of parang fuelled by excesses of food and drink – usually takes place on May 17, though a shift to July has been known.

ing house, a dirt oven and a cave. The estate makes a good spot for watching birds such as the white-shouldered tanager, the bare-eyed thrush and the violaceous euphonia. Inside the great house, a small **museum** is dedicated to the culture of local residents. The community, relocated here when the Caura dam was proposed (see p.160), is of Spanish, African and Amerindian descent; it has spawned some of Trinidad's finest parang players, inspiring villagers to call Lopinot the "**home of parang**". The village is one of the few places where each Christmas, a band of roving players still serenade each household. Site caretaker Martin Gomez is a parang master who delights in treating visitors to a song, accompanying himself on the cuatro. The museum displays photographs of local parang elders as well as a couple of dusty Amerindian artefacts and the dried-out husks of large grasshoppers and tarantulas, presumably on show to scare the tourists.

For more on the parang tradition, see p.341.

The boxy, cut-stone **La Veronique RC church**, by the roadside on the other side of the playing field, was originally built in Caura in 1897, but was taken piece by piece from the neighbouring valley during the Caura evacuation and reassembled here. Past the church and the primary school, lichen-smothered cocoa trees line the road, and a downhill turn-off leads to the **La Pastora** chapel and shrine, one of many on the island to share the title. This dedication to the Virgin of Shepherds stems from Capuchin monks who established several missions during the late seventeenth century, instilling devotion to La Pastora in their Amerindian converts. Carved in the 1940s, the plain white shrine inside depicts the Virgin Mary, and is said to have been chipped directly from the mountain.

The route taxi fare from Arouca to Lopinot is TT\$3; cars are fairly frequent (Mon–Sat 5am–6pm), but the service is reduced on Sundays.

After passing several small, friendly villages, the road eventually forks; a left down San Francisco Road brings you to a series of deep, swimmable **pools** on the river. There is good **hiking** in the surrounding mountains; Martin Gomez can arrange a guide who'll take you to nearby bat-filled **caves** – Mr Gomez discovered one of them himself, and it bears his name.

Should you find a need to stay overnight, you might try *Sadila House* (Waterpipe Road, Five Rivers ☎640 3659, fax 640 1376, *www.sadila.com*; ⑤); ring first for directions as it can be difficult to find. Rooms are clean and comfortable with a/c, en-suite bathroom and a shared communal area with TV. Breakfast is in included in the rates.

Arima and around

Past Lopinot, the EMR takes on a distinctly more rural aspect, with the shops and offices interspersed with the odd cattle pasture or overgrown empty lot. At the diminutive village of **D'Abadie**, the EMR wreathes through the pines and cocorite palms of **Cleaver Woods**. On Cleaver Trace, there's a gravel car park and the entrance to an **Amerindian museum** (daily 7am–6pm; free). Though the museum, housed in a thatch-roof ajoupa hut, is a bit neglected, the displays are interesting: including pottery, hunting traps, bows and arrows and equipment used to process cassava, which was farmed by Amerindians and formed a major part of their diet. The surrounding forest has a few short **trails** and picnic tables, and on the southern side of the road there's a small spring popular with local Rastas.

Named "Naparima" by the Amerindians who were the first to settle in the area, **ARIMA** is situated smack in the middle of the East–West Corridor. The largest town in the area, it's also one of the easiest places to get lost, as the EMR departs from its normally ruler-straight path and gets swiftly swallowed up in the urban clamour of endless shops, banks and wandering pedestrians.

The town has a far deeper history than its commercial facade would suggest, however, being home to what's left of Trinidad's **Carib** community, most of whom live around the crucifix-strewn **Calvary Hill**, a precipitous thoroughfare that overlooks the town and connects to the Arima–Blanchisseuse Road. You can still see remnants of Indian features in these distant relatives of the Carinepogoto tribe who once inhabited the Northern Range, but links are becoming ever-more tenuous as intermarriage slowly erodes the physical aspect of the **Karina nation**, as they like to be known – Carib is regarded as a European corruption of their correct title. However, Carib culture still has a stronghold here, and **the Santa Rosa Carib Community Association** was formed in 1974 to look after the interests of the dwindling tribe. Their headquarters on Paul Mitchell Street, behind the cemetery, sells good quality traditional Amerindian craft such as woven baskets or carved calabashes, as well as giving information about local Carib culture. The only remaining **ajoupa** – the traditional Carib thatched building – on Calvary Hill sits in the front yard of Christo Adonis, the local Carib shaman and vociferous defender of his people; if you can catch him at home, he's a mine of information on Amerindian medicine and all things pertaining to the Karinas.

Exploring Arima is best done on foot, as the one-way street system is confusing; there's a free car park behind the blue bus terminus. Walking is a good way to see the odd old house and soak up the hustle and bustle of town life – even the library has loud speakers mounted in front of it playing the latest soca/reggae tunes. Arima's main landmark and traffic roundabout, the **Arima Dial**, was knocked down by a truck in 2000; plans are afoot to restore the unreliable four-faced timepiece, originally presented to the townspeople in 1898 by their mayor, John Wallen. On **Hollis Road**, the statue of venerated calypsonian **Lord Kitchener** will hold your attention briefly before you're drawn to the fabulous open-air **market** nearby; it's liveliest on Fridays whilst the adjacent Arima Velodrome is the setting for many a wild Carnival fete. Weekend evenings are especially busy, with locals tending to lime by the savannah wall and engaging in a little "ol' talk". On the town end of **O'Meara Road**, the route from central Arima to the highway, a semi-permanent **children's fun park** known as Coney Island (daily, no set hours; free) has a ferris wheel, merry-go-rounds and some more adult-oriented fairground rides, while the **Santa Rosa Race Track** (☎646 2360), off the highway, holds occasional **horse racing** meets. Leaving town along the Eastern Main Road, you pass **Nutones panyard** on the right, whose dedicated beaters brought unexpected glory to Arima in 1998 when they won the **National Panorama** title with their arrangement of David Rudder's "High Mas".

Practicalities

As the region's main transport hub, Arima has three **petrol stations**, a few banks and **Internet** access (TT$9 per hour) at the shop Eastech (☎667 4556; Mon–Sat 9am–7.30pm, cnr Queen and Farfan streets). **Taxis** to Sangre Grande (TT$4) and Valencia (TT$2) leave from the roundabout, and taxis to Port of Spain ($TT5) can be caught on Broadway. Alternatively, catch the ECS **bus** to the capital outside the courthouse on Hollis Avenue ($TT4). **Maxis** for Port of Spain leave from the northern end of St Joseph Street ($TT4), whilst maxis for Sangre Grande ($TT3), Manzanilla ($TT3), Toco ($TT7), Mayaro ($TT7) and Grande Riviere (TT$15) leave from the corner of Raglan Street and Broadway.

Arima is full of fast **food** and low-key eating places, but its street food is tastiest and great value. Coconut water can be bought from vendors on Hollis Avenue, and doubles and roti are always available by Arima's excellent outdoor fruit and vegetable market. At **night** delicious punches can be bought from the stalls on Queen Street, and further up delicious doubles are cooked while you wait by roadside vendors.

There's no shortage of **entertainment** in the town, with plenty of rum shops, pool halls, two cinemas and various nightclubs. Well patronized by the locals – its rare you'll see a foreigner in these places – they are a good place to come if you're tired of the glitz of the more upmarket tourist-orientated places in Port of Spain. The two **cinemas** *Kabsco* (☎667 4003) on Sorozano Street and *Windsor* (☎667 3274) on Hollis Avenue both show double bills of the usual Hollywood action fare at around 4pm and 8pm (TT$10–15); check the papers for details. The brand new *5th Element* nightclub on the corner of Queen and Sozano streets, has a student night on Thursdays, after-work limes on Fridays, and dub/dancehall/hip-hop on Saturdays that attracts a young and trendy crowd. *The Abyss*, on the corner of Pro Queen Street and Malabar Road, features eerie cave-like décor; the sports bar has pool tables upstairs and a dancefloor downstairs. Local food is also available on Thursday, Friday and Saturday. Thursday is Caribbean night with local music and performances. For the more mature crowds, *Czar*,

For good craft work, sandals, belts and such, visit the stalls behind the market on the edge of the savannah or those on the northern end of Woodford Street.

The Feast of Santa Rosa

During the last weekend of August, Arima's Carib community celebrates the Feast of Santa Rosa de Lima, making the town the only place in Trinidad where the first canonized Roman Catholic Saint of the "New World" is honoured. Following a morning of church services, a Carib King and Queen are crowned, and a white-swathed statue of Santa Rosa is paraded through the streets, the procession bedecked with white, yellow, pink and red roses. An all-day party ensues; rum flows, and traditional Amerindian foods such as pastelles and cassava bread are eaten. The origins of the festival are somewhat murky, but in fairytale style, Carib elders relate that three hunters chanced upon a young girl lying in the woods, and brought her back to Calvary Hill. She disappeared three times, only to be returned to the community. A local priest told the Caribs that this was no normal child, but the spirit of Santa Rosa, and that they should make an image of her while she was still with them, for if she vanished again, her physical body would never again be seen. They made the statue, and Santa Rosa duly disappeared, leaving only a crown of roses at the spot where she had first been discovered. Ever since, Santa Rosa has been the patron saint of the Carib community.

opposite *5th Element*, plays "back in times" music and has a regular ballroom dancing instructor. *Sylvesters*, St Joseph Street, is another sports bar with pool tables and a nice open-air section, and serves tasty local food such as souse, and bake and shark.

The only place to stay is *Hotel California* on Nelson Street (☎667 2209; ③), on the southern skirts of the town. A well-maintained yellow-and-brown building, its carpeted walls, dark rooms and music are perfect for the hotel's main guests – lovers with nowhere else to go. The rooms are clean and cheerful, and there's a friendly bar downstairs.

Heights of Guanapo Road

On the eastern outskirts of Arima, the EMR switches abruptly from commercial thoroughfare to rural road, dominated by farmlands and cattle pastures rather than shopfronts and honking traffic. Just after the Arima Bypass meets the EMR, a turn-off at the WASA Guanapo Waterworks sign brings you to the **Heights of Guanapo Road**. Striking through thick forest, this is a hikers' paradise, but it's not a place to explore without the help of a knowledgeable **guide**; Laurence Pierre is recommended (see p.48). To get to good walking territory, drive past the waterworks along a country lane that's recently been partially wrecked by the huge wheels of logging vehicles; expect a lot of mud if you arrive in rainy season, when it's best to have a four-wheel drive. Though you can drive further uphill to **La Laja Heights**, which gives lovely views over the Guanapo Valley, it's a good idea to park in the large clearing where logging workers have built a hut, as from here onwards the road becomes treacherous with potholes; there's also a nice swimming spot in the Guanapo River, next to a concrete bridge. The main attractions of the area are the breathtaking **Guanapo Gorge**, and **the La Laja** and **Sombasson waterfalls**. With effort, you can see both the falls and the gorge in a day, but you'll need to be pretty fit.

Guanapo Gorge

A little nearer to the EMR than the waterfalls, **Guanapo Gorge** is a narrow channel whose vine-wreathed walls of smooth grey rock rise 15m to 30m above the water. Dark and cool even on a hot sunny day, the gorge runs for some 400m; exploring it – wading and swimming all the way – can be quite hard work. Though you can start the trek from the southern (downstream) end, a far more exciting option is to begin upstream, where a large boulder blocking the river has created a small waterfall. From here, you enter the gorge by jumping from the boulder into a deep pool and swimming for a few yards before your feet meet the riverbed. Water levels vary according to the time of year, but you should have to swim for no further than 25m at any point, travelling from one end to the other is quite simply one of Trinidad's most thrilling journeys due to the sense of danger it provokes. The tiny **Tumbason River** threads through rocks to meet the Guanapo at the southern end of the gorge; if you walk up for about 45min, you'll come to a small **waterfall** with a deep **pool**.

*Reputable
hiking guides
are listed in
Basics, pp.48,
244 and
throughout the
Guide.*

The La Laja and Sombasson waterfalls

The **La Laja and Sombasson waterfalls** are hidden deep in the folds of the Northern Range. Getting to them necessitates a long and difficult hike, passing through abandoned cocoa plantations and forests of bois cano, sandbuck, nutmeg, balata and silk cotton. The trail dips and climbs constantly, but frequent use by hunters, who come here for the rich stocks of wild meat, have kept the majority of the trails fairly free of bush, though you may need to blaze a trail in the last stages of the walk, marking your path by slashing the undergrowth or leaving other easily recognizable marks. The first of the falls, **La Laja** is the smaller at about 20m high, with a couple of good pools below; the water is kept icy cold by the overhanging cliffs and dense foliage. Above La Laja, you're in virgin forest, and the trek to **Sombasson falls** is harder, but the three-tiered fifty-metre cascade with deep pools is worth the effort.

Aripo Caves

Yet more lonely fields line the EMR east of Guanapo, where the nondescript-looking **Aripo Road** runs north into the mountains following a valley cut by the Aripo River. A pretty, meandering uphill route leads deep into the bush for some 14km. Its end marks the start of a hike to Trinidad's largest system of caverns, **Aripo**

Caves, which support one of the island's few **oilbird colonies**. It's also a main starting point for the climb to Trinidad's highest mountain, **El Cerro del Aripo**. At 941m, the peak is covered with prehistoric-looking elfin forest; short, scrubby and smothered with lichen, mosses and epiphytic growth. It's a tough full-day hike, but as the temperature at the peak is some ten degrees lower than in the lowlands, overheating is one thing you don't have to worry about. As the Aripo Road is rough and periodically pot-holed, you'll need a car with high clearance if you're driving; in the wet season, a four-wheel drive is a good idea. It's a pretty route, tracing the valley and passing through some quiet rural communities; artist **Leroy Clarke** has a home up here. If you're in the mood for a **river swim**, look out for a metal arch with the inscription "Jai Guru Data" soldered from iron rods; take the steps down the hill to a deep **pool**.

You can still make out the forestry department signs along Aripo Road – though they're weather-beaten and battered – which point the way to the caves; follow them past **Aripo**, the last village, where you should be able to hire a guide if you haven't travelled up with someone who knows the way. After a cocoa grove sporting fruits that turn purple when ripe rather than the usual orange, there's a final cave sign by a grassy clearing where you can park. The signs end here, and as parts of the original trail have been obscured by large, messily cut logging tracks, an experienced guide is essential to get to the caves. As the Aripo savannah is a scientific reserve you're supposed to get special permission to visit – your guide will sort this out. The fairly taxing two- to three-hour trek, with plenty of hills and gullies to navigate, is best under-taken in the dry season (Jan–March), when the three rivers that cross the path usually slow to a trickle; if it's been raining, you'll have to wade them. In the rainy season, you'll also have to get wet to enter the caves, as a river courses straight into the mouth; take care, as the going can be slippery.

The forest is thick, but if you squint through the leaves you can get the occasional view of the Central Plains below. On near-ing the main entrance of the caves, you'll start to hear the unearth-ly rasping shriek of the **oilbirds** inside (for more on oilbirds, see p.351). The **mouth** is large and dramatic, with a musty mist rising constantly from the depths. Water drips from the limestone roof, and every surface is covered with fruit stones dropped by oilbirds returning from night-time feeding forays as well as a thin film of guano. With a good torch, you can navigate the rocks and go fair-ly deep inside, but doing so increases the oilbirds' cries to an ear-splitting pitch; it's not difficult to imagine why the Amerindians named them "Guacharo", meaning "the one who wails and mourns". If you want to go any further into the cave, you'll need rope, a compass and some spelunking experience.

The East–West Corridor

Courtenay Rooks (☎ 622 8826, fax 628 1525, www.pariaspings.com) leads a day-long hike to El Cerro Del Aripo summit for US$65; a moderately difficult hike to the Aripo caves through abandoned cocoa estates (1 day, US$65); and easy walking tours of the Aripo savannah area (1 day, US$45).

The Northeast Tip

Stretching from **Matura** in the east to **Matelot** in the north, the wild and rugged coastline of Trinidad's **Northeast Tip** has a far more remote feeling than anywhere else in the region; it takes a minimum of three hours to drive from Port of Spain to Matelot, where the paved road ends. Cut off by a break in the coast road and by the rainforests of the Northern Range, the region seems suspended in a time warp; people and houses are few and far between and an air of hypnotic quiet pervades. The villages strung along the coast are close-knit and spirited communities, with proud residents clipping verges and planting flowers in voluntary beautification projects and making their own entertainment at the **rum shops**, country parties and fishermen's fetes. The residents have the only community radio station on the island – Radio Toco 106.7FM – which is great for giving you a taste of local life. **Farming** and **fishing** are the mainstays of the economy, and you'll lose count of the signs advertising shark oil, salt fish and sea moss for sale, while tiny roadside stalls offer fresh fruit and vegetables at knock-down prices.

The narrow Matura Road loops through neat farmlands and stark, untamed bush, with unreachable rocky coves enticing you to scramble down the cliffs. Warnings against frequent landslides and collapsing tarmac are clearly signposted and long-standing potholes thoughtfully circled with white paint. At wind-whipped **Matura**, **leatherback turtles** lumber up the sand to lay eggs, while the eastern headlands provide plenty of sheltered spots for a dip in the foaming Atlantic. At weekends, sublime stretches of yellow sand such as **Saline** and **Balandra bays** become popular retreats for seclusion-seekers, as does the reef-fringed seashore adjacent to **Galera Point**, where a lighthouse guides ships through the treacherous waters between Trinidad and Tobago. Inland, **Salybia Waterfall** is one of the island's best, and you'll usually have it all to yourself. The largest town in the area, **Toco**, is relatively tiny, but has lent its name to the surrounding region, with its awe-inspiring untamed coastline of weather-beaten cliffs and crashing sea. **Surfers** ride the breakers at **Sans Souci**, and the **rivers** and **waterfalls** inland from **Grande Riviere** and Matelot make jungle hiking a rewarding adventure.

As most people see the coast in a day trip, there aren't a lot of **accommodation** options, though there are more springing up each year. The fabulous hotel on the beach at Grande Riviere is one of Trinidad's best, however, and there are plenty of **beach houses** advertised for rent in the classified pages of the national newspapers. To explore the Northeast Tip easily you'll need your own car; though there is a rural **bus** service –– with buses concentrated at peak periods – and the occasional **maxi** and **taxi**, service is somewhat sporadic. Bus service to Matelot was suspended in 2000 when a bus driver lost his life in a landslide, and bus drivers are refusing to com-

Stakeholders Against Destruction (SAD ☎ 670 1452, www.opus.co.t t/toco) are a good source of information on the Northeast Tip, ranging from community-based eco-tours to accommod-ation, food services and features of local interest.

> **Transport to Toco and beyond**
>
> Sangre Grande, in Central Trinidad, is the region's main transport hub; all
> public transport to Toco starts here. The rural bus service has seven buses
> a day during the week (3.30, 5.30, 7.30, 9.30, 13.30, 15.30, 17.30) and
> four on weekends (5.30, 8.00, 13.00, 16.00) costing TT$8 to Grande
> Riviere. They are currently not running to Matelot. Maxis leave regularly
> from Sangre Grande for Cumana (TT$6), Toco (TT$8) and Grande Riviere
> (TT$9), and they also run to Matelot (TT$20) twice a day – in the early
> morning and evening (TT$20); route taxis run with the same frequency to
> Cumana (TT$7), Toco (TT$8), Grande Riviere (TT$10) and Matelot
> (TT$20). A cheaper and quicker option for Matelot is to take the rural bus
> from Sangre Grande to Grande Riviere, then take a taxi to Matelot from
> there (TT$4).

plete the route until the road is repaired. If you're **driving** from Port
of Spain, it's quicker to avoid the car-choked EMR and take the
Churchill Roosevelt Highway; turn left at the end of the highway, and
then right onto the quiet portion of the EMR to Valencia, from where
the Valencia Road swings north to the Toco coast.

Valencia and Matura

Straight and smooth, the **Valencia Road** swings through mile upon
mile of open country; other than the odd home or small provision
field, signs of human habitation are few and far between and it's rare
to pass another car. The quiet town of **Valencia**, about five miles
from Arima, has a few shops, a petrol station and plenty of coconut
vendors to refresh your thirst. The **Hollis Reservoir** – a serene spot
good for birdwatching if you go early in the morning – is on the eastern side of town; take the Quare Road turn-off from the Valencia
Road – watch out for the "North West Water Project" sign. There's a
river by the road past the entrance that has some good bathing spots.
You'll need a permit from the Water and Sewage Association (WASA)
to enter – call ☎662 2301. Further east is the well-posted North
Oropuche River recreational facility – a rather grand name for picnic
tables by the river; a popular place for families on weekends taking
a river swim and having a barbecue. Though there's a sign, the sharp
left-hand **turn** for the **Toco Main Road** is easy to miss – watch out for
the large Radio Toco sign; carrying on takes you straight to Sangre
Grande (see p.199).

Twelve miles away, the one-street town of **MATURA** consists of
little more than a police station, a school, a health centre and a few
modest houses slung along the tarmac. Other than stopping for a
drink at the rum shop, the only reason to spend any time in the area
is the **beach**, a windswept, four-kilometre stretch of fine yellow sand
strewn with coconut husks, chip-chip shells, driftwood and the odd
bit of flotsam and jetsam washed up by the fearsome waves. Though

local people often take a dip, it's not a place for the uninitiated to swim, as the currents are extremely powerful. The real attraction is the **leatherback turtles** which haul themselves on to the sand to lay eggs. The beach is a prohibited area during the laying season (March 1–Aug 31), and you need a permit to enter (see p.203). If you visit at the right time of year and want to see the turtles, check the offices of **Nature Seekers Incorporated** on the main road; they have trained guides who take you on to the beach to watch the amazing process (for more on turtles, see p.349). There are two entrances to the beach, both marked by Forestry Division signs. The first is in the centre of Matura; follow a challenging tarmac and gravel road to the right. The other end of the shore, reached from the far side of town down a dirt track, is known as **Rincon Beach** – also popular with turtle watches and well signposted.

Rio Seco Waterfall

Past Matura, the Toco Road meets the east coast for the first time. The view is often obscured by a thick cover of bush, though you do get some stunning views of small, wave-battered coves. The first safe place to swim is a beach just past the tiny village of **Salybia**, which consists of little other than a government school, *Friday's Grocery & Rest* bar and the *Silver Gates Recreational Club*. Just past the buildings, a large concrete bridge crosses the Rio Seco, flanked by a hut selling crafts. A turn-off to the right leads down to **Saline Beach**, a popular chill-out spot during the weekend when families come to bathe and picnic.

Opposite the beach turn-off is the clearly signposted **Rio Seco waterfall trail**, the route to one of the area's more spectacular **waterfalls** (known locally as Salybia Waterfall), beautifully placed in the **Matura Forest Reserve**. You can drive up for about ten to fifteen minutes if there's been no recent rain, but if the ground is wet, it's best to leave your car at the beach and tackle the rocky, uneven road on foot. It's a pleasant walk up a gentle incline enclosed by thick forest. Look out for a tall royal palm just before the pink house; on the tree are several of the teardrop-shaped **nests** of the black and yellow **crested oropendola**.

Past the house, the road has been churned into a muddy, rutted track by the wheels of forestry department vehicles. After 10 minutes, you should pass a wooden house on a hill to the left; carry straight on, skirting a small field of dasheen and sweetcorn and passing signs warning "Take only pictures, leave only footprints" and "Stay on the trail". After ten minutes' walk through the forest, the trail splits; left heads to the river and an attractive, fairly deep swimming pool, while the right-hand, uphill track leads to the falls. A mossy picnic table and chairs carved out of felled trees and some rather incongruously placed signs punctuate the path; for no discernible reason, one of them declares the place a "nature habitat".

You cross a river tributary and climb another hillock before descending to the falls – it's possible to follow the river all the way up to the main waterfall, passing some small cascades. The last stretch, bordered by rickety rails, is steep, but you get a good prospect of the waterfall below. The trunk of a huge silk cotton tree forms a bridge over the riverbed rocks and into a blue-green pool, 7m deep and 12m wide – a great place to bathe. The waterfall itself tumbles some 8m down the rocks, with plenty of handholds for an easy climb up and a dive from the top. Emerald light filters through the surrounding canopy, while a break in the cover above the water provides some direct sunlight. From the road, the walk should take about an hour, and the falls make a great picnic spot.

Balandra Bay

After cutting inland across some wild and undeveloped bush, the Toco Road rejoins the coast at **BALANDRA**, a pretty fishing village with a popular beach. Before the town, you pass a large sign for *Balandra Beach Resort*, now a private residence; a shame, as the location on a bluff overlooking the beach provides some marvellous coastal views. The main entrance to the **beach** is at the western end, and is marked by a small sign; you should be able to find a space in the car park unless you visit at a weekend, when cars line the path to the road.

Backed by the fishing village and fringed by palm trees and Indian almonds, the beach is wide and inviting, with clean yellow sand and moderate waves. Most of the weekend crowds swim by the sheltered walled area past the car park, though swimming is safe along the whole length of the beach. A small shack by the car park sells soft drinks, pies and pholouri and a rudimentary shower is located behind the fishing depot.

Rampanalgas and Cumana

The next settlement along the coast, the sizeable village of **RAMPANALGAS** clings to the landward side of the road. It's a friendly sort of place – the local hot-spot is *Arthur's Grocery* on the outskirts of town, boasting a lively bar with a pool table, a grocery that sells cakes and snacks, and a postal agency. From a backroad which strikes off the Toco Road just past the village name-sign, a trail leads to the **Cirra Falls**. The path crosses a stream and winds uphill, passing a rather grand wooden board house on the right; after a ten-minute walk you'll come to a river, where crazy paving put in by the villagers leads to the cascade. The waterfall is small but attractive, with a deep, greenery-wreathed pool and a tree stump which forms a diving board for local kids. You can climb up the bank to the top of the falls, where there's another, smaller cascade.

The next village along the Toco Road, **CUMANA**, manages the dizzy heights of a **petrol station**, several noisy **bars** – where rum-drinking patrons tend to be incredibly friendly – and a good **roti shop**, *Rose's*, on the western outskirts. A turning by an unattractively stone-clad Catholic church leads to a scrappy fisherman's beach, but it's not a place for swimming; vultures wait patiently for fish innards and there's a distinctly briny aroma.

These two sleepy villages are slowly changing as upmarket hotels are built in the area. *Jasmine's Ocean Resort*, 1 Simmons Drive, Rampanalgas (☎670 4567 or 625 8385, from the US 877/202 5567, from Europe 888/509 9852, fax 670 0992, *www.jasmines.net*; ⑦) is a plush hotel with tight security and little atmosphere, a large pool, bar and sundeck and a reasonably priced restaurant overlooking Balandra Bay. The somewhat plain rooms have satellite TV, phone and en-suite bathroom. The tiny balcony for the more expensive "standard" rooms do not justify the rates, but nature trails are on the grounds, and it's a five-minute walk to the beach.

Cumana is currently the last place to fill up with petrol before Matelot, as Toco's tiny petrol station is being refurbished. Opening hours are Mon–Sat 8.30am-6pm, Sun 8.30am–noon.

Further down the road in Cumana is the French-style villa *Hotel Esterel* (☎ & fax 662 4084 or 670 4767, *stay@hotelesterel.com*; ⑧), sister hotel of *Pax Guesthouse* in Mount St Benedict. The rooms in this spa resort are furnished with French antiques and come with a/c, mini-bars, TV and verandahs overlooking the sea. A secluded hotel garden, good for turtle- and birdwatching, as well as massages, whirlpools and a nearby beach complete the resort's offerings.

Toco and Galera Point

The largest community along this stretch of coast, **TOCO** is an attractive, quiet fishing village which retains a distinctly antiquated air. A proud, close-knit community it has one of the largest concentrations of Baptists in the Caribbean, inspiring one of its sons, the great Trinidadian writer Earl Lovelace to write *The Wine of Astonishment*, a novel about Baptist persecution under colonial rule. Most of the buildings are dilapidated gingerbreads, and weather-beaten wood reigns supreme. Though most residents make their money from fishing or farming, many have recently begun to sell off family land to prospective developers, tempted by the high real-estate prices brought about by the often-mooted suggestions to build a **ferry terminal** here, forming a second sea bridge to Tobago, a mere 20km away and easily visible on clear days. The plan would have entailed oil bunkering facilities, docks for cruise ships and trawler traffic, but local protest, particularly from action group Stakeholders Against Destruction has shelved it for now. SAD has proposed instead the development of Salybia beach, with an eco-tourism centre and a sporting complex run for and by locals. (For details on the group's visitor services, see p.168.)

Apart from the rural bus service (see p.26) maxis to Toco (TT$8) and Cumana (TT$6) leave from Sangre Grande. Route taxis also leave from Sangre Grande for Toco (TT$8) and Cumana (TT$7); see also p.199.

Most of the route taxis from Sangre Grande turn around at Toco; if you're heading further west, you may have to wait here for quite a while, or hitch a lift. Unless you want to spend time in the town or see

Galera Point, it's a good idea to try and find a ride to Matelot in "Grande" (see p.199).

There are some basic places to stay in Toco catering for local surfers – ask in the village. The *Blue Haven Resort* (c/o Marlene Clark ☎670 1563; ⑦) is a blue-and-white wooden apartment above *Annifar's Snack Bar*. The spacious three-bedroom unit sleeps up to six people and has fully equipped kitchen, bathroom, TV, wooden floors and a verandah decorated with a colourful mural. The snack bar downstairs serves good local food at bargain prices, if you can't be bothered cooking.

As you enter the town, **Galera Road** strikes off to the right; this is where Radio Toco is based, a local landmark and an integral part of island life. Behind the station is *Wad-P's Kitchen*, a good place to stop for a local lunch. The road continues past the Toco Composite School, site of the **Toco Folk Museum** (open during school hours 8am–3.30pm, or ring to make appointment ☎670 8261, TT$3 adults, TT$2 children). Started as a school project this small museum houses Amerindian artifacts, local shells, snakeskins, butterflies and insects, and household items, including a gramophone and some rare 78rpm calypso records, which can be played if especially requested. The curators, mainly school teachers, are an excellent source of local history. The road continues to a good **beach**. A gorgeous double horseshoe of yellow sand scattered with white fragments of finger coral, the beach is busy on weekends, when it's a popular spot for a cook-out, and fried fish, soft drinks and local sweets are sold from a thatch-roofed stall. Surfers skim along beyond the reef, but the water close to the shore is translucent and pretty calm.

Past the beach, the road meanders to **Galera Point**, the island's extreme eastern tip and site of the Galera **lighthouse**. A stocky tower built in 1897, the lighthouse flashes its red beacon over a notoriously treacherous stretch of sea known to fishermen as the "graveyard". If the keeper is in a good mood, he'll let you climb all eighty-three rickety steps to the top for a fantastic view over inland coconut estates and down the coast to Matelot. Below the lighthouse is a windblown, rocky bluff – known as Fishing Rock – pounded by crashing waves that send up mists of salty spray; several currents swirl in the shallows, a blowhole under the rock gives off occasional moans, and the point where the royal blue Caribbean sea meets the murky, pastel-blue Atlantic Ocean is easily visible far out to sea. It's a strange, wild spot, filled with an uneasy energy; the lighthouse keeper maintains that the point is haunted, relating tales of car doors slamming when there is no car, and ghostly wails in the still of the night. He might be right; during a 1699 **rebellion** at a Spanish encomienda in San Rafael, Amerindians killed three Capuchin monks. Incensed, Spanish forces pursued the culprits to Galera, where they leapt off the cliffs to their deaths rather than be killed by their slave-masters.

*Tune into
Radio Toco
106.7FM for a
taste of local
life.*

Sans Souci and around

Past Toco, the road Toco Main Road becomes **Paria Main Road** as it rounds the end of the peninsula onto the north coast, running perilously close to the cliffs. Shattering all illusions of what a Caribbean seashore should look like, huge waves crash onto the wild and rugged coast, and jagged rocks poke out of a surging ocean in which only the suicidal would swim. There are several relatively safe beaches, however, around the next village, **SANS SOUCI**, all boasting waves large enough to make this the island's **surfing** capital and a regular venue for competitions. The largest is known simply as **Big Bay**; here, the waves are a little smaller and there are two places to eat on the road, both serving excellent food. *The Beach Break Café* serves up sandwiches and cold drinks, while the adjacent *Beach Break Rest & Bar* serves inexpensive Creole dishes and is the centre of the village's nightlife.

There's a few places **to stay**: Kathleen Manswell (☎670 1345, ③) rents out a simple but roomy apartment with two bedrooms sleeping up to four, with furnished kitchen, lounge and verandah, two minutes from the beach. A little further away from the sand, but right on the river, on the western side of the village Carmen Joe (☎670 1867; ②) is the caretaker for a basic wood and brick cottage with three bedrooms sleeping up to nine people – a real bargain. Past the bay, Paria Main Road winds inland through impossibly lush jungle which lets up only at the tiny **Monte Video** village, notable mostly for the cold beers on sale at the lone bar. Further west, so small it's not even marked on the map, the village of L'Anse Noire is home to *Violet's Holiday Resort* (☎637 3973; ②), a spacious two-bedroom house with 1960s wooden furniture and a dark kitchen, just ten minutes' walk from the beach. Beach house rentals are advertised by weather-worn signs on placards and houses along this stretch of road if you're looking for other options.

Grande Riviere

One of the most appealing villages of the Toco coast, **GRANDE RIVIERE** is also the only place with any kind of tourist infrastructure. A beautiful **hotel** right on the beach has spurred a host of local residents to open up **guesthouses**, but the remote location has kept development low-key, and the town remains one of the most unspoilt, idyllic places you'll find anywhere on the island. Interaction between visitors and local people has none of the money-oriented duplicity of other resorts, and local people tend to be incredibly welcoming, often throwing parties when a set of guests leave.

Named after the wide, fast-flowing river which originates deep in the Northern Range and runs down to the sea at the eastern end of town, Grande Riviere also boasts a superlative **beach**, a wide, gentle curve of coarse yellow sand with a few unobtrusive buildings blending seamlessly into otherwise unbroken jungle. Tall forested headlands border the sand to the east, where you can take a freshwater bath in the river, while a good kilometre away, the western end is sealed from the rest of the coast by rocky outcrops. Strong waves provide passable surfing or an invigorating swim, and give **leatherback turtles** the extra push they need to haul themselves up the sand at laying time. This is one of the best places to see turtles, and at the peak of the season, it's common for 150 or more to lay simultaneously. As in Matura, the beach is a prohibited area between March 1 and August 31, and you need a permit to enter between dawn and dusk during the rest of the year. Local residents have formed a voluntary patrol, the Grande Riviere Environmental Awareness Trust, to guard against poachers. Based in a little hut on the beach, they are the best and most knowledgeable turtle-watching guides in the village; ask for Francisco or Carlos Chance at the hut or at the reception of the *Mount Plaisir Estate* hotel; adults pay TT$18, children TT$10.

*For more on
leatherback
turtles, see
p.349.*

The liveliest part of the beach centres around the *Mount Plaisir Estate* hotel, where the **bar** is everyone's favourite liming spot. Most people who stay in town divide their time between the beach and the interior, where there are hosts of **waterfalls** and **river walks** as well as excellent **bird-watching** – the rare **piping guan**, a kind of wild turkey that has died out in more developed areas, is quite common in the area. Other activities include horse riding – ask at the hotel – snorkelling and boat trips. Most guides in the village work through the hotel; it's best to ask here for a reputable one. Nigel Spencer (☎756 8496) based in the bamboo hut on the beach next to the hotel is particularly good. His trips in his 9-metre pirogue to deserted beaches and the wonderful Paria Waterfall are enthralling, but not for those without their sea legs (TT$700; 5hrs). He also conducts nature trails in Grande Riviere and Matelot (TT$50), fishing trips (TT$150 for 1hr 30min) and sailing trips ($TT900, 2hrs one way) to Tobago. He's also the resort's only watersports operator, renting out jetskis (TT$300, 1 hr, TT$150, 30min) and kayaks (TT$20 1hr). If you're lucky he may even cook up some wild meat and green fig on a three-stone fire in front of his shack on the beach – where you can rest in his hammocks free of charge. Another guide is Cyril James (see *Le Grande Almandier* below) who organizes a night's **camping** in the bush, which includes building a treehouse at the end of a day's hike. Local character Jakatan, the originator of the "**Earth People**", a loose family group who live the natural life deep in the bush according to their own set of customs, also takes groups to "Jakatan Falls", a waterfall that he "discovered" and which has been locally named in his honour. Jakatan makes an excellent source of information on local folklore and is working on a campsite in the hills. Most tours cost around TT$100 per person. Another option is a **snorkelling** trip to nearby Langosta Cove or **boat trips** to remote beaches; ask at the hotel.

Practicalities

By far the best place to **stay** is right on the beach at *Mount Plaisir Estate* (☎670 8381, fax 670 0057, *www.mtplaisir.com*; ⑥). Overflowing with easy style, the rooms are fitted with solid, locally made furniture, while beautiful paintings hang on the walls and surfaces are decorated with driftwood oddities. Most rooms sleep four people, some six; try and get one with a stable door overlooking the beach. The hotel is also the best place for a sit-down meal, and the food could easily hold its own in the swankiest of Port of Spain's eateries: home-made bread, local-style meat or chicken and imaginative vegetarian options. Breakfast and lunch are available, and three-course dinners cost between TT$100–175. The hotel will also take you to the airport in their Mercedes coach (TT$450). Across the track which leads to the beach is *Le Grande Almandier*, Hosang Street (☎670 1013, *www.legrandealmandier.com*; ⑥), owned by Cyril James. Most rooms can sleep four and have fan and en-suite bathroom, and rates include breakfast. The bar downstairs is a good place for an evening drink, and chips or hot dogs for snacking on the beach. The restaurant serves contemporary Creole-French cuisine from 7am–11pm for slightly cheaper than *Mt Plaisir* next door. The newest addition to the village is *McEachnie's Haven* (Bristol and Thomas streets ☎670 1014 or 642 0477; ⑤), turn left at the *Mt Plaisir* turn-off. This yellow guesthouse perched on the hillside provides clean, homely rooms sleeping up to four, with fans, mosquito nets and en-suite bathroom. The owner, Ingrid, cooks delicious, inexpensive meals, such as chicken in coconut and ginger sauce, on request for both guests and nonguests – just order in advance. Meals are served in the family home and are a good opportunity to chat to a local family; her husband, Eric, is "Roots" of the local band Roots and Branches, which started the careers of many famous local musicians, and their children are all licensed tour guides. In the village, you can stay at the dingy but economical apartment above *Guy's Rec Club* (☎670 0048; ②); there are three bedrooms, a living room and a kitchen. The bar downstairs is a lively liming spot, with music (turned down if guests request it) and a pool table. You'll need to ask around to find the other options; check at Mt Plaisir. Opposite the community centre and playing field, Miss Freda (no phone; ②) has

---

Getting to Grande Riviere

The rural **bus** service runs seven buses a day during the week from Sangre Grande to Grande Riviere (3.30am, 5.30am, 7.30am, 9.30am, 1.30pm, 3.30pm, 5.30pm) and four on weekends (5.30am, 8am, 1pm, 4pm) costing TT$8. Maxis also leave for Grande Riviere from Sangre Grande (TT$9) as do route taxis (TT$10); see also p.199.

Most **maxis** stop at Grande Riviere but **route taxis** ply the Matelot route; from Sangre Grande the fare is around TT$20; see also p.199.

several simple double rooms above her home; bathroom and kitchen are shared. Mr Roseman (no phone – ask for him in the village or at Mt Plaisir) has a pink, two-bedroom house on a hill overlooking town with two bedrooms, a kitchen, outside shower and toilet, and a verandah with a gorgeous view; the rent is TT$200 per week.

You'll have to make your own **entertainment** here; apart from the strains of Roots and Branches, Grande Riviere's local band, whose nightly sessions echo over the village from the rehearsal hall on top of a hill above *Guy's*, things are quiet in the evening. *Jamesy's Stone Wall Bar* on the main road is a friendly spot, though, as is the *First and Last Bar*. You can buy **snacks** and **food** from *Guy's Grocery*. **Transport** in and out the village is via Sangre Grande.

Matelot and around

The stretch of Paria Main Road on the way to Matelot is currently beset by landslides, depressions and giant potholes, all reasons why the rural bus service stops at Grande Riviere. It's still passable, however, – just take it slowly – and there's talk that it will be resurfaced soon.

Of the many plank-lined bridges that pepper the Paria Main Road past Grande Riviere, the one crossing **Shark River** is the largest. The river is a popular swimming spot, with a couple of deep **pools** just before the water meets the sea and plenty more upstream; during holiday weekends, campers pitch tent along its banks. Walking upriver makes a great excursion, though you have to clamber over some mighty rocks to reach the best pools, and you'll need a guide (contact the local *Pawi Culture & Eco Club* (☎670 1816) to negotiate several tributaries and the occasional swing off into the bush.

Beyond the river and past the tiny village of **St Helena**, a ten-minute scenic coastal drive takes you to the fishing hamlet of **MATELOT**, the last settlement on the Paria Main Road. The village square is flanked by a plain Catholic church and a couple of rum shops; from here, a track leads down to the fishermen's beach. Houses, some of them quite grand, meander up the hillsides. The best recreation round here is swimming in the **Matelot River**; follow the main road to the left and bear right. There's a wooden bridge, and the water runs crystal clear down to the sandy **beach**. A sparse thatched hut provides an outdoor cooking space. The adjacent football field sees plenty of action at dusk; in one corner a large TIDCO sign points the way to the Madamas River Nature Walk, the start of the bench trail to Blanchisseuse. A Glasgow University research project has inspired locals to form the *Pawi Culture & Eco Club* (☎670 1816), a group of fourteen licensed **tour guides** who can take you into the forest interior, to the Paria and Matelot waterfalls and the undeveloped beaches between Matelot and Blanchisseuse. They are also planning the construction of a guesthouse in the village and will be part of the monitoring and protection programme of the leatherback turtles. **Entertainment** is focused around the *Sea Breeze Recreational Club* (☎670 1724; ②) on Pyke Street, the main bar in the village. The owners – Janet and Raymond Joseph – also rent out two rustic wooden **cottages** in the village for bargain prices. One overlooks the river and the other has a sea view, and both come with equipped kitchen, fan and bathroom. Other rooms are available in the village – ask at *Sea Breeze* for more information. There are no restaurants here, but if you don't want to cook, Mr James, who runs the grocery shop opposite the church, prepares excellent local **meals** for reasonable prices. Though the rural bus stops at Grande Riviere, **transport** is available if you're patient – maxis run to the village twice a day (early morning and evening) from Sangre Grande (TT\$20) as do taxis (TT\$20); see also p.199. Alternatively, catch the rural bus from Sangre Grande to Grande Riviere then take a taxi from there to Matelot (TT\$4).

Past here, the road ends; there's nothing but a bench trail along the wild and undeveloped coast to Blanchisseuse, 19km to the west (see p.142). Local fishermen can usually be persuaded to take you along the undeveloped coast from Matelot, Paria, Madamas or Blanchisseuse; a round trip will take about four hours depending upon conditions, route and number of people travelling (around TT\$700 per boat for the whole stretch). Ask at the fishing depot in Matelot. The forest inland of Matelot is riddled with hunters' trails, including a half-day trek to the 3-metre **Matelot Waterfall**, with its wide, deep pool. Guides are available from *Pawi Sport Culture & Eco Club* (☎670 1816, or ask around in the village).

Chapter 3

Central Trinidad

Spanning a compact area of roughly 350 square kilometres, **central Trinidad** encompasses an astonishing variety of landscape and settlement. The **west coast** is gritty and industrialized, punctuated by brash commercial towns such as **Chaguanas**, but even here you can find the **Caroni Swamp** – home of the scarlet ibis – and, further south, the **Pointe-a-Pierre Wildfowl Trust**, its pristine pools nestled incongruously on the grounds of a huge oil refinery. Inland, the flatlands of the agricultural **Central Plains**, dotted with somnolent villages, rise gently to the wooded, limestone Montserrat Hills in the south, **home** of the awesome **Tamana bat caves**; to the north and south of these hills are the two largest dams and reservoirs in the country, **Arena** and **Navet**. In the **east coast** region, there's only one town of any size, the busy market centre of **Sangre Grande**; south of here, there's just the stunning **Manzanilla Beach** with its seemingly endless avenues of palms, and the starkly beautiful open space of the protected **Nariva Swamp** wetlands.

The population is mostly descended from Indian indentured labourers who came here in the 1840s to replace freed slaves. You'll see Hindu shrines in every other yard; Indian delicacies are sold in shacks along the street and Indian music blasts out of roadside cafés and bars. In places such as the **Waterloo Temple**, on the west coast, and the odd isolated village, you'll easily imagine that you're in India rather than the southern Caribbean.

Away from the west coast and the country's only airport at **Piarco** to the north, much of central Trinidad remains deeply traditional or, as Trinis put it, "countrified". On the Central Plains, wide, flat expanses of sugar cane and coconut estates stretch as far as the eye can see, while in the heart of the island around the Montserrat Hills, huge reserves of awe-inspiring **rainforest** shelter countless species of flora and fauna. **Wildlife**, including scarlet ibis, manatees (sea cows), red howler monkeys and caimans, can easily be seen by visiting the swamps, reserves and reservoirs, and with many of the island's 420 species nesting in the protected areas, the region is excellent for **birdwatching**.

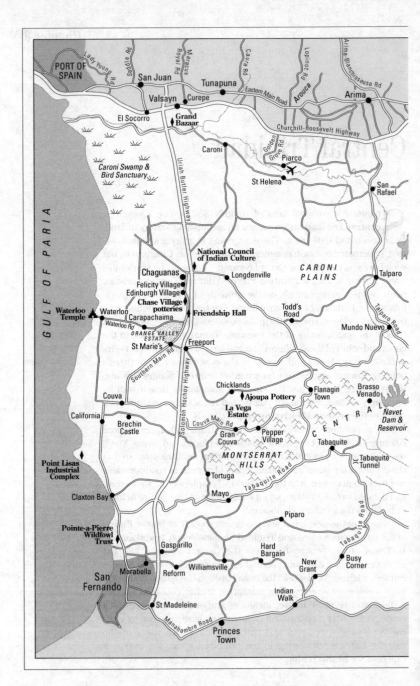

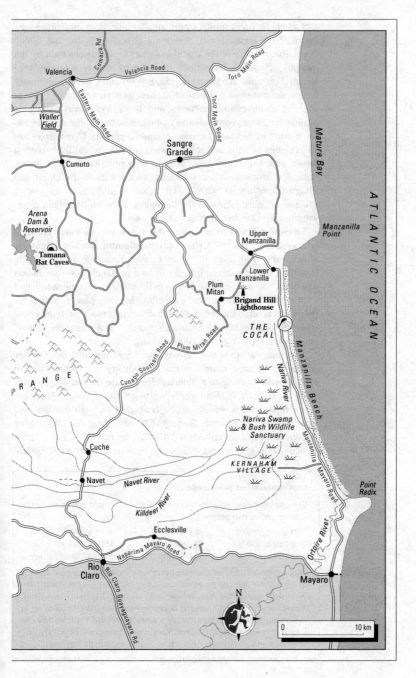

Some people still subsist by growing breadfruit, ground provisions and dasheen bush, though things are changing. In the last fifteen years, the majority of the traditional mud *tapia* houses built by the indentured Indians have been replaced by concrete homes constructed on stilts as a protection against flooding, which is frequent during the wet season. Mechanical harvesters now reap the fields in place of labourers with machetes, and the sight of a man leading his buffalo cart is less common now that much of the produce is taken to the market or factory in trucks. And while country Christmases are still celebrated with wild meat, home-made wines and lively parang music, even this tradition is declining in popularity. **Indian culture**, though, remains dominant, with religious festivals such as Diwali and Phagwa celebrated with much more vigour than up north; Chaguanas, particularly, is the best place to be on the island if you want to take in either of these celebrations.

Transport is no problem along the west coast; its towns are easily accessible from the **Uriah Butler–Solomon Hochoy Highway**, which runs from Port of Spain to San Fernando in the south. Reaching the rural areas inland can be a problem, however. **Maxis** and **taxis** take long circular routes to the villages, and the absence of road signs can make driving confusing. In many places, asking for directions is often the only way to find the right road, although country directions are often frustratingly vague – "just round the corner" could mean anything from 100m to 5km.

Accommodation in this little-touristed region is minimal. The few hotels are geared more toward oil industry personnel than to tourists, with nothing of a "holiday" feel, or are the motel type rented by the hour by Trini couples trying to get some privacy. There are a few **host homes**, which can be contacted through the Bed and Breakfast Co-Operative Society (☎ and fax 663 4413) or Accommodations Unlimited (☎628 3731, fax 628 3737, *owl@opusnetworx.com*). It is not necessary, however, to stay in central

---

Accommodation price codes

All accommodation listed in this guide has been graded according to the following **price categories**:

① under US$10	② US$10–20	③ US$20–35
④ US$35–50	⑤ US$50–70	⑥ US$70–100
⑦ US$100–150	⑧ US$150–200	⑨ US$200 and above

Rates are for the cheapest double or twin rooms, including 10 percent tax and 10 percent service charge where applicable. In Tobago, rates quoted are those used during the high season, normally mid December–mid April. During low season (mid April–mid December) rates are liable to fall by up to 25 percent. There are no high and low seasons in Trinidad, but rates may rise by up to 70 percent during Carnival. Many hotels give rates in US dollars – we have followed suit. Payment can be made in either US or TT currency.

Trinidad to visit; even the remotest areas can be reached from Port of Spain in less than two and a half hours. If you wish to get away from the bustle of the capital, there are various places to stay in Mayaro and San Fernando in the south (see Chapter 4, pp.232–234 & 206–215) that are also convenient for visiting central Trinidad. **Restaurants** and **nightlife** are very limited, though there are plenty of **fast-food places** serving cheap, filling meals, especially Indian and Chinese food, while the many small **bars** and **rum shops** provide friendly conversation and a good night out.

The west coast

Trinidad's **west coast** is a sometimes rather uneasy mix of nature and industry. Oil refineries and cement factories rub shoulders with workers' dormitory suburbs along the Uriah Butler–Solomon Hochoy Highway, which runs down the coast from Port of Spain past the rapidly developing commercial town of **Chaguanas** and the industrial zone of **Point Lisas**. Yet despite its inauspicious appearance, the coast harbours a couple of rich habitats for birds and other fauna: the huge **Caroni Swamp** in the north, and the **Pointe-a-Pierre Wildfowl Trust** to the south. The predominance of Indian culture is immediately noticeable from the highway, as the 12-metre statue of Swami Vivekananda that presides over the **National Council of Indian Culture** complex looms into view on the eastern side of the road, while **Waterloo Temple**, picturesquely built out over the sea, is one of the country's most well-known places of Hindu devotion.

As there's currently no signpost, the junction of the Uriah Butler–Solomon Hochoy and Churchill Roosevelt highways is easily missed; to find it watch out for the arches of the Grand Bazaar shopping mall, set back from the road.

Central Trinidad isn't the place to go for fine dining, but there are a few high-class **restaurants** at the **Grand Bazaar Mall**, its ostentatious arches and turrets poking into the sky at the junction of Uriah Butler–Solomon Hochoy and Churchill Roosevelt highways, about 10km east of Port of Spain. The *Imperial Garden* (Mon–Thurs 11am–10pm, Fri & Sat 11am–11pm; moderate–expensive; ☎662 6971) is a swish, Chinese restaurant that serves up reliable fare. *Botticelli's* (Mon–Sat 11am–11pm; ☎645 8733), decorated in ostentatious Italian style with Roman columns and a fountain outside, serves a wide variety of delicious Italian dishes, some given a Creole twist by the use of local fish and vegetables. Equally pricey *Apsara* (Mon–Sat 11am–11pm; expensive; ☎662 1013) is a magnificently furnished North Indian restaurant serving excellent food. An exclusive kind of place, with a doorman in traditional Indian dress, it's diagonally opposite the *Imperial Garden*. Reservations are recommended for all these places, which tend to be packed with residents from the chi-chi nearby community of Valsayn. Otherwise, Grand Bazaar is good for a wander, with an array of shops selling everything from books to swimwear; there's even one outlet devoted exclusively to Carib beer merchandise.

Most Grand Bazaar shops open Mon–Sat 10am–5pm.

Caroni Swamp and Bird Sanctuary

Trinidad's most heavily promoted environmental attraction, and deservedly so, the **Caroni Swamp** and **Bird Sanctuary** is the only roosting place on the island of the spectacular **scarlet ibis** – the national bird, an elegant, long-billed specimen sporting amazingly bright red plumage (see also pp.192–193). These sixty square kilometres of tidal lagoons, marshland and mangrove forest bordering the Gulf of Paria between the mouths of the Caroni and Madame Espagnole rivers are home to 157 species of birds, including white flamingos, egrets and blue herons, while caimans, snakes, opossums, racoons and silky anteaters can be observed in the water and the surrounding mangroves. Caroni Swamp was designated a protected wildlife area in 1953, but illegal hunting still occurs, and the reserve continues to suffer the effects of pollution from industrial waste. Nonetheless, it remains a quiet, mysteriously beautiful place, and well worth a visit. The mangrove trees themselves have an otherworldly appearance: some have twisted, triffid-like aerial roots growing downwards into the water, while others have roots that grow upwards, emerging from the murky depths like stalagmites.

Tours of the Caroni Swamp (TT$60/US$10) leave daily between 4–4.30pm and last two and half hours; advance booking is advisable. Contact Nanan (☎645 1305) or James (☎662 7356) for tours.

To visit the swamp you must take a boat – usually a 15-seater wooden pirogue – with either James or Nanan tours. The boatmen know the swamp and its wildlife well, and will point out birds, plants and animals of interest as they lead you through a maze of tunnel-like channels to the mangrove islands where the scarlet ibis roost at dusk. Once the boat engines shudder to a halt, a spectacular scene unfolds: as the birds flock in, an area of green mangrove gradually turns a vibrant red. It is not possible to get close to the birds' roosting spot without disturbing them, so bring binoculars or a powerful zoom lens, or you'll see little more than red specks against the dark green foliage.

Just past the turn-off for Caroni Swamp from the Uriah Butler–Solomon Hochoy Highway, look out for vendors selling strings of armoured cascadura catfish (see p.200).

The ibis's intense red plumage owes its pigment to carotene, derived from the birds' main prey – shrimp, worms and the tree-climbing **fiddler crabs** which inhabit the swamp in their millions; carotene substitutes don't do the trick, and in captivity the birds turn a faded pink. During the day the scarlet ibis fly to Venezuela to feed, returning at dusk to roost in the upper branches of mangrove islands in the midst of large lagoons. After a prolonged absence, possibly due to the impact of pollution on its food source, the scarlet ibis appear to be nesting in the area once again. In April and May, breeding pairs construct flat, open nests in the mangroves from twigs and their own droppings. Once laid, the eggs incubate for just under a month before all-black hatchlings emerge – it's another few months before their diet replace the dark feathers with brilliant crimson.

Driving to the swamp from Port of Spain, you'll need to leave at 3pm to catch a 4pm tour, as rush-hour traffic can be terrible. The exit off the Uriah Butler–Solomon Hochoy Highway is well signposted. **Maxis** and **route taxis** run from Port of Spain to Chaguanas; ask them to drop you at the Caroni Swamp exit, from where it is a five-minute walk. Aside from an incongruously large car park, facilities at the swamp are limited: there are toilets, and some drinks are sold from coolers in the boats, but you should bring your own water. Lashings of insect repellent are a must in rainy season, when mosquitoes go on the offensive.

Chaguanas

Halfway down the Uriah Butler–Solomon Hochoy Highway, the sprawling settlement of **CHAGUANAS** is one of Trinidad's oldest – the third largest town and the country's **shopping centre**, with a couple of glitzy shopping malls alongside its rambling old market. As a sign of the area's growing prosperity, there's a spanking new sport stadium on the outskirts of town. Chaguanas is also one of Trinidad's great centres of **Indian culture**: just outside town is the **National Council of Indian Culture**, one of the country's most important religious sites, while the elegant **Lion House** on Main Street is the birthplace of the acclaimed Indo-Trinidadian novelist V.S. Naipaul.

Some history

The town derives its name from an Amerindian tribe, the Chaguanes, which once lived in the region, but was pretty much a one-horse place until Indian indentured labourers came to work on the sugar and cocoa estates in the area in the 1840s; by the 1880s it had become the most important **market town** in central Trinidad, with good transport connections to Port of Spain, including rail and steamer. As the sugar industry declined in the early decades of the twentieth century, many Indians moved into professions such as journalism and the law, creating the middle-class intelligentsia from which **V.S. Naipaul** emerged and that would serve as the milieu for some of his early novels. Though the trains and steamer are long gone, the construction of the Uriah Butler–Solomon Hochoy Highway in the late 1940s ensured that the town would remain easily accessible. The oil boom of the 1970s brought a new lease of life to Chaguanas; conveniently located near the oil-rich south, it has developed rapidly into a shopping centre for those who prefer not to travel all the way into Port of Spain, and its swanky suburbs such as Lange Park, home to some lavish dwellings, are testament to the area's growing prosperity.

Arrival and information

There is no **accommodation** to speak of in Chaguanas, though the town is easily reached from the capital. **Maxis** from City Gate, Port of Spain, take you to the maxi stand next to Mid Centre Mall in Chaguanas for TT$3. **Route taxis** from Broadway, Port of Spain, will drop you on Chaguanas Main Road by *KFC* for TT$5. Maxis and route taxis to the rest of the west coast can be taken from here.

Buses leave City Gate, Port of Spain, for Chaguanas every 20–25 minutes and cost TT$2–3. The **post office** is located on Railway Road, opposite the **police station**. There are several **banks** in the town centre, including First Citizens on Market Street, Republic in City Centre Mall and Royal in Medford Plaza on Chaguanas Main Road. Computer Vision, in Centre Point Mall, offer inexpensive **internet access**.

The town

Chaguanas' busiest trading days, and the best times to visit even if you're not shopping, are Friday and Saturday.

Ranged around the junction of Chaguanas Main Road and the old Southern Main Road, the centre of town is a busy amalgam of new shops, hand-painted signs and street-side clothes stalls. It is dominated by two large malls: the **Mid Centre Mall** and **Centre Point Mall** (also known as Ramsarran Plaza), both great places to find bargains in shoes and clothes imported direct from New York and India. The big old-fashioned **market area**, lining the southern edge of Chaguanas Main Road, offers a complete – and far more absorbing – contrast: the pavements are chock-a-block with countless wooden stalls selling dirt-cheap clothes, ornaments and fashion accessories.

The beautifully illustrated Camps-Campins historical greetings cards, found in most book and gift shops, include an excellent "Lion House" edition, with background on the house's history, and photographs of the Capildeo family.

Plastic hair-slides, necklaces and earrings are displayed in their hundreds, and you can buy anything from locally made leather sandals to cheap plastic slippers or the latest Nike trainers. Behind the main road, narrow alleys wind their way through covered malls lined with fashion stores, but whatever you're after, you're more or less guaranteed to get it cheaper here than in Port of Spain. Be prepared to haggle, though – it's expected. The stalls start to thin out as you approach the **fruit and vegetable market**, an ambitious, industrial-style hangar bedecked with bright red wrought-iron arches; inside, old women sit behind stalls groaning under the weight of plantain, dasheen, chillies, ground provisions and artfully arranged piles of fruit.

The imposing **Lion House**, a stocky, arch-fronted edifice a few hundred metres further down Chaguanas Main Road from the market, was the birthplace and childhood home of Trinidad's most famous writer, V.S. Naipaul (see p.361). It's a fine, glaringly white-painted example of North Indian architecture and takes its name from the lions that adorn the stout columns supporting its grand arcade. Built in 1926 by the Pundit Capildeo, it became the residence of the Naipaul family when the writer's father Seepersad married Capildeo's daughter Droapatie. In his 1961 novel *A House for Mr Biswas*, Naipaul describes his experience of growing up in this house, surrounded by his mother's wealthy, religious and domineering family. Still a private residence, the Lion House is not open to the public, although the exterior can easily be viewed from the road.

National Council of Indian Culture

The large complex of the **National Council of Indian Culture** (also known as the **Diwali Nagar** site) on the Uriah Butler–Solomon

Phagwa

A lighthearted, joyous celebration of the new year and the arrival of spring, the Hindu Holi festival – known in Trinidad as Phagwa (pronounced "pag-wah") – is held around the first full moon in March to mark the end of the Hindu calendar's twelfth month (Phaglun). Upbeat and carnivalesque – to the horror of more traditional Hindus, who see the party aspect as *adharamic* (anti-religious) – Phagwa celebrations are massive outdoor parties that represent a symbolic triumph of light over darkness and happiness over suffering. In Indian religious mythology, the festival commemorates the death of Holika, the sister of an evil king, Hiranyakashyapu, who repeatedly tried to murder his son Prahalad, because of his insistence on worshipping Vishnu as the only God. Immune to flames, Holika was persuaded to do the deed by carrying Prahalad into a fire, but the gods ensured that she burned to death; her brother was later slain by Vishnu. Holika's conflagration is re-enacted the night before the main festivities, when sins amassed in the previous year are ceremonially consumed by the flames of large bonfires.

The main festivities revolve around traditions such as the singing of devotional folk songs called **chowtals**, composed specifically for Phagwa to tell the story of the festival and accompanied by goatskin *dholak* drums and brass cymbals called *ghanj*. Local businesses sponsor *chowtal* competitions in the weeks preceding Phagwa, and the winners perform on the main day. The main focus of the festival, though, is an intense fuschia pink dye known as **abir**, which is strewn about as powder or mixed with water and squirted from a plastic bottle renamed a *pichakaaree*; participants wear white to make the most of the ensuing glorious mess. Accompanying the *abir* squirting are **pichakaaree songs**; topical ditties sung in a mix of English and Hindi which relate current issues to religious concepts, while classical Indian dancers display their movements and chutney soca fuels the more risqué dancing. Games add to the fun; adults participate in **makhan chor**, where teams form a human pyramid in order to grab a suspended flag, while children compete in roti eating contests, the source of much hilarity; skins are strung through the middle and tied in a line to be eaten; no hands are allowed.

Chaguanas hosts one of the largest celebrations in Trinidad, the **Kendra Phagwa Festival**, in an open space off Longdenville Old Road. There are other gatherings at Aranguez Savannah in San Juan and at Couva, but none is widely publicized – to find the exact date, you'll have to scan the community events listings in the newspapers, or call TIDCO (☎ 623 6022).

Hochoy Highway at the Endeavour overpass, just north of Chaguanas, is dominated by a 12-metre **statue of Swami Vivekananda**, a nineteenth-century Calcutta-based thinker held in high regard in Trinidad for his insistence that Indians should find freedom through education, technology and physical fitness.

For an explanation of the religious significance of Diwali, see p.47.

The complex was set up as a venue for traditional Indian festivals. In itself, the place consists of little more than the statue, a large fenced-off area, a portakabin office and a concrete structure where stalls can be set up. But during the many festivals that punctuate the Indian year – all of which are attended by many of the country's top dignitaries –

For exact
dates of
festivals at the
National
Council of
Indian
Culture, call
☎ 656 6733 or
671 6242.

the place is utterly transformed. The highlight of the year is **Diwali** (the festival of lights), nine days and nights of celebration at the end of October. All aspects of Indian culture in Trinidad are represented: the complex is decorated with paintings and statues of Hindu gods; every type of music, from Indian classical to chutney (the Indian version of soca) is played; and there are performances of Indian folk theatre and modern dramas. The stalls – more than sixty of them – provide a fascinating mix of culture and commerce: at the Hindu Credit Union a man in a Lakers basketball hat gives free palm readings, while stalls selling burglar alarms and furniture do a roaring trade alongside those packed with people trying to find their Diwali souvenir trinket.

Christian and Muslim Indians also have their own festivities at the site for Christmas and Eid-ul-Fitr (see p.48), while **Indian Arrival Day** (May 30) re-enacts the docking of the *Fatel Rozack*, which carried the first 225 Indian immigrants to Trinidad in 1845. Displays reveal the way of life and working conditions of the indentured labourers.

Eating and entertainment

There is no shortage of **fast-food outlets** in Chaguanas: along with *KFC*, *Royal Castle* and the like on Main Road, there is a plethora of roti and doubles stalls and Chinese food vendors on the two main streets. For something slightly more upmarket, there are also a few **restaurants**: *Eagles*, 44 Eleanor St, Chaguanas (Mon–Thurs 10am–10pm, Fri & Sat 10am–11pm), is a dark Chinese eatery serving inexpensive standard fare. The haunt of the Indian elite, glitzy *Kam Po*, opposite Mid Centre Mall at 55 Ramsaran Park (Mon–Thurs 11am–10pm, Fri & Sat 11am–11pm; ☎665 4558) has a hugely varied menu ranging from steaks to classic Chinese dishes – service is excellent, and there's even Tsingtao Chinese beer available. For the best Indian food in town, head to the canteen-style *Indo-Chinese Vegetarian Restaurant*, on Ramsaran Street, but across the road at no. 98 (Mon–Sat 10.30am–8pm). Delicious dishes include all kinds of roti, from sada to buss-up-shut, with all the fillings, as well as veggie burgers, won tons and spring rolls.

We've listed
phone
numbers only
for
restaurants
where you
might need to
book a table.

Chaguanas also has central Trinidad's only **nightclub**. The *Tunnel*, Ramsaran St (Mon–Thurs noon–midnight, Fri & Sat 10pm–4am; ☎671 4819), is a sports bar where pool and darts are played during the week. At the weekend it becomes a lively club playing dancehall, calypso and hip-hop to a young, mixed, entirely Trini crowd. Cover charges are minimal. Otherwise, you can take in a **movie**; the Jubilee, 13 Main Rd (☎665 5812) screens Bollywood films; and the Globe on Market Street (☎665 1463) shows new releases from the United States.

Felicity and the Chaguanas potteries

South of Chaguanas town, the buildings that line Southern Main Road (at this point known as the Felicity Main Road) thin out, and the tarmac is bordered to the left by acre upon acre of undulating sugar cane. To the right, backstreets lead into **Felicity Village**, an almost entirely Indian community where you'll see a mini-temple outside every other home. Come **Diwali**, Felicity residents are particularly lavish with their decorations; thousands of *deyas* (pottery lamps produced for the festival) as well as strings of fairy lights set off an incredible glow in the evening, and it's one of the best places on the island to take in the celebrations, with tassa drummers, Indian dancers and loads of delicious food to sample. As traffic slows to a standstill around here during Diwali, you'll need to park up fairly close to Chaguanas and walk to Felicity.

The west coast

Past Felicity, the Southern Main Road winds through a string of indistinguishable Indian communities, best seen at night when neon shopsigns flash innumerable garish colours over the traffic. As you pass through the otherwise unremarkable Edinburgh Village, look out for the ornate, white-painted **Edinburgh Temple** on the right, its walls, arches and turrets richly embellished with plaster reliefs and with a colourful shrine to Kali outside. Five kilometres south of Chaguanas, the Southern Main Road enters Chase Village, where a number of stalls line the road. These stand in front of the famous **Chaguanas potteries**, the oldest and most famous of which is Benny's Pottery Works (daily 7am–6pm; ☎671 1763), at the back of Radika's Pottery Shop. The thousands of *deyas*, windchimes, wall plaques, pots and ornaments on sale in the shop are all produced here by traditional Indian methods passed down from the present owner Sylvan Benny's grandfather, who learnt his craft in India.

Caribbean Discovery Tours (☎624 7281; see p.48) can arrange a tour of the interior of Edinburgh Temple, which includes a chat with the eloquent and interesting pundit.

It's a fascinating process to watch. The clay, dug from the nearby Carlsen Field (the site of a World War II US airbase), is soaked, and kneaded by foot to remove all stones and lumps. It is then hand rolled or shaped on a wheel before being fired in the large open kiln that dominates the centre of the workshop. Fuelled by wood, the kiln has no temperature gauge – the process relies entirely on the potter's experience and judgement. There is something for every budget in the shop, and if you can't see what you want, Sylvan Benny will make it for you.

Friendship Hall

A little further down the Southern Main Road on the eastern side, halfway between the sign for Chase Village and the turn-off to Waterloo Village, is the grandiose **Friendship Hall**. With its elaborate balconies, steep gables, corner turret and fanciful roofscape clad in rusting galvanized iron, it's a fine, if rather dilapidated, example of the estate houses that were common throughout Trinidad in the mid-nineteenth century. It was built in 1864 by a Scotsman, Hugh MacLeod, whose fascination with Indian imagery led him to create most of the house's ornate exterior plasterwork by hand. On his deathbed he bequeathed it to his estate agent, whose family still live there today. Though the house isn't open to the public, the owners will usually let you poke around the splendid exterior if you ask.

Waterloo and Waterloo Temple

*The mudflats
around
Waterloo are
excellent for
birdwatching,
with a rich
array of
waders feeding
here
throughout the
year. For
birdwatching
tours, contact
Paria Springs
or Caribbean
Discovery
Tours (see
p.48).*

About a kilometre south of Chase Village, the Orange Field Road cuts west off the Southern Main Road through the **Orange Valley Estate** to join the signposted Waterloo Road down to the sea. This is prime sugar territory: fields of cane stretch out on either side, and graceful royal palms tower over the road as they have done since the early plantation days, when the land was owned by the Tate and Lyle sugar company. Look out for an old and pretty former railway station on the right; now a post office, it's a remnant of the days when Waterloo was a stop on the Port of Spain–San Fernando train line. Passing through a cluster of neat bungalows built in the 1920s for estate managers, you come to sleepy **Waterloo Village**, where Hindu prayer flags flutter in the gardens next to trees with blue plastic bottles hanging from their branches – an old Trinidadian superstition to ward off maljo, or bad luck.

This superb drive culminates half a kilometre down the road where, as you emerge at the sea, you'll be greeted by an remarkable scene. Opposite an old Anglican cemetery where buffalo graze between the headstones, and a plot reserved for Muslim burials, the gleaming white, onion-domed **Waterloo Temple** stands on a pier, surrounded, at high tide, by fishing boats bobbing in the waters of the Gulf of Paria, or by extensive mudflats at low tide. The flatlands, the funeral pyres at the water's edge and the flags (*jhandes*) – representing prayers and offerings – flapping in the breeze, all contribute to the impression that you are standing by the River Ganges rather than on a Caribbean island.

*The Waterloo
Temple is open
on Saturday
and Sunday
from 7am to
7pm. The
grounds are
open daily
between 7am
and 7pm.*

In the middle of the car park outside the temple is a life-size statue of **Seedas Sadhu**, an Indian labourer to whose zeal and persistence the place owes its existence. Sadhu built the original temple on the seashore in 1947, but since the land was the property of the state sugar monopoly Caroni, the government bulldozed the structure five years later, and sent him to jail for fourteen days. Sadhu then decided to rebuild his temple in the sea, where no permission was required. A lonely, determined figure, he struggled single-handedly for the next 25 years to build the shrine, using a bicycle to carry the foundation rocks out into the water; at low tide he placed barrels on the sea floor and filled them with concrete. No sooner had he constructed one part of the building than the sea would erode his previous work, ensuring that the shrine was never completely finished.

Help finally came in 1994, when the 150th anniversary of the arrival of Indians in Trinidad inspired the government to declare the temple an Unemployment Relief Project (URP). With labourers paid by the state to rebuild the structure, the temple was swiftly completed. The octagonal shrine covers an area of more than 100 square metres, with coloured glass windows that enable you to see the brightly painted stone and marble gods inside. The pier – planted with hibiscus and bougainvillea – allows visitors to walk to the temple at all times (it was previously only accessible at low tide). The local Hindu community uses the temple for weddings and puja ceremonies, in which fruit and flowers are offered to the gods. Anyone can enter the temple, provided they remove their shoes first.

To get to the temple by **public transport**, take a route taxi from Chaguanas to the start of Orange Field Road (TT$2–3), where you pick up another taxi (TT$3) to the temple.

Inland to Ajoupa Pottery

Back on the Southern Main Road, a signposted left-hand turn-off 1km south of Orange Field Road takes you into Freeport, a relatively bustling little village. From here, another signposted minor road heads for **Chicklands**, a rural community that's home to the **Ajoupa Pottery** (☎673-0604; by appointment), producers of the distinctive, classy ceramics you'll see on sale in most of T&T's gift shops, decorated with beautiful, deep-coloured glazes and featuring all maner of local animal life – the lizards-on-a-plate series are worth looking out for, but they sell fast. A family-owned concern presided over by the friendly Bunty O'Connor, Ajoupa produce all their ceramics here in an open-sided workshop packed to the gills with mounds of plastic-covered clay, moulds and tray upon tray of pottery in various stages of completion. Tours are very informal, with a quick explanation of ceramic production from sourcing and blending clay to the exquisite glazing that Ajoupa is known for, and usually finish with a visit to the main house, a beautifully restored wooden former estate house. Inside is a small shop where you can buy the pottery – and pay far less than you would in Port of Spain.

Couva and around

Of the smoggy, industrial towns that line the west coast below Chaguanas, the liveliest is COUVA, with its beautiful old gingerbread houses gradually deteriorating on the main road. The **Holy Faith Convent**, on the northern side of the road beyond the police station, occupies a fine old colonial house originally built for a plantation overseer. As in many other parts of Trinidad, however, the old buildings are being torn down in favour of cheap, concrete structures: the old Anglican church at Couva junction, for example, has been marked for demolition to make space for a housing development.

Just south of Couva is **Brechin Castle Sugar Factory**, a blackened, smoke-spewing factory which processes most of the cane grown on the surrounding Caroni Plain, a vast belt of sugar cane fields. Owned by Caroni 1975, Ltd, it's a strangely compelling sight amongst the rolling, cane-covered hills and lines of graceful royal palms.

The nicest **restaurant** in Couva is *Bal Tar Zzar*, on the corner of Edgar Street and the Southern Main Road (Mon–Thurs 11am–10pm, Fri & Sat 11am–midnight; ☎636 1294) which serves standard, inexpensive Chinese fare. *Bougainvillea*, 85 Rivulet Rd, Brechin Castle (Mon–Sat 11am–10pm), is an intimate, comfy restaurant serving moderately priced Chinese dishes, steaks and seafood, as well as daily themed buffets: Spanish, Italian, Creole and such. The adjoining **bar** can get quite busy at the weekends.

Point Lisas

Just south of Couva is **California**, a drab residential suburb of the massive **Point Lisas Industrial Complex**, whose belching chimneys are already visible from the Southern Main Road. The complex was built as a flagship for the Trinidadian economy during the oil boom years of the 1970s, and no expense was spared in creating the factories, which produce liquefied natural gas, steel and fertilizers; the complex has the unfortunate distinction of being the largest exporter of fertilizer in the world. Industrial it may be, but Point Lisas still has its wildlife. Every year between December and June, thousands of **blue crabs** make the hazardous journey from the swampland beside the complex across the highway to lay their eggs in the sea. During these months, the only noise you're likely to hear as you drive past Point Lisas is the crunch of crabs under car wheels.

To get to Couva, take a Port of Spain–San Fernando **bus**, **maxi** or **taxi** and get them to drop you at the relevant exit on the Uriah Butler–Solomon Hochoy Highway, and then hail a route taxi and persuade the driver to take you to your destination. **Maxis** also run to Couva **from** San Fernando (main stand opposite the hospital).

Pointe-a-Pierre Wildfowl Trust

Past **Claxton Bay**, an industrial suburb cloaked in dust from the nearby cement factory, you come upon a stunning oasis of nature, located on the extensive grounds of the Petrotrin Oil Refinery at Pointe-a-Pierre. The only nature reserve in the Caribbean maintained by the oil industry, the **Pointe-a-Pierre Wildfowl Trust** came into being in 1966, when a hunter who worked at the refinery realized that wildfowl stocks were diminishing, and set aside an area within the complex to breed the birds. In time it became an established reserve, supported (though not financially) by the refinery.

The Wildfowl Trust consists of 250,000 square metres of attractively landscaped grounds around two lakes filled with waterlilies and lotus flowers. Many rare species of bird can be found here, including the wild **Muscovy duck**, the **red-billed whistling duck** and **white-cheeked pintail**. Some of the rarer birds, including **scarlet ibis**, are caged to allow breeding programmes to continue; the ibis breeding programme has been something of a landmark project, particularly as the released birds have chosen to stay on the site, allowing you the only chance you'll get in Trinidad to see wild ibis up close. (For details on visiting Caroni Swamp, home of the scarlet ibis, see p.184). The well-maintained learning centre at the entrance has good photographic displays of flora and fauna found on the reserve, a collection of shells and insect specimens, and a small collection of Amerindian artefacts, with a very informative account of the culture and belief systems of Trinidad's original inhabitants. The guides are vastly knowledgeable not only about the bird life, but also about the **medicinal qualities** of the indigenous plants: a chemical in the white periwinkle, for example, is used to fight leukaemia, while certain mango leaves are used to reduce nervous tension.

The Trust may be viewed **by appointment** only, to ensure that the birds are not scared away by overvisiting. To **drive** to the Trust from Port of Spain or San Fernando, leave the Uriah Butler–Solomon Hochoy Highway at the Gasparillo exit and follow the signs to the Petrotrin Oil Refinery. On **public transport**, take a Port of Spain–San Fernando maxi, route taxi or bus, and get out at the Gasparillo exit, from where the refinery is a two-minute walk. Once inside, it's another fifteen-minute walk to the Trust. The best time to visit is before 11am or after 3pm, as the animals hide in the shade during the hottest part of the day.

The few **hotels** around Pointe-a-Pierre cater mainly for oil workers and businessmen. For the widest choice of accommodation, your best bet is to stay in San Fernando (see pp.206–213), just a ten-minute drive away. If you're stuck, or want to stay near the Wildfowl Trust, the quiet, excellent-value *Mikanne*, 15 Railway Ave, Plaisance Village, Pointe-a-Pierre (☎ & fax 659 2584, *mikanne@tstt.net.tt*; ④), has TV, a/c and en-suite bathrooms in all rooms, a small swimming pool, sun lounge and an inexpensive restaurant. Unless you're with what Trini's call your "outside" man or woman, avoid *Reflections* guesthouse, just opposite the turning for *Mikanne*; rooms are rented strictly by the hour, and a computer-operated door system is in place – presumably to keep irate spouses at bay.

The west coast

The Pointe-a-Pierre Wildlife Trust is open Mon–Fri 8am–5pm, Sat & Sun 10am–4pm; contact Molly Gaskin (☎ 628 4145) or the office (☎ 658 4200, ext 2512, www.trinwetlands.org) forty-eight hours in advance for an appointment. Admission, including guided tour, is TT$5.

The Central Plains

The **Central Plains**, just one to two hours from Port of Spain, are an ideal place in which to enjoy Trinidad's countryside and escape from the city. Most of the island's sugar cane is produced here, and apart from **Piarco International Airport** and its immediate environs, the area is deeply rural. The plains are bounded to the south by the low, rolling **Montserrat Hills** (part of the Central Range), which shelter huge cocoa estates; on and around the hills, kilometres of protected rainforest enfold the grandeur of the **Arena** and **Navet dams** and **reservoirs**. There is little in the way of tourist infrastructure, but that's part of the charm: the area is perfect for peaceful afternoons, picnicking and watching wildlife.

Public transport is slow and difficult, and the only **accommodation** is located around the airport. The *Bel Air International* (☎ &
fax 669 4771, *belair@tstt.net.tt*; ⑥), a 1940s hotel close to the airport exit, is mostly frequented by in-transit passengers and businessmen. All rooms have a/c, phone and en-suite bathroom; there's a
swimming pool and a restaurant/bar with live entertainment on
Saturdays. During Carnival season breakfast is included. On the
approach road to the airport, the *Piarco International Hotel*, 8–10
Golden Grove Rd (☎669 3030, fax 669 1739, *piarcohotel@mailcity.com*; ⑨), is newer, with a pool, restaurant, three bars and comfortable rooms with all the amenities; airport shuttles are complimentary. The *Airport View Guesthouse*, opposite the gas station on
the main crossroads of the small village of St Helena (☎669 4186,
fax 669 5104; ④), provides free transport to and from the airport (a
ten-minute drive). Basic and rather dark but spacious and functional, all rooms have a/c, TV and en-suite bathroom, and there's a 10
percent discount for stays longer than a week.

Entertainment revolves around village rum shops, and if you are
not taking a picnic, **food** can be bought at the numerous fast-food
outlets at the airport in Piarco or at snack parlours along the roadside. Alternatively, street vendors in the villages sell roasted corn,
aloo pies, snow cones and doubles.

The Piarco area

Although best known for its airport, the **Piarco area** in the northwest
of the Central Plains is an overwhelmingly rural landscape of winding country roads and small villages. Piarco itself consists of very little except for the airport and a few small houses, the homes of the
airport workers. Established in 1931, **Piarco International Airport**
(*www.airporttnt.com*) is the base of British West Indian Airlines
(BWIA), fondly referred to as "Bee wee" by locals. The company was
set up during World War II to provide a transport route that avoided
the German submarines that prowled the Caribbean. Piarco has
recently been given a multi-million dollar facelift courtesy of a brand
new terminal, all glass roofs and state-of-the-art technology, which
has replaced the rather scruffy original. It was an expensive and
lengthy project, with opening dates continually put back as the
details were fine-tuned, but with loading bridges straight into the terminal and several more luggage carousels, arrivals and departures
are a far more hassle-free affair. As this book went to press, details
were still being worked out, but already in place are a food court,
currency exchange booth, taxi rank and car rental desks adjacent to
the arrivals area.

St Helena, a somnolent village 1km south of the airport, consists
of little more than a cluster of houses, but is slowly expanding as a
result of airport trade. On the outskirts by the airport you'll pass a
few traditional, whitewashed *tapia* houses, built of mud on a bam-

*For
information
on flights to
and from
Piarco
International
Airport see
p.65.*

boo frame, though most of these have now given way to concrete buildings. **San Rafael**, 9km to the east through a flat landscape of cane fields and citrus groves, is scarcely larger – a church, a school and a few old board houses. Its peaceful aspect hides a violent past, however. In 1699, the local Amerindians rebelled against Spanish missionaries' who tried to force them to convert to Christianity and use them as slave labour in the construction of churches. The Amerindians killed the priests, dumping their bodies into the foundations of the church, and then laid an ambush for the Spanish governor, José de León y Echales, and his party, whom they successfully captured and killed. In retaliation, the Spanish massacred the region's entire Amerindian population. Ironically, today a statue of St Raphael, the healer of all wounds, presides over the village's main junction in front of the church.

Waller Field, 9km to the northeast of St Helena, recalls more recent conflicts. When it was occupied by the Americans during World War II, this was the largest and busiest airbase in the world, but the hangars, barrack blocks and control rooms are long gone, and what's left of the airstrip is used for weekly drag racing. Further on, the plains are dotted with small villages. **Cumuto** is typical of the area: a quiet place with the odd bar and shop, it has declined since its heyday in the early twentieth-century when it was the centre of the region's large-scale cocoa cultivation. In the 1940s, the community was given a new lease on life by its proximity to the US base at Waller Field, but like Carenage (see p.114), its reputation suffered as the village became the playground for lonely young soldiers, and rumours of wild parties and immoral behaviour ran rife. Not all Trinidadians regard the US occupation as entirely negative, however; it is said that the money earned from the Americans during these years funded new housing developments in the region during the 1970s.

The Arena Dam and Reservoir

From San Rafael, Talparo Road runs south through serene rainforest where you'll rarely meet another car. This is the beginning of the area designated as the **Central Range Wildlife Sanctuary**, though you'd scarcely notice the first low foothills beneath the luxuriant vegetation, as bamboo thickets jostle with papaya, mango, banana, cashew and breadfruit trees. The blooms of the golden poui dominate the woodlands in April, while from December to March the magnificent immortelle trees blaze a fiery red. In the seventeenth century, the forests sheltered Amerindians fleeing Spanish persecution – many of the Amerindian artefacts in the National Museum in Port of Spain (see p.83) were found here.

Within the sanctuary, the **Arena Dam and Reservoir** (daily 9am–2pm) lie 9km west of Cumuto and 3.5km south of San Rafael on the Arena Road. They are well signposted by the Water and Sewerage

Waller Field and its surrounds offer some excellent birdwatching; you can also hike to the Cumuto to see an oilbird colony; for tours, call Paria Springs (☎ 622 8826).

Route taxis to St Helena and Piarco (TT$2) leave from Arouca Junction on the Eastern Main Road.

*Visiting
permits to the
Arena Dam
(TT$5.75)
must be
purchased in
advance from
WASA offices at
Farm Rd, St
Joseph (☎ 662
2302);
Southland
Mall, San
Fernando
(☎ 652 4492);
or Kew Place,
Port of Spain
(☎ 625 8568);
all offices are
open Mon–Fri
8am–4pm.*

Authority of Trinidad and Tobago (WASA), but the road is bumpy and, in local parlance, "mash up" – after heavy rains it is often impassable, so check with WASA before starting out. Built in 1975, the dam is an awesome 760 metres long, the largest in Trinidad after Navet (see p.198); the seven square kilometre reservoir it created provides 75 percent of the nation's water. It's a favourite weekend spot for families, with picnic tables, swings and climbing frames, but swimming is not allowed in the reservoir. The wildlife is astounding: **parrots**, **hawks** and **white egrets** fly around the dam; **blue emperor butterflies** flutter among the bamboo and settle on the reeds by the water's edge; **caimans** lurk in the swamps that border the reservoir, while **red howler** and **capuchin monkeys**, **toucans** and **tree porcupines** inhabit the surrounding forest.

There is no **public transport** to the Arena Dam; you can either book a **taxi** for the day from Arima or Port of Spain (around TT$150), or **rent a car** (see p.29).

The Montserrat Hills

South of the Arena Dam, the Central Range becomes more noticeable as you ascend through the forests into the rolling **Montserrat Hills**. The Talparo Road peters out after the village of Mundo Nuevo, where you have to detour westwards to skirt the highlands. This is real backwoods country, full of winding roads with rickety wooden bridges, small villages and run-down banana, cocoa and coffee plantations. The scenery is wonderful: the nineteenth-century English novelist Charles Kingsley, who visited the region in 1870, described "the panorama from the top of Montserrat" as "the most vast and most lovely which I have ever seen".

Most of the villages have little specific to recommend them apart from the odd picturesque colonial house, a few faded board houses, and a great deal of rural charm. Life focuses around the football field and the rum shop. Quiet during the day, these little places liven up in the evening, when people return from work and take a drink with their neighbours on street corners. The history of **Flanagin Town** is characteristic of central Trinidad's minor settlements. In the early years of the twentieth century, when it was surrounded by highly productive cocoa estates, the place bustled with labourers and traders who poured into its train station. But most of the estates have long since returned to the forest, their location marked only by the red blaze of the immortelles planted to shade the cocoa trees; the trains are long gone; and many of the youth have moved to the capital or down south to the oilfields. All that remains of Flanagin Town's prosperous past is the old stationmaster's house behind the community centre.

La Vega Estate
An experimental commercial nursery dedicated to cultivating exotic plants, with a few recreational activities for visitors as well, the **La**

Vega Estate (☎679 9522) lies about 7km west of Flanagin Town on the Couva Main Road, between Pepper Village and Gran Couva. The on-site nursery has the largest variety of ornamental plants in Trinidad, including fifty different species of **bougainvillea**, spiky-fruiting rambutan trees from Malaysia, and caryota plants, bedecked with distinctive mop-like tendrils. The whole estate covers about a square kilometre, of which nearly a quarter consists of exquisitely **landscaped gardens** devoted to public recreation. Guided tours (TT$15) and nature trails highlight the work of the estate and the variety of flora, and provide an opportunity to spot local wildlife such as **manicou**, **agouti** and **wild deer**. There are large ponds for **canoeing** and **fishing** (TT$20), a childrens' play area, a meditation space, bromeliad and Japanese gardens and picnic tables in sheltered bamboo groves.

Route taxis set out for La Vega Estate from KK Plaza at Couva (TT$4); they're rather infrequent, however. To get there by **car**, take the Gran Couva exit from Uriah Butler–Solomon Hochoy Highway and follow the road past Gran Couva for about twenty minutes.

The La Vega Estate is open daily 9am–5pm. Entry is free if you're here to shop; otherwise, it's TT$10 to picnic and to walk the signposted nature trail.

Tamana bat caves

The distinctive, flat-topped **Mount Tamana**, topping the Monserrat Hills at 308 metres, and visible from as far as the Northern Range, was created thousands of years ago when geological shifts pushed what was a coral reef out of the sea. Over the centuries, underground water flows eroded Tamana's porous limestone core, creating a series of lengthy **cave systems** which provide the perfect home for the huge colonies of **bats** that inhabit the caverns today. The gentle walk up Tamana's slopes is pleasant enough, threading through shady groves of lichen-covered cocoa trees and under giant silk cotton trees and moras, with the occasional eye-popping view over the Central Plains. However, the real draw here are the bats, which make a spectacular exit en masse at dusk to feed. It's best to arrive around 4pm, which gives you time enough to walk up and enter the first of the caves, peek at the ceiling – almost every inch is covered with roosting bats – and exit before the sun goes down. As dusk approaches, the first stragglers make their way out, and as the darkness thickens the trickle becomes an ever-increasing stream as Tamana's three million strong population of furry, flapping balls shoot past, the bats' sonar clicking away as they avoid flying into you.

Though it's bang in the centre of Trinidad, Tamana is easiest to reach from Sangre Grande in the northeast of the island (see p.199), via the Cunapo Road. From there, it's a precarious journey along winding, heavily potholed and landslide-wrecked minor roads, but as the route isn't signposted, and there's no easy way to find the path to the caves unless you know it, it's practically impossible to visit Tamana independently. Paria Springs (☎622 8826), Nature Seekers (☎668 7337; ask for Abbeyraj) and Caribbean Discovery Tours (☎624 7281) all offer guided trips; for more details on these operators, see "Basics", p.48.

*Route taxis for
Flanagin
Town, Tortuga
and
surrounding
areas leave
from
Chaguanas
Main Road.*

Tortuga

TORTUGA, which sprawls up the slope of the Montserrat Hills just fifteen minutes from the busy Uriah Butler–Solomon Hochoy Highway, is another collection of old board houses interspersed with the odd rum shop. At the top of the village stands the Catholic **Church of Our Lady of Montserrat**, a grand, green-painted wooden gingerbread house built in 1872 with a big gable and a graceful arcade. Inside are many old plaster statues, carved wooden Stations of the Cross and, to the left of the altar, a shrine containing a **Black Virgin**. The small statue, half a metre high and swathed in an over-sized white dress, was brought to the island by the early Capuchin missionaries.

From the church, you get an excellent view over the rolling plains of central Trinidad, with the distinctive, half-flattened San Fernando Hill in the distance (see p.211).

Navet Dam and Reservoir

*The Navet Dam
is open daily
9am–2pm.
Visiting
permits
(TT$5.75)
must be
purchased in
advance from
WASA offices.
See p.155 and
p.196 for
locations.*

South of Tortuga, you hit the Tabaquite Road, which runs eastwards along the southern slopes of the Montserrat Hills. Sugar cane, cocoa and coffee estates border the road, while the undulating slopes are clad in seemingly endless tropical rainforest. Past the tiny village of Tabaquite, you come to an abandoned **railway tunnel**; an attempt in the early 1990s to turn it into a recreation centre was defeated by vandalism and neglect. A few kilometres further on, the road edges up a valley towards the towering **Navet Dam**. Constructed in the early 1960s, the dam is 320 metres long, while the **reservoir** behind it forms an intricate pattern of inlets and coves, some 2km in length and 3km across at its widest point. With only the minuscule hamlet of Brasso Venado nearby, it's an isolated place, excellent for quiet picnics and birdwatching – many species of wildfowl frequent the reservoir in the early mornings and late afternoons.

The public facilities are not as good as those at the Arena Dam, however: just one picnic table and some toilets. Nor is there any **public transport** – your options are to make friends with a car-owning Trini, rent a car or book a taxi.

The east coast

South of **Sangre Grande**, the largest town on this side of the island and a transport hub of considerable commercial vigour, central Trinidad's **east coast** is dominated by the **Cocal**, four spectacular kilometres of unbroken sand, lined by grove upon grove of swaying coconut palms, that begins at **Manzanilla** and stretches south as far as Mayaro (see pp.232–234). The lure of the seashore and a slow but steady increase in tourism has ensured a couple of places to stay around Manzanilla Village, but otherwise, the area is pretty much devoid of human development. The Manzanilla–Mayaro Road runs the length of the beach, fringed inland by the pristine rainforest and mangrove-smothered wetlands of **Nariva Swamp**, a primary breeding ground and habitat for all manner of rare and exotic animals and birds.

The east coast is also the source of most of the **coconuts** sold in Trinidad. The coconut estates add to the breathtaking environment, with their deserted beaches and waving palms reminiscent of exotic film backdrops and high-class fashion magazines. Sadly, it is unlikely to stay this way for long as a result of the increased tourist trade, though its beach is less appealing for swimming, it will probably suffer less than Mayaro Bay. So far, though, the owners of the east coast coconut estates have declined to sell the property to hotel developers, and the beach and protected swamp retain their idyllic seclusion.

Sangre Grande

A thriving market town slung along the Eastern Main Road, **SANGRE GRANDE** ("big blood", after a long-forgotten battle) – pronounced "sandy grandy" but usually just called "grandy" – is the largest town in the east, a bustling transport depot and the only place in the region where you can get to a bank or ATM. Residents of surrounding villages crowd the pavements every Friday, descending to deposit their wage cheques, shop at the **market** stalls or take a fast food fix at the conglomeration of neon-flashing takeaway chains along the main street. Friday evenings see Grande at its liveliest, as wages are spent at the rum bars and roadside food stalls do a roaring trade in doubles, jerk chicken, corn soup and roti.

Maxis and route taxis from Sangre Grande to Manzanilla Beach cost about TT$8.

Most people pass through Sangre Grande to change taxis and maxis, and aside from the shopping, there's no real reason to spend much time here unless you need to stock up on food, fill your gas tank or exchange money. Most **route taxis** and **maxis** leave from the square behind *Royal Castle* in the middle of the main drag; ask around to find the correct queue. The banks and petrol stations (one of which is open until midnight) are also nearby along the main road.

The Cocal

South of Sangre Grande, the Eastern Main Road cuts a picturesque but sometimes rather hair-raising 8km toward the Cocal; underground waterflows regularly cause substantial subsidence below the tarmac, and if you're driving, take things slowly, as dangerous spots can be poorly signposted and the lavish verges and gorgeous gingerbread homes are a constant distraction. The collective name for the large coconut estates that line the Manzanilla–Mayaro Road, the **Cocal** offers an awe-inspiring drive – 24km of graceful, leaning

*Mayaro village
and beach are
covered in
Chapter Four,
pp.233–234.*

coconut trees dancing in the wind, with unspoilt, wave-pounded beach to one side and preserved rainforest and wetlands to the other. If you're lucky you may see an experienced coconut picker climbing up and down a tree in the flash of an eye. The docile long-horned animals grazing between the coconuts at the edge of the road are **buffalypso**, kept for their meat and milk. The result of selective breeding of water buffalo, they are highly profitable; a farmer can raise four of them for the same cost as one cow, and each will command a higher price than a cow at market.

Nearing Mayaro, the road runs past a small grove of huge coconut palms, their nuts processed at a plant recognizable by the huge mounds of husks that surround it. After miles of bendy, leaning palms, these tall upright specimens stand out in firm resolution against the sea breeze that whips in constantly from the Atlantic; the palm-thatch fences that border the road in parts are not windbreaks, but an attempt to combat theft of the coconuts. Between 5.30pm and 6pm every night the air is raucous with the calls of the **red-chested macaws** that come to roost in the trees (telescope-toting birdwatchers usually mark the spot), while the surrounding swampland is a popular spot for southern lapwing and the rare red-breasted tanager. The ponds in this area are full of **cascadura** (also known as cascadoo), a small brown freshwater fish, properly known as an armoured catfish, with a tough skeletal covering. They can be spotted by circles appearing on the pond surface, and are caught on a line or by using nets. It's said that if you eat their chewy brown, tuna-like meat (invariably served curried), you'll return to end your days in Trinidad, but it's a messy business as you have to pick and suck the flesh from beneath the armour.

There are no hotels or restaurants anywhere along the road between Manzanilla and Mayaro, but there are a few stalls selling the shellfish known as chip-chip, while young boys and men sell freshly caught crabs, black conch, fish and, in season, watermelon by the roadside.

Coconuts

Grown on estates throughout eastern Trinidad, **coconuts** are in constant demand on account of their sheer versatility. Depending on when they are harvested, they can be a source of drink, food, flavouring, oil, soap and animal feed, while their fibrous husk makes an alternative to peat for potting plants. Green young nuts are full of sweet **water**, a popular drink sold fresh from the fruit from many an old Bedford van around the country. As the nut matures, much of the liquid is replaced by an edible white **jelly**. A few weeks later, the jelly solidifies into firm white flesh, which can be grated, dried and roasted in cooking. Later still, a bread-like substance grows in the centre of the fruit; if caught at the right time, it makes a tasty snack. Soon afterwards, it develops into a sprout, from which a new tree will grow. Depending on the type, a tree will take five to ten years to mature; it will live for many years, and produce nuts all year round.

Manzanilla

A quiet and attractive village strewn with gingerbread houses at the northern end of the Cocal, **MANZANILLA** is divided into Upper and Lower sections, interspersed with lush swathes of coconuts, banana and mango trees. The section of **beach** near to the village is the most popular part of the whole four-kilometre stretch; if you're after a swim, go through Upper Manzanilla along the Eastern Main Road and turn left opposite Plum Mitan Road. After passing a handful of small groceries and rum shops, you'll find yourself on the seashore, at the beginning of the Manzanilla–Mayaro Road. Behind the first stretch of beach is an open tract of land that's been cleared for development by the owners of *Calypso Inn* (see below), and is used as an impromptu car park when beach parties take over the main one.

South of here, the beach runs the whole length of the east coast, with only the odd decrepit building interrupting palm groves that line the wide, expansive stretch of fine, brownish-grey sand. Windswept and exposed, Manzanilla is usually deserted during the week, but becomes a popular swimming spot at the weekends. The water is often quite bracing, and you should take care while swimming as the undercurrents can be dangerous. The beach has experienced something of a renaissance in recent years; TIDCO have put in changing and showering facilities at the northern end (daily 10am–6pm; TT\$1) as well as a car park that rivals Maracas in capacity. Manzanilla is fast overtaking Maracas as the island's most popular Ash Wednesday chill-out spot, as well as a venue for massive Easter beach parties, with more space for the crowds of revellers to sunbathe or dance to the sound systems that set up in the northern section. Beyond the northern section, there are no facilities at all.

If you want to **stay** near Manzanilla Beach, there are a couple of options. *Calypso Inn* is closest to the sand (☎678 2315 or 668 5113, fax 668 5116; ⑤), at the end of a dirt track at the extreme northern corner of the beach. Beautifully located on a stretch of beach protected by the headland separating Manzanilla from Matura Beach (see p.169), the hotel has smart double rooms with a/c, TV and a balcony overlooking the sea. There's a bar and restaurant with outdoor and indoor eating and drinking areas (good for lunch even if you're not staying), and hammocks slung between the seashore palm trees. A less expensive option is *Dougies* (☎668 1504; ②), a large block of rooms adjacent to a rum bar and grocery, and a five-minute walk from the beach in Lower Manzanilla. Basic rooms have fan and private bathroom, but self-contained two-bedroom apartments with full facilities are also on offer; the place is friendly and the rum shop is a lively liming spot after dark.

Brigand Hill Lighthouse

Built in 1958, the stubby white **Brigand Hill Lighthouse** (8am–5pm; free) is one of only three in Trinidad. It's not possible to enter the

If you're planning to visit Manzanilla for the Ash Wednesday or Easter beach parties, try to get there early – it's not unknown for the traffic jams to start as far back as Valencia.

To visit
Brigand Hill
Lighthouse,
large groups
and those with
young children
need first to
gain
permission
from the
Ministry of
Works
Maritime
Services
(☎ 625-3858).

lantern itself, though you can climb the twenty-odd iron stairs that run up the outside for a magnificent view from Toco in the north to Galeota Point in the south, taking in the Central Plains towards the Northern Range, and the flatlands of Nariva Swamp. Red howler monkeys inhabit the trees around the lighthouse, and if you're lucky you'll see a troop passing by. To reach the lighthouse from Manzanilla, take the Plum Mitan Road off the Eastern Main Road after Upper Manzanilla, and turn off at the signpost. It's a steep climb; a hard thirty-minute walk or a five-minute drive. A word with the security guard will gain you entry at the gate.

Nariva Swamp

One of Trinidad's most significant wildlife areas, the internationally recognized wetland of **Nariva Swamp** covers 15 square kilometres behind the coconut estates along the coast south of Manzanilla. The area is made up of agricultural land (rice and melons are the main crops) as well as reed-fringed marshes, eerie mangroves between the Mayaro–Manzanilla Road and the swamp and, deep in the south-western corner of the swamp, **Bush Bush Island**, actually a peninsula standing around three metres higher than the surrounding land, bordered by palmiste and moriche palms and covered in hardwood forest and silk cotton trees. Nariva isn't really explorable independently (in any case, you need a permit to enter; see opposite), but if you're just passing by, it's worth taking a stroll along one of the paved roads that swing in from the Manzanilla–Mayaro Road, connecting the residential **Kernaham Village** with the coast. Reachable via the signposted Kernaham Trace, the village is little more than a widely dispersed collection of picturesque board houses, most on stilts, that are home to a friendly, overwhelmingly Indian community of small-scale rice farmers and fishermen. It's a beautiful scene, with the flatlands opening up huge expanses of open sky. Most of the homes and cultivated areas are on the edge of the swamp; further in is a unique freshwater ecosystem that harbours large concentrations of rare **wildlife**, with some 58 species of mammals, 37 species of reptiles, and 171 species of birds. The swamp also harbours 92 species of mosquito, so remember to bring your insect repellent.

The 1996 **Ramsar Convention** – to which Trinidad and Tobago is a signatory – designated the swamp a wetland of international importance, placing a legal obligation on the government to ensure the area is protected and maintained. In an area of low employment, however, it is not always easy to reconcile human economic needs with the demands of conservation. Many people turn to hunting as a means of subsistence, and large-scale illegal rice farming has destroyed some of the habitat. The government eventually expelled the big rice farmers after pressure from environmentalists, but small-scale cultivation continues. In addition, **bush fires**, often deliberately set by farmers to clear land, have ravaged almost half the territory in recent years, and as a result, access is often prohibited during the dry season.

Nariva is the only place in Trinidad to see the cute but threatened **manatee** or sea cow, a peculiar elephantine mammal that once fuelled rumours of mermaids lurking in the brackish depths. These shy, bizarre creatures can grow up to three metres in length, weigh over 900 kilograms, and live in freshwater ponds, where they feed off water hyacinth, moss and waterlilies. They are currently in danger of extinction: in the 1970s hundreds inhabited the swampland, but their numbers are now down to around fifteen as a result of increased human activity in the area. The swamp is also an excellent place to view **caimans**, **freshwater turtles**, **red howler monkeys** (whose rather alarming, otherworldly roars reverberate around the forest), white-fronted **capuchin monkeys** (which have been known to shower human intruders with a hail of twigs), three-toed and silky **anteaters**, **opposums**, **porcupines** and a wide variety of birds including **savannah hawks**, **dicksissels**, **orange-winged parrots** and the **yellow-capped Amazon parrot**. Its most alarming inhabitants, however, must be the **anacondas**, reputedly washed here from South America on the current of the Orinoco River. These terrifyingly large greenish-brown, black-spotted snakes grow up to nine metres long; they're the heaviest reptiles in the world, and the largest in the Americas.

If you want to visit the sanctuary, you must first obtain a free permit from the **Wildlife Division** of the **Forestry Department** in St Joseph or in Port of Spain; the division will advise you about which guides to contact. Alternatively you can ring the guides directly; they will get the passes for you and organize your trip. For those with a more amateur environmental interest, a limited budget and desire to gain some knowledge about the human residents of the area as well as the wildlife, South East Eco Tours (☎644 1072) offers excellent, well-rounded day-trips involving hikes into the swamp, boat rides up the nearby Ortoire River, lunch with local residents and trained guides from the local community. Caribbean Discovery Tours (☎624 7281) offers a marvellous Nariva trip, with a walk through Bush Bush, kayaking if water levels permit and an excellent Indian lunch cooked by residents of Kernaham Village and served in a private home. If you're a serious ornithologist, opt for the excellent birding tours offered by Paria Springs (☎622 8826).

Permits for entry to Nariva Swamp are available from the Forestry Department's Wildlife Division on Farm Road, St Joseph (☎662 5114) and Long Circular Road, Port of Spain (☎622 4521). Both offices open Mon–Fri 8am–4pm.

San Fernando and the south

Geographically, Trinidad's **south** presents a mirror image of the north: a long littoral extending beyond the main body of the island, with the low ridge of the forested Southern Range

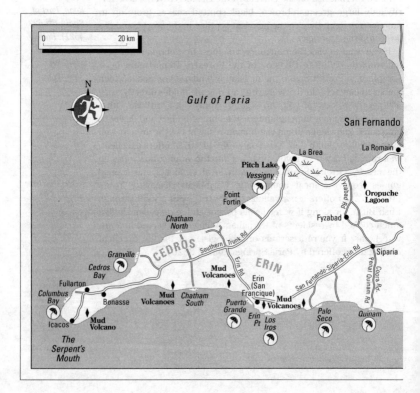

as its spine. In the Gulf of Paria, where the southwest peninsula crooks a finger towards Venezuela, Trinidad's second city, precipitous **San Fernando**, sits at the base of its oddly shaped landmark hill.

That's as far as the comparison goes, however; San Fernando is a serious, booming business town, but beyond its city limits the region is the most sparsely populated in Trinidad. Although many inhabitants still earn a living from agriculture – mainly sugar and rice – and from fishing, the economy is based around **oil**. This, ironically, is what has left the region so unspoilt; with its well-paid jobs, oil money means that the local population do not have to pander to the tourist dollar – a refreshing experience for holidaymakers in the Caribbean. In addition, the petroleum business leases large expanses of forest from the government; these remain largely undeveloped apart from a few discreet oil pumps.

Most of the land is covered with untouched rainforest – an environmentalist's dream. In the deep **southeast**, the protected rainforest of the **Trinity Hills Wildlife Reserve** shelters countless species of bird and exotic mammals such as the ocelot, while the **Oropuche Lagoon** on the southwest coast is a wildlife-rich mangrove swamp seldom vis-

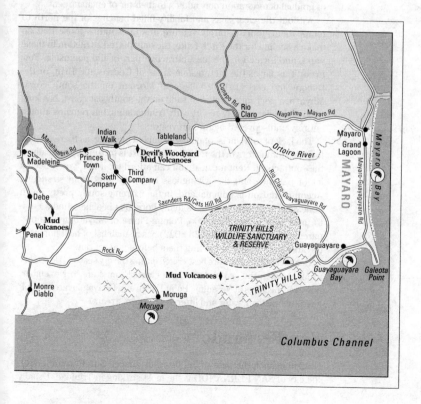

ited by tourists. Development is never far away, though, and in the built-up areas, the architecture, like elsewhere in Trinidad, is changing rapidly – brand new out-of-town malls are springing up all over the place – but many old colonial gingerbread buildings remain, their state of gradual deterioration only adding to their air of enchantment.

Without the clear seas and facility-filled beaches of the north to tempt them, tourists rarely venture this far south – those that do make a beeline for the **Pitch Lake**, the only potted attraction in these parts, and located in the least attractive part of the peninsula. Few make it as far as the picturesque areas of **Cedros** and **Erin**, or the remote and eerie fishing village of **Moruga** on the south coast. **Mayaro**, a gorgeous swathe of sand on the southeast coast, has long been a popular holiday resort with Trinidadians, but remains almost entirely undiscovered by foreign visitors.

The lack of tourism is, of course, a mixed blessing, as there are few facilities for visitors in the region. **Transport** is tortuous, especially to the south coast. Rent a car, if you can afford to; if not, you'll need a lot of patience and the willingness to accept lifts from strangers. **Accommodation** is minimal and, in the extreme south, pretty much nonexistent, despite the area's many gorgeous beaches; find a comfortable base in San Fernando, Point-a-Pierre or Mayaro and be prepared to travel. TIDCO (☎623 6022) has a small list of host homes in the area – it's worth contacting them before you set out.

Beaches in the south are best visited during the dry season (December to May) when the sea and sand are clear. From June to November, however, beaches at Vessigny, Point Fortin and Guayaguayare are polluted by brackish water and litter swept downstream.

San Fernando

Nestled against the base of the bizarrely shaped **San Fernando Hill**, the city of **SAN FERNANDO** is the most striking in Trinidad. Usually referred to as the industrial capital of Trinidad and Tobago, it has an old-fashioned charm that comes as some surprise. Its steep streets and sea views are reminiscent of a miniature, low-key San Francisco, while a warren of old winding lanes are studded with charming gingerbread buildings that have survived the city's rapid development in recent years.

San Fernando – usually referred to as "**Sando**" by Trinis – is far quieter than Port of Spain; life moves at a slower pace, there are fewer people on the streets, and the interaction between them is far friendlier. Long ignored or belittled by the capital for which it, in turn, has scant regard, San Fernando has always maintained an independent spirit. It is scarcely promoted as a tourist destination; a commercial city first and foremost, it gets many business visitors but few sightseers. You will be overwhelmed by local attention, although there is no need to feel intimidated; it is entirely well meant.

San Fernando has plenty of **restaurants**, **shops** and the odd **nightclub**. It is the hub of the region's **transport** system, just one hour's drive from the beaches of the south coast.

Some history

Amerindian legends, dating back to 8000 BC, emphasize the sacred nature of San Fernando Hill. It was the final resting place of **Haburi the Hero** and his mother, who were fleeing from the **Frog Woman** in the Orinoco Delta in Venezuela. They reached Trinidad safely, only to be turned into "**Anaparima**", the original Amerindian name for the mount. Amerindian tribes from the South American mainland made an annual pilgrimage to the site from 6500 BC to the early 1900s.

The settlement's first European contact was the arrival of **Sir Walter Raleigh** in 1595 – he was unimpressed and sailed on. Nearly a hundred years later in 1687, **Capuchin priests** established a mission here. However, it was between the years of 1784 and 1792 that the settlement began to flourish. French plantation owners attracted by the *cedula* of 1783 (see p.328) were allocated land in the area, and established the first estates. In 1784, José Maria Chacon, the last Spanish governor of Trinidad, renamed the town San Fernando de Naparima in honour of King Carlos III's new son. By 1797, when the British captured the island, San Fernando had more than a thousand inhabitants, twenty sugar mills and eight rum distilleries. Surrounded by fertile agricultural land, the town continued to grow, and by 1811 the population had trebled. In 1846, "Sando" was officially recognized as a town.

San Fernando became the **hub of the south**, a busy trading centre for successful planters, with a regular coastal steamer to Port of Spain – the overland route took three days of rough riding through forests and swamps. The arrival of the **railway** in 1882 led to another population increase, and by the late 1880s San Fernando had been thoroughly modernized. Suburbs grew as the plantations disappeared – the result of falling sugar prices in the 1920s – and the town

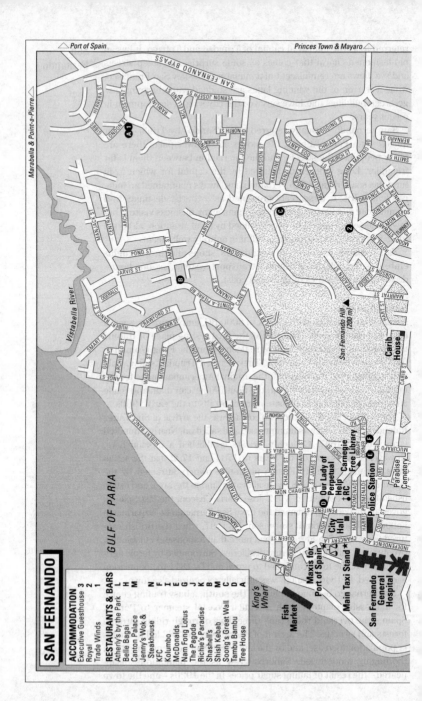

SAN FERNANDO

ACCOMMODATION
Executive Guesthouse 3
Royal 2
Trade Winds 1

RESTAURANTS & BARS
Atherly's by the Park L
Belle Bagai H
Canton Palace M
Jenny's Wok &
Steakhouse N
KFC F
Kolumbo I
McDonalds E
Nam Fong Lotus G
The Pagoda J
Richie's Paradise K
Shashell's B
Shish Kebab M
Soong's Great Wall C
Tambu Bambu D
Tree House A

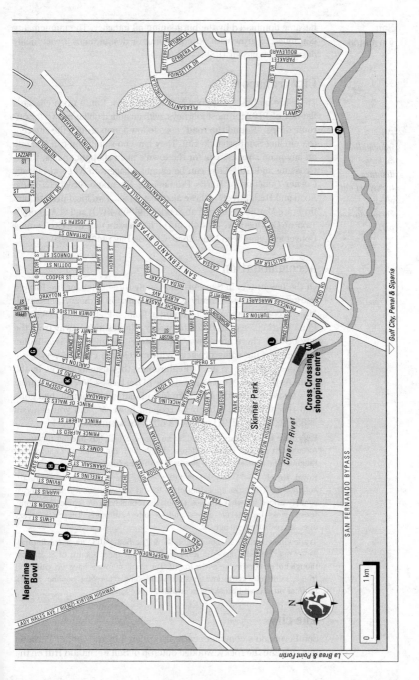

Naparima Bowl

Cross Crossing shopping centre

Skinner Park

Cipero River

SAN FERNANDO AND THE SOUTH

209

became dominated by the burgeoning oil industry. The municipality continued to grow with little planning or design, until it was finally designated a city in 1988.

City transport

There are no buses or maxis in San Fernando. **Route taxis** charge a flat fare of TT$2 for most journeys, with an added dollar or two for off-route drops. "**Round the road**" taxis follow a loop around the city centre, circling San Fernando Hill. They have no stand; you can hail one on any main street. Taxis for the town's main shopping malls, **Cross Crossing** and **Gulf City**, can be caught adjacent to *KFC* on **Library Corner** (junction of Harris Promenade, Mucurapo Street, La Pique Road and High Street) – these also cost TT$2. Two local **private taxi** firms are Mattadeen's Taxicab Service (☎658 4973) and St Anthony's Taxicab Co-Operative (☎648 3941). If you want to **rent a car**, contact Convenient, Southern Main Road, Claxton Bay (☎659 3015).

For information on long-distance transport out of San Fernando, see p.216.

Accommodation

Of the few **hotels** in San Fernando, only three cater for the foreign market – and these mainly geared toward oil industry personnel. More accommodation can be found in Point-a-Pierre (see p.192) and Point Fortin (see p.223), ten to twenty minutes' drive away from the city centre. There are a few "love hotels" designed for Trinidadian couples seeking some privacy. With motel-style chalets, very basic facilities and nonstop music in all rooms, they usually charge by the hour. As this book went to press, one of the largest hotels in the area, *TJ's by the Sea* on the Southern Main Road in La Romain, had gone into receivership; it's likely to reopen, however, and you can call ☎657 9278, or TIDCO on ☎623 6022 for an update.

Executive Guesthouse, 11 Todd St; no phone. Small, box-like but functional rooms with painted concrete floors, double bed, fan, toilet and shower, all ranging off a central corridor plastered with rules for guests. ③.

Royal Hotel, 46-54 Royal Rd ☎652 4881, fax 652 3924, *www.royal-hoteltt.com*. The most appealing place to stay in town, comfortable and reasonably priced for what you get: the bright rooms have a/c, cable TV, phone, fridge, jacks for internet access and en-suite bathrooms. There's a breezy open-air restaurant on site. ⑥.

Tradewinds Hotel, 38 London St ☎ & fax 652 9463, *www.tradewind-shotel.net*. Friendly place on a breezy hill in the quiet suburb of St Joseph, though not as good value as the *Royal*. The smallish rooms have a/c, cable TV, fridge, mini bar, kettle and en-suite bathrooms. There's a popular restaurant/bar on site, and breakfast is included in the rates. ⑥.

The city

San Fernando's compact centre is bordered by the Gulf of Paria on one side and the rocky, wooded outcrop of **San Fernando Hill** on the other. Most of the historical sights, shops and transport stands are located on and around the **Harris Promenade**, a broad, elegant boulevard running west from the foot of the hill. The wider urban area is defined by two main roads, **Lady Hales Avenue** (also known as Rienzi-Kirton Highway), which skirts the coast, and the **San Fernando Bypass** inland. The environs, such as the well-to-do suburb of **St Joseph Village**, sprawl up the slopes of San Fernando Hill, while more recent developments such as **Pleasantville** and the large shopping malls are located on the outskirts, beyond the bypass.

San Fernando Hill

At 200 metres high, **San Fernando Hill** overshadows the town centre. For many years the hill was quarried to provide gravel for the building of the city's streets, giving it its strange profile – half the hill is flattened with steep protruding points, while the other half maintains its natural outline. In 1980 it was declared a national park, providing a pleasant recreation area with picnic tables, planted flowers, a childrens' playground, a fountain, public toilets and several lookouts from which to enjoy the panoramic views. The clearly signposted road to the summit lies next to *Soong's Great Wall* restaurant. Though you can drive a car to the top, it's only a twenty-minute walk, or ten if you take the footpaths – popular with young couples and dog walkers – that provide a shortcut. Once at the top you get a good view of San Fernando, Tarquaba Bay and the flaming Petrotrin chimneys, or, to the other side, across the undulating sugar cane flats and agricultural plains of the interior.

*San Fernando
Hill road is
open daily
9am–6pm.*

Harris Promenade and around

The centre of civic life and the location of San Fernando's official buildings is the **Harris Promenade**, named after the British governor of Trinidad from 1846 to 1854, running from the long 1950s facade of **San Fernando General Hospital** to Library Corner in the east. It consists of two parallel streets with a paved centre lined with benches and tables, the odd statue and an ornate Victorian bandstand. Like the Brian Lara Promenade in Port of Spain (see p.77), it's been beautified to provide a pleasant hang-out for the city's residents, but is more picturesque than its equivalent in the capital, lined with attractive colonial buildings.

On the south side of the promenade towards its western end stands an old-fashioned, round-arched yellow stone building reminiscent of an English parish church or country mansion – the bright blue postmodern extension behind it more accurately reflects the building's function as the city's **police station**. Across the road, the grand neoclassical **City Hall** was built in 1930, and dominates the western end of the promenade – though it faces stiff competition from the Catholic **Church of Our Lady of Perpetual Help** one block to the east, a huge white modern building with a tall clock tower that can be seen from most places in the city. The interior is unusually stark for a Catholic place of worship.

At the centre of the promenade is the **Mahatma Gandhi Statue**, brought to Trinidad in 1952 from India. On Gandhi's birthday (October 2), the day of his death (January 30) and Diwali (see p.47), the local Gandhi Seva Sang Organization holds a commemorative service on the promenade below the statue. The aspirations of the Afro-Caribbean population are acknowledged by a brightly painted statue of Jamaican black rights activist **Marcus Garvey** at the eastern end of the promenade, typical of Trinidad's more modern monuments.

Here, the promenade's two roads converge, in front of the **Carnegie Free Library**, a large, ornate terracotta building built in 1919 and financed – like many others the world over – by the Scottish philanthropist Andrew Carnegie. In front of the library, an old **steam locomotive** recalls the last run from Port of Spain to San Fernando in 1968. People packed the carriages, hanging out the windows to be part of this historic occasion, which was subsequently immortalized by the late Lord Kitchener's famous calypso *Last Train to San Fernando*. Engine 11, which stands on the promenade today, is not the actual machine that pulled the last train, but one of the last to be used by the sugar estates. The chaotic junction of seven roads just beyond the library is known as **Library Corner**. At its centre stands a modern four-faced clock, of which only one face is currently working. This spot is a popular rendezvous – "meet meh library corner" is a common refrain among the city's residents.

Walking down the **High Street** from Library Corner brings you into the busiest part of town. This is San Fernando's main shopping street, lined with clothes stores and shops selling household goods, while street vendors hawk plastic trinkets and leopardskin underwear on the pavement. At its southern end, as the High Street doglegs into Queen Street, the sea comes into view. The area, ironically known as **Happy Corner**, is the most run-down in the city, but a few renovated colonial buildings give some architectural interest, while the patrons of the local rum shop add a touch of raffish life. Happy Corner gives on to **King's Wharf**, a scruffy tarmac dock lined with dilapidated wood and galvanized iron huts overlooking a small harbour where fishing boats bob up and down on the swell. In the **fish market**, a plain whitewashed building that has changed little since it was built in 1924, the fishermen gut, clean and sell their catch – snapper, kingfish and shark, alongside the occasional deep-sea monster.

Carib Street and "The Coffee"

To the south of San Fernando Hill runs **Carib Street**, fringed by ramshackle old colonial houses. Though less picturesque than its wooden neighbours, the stuccoed **Carib House** – on the corner of Upper

---

Dining prices

Each restaurant listed in this guide has been categorized according to the following grades: **budget** (under TT$25); **inexpensive** (TT$25–70); **moderate** (TT$70–150); **expensive** (TT$150+). These ratings relate to the price for a starter and main course.

Hillside Street and Carib Street – is the oldest in San Fernando, an eighteenth-century Spanish colonial building. Despite its age, there is no plaque or sign indicating its history or date of construction.

The Skiffle Bunch and Fonclaire panyards are usually open after 4pm from November until Carnival – ask someone local for the time of the next rehearsal.

Coffee Street, which turns off Carib Street towards the south, takes its name from the coffee plantations that once grew here. "The Coffee" – as the street is familiarly known – was the original home of many of the south's **steel bands**, including the highly acclaimed **Fonclaire**, led by inimitable panman Ken Professor Philmore. A brightly painted statue of a pan player at the junction with Cipero Street celebrates the area's musical heritage. A little further down on the left is the **Skiffle Bunch** panyard. Behind a small empty patch of rough ground, a narrow decaying building houses the pans, and the crumbling walls that flank the open space are decorated with frescoes. Known as the **Dancing Walls**, these fading images were painted in 1994 by local artist Glen Steel. The animated figures – executed in spiky black outline – capture the energy and excitement of the steel band as they trace its development from the tamboo bamboo of the 1940s (see p.342) to the present day. Interwoven with the pan players are traditional Carnival characters such as Jab Molassis and the sailors (see p.334). The panyard itself, a big open space hung with bunting and strings of lights, is at the back, and doubles as the parking lot for the Southern Food Basket grocery across the road. The Coffee is particularly lively during the run-up to Carnival, when practice sessions ring out into the street; it's an excellent time to be in the area.

Eating

There are few **restaurants** in San Fernando, most of them serving reasonably priced international cuisine or ever-popular Chinese food. If you fancy something different (pizza, pasta or felafel alongside easy-access Creole, Indian and Chinese), head for the expansive food court of Gulf City Shopping Complex.

Atherly's by the Park, 104 Gooding Village, near Cross Crossing Shopping Centre. Roadside diner close to Skinner Park with an air-conditioned main room and a couple of tables outside, serving solid, reliable Creole and Indian dishes. Daily 10am–late. Inexpensive.

Belle Bagai, 20 Gransaul St. Nice place for lunch or for dinner and drinks, with a simple menu of snacks – wontons, fish and chips, burgers – as well as more substantial steaks or fish dishes. Good service and relaxed atmosphere in a pretty, old colonial house. Mon–Sat 3pm–late. Inexpensive/Moderate.

We've listed
phone
numbers only
for
restaurants
where you
might need to
book a table.

Canton Palace Restaurant, Cross Crossing Shopping Centre, Lady Hales Ave ☎652 5993. Large Chinese restaurant with pleasant decor, recommended for its crab and pepper shrimp. Takeaway available. Mon-Sat 11am-10pm. Inexpensive/Moderate.

Jenny's Wok & Steakhouse, 175 Cipero Rd ☎652 1807. Opulent fine dining establishment serving Chinese food, steaks and seafood. Mon-Thurs 11am-10pm, Fri & Sat 11am-11pm. Expensive.

Kolumbo Restaurant, 34 Sutton St ☎653 7684. International cuisine with gourmet burgers and patés. Set in a restored colonial building, this stylish restaurant is very romantic at night, with live piano music on the upper level. Also serves afternoon tea. Mon-Sat 11am-10pm. Moderate.

Nam Fong Lotus Restaurant, 91-93 Cipero St ☎652 3356. Serves huge Chinese lunches and dinners at inexpensive prices. A relaxing, comfy and more upmarket atmosphere than the usual plastic tables. Mon-Sat 10am-10pm. Inexpensive.

The Pagoda, 59 Independence Ave ☎657 6375. Cosy restaurant serving usual Chinese fare; the steamed fish is recommended. Mon-Thurs 10.30am-10pm, Fri & Sat 10.30am-10.30pm. Inexpensive.

Royal Hotel Restaurant, 46-54 Royal Rd ☎652 4881. Typical in-hotel restaurant serving Creole and international breakfasts, sandwiches at lunch, and steak or fish dinners, all on a pleasant patio. Mon-Sun 6am-10pm. Moderate.

Shish Kebab, Top Floor, Cross Crossing Shopping Centre, Lady Hales Ave ☎652 4069. Intimate restaurant decorated in cosy Mediterranean style, serving creative international cuisine from kebabs to steaks and seafood platters. Mon-Sat 11am-10pm. Expensive.

Soong's Great Wall, 91 Circular Rd ☎652 9255. High-quality Chinese food - as well as the obligatory steak dinners – served in an ornate pagoda-shaped building with some outdoor seating. Buffets each Wednesday. Mon-Thurs & Sun 11am-10pm, Fri & Sat 11am-10.30pm. Moderate/Expensive.

Tambu Bambu Restaurant, 778 High St ☎657 2435. Huge, satisfying Creole buffet meals in dark dining area. Mon-Sat 9.30am-4pm. Budget.

Tree House, 38 London St ☎653 8733. Pleasant, friendly place inside the *Tradewinds Hotel* that's a popular haunt amongst locals, ranged over a plant-bedecked balcony overlooking the city. Food is reliably good and the menu varied, from crab backs and shrimp bruschetta to seafood, steaks and Mexican and Cajun dishes. Open very early for local and international breakfasts; reservations recommended for dinner. Mon-Thurs 4am-10pm, Fri-Sun 4am-2am. Moderate/Expensive.

Nightlife and entertainment

Clubs and **nightspots** are fairly limited in San Fernando, but there are plenty of **rum shops** to choose from, with loud music and lively conversations. Since *TJ's by the Sea* hotel went into receivership, its *Submarine Club*, formerly one of the area's liveliest spots, has been closed; it's worth calling ☎653 2980 to see if it has reopened.

Atherly's by the Park, 104 Gooding Village, near Cross Crossings Shopping Centre. Popular, friendly bar that's good for a low-key drink, either in the softly lit a/c indoor section, or at the tables outside. DJ plays a nice selection of calypso, reggae and old hits nightly. Daily 10am–late.

Belle Bagai, 20 Gransaul St ☎657 5353. Elegant bar/restaurant in a wooden gingerbread house, all creaky floorboards and polished mahogany. Good for a low-key lime or a game of pool; Fridays and Saturdays are busiest. Mon–Sat 3pm–late.

Club Celebs, Top Level, Gulf City Shopping Complex ☎652 7641. The most popular nightspot in the city – a modern club and sports bar playing a wide variety of music to a young crowd. Entrance fee varies. Sun–Thurs 3.30–11pm, Fri & Sat 11am–4am.

Naparima Bowl, 19 Paradise Pasture ☎657 8770. Comfy theatre and outdoor amphitheatre hosting plays, which regularly come here after showing in Port of Spain, and big calypso and steel band events. Ticket prices vary depending upon what's on.

Richie's Paradise, Cipero St ☎653 0711. Bar-cum-club with a big dancefloor that attracts a mature crowd and lots of couples; music ranges from back-in-times to dance. Moderate cover charge. Weds–Sun 6pm–late.

Shashell's, 137a Lambie St, cor. Point-a-Pierre Rd ☎652 5836. Lively bar and club playing tunes for a party crowd; Fridays see a younger crowd for the soca and reggae, while Saturday's calypso and soca draws more mature revellers. Moderate cover charge. Mon– Sat 5pm–late.

Tree House (see above) The restaurant's friendly, intimate cocktail bar is good for a drink and a lime; there's a pianist on Mondays and live bands at the weekend.

Shopping

The best place for shopping is the **Gulf City Shopping Complex** (Mon–Thurs 9am–8pm, Fri & Sat 9am–9pm), a typical mall on the Link Road on the southern outskirts of the city stuffed with every shop you can imagine. Another mall with fewer outlets is the **Cross Crossing Shopping Centre** opposite Skinner Park on Lady Hales Avenue. For more local produce, the **Chancery Lane Market** at the western end of the High Street features a number of stalls selling local arts and crafts made by Rastafarians, who make up a significant proportion of San Fernando's residents. Sandals, hats, jewellery, belts and straw goods can be found here for very reasonable prices; particularly good quality items and friendly service can be found at the **Junior Roots** stall.

Listings

Banks Bank of Commerce, 1-3 Coffee St ☎652 4519; Republic, 92-94 Cipero St ☎652 4627; Royal, 11 High St ☎652 2233.

Cinema Hobosco, 21-23 Mucurapo St ☎652 4543; National Cinema, cor. Gomez and Keate streets ☎652 2343; Metro, 41-43 Harris Promenade ☎652 4107.

Hospital San Fernando General, Independence Ave ☎652 3581.

Internet You can get inexpensive Net access at Browwwser's, Library Corner; and *The Internet Café*, Ground Floor, 20d Gulf City Shopping Complex.

Laundry Chee's, Gulf City Shopping Complex ☎657 5505; Ng Pack Laundry, 4 Mucurapo St ☎652 3276.

Police The main police station is at the western end of Harris Promenade ☎652 2561.

As in Port of Spain, taxi and maxi fares around San Fernando do change; it's best to offer a TT$10 bill and wait for your change.

Moving on from San Fernando

The main transport stand for rides out of the city to the rest of the south (and the arrival point for maxis and taxis from Port of Spain) is adjacent to the San Fernando General Hospital in Chancery Lane. **Maxis** go from here to La Brea (TT$4), Vessigny (TT$4), Penal (TT$3.50), Siparia (TT$4), Fyzabad (TT$3.50) and Point Fortin (TT$5). For Palo Seco, you will have to take a maxi to Siparia and then change. **Route taxis** from this stand run to La Brea (TT$6), Vessigny (TT$6), Erin (TT$8), Siparia (TT$6), Palo Seco (TT$7), Fyzabad (TT$4) and Point Fortin (TT$8).

Other destinations have their stands located around the city centre. Maxis for **Port of Spain** (TT$5) leave from behind the Chancery Lane Market; for **Couva** (TT$3) and **Chaguanas** (TT$4) they depart from St James Street, and for **Princes Town** (TT$3) they go from Coffee Street. Route taxis to **Penal** (TT$5) leave from High Street, those to **Princes Town** (TT$3) depart from the top of Harris Promenade, next to *McDonald's*. To go to **Granville** and **Icacos** you have to change at Point Fortin. To reach **Mayaro** you need to go via Princes Town or Sangre Grande in the northeast.

The **bus depot** and **ticket office** (Mon–Fri 5am–8pm, Sat 6am–7pm, Sun noon–7pm) are at the bottom of **Queen Street** by the fish market. For information ring ☎652-3705. Buses run from here to Port of Spain (ECS: 5am–8pm, 15min, TT$6. Transit 4am–9pm, 45min, TT$4), Chaguanas (ECS: 5am–8pm, 15min, TT$3. Transit; 4am–9pm, 45min, TT$2.50), Point Fortin (Transit; 2.30am–9pm, 1.5hr, TT$3) and La Brea (Point Fortin bus, TT$3).

Post office King St ☎652 3431. Mon–Fri 8am–4pm.

Sports Skinner Park, Lady Hales Ave ☎657 7168; hosts local football and basketball games and the odd concert, as well as Carnival fetes and events. Entrance tickets vary.

For details of transport to the southwest from San Fernando, see above.

The southwest peninsula

Trinidad's **southwest peninsula**, known locally as the "deep south", offers a mix of gritty oil towns and marvellous drives through sleepy backwaters, forested hills, and teak and coconut plantations, down to beaches of soft brown sand backed by red-earth cliffs and lapped by calm seas. The pace of life is very slow, so take time to enjoy the relaxed atmosphere and incomparable countryside.

Despite its proximity to San Fernando, the mangrove swampland of the **Oropuche Lagoon** is a seldom-visited wildlife haven teeming with birds. Indeed, it's rare for tourists to explore beyond the well-publicized **Pitch Lake** at **La Brea**, but it is worth travelling on south to the areas of **Cedros** and **Erin** at the tip of the peninsula. Small fishing hamlets line the coast, while the beaches are an escapist's dream – small sheltered coves, usually deserted apart from the odd fisherman or truant child. The road down to **Icacos Point**, the extreme southwest tip, is one of the most spectacular drives in Trinidad, lined with coconut plantations where herds of buffalypso graze.

Trinidad's oil industry

When oil was first discovered in Trinidad in 1819, in Guayaguayare in the southeast, the samples were reported to be "of such fine quality that the chemists regarded them as artificial". Exploration was begun in earnest in 1857 by the Merrimac Company, and ten years later they drilled the first oil well in the world in La Brea. The English novelist Charles Kingsley – author of *The Water Babies* – visited the site in 1870 and was appalled, denouncing the sputtering well as an interference with God's work and declaring that "man should mind his own business". The success of the well was short-lived, however, and the industry didn't really take off until 1893, when Randolph Rust, an entrepreneur of disputed nationality, started prospecting. With Canadian funding he established a well on the banks of the Pilot River in Guayaguayare in 1902, and persuaded the British government – which was converting the Royal Navy to oil-powered ships – to invest in the industry.

World War I boosted demand, and by the 1920s there were dozens of oil companies on the island. By 1932 the black gold made up 50 percent of the nation's exports, and by 1946, Trinidad accounted for 65 percent of all the British Empire's oil production. The situation remained stable until the 1974 international oil crisis, when prices went through the roof. Prime Minister Eric Williams declared that "money was no problem", and the country went on a wild spree with the government spending millions on lavish and ambitious projects. The most infamous was the proposed horse racing complex – including air-conditioned stables – to be built on the Caroni Plains. Escalating costs and the opposition's cry of "houses before horses", saved Trinis the estimated TT$400 million it would have cost, but not before substantial sums had been spent on negotiating contracts and designing the facilities.

Trinidadians speak of these days with a mixture of disgust and nostalgia. Stories abound of people who went to work at 8am, returned at 10am and were paid a full day's wage. Everyone seemed to have money and the latest consumer goods, but the traditional Trinidadian collective values were eroded by greed, individualism and corruption. Not all the money was wasted though. The Point Lisas Industrial Complex (see p.192) was established on the west coast, improvements were made to the infrastructure and educational grants were provided for T&T citizens. Trinidad's good fortune did not last long, however; declining oil prices in the 1980s forced people to realize that the easy life was over. Over-ambitious projects had drained public resources, unemployment had risen and crime increased. Harsh measures such as the devaluation of the dollar were required to put the economy back on track.

Although the boom is over, oil has remained the mainstay of the economy, employing more than 16,000 people and providing 25 percent of the nation's GDP; around 129,000 barrels are still produced each day, many from offshore reserves discovered in the late 1990s. It has ensured that Trinidad remains one of the strongest economies in the Caribbean. Ironically, this has helped to preserve the island's natural environment – unlike other Caribbean nations, Trinidad has not been obliged to develop an extensive tourist trade, leaving the coastline free of multinational hotel chains and the rainforests to grow unabated.

The southwest peninsula

The larger towns, such as **Point Fortin** and the **Siparia-Fyzabad conurbation**, revolve around the oil industry; they come to life after 4pm when people finish work. Though of little interest in themselves, they do provide the only **accommodation** and **restaurants** in the area.

Oropuche Lagoon

Caribbean Discovery Tours (☎624 7281) will take you into the Oropuche Lagoon by kayak; Wildways (☎623 7332) and Paria Springs (☎622 8826) arrange birdwatching and wildlife tours.

The **Oropuche Lagoon** – 56 square kilometres of tidal mangrove swamp alongside the Southern Main Road (SMR) 6km south of San Fernando – features on the itineraries of very few tour companies. That's just how the government plans to keep it – a sanctuary for fish and endangered wildfowl bred in the Point-a-Pierre Wildfowl Trust (see p.192).

Oropuche's inaccessible location amid swampy marshland discourages hunters as well as visitors, and as a result it teems with animals and birdlife. It is an excellent place to view **butterflies**, as well as **birds** such as egrets, black-bellied whistling duck, American bittern, ringed kingfish and a variety of herons. The swamp is home to a variety of fish including tarpin and catfish, and the area is known for its shrimping grounds. Though it is less disturbed than the Caroni Swamp (see p.184), the lagoon is under threat from pollution due to oil leaks from pumping jacks – there are more than 1600 scattered around the south, and damaging oilspills occur fairly frequently.

The Siparia-Fyzabad conurbation

Some 10 to 13km south of San Fernando, surrounded by the rolling pastures and endless sugar cane fields of the **Philippines Estate**, is the **Siparia-Fyzabad conurbation**, powerhouse of the country's oil industry. The government has designated the magnificent untouched forest on either side of the road as the **Palmiste National Park**. The small agricultural town of **Penal**, which produces a large proportion of the country's rice, holds little of interest for the visitor, but it marks the beginning of the built-up area; from here it is easy to drive into the lively old Spanish town of **Siparia** without noticing where one starts and the other ends. To the north, the urban area also encompasses **Fyzabad**, a gritty place that played a crucial role in the development of Trinidadian trade unionism and the struggle for civil rights. These hectic towns are excellent places to buy **Indian** sweets, pies and snacks that are sold on roadside stalls in little wooden glass cases known locally as "safes".

Siparia

Action in **SIPARIA** is focused on the main street, lined with attractive colonial houses interspersed with more modern constructions and fringed by rickety market stalls. It's a lively place full of shoppers and market vendors, though there are few specific sights, unless you are interested in the variety of vegetables, ground provisions and fruit on offer.

The town was originally settled in 1758 by Capuchin priests from Spain, who established a mission to convert the Amerindians in the area.

The Festival of La Divina Pastora

Held on the second Sunday after Easter in Siparia, the Festival of La Divina Pastora – the divine Shepherdess – was brought to Trinidad from Andalucia by way of Venezuela in the eighteenth century. Decked out in new clothes, the locals make offerings to the **Black Virgin** statue, carried in procession through the streets, and celebrate with general feasting and merrymaking. Some believe that the wooden statue was in fact the prow of the ship in which the priests travelled from the mainland, and found in refuse from a shipwreck on Quinam Beach by passing Warwarrhoons Indians. Others claim it was brought to Siparia from Venezuela by a Spanish priest whose life it had saved. Whatever its origins, many miracles have been attributed to the statue. In the 1890s, Hindu indentured labourers saw in the statue's dark features the Hindu goddess Kali, the destroyer of sorrow. Renaming the statue Soparee Kay Mai, the Hindus started their own form of worship – if Kali answered their prayers, Hindu women would offer the statue locks from their children's first haircut. The Catholic Church attempted to discourage this devotion in the 1920s, but the cult had already grown too strong, and to this day, Hindu devotees are well represented at the festival.

The legacy of Catholicism is still very much in evidence in the feast day of **La Divina Pastora** (see box p.219) held in Siparia three weeks after Easter. The **Black Virgin**, a small statue of the Virgin Mary normally housed in the church at the top of the hill (follow the road that branches off the SMR opposite the Republic Bank), is carried through the streets to the beat of tassa drums and showered with offerings of gold bracelets, flower, olive oil and money. The festival is one big street party, with the whole town coming out to celebrate in their best clothes. Despite the festival's Catholic origin, Trinidadians of all denominations now participate – Hindus also worship the statue, calling her Soparee Kay Mai (Mother Kali), while local Baptists attribute mystical powers to the Black Virgin.

Quinam Beach

A well signposted, if rather bumpy, 7.5km drive down the Coora Road/Penal Quinam Road, through teak plantations and forest inhabited by deer, takes you to **Quinam Beach** on the south coast of the peninsula. The sands are fine and brown, though at high tide they disappear beneath the waves; the waters are calm and good for swimming; and Baptist flags flap in the breeze on the seashore – followers of the faith believe the sea here has mystical qualities.

This is the most popular beach on the south coast – on weekends the small car park on the seafront is packed with Trinis coming to take their "seabath". Families and friends chill out under the palm huts, tending barbecues and eating large picnic lunches, while the babble of lively conversation and music from stereos fills the air. The **Quinam Bay Interpretive Centre** (daily 9am–6pm) just by the beach, displays pictures of the local flora and fauna, and also provides sheltered picnic facilities, firewood cooking stoves and a special praying area for Hindus, Muslims and Spiritual Baptists. You'll need to bring your own food and drink unless you want to buy aloo pies, snow cones or soft drinks from the beach vendors. There is no

Uriah Butler

Tubal Uriah "Buzz" Butler – Trinidad's foremost trade union activist – was a Grenadian who came to work in Trinidad's oilfields in 1921. After an industrial accident in 1929 left Butler unfit for oil work, he joined the Moravian Baptist church and became a preacher, developing the rousing oratorical skills that characterized his political career. Disillusioned with Cipriani's Trinidad Labour Party (see p.330), after it failed to support an oilworkers' strike in 1935, he established the **British Empire Workers** to further the "heroic struggle for British justice for British Blacks in a British colony".

The BEW campaigned for better pay and working conditions in the oilfields, where many of the managers were white South Africans who had instituted an apartheid-type regime. Among the workers' many grievances were low wages, long working hours, and the frequency of industrial accidents, for which there was no compensation. Workers were liable to be dismissed on the spot and, once sacked, a blackballing system made it impossible for them to find work elsewhere.

In June 1937 strikers started a **sit-in** at the **Forest Reserve oilfield**. The police broke up the protest, and in response the strikers set fire to two wells in the Apex oilfield. When the police arrived at Fyzabad to arrest Butler on a charge of agitation, they found him addressing a large crowd. As they attempted to serve the warrant, a riot broke out. One plainclothes officer, the deeply unpopular **Charlie King**, fled into a nearby shop, found himself trapped, and jumped from an upstairs window, breaking his leg; the furious crowd burned him alive, and when his colleagues tried to retrieve his body, a British police officer was shot dead. A 1938 calypso caught the popular mood: "Everybody's rejoicing, How they burned Charlie King, Everybody was glad, Nobody was sad, When they beat him and they burned him, In Fyzabad."

Strikes spread like wildfire, and became increasingly violent, with a mounting death toll on both sides. Butler, in hiding after the riot, was soon discovered and sentenced to two years in prison. But the strikes won important concessions: public workers were granted an eight-hour day and a higher minimum wage. The government recognized the trade unions, though the police continued to harass trade union officials. On his release in 1939, Butler was given a hero's welcome, but during his imprisonment the BEW had changed, adopting a more mainstream position. After Butler agitated for a strike in defiance of a Union Executive decision, he was expelled from the BEW. In September 1939 he was once again incarcerated for sedition, and remained behind bars till the end of World War II.

Butler continued to be politically active after his release in 1945, campaigning in the national elections; but though his party won the largest block of seats in 1950, he was outflanked by the rise of Eric Williams's nationalist politics (see p.331), and his star faded. In remembrance of his role in defending workers' rights, the Princess Margaret Highway linking north and south Trinidad was renamed in his honour in the 1960s. In 1971 the government awarded him the Trinity Cross – the highest honour in the land, and June 19, the day of the riots, was declared a public holiday.

transport to the beach, but you can persuade a Siparia taxi driver to take you there for an agreed fare (around TT$10–20).

Fyzabad

The bustling town of **FYZABAD**, on Fyzabad Road 5km north of Siparia, occupies a unique place in the history of **trade unionism** and the struggle for equal rights in Trinidad. Established in the nineteenth century by Canadian Presbyterian missionaries, Fyzabad took its name from the district in Uttar Pradesh, India, where most of its settlers originated. After oil was discovered in the area in 1917, however, the town's character changed dramatically. Fyzabad quickly developed into a busy industrial town, the centre of the emergent labour movement, while the original Indo-Trinidadian Presbyterian community were soon outnumbered by migrants who came from Grenada and St Vincent to work on the oilfields, and whose descendants still make up the majority of the town's population.

The compact commercial centre, a blend of dilapidated colonial buildings and modern concrete, clusters around Charlie King Junction. **The Oil Workers' Trade Union Hall** and the painted statue of the workers' leader **Uriah Butler** (see box opposite) in his black suit and bowler hat, dominate the junction, ironically named after **Charlie King**, the policeman killed when he tried to arrest Butler for political agitation. The junction is also the focus of the **Labour Day** (June 19) celebrations organized by the OWTU every year. The streets are blocked, a stage is erected and a street party, with a political message, ensues – union leaders make fiery speeches, a wreath is laid on Butler's grave and DJs entertain the crowd.

La Brea and around

Eighteen kilometres south of San Fernando on the SMR, a turn-off winds through rainforest and teak plantations to **LA BREA**. The village's name, Spanish for pitch, announces its main claim to fame: the nearby **Pitch Lake**. There's little else to see – the most memorable feature of the village itself is its excruciatingly bumpy roads – a car suspension's nightmare, caused by the underground volcanic eruptions that replenish the lake. La Brea's residents put up with it, finding compensation in the free pitch that bubbles up all over the place, used as rather unattractive paving for driveways and as an unusual garden weedkiller.

The Pitch Lake

Some of the world's finest quality asphalt comes from the **Pitch Lake**, well signposted 1.5km south of La Brea on the SMR. Trinis may claim it as the eighth wonder of the world, but to the sightseer it bears a remarkable resemblance to a car park or the wrinkly hide of an elephant. It is a genuine curiosity, however – there are only three such lakes in the world, the other two being in Los Angeles (Rancho La Brea) and Venezuela (Guanaco).

Between the SMR and La Brea, look out for the displays of pepper sauce outside Angie's, a small shop on the left; produced on the spot, the pepper and tamarind sauce are some of the best in Trinidad.

The southwest peninsula

Five to six million years ago, asphaltic oil flowed into a huge mud volcano, developing over time into the asphalt that is now extracted from the lake and used to pave roads all over the world. The asphalt is continually churned up from an estimated depth of 80 metres – a measuring attempt in 1910 was foiled when the cast-iron measuring pipe was snapped by currents 50 metres down.

According to local **legend**, a Carib tribe who killed and ate the sacred hummingbird to celebrate a tribal victory angered the Great Spirit of the Amerindians. The spirit punished them by trapping them forever under the Pitch Lake – a story reinforced by the many Amerindian artefacts yielded up by the lake over the years, and now displayed on shelves in local homes as well as in glass cases in the National Museum in Port of Spain. **Sir Walter Raleigh** discovered the pitch lake in 1595, used the pitch to caulk his ships, and reported on its quality to Queen Elizabeth I. The lake was not commercially exploited until the 1860s, however, when it was developed by the British, who continued to control the excavation of pitch until 1978. The National Museum (see p.83) has a collection of photographs of streets from London to Australia, India and Singapore, surfaced with Trinidadian pitch.

The Pitch Lake is open daily 9am–5pm. Admission TT$30/US$5.

Covering more than 40,000 square metres, the lake probably represents the largest deposit in the world. Bird of paradise flowers grow around its edge, in stark contrast to the unsightly factory that excavates 180 tonnes of pitch daily. If you visit between 8am and 4pm, you'll see the workers loading the substance onto trolleys and dragging their load across the surface to the factory. The "**mother of the lake**" – the soft centre where the pitch is replenished – is firm enough to walk on in most places, though not in high-heeled shoes. The pitch is extracted from the "mother of the lake" by peeling off the hardened top layer. Cracks that form in the surface are often filled with sulphuric water reputed to be excellent for mosquito bites, rashes, skin conditions and for cleaning jewellery. Natural springs appear at the lake's centre during the June-to-November wet season, and after working hours, local people descend for an evening dip, most to capitalize on the healing qualities of the waters.

Until recently, **visiting** the Pitch Lake was a rather chaotic experience, with prospective guides rushing up to your car from as far away as the SMR junction. Thanks to the strident efforts of TIDCO, though, it's a bit more organized these days. Unauthorized guides and touts are banned, and you simply go to the main booth, where you pay your TT$30 and are allotted an authorized **guide** (who'll be wearing a badge). Guides give a rundown of the lake's history, and demonstrate the various textures and fluidity, posing for photographs with sticks covered in runny pitch. Expect to leave a tip. Wear shoes with low heels and be careful not to let the pitch touch your clothes – it is a nightmare to clean off. It's not advisable to strike out onto the lake alone; soft patches are difficult for the uninitiated to recognize, and a picture of a hapless Trini youth in the guide booth, covered from head to toe in pitch, warns of the consequences of unguided exploration.

Vessigny Beach

Three kilometres past the Pitch Lake, **Vessigny Beach** (facilities open 10am–6pm; small fee charged) is a delightful little cove of brown sand lapped by calm seas. It's a popular spot with Trinis at the weekends, and the destination for evening excursions that turn into high-spirited beach parties. There are no lifeguards on duty, so be careful when swimming. This is the only developed seaside on the south coast; its well-maintained facilities include a snack bar (open at weekends and during school holidays), changing rooms and picnic tables. Trinidadians sometimes camp on the grass by the beach – it is not an official campsite, and there is no charge if you wish to do the same.

Point Fortin

Five kilometres on from Vessigny beach, through forest, bamboo groves and small villages, is the oil town of **POINT FORTIN**. Evidence of the industry is everywhere: large storage tanks pop up in the suburbs, and the rhythmic motion of an oil pump will catch the corner of your eye from a side street. Shell, which once owned the refinery and tank farm, built extensive facilities for its expatriate management; scattered around town are tennis courts, a golf course and an old country club, while the suburbs are full of large houses with satellite dishes and barking dogs. In some roads, the old **workers' houses** can be seen – rough concrete boxes that are a far cry from the luxurious mansions of the managers.

There is little to see in Point Fortin unless you have a personal interest in the oil industry. The place only comes to life after 4pm, when the workers come out to lime in the bars and hang around the main junction. Locals go to swim at **Clifford Beach**, by the oil storage tanks. It must have been a nice spot once, but the bar has closed down, leaving only the tables with their thatched palm canopies as a reminder.

There's not much in the way of **accommodation**. *Cinnamon House*, 118 Cinnamon Drive, Clifton Hill (☎648 2349, fax 648 1419; ④), is an attractively decorated small hotel with a/c and cable TV in all rooms, most of which are en suite. The comfortable **restaurant** serves good Creole/international food. The place is hard to find – ring first for directions.

The best time to visit Point Fortin is for the annual Borough Day in May, a mini-Carnival event. Contact TIDCO (☎623 6022) for exact dates.

Cedros and Erin

The areas of **Cedros** and **Erin**, occupying the extreme tip of the southwestern peninsula, are some of the most picturesque and untouched in Trinidad. The **environment** is stunning, as the teak plantations that line the Southern Trunk Road (as the SMR is known from here on) to the north are replaced by miles of palm and coconut trees. There are some appealing beaches here, too: lovely sheltered coves lapped by a calm sea and – unimaginably in the tourist-focused Caribbean – you'll usually find them practically deserted. At the furthest tip of the southwest peninsula, **Icacos Point** looks out across

*Paria Springs
(☎ 622 8826)
conduct
excellent
birdwatching
and mountain
biking tours
around Icacos
Point, and can
also arrange
host home
here.*

the swirling waters of the **Serpent's Mouth** to the South American mainland just 11km away.

Residents earn their living by fishing, indifferent to the region's growing tourist trade – though even this is relatively low key, as few visitors make the three- to four-hour drive from Port of Spain. Charming **board houses** line the road, their occupants watching the occasional passer-by from their verandahs. Small groceries sell traditional snacks such as fruit preserved with salt, lime, pepper and herbs. Village life centres on the bar and the football field, where lively games take place in the cool light of dusk. In the evenings villagers catch the breeze on the seafront beneath the red, orange and green almond trees, while snow cone vendors ride their bicycle carts along the promenade, ringing their bells to drum up business. At night the bumpy streets are quiet and often unlit. Animals rule here, not cars; the occasional **buffalypso** herd will wander across your path, or you may come head to head with an unruly goat.

Cedros

Cedros takes its name from the **giant cedar trees** that lined the bays in the early 1700s, though sadly none of these have survived. It was first settled by Spaniards, whose influence lingered longer in this isolated region than in the rest of the island; despite an influx of Indian indentured labourers, Spanish was still widely spoken until the 1880s, almost a century after the British had captured Trinidad. A hundred years ago, during the nineteenth-century heyday of the sugar estates, Cedros was a bustling place with a population twice as large as it is today. Famed for its rum, this small district boasted no less than seven distilleries, though now that these have shut down, there's little industriousness today.

Every bay in Cedros seems to have a picture postcard **beach**, usually a small sheltered cove with soft brown sand and calm waters. The idyllic settings more than compensate for the total lack of facilities. The beach at **Granville** is so far off the beaten track – 5.5km from the Southern Trunk Road through the well-kept village of the same name – that it's often completely deserted. Its fine sands are a very light brown and the waters are calm, though underwater currents that drag sand from the bottom give the water a somewhat murky aspect. Unless you fancy walking to the sea from the main road (not much fun in the heat of the day), you'll have to negotiate a fare with a taxi driver from Point Fortin.

.Though Cedros is actually the name of the whole area south of Granville, many people from outside the district use it to refer to **Bonasse**, a sleepy, charming village on **Cedros Bay**, a 10km beach used mainly by local fishermen. Two kilometres from neighbouring **Fullarton** is the lovely 3km beach on **Columbus Bay** – an excellent spot to find interesting pieces of driftwood. This is very quiet during the week and large enough to avoid bumping into people at the weekends. The view has changed little from the one that greeted Columbus when he visited these sands after his landing at Moruga in 1498.

From Columbus Bay the road winds on through a huge, spectacular coconut estate, down to the sleepy little village of Icacos (Ih-*car*-cus); a little further on it comes to an end at **Icacos Point**, the southwesternmost point in Trinidad. There's nothing much to see at this faraway spot apart from the crumbling sea wall, the pelicans, the buffalypso herds and the vague outline of the Venezuelan coast. The dividing channel is called the **Serpent's Mouth** – an apt description, for the bay forms the shape of an open mouth, while the three rocks jutting out at sea at the northern end resemble the serpent's fangs. The serpent fails to scare the drug smugglers who use these beaches to bring in cocaine from Colombia via Venezuela. Rumours abound that the area is awash with drug money now that the Caroni Swamp – the smuggler's previous entry point – is well patrolled by the T&T coastguard.

Nine kilometres to the west, you can see the craggy silhouette of **Soldado Rock**. This small, 60-metre high island marks the division between Venezuela and Trinidad's territorial waters – its name means "the soldier". The only major seabird breeding site in Trinidad, it has been a wildlife sanctuary since 1934, and is home to frigate birds, grey-breasted martins and brown pelicans, and the nesting site of sooty and noddy terns. During nesting season – March to July – these birds lay over 5000 eggs on the rocky protrusion. Its varied and dramatic rock formations are of great interest to geologists, and even amateurs can spot the many fossil beds. Those interested in visiting the island should negotiate with one of the fishermen from Icacos. It is difficult to land on the rock, however, and you must be careful not to sail into Venezuelan waters unless you fancy a night in a South American jail. Paria Springs (☎622 8826) organise birdwatching tours of Soldado.

To reach Icacos by public transport, take a maxi from Point Fortin to Bonasse, a route taxi from Bonasse to Fullarton (TT$2) and then another route taxi to Icacos (TT$5).

Erin

Rounding the tip of the peninsula to **Erin Point**, you pass many quiet villages where the only noise comes from the school playground. **Erin** (**San Francique** on many maps) is one of the most picturesque, with old board houses set in flowering gardens and colourful fishing boats bobbing on the seashore. Little changes here – the population is roughly the same size as it was a hundred years ago, when it had the reputation of producing some of the finest cocoa in the world. These days it's Trinidad's most important **fishing village**, with the biggest catches in the country. During the Erin fishing season (June to December), the village is frenetically busy with fishermen landing their catch and buyers and sellers haggling on the shore. From January to May the community returns to a more peaceful existence, as the fishermen depart for Moruga where the catch is greater.

Erin's beach, known as **Puerto Grande**, is the centre of its fishing activities. Fishermen painstakingly mend their nets with huge needles, weigh fish on large old-fashioned scales and discuss prices in discreet tones. It is a busy working beach, with a fishy scent to the air, and not really the place to take a swim. It is the best place in the region to buy fresh fish, though; you can watch your purchase being pulled out of the water and you will pay half the price advertised in the supermarket in town. There are a few snack parlours and bars on the waterfront, catering to the fishermen.

If you want a more private bathing spot, try the pretty cove of **Los Iros** 2km east of Puerto Grande. The water is calm and clean, and though the beach is popular at weekends, you'll find it deserted during the week apart from the odd fishing boat. There is a small snack parlour and a bar nearby, but if you are planning to spend the whole day, follow the Trini example and bring your own food; at weekends it is common to see whole families with pots, containers and coolers, as they bring their large Sunday lunch down to the beach.

Los Iros cove boasts the only **accommodation** in Erin or Cedros. The *Beach Boys Guest House* (☎657 9826; TT$100 per night Mon–Thurs, TT$200 per weekend including Fri) consists of four basic but functional self-catering apartments 15m from the beach. Each has two bedrooms with double beds, a lounge with TV and fans, and a kitchenette. Book early, especially for the holiday weekends, and remember to bring your own food.

Eight kilometres east of Erin is another marvellous **beach** at Palo Seco Bay. Turn onto **Beach Road** by the YKC & Son supermarket at Palo Seco village. This takes you past the Petrotrin beach club, where it is best to park, as beyond it the road degenerates into a steep dirt

---

Trinidad's fishing industry

Fishing in Trinidad is big business. Over the last twenty years the industry has developed from local self-sufficiency to an organized business, becoming an excellent earner of foreign exchange. Its potential persuaded the government in 1977 to provide incentives to encourage people to become fishermen. The policy was highly successful: the industry now employs 9000 people, and the catch weighed 8.7 million kg in 1996. As well as providing for the domestic market – it is estimated that every Trinidadian eats 18kg of fish per year – Trinidad exports TT$70 million worth of fish annually, mostly red snapper, carite and kingfish.

This success story has brought its problems, however. T&T's fishing grounds are becoming seriously depleted, and disputes regularly arise when Trinidadians are caught in Venezuelan waters. Declining fish stocks are variously blamed on increasing pollution and the large foreign trawlers that haunt T&T's waters, though some point the finger at the use of "ghost" nets – transparent plastic netting banned in many other countries – by their own countrymen. The fishermen argue that they are obliged to use ghost nets to ensure a decent catch during the day, since increasing crime has prevented them from fishing at night, when most fish feed and hence larger catches can be hauled.

track. This leads to a 4km beach scattered with driftwood and lapped by the typical calm seas of the region. It is a fifteen-minute walk from the San Fernando–Siparia–Erin Road, the route of the maxis from Siparia or taxis from San Fernando.

The southern central region

The **southern central region** is one of the most impenetrable in Trinidad. The only transport artery, made up of the Manahambre, Naparima and Mayaro roads, runs from the west to the east coast, through rolling plains of sugar cane, linking the region's two main towns, **Princes Town** and **Rio Claro**. The road is dotted with Hindu temples, Muslim mosques, Christian churches and agricultural villages, with little to interest the visitor beyond the well-publicized **Devil's Woodyard** with its over-hyped mud volcanoes, and a predilection for bizarre place names.

South of the main road, much of the landscape is swathed in wild forest dotted with the occasional oil well. There are very few passable roads, signs are almost nonexistent and trying to follow a map is a lesson in frustration – what is marked as a road may turn out to be no more than a dirt track. If you need directions, it's best to ask how to get from A to B – few locals know the official names of the roads. You may have problems finding anyone to ask, as the area is largely uninhabited – when you do stumble on someone, they will usually turn out to be oil workers mending leaks, or loggers working in the forest. It's best to stick to the main roads and not venture onto the dirt tracks – many are dead ends, or lead to no more than an oil pump. Just one decent road penetrates this wilderness, running down to the small fishing village of **Moruga** on the south coast – a strange, isolated place, undisturbed by visitors and steeped in ancestral African faiths that give the place an eerie and mystical atmosphere.

Maxis and taxis are frequent along the Manahambre Road from **Princes Town** to **Rio Claro** (TT$4/5). To go to **Devil's Woodyard** take a maxi from San Fernando to Princes Town (TT$3), change here and get a taxi to take you to Hindustan Road (TT$4). You will then have to change again or cajole your driver into taking you to the seldom-visited site for another TT$4. You can get a maxi or taxi to **Moruga** from Princes Town for TT$5.

Accommodation is extremely limited in this area, but the two nearest concentrations of hotels, in San Fernando and Mayaro are easily accessible. South East Eco Tours (☎644 1072) can arrange accommodation in a few **host homes**. Restaurants in the American or European sense are nonexistent, but there are many Chinese fast-food parlours and the usual roadside stalls selling snacks, home-made pies and preserved fruit.

Princes Town and around

The unremarkable **PRINCES TOWN**, 7km east of San Fernando on the Manahambre Road, resembles a permanent traffic jam. En route you pass the blackened chimneys of the **St Madeleine Sugar Factory** a rather incongruous sight in the midst of rolling fields and lines of palm trees – during harvest season, the smell of burnt sugar fills the air along with ominous billows of smoke. Princes Town itself is developing faster than its infrastructure can cope with. New buildings are springing up in every imaginable style, competing with traditional places of worship such as the grand mosque with its copper dome and steel-plated minarets on the east side of the town centre. The town's most curious feature, however, best glimpsed when driving in from the west, is **Randy's Enterprises**, a large electrical goods shop covered in murals and reliefs of Hindu gods and the Statue of Liberty. Around the corner on the left stands the Anglican **St Stephen's Church** – its two poui trees were planted by Prince Albert and Prince George in 1880. It was this visit by the future kings Edward VII and George V that led to the village, previously known as Mission, being renamed in their honour. The English novelist Charles Kingsley visited the town in 1870, and is commemorated in a street name.

You can get internet access at Cyberspace Network in Shopper's World Plaza in Princes Town.

The tiny villages of **First**, **Third**, **Fourth** and **Fifth Company** surrounding Princes Town are a legacy of the black American **soldiers** of the War of 1812. These former slaves had fought on the British side in return for promises of land, and after the British defeat they were allocated lots in Trinidad. There is no village called Second Company – this unit was lost at sea on the voyage to Trinidad.

The soldiers settled here in 1816, bringing with them the Baptist faith that still has a strong influence on village life. They cleared the land and established successful plantations in uncharted jungle, earning themselves the reputation of pioneers. They complained bitterly to the then governor, Ralph Woodford, about the condition of the land they had been granted, but without success; he wanted to open up the interior, and also to keep the radical black soldiers far away from potentially rebellious slaves.

The small village of **Indian Walk**, 5km east of Princes Town, is of little interest except for its unusual name, which recalls the many Amerindian traders who travelled this route selling parrots, food and ornaments. Seven kilometres to the east, the small village of **Tableland** has what is claimed to be the second oldest Hindu temple in the western hemisphere (the oldest is in Martinique). Pundit Mahant Moose Bhagat Dass, an indentured labourer who had migrated from Bharat Desh in India, built the small temple on the northern side of the road in 1904. The pundit had removed some stones from a stream and placed them near his house. That night in a dream, the spirit Shiva Bhagwan asked him to build a temple, as his previous home in the stones had been disrupted by the pundit's action. To this day the stones remain in the temple, housed in the shrine of Shiva.

Devil's Woodyard

Devil's Woodyard, with its **mud volcano** is marked on all the tourist maps, but despite the intriguing name, the sight is disappointing, a series of metre-high hillocks oozing gunge. The route down Hindustan Road, 3km past Indian Walk, is well signposted; it's a pretty but very bumpy drive through rolling pastures, and teak and citrus plantations. The name came about in 1852 when a large eruption shook the surrounding houses, scattering the planks like matchsticks.

The local Amerindians believed the mud volcanoes were passages between this world and the one below, and that the explosions were the Devil coming out to shake the earth. The present reality is less dramatic – little more than a few small mounds of earth with grey mud bubbling lazily to the surface. If you are curious to see a mud volcano, though, this is the most accessible, and has the best facilities, including a children's playground, picnic tables, toilets (though the latter are often locked). Bear in mind that like all natural phenomena, its level of activity can vary; most of the time the eruptions splutter harmlessly, though in some years the eruptions have been violent enough to shower the picnic tables with mud. The cracked, heavily indented earth around the volcanoes is the result of earlier explosions.

Moruga

MORUGA is a pretty, isolated village on the central south coast, 21km from Princes Town, by a sheltered cove lined with soft brown sand. The place seems to have changed little since it was first settled: the bright, contrasting colours of the old board houses have weathered to pastel shades; colourful wooden fishing boats lie on the seashore; and fishermen while away their spare hours liming outside the two shops on the main road.

Mud volcanoes

The many **mud volcanoes** scattered around southern Trinidad are promoted as environmental curiosities by TIDCO, which highlights them on its maps. The majority are largely inaccessible – unless you like taking hikes through dense forest – and in most cases it's not worth the effort. The volcanoes are small mounds less than a metre high that seep and bubble grey sulphuric mud, which is believed to be good for skin conditions.

The volcanoes can appear anywhere: in the middle of the bush, in people's back gardens and by the road. They are usually ignored, though those who live near them do so at their peril, for they have a tendency to explode every few years. The most recent and damaging explosion was in Piparo in central Trinidad in 1997, where a road was completely destroyed; the villagers had to endure repeated tremors and the pungent smell of sulphuric gas, while the mud-filled gutters provided an excellent breeding ground for mosquitoes.

The
southern
central
region

The Catholic church on the seafront dominates both the surroundings and the life of the village. This is a place of strong – but heterodox – beliefs; villagers may avow allegiance to Catholicism, to the Baptist faith, or to obeah, but many will believe in aspects of all three. A religious, almost superstitious atmosphere pervades the village. Locals speak of **obeah spells**, and stories abound of **Papa Neiza**, an African herbal doctor, immortalized by the calypsonian Sparrow in his song *Melda*, who allegedly could exorcise devils – and instil them in people as well. An obeah woman, **Madame Cornstick**,

*For more
information
on obeah and
other ancestral
beliefs, see
p.339.*

is said to still live in the village, though she is rarely seen nowadays. Her powers are reputed to be great, and many people still come to Moruga to consult her in the hope of solving their romantic or financial problems. Residents mumble that she does more harm than good, though no one speaks too loudly for fear of falling victim to one of her curses.

The village's main event is its **Columbus Festival**, held on August 1 each year. Situated near the spot where Columbus landed in 1498 (see box below), Moruga is the only place left in Trinidad to celebrate **Discovery Day**, which has been replaced everywhere else by

*For more on
the early
history of
Trinidad, see
p.327.*

Emancipation Day (see p.47). The organizers hold the controversial view that without Columbus, the majority of Trinidadians would not have the benefit of living on the island, or of the Catholic faith. Besides, the yearly festival brings much-needed money, and provides the locals with a good party and street bazaar. The festivities take place on the beach, where three boats are decorated as fifteenth-century galleons and locals play the part of Columbus and the

---

Columbus in Trinidad

Christopher Columbus had nearly run out of drinking water when, on July 31, 1498, he sighted the three peaks of the Trinity Hills (see p.234), said to have inspired him to name the island Trinidad. He landed near present-day Moruga, where he gathered fresh water from the river. His crew reported seeing fishing implements that had clearly been abandoned in haste, and realized that they had arrived in a region that was already well populated. In fact, there were some 35,000 **Amerindians**, from the Arawak, Shebaio, Nepoio, Carinepagoto and Yao peoples, then living on the island which they called "Ieri", the land of the hummingbird.

Columbus encountered the island's residents the next day while he was anchored off Icacos Point. Twenty-four Amerindians armed with bows and arrows set off in a large canoe to investigate the foreign ship. Upon sighting them Columbus ordered a drum to be played and the sailors to dance, believing the indigenous population would be entertained by this spectacle. However, the Amerindians mistook it for a war dance and rained arrows on the Spaniards; as the latter returned fire, the Amerindians fled. That night, Columbus had little sleep as strong currents tossed the ship. Huge waves crashed against the boat, rocking it so violently that the anchor broke. A bewildered and fearful Columbus named the passage the Serpent's Mouth, and quickly sailed away.

Amerindians who greet the explorer peacefully and exchange gifts – hardly an accurate account, but it makes an entertaining spectacle.

Catholicism also inspires the two other celebrations in Moruga. On **St Peter's Day** (the last Sunday in June) the fishermen's boats are blessed, and there is also a street festival on the Sunday after **Easter**.

Rio Claro

Located on the Naparima–Mayaro Road 24km east of Princes Town, **RIO CLARO** is the administrative hub for the central and southeastern region. This makes it a busy place compared to its surroundings – but that's not saying much in this somnolent corner of the island. The town enjoyed a period of prosperity between 1914 and 1965, when it was connected to Trinidad's major cities by the railway, but once that closed down, the place went into decline as young people abandoned agricultural work for more profitable jobs in the oilfields and the bigger cities.

As you enter Rio Claro from the west, you'll pass between a grand wedding-cake-pink and ice-blue **Catholic church** and a resplendent white **Hindu temple** with a stepped dome and gold and blue trimmings. After this majestic entrance you come upon the main junction and town centre, with its lively stalls, maxi stand and four-armed signpost pointing to all the corners of Trinidad. A large mosque commands the main road going out of town to the east, amid a cluster of businesses and banks. The town's Spanish heritage emerges towards Christmas, as Rio Claro's famous **parang** singers (see p.341) come out and entertain the clientele of the local bars and clubs.

You can check your email at the Cyber-Surf Internet Café, *on the corner of Mayaro and Cunapo roads in Rio Claro.*

The southeast

Trinidad's **southeast** is bounded on its Atlantic coast by **Mayaro Bay**, the longest beach in the country, an astonishing – and astonishingly undeveloped – 22.5km of palm-fringed sand running from Point Radix in the north down to **Galeota Point**, a small peninsula that marks the country's southwesternmost extremity. Just inland, the low Southern Range rises to the **Trinity Hills**; swathed in dense rainforest, they are part of a rugged, unspoilt and seldom-visited **wildlife reserve**. Despite the presence of the oil industry in and around Galeota Point and the nearby town of **Guayaguayare**, the southeast has a holiday ambience, and many Trinidadians take their vacations here. It is the ideal place to get away from it all, soak up the sun and, as the Trinis say, "just chill".

Accommodation consists mostly of beach houses and self-catering apartments on Mayaro Bay – as yet there is only one hotel in the area; South East Eco Tours (☎644 1072) can arrange host homes. **Public transport** to the region is tortuous and slow; travelling from Port of Spain can take three to four hours, as opposed to two by private car.

Mayaro Bay

Mayaro Bay's greatest attraction is its beach, a gentle, coconut tree-lined curve of clean, soft brown sand. The only settlement of any size is the holiday village of **Mayaro**, towards the northern end of the beach – though the upmarket resort of **Grand Lagoon**, 2km south on the Mayaro–Guayaguayare Road, is rapidly sprouting new beach houses in anticipation of the growth in the area's tourist trade. Continuing south, you will see, with increasing frequency, the large luxurious houses built by the oil companies for their managers and workers. Men sell fresh fish by the roadside, and small boys will tempt you with strings of crabs and conch; sadly, these delicacies are rarely served in restaurants. Despite its stunning setting and wonderful beach, Mayaro remains practically undiscovered by foreign visitors; enjoy the peace and quiet while you can.

Some history

Originally inhabited by the Amerindians, the bay was settled by French royalist planters fleeing the wars and rebellions that ravaged the West Indies in the 1790s. The place boomed in the nineteenth century on the strength of its cotton and coconut estates. With the opening of a train service in 1914, it began to flourish as a seaside resort, but after the railways were closed down in 1965, the village went into economic decline. Its fortunes revived during the oil boom of the late 1970s, when it once again became a popular holiday resort with Trinidadians, and hotels and beach houses lined the coast. After the boom went bust in the mid-1980s, many of these fell into disrepair, and the largest hotel was taken over by an oil company as a retreat for its workers.

Arrival and accommodation

If you're **driving** to Mayaro from Port of Spain, the quickest route is via the Churchill Roosevelt Highway to Valencia, through Sangre Grande and down the east coast via Manzanilla (see p.201). This is also the quickest way if you are going by **public transport** – take a maxi to Arima, then one to Sangre Grande, and then one down to Mayaro. If you're coming from San Fernando and the west coast, drive east along the Manahambre, Naparima and Mayaro Roads. Maxis go from San Fernando to Princes Town; change here for a maxi to Mayaro.

There are a variety of **beach houses** to rent, from the most basic to the most luxurious – look out for the hand-painted advertisements along the main road. Advance booking isn't necessary unless you plan to visit during a public holiday. Most Trinidadians go on holiday in large groups, and the accommodation caters for this – plenty of spare mattresses are provided. *Westside House*, Beaumont Rd (☎652 8276 or 662 2494; ③) is a three-bedroom house sleeping a maximum of twelve people, two minutes' walk from the beach. It's clean but basic, with no a/c or fans, and you'll have to bring your own dishes and linen. *Amar's Beach Resort* (☎663 4961; ⑤), well signposted on a dirt track off the main road in Mayaro and is built directly onto the beach. The clean, fully furnished house has three bedrooms that can sleep up to seventeen people, but again, you'll have to bring your own linen. Well-signposted *Queen's Beach*, right on the sea in Radix Village (☎630 5532, fax 630 5607; ④) is one of the largest beachside properties, a full-blown but friendly place with a personal touch. The large rooms have a/c, TV, fridge and en-suite bathrooms, and there's a restaurant and a lively bar with a pool table. Equally well signposted and also on the beach, *RASH Resort* on Church Road (☎630 7274, fax 656 0193, *rashresort@tstt.net.tt*; ④), a collection of brightly painted one- to four-bedroom self-contained apartment with a/c, full kitchens and TVs; you'll need to bring blankets and towels, though linens are provided. There's a plunge pool and a covered, hammock-slung gazebo for barbecues and chilling out, and recliners for relaxing on the beach.

For details of the accommodation price codes used in these listings, see p.206.

Azee's Guest House, 3 1/2 mile marker Guayaguayare Rd (☎630 4619, fax 630 9140, *azees@tstt.net.tt*; ④) is a small, friendly hotel just two minutes' walk from the beach. All rooms have a/c, cable TV, telephone, fridge and en-suite bathrooms, and there's a homely bar and a restaurant, good for meals even if you're not a guest. *B's Host Home*, 4/5 mile marker Guayaguayare Rd (☎630 8510; ④) – the third house after the fenced Amoco complex – is run by Beulah Parriag, a pillar of the local community and an informative and friendly host. Rooms have a/c and cable TV; an excellent breakfast is included.

Mayaro village

MAYARO – 16.5km east of Rio Claro and 24km south of Manzanilla – has grown out of two old French villages, Pierreville and Plaisance, and is still marked as such on some maps. **Pierreville**, on the main Guayaguayare Road, is the business end of town, a small nexus of shops and local businesses. A side road cuts east to the seaside quarter, **Plaisance**, a lovely place with a thoroughly relaxing atmosphere. Residents and day-trippers eat and drink at the roadside cafés and bars, people wander on and off the beach, towels round their necks and a sprinkling of sand on their casual clothes, while music, lively conversation and the odd burst of raucous laughter drift on the air.

Each mini-community along the Mayaro–Guayaguayare Road is marked by signs paid for by the oil companies.

The beach here is one of the most popular bathing spots on Mayaro Bay. There are no changing facilities or toilets, but there is a lifeguard on duty from 10am to 5pm. The sea in this area has **strong currents**, so it is important to exercise caution.

Eating and drinking

There are not many places to eat in Mayaro – Trini holidaymakers tend to barbecue their own food on the beach – except for a few **fast-**

food outlets, mostly selling roti, and snack parlours. For more formal dining, the **restaurant** in *Azee's Guest House* (see p.233) serves delicious, inexpensive Creole food, while the larger air-conditioned restaurant at *Queen's Beach Resort* does a good Sunday brunch (11am–2.30pm; TT$50), as well as lovely breakfasts, and lunches and dinners: fish broth, salads, chicken and fish. There are also a few lively **rum shops** if you feel like a drink and a lime.

Galeota Point and Guayaguayare

Galeota Point, the southeast tip of Trinidad, is the domain of American oil companies. The area is dotted with oil storage tanks, and many oil wells can be seen offshore. The point itself is owned by Amoco, who do not permit public access to the end of the peninsula.

Two kilometres past Galeota Point on the south coast is the small town of **GUAYAGUAYARE**. The sea has been eroding the coast here for centuries, but the growing population seems unconcerned; the inhabitants build their houses away from the seafront, and a sea wall has been erected. The brown sandy **beach** is 4km long, with good calm seas for swimming.

Guayaguayare changed the fortunes of Trinidad, for it was here that oil was first discovered on the island in 1819 (see p.217), and the village blossomed in the early twentieth century when the petroleum industry really got going. Unless you are here in connection with the oil business, however, it's a quiet and uneventful place. Local residents still remember the big day a few years ago when a smuggler's ship, chased by the T&T coastguard, abandoned its cargo of cocaine. Large quantities of the drug were washed up on Guayaguayare beach, giving some of the locals an opportunity to make a quick killing before law enforcerment arrived.

The *Sea Wall Beach Resort* (☎630 9255; ②) on the Guayaguayare Main Road west of the village has three cheap and very basic rooms overlooking the sea. It is also a lively **bar** and nightspot, serving inexpensive **meals** of freshly caught fish. Three times a year at Easter, August and November they hold large **parties**, attracting heaving maxis full of people from all over the country. The owners also run The Eastern Diving Company (☎630 8572). Though this business is mainly directed at the oil industry, its internationally qualified (PADI) instructors can teach you to **scuba dive**; there are no spectacular reefs around here, but they do offer unusual trips under oil rigs, and will teach you **spear fishing** out on the open seas.

Trinity Hills Wildlife Sanctuary

The **Trinity Hills Wildlife Sanctuary and Reserve** encompasses 65 square kilometres of evergreen forest in the extreme southeast of Trinidad, running alongside the Rio Claro–Guayaguayare Road down to the sea. Situated in the highest part of the Southern Range, it includes the famous Trinity Hills and Mount Derrick, at 314 metres the tallest peak in the south. The hills form a watershed that's vital to the nation's water supply, ensuring that the area was declared a reserve as early as 1900; it received wildlife sanctuary status in 1934.

The many **rivers**, **streams** and **waterfalls** are excellent for bathing. The lush forests of **carat**, **redwood**, **cooperhoop** and **bois pois trees** shelter wild animals such as lappe, agouti, quenk, tatoo and red howler monkeys, and you may even see such rare creatures as ocelots, capuchin monkeys, buck deer, armadillos and opossums. The wide variety of birds includes the **mountain quail dove**, while deep in the hills, mysterious caves harbour many species of bats. A 45-minute hike from the road is a **mud volcano** and lake known as **Lagoon Bouffe**, at 100 metres wide one of Trinidad's largest.

Information on the reserve is hard to find due to its remoteness and the paucity of visitors. A few tour companies do visit the area, however, and though it is possible to visit independently (you'll need to get a permit from Petrotrin, who have a pipeline running through the reserve), it's far better to go with a guide. There are, it's alleged, marijuana fields in the hills, so it is wise to go with a local to avoid stumbling into dangerous areas. South East Eco Tours (☎644 1072) offer trips, ranging from easy to strenuous, guided by trained local people, for US$35–80; they need 48 hours (working days) notice to arrange the permit.

The southeast

For a permit to visit Trinity Hills, ring Petrotrin ☎649 5539, after 4pm Mon–Sat; on Sundays and public holidays call ☎649 5500 or 5501.

Chapter 5

Tobago

A n elongated oval of just 41 by 14 kilometres, **TOBAGO** features an astonishing richness within her craggy coastal fringes. Abounding with natural allure – deserted palm-lined beaches, pristine coral reefs and a wealth of lush rainforest – the island really is the last of the "unspoilt Caribbean", a tropical idyll largely unfettered by all-inclusive resorts but suitably geared toward visitors nonetheless. Tourism has taken root with breathtaking speed – 40,000 people now visit the island each year – and the subsequent reliance upon foreign dollars has inevitably had some negative effects, eating away at the very attributes which make the island so special. Huge resort developments are springing up along hitherto undisturbed seashores, and in the tourist strongholds, the traditional values held high in the otherwise deeply religious, close-knit communities are being replaced by a hustler mentality.

Tobago is hardly the typically jaded resort island, though. Local people and tourists co-exist in an easy equilibrium. Everyone frequents the same beaches, bars and nightclubs. Moreover, celebrations such as the Easter **goat races** are attended by more Tobagonians than tourists, and local culture is honoured at the annual **Heritage Festival** each August. The uniquely friendly and collective Tobagonian mentality can be seen at **Harvest Festivals**, where entire villages open their doors to passing revellers, and the marvellous **fisherman's fetes**, usually held around St Peter's Day at the end of July, where huge vats of fish tea are cooked up on the beach and served to the strains of booming sound systems.

Nevertheless, tourism *is* changing Tobago: helping hands sharing the labour of pulling in seine fishing nets are still called by a resonant toot on a conch shell, but nowadays the fishermen often wait until they've captured an audience before hauling the catch onto the sand, and the African drumming that forms a major part of local **Orisha** and **Spiritual Baptist** ceremonies (see "Religion," p.336) is now the soundtrack of many a hotel floorshow. However, Tobagonians take their culture – and their heritage – very seriously, and it's difficult to penetrate very far beneath the surface of this clannish, almost insular small-island community.

This close sense of community also means that Tobago is very safe – especially outside the Crown Point area, and if you use your common sense you should be fine. Ignore the warnings of all-inclusive hotels, such as *Turtle Beach* and the *Grafton*, which encourage tourists to stay on-site with tour operators, claiming that Tobago is dangerous. The best food, entertainment and scenic areas are outside the hotel complexes, so be adventurous, explore and keep the locals in business.

Physically, Tobago is breathtaking; heavy industry is confined to Trinidad, so the beaches are clean and the landscape left largely to its own devices. The flat coral and limestone plateau of the southwest – the **Lowlands** – is the island's most heavily developed region, comprising commercialized powder sand beaches such as **Pigeon Point** and **Store Bay**, where watersports, frothy drinks and suntanning are the order of the day, as well as quieter stretches of sand along the smart hotel coast of the southwest, where glass-bottom boats head for **Buccoo Reef**, palms sway over the **Mount Irvine** golf course, visitors puzzle over the "**mystery tombstone**" in residential **Plymouth** and hotels run night excursions to watch giant **turtles** laying eggs on the beach. Strong currents also provide some excellent **surfing** possibilities; rough seas between November and February (the height of the tourist season) provide massive breakers at bays like Mount Irvine. However, the tourist clamour is kept in check by the mercurial rush of the capital, **Scarborough**, a lively, picturesque port town tumbling down a lighthouse-topped hillside.

Pummelled by the dark-green, wave-whipped Atlantic, the island's rugged **windward** (south) **coast** is lined with appealing fishing villages; **Speyside** and **Charlotteville** in the remote eastern reaches have **coral reefs** as ornate and lively as you'll find anywhere in the Caribbean – Jacques Cousteau declared them the third finest in the region, and **scuba diving** is a burgeoning industry. Tobago is an excellent and inexpensive place to learn to dive, and there's plenty of challenging drift diving for the more experienced, while the many reefs within swimming distance of the beaches make for fantastic **snorkelling**. Coral sands and glassy Caribbean waters along the **leeward** (north) coast provide some of Tobago's finest beaches; some, like **Englishman's Bay**, are regularly deserted, while at **Castara**, **Parlatuvier** and **Bloody Bay**, you'll share the sand with local fishermen.

The landscape of the eastern interior rises steeply into the hillocks and rolling bluffs which make up the central **Main Ridge**. These mountains shelter the **Forest Reserve**, the oldest protected rainforest in the western hemisphere, an absurdly abundant tangle of mist-shrouded greenery dripping down to fabulous coastline with – in places – neither building nor road to interrupt the flow. Ornithologists and naturalists flock in for the **bird** and **animal** life that flourishes here; David Attenborough filmed parts of his celebrated *Trials of Life* series at **Little Tobago**, a solitary seabird sanctuary off the coast of Speyside.

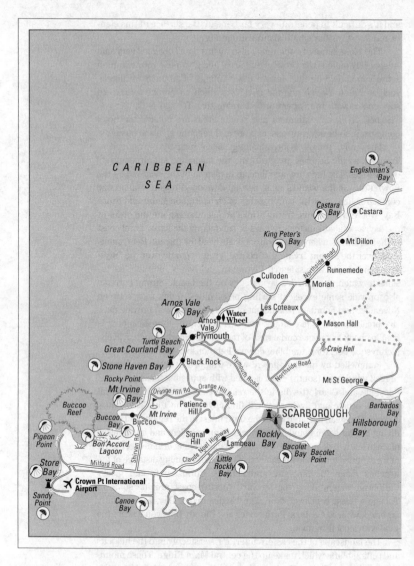

For more casual visitors, the squawking, chirruping forest offers plenty of opportunities for birdwatching or a splash in the icy **waterfalls**.

Some history

Though treated with indifference by the Spanish, Tobago has been hotly contested by other nations over the centuries. The original

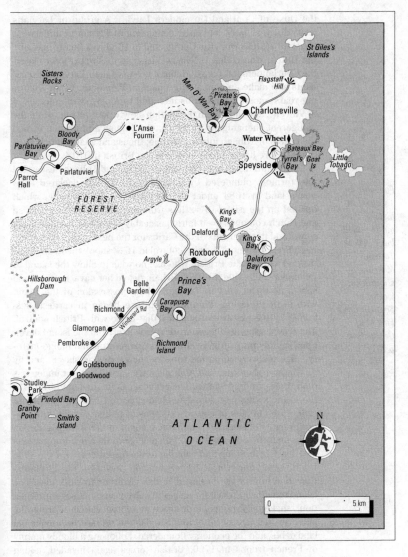

Carib population fiercely defended their paradisical *Tavaco* (the name is derived from the Indian word for tobacco) against other Amerindian tribes, and drove off several attempts by European colonists throughout the late 1500s and early 1600s. English sailors had staked Britain's claim in 1580, tacking a flag to a tree trunk during a water stop en route to Brazil, and in 1641, England's King Charles I presented Tobago to his godson James, the Duke of Courland (in modern Latvia). A group of **Latvians** arrived a year later, but their settlement at Plymouth underwent constant attacks from the Caribs, and in 1658 was finally taken by the Dutch, who called it "Nieuw Vlissingen". Twenty years later, the Courlanders left for good, but a group of their Latvian descendants still make an annual pilgrimage to Plymouth. In the following years, most of the Caribs migrated to Amerindian colonies in St Vincent, and the Indian population slowly petered out, while the belligerent shenanigans of the Dutch, English and French turned the coasts of Tobago into a war zone; the island changed hands 31 times before it was finally ceded to the British in 1814.

Forts sprang up at every vantage point, and Tobago descended into turmoil, plundered by **pirates** and officially declared a no man's land in 1684 under the treaty of Aix La Chapelle, which opened up the island to settlers from any nation. French, British and Dutch colonists lived fairly peaceably alongside free Africans, slaves and the remnants of the Caribs for the next eighty-odd years, but a French attempt to seize control in 1648 shook the neutral status and worried the British, who had no wish to allow the island to fall under Gallic rule. In 1672, Britain flexed her naval muscles and sent a powerful fleet to Tobago, taking possession of the island with swift precision. **Plantation culture** began in earnest, sustained by the promise of stability that came with British control. The crown appointed a **governor** a year later, and the island developed rapidly into a highly efficient sugar, cotton and indigo factory. Africans were imported to work the estates as slaves, and by 1772, three thousand-odd Africans were sweating it out under less than three hundred whites. The economy flourished, and by 1777, the island's eighty or so estates had exported 160,000 gallons of rum, 1,500,000lbs of cotton, 5,000lbs of indigo and 24,000 hundredweights of sugar. The numerical might of the slave population led to many bloody **uprisings**, with planters doling out amputations and death by burning and hanging to the dissenters.

For more on Tobagonian history, check out the small but excellent Tobago Museum, stunningly located at Scarborough's Fort King George (see p.293).

In 1781, however, the **French** again prevailed, razing plantations and forcing the besieged British governor to surrender. The island remained French for another twelve years, but sugar production, shaken by rampant destruction of the estates during the takeover, fell into decline. English planters refused to honour old land debts, and the economy floundered. Following a bloody mutiny of French troops in 1790, British forces again invaded, taking Tobago in 1793 only to relinquish her back to their enemy less than ten years later. Following Britain's formal declaration of war against France in 1802, the island was finally ceded to the British under the 1814 Treaty of Paris, and another phase of successful sugar production ensued.

Tobago prospered until the 1840s, her newly emancipated African population taking to the bush to plant small-scale farms, forming coastal fishing communities or continuing to work the estates as free men and women. **Moravian missions** began to provide them with education, and many converted to Christianity; the faith has been incorporated with African belief systems to form the Spiritual Baptist sect (see p.337), and today, Tobago boasts T&T's strongest concentration. When Britain removed its protective tariffs on sugar sales, however, Tobago's unmechanized industry was unable to compete with more efficient producers. A severe hurricane in 1847, along with the collapse of the West India Bank which underwrote the plantations, marked the beginning of the end of the sugar trade in Tobago. In the aftermath of the **Belmanna Riots** (see p.311), Tobago's Legislative Council relinquished its tenuous rule, and the island became a Crown Colony in 1879. Having reaped all it could from the island and its sugar industry, England had little further need for troublesome, ailing Tobago and washed her hands of the island. In 1899, Tobago was made a **ward** of Trinidad, effectively becoming the bigger island's poor relation with little control over her own destiny. With the collapse of the sugar industry, the islanders fell back upon other crops, planting the acres of limes, coconuts and cocoa that still stand today; boosted by the arrival of **free Africans** in the mid-1800s, the black population clubbed together to farm the land, tending their food crops in the efficient **"Len-Hand" system** of shared labour that is still celebrated in the annual round of Harvest Festivals. By the early 1900s the island was exporting fruit and vegetables to Trinidad, and in 1927, the island was granted a single seat on the legislative council.

In 1963, **Hurricane Flora** (see p.303) ravaged Tobago, razing whole villages and laying waste to most of the island's crops. In the restructuring programme that followed, attempts were made to diversify the economy and the first tentative steps towards developing a tourist industry began. By 1980, the island had her sovereignty partially restored when the **Tobago House Of Assembly** (THA) was reconvened, but it had authority only over the island's more mundane affairs while the main decisions were still made in Trinidad. The lobbying of Tobagonian-born former Prime Minister **Arthur Robinson** gave Tobago a stronger profile in the republic's affairs but Tobago is still looked down on by the bigger isle, much to the resentment of the local populace. With agriculture on the decline and tourism slowly becoming the main earner, the island's economic future is still uncertain; in spring 1998, Tobago was officially declared an underdeveloped and low-income region in order to qualify for aid from the UN and EC. However, as Tobago and her people have so often demonstrated formidable strength in the face of adversity, the island seems set to prosper, despite the challenges.

If you're interested in keeping informed on local issues, Tobago's Radio Tambrin – 92.1FM – has an excellent call-in morning show (7–9am) that even the local politicians use to keep abreast of the population's concerns.

Arrival and information

Most people arrive via **Crown Point International Airport**, an airy, open-plan affair that despite expansion remains small enough to feel overwhelmed by the arrival of a single jet. Opposite is a row of shops; among them is a branch of the Republic Bank (Mon–Thurs 8am–3pm, Fri 8am–1pm & 3–5pm) for **currency exchange**, a small newsagent and two restaurants – the fast-food chain *Royal Castle* and the cheerful and busy *Tri-Star Restaurant*. Local and Companion **phonecards** (TT$20, $30, $60, $100 + VAT) are available from the stationery shop opposite the airport.

All visitors must pay TT$100 departure tax, in local currency, at the smoked-glass window at the front of the airport complex (daily 6am–10pm)

For **information**, head to the tourist board office; the last shop to the left of the parade (daily 6am–10pm; ☎639 0509). Staff can advise on accommodation, transport and activities. The B&B Association is also based out of this office. If you're heading anywhere further than Plymouth or Scarborough (eg Charlotteville or Speyside), this is well worth doing, as chartering a taxi is quite expensive and many hotels throw in free airport pick-ups as an incentive to choose them over the many alternatives. The tourist board also have copies of the free, tourist-oriented *Tobago Today* listings newspaper as well as the latest version of the more detailed *Discover Trinidad and Tobago* booklet. Internet access is available as well, payable by credit card.

Travel between Tobago and Trinidad

Since Air Caribbean closed down in 2000 the only airline that flies regularly between the two islands is BWIA – though LIAT also makes the occasional flight. Currently, BWIA offer seven to ten flights daily (TT$150 one way, TT$300 return; in Trinidad ☎627 2942, in Tobago ☎660 2942).

Getting around

Tobago's **public transport** system is not as comprehensive as Trinidad's, and **renting a car** is essential to see the island independently and avoid the hassles, confusion and long waits that inevitably ensue if you rely on route taxis or buses. Blue-banded **maxi taxis** (see "Basics", p.27) are rare, most operating private school runs or attempting to ferry tourists at inflated prices; the only regular route runs from Scarborough to Charlotteville (see Scarborough, pp.285–296). However, the **route taxi** network is extensive and convenient for short hops in the western portion of the island: taxis run along all the main roads, and travelling between Crown Point, Buccoo, Mount Irvine or Plymouth simply involves standing on the right side of the road for your destination, sticking out your hand and asking the driver where they're heading: note that in Tobago, not all route taxis have the usual "H" taxi registration plate; the best way to recognize one is to watch out for a car with multiple passengers and

Parlatuvier Bay, Tobago

The Pitch Lake at La Brea, Trinidad

Rasta hats, Scarborough

Argyll Waterfall, Tobago

Scarlet ibis, Point-a-Pierre, Trinidad

Pepper stall in southern Trinidad

Castara, Tobago

Turtle Beach, Tobago

Tobago rum shop

Englishman's Bay, Tobago

Rainforest on Little Tobago

Liming on the pier, Charlotteville, Tobago

a driver clutching a wad of dollars. If you're heading further afield, say to Castara, Charlotteville or Speyside, you'll need to travel into Scarborough, where route taxis and buses depart to the rest of the island; see p.288 for details.

Taxis

You can **walk** to most of the hotels in Crown Point, but if you're travelling further, such as Mount Irvine, Plymouth, Charlotteville or Speyside, check the taxi price list on the wall of the arrivals lounge. The rates are used by all the **licensed drivers** who meet each flight – they're high, but not wildly so. If you're on a budget, you can cross the street and haggle with the drivers who are not part of the authorized airport queuing system; they may reduce their rates (to the wrath of the licensed guys). For reputable operators to call (including a woman driver), see "Listings", p.321.

Buses

Tobago's public transport has greatly improved in recent years. Cumbersome, diesel-billowing Public Transport Service Company (PTSC) buses and confusing and often contradictory timetables made getting around the island a slow and frustrating experience. The company has since bought a new fleet of buses and improved its timetables, making public transport a convenient and inexpensive option. There's an hourly shuttle service between Crown Point (there's a stop just outside the airport complex) and the main Scarborough **depot** on Greenside Street; buses run half past the hour from Crown Point and on the hour from Scarborough.

From Scarborough, buses run along the windward coast to Mount St George, Studley Park, Glamorgan, Argyll Falls, Roxborough, Delaford, King's Bay, Speyside and Charlotteville (6 daily; 4.30am–6.30pm, variable times). The leeward coast route extends from Scarborough to L'Anse Fourmi via Moriah, Castara, Englishman's Bay, Parlatuvier and Bloody Bay (6 daily, 4.30am–6.30pm, variable times). In the Lowlands, buses run from Scarborough to Mount Thomas via Les Coteaux and Golden Lane (8 daily, 5am–6pm, every two hours); they also go from Scarborough to Plymouth via Mount Irvine and Black Rock (hourly, 5am–8pm). All

---

Bus prices

Scarborough to:

Belle Garden: TT$5	Mason Hall: TT$2
Castara: TT$5	Mount St George: TT$3
Charlotteville: TT$8	Parlatuvier: TT$6
Crown Point TT$2	Pembroke: TT$4
Delaford: TT$6	Roxborough: TT$5
Glamorgan: TT$4	Speyside: TT$8

ORGANIZED TOURS

Several established tour companies offer rather sterile itineraries of Tobago's main sights, ranging from snorkelling on the Buccoo Reef and a barbecue at No Man's Land to trips to Scarborough, Fort George, Little Tobago, the Forest Reserve, Plymouth and the mystery tombstone. These tours are great if you want a zero-hassle overview of the island, but at worst, you can feel completely distanced from what flashes by through the window. Full-day tours almost always include lunch and cost US$55–70 per person; groups must be of four or more. Most people book through reps who visit the main hotels or trawl the beaches, but you can sign up individually as well. Classic Tours (☎639 9891, fax 639 9892) and Sun Fun Tours (☎639 7461, fax 639 7561, www.sunfuntour.com) are the best of the bunch.

Hiking and wildlife tours

For more information on Forest Reserve tour guides, see p.304.

Margaret Hinkson's thoughtful Educatours (☎639 7422, magintob@hotmail.com) organizes excursions with local guides, custom designed to suit your interests. Prices start from US$65 for a guided trek through the rainforest and on to Argyll Waterfall (6hr), including lunch. Renowned naturalist David Rooks (☎ & fax 639 4276, www.trinidad.net/rookstobago) leads informed and professional tours to **Little Tobago** (Thurs, 8–9hr; US$65) and the Forest Reserve (Sat, 7hr; US$45), though you may have to share him with up to fifteen others. Pioneer Journeys (☎660 4327, *pturpin@tstt.net.tt*) offer more rugged jaunts, including a hike along the **Louis D'Or River** to see crayfish, crab and wetland birds; prices start from US$30–40 for transport to the hike area. Mark Puddy (☎639 4931) leads fabulous offbeat **hiking trips** to deserted beaches (6hr; US$40) or seldom-visited waterfalls (4hr; US$25); rates include transport to and from your hotel as well as drinks and snacks. Darren Henry (☎639 4559) is a trained forester and licensed tour guide who takes trips into the **forest reserve** (1hr 30min–2hrs; US$25) and to Little Tobago (2 hrs; TT$150), a short tour of the Botanical Gardens (45mins; TT$50) and a hike to Mason Hall Waterfall (2hr 30min; TT$80). Adolphus James (☎639 2231, fax 639 3249) is an excellent guide for serious birders, specializing in a rainforest tour for up to four people (US$120). Part-time Store Bay lifeguard Harris McDonald (☎639 0513) does a lively, informative all-day Leeward coast, forest reserve and Little Tobago tour (US$70, plus US$15 for the boat to Little Tobago). Trained by David Rooks, Ali Baba (☎639 1096, alibaba@scholzkom.de, www.scholzkom.ce/alibaba) is an excellent tour operator working from Castara. In addition to the standard island trips (Little Tobago and such) he

tickets must be **pre-purchased** as drivers will not accept cash; they are available from the shops opposite the airport complex or from bars and mini-marts throughout the island. For information on bus times and where to buy tickets locally call ☎639 2293.

Car and bike rental

Most of the international **car rental** firms and the local guys with two or three vehicles are clustered around the airport; prices for standard jeeps and manual/automatic cars can vary; stick-shift cars and takes people **dolphin watching** (US$50) and camping on Englishman's Bay (US$60), where under the starry sky he will serenade you with his guitar by an open fire. He also does off-trail hikes in the rainforest and birdwatching trips (both US$50).

Jeep and dirt bike safaris

Jeep and dirt bike safaris booked through *Coconut Inn* (☎639 8493, fax 639 0512) take you to less accessible parts of the island, along ancient trails through deserted plantations, stopping at beaches and waterfalls; you can ride pillion on request. All-day bike and jeep tours cost US$65; both include food and drink. Tobago's only female taxi driver, Liz Lezama (☎639 2309 or 758 1748) offers an extensive island tour including lunch for US$60 with plenty of stops at small rum shops and a good local perspective.

Sea safaris

Adventurous **sea safaris** aboard hobie cat mini-catamarans are available from Cool Runnings (☎639 6363, fax 639 4755, www.outdoor-tobago.com). A No Man's Land picnic costs US$95, a trip to Castara is US$155 and an Englishman's Bay safari that includes all meals and a night's camping on the beach is from US$235 for two boats, depending upon group size; for an extra fee a dive or water-skiing can be included. They also offer a variety of three-, four- and seven-night packages as well as horseback riding, mountain biking tours for all levels of experience and offshore charters to the Grenadines.

Aerial tours

If you want to do a little **aerial sightseeing**, you could consider chartering a small plane or helicopter from Hummingbird Helicopter Services in Crown Point (☎639 7159 or 622 7159, hummingbird@ hummingbirdheli-copters.com), who offer twenty- (US$300) and forty-minute (US$500) tours of the island for a minimum of four people. Romantics can opt for their sunset soiree tour (US$300 per couple), which includes a bottle of wine with the flight.

Horseback riding tours

Those who prefer a slower, more earth-bound tour can go horseback riding with Essentially Tobago (☎639 9379, tobago@pobox.com, www.essentially-tobago.com); a two-hour tour costs US$50.

jeeps are less expensive than automatics. Local operators tend to be cheaper, but the smaller the company, the less likely you are to be offered 24-hour assistance and adequate coverage in case of an accident; the most reliable among them is Sherman's, based in Lambeau (☎639 2292). Friendliest amongst the internationals is the local franchise of Thrifty (☎639 8507), which offers efficient service and a wide selection of vehicles. Most companies ask for some kind of **deposit**, usually a credit card imprint; a notable exception is Auto Rentals (☎639 0644), which has one of the largest fleets in Tobago.

Scuba diving and snorkelling

Tobago is one of the best **diving** spots in the southeastern Caribbean, yet it has relatively few divers visiting its pristine coral reefs, volcanic formations and marine wrecks. The island is internationally recognized for its exciting, though difficult, drift dives, caused by the Guyana current, a result of the confluence of the Caribbean Sea and the Atlantic Ocean. The island's aquamarine seas are home to three hundred species of South Atlantic coral and a variety of spectacular multicoloured fish, including the neon orange-and-blue parrot fish, the black-and-yellow-striped sergeant majors and every species of angel fish. Larger species such as whales, stingrays, sharks, dolphins, turtles and squid are also present. While it's even possible to see rare species such as toadfish and shortnose batfish, the island is best known for is the enormous number of manta rays that are frequently encountered on diving trips. Equally thrilling is the large variety of plant life, huge corals, thousands of giant barrel sponges, Venus sea fans and orange elephant ear sponges among others. Adding a touch of history to underwater encounters are the sunken pirate ships, Spanish galleons and dozens of World War II troop and supply carriers that litter the sea floor. Speyside (see pp.312–317) is known as "the Disneyland of diving", offering a variety of spectacular sites surrounding the offshore islands: Goat Island is popular for drift dives, St Giles for its rocky pinnacles and underwater canyon and Little Tobago, where 70 percent of dives encounter manta rays. Popular dives in this area include London Bridge, Bookends, Angel Reef, The Cathedral and Kelliston Drain – the site of the single largest brain coral in the Caribbean, and at six metres across and four metres high, possibly the world. For more advanced divers Sisters Rocks – with the sea shelf falling to 667 metres – is especially popular for larger species of fish including hammerhead sharks.

Tobago's **diving industry** was only established in the 1980s but since then scuba diving operations have multiplied with every hotel, beach and guesthouse sporting their own centre. There's some excellent diving to be had in the west, particularly around Buccoo reef, the Mount Irvine wall – popular for night dives – and Arnos Vale, which has a multitude of eels and rays. Prices vary slightly between operators; in general one to three dives cost US$30–35 each, one-day resort courses US$55–65, five-day PADI open water certification courses from US$350–375, advanced open water from US$225 and skin diving at around US$35.

When deciding who to dive with, **safety** comes first. Always check for the prominent display of a dive affiliation, such as NAUI, PADI, SSI or BSAC. A good operator will always ask you to fill in paperwork and present a diving certification card. The rental equipment should be well rinsed; if you see sand or salt crystals this may indicate careless equipment care.

Scooters are available from some beach outlets and cost approximately US$20 a day. **Motorbikes** are catching on fast and there are several places offering dirt bikes for about US$30 per day. Some places offer discounts for extended rental (take a bike for six days and you get a seventh free), and most also offer accompanied tours along off-road trails. Check your bike and helmet before you ride away, as some are less than perfect. With a car or bike, it's

Inspect all equipment thoroughly, check hoses for wear, see that mouth-pieces are secure and ensure they give you a depth gauge and air-pressure gauge. Listen for air leaks when you gear up and smell the air, which should be odourless. If you smell oil or anything else, search for a different operator. Reliable operators include SubLime (sublime@tstt.net.tt), based at one of the west's best dive sites, sheltered Arnos Vale Bay (☎639 9386) and the *Tropikist Beach Hotel* in Crown Point (☎639 9642 or 8512), R & Sea Diving Company (☎639 8120 rsdivers@tstt.net.tt), a locally run oper-ation based at Spence's Terrace on Milford Road and Pigeon Point; Tobago Dive Experience (☎639 7034); Sal's & Stina Scuba (☎639 1142, salsti-nascuba@tstt.met.tt) based at *Conrado's* on Pigeon Point offer special accommodation rates for divers at the hotel; Dive Tobago at Pigeon Point, whose catchphrase is "go down with a local" (☎639 0202 or 2150, cohel@tstt.net.tt); while Proscuba (☎639 7424 or 682 9673, www.diveg-uide.com/proscuba), based at *Rovanel's* resort on Store Bay Local Road and *Surfside* on Milford Road, offer "scuba phones" for easy communica-tion underwater, as well as Dutch-, German- and French-speaking dive masters. Once a week they go to Speyside and Sisters Rocks. Two newer reputable firms are Manta Dive Centre (☎639 9969 or 9209, man-taray@tstt.net.tt, mantadive.com) based on Pigeon Point Road and oppo-site the *Crown Point Beach* hotel and Scuba Adventure Safari (☎660 7333 or 7767, infodivetobago.com, www.divetobago.com) on Pigeon Point Road. Adventure Eco-Divers Ltd, based at Stone Haven Bay (☎639 8729, eco-diver@tstt.net.tt), offer the standard dive packages and equip-ment rental. World of Watersports (☎660 7234, info@worldofwater-ports.com, www.worldofwatersports.com) operate from *Tobago Hilton*, *Blue Haven* and *Arnos Vale* hotels, and their staff speak English, German, Afrikaans and Dutch. For dive operators in Speyside see p.316. Man Friday (☎660 4676, mfdiving@tstt.net.tt) near Man O' War Bay beach in Charlotteville offer resort and certification courses, single dives and pack-ages, and rent out snorkelling equipment. If anything does go wrong, Tobago has a recompression chamber in Roxborough (☎660 4000).

Much of the exotic plant and fish life in Tobago's waters can also be seen **snorkelling**. Recommended sites include Pirate's Bay in Charlotteville, Arnos Vale, and Englishman's and Great Courland bays. Many local tour operators, such as Natural Mystics (☎639 7245, fax 639 7888, mystic@tstt.net.tt), offer day cruises, with snorkelling included, at deserted bays or at excellent sites which can only be reached by boat – around Goat Island, for example. Most dive operators rent out snorkelling equipment for US$10 a day, so if you plan to do plenty it's cheaper to bring your own.

imperative that you take note of every bump and scratch as well as checking the tyres (especially the spare and the jack), headlamps and indicators. If the car is damaged, let the company know imme-diately, and on no account let anyone unauthorized drive the car; as Tobago is so tiny, someone is bound to catch you at it, and you are liable for any damage. For details of reputable operators, see "Listings", p.321.

Shopping in Tobago

The widest variety of local crafts – carved calabashes, Rasta hats and such – are sold at the huts adjacent to Store Bay beach, but you'll get better deals at the vendors' mall in Scarborough; good carvings are on offer from a lone vendor who sets up in A.P.T James Park. Also in town, Tobago Treasures on Carrington Street sell a nice line in colourful fish carvings. On the Arnos Vale Road, inland of Plymouth, keep a sharp eye out for a small, brightly painted shop selling drums and beautifully tailored African-style clothing. The Doux Doux shop on Milford Road, adjacent to Viewport Supermarket stocks good handmade sandals, clothing and knick-knacks, whilst Shore Things on Old Milford Road in Lambeau sells high-quality crafts and furniture, and serves lovely light lunches as well. Drum lovers should head straight for the Culture Barn (☎639 9022, Mon–Sat 8am–7pm) at Fort Bennett, Black Rock, where Malcolm Melville crafts beautiful, innovative drums from mango, mahogany, cedar and breadfruit woods; he also sells drums at booth nine at Store Bay beach. The Art Gallery (artgal@tstt.net.tt), just off the Claude Noel Highway opposite the *Tobago Hilton* entrance has an ever-changing collection of Tobagonian art, including gorgeous watercolours of gingerbread homes and local life, oils, prints and crafts. Sculptures and gifts imported from a dozen African west coast countries are on sale just up the road at the African Art Gallery and Gift Shop. Tobago Fine Art – on the Claude Noel Highway between the Shirvan Road and Canoe Road turn-offs – is run by a local artist and has a variety of inexpensive paintings of local culture.

Funky and distinctive **clothing** can be bought from Radical Designs on the corner of Main and Bacolet streets in Scarborough; their trademark T-shirts are far more chic than your average souvenir specimen – you'd actually want to wear them at home. Reflections, next to *Hendrix Bar* in Buccoo village sell a stylish range of natural linen clothes alongside their selection of cool Tobago T-shirts. For batik lovers, The Backyard on Airport Road, Crown Point, has a good selection and if you're hungry they also serve up delicious sandwiches. Also known for its wide range of batiks is the Cotton House on Bacolet Street; their selection is much wider than The Backyard's but more expensive.

While duty-free goods are sold at Stetchers in the airport departure lounge, local jams and honey are best bought from supermarkets. Zoom Caribbean on Pigeon Point beach carry quality T-shirts and Carib memorabilia, and calypso, soca and reggae records, tapes or CDs are available from One World Music Shop on Airport Road, opposite *Dillon's* restaurant.

Lowlands: Crown Point to Plymouth

Tobago's flattest, most accessible portion is focused around a crowded 5-kilometre stretch of **Milford Road** from the airport and Store Bay beach – a tiny area known as **Crown Point** – through **Bon Accord, Canaan** and **Mount Pleasant**, and 10 kilometres north along **Shirvan Road** to **Buccoo, Mount Irvine** and **Plymouth**. Usually lumped together as "the **Lowlands**", the low-lying western tip is the island's most heavily developed region, home to most of its residents as well as the vast majority of hotels, restaurants, nightclubs and the most popular beaches. A highly commercialized hotchpotch of concrete and neon around Milford Road (bar the **birdwatching** paradise of Bon Accord Lagoon wetlands) combined with the less frenetic beaches and smart hotels that shoot off Shirvan Road, the area is hardly the "real Tobago", but its animation and sense of industry more than make up for an occasional lack of aesthetic charm and, whether you like it or not, the concentration of facilities and activities mean that you'll inevitably spend a lot of time here.

Tobago's most popular **beaches** are within shouting distance of the airport – **Store Bay** is a couple of minutes on foot, and **Pigeon Point** is about ten minutes further. The terrain between the two is jam-packed with all the familiar tourist trappings – craft stalls, restaurants and bars advertising specials or happy hours, and the hoardings of endless resort hotels – and many people (especially the notoriously unadventurous Trinidadian holidaymakers) never make it any further. East of the beaches, Milford Road continues in the same vein, cutting through Tobago's tourist heartland to quieter stretches of sand; you'll rarely have to share **Canoe Bay**, and past here, the vacation ethic slackens a little; **Lambeau** and **Signal Hill** communities are the almost exclusive preserve of locals. Set atop the foothills of the island's modest mountains, both villages provide beautiful views of the unravelling flatlands to the west, and **Little Rockly Bay** is a pretty cove below.

Another rash of tourism development lies along Shirvan Road, which cuts north from Milford along the coast. **Buccoo** harbours two main attractions: an abundant **reef**, trawled by fleets of glass-bottom boats carrying snorkellers out to the coral and the **Nylon Pool**, a metre-deep bathing spot on a sandbar in the middle of the bay, as well as **Sunday School**, Tobago's biggest, brashest open-air party. Dominated by a palm-studded eighteen-hole **golf course**, **Mount Irvine** heralds the start of a series of glorious **beaches**, while historic **Plymouth**, with its cluster of **forts** and **mystery tombstone**, is also heavily visited. Potted attractions like the **Arnos Vale water wheel** complex and the Kimme **art exhibition**, as well as plenty of restaurants and the fabulous prospect of watching a **turtle** lay eggs metres from your hotel room draw enthusiastic crowds of locals and tourists alike.

Accommodation

Though the sheer number of **hotels** and **guesthouses** crammed into Crown Point makes choosing accommodation mind-boggling, the tourist-friendly location keeps prices relatively high; you pay less for the same standard of room in more remote areas, and there are few bed and breakfasts or host homes here; most are

Tobago's best beaches	
Bloody Bay	p.302
Castara	p.298
Englishman's Bay	p.301
King Peter's Bay	p.298
Pirate's Bay	p.319

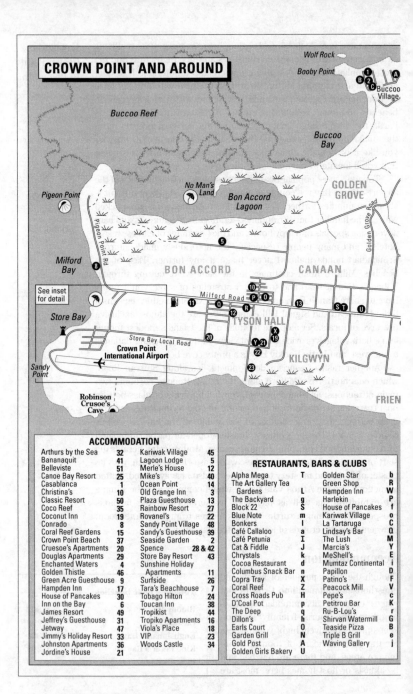

CROWN POINT AND AROUND

Wolf Rock

Booby Point

Buccoo Village

Buccoo Reef

Buccoo Bay

GOLDEN GROVE

Pigeon Point

No Man's Land

Bon Accord Lagoon

Golden Grove Road

Milford Bay

Pigeon Point Rd

BON ACCORD

CANAAN

See inset for detail

Store Bay

Milford Road

Sandy Point

Store Bay Local Road

Crown Point International Airport

TYSON HALL

KILGWYN

Robinson Crusoe's Cave

FRIEN

ACCOMMODATION

Arthurs by the Sea	32	Kariwak Village	45
Bananaquit	41	Lagoon Lodge	5
Belleviste	51	Merle's House	12
Canoe Bay Resort	25	Mike's	40
Casablanca	1	Ocean Point	14
Christina's	10	Old Grange Inn	3
Classic Resort	50	Plaza Guesthouse	13
Coco Reef	35	Rainbow Resort	27
Coconut Inn	19	Rovanel's	22
Conrado	8	Sandy Point Village	48
Coral Reef Gardens	15	Sandy's Guesthouse	39
Crown Point Beach	37	Seaside Garden	2
Cruesoe's Apartments	20	Spence	28 & 42
Douglas Apartments	29	Store Bay Resort	43
Enchanted Waters	4	Sunshine Holiday	
Golden Thistle	46	Apartments	11
Green Acre Guesthouse	9	Surfside	26
Hampden Inn	17	Tara's Beachhouse	7
House of Pancakes	30	Tobago Hilton	24
Inn on the Bay	6	Toucan Inn	38
James Resort	49	Tropikist	44
Jeffrey's Guesthouse	31	Tropiko Apartments	16
Jetway	47	Viola's Place	18
Jimmy's Holiday Resort	33	VIP	23
Johnston Apartments	36	Woods Castle	34
Jordine's House	21		

RESTAURANTS, BARS & CLUBS

Alpha Mega	T	Golden Star	b
The Art Gallery Tea		Green Shop	R
Gardens	L	Hampden Inn	W
The Backyard	g	Harlekin	P
Block 22	S	House of Pancakes	f
Blue Note	m	Kariwak Village	o
Bonkers	l	La Tartaruga	C
Café Callaloo	a	Lindsay's Bar	Q
Café Petunia	I	The Lush	M
Cat & Fiddle	J	Marcia's	Y
Chrystals	k	MeShell's	E
Cocoa Restaurant	d	Mumtaz Continental	i
Columbus Snack Bar	n	Papillon	D
Copra Tray	X	Patino's	F
Coral Reef	Z	Peacock Mill	V
Cross Roads Pub	H	Pepe's	c
D'Coal Pot	p	Petitrou Bar	K
The Deep	q	Ru-B-Lou's	r
Dillon's	h	Shirvan Watermill	G
Earls Court	O	Teaside Pizza	B
Garden Grill	N	Triple B Grill	e
Gold Post	A	Waving Gallery	j
Golden Girls Bakery	U		

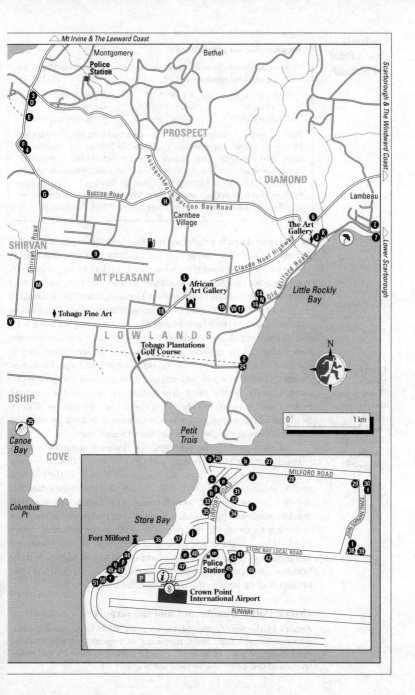

Montgomery
Bethel
Police Station

PROSPECT

Scarborough & The Windward Coast △

DIAMOND

Lambeau

Auchenskeoch Buccoo Bay Road

Buccoo Road
Carnbee Village

The Art Gallery

Little Rockly Bay

SHIRVAN

Claude Noel Highway

Old Milford Road

Lower Scarborough △

MT PLEASANT

African Art Gallery

Shirvan Road

♦ **Tobago Fine Art**

L O W L A N D S

N

Tobago Plantations Golf Course

DSHIP

COVE

Canoe Bay

Petit Trois

0   1 km

Columbus Pt

Store Bay

Fort Milford ♣

MILFORD ROAD

AIRPORT ROAD

JOHN GORMAN TRACE

STORE BAY LOCAL ROAD

Police Station

P

ℹ

Ⓢ **Crown Point International Airport**

RUNWAY

Lowlands: Crown Point to Plymouth

located around Scarborough (see pp.285–296). Space is at a premium and many establishments are built back to back with little individuality and scant regard for aesthetics; rooms are kept dark to keep them cool. You'll miss out on solitude; discos blare soca into the night air and road traffic is pretty constant, scaring away bird and animal life and making the place feel like the Costa Del Sol rather than an unspoilt Caribbean paradise. However, there are definite advantages to staying in the area; you'll be within walking distance of the busiest beaches, restaurants and bars, and among the uniform, you'll find some of Tobago's most appealing hotels. The proximity of the airport (jet noise isn't a problem) also means that you can often walk straight from the tarmac to your room, though many hotels offer free transport from the airport or Scarborough sea port; call ahead and check from the tourism office or from one of the airport phone booths; phonecards are available from the small newsagents shop opposite the arrivals lounge.

Accommodation in Crown Point and the surrounding areas are shown on the map on pp.250–251.

Tobago's most **upmarket** hotels are clustered along the beaches between Buccoo and Plymouth, and the exclusive **villas** (see opposite) around the Mount Irvine golf course offer some of the plushest private accommodation you'll find, but not all the accommodation is the exclusive preserve of the well-heeled. There are plenty of middle bracket hotels and guesthouses, and the area makes one of the most appealing bases on the island; you're close to the action of Crown Point without being stuck right in it, transport is easy (taxis run along Shirvan Road from early mornings to late at night), and the beaches are marvellous. You will, however, need a car in Arnos Vale, or be reliant on taxis in Buccoo to visit the better beaches.

Crown Point, Bon Accord and the airport

Arthurs by the Sea, Airport Rd, Crown Point ☎639 0196, fax 639 4122, www.trinidad.net/arthurs. Small, simple and dark rooms, each with a balcony overlooking the pool; all have a/c, en-suite bathroom, cable TV and fridge. Overpriced despite the nice sundeck and pool area. ⑦.

Bananaquit, Store Bay Local Rd, Crown Point ☎ & fax 639 9733, www.bananaquit.com. Friendly Trinidadian-Geordie hosts run these large, clean studio rooms that include kitchenette, en-suite bathroom, a/c and cable TV. Some rooms sleep up to six. Guests can use the pool at the adjacent *Store Bay Resort*. ④.

Belleviste, Sandy Point, Crown Point, PO Box 69, Scarborough ☎ & fax 639 9351, www.trinidad.net/belleviste. Unattractive block-like exterior masking spacious, well-designed apartments. All have wooden fittings, a/c, cable TV and full kitchen. Outside is a garden with barbecue pits, pool, children's play equipment, gazebo overlooking the sea and a path to the beach. Directly opposite the airport runway. ⑥.

Canoe Bay, Canoe Bay Resort, Friendship ☎639 4055. Three apartments, each with two bedrooms, a/c, furnished kitchen and bathroom, set in the beautifully landscaped grounds of Canoe Bay. A quiet, clean beach with changing facilities and a bar is on your doorstep. ⑨.

Christina's, Roberts Street, Bon Accord ☎ & fax 639 7834. Good value and German-owned guesthouse set in a peaceful backstreet behind Milford Road, ten minutes' walk from Pigeon Point beach. Huge rooms have a/c, radio, TV, fridge, phone and en-suite bathroom. On-site restaurant serves German cuisine, and breakfast is included in the rates. ⑥.

Classic Resort, Sandy Point, Crown Point ☎639 0742. Tiny place with small, basic rooms that have seen better days, and shared bathroom and kitchen facilities. Good for Tobagonian ambience. ③.

Coco Reef, Airport Rd, Crown Point, PO Box 434, Scarborough ☎639 8571,

---

Villas

Though **villas** are conventionally seen as luxury accommodation, they can work out to be quite cost effective if you're travelling in a large group. Recent years have seen an explosion of villa building aimed at the well-heeled traveller, ranging from packed, estate-type complexes – the majority are set around the Mount Irvine golf course – to the secluded villa of one's dreams. For reviews, see the accommodation listings on pp.252–261. A useful go-between is the Tobago Villas Agency on Shirvan Road (PO Box 301, Scarborough ☎ & fax 639 8737), which represents properties throughout the island. Their villas rent from US$110 per day for a very basic one-bedroom unit to palatial residences with up to five bedrooms and every conceivable luxury at US$600 per day. Essentially Tobago (☎639 9379, tobago@pobox.com, www.essentiallytobago.com) are agents for five large, plush villas overlooking Mount Irvine golf course. They also organise tours and watersports. Prices for villas start at US$395 per night.

For further villa listings – including the exclusive *Being Villa*, a snip at US$1200 a night – visit the See Tobago website (www.seetobago.com), a font of accommodation information. You might have trouble finding reasonably priced villas from outside the island as they're unlikely to be advertised by foreign travel agents. If you're prepared to take a risk, it's feasible to find a house once you've arrived, often at bargain rates. Book yourself into a nice hotel for a few days and start making local friends; these inexpensive houses are unlikely to be on any agency books.

fax 639 8574, in US and Canada 1-800/221 1294, cocoreef-tobago@trinidad.net. Peach-painted enclave of contrived luxury with perimeter walls beside an artifical white sand beach. Two restaurants, two bars, health spa, gym, pool, watersports and rooms with every associated frippery offer opulence at the expense of atmosphere, due mainly to package tour bookings and overworked staff. Restaurant food is good but overpriced. ⑨.

Coconut Inn, Store Bay Local Rd, Bon Accord, PO Box 329, Scarborough ☎639 8493, fax 639 0512, www.coconut-inn.com. Distinctly Teutonic ambience – clean lines, spotless rooms, well-mown lawns and no-hassle atmosphere – nestled behind the *Copra Tray* bar. Apartments have kitchenette, a/c and verandah, and there's a pool on site. The seriously spacious "budget" rooms are set in another block; all have fans, and sink, and shared access to showers, a large kitchen and TV lounge. Standard ⑤/budget ④.

Conrado, Milford Extension Rd, Pigeon Point ☎639 0145, fax 639 0755, *conrado@tstt.net.tt* The closest you can stay to the much-vaunted Pigeon Point; modestly proportioned garden or sea view rooms with carpet, a/c, cable TV, phone and balcony. Busy with its own stretch of beach, as well as a restaurant, bar and entertainment area. ⑥.

Crown Point Beach, Store Bay Rd, PO Box 223, Crown Point ☎639 8781, fax 639 8731, www.trinidad.net/crownpoint/. The largest hotel at the westerly side of Store Bay beach, with unsightly concrete room blocks softened by sprawling cabana-filled gardens overlooking the sea; cabanas are the better option. Both have kitchen, a/c, phone, cable TV and small patio, and there's a pool, restaurant and tennis courts on site. Usually busy with a Trinidadian/European crowd. ⑥.

Cruesoe's Apartments, Store Bay Local Road, Bon Accord ☎639 7789, fax 631 0155, *janmarc@tstt.net.tt*. Spacious self-contained apartments, tastefully decorated in blue and orange with a/c, cable TV, fully furnished kitchen and pool. Excellent value. ⑤.

Douglas Apartments, John Gorman Trace, Milford Rd ☎ & fax 639 7723, *dougapp@tstt.net.tt*. Sparkling clean, spacious and varied apartments at the Bon Accord end of Milford Road, with one and two bedrooms – each with a couple of double beds for large groups – as well as a lounge, full kitchen, patio, a/c, TV and priceless family atmosphere. Car rental is available on site. ④.

Golden Thistle, Store Bay Local Rd, Crown Point ☎ & fax 639 8521, www.caribbean-connexion.com/hotels/thistle.htm. Tucked away behind Store Bay Local Rd, and good for groups who want relative seclusion with middle-bracket luxury, rooms have a/c, TV, phone, kitchenette and a patio; there's also a pool, bar and infrequently functioning restaurant on site. Discount available for four nights or more. ⑥.

House of Pancakes, cor. Milford Rd and John Gorman Trace, Bon Accord ☎639 9866, *kittycat@tstt.net.tt, geocities.com/originalhouseofpancakes_tt*. Three rooms at the back of this Milford Road restaurant, all very home-style with varied decor and double, single or bunk beds, TV, a/c or fan, and shared or private bathroom. Clean, comfy but cramped and not the prettiest of places. ④.

James Resort, Sandy Point, Crown Point ☎ & fax 639 8084. The units are about as varied as you can get within walls of concrete, but the Tobagonian owners are friendly and you're close to the action without being right in it. Rooms are cramped but neat and serviceable with a/c, satellite TV and balcony while apartments (1–3 bedrooms) have a kitchen and more space. Mini-mart, car rental and pool available on site. ④.

Jeffrey's Guesthouse, Airport Rd, Crown Point ☎639 0617, *hsorace@hotmail.com*. Close to Store Bay and Pigeon Point, these very sparse rooms with a/c and en-suite bathroom share a communal kitchen and lounge. Clean and inexpensive with amiable Tobagonian hosts. Discounts are available for stays longer than a week. ③.

Jetway, Crown Point ☎ & fax 639 8504. Directly opposite the airport (1min walk), this is a good place to get your bearings. Clean and functional rooms with a/c and kitchenette; friendly atmosphere but expect some airport noise. ⑤.

Jimmy's Holiday Resort, Airport Rd, PO Box 109, Scarborough ☎639 8292 or 8929, fax 639 3100, *jimmys@tstt.net.tt*. One-, two- and three-bedroom self-contained apartments right on the road between Store Bay and Pigeon Point. Functional, clean and drably decorated with sitting room, kitchenette, a/c, TV and phone, and a mini-mart on site. ⑤.

Johnston Apartments, Store Bay Rd, Crown Point ☎639 8915, fax 631 5112. Set right above Store Bay and sharing the pool and restaurant of its larger neighbour, *Crown Point Beach*, these studios and one- and three-bedroom apartments are huge (some sleep eight) with fully equipped kitchen, living room, a/c, cable TV and phone, and instant access to the sand and sea. ⑥.

Jordine's House, Store Bay Local Rd ☎ & fax 639 1032. Good value, spacious self-contained apartments with fan, a/c and kitchenette, set in a residential section of Store Bay Local Rd, and a 5min walk to the supermarket. ④.

Kariwak Village, Store Bay Local Rd, PO Box 27, Scarborough ☎639 8442, fax 639 8441, www.kariwak.co.tt/. A jewel in the middle of bustling Crown Point: the lush gardens, thatched-roof cabanas and peaceful atmosphere give a real feeling of retreat. Cabanas are split in two and furnished using local wood crafted on the premises; each has a/c and phone. There's also the option of larger and more luxurious garden rooms, and facilities include a pool, jacuzzi and fabulous restaurant/bar, and excellent and personal service, though there is intermittent airport noise. ⑧.

Lagoon Lodge, Bon Accord Lagoon – left off Milford Rd by Calvary Road Deliverance Temple, PO Box 1054, Bon Accord ☎639 8555, fax 639 0957, www.lagoonlodge.com. Upmarket and unique private nature reserve on the edge of the lagoon. Seven acres of beautifully landscaped grounds include a boardwalk traversing the mangrove to the sea, and peacocks, parrots, doves and an ostrich strolling the grounds. Complete luxury and privacy in one of two creatively decorated self-contained houses with all mod cons (and a cook during the week), as well as use of kayaks, sailboat, pool, jacuzzi and mountain bikes. Rates include a car or jeep. Bliss for well-heeled seclusion-seekers and great value for money, though no children are allowed. ⑨.

Merle's House, 7 Kilgwyn Bay Rd, Bon Accord ☎639 7630 *imarcell@tstt.net.tt*, *imarcelle@hotmail.com*. Homely rooms all with a/c, kitchenette, en-suite bathroom and porch. Tobagonian run, this guesthouse is basic but a good value. ③.

Mike's, Store Bay Rd, Crown Point ☎639 8050. Excellent value and two minutes from the airport, this busy Tobagonian-owned place has small but clean and inviting one-, two- and three-bedroom apartments with a/c, cable TV and kitchenette. There's a mini-mart on site and the atmosphere is relaxed. ④.

Plaza Guesthouse, Friendship Estate, Milford Rd, Canaan ☎639 9269. Very basic rooms in a friendly Tobagonian-run guesthouse right on the road. You pay for what you get; a bed, fan and en-suite bathroom, all somewhat down at heel. ②.

Rainbow Resort, Milford Rd ☎639 8271, fax 639 9940, *Ratt@tstt.net.tt*. Unimaginative concrete exterior contains clean, functional white-tiled rooms with kitchenette, en-suite bathroom, cable TV, a/c and radio. Some rooms are adapted for disabled guests. Car rental is available, and there's a pool on site. Pigeon Point beach is a 5min walk. ⑤.

Rovanel's, Store Bay Local Rd, Bon Accord ☎639 9666, fax 639 7908. Palatial splendour set in landscaped gardens, with a pool, restaurant and bar, as well as a mini-zoo of sorts featuring a monkey, deer and some rabbits in tiny cages. Rooms have phone, TV, a/c, hairdryer and patio; some have kitchenette. ⑦.

Sandy Point Village, Sandy Point ☎639 8534, reservations 639 8533, *sandypt@tstt.net.tt*. Large, clean studio apartments with fully equipped kitchen, en-suite bathrooms, satellite TV, a/c and phone, furnished in wicker and teak. Good value for facilities that include a mini-gym, two jacuzzis, two pools (30m & 15m), a dive shop and car rental. The restaurant has stunning views over Sandy Point beach. ⑤.

Sandy's Guesthouse, Store Bay Local Rd, next to *Toucan Inn* ☎639 9221. Very simple and inexpensive rooms with en-suite bathroom, fans and a communal kitchen, overseen by good-natured Tobagonian hosts. ③.

Spence, Store Bay Local Rd, also a branch on Milford Rd ☎ & fax 639 8082, *myorkeol@hotmail.com*. Simple, faded rooms, but inexpensive and close to the airport with a pool and restaurant. Eclectic design: some are split level, some have bunk beds, others are doubles; and all have a/c, TV and kitchenette. Popular with a German clientele. ④.

Store Bay Resort, Store Bay Local Rd ☎639 8810, fax 639 7507, *sbaymair@cablenett.net.tt*. Clean and well-maintained apartments with kitchen, living room, a/c and cable TV, and a hotel pool. Genial owners and five minutes from the airport and beaches to boot. ⑤.

Sunshine Holiday Apartments, Milford Rd, Bon Accord ☎639 7482, fax 639 7495, *sunapt@tstt.net.tt*. A ten-minute walk from Pigeon Point beach, these good-value rooms all have high ceilings, kitchenette, en-suite bathroom and porch, and phone, a/c and cable TV. A pool is also available. ④.

Surfside, Milford Rd ☎ & fax 639 0614, *surfside@tstt.net.tt*. Set on the road to Pigeon Point beach, with wall murals and truly Trinbagonian decor in roomy units with kitchenette, a/c, fan, cable TV, and patio area and pool. Vibrant and popular with Trinidadian holidaymakers, and and well located on the road to the beach. Discounts are available May–Nov for stays over a month. ④.

Toucan Inn, *Bonkers* restaurant, Store Bay Local Rd, PO Box 452, Crown Point ☎639 7173, fax 639 8933, *bonkers@trinidad.net*. This recently expanded hotel still maintains a welcoming feel. Some rooms are poolside, octagonal wood cabanas chopped in half to make a cramped but comfy double room; all have a/c and fittings made from local teak and pine. Breakfast is included for stays of seven nights or more. ⑥.

Tropikist, Store Bay Rd, Crown Point ☎639 8512, fax 639 9605, www.tropikist.com. Popular with British tour groups and a real holidaymaker kind of a place with volleyball nets, pool and a large grassy tanning area overlooking the beach. White tiles, a/c, phone, radio, fridge and glass patio doors give rooms a handsome degree of luxury, and there's a restaurant, bar and car rental on site. ⑦.

VIP, Store Bay Local Rd. c/o PR Contracting, 119 Cacandee Rd, Chaguanas ☎639 9096, fax 639 0581. Slightly out-of-the-way apartment block offering peace and competitive rates for the self-contained units; studios and one- and two-bedroom apartments have full kitchen, TV, phone, a/c and balcony. Car rental is available on site. ③

Woods Castle, Airport Rd, Crown Point ☎639 0803. Right in the centre of the action, rooms are dark and run down; all have a/c, TV, en-suite bathroom and some have kitchenette. There's also a restaurant and bar on site. ④.

Lowlands and Little Rockly Bay

Coral Reef Gardens, All Fields Crown Trace – off Old Milford Rd, Little Rockly Bay ☎639 2536, fax 639 0770, *janicejo@tstt.net.tt*. Clean, simple and somewhat cramped room with 1960s furniture; some have a/c, others have fan only. Studio apartments have kitchenette and TV. Special rates for groups of ten or more, and meals are available on request. There's also a small pool. ③.

Green Acre Guesthouse, Daniel Trace, Carnbee Village ☎639 8287. Slightly north of the Lowlands area, this recently renovated Tobagonian-run guest-house has basic rooms with en-suite bathroom and ceiling fan. Some apartments have kitchenettes, but meals are available on request. ④.

Hampden Inn, Old Milford Rd, Lowlands ☎ & fax 639 9866, www.seetobago .com/tobago/resorts/hampden. Efficient, friendly and German-run (popular with German clientele as well) but stuck in the backwoods. Large rooms are scattered around a landscaped garden, all with a/c, cable TV, a huge bathroom and patio with hammocks. There's a good restaurant on site. ⑥.

Inn on the Bay, Old Milford Rd, Little Rockly Bay, Lambeau ☎639 4347, reservations ☎639 7173, *bonkers@trinidad.net*. Toucan Inn's sister hotel is set in sleepy Lambeau across the road from a narrow strip of beach. The vanilla-painted hotel has rooms with mahogany furniture and teak floors; all have phone, a/c, en-suite bathroom, balcony and sea view, and TV on request. There's a small deep pool and sundeck as well. ⑦.

Ocean Point, Old Milford Rd, Hampden Lowlands ☎ & fax 639 0973, www.oceanpoint.com. Self-contained, spotless and semi-plush studios and suites on quiet Old Milford Road, with a/c, cable TV, full kitchen and wood fittings. All rooms have a sea view, and there's a small pool and sundeck, and a restaurant on site. ⑥.

Tara's Beachhouse, Old Milford Rd, Little Rockly Bay, Lambeau ☎639 1556, margaret@wow.net, www.tarasbeachhouse.com. Ugly red-brick building with spacious but simple and clean apartments and a small pool, perched on the hillside overlooking Little Rockly Bay. All with kitchenette, TV, small bathroom and innovative chairs made from car seats. ⑤.

Tobago Hilton, Lowlands, PO Box 633, Scarborough ☎660 8500, fax 660 8503, www.hilton.com. Subject to gusty sea winds, this sprawling mock colonial three-storey hotel in sickly pink and pistachio has all the mod cons expected of the *Hilton* chain. All rooms have a sea view and striped circus tent decor. Facilities include a small gym, sauna, tennis courts, swimming pool, children's activity centre, and all nonmotorised watersports are free. Excellent local art adorns the walls, but the rooms do not justify the high rates. ⑨.

Tobago Plantation Villas, Lowlands, Level 2, West Mall, Westmoorings, Trinidad ☎639 8000 or 1025, fax 637 1025, www.tobagoplantations.com. Situated in Lowlands near the *Tobago Hilton*. Choose from two- and three-bedroom condominiums or luxurious three- and four-bedroom villas with their own pool. The complex borders a golf course, but the nearby beach is one of the most windswept and dirty on the island. ⑨.

Tropiko Apartments, 26 Old Milford Rd, Hampden Lowlands ☎660 8724, stay@tropiko.com, www.tropikotobago.com. Two spotless and tastefully decorated apartments with large kitchen, lounge and dining area, and two white and pine bedrooms. Some rooms have TV and a/c. Guests can use the pool at nearby *Ocean Point* hotel, and the *Tobago Plantations* golf course is five minutes' away. Excellent value. ⑤.

Viola's Place, Birchwood Triangle, Hampden Lowlands ☎639 9441, fax 624 8765, www.violasplace.com. Just off the Claude Noel Highway opposite the *Tobago Hilton* entrance, these spacious, comfy apartments – for two to eight people – come with fully equipped kitchen, bathroom, a/c, phone, cable TV and iron. Meals are available on request, and there's also a pool. Excellent value, with a friendly atmosphere and popular with Germans, though there is some noise from the nearby highway. Five minutes from the *Tobago Plantations* golf course. ⑤.

Buccoo and Mount Irvine

For an account of Buccoo, Mount Irvine and the surrounding area, see p.280.

Blue Horizon, Jacamar Drive, Mount Irvine ☎639 0433, fax 639 0432; in US ☎305/592 1434, fax 305/592 4935, www.blue-horizonresort.com. Commanding great views over the golf course and the sea from a hilly setting (you'll need a car), these spacious, shady rooms have a/c, cable TV and phone, living room, patio and full kitchen; some can sleep up to six. The atmosphere is friendly, and the service laid-back but efficient. There's also a pool. Free airport pick-up. ⑥.

Casablanca, Battery St ☎ & fax 639 0081, *peiser@tstt.net.tt*. Brand-new rooms with fan, sink and cable TV, kitchenette and en-suite bathroom. For those on a limited budget, there's a dormitory with bunk beds and shared kitchen. All rooms have wheelchair access. ③.

Enchanted Waters, Shirvan Rd ☎ and fax 639 9481, www.kpresorts.com. Adjacent to *Patino's* restaurant, these luxurious rooms are a bargain; all have a/c, cable TV, phone, radio, hairdryer, en-suite bathroom and an open-air, but covered kitchenette on the balcony. The beautiful honeymoon suites include a four-poster bed and jacuzzi. Recently landscaped grounds feature a pool and a 75ft-wide waterfall, and the location is convenient for Mount Irvine beach and route taxis. ⑥.

Golf View, Buccoo Junction, Mount Irvine, PO Box 354, Scarborough ☎639 9551, fax 639 0979. Good value for these clean and spacious rooms with a/c, TV, phone and optional kitchenette. There's a restaurant and bar on site, and a large pool in a pretty garden out front, though it's a bit close to the road. ⑤.

Hillcrest, Buccoo Rd, c/o Max Baden-Semper; in UK ☎020/8741 9264 or 563 0425, fax 748 6511. Set on a hilltop off Shirvan Road near *Morshead's* deli, the verandah of this sumptuous five-bedroom villa commands a panoramic view of Buccoo Reef and the southwest coast all the way to Scarborough. A living room, dining room, full kitchen, pool and spacious grounds complete the perfection. Rates cover ten people. ⑨.

Mount Irvine Hotel and Golf Club, Mount Irvine. PO Box 222, Scarborough ☎639 8871, fax 639, www.sputnick.com/mtirvine/. Built around a coral stone sugar mill and other plantation remnants, this grand old lady of Tobago hotels maintains a sophisticated elegance. Amenities include tennis courts, sauna, huge pool, three restaurants, five bars plus a private stretch of beach and an 18-hole golf course (guests get a 30 percent discount on green fees). Rooms are luxurious with a/c, phone, satellite TV and patio; self-contained two-bedroom bungalows are available as well. ⑨.

Old Grange Inn, Buccoo Junction, Mount Irvine. PO Box 297, Scarborough ☎ & fax 639 9395, www.trinidad.net/grangeinn/index.html. Appealing rooms with wooden floors, a/c, phone and fridge or else rather gloomy self-contained units with kitchenette, phone, a/c, TV and small patio. There's also a large pool and a good restaurant, and a golf course is close by. ⑤.

Rolita, Jacamar Drive, Mount Irvine ☎ and fax 639 7970. Extremely friendly and accommodating atmosphere with great views down to Pigeon Point. The good-value rooms are plain, clean and breezy with fan and double bed, There's also a pool and meals are available on request. ③.

Seaside Garden, Buccoo Bay ☎ & fax 639 0682. Clean rooms with mosquito nets, ceiling fans and en-suite bathrooms, all within staggering distance of the Sunday School venue. ③.

Villas on the Green Jacamar Drive, Mount Irvine ☎ & fax 639 9748, www.golftobago.com. Each villa has three bedrooms, three bathrooms, a small pool and a jacuzzi, and every imaginable amenity. There's also a large communal pool. ⑨.

Black Rock and around

Grafton, Black Rock ☎639 0191, fax 639 0030, www.grafton-resort.com. Now an all-inclusive hotel – most guests arrive on package tours – this resort hotel dominates Stone Haven Bay. Comprehensive amenities include pool, tennis and squash courts, games room, two restaurants and a beach bar, nightly entertainment, watersports and a scuba centre. Rooms are tastefully decorated with balcony, a/c, fan, safes, TV and phone, but don't justify the high walk-in rates. ⑦.

For an account of Black Rock and the surrounding area, see p.281–284.

Indigo, Pleasant Prospect ☎ & fax 639 9635, *http://homepage.eircom.net /~indigo/*. Nestled above the bar and restaurant of the same name, Caribbean colours and batiks decorate these basic but pleasant rooms which have a/c, mosquito nets, fridge, tea/coffee-making facilites and en-suite bathroom. Each has a balcony, some overlooking the beautiful Stone Haven Bay. A family room with TV is also available, and breakfast is included in the rates. ⑥.

Jemma's, c/o Ashaki Thomas, Black Rock Post Office ☎639 7724. Tucked behind Turtle Beach, this three-bedroom, Tobagonian/German-run outfit is beautifully decorated with rattan furniture and a nice verandah. Rooms are simple with mosquito nets and fans; the kitchen and bathroom are shared, and breakfast is available on request. ④.

Le Grand Courlan, Stone Haven Bay Rd, Black Rock ☎639 9667, fax 639 9292, in US 800/468 3750, www.legrandcourlan-resort.com. Favoured by airline crew and package tour operators, this all-inclusive, swish pink-and-blue resort features an extensive spa, gym overlooking the sea and all the mod cons of a luxury hotel. There's a large sundeck area and pleasing decor but no atmosphere. Rates include one spa treatment a day. ⑨.

Over Seas Cottage, Fort Bennett, Black Rock ☎639 7995 or 0819. These three Tobagonian-run apartments are basic with kitchen, lounge, bedroom with fan, bathroom and small verandah/sundeck. Steps lead down from the apartments to Stone Haven Bay. ⑤.

Plantation Villas, Stone Haven Bay Rd, Black Rock, PO Box 435, Scarborough ☎639 9377, fax 639 0455, www.wow.net/villas. Gorgeous colonial-style three-bedroom villas with gingerbread fretwork, wraparound verandahs overlooking the sea, beautiful fittings (four-poster beds, rocking chairs) and all mod cons, as well as washing machine and dryer, dishwasher, well-equipped kitchen and spacious living room. Bar and pool are on site and the sea is a minute away. ⑨.

Sanctuary Villas, Grafton Estate, PO Box 424, Scarborough ☎639 9556, fax 639 0019, www.sanctuaryvillass.com. Attractive and well designed, these 25 two-, three- and four-bedroom villas have all mod cons, TV, a/c, phone, verandah, full kitchen, beautifully decorated living room and private pool,. Opposite Grafton Beach and there's plenty of peace and quiet. ⑧.

Seahorse Inn, Stone Haven Bay Rd, Black Rock. PO Box 488, Scarborough ☎639 0686, fax 639 0057, seahorse@trinidad.net.tt. Small and right on the beach, these three spartan but attractive rooms have appealing quirks like arched windows and teak floors. All have a patio with sea view, a/c, fan and en-suite bathroom. There's a good restaurant on site (rates include huge breakfast) and evening entertainment during the high season. ⑦.

Stonehaven Villas, Grafton Estate, Black Rock, PO Box 1079, Bon Accord ☎639 0102 or 9887, stonehav@tstt.net.tt. Fourteen huge colonial villas fitted with mahogany, marble and granite and every conceivable luxury: four poster beds, a maid's room for those travelling with servants, personal pool and stunning views over Stone Haven Bay. The complex includes a club house with bar and open-air restaurant and a conference centre. ⑨.

Two Seasons, Pleasant Prospect, Shirvan Rd ☎639 7713. Bargain accommodation set back from the road between Mount Irvine and Stone Haven beaches. Rooms are plain with wood floors, fan, mosquito net and a bed, but the atmosphere is friendly and this is an excellent budget choice. Meals are available from the restaurant downstairs, and there's also a communal kitchen, lounge and bathroom. Guests must like animals as there are cats and dogs on the premises. ②.

Turtle Beach, Turtle Beach/Stone Haven Bay. PO Box 201, Scarborough ☎639 2851, fax 639 1495; in UK ☎020/8741 5333, fax 741 9030; in US ☎800/255 5859, fax 305/471 9547. A member of the *Rex* chain, this 1970s-style concrete edifice is right on the beach and is predominantly all-inclusive. Popular with tour groups, the rooms with sea vew are suitably well equipped with a/c, phone, king-size or twin bed and balcony. Amenities include tennis courts, pool and watersports, and there's also a restaurant on site. The first child under 12 stays free; additional children are charged the adult rate. Pleasant accommodation, but does not justify the expensive walk-in rate. ⑨.

Plymouth and Arnos Vale

For an account of Plymouth, see p.284–285; for Arnos Vale, see p.285.

Adventure Eco Villas, Arnos Vale Rd, Plymouth ☎639 2839, fax 639 4597 or 4157, www.adventure-ecovillas.com. Two wooden wendy house–type villas overlooking the Adventure Farm and Nature Reserve (see p.285), with kitchen, a/c, satellite TV, iron, hairdryer and double bed, plus sofa bed – a cot is available on request. ⑨.

Arnos Vale, Arnos Vale Estate, PO Box 208, Scarborough ☎639 2881, fax 639 4629, www.arnosvalehotel.com. Faded grandeur 1970s-style, set on a hillside (you'll need strong legs to reach there) in 400 acres of beautiful bird- and flower-filled private land. Close to a gorgeous protected cove of brown sand and reef-filled sea, which is great for snorkelling. Popular with Italians, the rooms are chintzy with rattan furniture, phone, TV, a/c and balcony; some are in need of redecoration. Plastic bird feeders in the restaurant attract the local birds. Buffet breakfast (included in the rates) and lunch are good but dinner can be bland and uninspired. ⑨.

Cocrico Inn, PO Box 287, North Street (☎639 2961, fax 639 6565, www.hews-tours.com. Comfortable, family-run and very friendly with a restaurant, pool and quiet location in residential backstreets. Eclectic accommodation ranges from clean, simple rooms with fan to larger units with a/c, fridge, TV and kitchen. They also rent basic or luxurious self-contained one-, two- and three-bedroom houses in Plymouth and a plush villa on Great Courland Bay. ⑥.

Footprints, Culloden Bay Rd, via Golden Lane ☎660 0118, fax 660 0027, in the US ☎868/660 0118, www.footprintseco-resort.com. Overlooking Culloden Bay, down a long, windy, pot-holed road, this remote, self-styled 62-two-acre "eco resort" has its own nature trails, saltwater and freshwater pools, excellent snorkelling just steps from the rooms and plenty of peace and quiet. Accommodation ranges from standard suites to self-contained villas with jacuzzi and pool, and a "lovers' retreat". There's an excellent restaurant, boutique, library, and a mini-museum displaying local artefacts. ⑦.

Seekei's Ville, North Street ☎639 1352. Friendly and comfortable family-run apartments with kitchen, fan and cable TV. Popular with Trini holidaymakers. ③.

Top O' Tobago, Arnos Vale Estate, c/o N.J. Walker, Fosse Cottage, Fosse Lane, Bath BA1 7NL, UK ☎639 3166; in UK ☎01225/859530, fax 859916, ticketsent@aol.com. Perched above Arnos Vale Bay with pretty gardens, a distant sea view and plenty of bird life. The comfortably opulent main two-bedroom house sleeps up to seven and has a large sitting room, two bathrooms, fully equipped kitchen, patio, cable TV, stereo, and washer and drier. Smaller cabanas are stylish with kitchenette and all have use of the pool. Cabana and house can be rented separately or as a package. Remote enough to merit a car but excellent value. Cabana ⑥; cabana/house ⑨.

The Runway to Store Bay

A two-minute walk from the airport brings you to the best place to swim in Crown Point, **Store Bay beach** (lifeguards on duty 10am–6pm, no set opening hours; free). Named after early Dutch settler Jan Stoer, this is some of the most popular sand in Tobago, and deservedly so; it's close to the airport and main hotels, has the best and most inexpensive food available and is a great place to buy crafts. Trinidadian holidaymakers consume vast quantities of curry crab and dumplin' (see below), fishermen pull in the odd seine net to the accompaniment of clicking cameras, soca thuds through the air and glass-bottom boat vendors prowl, making the stretch one of the liveliest places on the island.

Though fairly small and hemmed in by *Coco Reef* hotel and the rocks, the beach is excellent; tides govern the extent of the fine, off-white sand, and lifeguards patrol the areas flagged off for safe bathing. With a gentle shelf and crystal-clear, mirror-calm water, Store Bay is a good choice if you're travelling with children; occasionally, though, you'll see big breakers crashing against the mini-cave-riddled volcanic rocks which overhang the sand. The bars opposite are a popular liming spot, particularly during and after sunset. Opposite the beach is a car park, pristine shower/changing facil-

Store Bay is the finishing point for the annual Great Race power-boat contest each August (see "Festival Calendar", pp.45–48) as well as a venue for open-air parties around Easter weekend.

Store Bay dining

An essential part of any visit to Tobago is a plate of **crab and dumplin'**, **macaroni pie with callaloo**, or **curry goat and vegetable rice** from one of the row of shacks facing Store Bay beach. This strip of eateries (from right to left there's *Miss Jean*, *Miss Trim*, *Joycie's*, *Alma's*, *Silvia's* and *Miss Esmie*) are the places for a tasty local-style meal; in fact, you'll probably find yourself heading to Store Bay come lunchtime even if you aren't planning to grace the beach. The rewards of eating here are simple; it's inexpensive, convenient and almost always tasty, though the use of a microwave to heat up your selection from an over-ambitiously large menu is a bit of a disappointment, and many bemoan that the cooking has suffered in the move from the original lean-to beach-side location. The fare of bake with fish or eggs, buljol and smoked herring for breakfast and goat, beef, chicken or vegetable roti, stewed beef or chicken, conch or crab and dumplin', pelau, vegetable rice, stewed lentils, macaroni pie, callaloo and ground provisions varies little from stall to stall, and neither does the cooking; most popular is *Miss Jean*; but don't be discouraged from trying the others – *Miss Esmie* and *Miss Trim* are both well worth visits, too. All are open daily from around 8.30am to 8.30pm, but the flow of custom usually dictates.

---

ities (daily 10am–6pm; TT$1 per entry) with lockers for rent (TT$10 per day) as well as a couple of bars blasting reggae and soca, an ice-cream kiosk and the row of shacks housing the infamous cookshops – *Miss Jean*'s and *Miss Esmie*'s are local institutions – from which most people purchase their lunch (see box, above). If you don't fancy local staples, try the Tobago Taxi Co-Op café for generous portions of chicken or fish with fries, sandwiches and hot dogs. The purpose-built **craft shops** (8am–8pm) by the car park are one of the best places to buy souvenirs; Rasta-oriented jewellery, calabashes and carvings from "Father" – a local Rasta craftsman – nearby on Store Bay Road, next to First Class bike hire, are particularly well made.

Fort Milford to Robinson Crusoe's Cave

Though it linked the airport with Store Bay and Pigeon Point before the *Coco Reef* hotel was built, the road that shoots off toward the airport behind the Store Bay craft shacks is now the main route from the beach to hotel-filled Sandy Point and the **Fort Milford** stockade. Marked by a wall daubed with "It's nice to be nice", the fort was preceded by a Latvian settlement and a Dutch redoubt named Belleviste. Today's crumbling mass of gun-slitted coral stone was built by the British in 1777, and briefly appropriated by the French during their 1781–93 occupation of Tobago; five of the six cannons still pointing out to sea are British-built while the French contributed the other. Surrounded by bench-studded lawns that make a quiet chill-out spot for Tobagonians, the fort gives a panoramic perspective over Store Bay beach and Milford Bay right up to Pigeon Point.

Past the fort, the road swings left, skirting hotels and restaurants before meeting the fences of the airport runway. A right turn at this junction takes you onto what's known as NP Road, so called because there's a National Petroleum garage at its far reaches. As it circles the runway, the road passes the pretty and often deserted Sandy Point **beach**. Obscured by trees and shrubs, the beach is easy to miss; take the first dirt road into the bush (right opposite where the tarmac ends) and you'll emerge onto a picturesque strip of fine white sand and translucent sea bordered by sea grapes and palms. Swimming is safe if you stick to the left of the beach; currents get strong around the headland to the right which divides this stretch of sand from the more popular strip at Store Bay.

On the other side of the runway, NP Road takes you past a hand-painted sign marking the right turn to the ambitiously named **Crusoe's Cave**. A five-minute drive through cow pasture interspersed with the odd rambling home takes you to a clearing; ask for Mrs Crooks at the last house; her family own the land which leads to the cave, and she'll collect the entry fee (TT$3) and direct you down. The concrete steps and rocky pathway constructed for easy access do little for aesthetics and are treacherous, the cave itself is small, with craggy limestone walls stained green by mineral drips and a visible depth of about 4.5m. Successive earthquakes have reduced the cavern; it once stretched right back to Store Bay. The Crusoe con-

---

Robinson Crusoe's isle

"The Life and Strange Surprising Adventures of Robinson Crusoe of York, Mariner; Who lived eight and twenty Years all alone, on an uninhabited Island on the coast of America, near the mouth of the Great River of Oroonoque; Having been Cast on Shore by shipwreck, wherein all the Men perished but himself." Thus reads the introductory blurb to the first edition of Daniel Defoe's *Robinson Crusoe*, dated April 25, 1719, cited as the principal rationale of the claim that Tobago was the setting for Defoe's epic: the fabled island was situated, like Tobago, off the coast of (South) America near the mouth of the Orinoco River.

In the late seventeenth century, the then-sovereign Duke of Courland commissioned an Englishman, John Poyntz, to develop the island. Poyntz wrote a pamphlet praising Tobago's beauty and natural riches as well as giving a physical description of the island. Believers argue that Defoe got hold of the document and used it as the basis for his novel.

However, this clashes with the accepted notion that Defoe based the book on the experience of Alexander Selkirk, a crew member on the ship of English explorer and pirate William Dampier. During a voyage in the Pacific Ocean, Selkirk quarrelled with another crew member and, rather than continue in his company, he volunteered to be put ashore at the tiny island of Juan Fernandez, off the coast of Chile. He spent four years alone there before Dampier rescued him. After his return to England in 1711, his story became well known through various pamphlets, on which Defoe's novel was almost certainly based.

---

nection came about via the fertile imagination of the late Mr Crooks; having read Defoe's novel, he sided with the local rumour that Tobago was Crusoe's isle and concluded that this was as legitimate a base as any other on the island for the fabled castaway. Whatever the reality, it's a pretty spot with smashing views down to the white sand at Canoe Bay, but the cave itself is not spectacular.

Pigeon Point

Running north from the airport past the entrance to Store Bay, Airport Road becomes Milford Road as it swings to the right some 50 metres from the complex. Here, a left-hand turn (marked by the neon constellation of the *Golden Star* bar and restaurant) leads to **Pigeon Point Road** (also known as Milford Extension Road), taking you past the spot where the Atlantic Ocean meets the Caribbean Sea. The shoreline here – unlike the majority of Tobago's rugged beaches – is definitively Caribbean; powdery white sand with turquoise sea on one side and the ubiquitous swaying palms on the other, the latter an attractive remnant of the time when the area was part of a coconut plantation. Not surprisingly, you're advancing upon what some see as the island's best **beach**, though you have to pay for it – it's private land and an entrance fee is charged. The commercial trappings are ever-present; watersports outlets and souvenir stalls line the approach.

During the rainy season, mosquitoes from the nearby marsh have a field day – insect repellent is essential.

Set at the end of its very own road, **Pigeon Point** (daily 8am–7pm; TT$12) is an immensely popular strip of glaring sand backed by almond and palm trees, shady picnic spots, volleyball courts and a flotilla of yachts moored around Tobago's most photographed pier, a weathered wooden boardwalk with a thatch-roofed hut at the end. White sand on the sea floor lends the water that impossibly bright blue which typifies a postcard-style Caribbean beach, while gently shelving waters and tame currents make swimming benign, and there's ample space to stake out your niche without feeling cramped; you can take a long walk around the headland to another, less pretty, stretch of sand that borders the **Bon Accord Lagoon**. The busy central **bar** becomes a liming spot at sundown, when steel pans play away the last rays; cameras click, rum punch is downed and camcorders capture the best **sunset** view on the island. As picturesque as it appears, this beach has been the source of controversy among locals. It was the first beach to charge an entry fee, and regularly increases rents for beach vendors. Many locals now refuse to go there, especially after a fisherman was fatally shot when he tried to enter without paying. This history, and the tourist-driven development, have diminished the beach's appeal and natural beauty.

If you're driving into Pigeon Point, avoid parking under a coconut-laden palm – a single nut can cause a lot of damage if it lands on your vehicle.

Pigeon Point is one of the few places in the island to suffer from development. The shower blocks are shoddy and down-at-heel, piles of beach chairs are rented at TT$5 a day and fast-food chain *Pizza Boys* have ousted the local café; though it's sometimes possible to buy roti and the odd local dish from the food outlets on the beach for

Watersports in the Lowlands

The Lowlands are the best place to indulge in watersports, with a large variety of outlets and operators. Buzzing **jet-skis** have not yet become a regular feature amid the surf (though you can rent them from R & Sea Divers Den on Pigeon Point, US$25 for 20min), and nonmotorized watersports are freely available at the main Crown Point beaches and from the all-purpose outlet Essentially Tobago (☎639 9379, tobago@pobox.com, www.essentiallytobago.com) at Mount Irvine beach complex (see p.280). You can rent **snorkelling** gear from itinerant vendors or scuba concessions for US$5–15 per day, while **kayaking** costs about US$10 an hour at Pigeon Point. Wild Turtle (☎639 7936, info@wildturtledive.com, www.wildturtledive.com) at Pigeon Point rents out kayaks (TT$30 for 30min, TT$60 for 1hr). World of Watersports (☎660 7234, fax 660 8326, www.worldofwatersports.com) based at *Blue Haven*, *Hilton Tobago* and *Arnos Vale* hotels offer **water-skiing** and **inflatable bananas** (TT$80 for 15 mins) as well as **jet skiing** (TT$200 for 20min) and **windsurfing** (TT$200 for 60min). Water-skiing, windsurfing and sailing lessons are also available (TT$320 for 60mins). The most popular local **surfing** site is Mount Irvine beach – early morning sees as many as twenty to thirty surfers riding the waves. A well-kept secret, local surfers are trying to keep it that way, making it difficult to find places that rent equipment; keen surfers should bring their own. Note that the water here is shallow and directly over coral reef, so surf fins can be badly damaged and no protective footwear is allowed to protect the reef from overeager surfers jumping in and damaging the coral.

around TT$20–30. The groynes constructed to curtail beach erosion have reduced the water circulation, and this – along with general pollution and poor management – has allowed algae to flourish on the sea floor, making local people question the sagacity of swimming in what on a bad day resembles a rather milky soup. Though water quality is monitored by local environmental groups, and the chance of getting sick is pretty scant, try to shower off as soon as you leave the water and avoid immersing your head; there's little to see in any case.

East along Milford Road

Bisecting Tobago's low-lying southwest tip, ruler-straight Milford Road is the artery of the area, a busy main road traversing the Bon Accord, Tyson Hall, Canaan and Friendship communities. Trucks, cars and route taxis fly past, limers congregate on every corner – even the supermarket forecourt becomes a choice drinking spot on a Friday evening – and the whole stretch is the busiest you'll find away from Scarborough. One community melts seamlessly into another (boundaries seem to be a law unto themselves which only local residents can grasp), but as this is probably the most well-travelled thoroughfare on the island, the strip rapidly becomes familiar.

Taxis travelling along Milford Road are usually plying the Scarborough–Crown Point route, but some turn off at Shirvan Road to Buccoo, Mount Irvine, Black Rock and Plymouth.

Boat tours, activities and cruises

One of the most popular ways to explore the brine is a pleasure boat **cruise**. Several operators work the waters – their prices for a full-day trip vary little (US$70 per person for a 6–8hr cruise and around US$35 for a 2hr sunset trip) and usually include lunch, snorkelling at Bon Accord Lagoon, Englishman's Bay or other similarly deserted coves, and an open bar; private charters or sunset and moonlight dinner trips are also on the roster of most. Atmosphere varies from racy booze cruises to sedate sightseeing. Kalina Cats (☎639 6304 or 6306, kalina@trinidad.net, www.trinidad.net/kalina) offer touristy but fun catamaran cruises similar to those offered by the *Loafer* (☎639 7312; 7hrs US$60), a catamaran converted for partying. Best of the bunch is *Natural Mystic* (☎639 7245, fax 639 7888, mystic@tstt.net.tt), a 12m trimaran that unfurls its sails when the wind allows, cruising to deserted beaches for fantastic snorkelling and a sumptuous freshly cooked barbecue lunch and as much drink as you can handle. Exhilarating and not to be attempted after a rum punch session, **hobie cats** are mini-catamarans built for speed and balanced by the bodies of the passengers; hooked on to a trapeze, you swing out over the water when the craft reaches its highest speed. Trips are available from Cool Runnings at Mount Irvine Bay (☎639 6363, fax 639 4755, www.outdoor-tobago.com; 1hr with or without instructor US$50); they also offer all-day trips aboard the hobies, as well as water-skiing, snorkelling, windsurfing, kayaking, surfing of all kinds, deep-sea fishing, and tube and banana boat rides. Chartering a **sport fishing** boat is exciting but expensive; rich pickings of marlin, sailfish, tuna and dolphin are caught year round. A speedy boat accommodating up to six and equipped with rods, tackle and bait will cost in excess of US$275 per half day, US$400 for a full day; try Dillon's Deep Sea Charters (☎639 8765, *dillons@tstt.net.tt*), or local character Captain Frothy's boat *Hardplay* (☎639 7108, *hardplay@tstt.net.tt*). Ask around at Store Bay, Mount Irvine or Pigeon Point beaches if you're interested in joining a local fisherman aboard a pirogue; however, you'll get a better deal if you try one of the less developed fishing beaches, such as Castara or Parlatuvier (see pp.298–301). **Glass-bottom boat** tours of Buccoo Reef (US$20) leave from Store Bay, Pigeon Point and Buccoo.

Bon Accord

Following the right-hand curve of Airport Road/Milford Road takes you into **BON ACCORD** district, though it's an area as loosely demarcated as any of the mini-villages skirting this central thoroughfare. North of the road is **Bon Accord Lagoon**, a sweeping oval of mangrove swamp and reef-sheltered, shallow water which forms one of the most important fish nurseries on the island. Though the marine life has been adversely affected by run-off from a nearby sewage treatment plant (out of action for the last twelve years but now being repaired), the lagoon remains a sanctuary for conch, snails, shrimp, oysters, crab, urchins and sponges – if you can see them amongst the thick sea grass – as well as fish which spawn amidst the protective roots of the mangrove trees and provide rich pickings for the bird life.

Adolphus James (☎639 2231) is an excellent guide for birdwatching around the lagoon.

As most of the land skirting the swamp is privately owned – Britain's Princess Margaret stayed at one of the beach houses during a 1950s sojourn – access is problematic. You can get pretty close by turning down Golden Grove road from Milford (though the road becomes extremely bumpy after the small bridge, and is impossible without four-wheel drive in the wet season) and taking the first dirt track you come to – passing the crumbling remains of a windmill and cocoa drying house, once part of the Bon Accord sugar estate. Better to see it on a Buccoo Reef boat tour (see p.280) that includes a bar-becue at a deserted sandy spit on the lagoon's north side known as **No Man's Land**, an idyllic place to swim. You'll have to move fast to catch the area in its current unspoilt state, though, as the Golden Grove estate encompassing this land is slated for development, including a hotel, villa and golf course.

Canaan to Canoe Bay

Tyre shops, dusty rum bars and the obligatory coconut palms prevail as Milford Road continues eastward into **CANAAN**, an unremarkable district dominated by a row of shops in front of sprawling Milford Court, the southwest's largest housing scheme. The low-lying landscape made this part of the island a favourite amongst **sugar** planters; the entire area was once carved up into individual plantations; some – like Friendship Estate – have not yet shed their colonial names, while Canaan and Bon Accord received their unusual titles from Moravian missionaries who arrived in Tobago in 1789 to convert the populace. You can still pick out the odd bit of period architecture, such as the old windmills housing the *Peacock Mill* restaurant (well-signposted right turn). These days, though, this stretch of Milford Road with its peppering of rum bars is a nice place to stop off for a drink and a spot of "ol' talk", the inconsequential rum-fuelled banter which goes hand-in-hand with the liquor. Due to the presence of a roti stall and the renowned *Block 22* fried chicken outlet, it also stays comfortably busy during the evenings.

Just after the turn-off for Buccoo (see p.278), a right-hand gravel track signposted for **Canoe Bay Resort** leads to a pretty and seldom-visited **beach** (daily 9am–5pm; TT$12), once the site of a large Amerindian settlement; the English named it Canoe Bay after the Indian pirogue fleets moored here. Today, the 56 acres around the bay are beautifully landscaped and are an appealing place to spend the day if you desire some peace (or even overnight; see p.253 for accommodation). The entry fee covers use of the showers and bathrooms, and you're free to explore – you may even discover the odd artefact poking up from the sand. The main area boasts lawns, thatched gazebos, picnic tables and a supremely private beach of clean yellow sand and calm waters – the view stretches right down to Crown Point and there's some good snorkelling to be had.

If you have your own tent you can camp at Canoe Bay for US$15; security, lighting and bathrooms are included.

Lowlands to Little Rockly Bay

Back on Milford Road, the tarmac widens as you approach Claude Noel Highway, named after a local boxer and built in the late 1980s as a swifter route into Scarborough than the narrow and weatherbeaten Milford, which swings off right from the highway after the *Tobago Hilton* turn-off. This area, known as **LOWLANDS**, previously a swampy peninsula, has seen Tobago's biggest development in recent years – Tobago Plantations, a joint venture that has built exclusive villas, condominiums, a shopping centre and a 9- and 18-hole golf course (TT$95 for 18 holes; ☎631 0875, www.golftobagoplantations.com). The real centre of the development is the *Tobago Hilton*, opened in 2000, its sprawling pink and pistachio plantation-style buildings stretching across twenty acres of beachfront.

Leaving the *Hilton/Tobago Plantations* complex via the north east you end up on **Old Milford Road**, which runs along the coast. It is little more than a country lane; cattle graze, paint peels and signs of life are few and far between; look out for Tobago's only **mosque**. **Little Rockly Bay**, the small bay between the *Hilton* development and the village of Lambeau, used to be the site for horse racing before the Shirvan race track was constructed. The constant sea breezes make this a popular lunch spot, as the piles of fluttering take-away wrappers reveal – signs proclaiming "Thank-you for not littering" stand amid piles of trash. And though the white-tipped waves look picturesque, it's not the best place for a swim; the close proximity of Scarborough ensures that the murky brine is seasoned with a little sewage and the undercurrent can be dangerous. Past Lambeau, where Little Rockly Bay becomes Rockly Bay, the spot opposite the *Cat and Fiddle* is known locally as "warm pool". Enclosed by a reef, its shallow waters make it perfect for bathing, though the plastic bottles littering the shore are a little off-putting.

Along the highway

Just past the Old Milford Road turning, the highway scoots past a forest-like plantation of coconut palms to the left. From here, the road begins to climb; once you've passed the Auchenskeoch Road (a convenient shortcut to Buccoo and Mount Irvine), you come to a set of traffic lights marking a crossroads; right leads to the hilly residential community of **LAMBEAU**, a tight-knit and completely untouristed village, while turning left is the steep route up to **Signal Hill**, a great vantage point to take in the panoramic view of Crown Point and the Lowlands beyond the forest-like coconut plantations. Throughout Tobago's chequered history, Signal Hill has been used as a lookout point, notably by signalmen communicating out to sea to nearby forts. Today, the area is home to the local comprehensive school where Tobagonian footballer **Dwight Yorke** was educated, as well as a base for the Trinidad and Tobago Regiment; listen out for strains of their marching band at practice.

The next right-hand turn-off from the highway is the route to **Shaw Park football ground**, a sprawling facility which occasionally doubles up as a concert venue. Sport is the main focus of the place, though, with football taking precedence. Advertised on the radio, in *Tobago News* or by word of mouth, games are great fun to attend, and as most take place in the cool of the night, the floodlights are the best way to tell if a match is on. The hill overlooking Shaw Park is the home of an ugly yellow pipe sculpture known as "**the matchstick man**", a cryptic monument designed to be part of Tobago's millenium celebrations – the island spent more than TT$40 million on the sculpture and a large concert, only to have a dismally low turnout.

Turning left at the highway's next set of traffic lights brings you to quiescent **Orange Hill Road**, a rambling route to the leeward coast to Mount Irvine. Past the attractive Spring Garden Moravian church, the road splits as if in disgust at the vicious potholes; left takes you into **PATIENCE HILL**, an attractively quiet rural community that makes a pleasant drive and a great way to get completely lost along the winding country roads; if you can find it, there's a fantastic view of the Lowlands from the top of what locals call "Patience Hill Back Bottom Road". The right fork takes you into sparsely populated but pretty **ORANGE HILL** itself, its bougainvillea hedges and overgrown empty lots sliding loosely into Bethel and down to the coast.

Eating

While the highlights of Tobagonian food – crab and dumplin' or pacro water – are sublime, the available variety isn't particularly wide, particularly in the Lowlands, where it can be difficult to escape the expensive and bland tourist-oriented offerings; pasta or steak often take pride of place over *coocoo* or conch. It's not impossible to find good Tobagonian cooking, though, and even some of the smartest restaurants allow their callaloo to remain unadulterated by cream or a blender. If you're here in the slow season (April 15–Dec 15), bear in mind that many kitchens close at around 9pm. In the listings below, we've included phone numbers only for restaurants where you might need to book a table.

Most of the **restaurants** along Shirvan/Grafton Road are dedicated to the tourist palate, and many are quite flashy with prices to match, but you can get inexpensive local lunches from hole-in-the-wall eateries in Black Rock and Plymouth. All of the restaurants list-

Check whether menu prices include tax (up to 15 percent) and service charge (usually 10 percent). If a service charge is included, you don't have to leave a tip.

Dining prices

Each restaurant listed in this guide has been categorized according to the following grades: **budget** (under TT$25); **inexpensive** (TT$25–70); **moderate** (TT$70–150); **expensive** (TT$150+). These ratings relate to the price for a starter and main course.

Lowlands: Crown Point to Plymouth

In high season, beach barbecues at Pigeon Point or Store Bay are advertised by vendors distributing fliers. Flambeaux and a steelband provide atmosphere; US$35-plus covers drinks and all the freshly cooked seafood you can eat.

Tobago street food

Trinidad-style **street food** has yet to make an impact in Tobago – even in Scarborough, it's impossible to find a good corn soup, but one notable exception is *Block 22*, a hulk of concrete at the Canaan end of Milford Road that makes the best fried chicken in Tobago; spicy batter and rum shop ambience keep the cars double parked until 1–2am on the weekends. Also in this section of Milford Road, the popular morning stopoff *Golden Girls Bakery* makes excellent buljol or smoked mackerel and hops as well as sandwiches, pastries and a cracking carrot juice and peanut punch. You'll inevitably be drawn in by the local staples – "roti, conch and all kind ah ting" – served up by Miss Jean and co at Store Bay (see box, p262), while a few hundred yards up Airport Road, try *Triple B Burger Grill* for fish, beef or chicken burgers and fried potato wedges – usually open until 11pm. You'll find food stalls springing up wherever there is nightlife – the *Golden Star* restaurant and bar is a favourite place to pitch – where you can get chicken, souse, boiled corn and fish tea. For more familiar fast food, *KFC* and local burger joint *Royal Castle* are both in Scarborough.

---

ed below are good for a **drink**, but the most scenic place to sink a few beers in the area is the beautifully located *Ocean Edge* rum shop perched on a cliff top overlooking Stone Haven Bay; a great place to while away the sunset hours. There are plenty of friendly, low-key rum shops in Buccoo, Black Rock and Plymouth; a good bet is *Michael's* in Black Rock.

Crown Point, Bon Accord and the airport

Alpha Mega, Milford Rd, Canaan. Local-run, inexpensive café serving up fish and chips, roti, bake and shark and fruit juices. Open Mon–Sat 7am–10.30pm. Budget.

The Backyard, Airport Rd, Crown Point. Cosy café serving excellent, well-filled sandwiches on toasted French bread, as well as salads. The owners also provide takeaway and picnic lunches. A small shop on site sells beautiful local batiks. Affordable and easygoing. Mon–Fri 12–6pm. Budget/Inexpensive.

For details of the dining price codes used in these listings, see p.269.

Blue Note, cor. Store Bay Local Rd and Airport Rd by the police station. Appealing local-run bar and restaurant serving up tasty fresh fish and a variety of local vegetables done with an interesting twist. Lively atmosphere. Moderate.

Bonkers, *Toucan Inn*, Store Bay Local Rd, Crown Point ☎639 7173. Tasty Tobagonian food with the corners smoothed away, served under the shady pavilion or at poolside tables – customers can take a dip. Breakfast is local and European-style, lunch is sandwiches, soup (usually callaloo) with home-made bread, or pelau, chicken, fish, chilli con carne and salads. Dinner highlights are roast chicken with rosemary, pork in pimento sauce and salsa blackened shrimp. Moderate.

Café Callaloo, Pigeon Point Rd, next to *Surfside Hotel*, Crown Point ☎639 9020. A former *Hilton International* chef cooks up local dishes with an extravagant touch: caviar and truffles with Tobago produce. Ring ahead in high season to make reservations. Expensive.

Chrystals, cor. Store Bay Local Rd and Airport Rd. Low-key, inexpensive bar/café serving fruit juices, bake and shark, and flying fish. The sheltered tables outside make a good spot for street gazing. Budget.

Cocoa Restaurant, cor. Milford and Pigeon Point roads, Crown Point. Tastefully decorated restaurant serving local and international dishes for dinner. Live entertainment nightly. Moderate.

Columbus Snack Bar, Store Bay Rd, Crown Point. Popular drinking spot opposite the airport that also serves great Tobagonian staples: flying fish, buljol or smoked mackerel breakfasts; roti, fried chicken and rice or stew pork for lunch and dinner. The Friday night barbecue is popular, offering a good lime as you eat. Budget.

Copra Tray, Store Bay Local Rd. International menu, good for a light lunch – shrimp wonton, chicken wings, beef or fish salad, burgers and filled croissants – or a pre-drinking dinner of meatloaf, vegetable quiche, lasagne, calamari or pizza, served in a pleasant garden setting set back from the road. Inexpensive/Moderate.

D'Coal Pot, Sandy Point Rd, Crown Point. Adjacent to the *Tropikist* hotel, this Trinidadian-owned restaurant and bar serves up local staples for breakfast, lunch and dinner at extremely low prices, in a clean, simple environment with very welcoming atmosphere. Weekend entertainment and live music with meals. Inexpensive.

Dillon's, Airport Rd ☎639 8765. Busy seafood restaurant midway between the turn-offs for Pigeon Point and Store Bay beaches, with an air-conditioned dining room and outdoor tables. Sumptuous dinners of fish, lobster and shrimp carefully prepared with a Creole flavour; steak or chicken are alternatives. Live music most nights. Open daily. Moderate.

Golden Star, cor. Milford and Pigeon Point roads. Chiefly recommendable for its easy-access location. Food is mediocre – the fish, chicken, steaks, lobster and club sandwiches hold no surprises (or nasty shocks), but it's open late and service is cheerful. Moderate.

House of Pancakes, Milford Rd, Bon Accord. Medium-priced breakfasts of cinnamon- and nutmeg-laced pancakes with fresh bananas and walnuts; omelettes, bacon and eggs are also on offer. Dinner is Cajun-style: blackened fish or shrimp, shrimp jambalaya or seafood and okra gumbo. The roadside setting is noisy, but central and good for watching the world go by. Moderate.

Kariwak Village, Store Bay Local Rd ☎639 8442. Fresh herbs and spices, inventive slants on local staples and genuine love in the kitchen make this the best place to eat in Crown Point. Breakfast and dinner menus are set – usually with a meat, fish or vegetarian option – and everything is supremely fresh, succulently cooked and completely delicious. Accompanied by live music, the Saturday night buffet is particularly good. Great service and vegan food available. Reasonably priced snacks and sandwiches offered during the day. Expensive,

Marcia's, Store Bay Local Rd ☎639 0359. Completely Tobagonian, the genial owners make this one of the most welcoming small restaurants in the area. Open for dinner from 6.30pm (call the day before to order lunch) and offering great local food: red snapper Creole, lobster in coconut garlic sauce, stewed or curried conch and Sunday-style stewed chicken with macaroni pie and callaloo, all served with rice and ground provisions. Gorgeous cassava pudding for dessert. Inexpensive.

Mumtaz Continental Restaurant, Airport Rd, Crown Point, opposite *Jimmy's Holiday Resort*. Serves excellent Indo-Trinidadian food including rotis,

Korma and samosas, with steak, lobster and shrimp dishes available for tamer tastes. Simple surroundings with Indian kitsch decoration. Open for breakfast, lunch and dinner Mon–Sat; dinner only on Sunday. Budget.

Pepe's, Store Bay Rd, off Pigeon Point Rd ☎ 639 7304. Copious menu served in the open-sided downstairs section of this two-restaurant building. Usually full of foreign visitors gorging on sesame chicken wings or stuffed crab-back appetizers and a huge range of chicken preparations, including red wine and mushroom sauce and curry and coconut. The pepper shrimp is excellent, and soup, salad and rum punch are included with every evening meal. Moderate/Expensive.

Ru-B-Lou's, Sandy Point, opposite James Resort ☎639 8046. This extremely genial place offers hearty, inexpensive and flavoursome American-style breakfasts, and English fry-ups on request. Their simple dinner menu, served daily from 6pm until the last customer leaves, features fresh and tasty meat and fish dishes suitable for every taste. Small venue so come early or call ahead. Moderate.

Steak & Lobster Grill, *Sandy Point Village*, Sandy Point. ☎639 8533. Stunning setting overlooking Sandy Point beach, accompanied by the sound of the sea. A combination of mediocre local and international food, though weekly buffet (Tuesday) is good value for money. Nightly entertainment of local dancers and musicians livens up the atmosphere. Expensive.

Accommodation in Crown Point and the surrounding areas are shown on the map on pp.249–251.

Waving Gallery, Store Bay beach facilities. Upstairs dining spot offering no-frills food – fish sandwiches, hamburgers, hot dogs and salads and an extremely inexpensive buffet on Friday night, served to the strains of an in-house sound system. Excellent and least expensive grilled shrimp in Tobago. Barbecue on Sundays. Budget.

Lowlands and Little Rockly Bay

The Art Gallery Tea Gardens, Hibiscus Drive, Lowlands ☎639 0457. Set in the delightful gardens of the *Art Gallery* this intimate venue serves local teas accompanied by poetry readings, steel drum music and discussions on art. Open Thurs & Sun 5pm–9pm. Expensive.

Café Petunia, Old Milford Rd, Little Rockly Bay, Lambeau ☎639 6878. This delightful little café overlooking Little Rockly Bay has great atmosphere, because of the local and tourist mix, its excellent service and delicious home-made cakes, sandwiches, salads and cappuccinos. Especially popular on Friday nights for happy hour (6–8.30pm) when the good-natured owner, Petunia, entertains her guests with soulful singing accompanied by a cuatro band. Open daily 10am–10pm. Budget/Inexpensive.

Cat & Fiddle, Old Milford Road, Little Rockly Bay, Lambeau, ☎639 4347. Large restaurant with fishing boat decor in a breezy location overlooking Little Rockly Bay. Sister restaurant to the popular *Bonkers*, this eatery serves, among other things, crayfish, jalapeño conch and oven-roasted duck. Expensive.

Coral Reef, *Tobago Hilton*, Lowlands ☎660 8500. Expensive *à la carte* restaurant overlooking Little Rockly Bay specializing in seafood and international fare. Open Mon–Sun 6.30pm–11pm. Expensive.

Garden Grill, *Ocean Point Hotel* ☎639 7312. Informal restaurant serving reasonably priced chicken, steak and fish. Creole buffet on Monday, East Indian buffet on Wednesday and barbecue on Thursday. Open Mon–Sun 7am–11pm. Budget.

Hampden Inn, Old Milford Rd, Lowlands. Good in-hotel restaurant serving medium-priced European fare; American or continental breakfast, sandwiches, salads, burgers and soups for lunch, and pizza, spaghetti, curried or stewed fish, chicken and shrimp for dinner, accompanied by an African drumming show each Sunday. Moderate.

Shore Things, Old Milford Rd, Lambeau ☎635 1072. A delightful café in a brightly painted old house with verandah overlooking the sea. Serves delicious light lunches, pizzas, pastelles, quiches and salads plus fresh pastries and fruit juices. High-quality regional crafts and furniture also on sale. Mon–Sat 10am–6pm. Budget/Inexpensive.

Buccoo to Arnos Vale

Arnos Vale Waterwheel, Franklyn Rd, Arnos Vale Estate ☎639 2881. Set in the beautiful grounds of the water wheel park, this classy, romantic and expensive restaurant has an eclectic and delicious menu. Highlights are toasted lobster, mignon with brandy and peppercorn sauce, and duck in Grand Marnier sauce; prawns, squid and mussels in a lemon grass and curry sauce; or the chicken salad starter with peppers, gherkins, sultanas, almonds and basil in a balsamic vinegar dressing. There's a themed buffet each Wednesday and on Friday there are cultural shows. Expensive.

Black Rock Cafe, Grafton Rd, Black Rock ☎639 7625. Popular open-air restaurant on the town's outskirts serving medium-priced soups, salads and fabulous fish dishes for lunch and daily dinner specials of steak, chicken and fish. Moderate.

Blue House, Shirvan Rd ☎639 8242. Open in the high season from Dec to April, this pleasant restaurant set on the road serves reasonably priced meals inspired by Italian, German, American and local cuisine. Things liven up at the weekend with Latin dance and barbecue on Saturday and Steel Band and barbecue on Sunday. Moderate.

The Emerald, Pleasant Prospect ☎639 8272. Just off the road between Mount Irvine and Stone Haven bays, *The Emerald* has a breezy upstairs setting, good for moderately priced seafood, tender lobster, steaks and great Creole-style shrimp. For those with smaller appetites there is a kiddies' menu. Expensive.

Indigo, Pleasant Prospect ☎639 9635. Friendly restaurant and bar with changing daily menu specializing in seafood. The conch fritters and spicy black pudding is particularly good; for the main course they offer red snapper, dolphin, steak and chicken in the medium-price range. Food served from 7pm–11pm. Bar frequented by both locals and tourists for a lively lime, open 5pm till late. Moderate.

La Tartaruga, Buccoo Bay ☎639 0940. Tobago's best – and most expensive – Italian restaurant with an open-air patio near the sea, owned and run by a mercurial Italian émigré. For a set price of TT$165, you get three courses of authentic Italian fare; pesto a la Genovese, bruschetta, calamari and homemade pasta with a huge range of sauces. Puddings include a delicious passionfruit jelly. A more expensive meal at TT$250 serves up a large variety of appetizers. Afternoon tea is available. A shop upstairs sells Italian produce, gifts and wines. Closed Sun and Mon. Expensive.

Le Beau Rivage, Mount Irvine Golf Course, Mount Irvine ☎639 8871, ext 327. Located on the spectacular Mount Irvine golf course this exclusive, tastefully decorated restaurant features an international menu specializing in seafood such as lobster and shrimp at equally exclusive prices. Dinner from 7pm. Closed Tuesdays. Expensive.

MeShell's, Shirvan Rd ☎631 0353. Peach-painted restaurant serving expensive international cuisine with a Caribbean twist. Good for seafood, especially shrimp and lobster. Expensive.

Papillon, *Old Grange Inn*, Buccoo ☎639 0275. Classy – and expensive – dining in a leafy patio or an air-conditioned room. Huge menu adds pastelles, conch in coconut milk, lamb kebabs, and shark in rum and lime to the usual fish and chicken selections. Deeply satisfying pone with ice cream for dessert. Expensive.

Patino's, Shirvan Rd ☎639 9481. Friendly Trinidadian/Canadian hosts serve Polynesian-style food which works extremely well in a congenial setting. A waterfall wall with changing coloured lighting and garden patio provide romantic atmosphere to meals featuring seafood, ginger beef with Chinese mushrooms, hot and sour shrimp and lobster Polynesian. This upmarket restaurant has a different theme every night ranging from Thai to seafood – supremely fresh and tasty. Expensive.

Peacock Mill, Shirvan Rd, Friendship Estate ☎639 0503. Decorated in a multitude of greens this old windmill serves tasty light meals such as sandwiches and baked potatoes. Open Mon–Sun 3pm–11pm. Moderate.

Seahorse Inn, Stone Haven Bay Rd ☎639 0686. Imaginative menu based around international staples; sandwiches, fish, shrimp and a good tuna pasta salad for lunch, and more sophisticated offerings for dinner: stuffed peppers, chef's paté, lobster bisque or fish chowder to start and excellent seafood, steaks, pork chops and chicken for the main course. The chocolate gâteau is delicious. Expensive.

Shirvan Watermill, Shirvan Rd ☎639 0000. Upmarket restaurant with tables beautifully set under the cut stone roof of an abandoned water mill. The "inter-

---

Sunday School

A Tobago institution, **Sunday School** is most definitely not for the pious. A massive beach party that the whole island seems to attend, Sunday School is the highlight of the week's nightlife, completely taking over Buccoo village with swarms of people, food stalls and cars squeezed sardine-style into available space. The action begins at around 8pm, when the Buccooneers Steel Orchestra play pan for a couple of hours. The crowd begins to thicken at around 10–11pm, when the sound system at the covered beach facilities begins to play, competing for the highest decibels with the music pumping out of *Hendrix Bar* across the road; this is also a nice place to sit and watch the human traffic, though the bar does charge a $5 cover. Music policy at the beach is inevitably Jamaican dancehall with the most popular soca tunes thrown in alongside hip-hop and R&B, while you'll hear oldies (disco, Michael Jackson), soca, calypso and a little Jamaican reggae at *Hendrix*. Either dancefloor is jumping, as experienced winers display their skills, foreigners let loose or take a wining lesson and the gigolos (and tourists) scout for a partner – Sunday School is well-known as a kind of pick-up joint, so it's the ideal place to watch the intricate mating dance of thrill-seeking foreigners and those hard-working beach bums. Though Buccoo is busy every Sunday night, the largest Sunday School of the year takes place each Easter Monday, when several more sound systems add to the cacophony and parked cars back up all the way to the golf course. To avoid car parking hassles it's a good idea to book a taxi to collect you at a prearranged time.

---

national" fare (steak, lobster and so on) is beautifully cooked and the prices match the decor; cocktails are served at 5pm, dinner from 6pm. Expensive.

Teaside Pizza, Battery St, Buccoo Point ☎639 8437. Unpretentious, appealing and tucked away behind Buccoo Bay; the main dish is pizza, good and reasonably priced with seven standard toppings. Wholewheat bases are available, as are natural juices – fig (banana) is recommended. Toasted sandwiches and home-made cookies are good too; they'll deliver to hotels and guesthouses in Crown Point. Budget/Inexpensive.

Two Seasons, Pleasant Prospect ☎639 7713. Next door to *The Emerald*, the tasty, freshly made pizza comes with a white or wholewheat base and plenty of toppings. Brown rice and vegetables is a good option for non-meateaters. Local food and breakfasts are also served at bargain prices. Budget.

Under the Mango Tree, Black Rock ☎639 8964. Lovely yellow-and-green café on the roadside serving sandwiches, pizza, salads and hot meals including coconut crusted chicken in peanut sauce, all freshly made and served inside or under the shady mango tree. Delicious fruit juices and amusing signs, "Beware – falling mango", toilets marked "mango" and "womango" complete the atmosphere. Open 1pm–9.30pm for lunch and dinner. Closed Fri. Inexpensive.

Drinking and nightlife

Tobagonians tend to display less of the frantic party enthusiasm that characterises Trini "feting", and much of the local nightlife revolves around the **bar** scene, a mix of rum shops and more tourist-oriented dives like *Copra Tray*. Tobago isn't smothered with heaving dancefloors, and even the bright lights of Crown Point offer limited options after dark, but you can find some excitement most nights of the week – consult roadside posters or ask around to find the current and everchanging hotspots; Monday and Tuesday are often quiet as everyone recovers from Sunday School excesses. If you're looking for a place to **dance**, *Golden Star* is almost always lively – Thursday night parties and Scouting for Talent are the busiest nights – while *The Deep* is best at weekends. *Indigo* and the *Harlekin* bar are popular spots with both foreigners and locals alike and are well worth checking out for their more modern environs. Other than the weekly bacchanal of **Sunday School** at Buccoo (see above), Friday (pay day for locals) is the biggest party night – the Lowlands echo with bass notes and many locals head for Scarborough to the *Level Three* disco, the John Dial roadside dance at *Fairy Queen* bar or the market square sound systems (see p.296). Aside from a flirtation with soca during Carnival time, Tobagonian music policy is primarily dancehall reggae – singers Buju Banton and Sizzla are guaranteed floor-fillers – while only *The Deep* offers a more "international" playlist.

Larger hotels provide nightly **entertainment** for guests and nonguests alike, most of which manages to avoid the rather tacky limbo and fire-eating ilk of other Caribbean islands. Some, such as the *Arnos Vale* cabarets (Wed and Fri), or anything featuring the Les Coteaux cultural dancers or the entertaining Pleasure Pirates, are exceptionally good. Occasional **stageshows** are held at Shaw Park football ground or *Golden Star*; you'll see promotional billboards all around the island – this is also the method of choice for advertising the marvellous round of summer fishermen's **fetes**. Your only other entertainment options are a visit to the *Kaiso Club* casino in Canaan, or the **casino** or **cinema** in Scarborough (see pp.285–296).

Bars and clubs

Bonkers, Store Bay Local Rd. Pleasant wooden bar area by the pool with nightly entertainment; calypso singers (Tues & Sat), steel band on Wednesday, the Les Coteaux dancers on Thursday and a "Native Spirit" floor show on Friday.

Columbus Snack Bar, Store Bay Rd, opposite the airport. Known as "Uncle C's", this is an enduringly busy place to sink a few beers, with loud music over the weekends.

Copra Tray, Store Bay Local Rd. You'll inevitably grace these doors whilst in Tobago as this roomy, thatch-roofed bar with dancefloor is one of the most popular liming spots for locals and tourists. With pool tables (TT$10 for 30min), an outdoor patio to catch the breeze, a resident DJ and African drumming every Saturday night. Watch out for the prowling men-folk. Closed Sun.

Cross Roads Pub, Buccoo Rd, Carnbee. Expansive bar which comes to life each Saturday night for a "Back in Time" dance where an older set groove to '60s, '70s and '80s music.

The Deep, *Sandy Point Village* hotel, Crown Point. Air-conditioned subterranean disco popular with upwardly mobile locals and tourist crowds – good for a hassle-free dance. Moderate cover charge; women usually get in for free. Open Fri & Sat.

Gold Post, Buccoo Village. Set just off Buccoo's main road, this is a quiet and intimate place to have a drink, with a pool table and meals available.

Golden Star Restaurant and Bar, Pigeon Point Rd, Crown Point ☎639 0873. One of Tobago's busiest nightspots with an outdoor stage that remains popular with a young crowd of tourists, locals and especially those on the lookout for company. The entertainment varies every evening; karaoke, "Latin" night (Thurs), and the marvellous "Scouting for Talent" show, an annual competition for Tobagonians with stars in their eyes. TT$20 plus cover charge.

Green Shop, Canaan, Milford Rd, opposite Milford Court. Popular rum shop, good for a game of dominoes or a quiet lime.

Harlekin, Milford Rd, Bon Accord. Liming spot for locals and foreigners in a lemon-yellow building off the Milford Road. Friendly bar serves light meals. Open 5pm–midnight Tues–Sat.

Kaiso Club, cor. George St and Milford Rd, Canaan ☎631 1000. Tobago's latest casino and bar offers Caribbean poker, blackjack, American roulette and a few slot machines. Open Mon–Sun 7pm–3am.

Lindsay's Bar, Milford Rd, Bon Accord. Another Milford rum bar patronized mainly by locals, inexpensive and good for catching up with local gossip.

Lush, Shirvan Rd, Mount Pleasant. Former site of Tobago's only horse racing track, this popular pick-up joint is filled with locals and foreigners who come here for live music and DJs serving up ever-popular Jamaican and Trini tracks, alongside hip-hop, R&B and old-school soul. Tue–Sat 7pm–3am. Best night is Friday, when the crowd is at its biggest. Small cover charge.

Petitrou Bar, Old Milford Rd, Little Rockly Bay. Adjacent to the *Cat & Fiddle* this local liming spot, an open-air wooden board bar is good for its intimate atmosphere and prices lower than its neighbour's.

Waving Gallery, Store Bay Complex. Cool and breezy upstairs spot for a laid-back drink (cocktails as well as Carib) and a lime as the beach traffic passes below. A sound system plays on Friday nights.

North to Buccoo

A kilometre or so before Milford Road widens into Claude Noel Highway, Shirvan Road strikes off to the left. Bristling with signs tacked up by enterprising restaurateurs and hoteliers, this is the route to Buccoo Bay and its famous reef (see pp.278–280) as well as several wide yellow-sand beaches and the neat coastal town of Plymouth. The first stretch is bordered to the left by a plantation of towering coconut palms and to the right by thick hedges masking what was once Shirvan Park horse racing track. A fire in 1985 put a permanent stop to horse racing in Tobago, and the site then had a brief incarnation as Tobago's most popular nightspot *Starting Gate* before turning into *The Lush*, the place to "large it".

Studded with swanky restaurants, fruit stalls and simple board shacks, Shirvan Road continues north, passing turn-offs to quietly residential Mount Pleasant and Carnbee Village – the latter has a supermarket and petrol station. There's another cluster of tourist-oriented signposts at the next crossroads, known as Buccoo Junction. Here, route taxis running between Scarborough and the north coast pick up and drop passengers, so you'll often see beckoning hands if you're driving. The right turn at the crossroads is Auchenskeoch (pronounced or-kins-styor)/Buccoo Bay Road – take any left from here and you'll climb into the midst of one of Tobago's smartest residential areas; opulent villas sporting swimming pools, towering satellite dishes, the Mount Irvine golf course and fantastic views of Buccoo Reef/Pigeon Point. A little further up the road and you're at the outskirts of tiny BETHEL, a precipitously situated and completely charming rural village once home to infamously eccentric German artist Luise Kimme (see p.281); there are several wonderful views of the Lowlands and the Buccoo coast from the village. From Bethel, Orange Hill Road eventually meets Claude Noel Highway.

Tobago's most upmarket hotels are clustered along the beaches between Buccoo and Plymouth, and the exclusive villas (see pp.258–259) around the Mount Irvine golf course offer some of the plushest private lodgings you'll find, but not all the accommodation is the exclusive preserve of the well heeled. There are plenty of middle-bracket hotels and guesthouses, and the area makes one of the most appealing bases on the island; you're close to the action of Crown Point without being stuck right in it, transport is easy (taxis run along Shirvan Road from early morning to late at night), and the

For information on villa rentals in the area, see p.253.

beaches are marvellous. Accommodation details are listed under the relevant areas.

Buccoo

The left turn at Buccoo Junction takes you into the small settlement of **BUCCOO**, haphazardly built around a calm and beautiful bay. Fishing remains a major industry here – the day's catch is sold by the beach facilities when the boats return in the late afternoon – but since the nearby reef has become a premier attraction, this close-knit community has embraced tourism. Shopfronts are daubed with "Welcome to Buccoo", and the green space in front of the bay is the venue for the annual **goat races**, a highlight in Tobago's tourist calender – the scoreboard is left up year round as testament to the bitterly fought contests which take place each Easter (see box opposite). Buccoo gets a weekly energy injection when the masses descend for the **Sunday School** debauchery (see box, p.274) and the village is completely taken over. The rest of the week sees a quieter scene, with the community (and its posse of skinny dogs) tidying up the revellers' rubbish and enjoying their peace and quiet while they can; families chat over garden walls and small boys take pleasure in diving off the fishing pier, despite the scummy waves that lap against the coarse grey sand. The combined effect of a Sunday job as a urinal and a muddy sea bed make Buccoo a terrible place to swim, though the palm-lined western fringe of the bay is more appealing with cleaner water and plenty of shells and coral fragments to collect. There are run-down government-built beach facilities, but hardly anyone uses them these days. Several roads shoot off right from Buccoo's main street, all of them dead ends; the last – Battery Street – terminates at a grassy bluff that was the original venue for the goat races, but close proximity to the cliffs that give sweeping views over Mount Irvine Bay prompted a shift to safer ground.

Buccoo Reef and Nylon Pool

Covering around twelve square kilometres of Caribbean sea bed between Pigeon Point and Buccoo Bay, **Buccoo Reef** is the largest and most heavily visited reef in Tobago. Home to forty-odd species of hard and soft coral, the reef has taken around ten thousand years to grow into today's magnificent labyrinth. The predominant corals are hard stag and elkhorn, though you'll see waving purple sea fans and peach-coloured fire coral as well, all of which make good feeding for the brilliantly coloured trigger, butterfly, surgeon and parrot fish. To the south of the reef is **Nylon Pool**, a gleaming coralline sandbar forming an appealing metre-deep swimming pool smack in the middle of the sea. It's said to have been named by Princess Margaret during a stay in the 1950s; she remarked that the water was as clear as her nylon stockings.

Sadly, however, human interference is taking a devastating toll. Carelessly placed anchors and thoughtless removal of coral souvenirs – not to mention the inevitable pollution – mean that many parts bear more resemblance to a coral graveyard than a living reef. Large sections have died off completely, leaving white skeletons in their wake, while overfishing has reduced fish and crustacean populations, and misplaced spear guns have ripped chunks from the coral. The situation became so bad that Buccoo was declared a protected national park in 1973, but with scant resources to enforce

Goat and crab races

Easter weekend in Tobago is what Carnival is to Trinidad; an unofficial national holiday when the hotels are filled to the brim with Trinidadians on a weekend break and the island erupts with festivities. A succession of huge open-air parties and well-attended harvest feasts culminate at the **Buccoo goat races** on Easter Tuesday, introduced by Barbadian national Samuel Callender in 1925. Though attempting to race one of the most intractable and belligerent animals in the world may seem a little ridiculous to the uninitiated, these tournaments are taken very seriously by aficionados, who study the form (and character) of the sleekly groomed animals and place bets on their favourites. Kept separately from the run-of-the-mill roadside grazer and given fanciful names like Dance Hall King, Nobody Wants Me, Nasty Man or Ben Johnson, racing goats never end up in the pot, but instead undergo a rigorous training routine and return to the tracks year after year. Prize specimens live out their days as stud goats to breed more potential champions.

The preliminary round at the Mount Pleasant Family Fun Day on Easter Monday gives everyone a chance to see which goat is running best, and by Tuesday, Buccoo – still reeling from the two largest Sunday Schools of the year – is transformed; the track is clipped and fenced in, the scoreboard is resplendent with a new coat of paint and the starting gates are in place. Food vendors and craft stalls line the streets and a carnival atmosphere builds as fast as the crowds, who are kept entertained by dancing and drumming in between stakes. Suitably attired in white shorts and coloured vests, the jockeys limber up by the side of the tracks; a necessary exercise, as their ability to keep up with their goat (and keep hold of it) has more influence on their success or failure than the capabilities of the goat itself; animals are raced at the end of a rope, and guided or encouraged with the help of a long stick. Sponsored by local businesses and given grand titles like White Oak Classic or Penta Paints Stake A, the actual races are a joy to watch once the jockeys manage to manoeuvre their malignant charges into starting position. With wild-eyed stares, the goats tear haphazardly down the track, often taking a diagonal course that trips up other goats and runners alike to the delight of the spectators. The best of the bunch battle for supremacy in the final "Champ of Champs" race, while "Champion Jockey", "Champion Trainer" and "Most Outstanding Goat" prizes are also presented.

The equally improbable **crab races** are taken a little less seriously. Plucked from the ocean a couple of weeks before, the crustaceans are encouraged to run both by tugs on a piece of string and by temporary withdrawal of food; choice morsels placed at the end of the wooden alleys which keep the crabs on course are the incentive for the sideways dash to the finishing line. Once all the races are over, the final all-night party swings into action, and the dancing continues until dawn.

the law, the legal status meant little and the damage continued practically unabated. Today, glass-bottom boat operators are more conscientious, anchoring only on dead reef and warning visitors that touching or removing reef matter and shells is illegal, but they still hand out the plastic shoes, making it possible for a single footstep to damage or kill hundreds of years' growth. You can do your bit by standing on sea bed only and refusing to buy any coral trinkets. A donation to Environment Tobago is also a good way to help preserve Tobago's reefs.

If you want to see the reef, you'll have no difficulty in finding a **glass-bottom boat** to take you; they leave from Store Bay, Pigeon Point and Buccoo – though if you choose the former, snorkelling time may be reduced as it's a longer journey to the reef. Basic tours include a trip across the unscathed deep-water coral garden as well as snorkelling and a dip in Nylon Pool; a two– to three-hour trip costs around US$20. Some operators make a day of it by including a beach barbecue at No Man's Land for around US$40. Some of the most reliable operators are Buccoo-based Johnson and Sons (☎639 8519), Mr Power, who makes daily trips on his boat *POWER1* from Pigeon Point; or Hew's (☎639 9058) – just ask around on the beaches. These operators time their trips with the low tide, when snorkelling is at its best, while others will go anytime you want.

Mount Irvine

Though it lacks atmosphere the semi-private section of beach maintained by the Mount Irvine *hotel is a little superior to the public area; nonguests are welcome to swim, and you can use the showers if you're drinking from the bar.*

The swaying palms and shaven greens of Tobago's first **golf course** herald the outskirts of **MOUNT IRVINE**, the next coastal village past Buccoo. Straddled across Shirvan Road, the course was opened in 1968 as the main attraction of *Mount Irvine* hotel, which still owns and maintains the greens. At some six hundred metres, with several onerous water holes and some wicked undulations, it offers a challenging game and plays host to the Tobago Pro-Am tournament every January. Green fees are US$30 for nine holes, US$48 for eighteen – there's also a weekly rate of US$264.

Past the golf course, the hitherto hidden coast swings spectacularly back into view; yachts bob on the waves and craggy volcanic rock formations bordering Buccoo Point make an arresting backdrop to the west. There's a lovely section of yellow-sand beach behind a low concrete bulwark just past the golf course; known as Mount Irvine Wall, the wide, wavy beach is popular with local devotees of a restorative "sea bath" who sit chatting in the emerald-green. Around the next bend is **Mount Irvine Bay Beach**, a regularly busy slip of fine yellow sand with just enough room for beach tennis and volleyball, surrounded by cutesy covered gazebos and the ubiquitous palms and sea grape trees. The facilities (daylight hours; TT$1) are adequate if a bit run-down, and there's a bar/restaurant on site doling out mountains of fried shark and bake. During the summer months, the water is calm enough to make exploration of the ornate offshore **reef** a joy, but Mount Irvine becomes one of the island's best **surfing** beaches between December and March, when huge breakers crash against the sand and plain swimming becomes a bit redundant. Boards can be rented from Mt. Irvine Watersports (☎639 9379) right next to the beach complex; they also rent out windsurfing and snorkelling equipment as well as Sailfish boats.

Lowlands:
Crown Point
to Plymouth

Kimme museum

Nestled in the hills behind the beach along Orange Hill Road (take the right turn just past the Mount Irvine golf course then follow the signposts), the **Kimme Museum** is the private gallery of German sculptor Luise Kimme, who settled in Tobago in 1979. Her eerily beguiling wood sculptures are on display in the *Tobago Hilton* (see p.257) and the *Kariwak Village* hotel (see p.255), and her bronze head of local politician A.P.T. James graces James Park in Scarborough. Works are also dotted around the surrounds of her quirky, mural-decorated fret-worked home, the "Fairyhaus" – known locally as "the castle". The collection is stunning; three-metre-high figures carved from whole trunks of oak depict the subtlest nuances of Tobagonian dancing, and her interpretations of local folklore characters Mama L'Eau, La Diablesse and the Soucouyant are powerful.

The museum is well worth a visit (open Sun only, 10am–2pm, appointments taken for other days; TT$10; ☎639 0257, www.kimme.de). Meeting Luise Kimme – ever the eccentric artist – is an experience in itself; she's always on hand to provide further insight into her work. You can buy copies of her evocative Tobago diary, *Chachalaca* (see "Books", p.363), as well as photograph booklets of her pieces.

For more information on surfing in the islands, contact the Trinidad-based Surfing Association of Trinidad and Tobago (☎623 0920).

Black Rock and around

Past Mount Irvine, Shirvan Road becomes Grafton Road from this point on. Its narrower forefather, Old Stone Haven Road, ran close to the sea, and though potholed and semi-private looking, you can still drive or walk along it to access an excellent **beach** – often referred to as Grafton Beach after the resort hotel which dominates the sand from above. A glorious, wide swathe with coarse sand and year-round crashing waves that attracts turtles to lay eggs (see p.349), Stone Haven (as it's officially called) makes for marvellous swimming. The proximity of the hotel makes this a rather commercial beach in some ways, though; washing lines strung between the almond trees display pretty batik sarongs and you'll be periodically approached by roving craft vendors. Adjacent to the entrance to *Stonehaven Villas* on the main road is a sun-bleached sign marking the entrance to the **Grafton Caledonia Bird Sanctuary** (daylight hours; free). Now somewhat run down the sanctuary was founded by the late owner of the surrounding estate, Eleanor Alefounder, who began feeding hungry local birds following the

Marie's Place in Pleasant Prospect (downstairs from The Emerald restaurant, right on the road between Mount Irvine and Stone Haven bays) is convenient for basic supplies and batik (Mon–Sat 8am–8pm, Sun 9am–5pm). There's also a cash machine on site.

devastation wreaked by Hurricane Flora in 1963 (see p.303). Since then, 4pm is the regular feeding time for the flocks of mot-mot, cocorico, bananaquit and practically every other feathered specimen found on the island, many of which will peck right out of your hand. There are extensive trails through the property which make excellent, easy and scenic **hiking**.

Less than a kilometre beyond Grafton Beach is another, far less developed strip of sand, and a ravishing one to boot. Masked by a thick belt of bush between Grafton Road and the sea, **Back Bay** manages an uncanny remoteness despite its central location, and it's one of the few places on the island where you can discard your bathing suit without offending locals and risking prosecution; however, this solitary spot demands caution as rumours of robberies are rife. To find the beach, continue along the coast past Mount Irvine; after rounding a bend in the road, look for an expansive house on the inland side, where a dirt track leads into the foliage, forking after a few metres – either path will take you to the shore.

The Tobago hustle

Though tourist harassment in Tobago is far less of a problem than in many other destinations where the industry is a major earner, aggressive and unsettling attitudes are becoming increasingly common among a small number of people who seem bent on stressing you out, either through sexual harassment at the bars and clubs or over-insistent hustling of over-priced crafts on the more touristy beaches. It can be irritating and frustrating, especially if you're not in the best of moods, but it's important not to lose perspective. Many tourists do come to the island with a holiday romance in mind, so you can't blame people for trying it on just because it's not on your personal agenda; most hustlers are simply struggling to make ends meet in an island where unemployment stands at 25 percent (10 percent more than the national average for T&T) and career opportunities are severely limited. Be aware that HIV infection is high on the island, though, the result of earlier hedonistic holidaymakers, so if you do indulge make sure you use protection, otherwise you could be returning home with an unwanted souvenir.

Tobagonians on the whole are hugely generous hosts, warming to visitors with genuine respect and taking pride in showing you their island, but constantly having to pander to another's needs – especially those of comparatively wealthy tourists with little knowledge of conservative Tobagonian culture – must get frustrating, and it's hardly surprising that the usually gentle entreaties to buy some crafts or take a boat tour can occasionally boil over into heavy-handed hustling or downright rudeness.

If you do feel harassed, maintain your sense of humour, say no if someone's selling something you don't want, and make your intentions clear if someone offers themselves as your ideal Tobagonian partner; local women are not expected to dance with anyone but their lovers or friends, so you needn't feel pressured to accept an invitation. Should you be unlucky enough to need to report an incident to the police, do so at Old Grange police station (☎639 8888), off the Auchenskeoch/Buccoo Road.

The beach is wide and wild, with one main curve bordered by two smaller bays and a backdrop of trees which include a **manchineel**, a nasty tree with poisonous green fruits and sap that's a severe irritant to the skin; look out for the warning sign. At the western corner of the bay, smooth yellow sand that's seldom disturbed by a footprint surrounds magnificent craggy outcrops divided by tracts of rough water boiling against the rock; swimming is dangerous all along the beach, so stick to paddling.

Continuing northeast, the road narrows as it enters **BLACK ROCK**, a busy, friendly village with a couple of nice rum shops, a small supermarket and a large electricity substation. On the western outskirts of town is a signpost for **Fort Bennet**, a still-intact stockade first established by English mercenary Lieutenant Robert Bennet in 1680. During the plantation era, the fort was expanded by British troops, who built a red-brick oven to heat up the metal used to make cannonballs and placed two cannons to defend the bay against US warships during the American War of Independence. The THA have added a gazebo, and the view over Mount Irvine Bay and the Pigeon Point headland is spectacular, particularly at sunset. Close by is the Culture Barn (☎639 9022) a small shop run by Malcolm Melville, renowned internationally for his unique and innovative drums. Behind the shop is his workshop where he crafts drums from mango, cypre, cedar mahogany and breadfruit woods.

Turtle Beach

Beyond a grating section of potholes marking the end of Black Rock, the road swings round a blind bend before entering a straight stretch. Trees mask the lovely **Turtle Beach**, a good kilometre of picturesque, coarse yellow sand flecked with the occasional swathe of volcanic grey; there are several dirt tracks from which to enter the bay. The water shelves steeply from the beach and the waves are large, making for exhilarating swimming, while a river at the western end has possibilities for a freshwater dip, but it's often dammed up and stagnant in the dry season. Jealously guarding pole position in the centre of the bay (only guests are allowed to use the purpose-built sun shelters), the two-storey *Turtle Beach* hotel dominates the sand, and the constant presence of well-heeled guests has generated an ideal captive market for itinerant vendors. Like Grafton next-door, the sand is patrolled by craft and aloe-purveyors who offer their inflatedly priced wares with varying degrees of insistence, and the strip in front of the hotel is one of the few places in Tobago where you might feel hustled (see box opposite). If you do, head for a spot further away from the hotel; however, the centre of the beach is the only place where you can buy drinks and snacks; *A Team* (☎639 9136), a tour operator, also puts on a beach barbecue every Wednesday and Friday – for TT$200 you can have grilled fish, chicken, rice and salads, and rum punch whilst being entertained by limbo dancers and calypso music.

Though the beach is officially called **Great Courland Bay**, it acquired its colloquial title on account of the **turtles** that still lay eggs here in the dark of night (see box, p.349). The main laying season runs between March and August, and six weeks after the eggs are laid, hatchlings make a dash for the sea; both equally moving sights. All of the hotels along this stretch organize a turtle watch during the laying and hatching seasons, but if you're not staying in the area, contact Nick Hardwicke at *Seahorse Inn* (☎639 0686) for turtle watching expeditions.

Plymouth

A mile or so beyond Turtle Beach, Grafton Road meets a junction – straight on is the Plymouth Road, which leads scenically to Scarborough via Whim, a quiet interior village, while to the left, a narrow bridge over the Courland River signifies the outskirts of **PLYMOUTH**, Tobago's first European community, settled first by a group of roving Latvians usually referred to as Courlanders, then by the Dutch and finally by the British (see "Contexts", p.240). Today, it's an attractive little town, with neat board houses and an overabundance of rum shops lining the grid-patterned streets. Turning left from the main road at the phone box will take you to Plymouth's main attractions; the so-called **mystery tombstone** and **Fort James**. Well signposted and sitting alone on a concrete platform close to the sea, the tombstone is an enigmatic, if rather depressing, reminder of Tobago's history of slavery. The double grave of a child and her 23-year-old mother, Betty Stiven, wife of one Alex Stiven, the "mystery" is the inscription on the stone slab: "What was remarkable of her; she was a mother without knowing it, and a wife without letting her husband know it, except by her kind indulgences to him". Betty is said to have been the African slave (and lover) of Alex Stiven, a wealthy Dutch planter, and the general hypothesis has two strands. In the first theory, she gave birth to Stiven's mulatto child, and he took charge of it, raising it as his but not acknowledging Betty as the mother, giving her "freedom" to carry on as his lover and making her a "mother without knowing it". The other theory proposes that the affair between Alex and Betty was illicit and scandalous but passionate, carried out in secret to save the face of a white man. When she died giving birth to his child, he was so overcome with grief that he left this cryptic message as a commemoration of their love.

Opposite the tombstone, a road leads down toward the sea; turn right and you'll see the stark concrete blocks of the **Great Courland Bay Monument**, testament to the "bold, enterprising and industrious" Latvians – who colonized the area and lent their name to the bay. Carrying straight on past the tombstone brings you to Fort James, the oldest stockade in Tobago. The solid, roofed coral stone structure and four cannons that remain today are a British legacy, built in 1811, and there's an excellent view of Turtle Beach from the mown lawns behind. Life in Plymouth centres around the large grocery on the main street, opposite the *S&B Tasty Roti* parlour (Mon–Sat 11am–2pm). Jamaican dub blasts out from cars and shops bringing the street to life while the local youth hang out outside chilling and passing the time.

The Plymouth main road leads back onto the Arnos Vale Road, where, on the outskirts of town, a small weather-beaten sign on the left-hand side directs you to the **Adventure Farm and Nature Reserve** (Mon–Fri 7am–5pm, US$4). There's little adventure to be had on this twelve-acre site, though there is plenty of nature with mot-mots, green herons and chachalaca and other birds that regularly appear to feed in the late afternoon. There's also a butterfly garden, an organic farm where you can pick your own fruit and toy-like cottages in which to stay (see p.260).

If you're driving up the coast, it's wise to fill your tank at Plymouth's petrol station, as it's the only one for miles (Mon–Sat 6.30am–9pm, Sun 5.30am–9pm).

Arnos Vale

From the centre of Plymouth, a well-signposted but narrow road meanders through the greenery toward **Arnos Vale**, one of the few sugar estates to keep its land, and parts of the plantation have been opened up to the public while a resort hotel straddles the beachfront section of the property. The main point of access is at the old estate **water wheel**, now slickly packaged as a tourist attraction (daily 8am–11pm; TT$10). The wheel, pump and stream train that once transported sugar around the plantation have been restored, and you can view them from a wooden walkway. The modest **museum** is disappointing, displaying a small selection of Amerindian pottery and colonial artefacts – horseshoes, pipes etc – found on the estate, and there are several trails leading off into the hinterland, for which guides are available. It's a pretty spot, lavish with flowering plants and lush foliage and nice for a relaxing drink after you've toured the estate. Past Arnos Vale, the recently resurfaced road passes the tiny but attractive villages of **Golden Lane** and **Les Coteaux**; the latter is known as a centre for obeah, and rumours of witchery and potions abound – the community hosts spooky story sessions during the Heritage Festival celebrations. Road improvements have linked Arnos Vale with the rest of the leeward coast, but you can also get to Moriah and Castara from Scarborough via the Northside Road (see p.297).

Scarborough

Tobago's raucous, hot and dusty capital, precipitous **SCARBOROUGH** (population 18,000) is an immensely appealing place. Poking through the treetops, houses, roads and the canary-yellow facade of a furniture chain spill higgledy-piggledy down the hillside while the Atlantic provides a magnificent backdrop for the silhouettes of the

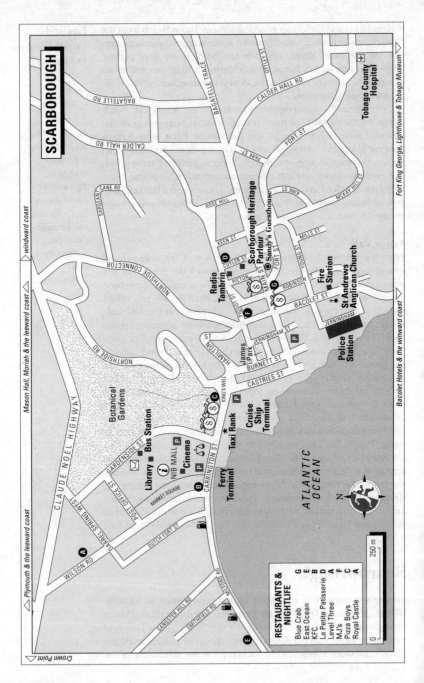

SCARBOROUGH

RESTAURANTS & NIGHTLIFE

Blue Crab	G
East Ocean	E
KFC	B
La Petite Patisserie	D
Level Three	F
MJ's	C
Pizza Boys	A
Royal Castle	A

Fort King George, Lighthouse & Tobago Museum

Bacolet Hotels & the winward coast

Mason Hall, Moriah & the leeward coast

windward coast

Plymouth & the leeward coast

Crown Point

ATLANTIC OCEAN

0   250 m

lighthouse and **Fort King George**, perched at the top of the hill. The island's administrative centre and its main **port**, Scarborough is a flourishing town, brimming with a brisk vibrancy. Devoid of touristic pretensions, the town throbs with activity; street corners swarm with liming locals, stalls draped with clothes are perused by the shoppers, while the **market**, with its artistically arranged displays of intensely coloured fruit and vegetables, and constant sales banter of the stall-holders, is irresistible.

Though it's the island's largest conglomeration of concrete, Scarborough is pretty tiny; the docking of the **ferry** from Trinidad is spectacle enough to draw crowds of onlookers – prospective passengers scurry by clutching parcels, cars and lorries inch along as they wait to board, bars spill over onto the pavement and food vendors fill the air with barbecue smoke. Away from the commercial clamour, the peaceful **botanical gardens** or the cool breezes and views from the port offer respite from the traffic and steep climbs that can make Scarborough a bit of an ordeal; visiting on an overcast day makes sightseeing more comfortable.

Some history

The **Dutch** were the first Europeans to settle in what became one of Tobago's most hotly contested pieces of land. They navigated the treacherous harbour rocks in 1654, constructed a fort and a few buildings, and named it **Lampsinsburgh**. Around the same time, a group of Courlanders (Latvians) were building up their stronghold on the opposite coast at Plymouth (see p.240). In 1658, the Dutch captured it – an act that was to lead to the destruction of their own settlement a few years later when, in 1666, a fleet of English ships came to the aid of the Latvians and blew Lampsinsburgh to smithereens.

The English officially won the island in 1672, but didn't maintain a presence, allowing the Dutch to return and build Lampsinsburgh into a more substantial settlement, with houses, a single street and a church as well as warehouses and wharves at the harbour and a new fort armed with cannons. However, during the French assault of 1677, the newly improved fortifications proved to be the undoing of the Dutch; a French cannonball hit the ammunition dump, and the resulting fireball destroyed the structure and killed the 250 occupants. Though it's still commemorated in the current name Dutch Fort Road, there's nothing left of the settlement.

The British bestowed the name **Scarborough** when they regained control of Tobago in 1762, establishing the House of Assembly and constructing Fort King George. After a 20-year lull, the struggle began anew; following a prolonged and bloody effort, during which they constructed the "French Fort" in nearby Calder Hall, the **French** took control in 1781. Scarborough was renamed Port Louis, while Fort King George – with finishing touches added by

French soldiers – became **Fort Castries**. The town ricocheted between the British and French until Tobago was finally ceded to the British in 1814. Though Scarborough was a thriving commercial centre during the plantation era, it was the first place to suffer when the sugar industry collapsed in the 1870s; the House of Assembly was disbanded, and not reconvened until 1980.

Arrival, getting around and information

Most people enter Scarborough by **road** along the Wilson Road turn-off from Claude Noel Highway, following the one-way system toward the wharves bordering Carrington Street, the docking point for **ferries** to and from Trinidad, which moor up at the central terminal (for departures and prices, see "Listings", p.321). There are two **taxi** stands on Carrington Street, a one-minute walk from the terminal (it should cost around TT$4–6 to Crown Point), while the **bus station** is located on Greenside Street behind the NIB Mall, walkable in five minutes. Buses to all corners of the island run daily between 4.30am and 8pm; for details see pp.243–244. Remember to purchase your tickets before boarding. As Scarborough is so small, there are no bus services within the town, but you can easily see all the sights by foot. For **information**, head to the offices of the Tobago House of Assembly, Division of Tourism on the third floor of the NIB Mall (8am–4pm; ☎639 2125 or 4636, fax 639 3566, tourbago@tstt.net.tt).

Practicalities

Free parking is available at the wharf lot on the corner of Carrington and Castries streets, in the NIB Mall car park off Greenside Street (strictly speaking for shoppers only) and the lot behind the cinema and KFC.

For **currency exchange**, you'll find the Bank of Commerce and Scotiabank on Carrington Street opposite the wharf, Royal and Republic banks on Main Street and First Citizens Bank on Lower Milford Road, of which Royal is the most efficient. All are subject to local opening hours (see "Basics", p.12). There are several late-opening **petrol stations** around town – see "Listings" (pp.322–323) for details. Scarborough is the departure point for **route taxis** serving the whole of the island, though finding where to catch your ride can be confusing. For Crown Point (TT$5–6), Mount Irvine (TT$5), Buccoo (TT$4), Carnbee (TT$3), Bethel (TT$4), Plymouth (TT$4) and Black Rock (TT$4) go to the "west end" taxi rank directly outside the ferry terminal. For Carnbee and Mount Pleasant (TT$4), go to the phone booth opposite *KFC* on Carrington Street. Taxis running the Northside Road to Castara (TT$6) and Parlatuvier (TT$10) leave from Carrington Street opposite the port, while cars going to L'Anse Fourmi (TT$12) leave from the NIB Mall car park on Greenside Street. Taxis to Speyside leave from Republic Bank, Main Street. (TT$10). **Maxis** to Charlotteville leave two or three times a day from outside the James Park on Burnett Street (TT$12).

Accommodation

Though Scarborough and the Bacolet suburbs were popular in the 1960s and 1970s during the early years of Tobagonian tourism, the Lowlands area are now the most tourist-developed areas. Some excellent options remain, though, particularly in suburban Bacolet. Prices are lower, and access to public transport is good. Staying in a host home or bed and breakfast (see "Basics", p.24) can be great if you're on a budget or fancy a little more intimacy with local lifestyles than a hotel can provide. The tourist board recommends a number of **host homes** in their standard accommodation listings booklet (available from offices worldwide) – most rent at around US$35–55 per person, but you can often get a room for less than this, particularly if you're visiting in the off-season. The best way to find a good **B&B** is through Ms Miriam Edwards of the Tobago Bed and Breakfast Association (☎639 3926; c/o *Federal Villa*, 1–3 Crooks River, Scarborough, *maredwards@hotmail.com*).

For details of the accommodation price codes used in these listings, see p.252.

Ade's Domicil, 19 Old Lighthouse Rd, Bacolet Point ☎639 4306, fax 639 3779, www.adesdomicil.de. This spacious white plantation-style house is a few minutes' away from the beach. All rooms have en-suite bathroom, a/c or ceiling fan, cable TV, fully equipped kitchen and a sea view. Good value. ⑤.

Bacolet Bay Apartments, Bacolet St ☎ & fax 639 2955, *cross@ Cariblink.ne*t. Past its heyday but very friendly, great value and just a step away from Bacolet beach. Studios have kitchen, TV, a/c and a patio, suites are much larger with a living room; all rooms are clean and serviceable. There's also a pool. ⑤.

Blue Haven, Bacolet Bay ☎660 7400, fax 660 7900, www.bluehavenhotel.com. The best luxury accommodation on the island, this historic hotel – former guests include Rita Hayworth and Robert Mitchum – has been recently restored. The lavish rooms have four-poster or sleigh beds, a/c, TV, minibar, phone and modern artwork, spacious bathrooms and a balcony overlooking stunning Bacolet Bay. There's a swimming pool with ornamental waterfall, mini-gym, spa and tennis court, and an excellent restaurant on site that serves organic vegetables. Close to restaurants, with Scarborough a ten-minute walk away. ⑨.

Della Mira, 36 Bacolet St ☎639 2531, fax 639 4018 or 5226. Set in a pretty colonial-style house overlooking the sea with a pool, bar and restaurant on site. The basic rooms with bathroom and a/c are somewhat down at heel, but the rates are reasonable. ④.

Federal Villa, 1–3 Crooks River, Scarborough ☎ & fax 639 3926, maredwards@hotmail.com. Home of the B&B Association, rooms are set in a private house in the Scarborough suburbs. All are basic with fan and shared bathroom, and have a pleasant atmosphere. ④.

Hope Cottage, Calder Hall Rd ☎639 2179, *hopecottage100@hotmail.com*, www.surfmaster.btinternet.co.uk. Set in a 100-year-old colonial building just before the hospital, this is one of the oldest guesthouses in Tobago and a great bargain. Rooms are plain with private bathroom and kitchenette, and there's also a three-bedroom cottage with shared kitchen in the two-acre grounds. ②.

Horizons Tobago, 89 Bacolet Point ☎0121 709 1648, *info@horizonstobago.com*. Cream-and-brown concrete building in a lush setting housing five one- and two-bedroom apartments furnished with rattan and decorated local artwork. All have a/c, phones, cable TV, equipped kitchens and mosquito nets. A shared utility area is available for washing clothes, and there's also a 37-foot swimming pool; maid service is also provided. Discounts for stays of over eighteen nights. ⑥.

Jacob's Guesthouse, Crooks River, Scarborough ☎639 2271. The small dark rooms are clean and simple; all have fans and washbasin, some have en-suite shower and toilet, and a few sleep four. Two minutes' from Scarborough's centre. ②.

Mt Pelier Cottage, Montpelier, Scarborough, c/o Mark and Zena Puddy, PO Box 14, Scarborough ☎639 4931, *puddy@tstt.net.tt*. Unique and utterly fabulous home away from home in the host's self-built wooden house perched on Scarborough's hillside. These airy rooms (double, twin or single) have lattice windows, creative hand-carved decor and shared bathroom. Meals are served on a balcony overlooking the forest in the company of mot-mots, blue jays and bananaquits. Rates include excellent home-cooked breakfast, huge evening meals and the owner as personal guide and driver. ⑦.

Noon's Holiday Cottage, 97 Bacolet Pt ☎639 5567, *pat_denoon@hotmail.com*. Spacious two-bedroom apartment with fully furnished kitchen, lounge and fan on the ground floor of the owner's home. Located in a quiet residential road five minutes' walk from Bacolet Bay the apartment has a back garden to relax in and is good value for the space. ③.

Old Donkey Cart, 73 Bacolet St ☎639 3551, fax 639 6124, www .donkeycarthouse.com. Spacious garden and superior rooms with fridge, TV, phone, fans, unusual decor and great views of Bacolet Bay; the open-plan penthouse suite is fabulous. There's an overflow pool and a restaurant on site; rates include continental breakfast. Airport transfers on request. ⑥.

Sandy's, cor. Fort and Main streets ☎639 2737, fax 660 7748. Run by hospitable owners of the *Blue Crab* restaurant, this cosy place has two pretty and spotless rooms with a/c and private bathroom. ⑤.

Seaview Guesthouse, Bacolet St ☎639 5613, fax 639 6243, verleen@tstt.net.tt. Overlooking the sea 50m down the road from *Old Donkey Cart*, this guesthouse offers superb value and a warm atmosphere. Sparklingly clean apartments with full kitchen, fan, hot water and beautiful views; all share a communal patio. Meals are available on request. ④.

Lower Scarborough: the mall and the market

Most vehicles enter town from the highway along car-choked Wilson Road, following the one-way system along Greenside Street, which takes you past the bus station and the back of **NIB Mall** to the right, and the botanical gardens to the left. The largest shopping centre in Scarborough, **NIB Mall** houses Christian bookshops, fast-food outlets and pharmacies, as well as the **library**, a cool and pleasant place to pore over the collection of Caribbean-oriented titles. Also on this stretch is a car park that doubles as a venue for Carnival celebrations and sound system dances as well as the main **post office** (Mon–Fri 8am–4pm) and the food **market**. Main trading days are Friday and Saturday, but throughout the week, vendors loudly hawk every tropical fruit and vegetable imaginable. The indoor meat section is an odoriferous melange of goat, beef, lamb, mutton and chicken, while fish on ice gleam at the back of the market, where stallholders attract customers by blowing on a **conch shell**. Trading reaches a peak on Friday, when the heavily scented fruits and earth-encrusted ground provisions are piled up alongside with leather sandals, incense, mounds of soap powder, clothing and dry goods, and carts selling snow cones, doubles and boiled corn do a roaring trade. It's a friendly and absorbing scene, great for bargains and interaction with Tobagonians away from the resorts. If you're after souvenirs, check out the **vendors mall**, a ramshackle collection of tarpaulin-covered stalls just south of the NIB Mall, where you'll find knitted Rasta hats, sandals, wood carvings and carved calabashes.

The Botanical Gardens

Opposite the bus station on Greenside Street is the back entrance to the **Botanical Gardens** (daily, daylight hours; free), a soothing oasis after the heat-retaining concrete and constant traffic fumes. Covering eighteen acres of former sugar estate, part of the Dal Fair and Rockly Vale plantations, the land was requisitioned by the British in the late nineteenth century with the intention of creating a public botanical garden, and the broad sweeps of lawn interspersed with planted beds and shade trees could pass for an English park were it not for the garish crimson of towering African tulips or flamboyant trees or the yellow and pink cascades of the poui trees, all bearing labels for easy identification. Near the botanical station is an **orchid house** displaying most of T&T's indigenous orchids as well as a few imported species. It's an enchanting spot, often deserted save for the odd office worker taking lunch under a shade tree. At its highest point a covered gazebo affords a nice view over town and the sea. There are no guided tours as such, but the team of gardeners are usually available on site to answer questions.

You can also enter the Botanical Gardens from the highway – pull in at the signpost marked "Botanical Gardens Layby".

Upper Scarborough: the wharf to James Park

Though some older buildings remain in Scarborough's steep heights, most of the waterfront has been overtaken by a glut of concrete. Souped up in 1990 by the addition of a deep-water cruise ship pier, the harbour is soon to be given a new lease on life when the **promenade** along Milford Road reaches its long-awaited completion, giving the thronging crowds around *KFC* and Market Square somewhere to hang out. Proceeding east from *KFC* along the bank and bar-lined Carrington Street, you reach a junction known as **King's Well**, originally the site of the town's main watercourse but now a rum shop and restaurant of the same name; a sharp left takes you out of town along Northside Road while the sharp right is Castries Street and ultimately Main Street. Between the two, steeply inclining **Burnett Street** is one of Scarborough's best places for knick-knack **shopping**, its tarmac decorated with white-painted palm trees and hibis-

Darren Henry (☎ 639 4559) trained forester and licensed tour guide does a 45-minute tour of the gardens for TT$50.

cus flowers by a local shopkeeper. As the road reaches a plateau, you enter **James Park**, once the town's main marketplace but now a scrap of grass decorated with Luise Kimme's bronze of A.P.T James, a former Minister of Tobago Affairs.

The park is bordered to the north by the imposing old **courthouse**, which has housed the administrative offices of the Tobago House of Assembly since the judiciary were shifted to their current Bacolet Street base in the late 1980s. Built between 1816 and 1825, the cut-stone structure – as a tourist board plaque outside proudly proclaims – was considered one of the finest examples of Georgian architecture in the Caribbean on completion. Subsequent alterations have, unfortunately, smothered the brickwork with white paint and removed the pillars, leaving it a shadow of its former glory. A small monument outside, dating from the reign of King Edward VII, bears the inscription "One flag, one king, one empire". On the opposite side of the park to the Burnett Street edge, **Jerningham Street** houses a paved mini-park with benches, a fountain and a relief map of Tobago which gives you a good idea of the island's topography.

Uphill to the Fort

Carrying straight on past James Park along Burnett Street brings you directly onto the bustling shop-and-office-lined **Main Street**. One hundred yards or so uphill are traffic lights marking the right turn on to **Bacolet Street**, the route to the fire station, the main police station (and only jail) as well as **Gun Bridge**. In commemoration of the town's historical discord, its stone walls are embellished with four cannons taken from Fort George, while musket barrels form the guard rails. A little further along is **St Andrew's Anglican Church**, originally built in 1819 but razed by Hurricane Flora in 1963 and reconstructed a year later. Further down Bacolet Street, the buildings thin out as you enter the quiet and attractive Bacolet suburbs (see p.294).

Fort King George

Back on Main Street and a few metres higher, well-signposted **Fort Street** forks off to the right, twisting its way up a steep hill to the fort, past the imposing Methodist Church and some attractive but dishevelled colonial architecture. A weathered sign pointing to Cuyler Street on your left leads you to the eclectic **Scarborough Heritage Parlour** (Mon–Fri 9am–5pm; free), which contains furniture from the old plantation houses, slave shackles, coins and antique uniforms – all allowing a glimpse of Tobago's social history. Near to the top of the hill, a vine-wreathed red brick building to the right is all that remains of an old **prison**, once part of the fort complex above; time and the elements have opened its tiny, dingy cells to shafts of sunlight. Round the next bend is **Tobago County Hospital**

If you drive yourself to the fort, you can almost always find a parking space in the lot adjacent to the museum and main fort.

and the start of the **Fort King George** complex. The first building on the left is the dome-shaped cover of an old **well**, built in 1926 to service the hospital. Opposite is the red brick **Officer's Mess**, now home to a local craft centre (Mon–Fri 9am–1pm).

A grassy path next to the Officer's Mess leads below the main fort to a landscaped **park**, lush with poui trees and colourful planted beds. Benches are perfectly placed for soaking up marvellous views back of Scarborough and the Orange Hill district. In the shade of a massive, buttressed silk cotton tree is the decrepit **powder magazine**, its inner walls blackened by fires. The main fortification above is the largest in Tobago, built by the British and initially composed of some thirty buildings but reduced to around ten by an 1847 hurricane. The fort was occupied by French troops between 1781 and 1793, who built the solid stone perimeter walls. Inspired by the French Revolution, the soldiers **mutinied** in 1790, imprisoning their officers and razing the town below.

Today, this peaceful spot 140m above sea level is favoured for its constant sea breezes and spectacular views of Bacolet Bay, Minister Point and the rugged interior to the west, and Rockly Bay and the north coast of Trinidad to the east. By night it's a suitably deserted destination for a bit of in-car canoodling. Despite the profusion of cannons that still point out to sea, the tranquil atmosphere of the place makes it hard to imagine its military history. Behind the old officers' mess is the **lighthouse**, a squat structure transferred from Galera Point in Trinidad in 1958; the Fresnel lens beams fifty kilometres out to sea and sweeps spectacularly over the Scarborough suburbs.

Tobago Museum

The rest of the fort's buildings are ranged around the tidy lawns of Barrack Square. The buildings house the Culture Division of the Tobago House of Assembly, as well as the unmissable **Tobago Museum** (Mon–Fri 9am–5pm; adults TT$5, 13–15 year olds TT$2, children TT$1). Collated by the Tobago Trust, the small but fascinating collection of idiosyncratically labelled artefacts includes Amerindian plates, cooking wares, tools and talismans (one shaped like a penis, presumably for fertility) dating back to 2500 BC as well as pre-Columbian nostril bowls, used to inhale the intoxicating tobacco water favoured by the Indians. One unnerving exhibit unearthed during construction work at Mount Irvine beach in the 1970s is part of the skeleton of a young Indian; teeth, skull and ribcage are all clearly visible. Satirical colonial prints depicting the exploits of "Johnny Newcome in the West Indies" are well worth a look, as are the shells, fish fossils and military paraphernalia. Upstairs, there's a gallery of ancient maps, imported African drums, sculptures and some fascinating logs of the colonial era including notes on the sale of plantation slaves.

You can buy refreshments at a kiosk opposite the hospital, but as it's often closed, it's a good idea to bring your own, particularly if you're walking up.

Bacolet

The main Scarborough post office is the best place to post mail, being far quicker than the small regional postal agencies.

For bus services to Scarborough, see p.288.

As Bacolet Street eases out of town along the coast past Sandy Hall and Fairfield Complex, the main administrative base of the Tobago House of Assembly as well as the Tobago Hall of Justice court and the island's main cemetery, the roadside homes become noticeably upmarket. Though the area suffered a lull when Bacolet Street was replaced by Claude Noel Highway as the main route to the windward coast – Bacolet Street is also known as Old Windward Road – this is still a suburb of choice for Tobago's elite; the grand structures built along Bacolet Point stand as testament to the wealth of their owners. The area enjoyed a heady prestige during the late 1960s and early 70s, when the **Beatles** frolicked on Bacolet Bay beach and the area boasted a couple of flashy hotels, the *Bacolet* and *Blue Haven*. The latter was once part of Tobago's battlements: a cannon still resides on the hotel's grounds and stone walls dating back to 1770 surround the base of the hotel. The hotels tried to cordon off the sand in the 1960s but Dr Eric Williams – the premier who once declared that he had no intention of ruling "a nation of waiters and bellhops" – intervened to keep the beaches public. To this day Bacolet Bay beach is a popular beach for local football matches. After twenty-five years of dilapidation new owners and changing times have restored the *Blue Haven* to its former glory.

Though you can stop off at the Cotton House to view expensive batik work, the best reason to linger here is the charm of crescent-shaped **Bacolet Bay Beach**, brought to the silver screen during the filming of Walt Disney's *Swiss Family Robinson*. It's a lovely spot, the black sand lapped by the vigorous green Atlantic (be aware of the occasional dangerous undercurrents) and shaded by palms and Indian almond trees; rough seas in winter also make it popular with surfers. From the road concrete steps down the cliff side lead to the sand, where the thatched beach bar *No Problem* serves up ice cold drinks for thirsty sun worshippers. Past the beach, the houses thin out as the road swings left to meet with the highway and the traffic on its way along the windward coast (see pp.304–321).

Eating and drinking

For details of the dining price codes used in these listings, see p.269.

Scarborough offers everything from excellent low-cost meals to the most exclusive eatery. Cafés for working men and women have food on a par with the exclusive restaurants, though the latter have a wider range of international options. The favourite **roti** outlet in town is at the coastal end of Dutch Fort Road in the small plaza, but many locals still opt for the foreign allure of *KFC* on Wilson and Carrington streets or stick with what they know best at *Royal Castle* on Wilson Road – the spicy fried chicken, fish or veggie burgers and fries are available till 1am Thursday to Saturday. Another fast-food favourite is the *Pizza Boys* chain, though their prices are not worth the stodgy dough and limited toppings that are available. For drinks there are plenty of rum bars along Carrington Street well worth checking out; *King's Well Inn* at the junction with Crook's River is the least salubrious.

Blue Crab, cor. Robinson and Main streets ☎639 2737. Bustling, open-air weekday lunch spot. The excellent Creole food is popular with an office crowd; highlights are the green fig salad, any style of fish and the unsweetened natural juices. Lunch Mon–Fri 11am–3pm, dinner by reservation only. Expensive.

E&F Health Foods NIB Mall. Tasty weekday lunch specials including roti, buss-up-shut and vegetables. Budget.

East Ocean, Milford Rd ☎639 4535. The best Chinese restaurant in Tobago, overlooking the sea and offering a menu of familiar dishes. Order takeaway or eat in the air-conditioned dining room; they also deliver large orders. Inexpensive.

Glendale's Local Cuisine Glen Rd, just outside town on the north side of the highway. Huge servings of local staples, pilau, chicken and goat lure a steady stream of cars from the highway. Particularly good for lunches. Budget.

Harriet's, Stall five, Indoor Market. Renowned breakfasts – fried or roast bake, smoked herring, saltfish or fried fish (6–10am). Lunch varies daily: chicken, vegetables and ground provisions, lamb or goat with dumplings or pelau. Saturdays mean soup, and on Sunday it's traditional chicken, macaroni pie and callaloo. Go before 1.30pm or it's all gone. Budget.

La Petite Patisserie, Cuyler St ☎660 7971. Delicious authentic French pastries, bread and coffee. Freshly made cakes are available from 11am – a must is their to-die-for rum-soaked chocolate cake. Mon–Fri 7am–4pm, Sat 7am–1pm. Budget.

MJ's, cor. of Bacolet and Main streets. Good for a fast snack, serving vegetable pies, pastries and pizza all day. Budget.

Mr D's, NIB Mall. Caters for vegetarians, with a daily changing menu including roti and buss-up-shut. Budget.

Old Donkey Cart, 73 Bacolet St, Bacolet ☎639 3551. Italian restaurant in the hotel of the same name offers good but expensive pasta as well as local and American-style breakfast and light lunches. Expensive.

Rouselle's, Old Windward Rd, Bacolet ☎639 4738. Stylish restaurant with hardwood decor, a breezy verandah setting and relaxed sophistication reminiscent of a Port of Spain hang-out. Food is chic and tasty, nouvelle cuisine-style, with correspondingly small portions. Dishes to try include lobster in lemon, white wine and garlic sauce, fish or chicken in Creole sauce, and charcoal-flamed pork chops with garlic and mustard; reservations are recommended for dinner. Tue–Sat 3–11pm. Moderate/Expensive.

Salsa Kitchen, 8 Pumpmill Rd ☎639 7426. Child-friendly, with an enticing menu of pizza, pasta, tapas and grilled food, along with fresh fruit juices and locally grown coffee. At weekends the café livens up with nightly entertainment, music and dancing. Mon–Thurs 11am–10pm, Fri–Sun 11am–2pm & 6–10pm. Moderate.

Shutters on the Bay, *Blue Haven Hotel*, Bacolet Bay ☎660 7400. On a par with any exclusive eatery in New York or London, with prices to match. A sophisticated setting with an international menu that changes daily and always includes a fresh fish, meat and vegetarian option. Expensive.

Entertainment and nightlife

Until recently, Tobagonians had to make do with hard chairs, a poor-quality screen and billows of cigarette smoke each time they went to the movies, but following a recent refurbishment the *Gate* **cinema** (☎639 2066) is luxurious if less atmospheric, a state which the owners are eager to maintain by confiscating cigarettes and chewing gum at the door (customers can retrieve them after the show). Programmes are usually double bills (daily 4pm and 8.15pm with a late weekend show at 11pm; TT$15, under-10 TT$10), and the box office closes one hour into the programme. Scarborough also has a **casino**, the *Crystal Palace* (Tues–Sun 7pm–3am), by the sea on the corner of Milford and Mount Marie roads. The blackjack, roulette and poker tables are usually busy, but most locals opt for a round of easy-to-learn "all fours" played at home, in the street and at some bars.

Dancing is best at the weekend; *Level Three* on Wilson Street, above the *Royal Castle* fast-food chain, have a busy **club night** every Friday and Saturday with reggae and soca spun for a mixed but predominantly local crowd (10.30pm–4am; small cover charge), while there's sometimes a sound system jam in Market Square on Friday and Saturday – late-night fun with plenty of reggae and best experienced in the company of locals. Another excellent Friday option is the dance at *Fairy Queen Bar* in the village of John Dial, a five-minute drive east of town along the highway. Cars line the road and the good-natured drinking and dancing spills out on to the tarmac.

The leeward coast and Tobago Forest Reserve

Beyond Plymouth, the leeward coast feels more remote than any other part of the island; curious eyes follow passing cars and tourist development is minimal, leaving the ravishing beaches at **Castara**, **Englishman's Bay**, **Parlatuvier** and **Bloody Bay** much the same as they were twenty years ago. These communities have made only minimal efforts to cater to visitors; clusters of bobbing pirogues in every bay or seine nets drying in the sun hint at the centrality of **fishing** to this area, and you'll often see machete-wielding fellows trudging the route to small-scale plantations or meandering along with a pack of hunting dogs. Inland of Castara, the protected **forest reserve** is traversed by the Roxborough–Parlatuvier Road, and thick vegetation rises sharply from the tarmac. Though the rainforest canopy looks thick and impenetrable, even the most confirmed city-dweller should find the managed trails.

From the look of most maps, you'd assume the most direct route to the leeward coast would be the coast road from Plymouth; however, this is actually the slowest route, because of twists and turns and though a new surface is currently being laid, you've best bet is to head for the leeward coast along the Northside Road from Claude Noel Highway at Calder Hall.

The Northside Road

Less than a kilometre east of Scarborough, the well-signposted **Northside Road** strikes into the interior, meandering straight across the middle of Tobago and connecting the windward with the leeward coast. A downhill right turn 50 metres or so from the highway (bear right at the bridge) takes you up a narrow, near-perpendicular road to **French Fort**, named after a Gallic invasion in 1781 and the site of a French garrison until 1787. It's now home to several towering radio transmitters and satellite pylons, and the only hint of its history is a plaque nestled in the trees, but the panoramic **views** of Scarborough, Fort King George, Rockly Bay and Lowlands, the northern coast around Plymouth and Arnos Vale, and the southeast as far as Granby Point make the journey up worthwhile.

Past the fort turn-off, the Northside Road swings past the armed guards and clipped hedges flanking the **President's House** (closed to the public), and continues its snaking climb, passing through the quiet villages of **Concordia** and **Cinnamon Hill**. Beyond them lies the larger and close-knit residential community of **Mason Hall**, home of the island's first government school – built in 1938 – as well as a massive football pitch, clusters of snug gingerbread homes and a few good drinking spots – *Mason Hall Recreational Club* and *Pub Unique* among them. The latter often has live music on weekends. A marvellous **waterfall** is hidden on the outskirts of the village. To find it, look for the roadside WASA sign for the Craig Hall water intake. Half an hour's walk from the road along the Sandy River will bring you to **Mason Hall Falls**, one of the island's tallest at about 50 metres. Taking the Craig Hall route leads you to the top of the main cascade, where there's another, smaller waterfall with a pool deep enough to jump into without touching the bottom.

Darren Henry (☎ 639 4559), a trained forester and licensed tour guide, does hikes to Mason Hall Falls (2hrs 30min, TT$80).

If you fancy staying in the area, *Oasis Apartments* (☎660 7218; ②) has a simple, somewhat shabby three-bedroom apartment with bathroom and kitchen; you can also rent on a monthly basis, though you'll need a car here if you're not to feel cut off.

Moriah

Continuing north, the road begins its winding ascent of the lumpy, egg-carton-like undulations that surround **MORIAH**, a roadside village teetering at the top of a particularly steep precipice; sheer drops plummet straight into a valley from the road, and the roofs of houses sit precariously parallel to the tarmac. Terraces on the surrounding hills support crops of pigeon peas and ground provisions, Baptist prayer flags flutter in the breeze and the views are superlative. A police station, clapboard parlours and a Moravian church – one of Tobago's earliest missions was located here – form the centre of the village. There are a couple of **rum shops** well worth a visit, if only for their eccentric names and interesting decor; the *Hardest Hard Rec Club*, on the road before you enter town, has a shady outdoor section, while *Man John's* bar, right on the other side of Moriah, is a popular, Rasta-owned drinking spot with colourful Rasta-inspired murals. Further down the hill is *Green Corner*, a lively spot on the weekends when the DJ plays the latest tunes. Tobagonian youths turn the road nearby into an impromptu disco, whilst lovers canoodle on the roadside wall.

A potholed downhill turn-off to the left as you leave the village leads to **King Peter's Bay**, a seldom-visited but beautiful yellow-sand beach named after a Carib cacique. Striking west into the bush over the next bluff takes you to an even more beautiful strip, with a good reef to boot. Beyond King Peter's Bay road, Northside Road heads for the coast, providing breathtaking views as you enter the tiny communities of **Des Vignes** and **Runnemede**. Look out for a truly monumental **silk cotton** tree at the roadside; its buttressed roots are said to be haunted by jumbies (ghosts). For an even better vista, ask for directions to find the correct right turn for **Mount Dillon**, where benches are set up to admire the unravelling coastline.

If you want a peaceful hideaway in the forest stay at *Cuffie River Nature Retreat* in Runnemede (PO Box 461, Scarborough ☎660 0505, fax 660 0606, www.cuffie-river.com; ⑥), a comfortable hotel on an old sugar plantation where the large airy rooms come with en-suite bathroom, radio and balcony; two have access to a shared kitchen. Its restaurant serves huge, delicious – if somewhat over-priced – meals, and breakfast is included in the rates. The changing menu features local staples, the chicken being particularly good. The hotel also organizes tours and hikes of the surrounding forest, including trips to nearby waterfalls.

On the outskirts of Moriah the *Immortelle* hotel (☎660 0896, www.immortelleresort.com; ⑨) has sixteen two-storey wooden cabanas spread over a hundred acres in the Woodland Hills forest behind the village. The cabanas are spacious with beautiful wood and stone fittings and offer prime views across the forest reserve; some have a pool and jacuzzi, and all have a/c. Facilities include a restaurant, squash courts, health spa with gym, two bars, small boutiques and a library. Worth it if you can afford it, though you'll need a car and patience to deal with windy roads if you want to go to the beach.

Castara

After yet another downhill plunge, Northside Road slides into **CASTARA**, an attractive, easygoing fishing village that's slowly developing a nonchalant tourist-friendliness; low-key guesthouses are scattered on a hillside, while visitors dribble in to swim at the marvellous **beach** or splash in the nearby **waterfall**. Although a couple of guesthouses have gone up in recent years Castara seems unlikely to be eaten up by resort hotels and beach bars; to ensure that development is in tune with the residents and actually benefits them, one German guesthouse owner has given locals a 30-percent share in his property. Fishing remains the main earner at present, and the beach is one of the best places to participate in the pulling of a **seine net**, still in constant use by the supremely friendly posse of Rasta fishermen. The village abandons its languid air each August, when the beach is packed with revellers attending the **Castara Fishermen's Fete**, one of Tobago's biggest; the drinking, dancing, eating and swimming start at about midday and continue until well after dark.

The leeward coast and Tobago Forest Reserve

A layby above Castara is a good spot to park and admire the view of the bay below.

Accommodation

Castara is the only village along this section of coast where you'll find a choice of places to stay, though almost all of the guesthouses are small and located on a bluff overlooking the eastern portion of the beach. The town is becoming increasingly popular, so it's wise to reserve a room before turning up. If you're stuck, finding someone to put you up in their home shouldn't be a problem.

Blue Mango, Second Bay Rd ☎639 2060, www.direct-marketing.com/castara1/b-m-home.html. More upmarket than the competition, these simply furnished, stylish one- and two-bedroom self-contained cottages have great bay views, cool breezes, well-equipped kitchens, mosquito nets and plenty of privacy; the owners also manage two cottages at nearby Little Bay and an old wooden house perched on a hill five minutes' walk from the beach. The "Sea Steps" cottage is the best – a tropical dream house, with indoor and outdoor shower, sundeck overhanging your own private cove, from where you can watch dolphins, and lilies growing over the entire cottage. Excellent restaurant on site. ⑥.

McKnight's Golden Palace, Castara Village ☎639 4664. Two rooms overlooking Castara on the eastern side of the village and run by an eccentric elderly couple. Spacious and airy basic studio apartments have kitchenette, fan and balcony, with great views of the forest. Restaurant on site. ③.

Naturalist, Castara Village ☎639 5901, fax 660 7166, www.seetobago.com/tobago/resorts/natural/. Right at the edge of the beach, rooms are small with aging decor but are well equipped and clean; all have radio, TV, private bathroom and a kitchenette; some have a/c. The staff are extremely genial and will cook for you on request – you can eat on their recently built porch overlooking the beach. The name refers to nature-lovers rather than potential strippers; "no nudity" was added to the roadside advertisements after guests got the wrong idea. ③.

Sandcastles, Northside Rd ☎635 0933. Opposite *Sundeck* (see below) this sand-coloured building houses two apartments: a family-sized one downstairs, and two rooms sharing a kitchen and lounge upstairs. Basic decor, large bathrooms and great views out to sea; the family apartment has a/c. Plans are afoot for twelve villas and a pool to be added within the next three years. ⑨ for one upstairs room per week.

Sea Level, Second Bay Rd ☎660 7311 or 7549, *irie_Horizon@hotmail.com*. Just up the hill from the *Naturalist*, this joint German/Tobagonian-owned guesthouse is the largest in the village. All rooms have a balcony, spacious bathroom, mosquito nets and fan; some have bunk beds for the backpackers while others have doubles and twins. Excellent value. ③.

Sundeck, Northside Rd ☎639 1410, www.sundeck.com. The first guesthouse you'll pass on entering Castara, this recently opened yellow-and-green hotel has compact studio apartments with low ceilings, fully fitted kitchen, huge bathrooms, TV and VCRs; most rooms have fans, one has a/c, and all have mosquito nets. Ask for apartments facing the sea, which have great views. Meals provided on request. Steep hike to a private beach or 15min walk to Castara beach. Lovely communal sundeck and two complimentary videos included in rates. Mini-mart on site. ④.

The village

Straddling the Northside Road, the main body of the village consists of weather-beaten rum shops and parlours interspersed with simple board homes. A bridge at the eastern edge of town crosses the **Castara River**; a ten-minute walk along the riverbed brings you to a small **waterfall** with a fairly deep swimming pool below. Crossing the playing field behind the bridge cuts the walking time, and the pool is popular among local lads cooling off after a game of football; these frenetic, foul-filled tournaments take place in the late afternoon, and often attract a small crowd of spectators. There's another waterfall on the river, about an hour's walk from the road; to find it, you'll need to hire a local guide in the village.

The main focus of the town, though, is its **beach**, a generous swathe of coarse, shell- and pebble-strewn sand divided in two by the fast-flowing Castara River, which turns the water a murky brown during the rainy season and disappears completely during the parched dry months. If there hasn't been rain, the water is a joy – crystal clear and relatively calm due to the protection of the surrounding forested headlands. Flotillas of seagull-infested pirogues bob out to sea, and there's always activity around the Fishermen's Co-Op building, where the day's catch is weighed, scaled and sold; impromptu gutting usually draws a posse of mangy pot-hounds that clear up the entrails with gusto. The changing facilities (daylight hours; TT$1) are opposite the Fishermen's Co-Op.

Of the enterprising locals who take visitors on tours, a few reliable operators are David Williams, also known as "King David" (☎660 7906) who offers snorkelling and fishing trips and sunset cruises, and barbecues from his sun-roofed boat, providing all equipment (US$50) – if he's not around ask in the village for colleague Charlie. Brenton (☎660 7354) leads excellent fishing and dolphin watching tours; he also rents out inexpensive, basic rooms on a casual basis and sings with the local band, Vintage, which plays every Friday at *Cascreole* restaurant. The *Bobo Shanti* wooden stall on the beach is where you'll find Rudi, who offers relaxing herbal steam baths ($US50) and more rigorous tours of the area ($US50), taking in waterfalls and prime spots for birdwatching. The stall, usually run by his wife, is open every day except Saturday, and sells locally made batik, tie-dye and jewellery.

Eating and drinking

There are a few places to eat on the beach; among them, the inexpensive *L&H Sunset*, set on a lofty patio next to the Fishermen's Co-Op, is most popular with locals. The classic Tobagonian cooking is excellent; usually revolving around fish, main dishes change daily – the traditional Sunday dinner of chicken, callaloo and macaroni pie is a gastronomic triumph, as is the cow heel soup. Right on the beach, *Cascreole* is more tourist-oriented, but the fish or chicken lunches and dinners are tasty nonetheless, and the prices inexpensive. The adjacent bar makes a good all-day **drinking** spot, and stays open as long as there are customers. There are a couple of general stores in the village, but the small bar-cum-parlour under *L&H* restaurant is convenient, open daily from 6am till very late; the religious/inspirational sayings painted on the walls make good reading too. Blended fruit drinks (and a rudimentary selection of fresh vegetables) are available from a stall on the hilly eastern edge of the village. *McKnight's Golden Palace* on the eastern side of town serves inexpensive lunches of fresh fish, rice and salad. Slightly more expensive but with the friendliest service and the best food in Castara – and a popular hang-out for locals and tourists alike – is *The Clay Kitchen* (Inexpensive/Moderate) at *Blue Mango* cottages. The verandah makes a fine setting for eating fish in various sauces, including delicious coconut and ginger marinades. *Wallace's* bar on the hill by *Sea Level* is another congenial hang-out for those who want to lime with the locals to the sound of "back-in-times" music.

Englishman's Bay to Bloody Bay

Past Castara, houses and shops melt away, and the Northside Road is flanked by enormous tufts of whispering, creaking bamboo, broken occasionally to reveal marvellous jungle-clad hilly prospects. The next worthy beach, **Englishman's Bay**, is hidden from the road by a thick cover of bush; look out for the blue and white sign. Utterly ravishing and completely undeveloped, the bay offers a perfect crescent of pure white sand, deep blue water, offshore reef and nothing else – from the sea, the forested hillside appears completely untouched, as the bush drips right down to the sand. The bay remains deliciously remote, the "deserted beach" destination of many a pleasure boat cruise. Hot meals (including roti on Sundays), soft drinks and bamboo craft are sold at Eula's stall near the entrance. Next door, Edwin and Dexter sell more of the same, at reasonable prices.

Past Englishman's Bay, the coast road climbs upward and inland, passing through the diminutive community of **Parrot Hall** before descending to reveal one of the most arresting views on the island; **Parlatuvier Bay**, flanked by an absurdly pretty hillside scattered with palms, terraced provision grounds and the odd house. Another crescent of pearly sand, the pier in the middle of the bay is

The leeward coast and Tobago Forest Reserve

testament to the village's dedication to fishing, as are the gulls which roost on the rocks at either side of the bay, patiently awaiting the return of the boats. **Swimming** is a vigorous experience; waves are usually quite strong and the water deepens sharply from the sand.

Built around the bay, the village consists of a few houses, a school and a couple of shops; one sells tourist souvenirs, while the other, presided over by local character Duran Chance, sells everything from floor wax to bread and rum. Above the shop, the excellent-value *Parlatuvier Tourist Resort* (☎639 5629; ③) has breezy apartments with fan or a/c, bathroom, kitchen and balcony overlooking a gorgeous beach. Inexpensive and delicious **meals** are available from *Gloria and Anthony Joseph's Riverside Restaurant* (☎639 4935) on the Northside Road, where you get lavish portions of local-style fresh fish, lobster or shrimp with ground provisions for about TT$50–100. Below the restaurant are a couple of dark, basic rooms to rent with fan and kitchenette (③). On the western side of the village is *Menu Board* a small roadside parlour selling rotis and hot snacks. Further west is Nature Cotton, a roadside stall selling beautiful batik and tie-dye bags and clothes.

The last accessible beach on the coast is **Bloody Bay**, named for a battle between English soldiers and African slaves here in 1771 that was fierce enough to turn the sea crimson with blood; Dead Bay River, which runs across the sand and into the sea, is named for the same event. The turn-off for the beach is at the large mango tree lookout. From here directly opposite the bay and clearly visible five kilometres out to sea, the **Sisters Rocks** form an attractive chain. The beach itself is fine brown sand, strewn with pebbles and driftwood and frequented by no one except the odd fisherman. Beyond Bloody Bay, the smooth tarmac continues to the lofty village of **L'Anse Fourmi**, remote enough to make the sight of a tourist a talking point. *Living Fountain* and the *Punnet* bar are two good places to refresh yourself before turning round, for from here on only the bravest of drivers and hardiest of four-wheel drives or dirt bikes can manage the track to Charlotteville – and you'd be foolish to attempt it if you're here in the rainy season.

See p.317 for information on Charlotteville, a pretty little fishing village.

Tobago Forest Reserve

Swinging inland from the Northside Road at Bloody Bay, the Roxborough–Parlatuvier Road is the route to **Tobago Forest Reserve** and the central mountain range, so things get pretty steep. Construction of the road began in 1958, but Hurricane Flora (see box opposite) ravaged it mercilessly five years later, and the road was not repaired until the mid-1990s. Now it's a beautifully quiet drive through the rainforest.

The reserve acquired its status as the oldest protected rainforest in the western hemisphere during the plantation era, when British scientist Stephen Hales began researching the relationship between rainfall and trees and communicated his findings to one Soame Jenyns, a British MP responsible for the development of Tobago. At the time, the island was a flourishing plantation, with most of the estates concentrated in low-lying areas. Gradually, though, the planters began encroaching on the more precipitous forest areas, felling trees for fuel or clearing land to make way for yet more sugar cane. It took Jenyns ten years to convince Tobago's planters that if they continued to cut down the forest, the island would soon be incapable of supporting the smallest of shrubs, let alone a massive sugar plantation. Ultimately, he was successful, and on April 13, 1776, 14,000 acres of central Tobago were designated a protected Crown Reserve.

There are two main points of access into the rainforest. **Gilpin Trace** is marked by a huge slab of rock by the road in front of a forestry division hut, housing a toilet and a water tank; it's also a great lookout point over the Caribbean, with views stretching all the way down to the Sisters Rocks below. A trail strikes straight into the forest from here, but unless you only plan to go a few hundred yards, it's advisable to hire a **guide**; you'll understand a lot more about forest dynamics, and you won't get lost. The forestry hut trail is an easy hike – though often very muddy – taking you through some spectacular forest dotted with mini-waterfalls. Huge bachac ant nests punctuate the trail, while lianas and vines block out most of the light. If

---

Hurricane Flora

On September 30, 1963, **Hurricane Flora** swept over Tobago and completely devastated the island. Most of the banana, coconut and cocoa plantations were wiped out, and large tracts of the forest reserve laid to waste, with 30-metre-high trees toppling like matchsticks; many still block the trails to this day. For Tobagonians, the hurricane was a total catastrophe; thirty people died, and hundreds of others suffered injuries. Sixty out of every hundred fragile board houses were razed to the ground. Moriah, Concordia, Argyll and Richmond were completely demolished, roads were impassable and there was no water or electricity outside Scarborough for more than six weeks.

A relief fund helped to repair the worst of the damage, and the United Nations provided foodstuffs that fed the population for nearly a year, while other Caribbean islands donated items as various as fevergrass (a bush remedy for colds and fevers) and roasted breadfruits. Though there are few signs of the damage left today other than some toppled trunks in the forest reserve, the hurricane had a profound influence on Tobago's future; a tentative agricultural economy was abandoned, and the island began to devote its energy to tourism. Tobagonians still remember Flora with a shudder, but thankfully her force has since not been repeated. However, in 1997, Tobago was shaken by another natural disaster of less catastrophic proportion; on April 22, an **earthquake** measuring 5.9 on the Richter scale shook the island, destroying four homes and causing structural damage to several more.

Rainforest Guides

Recent training programmes have greatly increased the number of knowledgeable guides in the area, most of whom are from local villages such as Parlatuvier and Roxborough. All are far cheaper than the hotel-arranged guides.

Good bets include David Rooks (☎639 4276, rookstobago@trinidad.net.tt, www.trinidad.net/rookstobago). At the *Birds Nest Café* on the Main Ridge road after the Bloody Bay junction you'll find "Parrot Man" – Curtis James (☎660 7893) who does a two-hour tour for TT$200 and a three-hour tour, with food and drink, for TT$500. His brother Dexter James (☎660 7852 or 639 6936) – in the second house after the Northside Road/Parlatuvier–Roxborough Road junction – is cheaper; his three-hour tour is TT$220 and 1hr 30min tour TT$120. Near Gilpin Trace, guides belonging to the *Nature Explorers* group offer a standard package of a three-hour trip for TT$200 and a 1hr 30min trip for TT$100: Junior Thomas (☎660 7847), Shurland James (☎660 7883 or 639 6936), Fitzroy Quamina (☎660 7836) and Darlington Chance (☎660 7828 or 7823). The only woman of the bunch, Shurland also does a five-hour hike to Charlotteville from L'Anse Fourmi (TT$450) and Fitzroy Quamina takes full moon nature hikes as well as an easy hike to Palm Tree Falls in Bloody Bay (TT$100).

you're feeling hardy, ask to be shown the Atlantic trail, two hours of hard walking. Before you enter the rainforest, at the main trail, order your roti from the *Rainforest Roti Shop* on the road and it'll be ready for you by the time you come out. Otherwise freshly made pies and fruit juice are sold at the forestry hut by Shurland James, one of the rainforest guides.

Away from the trail access points, the forest is pretty impenetrable, and the road continues south into Roxborough – where the *Riverside Fruits & Fruit Juice Bar* serve excellent, freshly prepared juices made while you wait.

The windward coast

Rugged and continually breathtaking, Tobago's southern shoreline is usually referred to as the **windward coast**. Narrow and peppered with blind corners and potholes, the Windward Road spans its length and sticks close to the sea, providing fantastic views of choppy Atlantic waters and tiny spray-shrouded islands. The parade of languid coastal villages is a complete contrast to the developed west; groups of limers congregate outside rum bars, ladies in curlers chat on the pavement and football games on salt-seasoned grassy pitches are the height of an afternoon's activity.

Though rip tides and strong undercurrents make some of the most attractive-looking beaches unsafe for swimming, there are plenty of sheltered bays to take a dip in the cool Atlantic. Some – such as **Kings**

Bay – have showers and changing rooms, but at most, you'll share the
sand only with fishermen. Tour buses make regular rounds, stopping
off at stock attractions like period plantation home **Richmond Great
House**, **Argyll Waterfall** or the famous *Jemma's* restaurant, perched
among the branches of an almond tree, but most of the windward traffic is heading for the tiny village of **Speyside** and its smattering of
guesthouses and small hotels. Nature is the main attraction here;
Speyside's **reefs** rank among Tobago's best, while the **Little Tobago**
island bird sanctuary has long been a magnet for ornithologists and
amateur bird-watchers alike. Fifteen minutes drive from Speyside and
directly opposite on the Caribbean coast, picturesque **Charlotteville**
with its attractive hillside houses and perfect twin beaches is the last
point of call on the windward route – the tarmac ends here, replaced
by a treacherous and often impassable stretch of coastal track which
divides the town from the rest of the leeward coast. Away from the
firmly beaten track, there's also plenty to see. You can **hike** to many of
the infrequently visited waterfalls scattered throughout the hilly southern interior, passing the crumbling remains of water wheels and sugar
boilers along the way, while the wetlands and rivers surrounding the
central **Hillsborough Dam** are great for bird and reptile watching;
Tobagonian cayman frequent the waters.

Mount St George and around

East of Scarborough, the first stretch of highway ends abruptly a couple of kilometres past the town, just after the Dwight Yorke football
stadium; the last fast and straight section of road then sweeps past
glorious **Hillsborough Bay** – sometimes called Hope by locals.
Though the long stretch of windswept sand looks inviting, stick to
paddling – the riptides are dangerous. Past the beach and over a narrow bridge, the road swings round a sharp corner and into tiny
MOUNT ST GEORGE, past roadside houses with attractive flowered
gardens. There's no discernible sign that this was once **Georgetown**,
the island's first British **capital**, named in honour of King George III.
The British began to develop Georgetown after they captured the
island in 1762, building houses and a base (now destroyed) for the
House of Assembly, which held its inaugural meeting here in April
1768. British occupation was short-lived, however; by 1769, they
shifted the capital to Scarborough. There's still one tenuous connection to sovereignty in the town, though; set at the top of a breezy
hillock overlooking the village below is the official residence of the
prime minister, a seldom-used, whitewashed structure that's closed to
the public. A little further into the interior is Mount St George Youth
Camp, where budding bad boys are forcibly sent to learn a trade.

If you're in the mood to linger, stop at the genial *Sparrow's Rest*
or else the easygoing *Hibiscus Bar*, right on the roadside for inexpensive and tasty lunchtime roti or a cool beer. You can also **stay** at
Vicky's Guesthouse (☎660 2089, *everace@tstt.net.tt*; ③), an

expansive building west of the village that's often used for local weddings. The basic but clean rooms are of varying standard, but meals are available, and all rooms have a/c, bathroom and kitchen.

Granby Point and around

Past the main body of Mount St George, the road is littered with the small white stones that fall from trucks travelling from the Studley Park Quarry, a busy commercial enterprise that's steadily eating into the surrounding hillsides. A fanfare of brightly painted wooden walls and blooming flowers just outside the next village of **STUDLEY PARK**, the *First Historical Café* makes an interesting stop even if you don't need refreshment (see also below). The pet project of charming retiree Kenneth Washington, the colourful café is a shrine to the history of the island. Every inch of wall space is covered with handwritten accounts of Tobago's turbulent past alongside local anecdotes: "Tobago's first shipment of sugar left the island from Studley Park aboard a ship named Dolly." Aside from soaking up the written word, this is a comfortable place to sit and watch pelicans taking rich pickings from the shoals of small fish which inhabit the bay; seine nets are sometimes pulled in at the small **beach** below, which you can reach from the bar.

Beyond the café, turn right along the track signposted for the *Dry Dock Pub* and you come to an open lot beside the sea with a small children's **playground**. Head up the flight of concrete steps and through some rather fly-infested bush and you've arrived at **Fort Granby**, built by the British to protect Georgetown and briefly occupied by the French between 1781 and 1787. Nothing remains of the original fortification; the cannons have long gone, replaced by pretty gazebos, mown lawns and picnic tables. The views of the sea and nearby **Smith's Island** are fantastic, and there is excellent swimming to be had on either of the **beaches** which flank the point. Barbados Bay to the left is the more populated; the fisherman's shacks on the sand make it a good spot to hang out, while the more deserted **Pinfold Bay** on the other side is a better bet if you fancy a spot of sunbathing; neither has any facilities, however.

Practicalities

If you're in search of **food**, the unmissable *Punnies Midway Bar*, a large yellow building on the roadside, is a good place for a drink, quick snacks and a lime with the locals; further down the road is the well-signposted *Eco Spot* (☎660 2470; Inexpensive/Moderate), a restaurant and bar serving local food and whose great view over Grandy Point makes up for its higher than average prices. The budget-priced *First Historical Café*, down the road from *Eco Spot* is a good, if often painfully slow, choice; they serve breakfast from 9am, and inexpensive salads, burgers and sandwiches for lunch. For a bout of serious **drinking** or a lime with the fishermen, head for the

Dry Dock Pub next to Fort Granby; tiny but with a great sea view and the chance to sink a Carib inside the converted hull of an old fishing boat. The only place to stay in the area is *Bougainvillaea Hotel*, which was undergoing management changes and refurbishment at press time.

Inland to Hillsborough Dam

The inland roads from Mount St George or Studley Park are routes to the birdwatchers' paradise of **Hillsborough Dam**, a 45 minute drive from the coast depending upon the condition of the often muddy and rutted Castara Road – you will need a four-wheel drive. The road doesn't actually go to Castara, tailing off into an undriveable and often impassable dirt track miles from the coast. To enter Hillsborough Dam, a man-made reservoir built to hold half of Tobago's drinking water, you are officially required to obtain a pass from the local water authority WASA, but hardly anyone bothers, clearing entrance with the security personnel on the gates instead. Though the concrete banks are pretty unattractive, they're overhung by the thick forest which provides an ideal habitat for the herons and other waterfowl which frequent the area. A more arresting sight are the cayman which heave themselves onto the banks to bask in the sun; obviously, this is not a great place to swim. There's usually somebody around to take you out onto the water aboard the dam's small rowing boat, a relaxing way to get close to the bird life. There are good possibilities for **river hikes** along the gentle streams which feed the dam, though it's best to go with a local guide as you can easily lose your way. Beyond Hillsborough, the road swings west, passing small-scale farms and homes to Mason Hall, from where you can head north for the leeward coast (see p.296–304), or west for Scarborough and Lowlands.

Goodwood to Pembroke

As the Windward Road swings into the tiny village of **GOODWOOD**, with its appealing gingerbread houses, primary school and neat playing field, the coastal views begin in earnest – starting with a spectacular panorama of the unravelling coast and distant **Richmond Island**. There's a track down to the beach from the centre of Goodwood; the greyish sand and ever-present palm trees are nothing to shout about, but it's a pleasant place for a swim, and popular with locals. On entering the village proper a large sign on the left-hand side directs you to **Genesis Nature Park & Art Gallery** (Mon–Sat 9am–6pm; US$5; ☎660 4668), where a variety of animals, including capuchin monkeys, a boa constrictor, cocoricos – the national bird of Tobago – and wild hogs (in small cages) are housed on the landscaped grounds; the gallery is fairly secondary. The entrance fee includes a complimentary drink and a tour of the grounds and the art gallery, which exhibits sculptures and paintings by the owner. A few kilometres up the road in **GOLDSBOROUGH** is the signposted left turn to **Rainbow Falls**, a series of privately managed cascades along the Goldsborough River. If you need a place to stay, *Rainbow Nature Resort* (☎ & fax 660 4755 or 6715, *sharilee@tstt.net.tt*; ⑤) offers spacious rooms with en-suite bathroom and fan; some have TV. The quiet hotel overlooks the Tobago Forest Reserve and is a twenty-minute walk from the falls. Rates include breakfast, and there's a restaurant and bar on site.

As the houses of Goodwood recede, the road climbs into yet another Lilliputian village, **PEMBROKE**, a serene fishing community spreading down to the sea from the road. It's a friendly place with a smattering of rum bars and a pretty clapboard Anglican church, St Mary's, set on cliffs overlooking the Atlantic. As the road dips down again, you can turn right to the **beach**, mostly dedicated to fishing as the fleet of pirogues and spread-out nets affirm, but nice enough for a swim. Pembroke is the venue for the annual **Salaka Feast** celebrations, now an important part of the July/August Heritage Festival. A kind of African thanksgiving to ancestors, the feast commemorates the community's founding by the first slaves brought to the area, and honours obeah spirits through dancing, singing, storytelling, drumming and offerings of fruit and other foods, followed by plenty of eating and drinking. It's a lovely place to absorb unadorned Tobagonian life, and if you want to **stay**, three self-contained apartments are available to rent at the *Paradise Villa* (☎660 4933; ⑤), signposted and set just off the road. None are the height of luxury but all are scrupulously clean with two small bedrooms, a bathroom, fans and a kitchen; the airy upstairs unit comes with TV and phone. Inclusive of a huge breakfast, this place is a real bargain. Even cheaper is the friendly *Rennalls White Castle* (☎ & fax 660 5287; ③), just two minutes from a small beach; rooms are simple with fan, en-suite bathroom and kitchenette, and breakfast – taken at the on-site restaurant – is included. A good place for a drink and reasonably priced seafood meals is the *Kountree Forest Cocktail Lounge* (☎660 5380; Inexpensive/Moderate) on the eastern side of Pembroke. This quirky corner building perched on the rockface beside the road was built by the owners themselves. The building is made from Roseau wood (a member of the bamboo family), coconut shell and coral stone, and makes a lovely place to while away the hours with fruit bats for company and a great view over the sea. You'll have to park down the road from the restaurant, or on the almost vertical incline of parking space, as the restaurant is located on a dangerous bend.

Mark Puddy (☎639 4931) leads fabulous hiking trips off the beaten track to deserted beaches (6hr; US$40) or seldom-visited waterfalls (4hr; US$25); rates include transport to and from your hotel as well as drinks and snacks.

Richmond Great House and Argyll Waterfall

A narrow bridge marks your entry to **Glamorgan**, a little bigger than neighbouring Pembroke and beautifully located atop its own hillock.

Stop for a snack at *Gee Bee's* bakery or scout around for the remains of an **old water wheel** behind the school, run by the adjacent Seventh Day Adventist church. Just out of town, the road widens, dipping down and up again through a small valley – this is *the* place to overtake if you're stuck behind a slow-moving truck. Before the road begins its descent, you can turn in to a little **park** to the left; benches and planted beds make it a nice place to take in the fantastic views over the rolling hills of the Main Ridge approaches.

On the other side of the valley is the signposted left turn for **Richmond Great House** (☎ & fax 660 4467, www.richmond-greathouse.com; ⑦), a hotel, restaurant and essential point of call for almost all of the tour buses that travel the Windward Road. Built of solid brick and whitewashed board in the eighteenth century, the house itself was the great house of the old Richmond sugar estate, and offers fantastic views over the jungle-smothered interior hills. It's now owned by Professor Hollis Lynch, a Tobagonian who used to lecture at Colombia University, and his extensive collection of African art and textiles is on display; tours (daily 10am–4pm; TT$15) are available. You can also visit for lunch, but you'll need to call ahead for dinner; prices are on the expensive side. The colonial-style bedrooms are gorgeous, cool with varnished wood floors and a private bathroom, and there's a pool and tennis courts on site. Rates include breakfast.

Past Richmond, the Windward Road passes the Richmond water works on the right. The small budget café on the left, *Caribbean Splendour* (Mon–Sat 7am–7pm), serves delicious roti, buss-up-shut and inexpensive local dishes and fruit juice. The road returns to the coast at the tiny village of **Belle Garden**. The next village is Argyll, just beyond which a cache of guides awaits at the entrance road to **Argyll Waterfall** (daily 7.30am–5pm), waving frantically for you to stop. The official guides, who carry ID and wear a khaki uniform, work for the Roxborough Visitor Service Co-Operative Society, set up in 1992 to co-ordinate guides and manage the area. To access the falls, turn off the road and follow a muddy but easily passable cocoa tree-lined path to a grassy parking lot where you'll see the clapboard booth of the Co-Op offices, the place to pay the entrance fee (TT$20) and hire a guide if you want one (TT$15); doing so will greatly improve your impression of the area, as they point out birds and flowers and show the way to the less accessible cascades – a tip is expected. Unofficial guides will charge anything from TT$30–80.

The falls are a pleasant fifteen-minute walk away, and you can hear the water long before you reach it. Argyll is the island's highest waterfall, tumbling 54 metres out of the greenery into a deep pool. It is also one of its most accessible, but to see the best parts you'll have to exert yourself a little and climb up the right-hand side along steep and sometimes bushy paths. There are three main cascades; the second is particularly strong – increased flow during the rainy season creates a constant fine mist that soon soaks you to the skin. The second tier is great for a dip in a natural jacuzzi, as there are plenty of rocky seats on which to perch and get a pounding shoulder massage. If you're feeling energetic, you can climb up even further to the deepest swimming pool – and the smallest section of waterfall – where you can dive or swing in Tarzan-style on a vine. If the climb doesn't appeal, you can drive right up to the highest swimming spot.

Roxborough

The **ROXBOROUGH** environs are **cocoa** country; just before you enter town on the main road, a left fork cuts straight through one of Tobago's largest plantations. Beneath deep green or rusty brown leaves, the cocoa's distinctive, gnarled limbs are smothered with lime-green or off-white lichen. The oval cocoa pods turn from bright green to brown, orange and sometimes purple as they ripen, at which point you can pick one, crack it open and suck sweet white pulp from the small black seeds. Sadly, cocoa is a declining industry these days, as local youth turn away from agriculture in favour of the easy money to be made in tourism. The cocoa estate road swings back to the Windward at the outskirts of town, adjacent to the expansive fire station and community centre, and the inland Roxborough–Parlatuvier Road, the route to the forest reserve and Caribbean coast.

Roxborough is the largest town along this section of the coast. The main drag runs parallel to the sea, although – unlike almost everywhere else on the windward parade – there are even a few residential streets stretching inland. Despite the profusion of small shops, and the presence of a post office, police station and even a petrol station, it's a peaceful place, though it hasn't always been so tranquil. In the hard times that followed emancipation, Roxborough was the scene of the infamous and bloody **Belmanna Riots** (see box opposite). Today, though, it's attractive, friendly and unused to a tourist presence. Apart from filling up your gas tank, there's no real reason to stay here; though it's fine for swimming, the **beach** is nothing special and beyond the low-key rum bars there's little to do. If you want to linger, you should be able to find someone who's willing to put you up. Ask for *Carter's* guesthouse on Roberts Street. Good places to eat are thin on the ground; try the *Pelican View Atlantic Beach* restaurant on the main road for budget chicken sit-down meals, *Mus Be Molly* for pies and fish and chips or *Beat the Heat* for ice cream. Delicious blended fruit drinks are sold from a roadside kiosk at the town end of the cocoa estate road. Village life centres around the *Sugar Loaf Recreational Club*, the local hall, at the eastern end of the village.

King's Bay

Turning inland past Roxborough, the Windward Road swings through the hilltop village of **Delaford**, making one almighty bend at

If you're driving, check your petrol gauge as you pass through Roxborough, as the nearest petrol stations are in Charlotteville and Scarborough.

You can get a good overview of local blooms and fruit trees at Louis D'Or Nursery, just outside Delaford (open daily, daylight hours; free).

The Belmanna uprising

Disgusted with the low pay and abysmal working conditions which dogged the ailing sugar industry after emancipation, African plantation workers from the Roxborough Estate **revolted** in 1876, burning down the home of the estate manager and rioting in the streets with such vigour that one of their comrades was killed in the struggle with police. Enraged, the workers surrounded the police station and demanded that the chief officer, Colonel Belmanna – whom they held responsible for the death – should come out and confront them. Unwisely, he did; the mob descended, gouging out his eyes, mutilating his body and beating him to death. As the ranks of the workers swelled with sympathizers from surrounding villages, the unrest continued. Hopelessly outnumbered, the police could do little but call for external assistance and retreat; it came a week later in the form of a British warship, which transported hundreds of the dissenters to Scarborough, where they were slammed into jail and put on trial, most receiving a life sentence or banishment from the island.

The riot left self-governed Tobago in turmoil. Feeling they had completely lost control of the island and its predominantly black population, and fearing total anarchy, the Legislative Council swiftly washed their hands of the whole affair and handed the running of Tobago back to the British. On January 1, 1877, Tobago became a Crown Colony, but the Belmanna repercussions were not to be quelled so easily. Continual unrest throughout the island contributed to the final collapse of the sugar industry and the overall economic decline which led to the official coupling of Trinidad and Tobago in 1879.

the outskirts to reveal a breathtaking view of the spiky coconut plantation surrounding beautiful, deep blue **KING'S BAY** below. In the midst of a cool green arbour of cocoa trees at the bottom of the hill is the spacious parking lot for **King's Bay Waterfall** (daily, no set hours; free). The most heavily manicured of any on the island, it was presented as a gift to the nation in 1987 by Delaford philanthropists James and Dorothy Rosenwald. It's a five-minute walk to the falls along a neat pathway well cropped by cattle. Sadly, the actual cascade is a disappointment; damming has drastically reduced the flow of King's Bay River, reducing the waterfall to a shadow of its former glory. The worn rocks are the only sign that a torrent once crashed down on them, but nowadays you're unlikely to see more than a trickle, even at the height of the rainy season. The once-deep pool at the base is murky and stagnant, and the only fun to be had is climbing the thirty metres to the top.

A far more satisfying time is to be had at **King's Bay beach** (daylight hours; free), one of the few along the windward coast to provide changing facilities (TT$1 to enter) – turn off at the large sign for *Pedro Point Rest & Bar*. With gentle waters, reefs and fine dark sand, King's Bay is one of the best beaches in the area, but apart from a handful of bathers, it's mostly favoured by fishermen, and is a great place to watch – and participate in – the pulling in of a seine net. The profusion of Carib Indian artefacts found here (on display at the Tobago Museum – see p.293) indicate that King's Bay was the site of a large settlement; some suggest that the bay is named after Carib cacique (chief) King Peter, though it's more likely that that honour goes to King Peter's Bay on the north coast.

Practicalities

For accommodation, there are a couple of basic places nearby. Just before the King's Bay cocoa plantation, a road branches off to the sea, identifiable by the signs promoting a variety of guesthouses. This road leads down to Delaford Bay – a smaller beach frequented by locals and fishermen. Follow the rocky road for a couple of minutes until you reach a junction opposite a bar; turn left to reach *Ocean View Cottage* (c/o Mrs Joslyn Orr ☎660 4220; ③), where the clean but basic small rooms have fan and en-suite bathroom, and are steps away from the sea. The owner of *Ocean View* also has rooms for the hard-pressed traveller at the *Sea Gardens Guest House* (signposted on the main road as *Restrite;* ③). Set on a rather raggle-taggle section of the otherwise beautiful Delaford Bay, the two rooms are a bit down-at-heel, small and dark but the waves lap on your doorstep. Both have patio space, two tiny bedrooms, shower and rudimentary kitchenette. *Crab Inn* (☎660 4285; ②) on the other side of the bay also has basic rooms for rent; ask for Mr James Edwards. If you don't want to feel isolated staying here, you'll need your own car – the nearest shops and restaurants are in Speyside or Delaford. At the latter, try *King's Bay Café* ("we specialise in freshness"), beautifully situated with a sweeping view of the bay from the back verandah, where hot meals, snacks, pastries, espresso and cappuccino are served at budget prices. A little further down the road behind *Liz Café & Bar* is the *Riverside Guesthouse* (☎660 4383; ③) where two rooms are available to rent. A five minutes' walk from King's Bay beach these clean pink rooms are basic with a fan and en-suite bathroom.

Speyside

Past King's Bay, the coast swings out of view as the road turns inland through lush hills and green valleys broken only by the odd roti shack. Constant hairpin bends and a steep incline make the going pretty treacherous, so if you're driving, don't let your surroundings become too much of a distraction. However, it's hard not to get side-tracked by the amazing view which opens up as you round the last corner before the descent into **SPEYSIDE**. From the bench-dotted **lookout** point, you get a marvellous panorama of the town, **Tyrrel's Bay** with its turquoise waters and the stunning sight of **Little Tobago** and **Goat Island**. There's good forest hiking to be had along Murchiston Trace, a tiny road that strikes off right from the main just before the Speyside lookout; ask in the village for a local guide.

Accommodation

With plenty of demand for rooms with marvellous views and the sea as background music, you'll need to book well in advance if visiting during the high season. If you get stuck without a roof over your head, you should be able to find someone who's willing to put you up in their home.

Blue Waters Inn, Bateaux Bay ☎660 4341 or 4077 or 2583, fax 660 5195, www.bluewatersinn.com. Speyside's largest and grandest hotel set around the semi-private and totally stunning Bateaux Bay. All rooms are spacious, with rattan furniture, batik decor, ceiling fan, a/c, porch and a sea view; choose from a standard unit or one- and two-bedroom self-catering rooms and bungalows. There's a restaurant, bar, dive shop and tennis court on site as well as 200,000 square metres of land sprinkled with nature trails. Free use of kayaks, wind-surfers and sun-tanning beds. Popular with divers, but shut off from the village by a steep walk. ⑧.

Clyde Denoon's, Speyside ☎660 5625 or 639 7069. Convenienty located on the eastern side of the village by the ragged end of the beach. Basic two- and three-bedroom apartments with a/c, TV and kitchen at bargain rates. ③.

Country Haven Guesthouse, Main Rd, Speyside ☎660 5901, c_haven99@hotmail.com. Three cramped rooms in a family-run guesthouse perched on Speyside's hillside; all have fan, mosquito net and en-suite bathroom, some have kitchenette. ③.

Davis Atlantic View, Main Rd, c/o *Jemma's* restaurant ☎ & fax 639 4066. Just opposite *Jemma's* and a good budget option, this guesthouse has three basic and clean rooms, two of which share a bathroom, kitchen and lounge and one with its own facilities. ⑤.

Kurt's, Housing Scheme ☎660 4232. Set in a quiet residential backstreet in Speyside *Kurt's* has two basic rooms with shared bathroom and kitchen. ④.

Manta Lodge, Main Rd, PO Box 443, Scarborough ☎660 5268, fax 660 5030, in US ☎800/544 7631, http.mantalodge.com. Colonial-style luxury catering for scuba enthusiasts. Standard rooms are small but stylish with ceiling fan and balcony; "superior" rooms provide more space and a/c, while the quirky attics have the lot plus a private sundeck on the roof. There's a good restaurant (breakfast included in the rates), pool and dive shop on site, and you can access the nature trails which network the grounds. ⑦.

Noon's Holiday Cottage, Main Rd ☎639 5567 or 660 5978, pat_denoon@hotmail.com. Cosy three-bedroom apartment has bathroom, fully furnished kitchen, TV, fans and great views of Speyside Bay. ④.

Seacrest, Main Rd ☎660 6642. Perfect bay views, lively and popular with a young crowd. Three of the four rooms overlook the sea; all have fan and bathroom. The bar below can mean late-night noise; breakfast is included in rates. Restaurant on site serves local cuisine. ⑤.

Speyside Inn, Main Rd ☎ & fax 660 4852, www.caribinfo.com/ speysideinn/. Simple and beautifully styled with priceless bay views, and accommodation varies from a circular tower to octagonal corner rooms; all have bathroom, balcony and fan. There's an excellent restaurant on site (rates include breakfast) and good swimming is just a step away. ⑦.

Top Ranking Hill View Guesthouse, Main Rd ☎ & fax 660 4904, www.toprank@caribinfo.com. Pink house in Speyside's hills. Spacious rooms in overbearing purple decor come with kitchenette and bathroom; some have a/c, others have fan. All have a porch. ④.

For details of the accommodation price codes used in these listings, see p2520.

The village

The last sizeable village on the windward coast, Speyside feels as remote as it is; just over ten years ago the road was little more than a dirt track, and the pace of life remains so slow that it's nearly at a standstill. Though the town is slowly adjusting to its latest role as a **scuba** paradise – and taking on some of the more negative aspects of such development – it still retains its fishing village atmosphere and small-town attitude. Everyone says hello on the street, and your face will be known to most of the locals after a day or two, as will your choice of hotel, what you had for dinner last night and who you ate it with. You'll find that forging genuine friendships here is not only inevitable but a lot easier than in the more commercialized west of the island. Interaction between local people and tourists is far more relaxed, but don't let go of all your common sense and assume that every smiling face means a friend.

As you descend into the village, a cluster of candy-floss coloured grocery shops and snack bars surround a large playing field to the right. This is a focal point for the community; regular football games draw crowds of spectators and it's a good place to get to know local people. A dirt track running between the playing field and the sea takes you to the **beach** facilities (daylight hours; TT$1 to enter). The sand here is slightly wider than in the central part of the bay, and the famous **reefs** are within swimming distance. It's also a good place to organize a **fishing** trip aboard a local pirogue; the fishermen will also be happy to take you to Little Tobago for in excess of TT$75, though if you're interested in birdwatching, it's probably better to go in more expert company (see opposite). Carrying on along the main road brings you into the main village, a minimal parade of small shops, a post office and a couple of bars. Past the next corner is what could loosely be termed the tourist strip, though it's a far cry from the conventional concrete and neon. In Speyside, tourism means diving, so the strip consists of several dive shops, a couple of restaurants, including the ubiquitous *Jemma's* – built into a tree over looking the sea – and a couple of hotels.

Just past *Manta Lodge* hotel, the road forks; left takes you across the interior and into Charlotteville (see p.317), while the right turn is the route to the astonishingly blue waters and rich reefs of **Bateaux Bay**, site of the luxurious *Blue Waters Inn*. The rutted road takes you past the Speyside **water wheel**, seemingly a remnant of the plantation era; however, this now-rusting iron contraption is a relatively recent addition, thought to have been built in the late nineteenth century, but since 1900 it's been allowed to slide into its current state of disrepair. Beyond *Blue Waters*, the coast is almost completely uninhabited. The road to picturesque Belmont and Starwood bays is often impassable; if so, ask a local fisherman to take you aboard a pirogue. Both bays offer great snorkelling and diving.

Little Tobago and Goat Island

Of the two misshapen islets sitting five kilometres or so out of Tyrrel's Bay, **Goat Island** is the closer. You'll see one white house nestled in the centre, built as the Tobagonian holiday home of Caribbean devotee Ian Fleming, author of the James Bond novels. The house and the island are privately owned and closed to the public. However, birdwatchers and hikers flock to the larger island, **Little Tobago**, a kilometre further out to sea. The most easterly point of the T&T republic, the two-square kilometre outcrop has been known as "Bird of Paradise Island" since the beginning of the twentieth century, when it was bought by keen ornithologist Sir William Ingram. In 1909 he transported 24 Greater **birds of paradise** (*Paradisaea apoda*) from Aru island in New Guinea. Over the years, however, the birds were slowly extinguished by hurricanes and hunters. When Sir William died in 1924, his heirs gave Little Tobago back to the government on condition that it receive protected status. It has remained a bird sanctuary ever since, uninhabited except for one of the largest seabird colonies in the Caribbean, which includes impressive flocks of frigate birds, boobies, terns and the spectacular red-billed tropic bird, the latter especially prevalent between October and June. You'll also hear the crows and clucks of feral cocks and chickens brought here by the now-departed resident caretaker, who was unable to catch his flock when he left the island.

Several trails cut during the island's brief spell as a cotton plantation mean there are good possibilities for **hiking**, though as Little Tobago is only 1.5km (1 mile) long at its widest point, these are hardly marathon treks. All the boats dock at a small beach facing the mainland, from where you get beautiful views of the town and Pigeon Hill above, one of Tobago's highest points. Here, there's a wooden shelter with toilets, benches, tables and a long list of dos and don'ts for visitors: no smoking, squatting or fires and so on. Concrete steps lead up the hillside, passing the ramshackle caretaker's house, long-deserted but still displaying framed posters of Little Tobago's most common bird species. Well-signposted trails lead off from here through the dry and scrubby landscape; head for the cliffside nesting grounds of the red-billed tropic bird, where a lookout point provides sweeping views and an opportunity to see birds in flight up close. Make sure you have enough drinking water with you, however, as no refreshments are available. To get the most from the island, hire an experienced guide such as David Rooks (☎639 4276, www.trinidad.net/rookstobago), the man who persuaded David Attenborough that Little Tobago was sufficiently unique to be included in his famous BBC *Trials of Life* documentary. For other firms, see the box on Speyside watersports, overleaf.

More good birdwatching is to be had at St Giles Islands, a few kilometres to the north. It's a major breeding ground for pelicans, terns and frigate birds, but currents make access difficult.

Speyside watersports

Speyside's main attraction are the amazingly rich coral **reefs** which net-work the bay. Generally pristine with little sign of bleaching or human damage, the reefs flourish on a rich diet of nutrients flowing in from Venezuela's mighty Orinoco River along the Guyana Current, ensuring a huge variety of marine life and some dazzling hues among the coral. Speyside also boasts one of the world's largest **brain corals**, an awesome four metres high and six metres across. Apart from the regular shoals of small fish – butterfly, grunt, angel, parrot and damselfish – the currents also attract a number of deep-water dwellers, including **nurse sharks, dolphins** and, most notably, **manta rays**. These regular visitors are usually around seven metres long, and are so accustomed to the divers' touch that it's now common practice to hitch a ride by grabbing on to the body just beside the horns – known as taking a "Tobago Taxi". Though this is not recommended, local operators claim that as the mantas make the first approach, they actually enjoy contact with humans, particularly a scratch on the back.

The most popular Speyside dive sites include Japanese Gardens, Angel Reef, Bookends and Blackjack hole, and most dives are of the drift variety. Operators to trust are Tobago Dive Experience at *Manta Lodge* (☎660 5268, info@tobagodiveexperience.com, www.tobagodiveexperience .com); the first operator to set up in the area, Aquamarine Dive at *Blue Waters Inn* (☎660 4341, amdtobago@trinidad.net.tt, www .aquamarinedive.com) who are also the most expensive; and Tobagonian-owned Tobago Dive Masters next to *Jemma's* (☎639 4697). For sample prices see box, p.246. All of these operators rent **snorkel** equipment for around US$10 per day, and Aquamarine offer snorkelling tuition for a rather inflated US$55 per person.

Glass-bottom boats are a good way to see the reefs if you don't want to get wet, though you can always jump overboard for a spot of snorkelling as well. Frank's (☎660 5438), based at *Blue Waters Inn*, offers a basic tour with snorkelling at Angel Reef for US$15, drift snorkelling at Little Tobago (US$17), as well as a boat tour around St Giles Island for US$35. Top Ranking Glass Bottom Boat (☎660 4904), also at the inn, offers reef and snorkelling and a trip to Little Tobago for US$17, reef tour and snorkel US$14 and reef tour alone for US$12. Fear Not (☎660 4654), based at *Jemma's*, also do inexpensive Angel Reef tours (1hr 30min; US$14).

Eating and drinking

Make dinner reservations for Speyside restaurants, during the high season; in the low season, some places won't cook unless guests are assured.

Even during the high season, Speyside isn't exactly a metropolis; in the low season, you'll find the town pretty much deserted as some of the cafés and dive operators close up shop.

Birdwatcher's Rest and Bar, Main Road. Unmissible red, gold and green café with indoor and outdoor eating areas. Friendly staff serve all the usual staples of chicken, fish and Creole dishes. Good food at good prices. Inexpensive.

Black Prince Sea Food & Pizza House, Main Road. Decorated with the motto "good over evil" on its green walls, this eccentric eating place serves delicious conch and the tasty local speciality, seamoss. Budget.

Fish Pot, *Blue Waters Inn* ☎660 4341. Designed with American package tourists in mind, the menu is somewhat bland resulting in average-tasting expensive seafood. The setting is pleasant though, decorated with fishermen's accessories and windows overlooking Bateaux Bay. Expensive.

Green Moray, *Manta Lodge* ☎660 5268. Well-executed seafood cooked for international tastes. The menu includes lobster, shrimp, kingfish and shark in an exclusive setting. Expensive.

Jemma's Treehouse, Main Road ☎660 4066. Popular with every island tour bus this place lurches crazily in the boughs of a tree, and the sea view is fantastic. Serves tasty Creole-style food. Breakfast (8.30–10am) is eggs, bacon or local fish dishes; lunch (available until 4pm) includes breadfruit or eggplant casserole, tannia fritters, fried plantain and salad; and dinner – fish, lobster and shrimp – is excellent, as are the puddings. No alcohol and closed from Friday night and all day Saturday. Moderate.

Paradise Cuisine & Beer Garden, Main Road, opposite *Seacrest* bar in the main village. Simple café/bar good for quick snacks, pies, rotis, alcohol and light refreshments. Budget.

Seacrest bar. Main Road. Popular with the local crowd, this bar, decorated with a fish and diving mural, is a lively place blasting soca music all day long. Dark interior, lively at night, when it becomes the local hotspot. Serves drinks only.

Speyside Inn, Main Road ☎660 4852. Delicious food with a dinner menu that changes daily, advertised by a chalked-up blackboard set on the roadside. Features lots of imaginatively cooked local ingredients: boneless chicken breast with mango and banana and excellent coconut shrimp, salsa as well as a mean chocolate cake and key lime pie. Moderate/Expensive.

Charlotteville

From Speyside, the Windward Road strikes inland on its way from the Atlantic to the Caribbean coast, climbing steeply upward through jungle-like mountain foliage before plummeting down to the opposite shoreline. Just before the descent, there's a stunning perspective of Charlotteville and the sea from **Flagstaff Hill**; take the signposted right turn from the main road – though it's quite bumpy and may be difficult without four-wheel drive in the rainy season. Tobago's most easterly portion of tarmac marks the last sign of "civilization"; north of here, the countryside is completely undeveloped, with no electricity or piped water for the hardy handful of small-scale farmers, bush hunters and fishermen. At the peak of the hill, the road opens up to reveal a battered coastguard's hut and tall pylon topped with a navigational beacon, a swathe of grass with a covered gazebo and a fantastic view of Man O' War Bay, Booby Island and Cambleton Battery with the Sisters Rocks deep out to sea. If you peek through the trees or risk climbing the pylon, you can make out the hills of St Giles Island. This excellent vantage point was utilized by British and French soldiers, who used mirrors to signal the approach of a ship to their colleagues stationed at Cambleton Battery below.

As the Windward Road begins its seaward plunge, the absurdly pretty fishing village of **CHARLOTTEVILLE** swings into view; houses tumble willy-nilly down a hillside met by calm Caribbean waters,

Jemma's *sells local flavoured coffee and food products, and two craft stalls opposite, the Greenlime Hacienda and Cliffs Craft Centre, carry the usual bamboo, calabash and coconut craft items.*

while frigate birds swoop overhead and hissing cicadas keep up a constant refrain. Snugly situated under the protective cover of two-kilometre-wide **Man O' War Bay**, Charlotteville is one of Tobago's foremost fishing communities – more than 60 percent of the island's total catch is brought in by local fishermen. Bordered on each side by steep forested hills, the town has an isolated feel, as though time were suspended and commercial concerns put aside. Though the tourist dollar is steadily encroaching upon this self-contained, tight-knit community, the atmosphere is so friendly that it's hard not to relax.

Despite the small-town atmosphere, Charlotteville is actually one of Tobago's oldest communities, first settled by Caribs and then by the Dutch in 1633 – for many years the bay was known as Jan De Moor Bay after an early Frisian occupant. During the plantation era, the surrounding area was divided into two successful estates, Pirate's Bay and Charlotteville; sugar shipments made regular departures from the bay, and the town prospered. In 1865, both estates were purchased by the Turpin family, who still own much of the surrounding land.

Accommodation

Between December and April it's wise to book ahead, as guesthouses fill up quickly in what is fast becoming Tobago's most popular retreat. To cope with demand, many local residents rent out rooms during high season, so if you find yourself without accommodation, ask around for possibilities, or call any of the numbers listed in the box on the page opposite.

Belle Aire Cottage, Belle Aire St ☎ & fax 660 5984. One hundred metres up the road from the Pirate's Bay track, these basic white-painted rooms have fan, en-suite bathroom and fridge. All have porches and shared kitchen and dining room. ④.

Charlotte Villa, North Side Rd, Cambleton ☎660 5919, *lutz@snafu.de*, www.tobagoholidays.com. This small simply decorated place, just two minutes from Man O' War Bay, has one apartment with two bedrooms (with double beds) and one bedroom (with twin beds), fans, kitchen and en-suite bathroom. ④.

Cholson Chalets, Man O' War Bay, c/o Pat Nicholson, Mount Pleasant ☎ & fax 639 8553. Completely charming green and white houses overlooking the beach at the Pirate's Bay end of town. The deliciously antiquated feel of the six simple rooms makes the basic romantic: muslin curtains and wooden floors, fans, private bathroom, optional maid service and a few kitchenettes; the upstairs flat is most appealing. Advance booking is recommended. ⑤.

Dr P's, Belle Aire St ☎660 5907. Excellent value one- and two-bedroom apartments with fan and bathroom, some with kitchen facilities. The small balconies have great views over the village and the bay. ③.

Man-O-War Bay Cottages, Man O' War Bay, c/o Pat Turpin, Charlotteville Estate ☎660 4327, fax 660 4328, *pturpin@tstt.net.tt*. Situated right on the bay in pretty landscaped gardens, the cottages are different shapes and sizes, with one to four bedrooms. All have fan, bathroom, hot water and kitchen, simple but attractive decor, books on the shelves, driftwood ornaments and an overwhelming feeling of peace. There's also a small commissary on site. Hiking tours are available and the maid/cook service is optional and costs extra. ⑤.

Mitchell Alleyne, Belle Aire St ☎660 4423. Pleasant rooms, simply decorated, with fan, shared toilet, shower and kitchen. Five metres from Pirate's Bay track and convenient to the best beach in the area, making this option a bargain. ②.

Moore's Guesthouse, Belle Aire St ☎660 4749. Large basic rooms and shared kitchen, lounge with plastic-covered sofa and simple bathroom can be rented as a two-bed apartment. Located on the hillside overlooking the bay, which means you'll need strong legs to get there. ④.

Ocean View, 11 Mission Rd ☎660 4891. Perched on Charlotteville's hillside these small cosy rooms have fan, en-suite bathroom and small kitchen, done in typical Tobagonian decor. The rooms overlook the serene Man O' War Bay. ④.

Uncle Man's Castle, c/o Sherryl, 29 Belle Aire St ☎660 6073. Two basic rooms in the friendly host's home overlooking Charlotteville harbour. Furnished with ceiling fan and shared kitchen and bathroom. ④.

Charlotteville's petrol station is open Mon–Sat 6am–8pm and Sun 6am–11am & 8.15pm–8.30pm.

The village

If you're seeking peace, quiet and great beaches, it's hard not to become utterly besotted with Charlotteville. The "town centre" with its hole-in-the-wall shops, petrol station, post office and sprinkling of restaurants sticks close to the sand; the streets that stretch uphill form the residential section. There's little to do but enjoy the sea, arrange a **fishing** trip aboard the many pirogues which moor up in the bay, or just while away the hours on the fine brown sand of **Man O' War Bay beach**. It's clean, calm and inviting, with good snorkelling and changing/shower facilities (daylight hours; TT$1) as well as a lively beach bar and restaurant. Just past the main swimming area is the busy Charlotteville **Fishermen's Co-Operative** building, with its blackboard displaying the day's catch alongside messages to its members. Benches along the sea wall, the fishing pier and a covered pavilion are popular liming spots, great for soaking up the village scene. Maurice Alleyne sells his beautifully handcrafted calabashes from a small stall called Jah One behind the pavillion.

In July, Man O' War Bay is the site of Tobago's most popular fisherman's fete, held to celebrate St Peter's Day.

Beyond the square, the coastal street turns inland, but a dirt track continues along the shoreline to the town's – and Tobago's – most attractive beach, **Pirate's Bay**. At the bottom of a flight of 165-plus concrete steps, you're rewarded with a stunning horseshoe of calm emerald green water and fine yellow sand, with a backdrop of

Bustin' the bamboo

In Charlotteville and other rural Tobago communities, music at open-air
celebrations and Christmas/Old Years' festivities is often given an ear-
splitting percussive accompaniment. Loved by small boys for the incredibly loud, cannon-like explosion that's produced, the tradition of "bustin'
the bamboo" remains a popular – and highly dangerous – sport, Tobago's
answer to the monumental bangs of firework displays in other countries.
To achieve the desired earth-shaking report, the prospective buster must
have the know-how to select a piece of bamboo of the correct age and
durability with at least four or five internal joints, cutting the section so
that joints seal each end. A hole is pierced at one end, and the bamboo is
filled with pitch oil (kerosene) from a slit at the opposite end. The fuel is
lit and fanned until it heats up sufficiently to blow out the remaining joints,
which creates the resounding boom and often results in the loss of eye-
lashes and moustaches.

trees, ferns and foliage. A tumbledown fisherman's hut and a smart
pair of pit toilets are the only buildings in sight, and a freshwater
rinse comes courtesy of a stream trickling down from the hills. There
is fantastic **snorkelling** to be had in the translucent waters of the
bay, but the pickings are particularly rich toward the left-hand side.
The seventeenth-century buccaneers after whom the bay was named
may have gone, but the bay still has its freebooters, a large colony of
frigate birds, which feed by snatching recently caught fish from the
beaks of smaller seabirds.

Cambleton Battery

Reached via a steep and potholed lane striking off from the main
road on the western outskirts of town, **Cambleton Battery** (no set
hours; free) was built by the British in 1777, who placed two cannons
to defend against attack from marauding American warships sailing
the Caribbean during the War of Independence; the sweeping views
of Charlotteville, Booby Island and Pirate's Bay explain why they
chose this site. It's a popular cooling-off spot for locals, who lime
away a few hours under the shade of the gazebo. Past the battery, the
track continues upward, but if you're driving, it's wise to go no further than the sign that warns "treacherous road – proceed at your
own risk". If you have a dirt bike or four-wheel drive vehicle, you can
proceed as far as the next bay, **Hermitage**, without too much trouble, but bear in mind that almost all of the island's rental companies
will hold you fully responsible for any damage incurred along this
stretch, and though it's attractively deserted with a shingle beach
and plenty of washed up flotsam, the bay isn't really worth the trouble; rip tides also make swimming precarious. If you do decide to
attempt the full stretch, it will take about an hour to cover the three
kilometres to **L'Anse Fourmi**, where the tarmac begins again.

Eating and drinking

Though most of the available accommodations are self-catering, Charlotteville offers only limited **food shopping**; basic needs are covered by two small mini-marts and shops along Man O' War Bay; you can buy fresh fish daily from the Fishermen's Co-Operative. **Restaurant** pickings have improved, though opening times can be erratic; in an emergency a couple of the grocery stores offer take-away lunches. *Gails*, by the Pirate's Bay track serves excellent, inexpensive local food for breakfast and dinner, while budget-priced *Eastman's* by the town square has a catch of the day with chips, burgers and sandwiches, served up on a verandah overlooking the fishing pier. Small parlours on the beach front sell roti and the popular fish or chicken and chips.

On the other side of town, *G's* is good and has a nice little blue and white bamboo shelter for those who want to eat whilst watching the waves and listening to the latest Jamaican dub. Local institution *Sharon and Pheeb's* across the way was known for some of the best food in Tobago until it was burnt down in 2000. The owners are rebuilding, in concrete this time. If you're lucky enough be in town when it opens, be sure to stop by for their fantastic breakfast, lunch or dinner. Michelle Jack (☎660 5206 or 4419) on Parrots Bay Road also serves local dinners from her home from TT$50 per person. Fries, fish or chicken meals, drinks and good company are on offer at the beach bar, which also puts on a lively sound-system party on Friday and Saturday nights.

Tobago Listings

Car and bike rental The most reliable companies for cars and jeeps are Sherman's (☎639 2292), Rattan's (☎639 8271) and Thrifty (☎639 8507). For motorbikes and bicycles try Baird's, who are another good bet for cars (☎639 2528). Bicycles are also available from First Class (pager ☎662 3377, ID1973), who ply on the Fort Milford approaches in Crown Point every day (7am–7pm), Glorious Rides at Pigeon Point junction (☎639 7124), Fun Rides (☎639 8889) on Shirvan Road and Marco Polo Tourism (☎639 7420) based at the car park at Mount Irvine beach complex. Scooters can be hired from R & Sea Diver's Company on Pigeon Point Road, who charge US$20 a day, with discounts for long-term hires.

Watersports in Charlotteville

If you want to visit the excellent **scuba diving** sights in the area, the only reputable local operator is Man Friday (☎660 4676, mfdiving@tstt.net.tt) near Man O' War Bay beach. They offer resort and certification courses, single dives and packages, and rent out single and double **kayaks** (US$30/45 per day) and **snorkelling equipment** (US$8 per day). Locally run Workshop Sea Tours (☎660 4262, wkshoptours@excite.com) offer fishing trips for US$25 per hour as well as offshore island tours and bird-watching expeditions.

Courier service As the postal service in Tobago can be anything but speedy, you might want to try the local branch of DHL in Lowlands (☎639 9244) if you need to send something abroad in a hurry.

Ferries Subject to periodical breakdowns, delays and a stomach-churning route that demands strong sea legs, the infamous ferry to Trinidad leaves Tobago Mon–Fri & Sun at 11pm, arriving in Trinidad about five hours later. Fares are TT$25 one way, returns TT$50–60 and cabin (TT$80); the latter sleep two, and should be booked at least two days in advance. Cars cost TT$115 or TT$138 depending on weight; call the Port Authority (☎623 2901) to confirm times and cost.

Internet access There's been an explosion of internet facilities in Tobago in recent years – focused mainly round Crown Point and Scarborough. Usually you'll pay between TT$20–30 an hour with 30-minute options also available and economy rates for longer periods. In Crown Point: *Cybercafe*, Crown Point – next to Sun Fun Tours by the airport , with a branch at the THA tourism information booth at the airport; and *House of Pancakes*, Milford Road, Bon Accord. In Scarborough: *J Putertech*, 20 Burnett Street, opposite James Park; *CIRC* in the Elias Building, Wilson Street; *CITI*, Bernard Street; and in Speyside at *NKY Internet Café*, 46 Tophill Street.

Laundry Machine washes are available at White and Bright on Milford Road (Mon–Sat 8am–5pm ☎639 0921), which charges TT$30 if you load the wash yourself, or TT$35 for a wash and dry service, detergent is TT$3; and at the recently opened Clothes Wash Café (Mon–Sat 9am–5pm) on Airport Road, Crown Point, next to *Coco Reef* hotel.

Medical Complete with an Accident and Emergency department, Tobago's only hospital is just below the fort complex in Scarborough (☎639 2551 or 2552). For an ambulance, call ☎990. If you need a doctor, try any of the physicians practising at the Triangle Building, Crooks River, Scarborough (☎639 1115) or Dr Melville (☎639 1722, 639 7586 or 678 8369). The best gynaecologist, according to local opinion, is Dr Francis Jacobs in Scarborough (☎639 5727). Late-opening pharmacies in Scarborough include Scarborough Drugs, opposite *KFC* on the corner of Carrington Street and Wilson Road (Mon–Sat 8am–7.30pm, Sun 8am–noon), and Tobago Pharmacy on Carrington Street (Mon–Thurs 8am–7pm, Fri 8am–8pm, Sat 8am–2pm). In Crown Point try Dove Drugs (Mon–Sat 8am–7pm, Sundays and public holidays 8am–noon) in the Real Value Plaza, located on Buccoo Bay Road, which runs from Claude Noel Highway to Shirvan Road, signposted for Auchenskeoch.

Money As there are no official bureaux de change in Tobago outside the hotels, all transactions must be made at the banks; there's one branch of Republic Bank at Crown Point airport, but all the others are in Scarborough (see p.288); all are subject to the same opening hours (Mon–Thurs 8am–2pm, Fri 8am–noon & 3–5pm). 24-hour ATM's are located at Crown Point airport and adjacent to the Scarborough banks, others are marked on the tourist board's map of the island; all provide cash advances on credit cards. Wire transfers can be collected at any of the banks.

Petrol stations In Crown Point, the Canaan garage on Milford Road is the only port of call (Mon–Sat 7.30am–1pm and 3–9pm, Sun 8am–2pm); you can also try the Carnbee petrol station (Mon–Sat 6am–9pm, closed Sun) – take the first right from Shirvan Road or the turn-off from the highway marked for Auchenskeoch. Roxborough petrol station is open Mon–Thurs & Sun 7am–9pm, Fri 7am–5pm, Sat 6pm–9pm, Plymouth's Mon–Sat 6.30am–9pm,

Sun 5.30am–9pm, Charlotteville's Mon–Sat 6am–8pm, Sun 6am–11am & 8.15pm–8.30pm. Scarborough petrol station on Milford Road is open Mon–Sat 6am–9pm, Sun 6am–1.30pm; the Taxi Co-Operative garage on Wilson Road and the three stations on Milford Road stay open until midnight daily. As a last resort, head for Hillsborough (Hope) Bay on the windward coast just outside Scarborough; ask around for directions to the man who keeps a reserve of (expensive) gas to sell to the desperate; fishermen often keep a container to fuel their boats as well.

Photography Fotomart have a shop on Burnett Street for film and developing (one-hour service available) as well as two easy-access booths (Mon–Fri 8am–6pm, Sat 8am–2pm), located at Mount Irvine beach complex and Store Bay. Their Crown Point branch is open Sunday 9am–6pm.

Police There are five police stations in Tobago; Scarborough (☎639 2512 or 4737), Old Grange (☎639 8888), Moriah (☎639 0029 or 0100), Roxborough (☎660 4333) and Charlotteville (☎660 4388). The island-wide emergency police line is ☎639 1200; alternatively, dial ☎999 for police ☎990 for fire and ambulance.

Supermarkets The best supermarket is Penny Savers on Milford Road at the Canaan end; it's competitively priced, well stocked and has lots of imported foods (Mon–Sat 8am–8pm, Sun 8am–1pm). In Crown Point, try the small but convenient Francis mini-mart just before Fort Milford in Crown Point (Mon–Sat 8am–6pm), or the View Port Supermarket (Mon–Thurs 8am–8pm, Fri & Sat 8am–9pm, Sun 8am–8pm), opposite the Tobago Taxi Co-Op in the Canaan section of Milford Road. The well-stocked All in 1 Tobago Supermarket at the corner of Glen and Darrell Spring roads is open late (daily 7am–11pm) – turn left from the highway just past the Scarborough turn-off. Morshead Delicatessen, on Buccoo Road (turn off Shirvan Road) sell imported cold meats and cheeses.

Taxis You can hail a car on almost all of Tobago's roads – make sure that you settle the price before getting in. Most large hotels have registered drivers, but they can be expensive. If you want to call a cab, try Tobago Owner Drivers' Association (☎639 2692) or Tobago Taxi Co-Operative (☎639 2659). Both have set rates which are pretty reasonable; drivers work until midnight or thereabouts. If you'd prefer a woman taxi driver, contact Liz Lezama (☎639 2309).

Telephones There are pay phones all around the island, most using the pre-paid TT$20 phonecards available from small stores and pharmacies – these can only be used for local calls. However, making a call in the remote eastern end of the island is difficult; the only call-boxes in Speyside and Charlotteville are often out of order, so you'll have to resort to a hotel, which usually means a hefty mark-up on local and international calls. You can always make interna-tional calls from the ferry terminal booths or buy a pre-paid companion card (TT$30, 60, 100 + 15% VAT) from local shops, which allows you to phone abroad from a private phone. The local phone company (TSTT) in the Caroline Building, Wilson Rd, Scarborough (Mon–Fri 8am–4pm) offers inexpensive international calls and a send-and-receive fax service.

Therapies and treatments Ayurvedic massage and reflexology are available from holistic practitioner Usha Innis (☎639 8442; US$50 per hour), while UK-trained Simon Abbot offers shiatsu (☎639 8442; US$50 per hour), and yoga classes are taught by Jacqueline Quesnel (☎639 8442; free to guests, for nonguests there is a charge of TT$30 per session.). All of them practice from

**Tobago
Listings**

Kariwak Village hotel in Crown Point. A few of the large hotels offer beauty treatments ranging from facials to massages. Contact *Blue Haven* (☎660 7400), *Tobago Hilton* (☎660 8500) or *Le Grand Courlan* (☎639 9667) for further details.

Weddings Since 1996 it has been possible for couples to marry in Trinidad and Tobago as soon as three days after their arrival. Many hotels offer sumptuous honeymoon suites, and *Tobago Weddings* (☎639 1400, fax 639 3253, *http://tobagoweddings.com*) will make all of the necessary arrangements. You will need passports, airline tickets, and if either you or your soon-to-be spouse is divorced or widowed, then the decree absolute or death certificate, along with proof of name change if it differs on the document.

Contexts

A brief history of Trinidad

For a history of Tobago, see pp.238–241.

Trinidad was the first inhabited island of the Caribbean, having been settled by Amerindians from South America as early as 5000 BC. The early settlers were Arawaks – peaceful farmers and fishers – though after 1000 AD they were joined by more warlike Carib tribes. The Amerindians called the island "Ieri", the land of the hummingbird.

The Amerindians and the Spanish

When **Christopher Columbus** "discovered" the island in 1498, the population numbered around 35,000, most of whom lived in the coastal areas. There was a structured society, with organized villages and chiefs, and a self-sufficient economy that exploited the abundant natural resources and extensive trade with the South American mainland. Sighting the three peaks of the Trinity Hills, Columbus is said to have renamed the island **Trinidad**, landing at Moruga on the south coast. Despite an initial skirmish with the local tribes, Columbus's sailors considered them the friendliest in the Caribbean islands. This didn't suit the Spanish **slave traders** who followed hot on Columbus's heels; despite protests from Spanish priests such as Bartolomeo de las Casas, they gleefully exaggerated the Caribs' occasional ritual **cannibalism** to justify enslaving them.

The first permanent **Spanish settlers** came to Trinidad in 1592, where they built the small town of San José – present-day St Joseph in the north of the island – complete with governor's residence, *cabildo* (council chamber) and church. Although the fledgling capital was sacked by **Sir Walter Raleigh** in 1595 as he headed for South America in search of El Dorado, it was quickly rebuilt, and the colony survived despite being vulnerable to foreign attacks and pirate raids, growing tobacco and cocoa for export to Europe. In 1687, Capuchin monks arrived from Spain, setting up several **missions** around the island. Alongside the proselytizing, the missions were also a means to control the Amerindians through the *encomienda* labour system, a kind of semi-slavery in which the Indians were forced to work on plantations and build more churches.

To evade this threat to their way of life, some Amerindians moved to the rainforested interior. Others rebelled: in 1699, a group of Amerindians killed three Capuchin friars at San Rafael. The reprisals were savage, as Spanish troops slaughtered hundreds of Amerindians in the ensuing **Arena Massacre**. Amerindians were further threatened by European diseases such as smallpox, to which they had no resistance. Consequently, three hundred years after Columbus's arrival, the indigenous population had been all but wiped out.

The arrival of the Africans and the French

The Spanish empire, however, had neither the desire nor the resources to develop the island, treating it as little more than a convenient watering-hole en route to the riches of South America. The governors of Trinidad did as they pleased; illegal trading of goods and slaves was commonplace; and the poorly defended island suffered repeated attacks from French, Dutch and English **pirates**. When Don Pedro de la Moneda arrived from Spain to take up the governorship of the island in 1757, he found his St Joseph residence practically in ruins, and decamped to Port of Spain.

After centuries of indifference, it became clear to the Spanish government that if it didn't develop this neglected colony, somebody else would. In

1783 it issued the **Cedula of Population**, a decree designed to encourage fellow Catholics, **French planters** suffering under Protestant discrimination in British Grenada and Martinique, to settle in Trinidad. The amount of land they were allocated depended on the number of slaves they brought with them. Immigrants of mixed European/African race (termed "coloured" by the Spanish) who brought slaves could also receive land (though only half as much as their white counterparts), thus opening the way for the development of a property-owning coloured middle class.

To implement this policy, Spain despatched a new governor, **José Maria Chacon**, in 1784. Under his energetic administration, the economy flourished, and people of French and African descent came to dominate the population. The island's culture also became increasingly French: it was during this period that **Carnival** was introduced, the French language created a local patois, and a society based on aristocratic principles of birth and connections developed.

As the repercussions of the **French Revolution** gave rise to civil and international wars throughout the West Indies, many more French – both republicans and royalists – sought refuge in neutral Trinidad. To Chacon's alarm, they brought their ideological conflicts with them. Along with the French came more coloureds, many with republican sympathies. Worried, the governor reported to Madrid that their radical ideas were encouraging the slaves to "dream of liberty and equality".

The British take over

The British, who already controlled much of the Caribbean, seized on the pretext that the island had become a nest of republicans and "bad people of all descriptions", despatching an invasion fleet under **Sir Ralph Abercromby** in 1797. The island had few defences: five ships compared to the British force of eighteen; two thousand men – many of whom had deserted – against seven thousand. The Spanish surrendered with hardly a shot fired, scuttling their own ships in Chaguaramas harbour, and Chacon was recalled to Spain in disgrace. It has been argued that, as a staunch royalist, he may have deliberately offered little resistance, preferring Spain's British enemies to her republican French allies.

The terms of defeat offered by Abercromby were lenient; residents could retain their property and Spanish law would remain in force. His

choice of governor, **Thomas Picton**, was less fortunate. Left in charge of the island with near absolute powers, this harsh military officer soon instituted a **reign of terror**, deporting and executing suspected subversives on the flimsiest evidence – frequently confessions obtained under **torture**. Slaves and freed coloureds – whom he regarded as dangerous republicans – bore the brunt of this oppression. Followers of African religious traditions were persecuted especially harshly; those suspected of practising obeah were hauled before a tribunal, and if found guilty were whipped, hanged, mutilated or burned to death. By 1802, Picton's activities had become an embarrassment to the British government, then facing an influential anti-slavery lobby at home, and he was demoted.

Trinidad presented the British government with a unique administrative conundrum. Other Caribbean islands such as Barbados were governed by colonial assemblies, but that was scarcely an option in Trinidad. Any such assembly would inevitably be dominated by planters, who would never tolerate the free coloureds sitting on the assembly; but since many of the latter were substantial property owners, it would have been difficult to exclude them under British law. The island therefore remained a **crown colony**, governed by French and Spanish law, with directions issued straight from the colonial office in London.

Various policies were tested in an attempt to curb the abuses of slavery, but these did little apart from infuriate the planters. Slaves were treated harshly, and a third of them died clearing the rainforests to make way for plantations. The slaves resisted by organizing secret societies with their own militias, and attempted several rebellions. One such society, led by a powerful obeah man known as **King Samson**, was discovered and crushed at Christmas in 1805.

The British abolished the slave trade in 1807, but the planters' need for labour meant that slave smuggling continued. Even after the **Act of Emancipation** in 1834, the freed slaves were required to serve as apprentices for a further six years, and remained tied to their owners since the latter provided their living quarters. When the apprenticeship system was abolished in 1838, many former slaves moved to urban areas. As few labourers could be found to work on the estates, field wages in Trinidad rose to become the highest in the Caribbean.

The Indians arrive

The increased wages were not sufficient to make up for the labour shortage, however, so the British government sanctioned the immigration of **indentured labourers from India**. In May 1845 the first 225 arrived from Calcutta aboard the *Fatel Rozack*. By 1917, when the indenture system finally came to an end, some 145,000 Indians, mainly from Calcutta, had come to the island. Fleeing from poverty and the increasingly harsh British rule in India, the immigrants had to sign contracts to work on the plantations for five years in return for their passage home at the end of that period. In 1854 the period of indenture was extended to ten years, and after 1895 the Indian immigrants had to pay a proportion of the cost of their return passage.

Though the system of indentured labour was better regulated and monitored than slavery, the working and living conditions of labourers and slaves were practically indistinguishable. Labourers lived in single-room **barrack houses**, unsanitary conditions meant that disease was rife, and the shortage of women immigrants heightened feelings of jealousy and possessiveness, resulting in many crimes of passion and domestic violence. The plantation owners failed to honour pledges on wages and working conditions, while breaches of contract by the labourers were treated as criminal offences punishable by imprisonment.

Many did not return to India, but accepted land in lieu of their passage home. Known as "East Indians" – the label is still used today – to differentiate them from the "West Indians", they formed the lowest rung of society, working in the agricultural sector scorned by the Afro-Caribbeans because of its link with slavery. They became a tight-knit community, maintaining many of their own traditions; this was (and still is) resented by many of the descendants of African slaves, who had been forbidden to practise their religion and culture. The white ruling class, on the other hand, saw the mainly Hindu immigrants as heathens and barbarians who worshipped false idols and ate with their hands. Their children were considered illegitimate as Muslim and Hindu marriages were not recognized until 1945. Many of these children remained uneducated – the schools were either Catholic or Presbyterian, and parents feared that their children would be converted.

Yet despite their persecution, the Indian indentured labourers contributed greatly to Trinidad's developing national identity. Just as the Europeans had brought Carnival, which was taken up and enriched by former slaves, Indians brought their own festivities and culture. The Muslims introduced **Hosay**; the Hindus brought **Diwali**. Indian food, such as roti and curry became staple foods for all Trinidadians. After their contracts had expired, many Indians turned to market gardening, broadening the country's agricultural base and making it less reliant on imports.

Other immigrants

Further adding to the ethnic mix in T&T were immigrants from other parts of the world. Several companies of **black American soldiers** who had supported Britain in its 1812 war against the US were given grants of land in southern Trinidad, where they founded villages named after the units in which they had served. After emancipation other immigrants, mainly freed slaves from other **Caribbean islands**, were attracted to Trinidad by the high wages. **Africans** liberated by the British Navy on anti-slave patrols settled in urban areas, becoming craftsmen and construction workers, establishing strong communities that maintained their own cultural institutions and heritage. The first **Chinese immigrants** arrived in Trinidad in 1853, brought by the government to meet the continuing labour shortage on the plantations. The plan failed on account of the high transport costs and an appalling mortality rate among the immigrants; those who survived tended to become shopkeepers, and their descendants constitute a small but visible minority. **Portuguese** labourers were brought to the country in the mid-1800s, but the practice was short-lived as the employment of Europeans in manual work was seen as a threat to the established racial hierarchy.

Except for a handful of **Jews** who settled in Trinidad during World War II, the last group of immigrants to join the island's melting pot were the **Syrians** who came in 1913, seeking refuge from religious persecution in the Lebanon. Though they only account for 0.1 percent of the country's population, their dominance of the cloth trade has given them a high profile. They form a tight-knit community, disapproving of intermarriage and often sending for spouses from their native land.

The people get organized

Trinidadian society remained deeply stratified on the basis of race and class, with the white planters at the top of the heap. In the 1880s and 1890s, however, reform movements began to challenge the status quo. An improved national **education system** and an enlarged franchise inspired the formation of political lobbying groups linked to the international labour movement. The **Trinidad Workingmen's Association** (TWA) – which had close links to the **British Labour Party** – and the **East Indian National Association** were both established in 1897; while the **Pan African Association** and the **Ratepayers' Association** were formed in 1901. Dominated by black, coloured and Indian professionals, these organizations lobbied the British Colonial Office for an elected governing body for the island.

In 1899, Britain made ailing **Tobago** a ward of Trinidad, though the larger island itself still had no effective form of self-government.. Resentment came to a head over the introduction of new **water rates**, and in 1903 a protest meeting in Port of Spain's Woodford Square erupted into a **riot**, in which eighteen people were shot dead by the police, and the Red House – seat of the colonial government – was burned to the ground. Eventually, in 1913, Joseph Chamberlain, the British Secretary of State for the Colonies, agreed to an **elected assembly** for Trinidad and Tobago, albeit one with very limited powers; it was more than ten years, however, before the first Legislative Council convened in the rebuilt Red House.

Trinidad's burgeoning **oil industry** and the aftermath of **World War I** politicized the populace. High inflation led to strikes, resulting in increased cooperation between Africans and Indians, while black **West Indian regiments** returned from the Great War with stories of discrimination at the hands of the British they had been fighting to defend. The **East Indian Destitute League**, established in 1916, fought to abolish indentureship, supported by the National Congress which was then fighting for independence in India. A 1919 **dockyard strike** erupted into violence, and the government, alarmed by the anger and unity of the population, called in British troops to restore order. The tide had turned, however. Socialism, national independence and the concept of black consciousness then being promoted in Jamaica by Marcus Garvey, were now firmly in the public consciousness.

In 1925, the TWA president **Arthur Cipriani** was elected to the new legislative council. A white French Creole who had fought with the British West Indians in the war, Cipriani campaigned hard for workers' rights and secured some important concessions, including compensation for industrial injuries. His essentially reformist politics had little effect on the underlying balance of power, however; wages were actually falling, malnutrition was widespread, living conditions grim and industrial accidents appallingly common. As the world economy nosedived into the **Great Depression** of the 1930s, Cipriani soon found himself outflanked by a new generation of radicals.

In 1932, after trade unions became legal, strikes broke out across the country. The oil workers soon found a charismatic leader in **Uriah Butler**, who broke away from the TWA to found the **British Empire Workers** in 1935. Black nationalism became popular after the failure of the west that same year to defend Ethiopia from Mussolini, while Indian race consciousness became heightened after the visit of several cultural leaders from their homeland.

One of the most influential groups of Trinidadian black intellectuals formed around the *Beacon*, a stridently anti-colonial, anti-government and anti-Catholic literary and political magazine that ran from 1931 to 1934, exploring issues of West Indian identity and attempting to instil a sense of pride among Afro-Trinidadians. In its regular "India section", Indo-Trinidadians wrote of their situation and the struggle for independence in India. Many of its contributors – who included Albert Gomes, C.L.R. James, Alfred Mendes and R.A.C. de Boisseiere – went on to become leading politicians.

Enter the Americans

World War II had a huge socio-economic impact on the island. Chaguaramas, the Bocas islands and Waller Field were leased to the **US military** in 1941 to provide a base for their Caribbean fleet. The Americans improved Trinidad's infrastructure and exposed the population to high-level technology for the first time. The **high wages** they were prepared to pay for the construction of buildings and roads lured workers from the agricultural sector and ensured the decline of many estates. The influx of so many young American soldiers also had a profound effect. Their racial attitudes, cruder than the more subtle racism of the British, and the aura of easy money that attracted many Trinidadian women, soon caused much of the populace to resent their presence.

The transition to Independence

In 1945 **universal suffrage** was granted to all those over the age of 21, though there were still property and income restrictions for those who wanted to stand as candidates for the legislature. Both the 1946 and 1950 elections were won by political parties linked to the trade unions. Britain, meanwhile, was not prepared to hand over total control while radical labour politics dominated the political arena.

In January 1956, a group of black intellectuals formed the **People's National Movement** (PNM) under the leadership of the Oxford-educated historian **Dr Eric Williams**. The party's black nationalist policies, and the charismatic leadership and immense intellectual authority of "the Doctor", soon gained widepread support among a population tired of colonial government and the divisions within the labour movement. The PNM's only serious opposition was from the **People's Democratic Party** (PDP), with its base among the rural Hindus.

A **new constitution** opened up the possibility of party government, and made it easy for the winner to maintain one-party rule. After a controversial campaign that raised racial tension by portraying the PDP as reactionary Hindus, the PNM won the most seats in the **September 1956** election. Though they lacked an outright majority the Colonial Office allowed them to form a government. The PNM were to remain in power for the next thirty years, with Williams as prime minister until his death in 1981.

Many Caribbean leaders saw a **federation of West Indian islands** as the way forward for the region, and at first Williams was an enthusiastic proponent of the idea. With British support, it was decided that Trinidad should be the capital, and in 1958 a federal government was elected, with the Barbadian premier Grantley Adams as prime minister. But political rivalries and the reluctance of the larger islands to subsidize the smaller ones resulted in a watered-down federation with no tax-raising powers. When Jamaica voted to leave the federation in September 1961, Williams announced that "one from ten leaves nought" after which Trinidad followed suit. In May 1962 the federation was officially dissolved.

Though the PNM adopted a radical stance during the early 1960s under the influence of Marxist intellectual C.L.R. James, persuading the US military to leave the country in 1961 and campaigning vigorously for independence, the party's essentially corporatist nationalism attempted to unite capital and labour, despite their conflicting economic interests. With the labour movement in disarray, politics was split along race lines, with government the preserve of Afro-Caribbeans, the opposition that of East Indians.

Independence was granted in 1962 as Britain eagerly rid itself of its colonies. After the PNM created a new constitution without consulting the opposition PDP, the country seemed to be heading towards civil war; only a last-minute compromise by the PNM pulled it back from the brink. As the 1960s progressed, disillusionment began to seep through Trinidadian society. Independence, it seemed, had done little to change the colonial structure of society.

Protest, wealth and disillusionment

The late 1960s were marked by repeated industrial unrest. The **Black Power** movement, which had already had a profound impact on the political life of the United States, caught the imagination of many disaffected Trinidadians. In 1970 its supporters launched a wave of marches, protests and **wildcat strikes** that shook Trinidad to the core. Businesses and banks were bombed, and when the police shot dead a young Black Power member named **Basil Davis**, 60,000 people took to the streets for his funeral. The government declared a state of emergency; an **army mutiny** in Chaguaramas was only quashed when coastguard vessels prevented the soldiers from marching on Port of Spain by shelling the main road; and rumours abounded that a bloody coup had been averted and plans had been discovered for mass executions of "enemies of the people".

The crisis proved cathartic. Many whites had fled the country; those who remained could no longer expect the deference to which they had been accustomed, while the government encouraged locals to be trained for jobs previously occupied by expatriates. The PNM owed its survival in office less to any strength of its own, however, than to the divisions in the opposition. "We are winning by default," PNM minister Hector McLean observed drily.

By the start of the 1970s, when Trinidad was practically bankrupt, vast reserves of **oil** were discovered off the east coast just as the world was sliding into the oil crisis of 1974, and the country found itself swimming in money overnight. Ambitious public projects were undertaken and the country settled back to enjoy the boom years. But this sudden wealth had its down side. People got used to the easy life, productivity fell, agriculture dwindled, inefficiency, bribery (locally known as "bobol") and corruption clogged the system. Williams – who had hoped to use the new wealth to improve the nation's economy and infrastructure – was criticized for "giving the people fish when he should have handed them a fishing rod."

When oil prices fell in the 1980s, the economy went into recession, unemployment rose sharply and inflation soared. Williams died in office in 1981, a disillusioned man with his policies in ruins; his former finance minister **George Chambers** took over the reins. As the population became increasingly dissatisfied, the opposition parties started to unify. In 1986, PNM was ousted for the first time in Trinidad's post-Independence history, in favour of the **National Alliance for Reconstruction** (NAR), led by the Tobagonian **A.N.R. Robinson**, who had resigned from Williams' government in 1970.

This unlikely coalition between the parties representing trade unions, big business, the rural Indians and the Tobagonians tried to resolve some of the more pressing problems facing the country, but within a year the government was breaking up into factions. Harsh economic measures, including **devaluation** of the TT dollar and a stringent IMF-inspired recovery programme, were widely seen as undemocratic and beneficial only to the rich. In 1990, the **Jamaat-al-Muslimeen** – a revolutionary Muslim organization – attempted to overthrow the government, holding Robinson and several of his cabinet hostage. Though the coup was crushed and Robinson released after a six-day siege, the government's authority was irreparably undermined, and the following year the PNM returned to power under the leadership of **Patrick Manning**.

Over the next five years, the PNM stabilized the economy and paid off the IMF, helped by increased oil revenues resulting from sales during the Gulf War. The 1995 election split the country down the middle, with the PNM and the Indo-Trinidadian **United National Congress** (UNC) both winning exactly seventeen seats. The two representatives of the NAR held the balance of power; they used it to support the UNC, making **Basdeo Panday**, the leader of the sugar workers' union, the country's first Indo-Trinidadian prime minister. The **2000 election** proved just as close a race but far more controversial. Initial results had the UNC winning 19 seats, the PNM 17 and the NAR 1; however, the PNM mounted a legal challenge against two of the UNC candidates for being foreign citizens. In return, the UNC argued that the PNM had improperly registered candidates as members of parliament, when they had not yet been re-elected. As legal wrangling continued well into 2001, Panday remained Prime Minister, pending the outcome of the court debates.

In Tobago, usually an NAR stronghold, the general election resulted in the PNM winning their first seat in Tobago in a long time, a victory owed for the most part to disillusionment with the NAR's leader, **Hochoy Charles**. The elections for the **Tobago House of Assembly** (THA) introduced new challengers. The UNC took part for the first time but found it so difficult to find candidates that they offered TT$25,000 and a rental car as incentive. Into this vacuum, a new political party emerged from the Tobago heartlands: the **People's Empowerment Party** (PEP). That too failed to make much of a dent, as the PNM won the elections by a landslide, with eight seats to NAR's four, leaving Tobago in the hands of the opposition party.

Current issues

In recent years the UNC have concentrated on fighting **crime** and the growing **drug trade** in T&T. Until the 1970s, the country was virtually crime free, and by international standards, crime is still low; there were just 115 reported murders in 2000, compared to 800 in Jamaica, a country with twice the population. But for Trinbagonians – used to leaving their doors unlocked at night – the emergence of "bandits" has given rise to crime paranoia, with lurid accounts splashed across the newspapers daily. **Domestic violence** is a major problem in the country, where the culture is predominantly macho and it's widely held that threats in relationships are natural and a way of "testing boundaries".

Corruption also continues to be a cause for concern; in this small country, nepotism is commonplace, and as politics divide along race lines this often causes racial tension. Though Trinidad and Tobago is promoted as a rainbow nation – its national anthem includes the phrase "every creed and race finds an equal place" – **race** continues to be an underlying issue. It is certainly subtler than in Europe or America – there are no race riots or racially motivated killings in T&T – but big business is still dominated by the minority of white Trinis. In addition, the continued rise of the Indo-Trinidadian population in economic, educational and numerical terms often arouses anxiety and resentment among the Afro-Caribbeans.

By international standards, however, Trinidad and Tobago is a model of racial harmony. It can also boast the most **stable economy** in the Caribbean; GDP has grown steadily since 1994, while unemployment and the level of external debt have declined. Oil continues to be an important source of revenue, but having learned from the heady days of the 1970s, the country is using the income it generates to develop other sectors, including manufacturing, finance, insurance and services. This does not mean life is easy for the majority by any means: high-tech malls co-exist with board shacks whose inhabitants live without water and electricity; the social security system is minimal and health care unaffordable for many. Life in Trinidad and Tobago is not easy for the majority, but compared with the rest of the Caribbean, the country is making progress, and its future holds some promise for a more even spread of wealth.

A brief history of Carnival

T&T's most **popular export** and main **tourist attraction**, Carnival originated in southern Europe with the Roman feast of **Saturnalia**, a midwinter celebration of birth and renewal, and the inversion of the norm. It developed during the Middle Ages into the **Feast of Fools**, in which the pretensions of the medieval Catholic Church were scabrously mocked. The Church, unsurprisingly, did its best to suppress the festival, but in the long run assimilation proved more effective, and Carnival was incorporated into the Catholic faith as a final binge (*carne vale* – "farewell to flesh") before the fasting period of Lent.

Today the vast majority of carnivals staged around the world are based on the Trinidadian model and were established by Trinis – they continue to export costumes and skilled craftsmen to these foreign carnivals.

Carnival comes to Trinidad

Introduced to Trinidad by **French planters** in the late eighteenth century, Carnival was initially the preserve of the white Creole establishment. Celebrated in the three days prior to Ash Wednesday, it was a comparatively decorous affair in which the gentry made house-to-house visits to attend masqued balls. The Carnival principle of inversion allowed the white ruling class a brief fictive escape from the "cares" of power and respectability: the men would dress as "negres jardins" (field labourers), the women as "mulatresses", representing their slaves or their husbands' mulatto mistresses.

The slaves also celebrated Carnival, in semi-secret, on the plantations, and after **emancipation** in 1834, the ex-slaves took their their own Carnival procession onto the streets in bands, protected by groups of *batonniers* or stick men. The revellers' costumes often satirized the affectations and eccentricities of their former masters with men dressing as fashionable planter's wives with large breasts and posterior. A number of characters drew on West African traditions and folklore: a little demon known as **jab jab** and the stilt-walking **moko jumbie**. The parade was enlivened by the use of **percussion instruments** and the introduction of **canboulay**, a procession of flambeaux carriers celebrating the former plantation workers' newfound freedom from the difficult and dangerous task of saving burning cane fields – the name is derived from the French *canes brulées*, or burning cane.

Satire and civil disobedience

Disapproving of what they saw as the "desecration" of the Sabbath by the first day of Carnival, the British authorities decreed in 1843 that the festivities could not begin until Monday morning. Since no time was specified, the carnivalgoers began to celebrate on the stroke of midnight – the origin of the wild procession known as **Jouvert** that begins Carnival today. Many of the masquerades acted out in the street processions took the form of trenchant satires of the colonial government, and in 1846 the authorities attempted to ban masking. Carnival found defenders in unexpected quarters, however: the French planters, keen to defend their own traditions in the face of increasing Anglicization, and the coloured middle class, whose desire for respectability kept them aloof from Carnival but who saw attempts to control it as an assertion of white domination.

Carnival continued to provide an outlet for irreverence and satire, with additional characters representing underworld archetypes: **jamettes** (prostitutes) and **jamets** ("sweetmen", or kept lovers), and the transvestite **pissenlets** (literally "wet-the-bed"). Masqueraders also outrageously parodied the British **sailors** stationed on the island by their colonial rulers. Bands organized **drumming** and **kalenda** (stickfighting), which is thought to have originated in the use of bamboo sticks to fight fires in the cane fields. None of this went down too well with the colonial administrators from Victorian Britain, and in 1877 **Captain Baker**, the island's police chief, began a campaign to tame Carnival. When British soldiers attempted to intercept a group of masqueraders in 1881, a riot broke out. Undeterred, the authorities went on to prohibit the jamets and pissenlets on the grounds of their lewdness. African-style drumming was banned in 1884, while canboulay and stickfighting – seen as a fire hazard and an incitement to violence respectively – were outlawed a year later under the **Peace Preservation Act**.

Carnival becomes respectable

Carnival was not so easily quashed, however, and a more sedate masquerade took to the streets in the following years. Social protest was channelled into the emerging labour movement (see p.331), and Carnival became an officially tolerated safety valve for social pressures, and the coloured middle class soon joined in. During the 1890s, Carnival became increasingly organized and socially acceptable with the introduction of a **competition** for best band by Port of Spain merchant and city councillor Ignatius Bodu – fondly remembered by today's masquers as Papa Bodi. Over the course of the twentieth century, practically every aspect of Carnival became the subject of a competition. In 1921, the calypsonian Chieftain Douglas opened the first organized calypso tent to preview the songs that would be heard in the forthcoming Carnival; the tents proliferated, and as they became established venues, the canvas tents gave way to permanent structures (though the name remains – see p.344).

During **World War II**, Carnival was suspended

For more on Carnival and a calendar of events, see p.104, for mas camps see pp.89–91 and for pan yards see box on p.97.

by the colonial government as a possible threat to public order, and when it returned on VE Day, 1945, it marched to the sound of a different drum – the **steel pan** fashioned from oil drums brought to the island by the US military. As the national independence movement gained momentum, Carnival, with its music, masquerades, bands and competitions, flourished. Recognizing its importance to Trinidad's cultural identity and sense of nationhood, Eric Williams's newly elected nationalist party established the **National Carnival Commission** in 1957 to organize and promote the festivities, and set up the competition in which a Calypso King is crowned.

Since then, Carnival has continued to reflect the state of Trinidadian society and politics. In 1970, as the Black Power movement gained widespread support, many of the masquerades explicitly addressed the topics of racism and white control of the economy. And as women have come to take a more prominent role in public life, they have become increasingly involved in Carnival, to the point where they now make up the majority of the masqueraders. And while Carnival has become a celebration of Trinidadian identity and nationhood, its world-famous mas makers don't shy away from tackling ambitious or controversial themes such as the environment.

Though the actual **construction** of the costumes is becoming increasingly specialized and skilled, commercialism and changing fashions have, sadly, led to the loss of many traditional Carnival characters as more and more mas camps turn to **bikini mas**, reducing their costumes to sequins, glitter and feathers attached to a basic bikini. A handful of designers are making a determined effort to preserve the link to Carnival's historic roots. Jason Griffith and his Sailor band ensure that **sailors** are still seen in the Carnival procession, "D" Midas Associates still produce costumes made by **traditional** methods, and Peter Minshall has ensured the survival of characters such as **moko jumbies** in the performance section of his band Callaloo. Recently, however, Minshall and Callaloo ended a three-year winning streak of the coveted Band of the Year award when it lost the title to arch rivals Masquerade in 1998 and 1999. Bikini mas experts, Legends, have recently usurped the well-established traditionalists with wins in 2000 and 2001.

Religion

Trinis sometimes joke that God must be from T&T, and it's easy to see why; deep faith and a laid-back attitude mean that while outsiders fret and panic, locals sit back calmly and wait with a belief that "God will solve all problems."

In this profoundly spiritual republic, most people hold some kind of religious conviction. Schoolchildren receive routine religious instruction and grow up making weekly visits to the church, temple or mosque. Adults are equally devout, with most people affiliated to one faith or another. Trinbagonian religion represents a polyglot of faiths as cosmopolitan as the population. Spain's long period of rule in Trinidad gave the **Catholic Church** a head start over other religions, and it retains the largest number of believers at 29.5 percent of the population. Most Indians remain **Hindu**, and devotees of that faith make up 23.8 percent of Trinidad's population, while **Anglicans** account for 10.9 percent, **Muslims** 5.8 percent, **Presbyterians** 3.4 percent and the remaining 26.6 percent are a mix of Pentecostals, Seventh Day Adventists, Moravians, Spiritual Baptists and followers of the Church of God and Yoruba **Orisha** faiths.

Indian religions

Brought to Trinidad by indentured Indian workers in the nineteenth century, **Hinduism** represents T&T's largest religious denomination after Catholicism. Though you'd hardly believe it judging by the proliferation of grandiose mosques, **Islam** has a smaller worship base, and much of the Muslim religious practice has changed little, save for the festival of **Hosay**, which has grown from a rather sombre affair to a carnivalesque party in which people of all denominations take part – much to the consternation of the Shiite Muslim faithful, who feel that the drinking and revelry that has become associated with the festival depreciates its solemn origins.

All Muslims must adhere to the **pillars of faith**: pray five times a day, make a pilgrimage to Mecca if circumstances allow, keep the Ramadan fast in the ninth month of the Islamic calendar, participate in the giving of alms, and – most importantly – declare their faith openly, accepting

that "There is none worthy of worship except God (Allah), and that Mohammed is His servant and His messenger." For more on Islam in T&T, visit *www.islam.org.tt*

Hinduism in Trinidad

Centred upon the worship of multiple deities rather than a single god (see box, opposite), the central tenets of Hinduism include **dharma**, the laws of duty and order in the universe and society, while one's position in life is determined by the eternal cause-and-effect repercussions of **karma**. Though the indentured workers all worshipped under the banner of Hinduism, their wide-ranging geographical and social origins reflected the huge **differences** in religious practice and status in India, and as they settled into their new life in Trinidad, they created a hybrid Hinduism that's unique to the island.

One of the main differences between Hinduism in Trinidad and in India is the lack of a **caste system** in T&T. The strong friendships forged during the passage, which gave rise to the term *jihaji bhai* ("ship brother") – transcended differences in social status, and many new-found friends chose to settle together and work the same plantations. Slowly, the caste system was eroded; only the priestly Brahman caste, whose **pundits** officiate at religious rites, has survived in Trinidad.

Rituals have also been modified. Whereas in India, prayers for blessing – called **pujas** – are lengthy processes, each with a specific meaning and directed toward a particular deity, in Trinidad several *pujas* are often combined, with several deities involved. Everyone who takes part must be ceremonially cleansed, and the list of articles necessary for a *puja* is long: oils, herbs, spices, ghee, incense, flowers, pictures (*murtis*) of the deity to be honoured, a bamboo flag pole and a **jhandi** (prayer flag) of the deity's assigned colour. Once the pundit arrives, he arranges the items and utters mantras that invoke the deity. The pole is then anointed and the flag raised, and all those present are considered blessed.

Daily rites include lighting **deyas**, reciting **mantras** and **throwing jal** (water); the latter is done by a designated child, who rises in the

Some Hindu deities

Shiva The God of creation and destruction, all-powerful Shiva (alongside Vishnu) rides his faithful bull Nandi, and is often depicted with several faces, each with a third eye in the middle of the forehead, and his hair wreathed with snakes.

Vishnu Blue-skinned, four-armed Vishnu holds a conch, discus, lotus and mace, and is often depicted in the coils of a large snake. He has manifested himself on earth nine times; his tenth visit as Kalki will bring deliverance to the pure and destruction to the wicked.

Durga This fierce female goddess is Shiva's consort. She wears a garland of skulls about her neck, blood drips from her mouth, and in her ten arms she holds various weapons and the head of a demon.

Ganesh Red-skinned Ganesh, the elephant God, sits chubby and benign astride a lotus or throne, holding a water lily, conch, discus and a club or bowl of sweets. The deity of learning and literature, he is the author of the 100,000-stanza philosophical poem, the *Mahabharata*.

Lakshmi The goddess of light and prosperity, Lakshmi is associated with Diwali festivities. She sits on a lotus flower and embodies beauty, grace and charm. Her form varies depending on the incarnation of her consort Vishnu.

Saraswati Taking her name from a sacred Indian river, the goddess of purification, fertility, music and eloquence sits on a water lily or peacock and plays a sitar or lute. She is also the inventor of writing.

Hanuman Depicted as a large monkey bearing a mace, Hanuman is a demon-fighter, the God of acrobats and wrestlers, and the inventor of Sanskrit grammar.

---

morning before the rest of the household and pours petal-laden water from a brass **lotah** near to a tulsi bush – a strain of basil that's planted in most Hindu gardens. Other Indian traditions that have acquired a Trini slant are the celebrations that now accompany the Phagwa and Diwali festivities (see pp.187 and 47).

During times of trouble, Hindus use two forms of healing magic. A **tabij** is a paper talisman inscribed with geometric designs of Sanskrit or Hindi lettering, which is folded and worn around the neck in a locket, while **totkas** are traditional ritual acts; sprinkling the first drops of a bottle of rum on the ground for the spirits (known to Hindus as **dih** rather than jumbies) or driving out evil by throwing five stones in different directions on the arrival of a groom at a wedding or a mother and new baby to the home.

For more on the Hindu faith in Trinidad, visit the excellent site run by pundit Bhadase Maharaj, which has features on festivals, deities and Hindu practices: www.trinihindu.faithweb.com

African religions

Brought to the island by enslaved blacks and further popularized by free Africans who arrived in their thousands during the nineteenth century, T&T's **African religions** centre upon the accep-

tance of a synthesis between the spiritual and temporal worlds. This belief in mystical powers – spirits or gods – which organize and animate the material universe is categorized in Western terms as **"animist"**. The two main sects – **Spiritual Baptists** and the more secretive **Shango** or **Orisha** – are widespread, with a particular concentration in Tobago. In both creeds, spirits are seen to have a distinct influence upon the living and must therefore be respected, pacified, praised and worshipped through ritual dances, chants, drumbeats, offerings and prayer. The YMIR Travel website, www.ymirtravel.com, has some absorbing information on African religion, including an account of an Orisha feast

Spiritual Baptists

More overtly Christian than Orisha, the **Spiritual Baptist** faith surfaced during the late nineteenth century, brought to the island by black Americans. Known as **Shouter Baptists** because of their propensity for loud and demonstrative worship, the sect was frowned upon by the British, who banned membership through the **Shouters Prohibition Ordinance** of 1917. **Shouter Baptist Liberation Day**, March 30, commemorates the abolition of this law in 1951 after years of campaigning. The day is still celebrated with ceremonies all over the island, and a convention at the Queen's Park Savannah in Port of Spain.

Spiritual Baptists ground their beliefs in the Bible and worship the **Holy Trinity** of the Father, the Son and the Holy Ghost as three separate entities. They are well organized, and have their own specially designed churches (unlike the more common sheds), with pews for the congregation, an altar from which the leader or priest preaches, and a **centre pole** decorated with flowers, jugs of water and candles to harness and attract the spirits. The characteristic white robes and colourful headwraps worn by followers (which signify their dedication to a particular saint or spirit) are a notable part of the Trinbago Sunday scenery, when you'll occasionally see bands of Baptists ringing their bells and chanting hymns in public. **Baptism**, where white-clad converts are ritually dipped into a body of moving water (usually the sea), is also commonly seen.

Lasting between three and six hours, **services** usually involve purification rituals designed to cast out **jumbies** (evil spirits) that might be lurking in the church: lighted candles are placed in front of doors and windows, incense is lit, brass bells are rung and perfumed water strewn about. Bible readings precede the chants and hand-clapping that intensify as **spirit manifestations** are brought about by a kind of hyperventilation known as **adoption**. Spirit possession – **catching the power** – is accompanied by bell-ringing and chanting called **trumpeting the spirit**, the origin of the "shouter" tag. Those who catch the power may grunt, gesticulate, speak in tongues or relay the counsel of the spirits in plain English, usually sharing their power by touching each of the assembled members.

Orisha

A Yoruba religion driven underground during British rule, **Orisha** (also Orisa or Shango) remains a somewhat clandestine cult. The faith centres upon worship of several deities called orishas, which are honoured through drumming, dancing, chanting and animal sacrifices. Each orisha's personality is described in stories that reveal their activities on earth, and each is assigned an individual drumbeat, colour, day of the week, favourite food and liquor, sacrificial animal (usually a chicken or goat) and an association with a Christian saint, a tradition which allowed Orisha worship to be syncretized with Christian festivals when the faith was outlawed. The patron orisha of Trinidad and Tobago, **Shango**, is one of the most powerful deities. The god of thunder, fire, war and drumming, Shango carries an axe, his colours are red and white, his patron St Barbara,

---

Traditional herbal medicine

One of the most widely practised aspects of the traditional African belief system known as obeah is herbal medicine. From boiling up bois cano leaves for a cold or bois bande bark and ruction root to revive a flagging libido, many Trinbagonians make use of **herbal medicine**, and most know the uses of the common plants, herbs, roots and barks that make up the materia medica of what's called **bush**. Concoctions are usually brewed into a **tea** and drunk or infused into the skin through a **bush bath**, and the curative power of the remedies is said to be for spiritual as well as physical health, getting rid of "blight" or maljo, the evil eye. Herbs must be picked during certain phases of the moon to ensure their effectiveness.

During the plantation era, every slave community had its **herbalist**, who doled out concoctions for every kind of ailment and presided over births long before Western midwifery was available, prescribing remedies to ease the pain of childbirth and seeing the mother through the week-long "lying in" period, when special tonics were administered.

Elements of these traditions remain strong in Trinbagonian attitudes to health, particularly in the customs of **cooling** and **purging**, which clean the blood and purify the system. After a dose of cooling herbs such as wild senna, caraili, mauby or pawpaw bark, comes a purge of aloes or castor oil, a monthly ritual that has whole families queuing up outside the bathroom door as the medicine takes effect. Other popular remedies include lemon grass, black sage, shandelay and Christmas bush for **colds**, zebapik, chadon beni and fever or carpenter grass for **temperatures**, lime or St John's bush for **itching**, and soursop and ti Marie leaves for **insomnia**.

Jumbies in Trini folklore

Douens The malevolent spirits of unbaptized children, these genderless waifs have backward-facing feet and hide their featureless faces beneath a wide-brimmed straw hat. They lurk in places where real children play; superstitious parents never call their child's name in the open, lest the douens remember it and lure the child away.

Jackalantern A mysterious light that misleads night-time travellers, luring them deep into the bush before vanishing.

La Diablesse An attractive female devil, La Diablesse (pronounced "jablesse") wears the floppy hat and flowing gown of French colonial times, and lures men (particularly unfaithful husbands) deep into the forest, never to return. At fetes, her frenzied dancing outshines the other women and attracts the men. The only way to distinguish her is by her feet; one is normal, the other a cloven hoof. She can only be avoided by wearing one's clothes inside out.

La Gahou Also known as lugarhoo, this spirit feeds on fresh blood. Iron chains slung about its body rattle and drag along the ground, and its sheaf of sticks function as a whip; it can alter its form (usually becoming a jackass or dog) as well as changing size from minute to monstrous. A pair of scissors opened to resemble a cross and a Bible placed at the head of the bed will force the hungry beast to revert to its human form.

Mama D'Leau Spirit and protector of rivers and lakes, Mama D'Leau (pronounced "mama glow") sits naked at the edge of running water, incessantly combing her long hair. Beneath the water, she has the lower body of a snake, which she uses to pull any man who comes along to a watery death. To escape Mama D'Leau, you must remove your left shoe and walk home backwards.

Papa Bois Tall and strong, his hair entwined with leaves, Papa Bois is the guardian of the trees, birds and animals that live in the forests. He imitates animal calls, leading hunters deep into the bush to become hopelessly lost. Papa Bois is assisted by douens, who lead him to animal traps so that he can release the captives.

Phantom The keeper of the roads, this impossibly tall jumbie is visible only from the waist down, as his torso and head are hidden in the trees. He uses his long legs to straddle roads, stopping travellers and crushing them to death if they attempt to pass.

Soucouyant This female vampire lives in villages as a reclusive old woman. At night, she sheds her skin to travel the country in the form of a ball of fire searching for victims, her skin kept in an overturned mortar bowl until her return at daybreak. She can only be stopped by dousing the skin in salt, which prevents her from re-entering it, or dropping piles of rice in homes and at crossroads; she is compelled to pick them up one by one until sunrise brings about her discovery.

---

and his favoured day Saturday (sometimes Friday). Equally respected is **Ogun**, Shango's brother and another war orisha, who represents blacksmiths and iron, but there are hosts of others, and each member of the faith is aligned with an individual god through a spirit possession when they first enter the cult.

Orisha worship takes place in a **palais**, an open space sheltered from the elements by a galvanized roof and decorated with the symbols of individual orishas – daggers, cutlasses, hammers, jugs of water and ritual items such as olive oil for anointing and offerings of flowers, fruit and foods. Known as **feasts**, most ceremonies take place over several days, and begin with the spe-

cialized drum patterns that summon Ogun. Drumming, dancing, chanting and hyperventilation encourage possession of devotees by various orishas, while sacrifices may be performed to honour the spirits that descend.

For online information on Orisha, including links to related sites, visit *www.geocities.com /shango_2000andbeyond/index.html*

Folklore: obeah and jumbies

A retention of African animist traditions, **obeah** (from the Ashante term *obayfoi*, meaning witchcraft or magic) is the belief in a spiritual power that can influence events in the temporal world, curing disease, providing good fortune or wreaking revenge. Though dismissed by most as mumbo-jumbo, obeah still has its followers, particularly in Tobago and in rural areas of Trinidad, where **blue bottles** (the locally available brand of milk of magnesia is commonly used) are placed over front doors or in gardens to ward off the evil spirits known as **jumbies** (see box overleaf).

Other superstitions include scrubbing the home with pumpkin leaves to drive out evil forces, avoiding sweeping the home after 6pm as doing so brushes away good luck, and entering the house backwards if you come home at midnight to avoid bringing in evil spirits. The **evil eye**, usually called **maljo** (*mal yeux*), is a widely believed concept; bad luck is commonly blamed on someone having "set maljo" on the recipient, and people wear red and black jumbie beads to fend it off.

Believers occasionally resort to hiring the services of an **obeah man** (or woman), also known as a bush doctor or herbalist, and an **ojhaman** or **seer-man** in the Indian community. Usually, the practitioner's extensive knowledge of natural medicines is the main reason for a consultation, and a variety of ailments are still successfully treated with bush baths, teas and decoctions of herbs, barks, leaves and roots (see box, p.338). Spiritual and physical problems are often viewed as part of the same thing: arthritis, for example, indicating that a curse has been placed on the sufferer.

In special circumstances, such as unrequited love, loss of an object or a string of bad luck, the obeah man may be paid to invoke or dispel a curse, doling powders comprised of roots and herbs, ashes, earth, blood, feathers, sulphur, cobweb, pitch oil, rusty nails, burnt toast or an ammonia-reeking plant gum called asafoetida, which are sprinkled, burnt, consumed or used in a ritual to bring on the desired effect – called **"working obeah"** – that is reversible only by a more powerful obeah man. Most obeah men and women today are hardly sinister characters cooking up bubbling potions under a full moon, but respected figures dispensing herbal medicines to rural communities.

Rastafari

Developed in Jamaica, **Rastafari** – particularly the well-organized, egalitarian **Twelve Tribes of Israel** sect, who now have branches in both islands – has become increasingly popular in recent years, attracting a very visible local congregation. Believers and nonbelievers flock to reggae parties known here as **nyabinghis**, "Jah" has become interchangeable with "God" in popular vocabulary, particularly among the youth, and the red, gold and green colours of the faith are everywhere.

With a mission of spreading love and unity, Rastafarians believe that Ethiopia's **Haile Selassie** is God or **Jah**, the 225th incarnation of King Solomon and a latter-day Christ. A second tenet is **repatriation** of all believers to the spiritual home of Africa and away from **Babylon**, the oppressive, corrupt society of the Western world and all that it represents.

Rastafarians live according to their interpretations of biblical readings; proverb 15:17 "Better is a dinner of herbs where love is, than a stalled ox and hatred therewith" directs their **ital** (natural and unprocessed) diet; no salt in cooking, no meat and few dairy products. Alcohol, cigarettes and chemical stimulants are also prohibited, though many Rastas see no problem with the odd drink or cigarette. **Ganja** (marijuana) is taken to aid meditations or used at prayer meetings: "He causeth the grass to grow for the cattle, and the herb for the service of man" (Psalm 104:14). **Reasoning** is central to the Rastafarian faith, designed to reveal truth and elucidate the wickedness of Babylon. **Dreadlocks** are directed by a loose interpretation of Leviticus 21:5; "They shall not make baldness upon their head, neither shall they shave off the corner of their beard", which Rastas read as meaning they should not tamper with their hair at all (when left to its own devices, uncombed black hair naturally forms locks).

Music

Trinbagonian music is some of the most exciting, entertaining and thought-provoking in the Caribbean. Most local people display a healthy dedication to their national musics: downtempo, lyrically based calypso (also called kaiso); the faster, more contemporary sounding, dance-oriented soca, in all its manifestations; and steel pan, that lilting tinkle that's synonymous with the region.

Most people have a direct connection with the industry as well, whether by entering the annual round of amateur calypso competitions to be crowned National Flour Mills or *Trinidad Guardian* **Calypso King** or **Queen**, or **beating iron** in the rhythm sections that spring up out of nowhere at the slightest hint of a celebration. A multitude of aficionados analyse the calypsos and soca hits released for Carnival season, when the professionals are pitted against each other in the **Calypso**, **Soca** and **Chutney Soca Monarch** competitions and pannists take over the Savannah in the quest for the **Panorama** title.

However, T&T's musical spectrum is far wider than just soca and calypso: at Christmas, you'll hear the Spanish guitars and nasal crooning of **parang**, while East Indian festivals such as Hosay and Phagwa take place to the sound of frenetic **tassa** drumming, and all forms of Indian music are put on show at the Mastana Bahar talent contest. Jamaican dancehall reggae – called **dub** – is popular among the youth, and has been fused with calypso-style political lyrics and hip-hop beats to create **rapso**, the republic's newest and most exciting genre.

Calypso to soca

The heart of T&T's music scene, **calypso** represents far more than catchy melodies and witty lyrics for the average Trinbagonian. Nearly everyone here is an expert scholar of the genre, capa-

---

Parang

Trinidad's answer to carol singing, **parang** is one of the last living vestiges of Spanish occupation. A traditional Christmas music, parang is performed during the festive season, when groups of roving players – called **parranderos** – descend on private households to perform **aguinaldos**, sentimental Spanish songs accompanied by rapid, Mediterranean-style strums on four-stringed instruments, usually **mandolins** and **cuatros**.

The Spanish **lyrics** can be romantic or humorous, though many are devoted to **religious** themes such as the exploits of saints and the birth of Jesus. Whatever the lyric, the music is always infused with a sense of joyous celebration, and the festivities are enhanced by the consumption of Spanish-derived dishes such as pastelles, arepas, pelau and strong draughts of rum or poncha crema, a spirit-laced eggnog.

Though the parang tradition has waned a little in recent years, it still remains strong in communities dominated by people of Spanish and Amerindian ancestry, such as Santa Cruz, San Raphael or St Joseph. At Lopinot (see p.161), site caretaker and master parrandero Martin Gomez is usually willing to give a demonstration at any time of the year.

ble of using the most obscure quote to illustrate an argument or make a moral point as well as singing along to classic compositions without skipping a single nuance. Trinbagonians analyse calypsos endlessly until the messages in each year's crop become ingrained in the national consciousness. The "poor people's newspaper", calypso has addressed every phase of T&T's development, commenting on shifts in society and attitudes to love, sex, marriage, masculinity, race and religion.

While many non-Trinidadians equate the genre with the glib Caribbean clichés of Jamaican Harry Belafonte's *Banana Boat Song* or *Island in the Sun*, to its home audience, calypso has always been their most accessible form of **social commentary**. Calypsonians use double entendre and allegory to make points that would get a politician arrested for libel, and it's widely believed that Eric Williams's PNM government would not have enjoyed thirty years in power without the support of the beloved calypsonian Mighty Sparrow. Recognizing the revolutionary potential of the "people's music", one of the first actions of 1990 coup leader Abu Bakr was to establish a television station given over exclusively to replays of political calypsos critical of the government.

Calypso developed from the songs of praise and derision performed in Africa by travelling troubadours known as **griots**. First known as **cariso** or **kaiso**, calypso as we know it first emerged on the plantations during the 1700s, where slaves used song as a means of covert communication as well as a rhythmic accompaniment to their back-breaking work. Cariso was also a form of entertainment for the planters; notorious Diego Martin estate owner Pierre Begorrat could be tempered only by the sweet verses of **Gros Jean**, his personal **chantuelle**, as these nascent calypsonians were known.

After emancipation, when the chantuelles were able to express themselves as free men for the first time, they entertained Carnival revellers with insurgent and satirical quips. However, the British found these uninhibited displays unsettling and associated calypso with vulgarity, barbarity and **civil disobedience**, a stigma that remained for many years. Clashes between revellers and colonial officers, as well as objections from the upper classes to "obscenity" in lyrics, led to the prohibition of African drumming in 1884. In the absence of drums, musicians were forced to be inventive, and created the **tamboo bamboo** – tuned sticks

of bamboo beaten on the ground to give a variety of percussive notes – to provide a legal rhythm for their mas and calypso.

Calypso's golden era

By the beginning of the twentieth century, calypso had entered a period of rapid evolution: English replaced French patois, and brass and string instruments took over from the basic rhythms of the tamboo bamboo. Armed with suitably boastful sobriquets, calypsonians such as **Atilla the Hun**, **Growling Tiger**, **Lord Invader**, **Lord Melody** and **Chieftain Douglas** refined their art and turned professional, performing for paying audiences at makeshift venues in downtown Port of Spain. Known as **tents**, these are still the best places to hear calypso at its most authentic (see opposite). Though veiled in metaphor and double entendre, much of the early material was as risqué and **controversial** as it is today; sex, religion, race and satirical portrayals of public figures were the meat of calypsos that usually included the patois disclaimer "**sans humanité**" – "without mercy".

During the 1930s, calypso also found an overseas audience, largely through the efforts of white appropriators such as Paul Whiteman, whose "Sly Mongoose" had been a huge US hit in the 1920s. However, local singers – including Atilla and Roaring Lion – took trips to the US to record, and the genre gradually gained a level of social acceptance. Nevertheless, the colonial government still had a vested interest in controlling what they perceived to be subversive lyrics, and the 1934 Theatre and Dance Halls Ordinance enabled the **censorship** of so-called offensive compositions and the outright **prohibition** of pieces deemed particularly seditious. Any calypso seen to undermine British rule (or champion black culture) was unceremoniously banned. Calypsonians were required to submit their compositions for government inspection before public performance, and officers stationed in the tents ensured that songs met with British approval.

During World War II, calypso got another boost through the support of **American troops** stationed at Chaguaramas. Entertainment-hungry soldiers responded enthusiastically to calypso-based nightclub floor shows and the tents were packed to the rafters, the lyrics now accompanied by sophisticated "**brass bands**", regular backing bands named for the emphasis given to the horn sections. Calypso's success overseas undermined British suppression, and the genre flourished, though the soldiers' preference for comedy and frivolity over politics or picong (private jokes that went over the head of a foreign audience) led to a trivialization of the lyrics. However, the brawling, fornicating habits of the soldiers did not go unnoticed, and calypsonians documented the morally bereft Port of Spain society during American occupation. Lord Invader's infamously cynical smash hit *Rum and Coca Cola* (see Chapter 1, p.116) gave calypso international acclaim, ironically through an Andrews Sisters cover which sold five million copies in the US. Denied a share of the profit, Invader successfully sued.

Dominated by **Mighty Sparrow** (www.mightys-parrow.com), and the inimitable **Lord Kitchener** (who passed away in 1999 and is sorely missed by the music fraternity; for more on him visit www.intr.net/goyewole/kitch.html), calypso continued to advance throughout the 1950s and 1960s. Tourists descended to experience this latest craze first-hand and the tents went from strength to strength, with new venues springing up each year. In 1956, Dr Eric Williams's newly elected PNM government created the **Calypso King** competition, and Sparrow swept to victory with the classic *Jean and Dinah*, which gloried in the fact that local women would have to fall back on Trini men now that US soldiers had departed. Crowned monarch so many times that he was eventually barred from competition and given the special title of "Calypso King of the World", Sparrow continued to overshadow his competitors, and calypso lyrics settled into two strands: praise or picong for the "Doctor" and his administration, and salacious references to love and sex.

Though Independence in 1962 saw calypsonians infusing their lyrics with optimism, by the late 1960s, a new radical politics shook Trinidad, and militant lyricists such as **Valentino**, **Black Stalin** and **Mighty Chalkdust** delivered incisive commentaries on post-colonial society. But despite some innovations – **Calypso Rose** became the first female "king" in 1978, and the competition was renamed **Calypso Monarch** – the 1970s turned out to be a decade of stagnation for calypso. As the anti-establishment, pro-black themes of Jamaican roots reggae held sway over Caribbean musical tastes and sensibilities, calypso lyrics sank to an all-time low of banality.

People wanted something lively to jump up to on the road and in the fetes, and from the early 1980s **soca** (see p.344) began to overshadow its parent during Carnival season. While soca took care of the nation's need to "wine and grind and have a good time", calypso was allowed the breathing space to return to its roots. The genre received a massive creative boost in the middle of the decade through the sensitive, thoughtful work of a single artist, **David Rudder** (www.davidrudder.co.tt). An accountant and session singer who worked with brass band Charlie's Roots, Rudder burst on to the scene in 1986, securing an unheard of triple victory in the Young King, Calypso Monarch and Road March competitions with his beautiful, down-tempo *Bahia Girl*; his other entry, *The Hammer* (a celebration of the life of Laventille pan legend, the late Rudolph Charles) was received equally rapturously, and became an enduring classic.

Rudder's victory sent shock waves through the calypso community. Previously, a budding calypsonian would only have dared to compete after a rigorous apprenticeship as a solo artist in the tents, earning the tacit blessing of the handful of established artists who had dominated the monarch competition since its inception. Rudder had no such patronage, and hadn't bothered to acquire a fanciful sobriquet or a wardrobe of sequinned stage clothes either. Though he entered Calypso Monarch the following year and was placed second with *Calypso Music* (acknowledged as one of the finest calypsos ever written), Rudder subsequently decided not to compete again, on the grounds that he preferred making music to winning prizes. It was a revolutionary and contentious gesture in a genre that tends to concentrate all its energy in capturing the attention of the Savannah judges, sticking to well-known formulas rather than attempting to evolve or develop. David Rudder has continued to release some of T&T's most original and thought-provoking compositions. Trinidad's answer to Bob Marley, he is also one of the few Trini singers to be embraced internationally while maintaining the support of his home audience.

Competitions and tents

Kaiso (the older term is preferred by purists) continues to underpin the soca scene. In the **tents** that provide a practice run for the Monarch competition, an older crowd of enthusiasts disentangle the metaphors and squeal at the jokes hinged on local references that are often unintelligible without a good knowledge of Trinbago affairs and gossip. Most artists concentrate on two numbers during the season, usually one with a political slant and another with a more lighthearted theme, be it picong or sex. Whether they get to perform them both is up to the audience; after the first few verses, kaisonians leave the stage, returning only if the claps and catcalls are deemed loud enough to bring them back on.

These days, the most established tents have a permanent location and a roster of well-known artists supplemented by the year's crop of promising newcomers; lineups change annually, and the lists below are not definitive. Traditional kaiso is best heard at **Calypso Revue**, the former home of Lord Kitchener, where the stalwart lineup usually includes Cro Cro, Crazy, Pink Panther, Denyse Plummer and Sugar Aloes. **Kaiso House** is equally good, with Black Stalin and Shadow topping a bill of Ella Andel, Singing Sandra, the United Sisters and Brother Resistance. A break from the norm, Nikki Crosby and Errol Fabian's **Maljo Kaiso** is a humorous cabaret-type performance, in which calypsonians' tunes are intermingled with skits – it's one of the best to attend if you're a first-timer, as the visual edge gives you more of a chance of keeping up with the jokes. **Yangatang**, marshalled by corrosively funny MC Sprangalang, also features lots of humour alongside the calypso; 2001 saw calypsonian Learie Joseph demonstrating the "police wine" whilst being held up by a jamette. A mix of classic kaiso and the years' hottest soca artists ensures that **Spektakula Forum** is one of the best attended tents, with MC Tommy Joseph and regulars such as David Rudder, Luta, Scrunter, Chalkdust and Funny, as well as comedienne Rachel Price, with the year's most popular soca artists. Spektakula occasionally moves to in the Savannah to accommodate its ever-growing audience, and most of the tents also participate in **clashes**, where kaisonians attempt to outwit each other with improvised material. (For addresses and practical information on the tents, see the Carnival calendar, p.104.)

Soca

Most attribute the birth of soca to the late calypsonian **Lord Shorty** (Ras Shorty I), who died in 2000. Distressed at the moribund state of his art

in the 1970s, he made a conscious decision to breathe new life into the genre. His souped-up rhythmic structure created an infinitely more danceable form that fitted in with the popularity of disco and took T&T by storm. Shorty wanted what he called **sokah** to reflect the soul of calypso, to deal with love and romance as well as the joys of feting, but his legacy is a party music, best heard during Carnival.

From January 1 until Carnival, soca artists release their new material in massive outdoor launch parties; one of the biggest is Crosby's launch, held outside the record shop in St James. Once released, the material does the rounds of the Carnival **fetes**, which whip the loyal listeners into a frenzy and provide a swift induction into soca culture; soon, everyone knows what to do when commanded to "wave yuh rag" or show that they know which dance step accompanies each song. Alongside piped soca from the DJs, fetes usually have a live show which will consist of **brass bands** such as Blue Ventures, Question or Charlie's Roots backing the year's most successful soca artists, who all perform **covers** of everyone else's hits as well as their own numbers.

Since Blue Boy's *Soca Baptist* became the Road March (the most heavily played tune as mas bands pass judging points on the Carnival route) of 1980, soca has dominated Carnival and become the music of choice among a nation of professional feters, sustained by more than 400 new releases per year. In 1994, the soca/calypso dichotomy was officially recognized when a separate **Soca Monarch** competition was set up. The climax of the soca madness that envelops pre-Carnival Trinidad, Soca Monarch has surpassed its parent event in terms of crowd numbers; it was won for several years running by **Super Blue**, the new name adopted by Blue Boy after he conquered cocaine addiction, and other recent holders of the title include calypsonian Shadow, who brought a welcome dose of traditionalism back to what had become a rather puerile "jump-and-wine" winners list. The **Road March** title has now become more or less a soca domain, and is often taken by **Xtatik**, a loose collective headed by heartthrob and expert winer **Machel Montano** (www.machelmontano.com).

Alongside a multitude of home-grown acts such as Destra Garcia, Rupee, Sanelle Dempster, KMC, Tony Prescott, Anslem Douglas, Iwer George and Traffik, soca's main names also include a strong contingent from **Barbados**; acts such as

TC or Alison Hinds' incredibly popular band **Square One** travel over for the season to headline at fetes. Successful soca (and calypso) artists are fostered in most eastern Caribbean islands, while Arrow, the man behind the world's most overplayed soca hit *Hot, Hot, Hot,* actually hails from Montserrat.

Chutney soca

East Indians have given soca their own slant through **chutney**, which mixes sparse, fast soca beats with sitars and thumping dholak drums. Sung in a mixture of Hindi and English, lyrics tend toward the lighthearted, and chutney fetes – attended predominantly by young East Indians – have become a showcase for sensual dance steps that combine athletic wining with the delicate arm and hand movements of classical Indian dance. However, many older Hindus dislike chutney, finding the overtly sexual dancing and sometimes risqué lyrics distasteful.

Established in 1996, the **National Chutney Soca Monarch** (www.southex.co.tt/chutney) competition is the annual focus for chutney artists, and the finals (usually held at Skinner Park in San Fernando) now attract up to 20,000 enthusiastic chutney converts. Chutney vocalists to look out for include the smooth **Rikki Jai** (usual winner of the Chutney Monarch competition), Heeralal Rampartap, Sonny Mann and Drupatee Ramgoonai; the late Sundar Popo also recorded some classic chutney tunes. Chutney has also influenced the conventional soca industry; white calypsonian Denise Plummer continues to flirt with the form, as does Machel Montano.

Steel pan

Said to be the only new acoustic instrument of the twentieth century, the **steel pan** evolved from the Trinbagonian propensity for using available materials as percussion instruments. During the Carnivals of the 1930s, **tamboo bamboo**-led kalinda music was supplied by bands of young men from deprived areas such as Port of Spain's Laventille and Belmont, who were unanimously viewed as "**bad johns**" or thugs by the more fortunate. With names such as Desperadoes and Invaders, these loosely organized bands supplemented the tamboo with "**rhythm sections**", beating steel rods against anything from brake drums and buckets to dustbin lids to satisfy the urge for rhythm.

It was only a matter of time before someone realized that discarded saucepans or biscuit tins – and later the **oil drums** brought over by US troops – could be hammered into concave sections that produced rough notes; these early raw materials explain why steel drums are known as **pans**. Depending upon who you believe, the first pan was played at some point in the late 1930s, either by **Winston Spree Simon** of the John John band (now Carib Tokyo), who tapped out *Mary Had a Little Lamb,* or **Neville Jules** of Hell Yard (now Trinidad All Stars) who managed the basic chords of a calypso called *Whoopsin, Whoopsin.*

By the end of the war, experimentation with basic pans had produced up to fourteen notes, and the 1946 victory Carnival was dominated by the ringing of steel bands. However, the associations of **violence** lingered, and the **panyards** that sprang up throughout the East–West Corridor were widely viewed – probably quite correctly – as seething dens of iniquity. Feuds were common, and in 1950 a bloody **pitched battle** between Invaders and Tokyo had Carnival revellers running for cover. Calypsonian Blakie documented the clash: "It was bacchanal/Fifty carnival/Fight for so, with Invaders and Tokyo/When the two bands clash/Mamayoe, if yuh see cutlass/Never me again/To jump in a steelband in Port of Spain."

However, the violence tailed off after this and the movement gained respectability (and respect) as the music became more polished and complex. Soon, bands of up to 200 pannists played a sophisticated repertoire of classical pieces as well as calypso, and the nation's dedication to pan began in earnest. In 1950, the **T&T Steelband Association** (now **Pan Trinbago**; www.pantrinbago.co.tt) was established to promote and coordinate the movement, setting up a round of competitions that eventually led to the first annual **Panorama** tournament in 1963; twenty-odd years later, the steel pan was officially declared the national instrument by then-PM Patrick Manning.

These days, the panyard calendar revolves around Panorama, a hugely popular affair that involves almost all of T&T's steel bands and attracts around 25,000 people to Port of Spain's Savannah stage, renamed in local vernacular as the "**Big Yard**" during the event. To qualify for the event, bands from the **regional zones** compete at regional venues; the Port of Spain Savannah for the north, the Orange Grove Savannah in

Tacarigua for the east, Skinner Park in San Fernando for central and south, and Shaw Park, Scarborough for Tobago. The bands that get the highest number of points qualify for the **preliminaries**, which are held a couple of weeks before Carnival (for more on Panorama and panyards, see pp.104 & 97). Other pan events include the October **World Steel Band Festival**, where bands from all over the world beat classical and calypso music pieces, while pan does sweet justice to jazz at **Pan Ramajay** in May, and at the **Pan Jazz Festival** in November (for details of these events, see "Basics" pp.45–48).

The steel band

Transforming a dirty old oil drum into a shiny playable **steel pan** demands skill and experience, and the **craftsmen's** job is further complicated by the poor quality steel used to make most drums. The high proportion of impurities can result in an effect called **damping**, producing short, dull notes rather than sustained, clear tones. Surprisingly, empty steel drums are not that easy to come by, and shortages are common; in 1997, Pan Trinbago resorted to importing from Venezuela.

Once the raw material is secured, the drum begins its metamorphosis. All pans other than the bass must first be **cut** to size, and a five-pound sledgehammer is used to beat the unopened end into a convex shape. The pan is then **heated** over a wood fire; oil is used to **temper** the metal, and a coating of **chrome** gives a better surface and a shiny finish. The **tuner** then takes over, marking the notes and beating them out with a hammer and chisel, an extremely specialized process that's usually achieved with the help of a keyboard. A finished pan will sell for around **TT$2500**.

In contemporary bands, different types of pan produce a variation of tones. The main melody is held by the **tenor** or **soprano** pan, which has the largest range of notes and the smallest skirt. **Guitar** and **cello** pans provide the background harmonies, and the booming **bass pan** underpins it all. However, no steel band would be complete without its rhythm section or **engine room**, as the percussion section is known. In addition to a conventional drum kit, cow bells, shakers and scrapers, there is the **iron**, assorted bits of metal beaten with iron rods – an old brake drum produces just the right metallic clank.

Known as **iron men**, the percussionists have to be pretty burly in order to keep up the repetitive beat for hours on end.

Each band is led by an **arranger**, who will adapt music from a variety of sources for the steel band. Though some arrangers work with more than one band, there are several long-standing relationships: Jit Samaroo and Renegades, Len "Boogsie" Sharp and Phase II Pan Groove, Pelham Goddard and Exodus, Ken "Professor" Philmore and Fonclaire, and Robbie Greenidge and Desperadoes. Though most bands used to play it safe and enter Panorama with calypsos familiar to audience and judges alike, original compositions have become popular since 1987, when Phase II won with a Boogsie Sharp original, *Dis Feeling Nice*. Lord Kichener was a master composer of pan music, and since his death many bands have entered his compositions for Panorama.

Most contemporary steel bands are comprised of between 50 and 200 volunteer pannists, who play one or two harmonic pans; with up to six instruments, bass pannists have to be pretty dextrous, twisting around to reach the right notes. A steel band is based at a **panyard**, usually a semi-open practice space where instruments are stored. As the band needs to be mobile, pans are housed in welded metal structures with wheels, plank floors and a galvanized canopy which can be pushed along by supporters; some bands also use flat-bed trucks to move through the streets. **Pan round the neck** bands are usually smaller, comprising 50 or so players who carry their instruments with a strap around the neck.

Reggae

After the bacchanal of Carnival, the nation gives up soca and calypso for Lent, and you'll find it difficult to pick up anything other than **reggae** or religious music on the radio. **Dub** to Trinbagonians, **reggae** has made massive inroads among the youth, who favour the "conscious" music of Rasta-oriented artists such as Capleton, Sizzla and Buju Banton as well as more upfront and lewd material from Jamaica. DJ families such as **Matsimela** and **Black Stone** play at large indoor parties, and their broadcasts are some of the most popular in T&T radio. Reggae has also lent its influence to soca, with many artists employing the vocal style (and the language and accent) or experimenting with the self-explanatory subgenre of **ragga soca**. The most popular ragga soca performer is **Bunji Garlin**, "the girls dem darlin" (www.triniweb.com/bunji), who thrills the ladies and bigs up the blokes with his smooth Trini-Jamaican cocktail.

Rapso

Trinbagonian artists have also created their own musical forms, and the most exciting genre is **rapso**, a politically conscious fusion of African-style drum beats, soca melodies and spoken calypso-esque vocals infused with the militancy of American rap. The movement was originated by **Lancelot "Kebu" Layne** and **Brother Resistance**, the "father of rapso" and the genre's main figurehead. Popularized by **3 Canal**'s 1997 and 1998 Carnival shots *Blue* and *Mud Madness*, and kept lively by their string of subsequent hits, rapso represents the freshest section of Trinbago

music, evolving in tempo and style each year. Artists such as Resistance, Ataklan, Black Lyrics and Kindred write poetic, haunting lyrics that centre upon black empowerment and resistance to oppression; as Brother Resistance states, "rapso is the power of the word in the rhythm of the word." The proselytizing is always backed up by the stinging, drum-dominated rhythms that have earned a huge following among the youth; Ataklan's reggae-influenced, dance-oriented tracks are essential plays at Carnival fetes, while 3 Canal remain the movement's most popular proponents. **Rapso month**, held at venues across Port of Spain in April or May, is a great opportunity to hear the rising stars of this newest expression of T&T's seemingly endless musical fertility; for more on events surrounding the festival, contact Rituals Records (☎625 3262, www.ritualsmusic.com).

Flora and fauna

Joined to the South American mainland during the Ice Age when sea levels were lower, Trinidad and Tobago only became separate entities when movements of the Caribbean tectonic plates submerged the Orinoco Delta some 10,000 years ago. The islands owe their immense environmental diversity to this period of attachment, which has left them with many South American plants, animals and birds, as well as the flora and fauna found elsewhere in the Caribbean. Few places of relative size harbour such variety.

A wide range of **habitat** supports the wildlife; **Tobago** boasts the oldest **protected rainforest** in the western hemisphere along its main ridge of mountains, as well as **marshes** and **lagoons** in the western tip, a network of ornate offshore **reefs** and the **bird sanctuaries** of Little Tobago and the St Giles islands. In **Trinidad**, the rich **wetlands** at Nariva Swamp support several plant and animal species found nowhere else in T&T, while Caroni Swamp offers easy access to **mangroves** and their inhabitants. The dry, treeless prairie at Aripo – the island's only remaining true **savannah** plain – sustains unusual plants and orchids as well as bird life. The islands' hills are afforded some government protection, and contain three state reserves; the **Northern Range Sanctuary**, the **Valencia Wildlife Sanctuary** in the northeast and the **Trinity Hills Wildlife Sanctuary** in the southeast. However, with only ten game war-

dens and six forest rangers to defend the forests, and the industrial wasteland of the west coast constantly encroaching on virgin land, the island's wildlife is under constant threat. For more on the T&T environment, visit the **website** of Environment Tobago (http://194.163.98.38/et), or The Trinidad and Tobago Field Naturalists Club (www.wow.net/ttfnc); the Environmental Management Agency's site is worth a browse too (www.ema.co.tt).

Fauna

With more than 100 species of **mammal** roaming the forests and flats (not including T&T's 52,000 goats), hunting remains a popular pastime and wild meat is consumed with gusto when available. Most hunters go after the most common varieties; aside from the burgeoning populations of **red squirrel**, the smallest quarry is the herbivorous **agouti**, a brown, rabbit-sized rodent that looks like a long-legged guinea pig and feeds on fruits and leaves, and its larger relative the **lappe** or **paca**, which has longer legs and a pattern of stripes and spots on its fur. Equally desirable for the pot is the **manicou** or opossum, an unattractive cat-sized marsupial with a rat-like tail and a long snout that forages for scraps and carrion. The nine-banded **tatoo** or armadillo is increasingly rare, as is the brown-coloured **red brocket deer** (extinct in Tobago) and the **quenk**, an aggressive wild hog with small sharp tusks that eats roots, bulbs and occasionally snakes; some say they are immune to the bushmaster's venom. Another threatened species, the metre-long **ocelot** wildcat has been extensively hunted for its beautiful spotted pelt.

Otters live in and around the Madamas and Paria rivers in Trinidad, but shy away from humans. Trinidad's cutest water-dwelling mammal, the herbivorous **West Indian manatee** or sea cow grows up to four metres long and can live for 50 years, but the destruction of its swampland habitat by development and by drainage for agriculture has decimated local populations; mature manatees need to eat as much as 400kg of weeds a day, and less than a hundred still live in the protected Nariva Swamp.

The islands' largest **monkey** colonies also live in Nariva; with red-furred, hulking frames and a bulbous, bearded larynx, troops of up to fifteen **red howlers** defend their territory with the eerie, deafening roars that prompted their name. Smaller but extremely intelligent, **weeping capuchin** monkeys live in the tree-tops in troops of up to twenty, and are able to use basic tools to crack open nuts as well as occasionally expressing their irritation at human intrusions by raining down a volley of sticks on curious heads. Around 60 species of **bat** inhabit T&T's forests and caves, most living on a diet of insects, fruit, nectar and pollen; however, the **vampire bat** prefers a more gruesome food source, creeping up to sleeping livestock and drinking their blood; anti-coagulants in the saliva keep the blood from clotting.

Reptiles and amphibians

The largest of the 70 species of **reptile** is an endemic sub-species of the **spectacled caiman**, a 3-metre alligator with an elongated snout that inhabits swamps, rivers and dams, and feeds on fish and birds. Among the 47 different **snakes**, only four are venomous. With the girth of a man's arm and a length of up to 3 metres, the **fer-de-lance** is particularly aggressive, and is identifiable

Leatherback turtles

Weighing in at up to 700kg and measuring three to four metres across, **leatherback turtles** have undergone few evolutionary alterations in their 150-million-year history. Named for the soft, leathery texture of their ridged, blue-grey **carapace** (which is more like a skin than a shell, and bleeds if cut), leatherbacks spend most of the year in cool temperate waters gorging on jellyfish, often eating twice their body weight per day. However, during the **egg laying season** (March–July), females swim thousands of miles, returning to the beach of their birth to lay their own eggs in the sand, a fascinating, moving two-hour process that takes place under the cover of night.

Choosing a spot above the water line, the turtle excavates a metre-deep **egg chamber** with her muscular back flippers, her body heaving with the effort and her eyes dripping mucous tears to protect against grains of sand. A trance-like state takes over during the laying of around 100 softskinned white eggs, about the same size as a chicken's. After filling in the nest and compacting the sand, leatherbacks may make several decoy nests with their powerful front flippers to confuse predators. The process over, the leatherback drags herself back to the water.

Leatherbacks often return to the same beach up to ten times per season – a necessary repetition, as only 60 percent of all eggs laid will mature into hatchlings – many are dug up by dogs or poachers – and only one or two of these will become fully-grown turtles. **Hatchlings** usually emerge from the sand about sixty days later and make a moon-guided dash for the sea. Many are eaten by dogs, birds and fish; these days, any that manage to emerge during the day are herded into groups by wardens until darkness provides a little more safety.

You can see leatherback egg laying at Grande Riviere, Matura and Fishing Pond in Trinidad or Parlatuvier, Stone Haven Bay, Bloody Bay and Turtle Bay in Tobago. Trinidad's turtle laying beaches are **protected areas** during the laying season, and you need a **permit** to enter after dark; these cost TT$10 and are available from the Forestry Division at Long Circular Road in Port of Spain (☎ 622 4521, 3217 or 5214), or from the District Revenue Offices in San Fernando (☎ 652 2556 or 2317) and Sangre Grande (☎ 668 3835). Alternatively, you can call Nature Seekers (☎ 668 7337), who patrol Matura Beach during laying season and offer sensitive and informative **turtle-watching trips**. GREAT (Grande Riviere Environmental Awareness Trust) at Grand Riviere offer the same service; though the group is younger and not as well organized, the beach is smaller and you have a greater chance of seeing several turtles (see pp.170, 175 for more details). Both of the above groups arrange permits for you, and if you don't have transport to get you to a laying beach, contact one of the tour operators listed on p.48, all of which offer turtle-watching excursions. In Tobago, most of the hotels along the Mount Irvine coast organize turtle-watching trips, and you can also contact Nick Hardwicke at the Seahorse Inn (☎ 639 0686). If you do go, keep quiet, stay 15 metres away and refrain from shining bright lights or taking flash photos until turtles have started laying; before this point, turtles are easily distracted and may return to the sea.

by its pointed head, yellow underside and chin, and orange/brown triangular markings. The **bushmaster** is slightly longer (up to 4 metres) with a burnt orange skin distinctly patterned by dark brown diamonds with smaller diamonds of orange within. Its venom can be lethal to the young, old or infirm, but most people manage to get the antidiote in time. For advice on dealing with snake bites, see "Health", pp.18–22. Both snakes are known as mapepire (pronounced "mah-pee-pee") and inhabit forest areas. The two varieties of **coral snake** are smaller, rarer and less aggressive; they're easy to spot, with black skin and red and white rings around the body.

Known as macajuel (pronounced *makka*-well), **boa constrictors** – including **anacondas** – are T&T's largest snakes, and can grow up to a fearsome 10 metres in length. Most are patterned with brown diamonds that provide camouflage. They are not venomous, but can easily crush a large mammal in their powerful coils.

Among more than twenty species of **lizard** are **geckos**, usually referred to as zandolie or ground lizards. The **twenty-four hour lizard** gets its name from a local myth which warns that if you disturb one, it will attach itself to your body and remain there for 24 hours – at the end of which you die. The bright green, spiky-backed, herbivorous **iguana** is a favourite delicacy, especially if it's carrying eggs; unsurprisingly, it spends most of its time hiding from human captors in leafy treetops. The metre-long, dark brown **matte lizard** relies on speed to stay out of the cooking pot, raising itself onto its hind legs to accelerate to 11kph in two seconds.

T&T's most common **amphibian** is the **crapaud** (pronounced "crappo"), a warty, hand-sized frog with a loud, booming croak. Another frog, the **colostethus**, provides a night-time chorus reminiscent of a demented guinea pig. Trinidad's only endemic amphibian, the **golden tree frog**, lives on the epiphytic plants that cling to the rainforest trees. In addition to the land turtle, or **morocoy**, five species of **sea turtle** lay their eggs on local beaches; the green turtle, the olive ridley, the hawksbill (illegally poached for its tortoiseshell), the loggerhead and – rarest and largest of them all – the giant leatherback (see box overleaf).

Birds

With more than 430 recorded **birds** (250 of which breed on the islands), Trinidad and Tobago rank among the world's top ten in terms of numbers of species, and offer the best **bird-watching** in the Caribbean (see "Basics", p.49). Adorning the republic's coat of arms, the **national birds** are the **scarlet ibis** (Trinidad) and the **cocorico** (Tobago); the latter is paradoxically classified as vermin. A native of Venezuela and best seen at the Caroni Swamp, the bright crimson ibis typifies the eye-catching colours of local species, while the golden-brown, pheasant-like cocorico has a fleshy, bright red turkey-style wattle at its throat and a raucous call.

The sugar-water feeders at most hotels are a great way to see smaller birds at close quarters. Before Trinidad got its European name, the Amerindians called it Ieri, the land of the hummingbird. There are fifteen different species of these brightly coloured miniatures in T&T, of which the most frequently seen are the **copper-rumped hummingbird** and the **white-necked jacobin**, both with fabulous iridescent feathers, but the most unusual hummer is the 6-centimetre **tufted coquette**, Trinidad's smallest bird and the third smallest in the world, with a red and yellow body, dark wings and a pretty red crest.

Both jet black, the blunt-beaked **smooth-billed ani** and the shiny **cowbird** with a sharper beak and beady yellow eyes are the local equivalent of pigeons. The audacious 10-centimetre black and yellow **bananaquit** is supposed to subsist on nectar, but has become a frequent visitor to hotel breakfast tables, dipping its sharp little beak into fruits and sweet preserves. Seen wherever there are cattle, **white egrets** roost on ruminating rumps in a mutually rewarding relationship that provides the egret with a constant supply of insects and the cow some relief from bloodsuckers.

In the forests and flats, frequently sighted birds include **white-bearded manakins**, which perform intricate courtship displays in designated areas known as **leks** (several other species also use leks), several intensely coloured **woodpeckers**, **antbirds**, **trogons** and **tanagers** – the palm tanager is a cool olive with black flecks on its wings, while the bay-headed variety is a brilliant emerald with a russet head. Various **honeycreepers** display dazzling hues of turquoise and black; the purple variety's near-black feathers only show purple in the sunshine.

Of larger birds, common varieties include multicoloured **toucans**, **parrots**, **yellow orioles** and **giant cowbirds** as well as the crow-like **crested oropendola**, black with a yellow tail, cream beak,

Oilbirds

Squat, mottled brown and whiskered, **oilbirds** have the honour of being the world's only nocturnal fruit-eating birds, and Trinidad supports eight breeding colonies. Spending the daylight hours inside their caves, oilbirds are unusually gregarious; up to forty birds will huddle on a single ledge, squawking and picking through each others' feathers for parasites. Mature birds venture into the open only at night, using sonar to assist their manoeuvres through the forests in search of palm, laurel and camphor fruits, often travelling as far as 120km from the colony in each foray. Fruits are swallowed whole and the seeds regurgitated, and in-flight consumption is an important agent of reforestation.

Oilbirds rear one **brood** of young each year, laying between two and four eggs over several days in nests constructed from regurgitated, cement-like matter that rapidly turns the snowy white clutch a dirty brown. Both parents share the 32-day incubation, after which the blind, featherless fledglings emerge, remaining immobile for up to three weeks and feeding on partially digested fruit pulp. Development is slow; a patchy cover of downy feathers grows after 21 days, and young birds do not fledge until they are 100 to 120 days old.

A young oilbird weighs twice as much as a mature one, due to the high **fat content** that gave rise to the name. The Amerindians and Capuchin monks used to boil the fledglings down for their oil, which they then used to fuel cooking fires and make flambeaux. The Amerindians also called the oilbird guacharo, "the one who wails and mourns", on account of the rasps, screams, squawks and snarls that make up its call; an eerie sound that also inspired the bird's French patois sobriquet, diablotin – devil bird.

beady blue eyes, a truly exotic call and a marvellous way of building nests: metre-long, teardrop-shaped constructions of dry grass that hang in groups from tree boughs. Though it can be hard to spot the **bearded bellbird**, you'll certainly hear its penetrating "bok, bok" call in the forests. Birds of prey include the **peregrine falcon**, as well as several **kites** and **hawks**, including the **ornate hawk-eagle**, the largest of the lot. The ubiquitous **vultures** – called corbeaux – perform a necessary if unsavoury function by devouring dead animals.

Tobago sustains a few species not seen regularly in Trinidad, such as the **red-crowned woodpecker**, **rufous-tailed jacamar** and the **white-tailed sabrewing**. The smaller island is also the best place to see **blue-crowned mot-mots** (locally called king of the woods), with deep orange breasts, green-blue heads and long flowing tail feathers, as well as seabirds such as the red-billed tropic bird. Offshore of both islands, **boobies** and **brown pelicans** trawl for fish, the latter being the only pelican to dive from great heights into the sea, scooping up its quarry in its large pouched bill. However, if a **frigate bird** is around, smaller sea birds often lose their catch, as the frigate feeds on stolen goods snatched from the beak of more efficient fishers.

Insects and spiders

With 92 varieties of **mosquito** in T&T, and far too many kinds of **cockroach** (ranging from 7-centimetre dark brown pests to the rare albino variety), you could be forgiven for doing your best to disregard the rest of the country's invertebrate life, but many species are vital to the local ecosystems. More than 600 varieties of **butterfly** flit between local flowers, ranging from the 2-centimetre crimson-and-black red devil to the commonly seen bright blue 7-centimetre emperor and the cocoa mort bleu, brown and mauve with eye-like spots on the wings.

Armies of black, brown or red bachac or **leaf-cutting ants**, with almost triangular heads and sharp, sizeable pincers, are divided into ranks. Large workers trim entire shrubs into coin-sized pieces and carry them on their backs to the nest, while smaller workers fend off any potential predators. The leaf-pieces are then shredded and chewed into compost for the cultivation of the fungus that feeds the colony. A single nest may discard as much as 20 cubic metres of waste material in five years, banking it up over the subterranean colony, which houses up to 2.5 million ants. Living in equally complex societies of up to one billion, **termites** attach their large, irregular earthen nests to the sides of trees; when crushed, termites give off the unmistakable odour of fresh carrots.

Aside from the spindly-limbed specimens that inhabit interior corners, the largest common **spiders** are black and red orb web spinners, about 8 centimetres long including the legs, which spin the classic hexagonal trap. More unusual is the **trapdoor spider**, which conceals its forest-floor burrow with a hinged doorway, springing out to drag passing prey into the hole. Ten species of **tarantula** range from a delicately hued violet and brown to hairy and black, and can measure between 8 and 15 centimetres including the legs. Apart from a bird-eating variety, most are nocturnal insect hunters that construct their basic, messy-looking web tunnels on grassy banks or in dead wood.

Marine life

Sediment flows from the Orinoco River have prevented the build-up of extensive **reefs** around Trinidad, but off Tobago, where visibility ranges from 12 to 50 metres, are some of the Caribbean's richest and most pristine reefs. Among the sixty or so **coral** varieties are rotund brains, patterned with furrowed trenches, branching umber elkhorn and staghorn, stalagmite-like pillar coral and cool green star coral. Extremely striking are the gorgonian group of intricate soft coral sea plumes, sea whips and purple sea fans while brilliant yellow anemones and red, brown, purple and green sponges provide a splash of colour, some growing up to three feet in diameter. **Caribbean spiny lobsters** and green or spotted **moray eels** lurk in the crevices between corals – if provoked, the eels can inflict a nasty bite.

Sand flats and seagrass fields between the reefs host spiny black **sea urchins**; the spines of round **white urchins** are too short to puncture skin. Long, thin and off-white, **sea cucumbers** sift through the sea floor to feed on deposited nutrients, while **starfish** and **queen conch** snails move slowly along the seagrass blades, hoovering up organisms that live there.

The reefs harbour a huge variety of multi-coloured tropical **fish**, including parrot fish, electric blue creole wrasse, queen and French angel fish, striped grunts and spiny puffer fish – which balloon in size if threatened – as well as tarpon and trigger fish. Giant seven-metre **manta rays** are best seen around Speyside in Tobago (see p.316); you'll also encounter smaller eagle, spot-

ted and Atlantic torpedo rays, and southern stingrays. **Dolphins** and **porpoises** are common, while the docile fifteen-metre **whale sharks** are occasional visitors, feeding on plankton and small fish. Other **large fish** include reef, tiger and nurse **sharks**, grouper, dolphin (the fish not the mammal), kingfish (wahoo), tuna, blackjack, marlin, blue cavalli, sailfish, bonita and barracuda.

Trees and shrubs

Although T&T's woodlands are disappearing at a rate of 2 percent a year, they still make up around 46 percent of the country's total land area. Several different forest types are found on the islands, including thick, warm and wet **evergreen** and **deciduous** woodlands. Higher elevations see **montane** forest, wet and cool with plenty of epiphytic growth, while the stubby 2-metre canopy of **elfin** forest occupies only the highest mountain peaks.

About **350 species** of tree grow in T&T, including the exotically named pink bark, gustacare, crapaud, saltfishwood, sardine, purpleheart, bloodwood, hairy cutlet and naked Indian. The main forest trees are **mora**, **teak**, **mahogany**, **cedar**, **cypre**, **Caribbean pine** and balata; the latter produces a milky latex used to coat golf balls. Immediately noticeable, the **bois cano** has large, deeply lobed leaves that dry into a distinctive claw shape while the mighty 40-metre **silk cotton** or kapok tree (its fruits contain the cotton-like kapok) boasts an impressive girth of buttressed roots spreading elegantly to meet the ground; Amerindians used entire trees for their dug-out pirogues. The spreading branches of the **samaan** are often employed to shade cocoa and coffee, while the **banyan** looks more like a collection of interweaved vines than a tree, as its boughs produce aerial roots that form secondary trunks when they reach the ground. The **tree fern's** diamond-patterned trunk and top-heavy crown of fern-like leaves lend a primeval aspect to high altitude forests.

Ornamental trees

A host of **ornamental** trees turn T&T's forests into a patchwork of colour in the dry months (Dec–May), when the intense orange-red flowers of the mountain **immortelle** compete with two varieties of **poui**, which shed their leaves to make way for cascades of dusky pink or bright yellow blossoms. The **cassia** also produces prolific cascades of deep yellow or pink flowers. Covering a flat, wide-spreading crown, the deep red **flamboyant** or poinciana flowers bloom in August as well as April; during the dry season, half-metre pods full of rattling seeds dangle from the leafless branches.

Flowering sporadically throughout the year, the 15-metre **African tulip** or "flame of the forest" produces clusters of deep red blooms along outer branches; unopened buds in the centre of the flower are sometimes used as natural water pistols, as they contain a pouch of water which spurts out at speed when pressure is applied. Creating patches of mauve throughout Trinidad's forests, the crown of the **crepe myrtle** is usually smothered with blooms, while **bauhinia** or orchid tree and **jacaranda** add to the purple hues.

Fruit trees

Among the huge variety of **fruit trees**, the most easily recognizable is the **mango**, with its rounded, dense crown of long, leathery leaves over a short trunk. Diminutive, twisty-branched **guava** trees grow wild throughout the islands; crack open one of its green-skinned, pink-fleshed fruit and you're sure to see a squirming contingent of small white worms. **Banana** plants are not trees in the strict botanical sense; their huge, tattered leaves grow from a central stem made up of overlapping leaf bases. Covered by large purple bracts, the flowers hang from the main stem and eventually develop into the fruit. **Plantain** trees are similar, with larger, less tattered leaves and bigger, more robust fruit. Equally easy to recognize, **pawpaw** (papaya) has a long hollow stem with large splayed leaves and fruit at the top. The fruit of **West Indian cherry** trees are bright red when ripe; they look similar to their temperate counterparts, but are much more sour. An excellent source of vitamin C, they are sweetened and juiced.

Still grown in groves for export, **cocoa** is easily identifiable by its lichen-smothered trunk, dark green shiny leaves and 20-centimetre ridged oval pods that grow from the trunk and turn from light green to brown, yellow, orange or purple when ripe. Covered with a sweet white gloop, the beans inside are sucked when raw, but are usually dried and roasted to make cocoa powder. **Cashew** trees, with their strongly veined oval leaves, are common; the familiar nut pokes out

of the bottom of a sweet-tasting, pear-shaped red fruit, whose shell produces an oily liquid that is a skin irritant. With dark, evergreen leaves, **nutmeg** trees produce a peach-like fruit that encases the nut, itself covered with a bright red network of mace.

The lifeblood of many a craft vendor, the fruits of the **calabash** tree grow to more than 35 centimetres in diameter and are traditionally halved and hollowed out to make bowls. Tall and compound-leaved, the **tamarind** tree bears a 10-centimetre brown pod; when ripe, the inner seeds are surrounded by an acidic pulp that's used to make tamarind balls, drinks and as a seasoning. Used as a vegetable but classified as a fruit, **breadfruit** was brought to the Caribbean by Captain Bligh aboard the *HMS Providence* as food for plantation slaves. With spreading branches decorated by large serrated leaves, the spherical fruits are lime green and pockmarked. Its close cousin is the chataigne or **breadnut**, a similar tree with smaller, spiky fruits that are eaten roasted.

Coastal trees and palms

Trinidad's swamps of red, black and white **mangrove** trees, with their dense tangle of aerial roots, protect coastal communities from hurricane surges, filter sediments that smother reefs and provide a nursery for fish and crustaceans.

Among the most common seashore plants is the **Indian almond**, with its symmetrical branches; the nuts can be eaten once the outer pods turn brown, though they don't taste like conventional almonds. On exposed shores, the **sea grape** lies low and twisted, but in less windswept conditions it's wide and spreading, and can attain a height of 15 metres. The flat, round leaves are distinctively veined and turn a deep red as they mature. Once they've turned purple, the grapes are edible if a little sour. Definitely one to avoid, the **manchineel** tree also grows to about 15 metres with a wide spreading canopy dotted with indistinct green fruits and flowers, all of which are extremely **poisonous** – even standing below a manchineel during rain incurs blistering from washed-down sap.

Commercial plantations on both islands have made the **coconut** T&T's most prevalent palm. It's an incredibly versatile tree; the water and meat are consumed fresh at the jelly stage, while the flesh of older coconuts is grated and used in baking or immersed in water and strained to produce the coconut milk that flavours a thousand local dishes. Coconut oil is used in soap, cosmetics and cooking, while the leaf fronds thatch roofs and make hats or floor mats, the husks are used to make floor buffers and pieces of hard shell are made into jewellery and cups.

There are many varieties of **ornamental palm**: often used to mark out driveways, the 30-metre **royal palm** is classically shaped with bushy fronds and a grey, ruler-straight trunk with a green section near to the top. Similar but even taller at an average of 40 metres, the **cabbage palm** has thicker, messier looking fronds. Squat and dominated by its spiky leaves, the **cocorite** is one of the most common forest palms. The ultimate in tropical splendour, the **traveller's palm** is actually a member of the banana family – the name refers to mini-ponds at the base of the trunk that provide a convenient water source. Fronds fan out from the base in an enormous peacock's tail shape as high as 10 metres.

Plants and flowers

Of T&T's various **wild plants**, some notable specimens include the **jumbie bead vine**, which produces shiny red and black poisonous seeds used in craft items and as good luck charms; they are said to ward off evil spirits, and a bead kept in a purse will keep it filled with money. A variety of mimosa with scratchy stems, **ti Marie** grows prolifically throughout the islands, and resembles a miniature bracken. It's also known as 'the sensitive plant' for its ability to curl back its leaves at the slightest touch.

The largest of the epiphytes that grow along tree branches, electricity wires and any available surface is the **wild pine bromeliad**, a spikyleafed relative of the pineapple that produces a battered-looking red flower. These "air plants" are not parasites – they draw their nutrients from the mineral-rich rainforest atmosphere – but host trees have been known to collapse under the weight of several of them. Ten-litre water reserves trapped between the leaves provide a habitat for insects and frogs. Other epiphytes include a 700-strong contingent of **orchids**, many of them so small that you'll need a magnifying glass to appreciate them. These chancers grow on living or dead plant or tree matter and in low-

land savannahs such as Aripo in eastern Trinidad. In the lowland forests, both the **monkey throat** and the pendulous **jack spaniard** with its trailing wasp-like petals are particularly distinctive, while the common **lamb's tail** grows horizontally from large trees, and has attractive maroon-flecked green petals with a white and pink stamen.

T&T's most eye-catching flora, however, are the 2300 varieties of **flowering plant** which provide beds, borders and hedges with a splash of colour, and you'll often see several varieties of multicoloured **croton** leaves in between the blooms. The national flower is the **chaconia**, a wild poinsettia which grows throughout the local forests, but the ubiquitous **bougainvillea** is the most spectacular ornamental, its red, white, orange and pink papery bracts spilling out into intensely coloured clumps. Distinguishable by its protruding pollen-tipped stamen, **hibiscus** takes on an abundance of hues and shapes; the lacy **coral hibiscus** has clusters of tiny curling red petals and a red frill at the end of the stamen, while the popular **Mexican creeper** provides a clambering shower of delicate pink or white. A dark-leafed shrub with clusters of small red flowers, **ixora** is another popular ornamental that flowers throughout the year.

Flamboyant **tropical flowers** are grown commercially in T&T as well as flourishing in the wild. Brush-like **ginger lilies** are one of the most common exotics; the deep pink or red bracts hide the insignificant true flower, and the shiny, bananalike leaves are used in flower arrangements. A close relative, the **torch ginger's** deep crimson cluster of thick waxy petals makes an impressively showy head. However, the queen of local exotics – and the symbol of the PNM political party – are the 40 vividly coloured varieties of **balisier**, all members of the heliconia family, which include the aptly named **lobster claw** and the red, yellow and green **hanging heliconia**, which looks like a series of fish hanging from a rod. Equally prevalent are the artificial-looking **anthuriums**, a shiny, heart-shaped red, pink or white bract with a long penile stem or spadix protruding from the centre. The flashy **bird of paradise**, a blue and purple flower that resembles a bird's head graced by a deep orange crest, is rarer.

Language

T&T's rich and varied vocabulary stems both from the republic's tumultuous history and from a love of wordplay. Amerindians, the Spanish and the French have all left their mark in the names of towns and villages around the country such as Arima, Sangre Grande and Pierreville. In isolated villages such as Paramin in Trinidad, French Creole (or patois) is still a working means of communication for village elders. Meanwhile Spanish surfaces in parang lyrics, and Hindi is still spoken in Indian communities.

The diverse ethnic mix of the nation has also influenced **Creole English**; Trinis will say, "its making hot" as the French would say "Il fait chaud". Terms such as *pomme cythere* (golden apple) and *dou dou* (sweetheart, from the French *doux doux*) are commonplace, and French patois phrases are still part of the vernacular; *tout bagai* and *toute monde* are catch-alls meaning "everything". Hindi words, such as *dougla* and *aloo* (potato), have also entered the language.

The language is often oblique and allusive. **Double entendres** – possibly a legacy of slavery, when people had to watch what they said – are common, especially in **calypsos** as a means of voicing political criticism to avoid libel actions. Nicknames, such as "Silver Fox" for Basdeo Panday, the current prime minister, are used, and if you are not well versed in local slang you'll need a Trini interpreter to appreciate the subtleties of the songs.

Some Trini expressions

Cockroach have no right in fowl party Don't involve yourself in situations where you are unwelcome or out of place.

Crab in a barrel Futile backstabbing, from the way crabs will pull one another down in their attempts to escape from a barrel, so that none succeeds.

Crapaud smoke your pipe You are in big trouble.

De fruit doh fall far from de tree Children often turn out like their parents.

Every bread have it cheese Everyone, no matter how ugly, will find his or her matching partner.

Get cage before yuh ketch bird Before you can ensnare a woman, you need a house to put her in.

If you play with dog, you must get fleas Hanging out with lowlifes will eventually rub off on you.

Like yuh went to school in August and yuh best subject was recess A description of someone who is not too intelligent.

Man plans, God laughs It doesn't matter what you plan to do, it never turns out that way.

Now yuh cookin' with gas When you finally understand something; getting the picture.

When cock get teeth Pigs might fly.

Yuh cyar play sailor an' fraid power If you're going to be controversial you have to accept the consequences.

Zandolie fin' yuh hole Disparaging advice meaning know your place and stick to it.

Glossary

Abir Pink dye thrown around by (and amongst) participants of the Hindu Phagwa festival.

Ajoupa Amerindian building with a palm-thatch roof and walls of clay and cow manure.

All fours Popular card game, often played for money.

Babash An illegal, extremely potent bootleg white rum, also called bush rum and mountain dew.

Bachac Large, black-brown leaf-cutting ant, which gives a nasty bite.

Bad head Being drunk or having a hangover.

Bad John Man of violent or criminal reputation, now a bit outdated.

Bamsie Bottom; backside.

Bandit A thief or mugger.

Bareback When a man is naked from the waist up. Also unprotected sex.

Bashment A big party, as in "de bashment fete for 98", or something very good.

Bath suit Swim suit.

Beastly Used to describe an extremely cold beer.

Beat pan To play the steel pan.

Big truck Large bottom, usually a woman's.

Big up To promote yourself and give thanks to others.

Big yard Trinidad's largest panyard; the Savannah at Panorama time.

Bill it To roll a joint.

Block A specific area, as in "he cool, he's from meh block"; also a liming spot for local youths, as in "mih see Harrison by de block las' night", and a place where weed is sold on the street.

Blue food Root vegetables such as dasheen or tannia.

Blues The TT$100 dollar bill.

Blunt A marijuana joint.

Bobo Cut, graze or scab.

Bobol Corruption, embezzlement.

Boldfaced Being pushy or demanding.

Boo No good, worthless, usually used in reference to low grade weed.

Bow To engage in oral sex.

Brush Sexual intercourse.

Brabadap Loud or uncouth person.

Brands Name-brand clothing, usually sportswear.

Brass band The bands that back live acts at fetes; traditionally, soca and calypso songs hinge on a repeated brass refrain.

Break a lime To leave when a lime is in full swing, causing others to think about leaving, and often used to guilt-trip the person who wants to leave.

Brethren Friends.

Buller Derogative term for a gay man.

Bump To get a light from someone else's cigarette.

Bumper Another word for backside, usually a woman's. Of Jamaican origin. (See also "big truck".)

Bush Generic term for forests and undeveloped countryside, as in "me doh trust de bush, not at all". Also medicinal herbs; a "bush bath", "bush tea".

Buss To do something; eg to "buss a lime". Also bust, broken.

Cascadura Scaly black fish with folklore behind it; if you eat it, you're destined to end your days in Trinidad.

Charged Inebriated; drunk.

Chinee Person of Chinese descent.

Chip-chip Mollusc found on Trinidad's beaches; see **pacro**.

Chipping Slow shuffling walk with a rhythm dictated by the music from trucks and steel bands during Carnival.

Commesse Confusion, controversy.

Cook up/cook out Food prepared in one pot, usually outside.

Coolie Derogatory term for someone of Indian descent.

Creole A broad term describing a person of mixed European and African descent born in T&T. Also classic Caribbean food, such as callaloo and coo-coo.

Cut eye A nasty look, also a "bad eye".

Cutlass Machete.

Darkers Sunglasses.

Dotish Stupid, ridiculous looking. Sometimes "doltishness" as well.

Dou dou Sweetheart.

Dougla Person of mixed Indian and African parentage.

Ease up To slacken, as in "ease up yuh mout'" (be quiet).

East Indian A person of Indian descent.

Ent Coined by Ronnie McIntosh's song of the same name, used at the end of a statement to mean "is that not so" or "that's true isn't it?"

Enviggle To persuade someone against their better judgement to do something.

Fatigue Witty repartee.

Fete A large, open-air party or concert; the biggest fetes are held around Carnival time.

Feting Attending fetes, partying.

Flambeaux A flaming torch made by filling a glass bottle with kerosene and lighting the cloth wick. Used by oyster salesmen to advertise their wares.

Flask A half bottle of rum.

Flex To let loose or party intensively, also a mode of behaviour, as in "I does flex positively".

Flim Film, movie.

Free up Relax, let go.

Fresh water yankee Mocking term for Trinbagonians who use foreign mannerisms picked up during short trips to the US.

Friending Having a sexual relationship with someone.

Frizzle-fowl Breed of chicken with rumpled feathers that make it look like it's been dragged through a hedge backwards.

Fronting Pretentious, false behaviour put on in order to impress others.

Funk The end of a weed joint, attached to a cigarette to make it last a little longer and give a subtle added high.

Gallery Verandah or porch where you can sit outside.

Get on bad To dance and jump up with abandon at a fete.

Goin' down Making a serious commitment in a relationship.

Ground provisions Root vegetable tubers (yam, dasheen etc), also just "provisions".

Gyal Girl, young woman.

Hard wuk Rough and passionate sex; wuk (work) is a general term for sex.

Hops Bread rolls, usually eaten as "hops an' ham".

Horning Two-timing, being unfaithful to your partner.

Horrors Lots of problems, bad vibes caused by anger.

Ignorant Quick to take offence, antagonistic.

Ital Rastafarian term meaning natural or pure, often used to refer to meatless food cooked with little salt.

Jackspaniard Large, aggressive hornet-like wasp which delivers a vicious sting; also called a jep.

Jamette Woman of questionable morals; also known as a jagabat.

Jammin' Working hard.

Jumbie Spirit or ghost, also a night person; "boy, you does favour a jumbie calling meh at this time in night."

Jump-up Frenetic partying or a frenetic party.

Kaiso Old-time word for calypso music, still frequently used in the calypso tents.

Ketch it To get high on marijuana.

Lackeray Gossiping.

Laginiappe Pronounced "lan-nyap", a little extra, a bonus.

Las' lap Final parade of revellers on Carnival Tuesday before the abstinence of Lent begins.

Licks To lash or hit someone.

Lickser Person who gets free things through sly methods, used with a tone of admiration.

Lime To socialize with friends on the street, in a bar, in a person's house, by a river, anywhere. T&T's favourite pastime.

Lock off Maintain a low profile for a while.

Lyrics Flirtatious sweet talk, usually from a man to a woman.

Maaga Skinny, slim.

Macco A busybody prying into other people's business.

Macco man Derogatory term for an effeminate and gossipy man.

Maljo Evil eye.

Malkadi Epilepsy. Having a fit.

Mamaguy To fool someone with smart talk, making false promises.

Mampy Fat woman.

Mas Short for masquerade; one can "play mas" (buy a costume and be part of a Carnival band), or "make mas" (create the costumes).

Mas camps Headquarters of Carnival bands, where costumes are made.

Mauvais langue Damaging gossip.

Melongene Aubergine, eggplant. Also called by its Indian name *baigan*.

Nannie Indian term for a woman's private parts.

Navel string Placenta, buried by the superstitious under a fruiting mango tree to ensure a prosperous life. Also used to denote someone's roots or a place they frequent, as in "yuh navel string eh buried in Carnival fete yuh know".

Ol' mas Raw and ready mas played on Jouvert morning.

Ol' talk Idle chatter.

One time Immediately, now.

Outside man/woman A person with whom you are committing adultery.

Pacro Sea barnacle cooked up into "pacro water", a thin fishy broth said to have aphrodisiac qualities.

Pan The steel drum as a musical instrument.

Panyard Headquarters of steel pan bands.

continued overleaf

Glossary continued

Pappy show From puppet show, meaning nonsense, something inconsequential and ridiculous.

Parlour Small grocery store.

Pelt To throw.

Petit carem Dry spell in the middle of the rainy season, usually in September.

Picong The tradition of making fun of someone through an exchange of witty comments.

Piper Crack user.

Pitch oil Kerosene.

Plam plam Vagina.

Planasse To hit someone with the flat part of a machete.

Pot hound Skinny mongrel dog.

Pressure General term for stress or problems, as in "it real pressure, man".

Prim To be high on marijuana.

Provision ground Vegetable garden.

Puja Indian prayer or offering to the gods.

Pum pum Vagina. Pum pum shorts are tight hot pants.

Puncheon High proof rum.

Ras Dreadlocks or a person with them.

Raggamuffin Borrowed from Jamaican slang, in T&T this describes a young, streetwise person.

Real Plenty.

Reds Someone of African descent but with a light skin colour, also known as high brown.

Respect Used as a greeting especially between Rastafarians.

Safe A multi-faceted term mainly used as an affirmation meaning all will be OK.

Saga boy Flashy dresser.

Salt fish Salted cod, as well as a crude euphemism for a woman's vagina.

Scheups A sign of irritation, disapproval or derision also known as kissing or sucking the teeth. Dating back to the 1800s, this common sound in Trinidadian conversation came from the French planters who used it as a way of undermining the authority of the new British rulers.

Scruntin' Penniless, broke.

Sea bath To go for a swim in the sea.

Semi demi Something unexpected, a little bit of magic.

Sensie Marijuana, short for sensimilla.

Sketel Usually a woman who sleeps around, but can also be used for a man.

Slackness Impolite, crude and low-down behaviour.

Sound system A crew of DJs operating the decks and providing the huge speaker boxes at fetes and parties.

Spranger Crack user, petty thief or volatile person.

Storm Getting into a fete without paying by climbing over the fence, sweet talking the doorman etc.

Stupidness The preferred term to describe ridiculous, slack, time-consuming actions or behaviour.

Sweetman A man who is financially supported by a woman.

Swizzle stick A whisk used for stirring callaloo or juicing fruits to make punch.

Tabanca The depression caused by the ending of a love affair. In extreme states, "tabantruck".

Tan-ta-na Excitement, confusion.

Tanty Aunt or a person who is like an aunt.

Tapia Hut made with thatch and mud walls.

Ting A thing, woman or a euphemism for all kinds of eventualities – "tings a gwan".

Tobago love Disguising your feelings for a loved one, possibly due to finding it difficult to express your emotions.

Torshont (pronounced "torshore") A loofah.

Totie Penis; the title of Errol Fabian's 1998 calypso "Ato Tea Party" was a play on the word; all those named in the song were strenuous in their efforts to deny that they wanted to taste some of "Ato tea" (Ato Bolden is Trinbago's most celebrated athlete).

Trace A road or street that once was or still is a dirt track.

Travel Using public transport.

Vex Angry or annoyed.

Vex money Extra money to take out with you, in case you have an argument with your partner and have to pay your own way home.

Wapie A card game.

Wassi Lewd, uninhibited behaviour and dancing at fetes; wining down to the ground.

We is we You are among friends.

Wine To dance by rotating hips and bottom in an erotic manner. Your wining bone is what allows you to move with suitable sensuality.

Wrapping paper Cigarette paper used for rolling joints.

Wutless Worthless, no good.

Yampie Matter that collects at the corner of the eyes after sleep

Yard fowl Chickens raised in someone's backyard.

Zaboca Avocado.

Zig zag Altering your opinions to fit the circumstances.

Other idiosyncrasies include a habit of using the part to refer to the whole, calling an arm a hand, or a leg a foot – when someone breaks their arm, for example, they'll say "meh han break". People will also describe the afternoon as evening – it's common to be greeted with "good evening" at 3pm, while "goodnight" is used as a greeting. "Local" is used to refer to the country as a whole, everywhere else is "outside" or "in foreign".

Trini Tidbits

When opening a bottle of rum, a capful is thrown onto the ground "for the spirit".

In memory of the dead, on the day of their wake, the street where the deceased lived is lined with candles on the pavement.

Trinis avoid walking on concrete manhole covers, not out of superstition but from a well-founded fear that they will collapse.

On hearing T&T's national anthem, all Trinis come to a direct halt and stand silently to attention – you are expected to do the same.

Meals are rarely eaten together in families unless it is a special occasion; usually a pot with food is left on the stove for each individual to dip into when necessary.

Trinis go everywhere with their "rags" – a facecloth or bandanna to wipe sweat, wave in a fete or place over their head as night falls – to prevent dew causing a head cold.

If it starts to rain, Trinis stop – waiting under shop awnings for the shower to pass. "It was raining" is a valid excuse for being late, even for a job interview.

All Trinis peel their oranges in the same way, using a knife in a circular motion from top to bottom, leaving the pith intact.

Expect a Trini goodbye to take half an hour from the point that they say they are leaving. If you're waiting for a lift, patience is essential while the goodbyes are done slowly and diplomatically to ensure no one is left out and a good vibe is kept.

Books

The following books should be readily available in the US, UK and/or T&T. Where a book is only published in one country we have specified which. It is also worth visiting the library in Port of Spain – many local authors whose work is unavailable abroad are well represented in its West Indian section. If you are staying for more than a couple of weeks, you can fill out a form, pay a TT$20 refundable deposit and borrow books. In Tobago they tend to be stricter – insisting that you be in the country at least three months before they lend you books.

Fiction and poetry

Michael Anthony *Cricket in the Road and Other Stories* (Heinemann, UK). An anthology of short stories evoking the atmosphere and lifestyle of Trinidad. Concise, thought-provoking pieces, rich in description. His novel *In the Heat of the Day* (Heinemann, UK) is centred on the period of industrial unrest that led to the 1903 water riots, while *The Year in San Fernando* (Heinemann, UK) is an acute portrayal of San Fernando in the 1940s, seen through the eyes of a teenage boy on a year's sojourn from his village home.

Robert Antoni, *My Grandmother's Erotic Folk Tales* (Faber & Faber). Outlandish – though not very erotic – tales of life on Caribbean island Corpus Christi (aka Trinidad), under US military occupation during World War II, as told by a saucy 97-year-old to her grandson. Wonderfully evocative of wartime Trinidad,

Kevin Baldeosingh *The Autobiography of Paras P* (Heinemann, UK). Biting satirical novel tracing the career of the entirely ludicrous Paras Parmanandansingh, with plenty of implicit references to society figures. Extremely funny.

Valerie Belgrave *Ti Marie* (Heinemann, UK). A romantic, passionate novel set in the late eighteenth century when Britain and Spain were fighting for control of Trinidad – a Caribbean *Gone with the Wind*, but far more intelligent and historically accurate.

Brother Resistance *Rapso Explosion* (Karia Press, UK). An excellent introduction to rapso poetry compiled by the father of the art form. These politically conscious poems describe the fears, hopes, dreams and lives of Trinidad's youth in contemporary Trini dialect.

Roslyn Carrington *A Thirst for Rain* (Kensington). Sensuous love story set in the St Ann's foothills, centred around food seller Myra and her relationship with saga boy Slim, ex-stickfighter Jacob and teenage daughter Odile, with some fabulous descriptions of Port of Spain in the summer going on rainy season.

Leroy Clarke *Douens* (Karaele, US). A book of unusual, intriguing drawings and poems that draw on Trinidadian folklore to explore issues of identity and conscience.

Earl Lovelace *While Gods are Falling* (Longman, UK). The author's first novel tells the story of a young man trapped by his family responsibilities and unfulfilled by his work as he struggles to survive in an impersonal city. *The Dragon Can't Dance* (Andre Deutsch, UK) is a powerful and passionate examination of the motivation behind Carnival – if you only read one book about Trinidad, make it this one. In *The Wine of Astonishment* (Heinemann, UK), Lovelace highlights the persecution of the Spiritual Baptists, while in *The Schoolmaster* (Heinemann, UK), a powerful and superbly handled allegory of colonialism, a repected schoolmaster abuses his position of power in an isolated and ill-informed country village.

Alfred Mendes *Black Fauns* (New Beacon, UK). An interesting and amusing book about the mainly female inhabitants of a barrack yard in the 1930s. As they attempt to cope with poverty, ambition and betrayal they reveal the sense of community that made barrack yard living bearable. The cleverly plotted *Pitch Lake* (New Beacon, UK) highlights the snobbery, racism and insecurity of a young middle-class Portuguese man that eventually lead to his moral, spiritual and physical downfall.

Sharlow Mohammed *The Promise* (Sharlow, T&T). A powerful and evocative account of the experiences of the Indian indentured labourers. *When Gods were Slaves* (Sharlow, T&T) follows the fate of Anyika – the name means endurance

– from his happy life in an African village through the trials of slavery in Trinidad.

Shani Mootoo *Cereus Blooms at Midnight* (Granta, UK). This Irish-Trinidadian-Canadian author's ambitious first novel deals with the relationship between an old woman dying in a Caribbean nursing home and her young gay nurse.

Pamela Mordecai and Betty Wilson (eds); *Her True True Name* (Heinemann, UK). Collection of short stories by women writers from the Caribbean. The T&T section includes work from Dionne Brand, Rosa Guy, Marion Patrick-Jones and Merle Hodge.

Trinbagonian Literature

It is scarcely surprising that with their diverse cultural heritage, opaque dialect and witty, imaginative use of language, the people of Trinidad and Tobago have developed a rich literary heritage, producing a stable of world-class writers far out of proportion to the size of the country. This unique literary tradition emerged in the 1930s with the publication of the *Beacon*, a radical journal that ran from 1931 to 1934. Featuring poetry and short stories by young Trinidadian writers and intellectuals such as **C.L.R. James** and **Alfred Mendes**, the magazine fostered the development of "yard literature", social realist stories such as Mendes's *Black Fauns*, describing the experiences of poorer Trinidadians.

Trinbagonian literature flourished after World War II with the emergence of a new generation of novelists. **Samuel Selvon**'s wryly humorous novels chronicle both the experience of growing up in Trinidad and the trials and tribulations of an emigrant in London, while those of **Earl Lovelace** are a lyrical celebration of Trinidadian life and culture, its "shacks that leap out of the red dirt and stone, thin like smoke, fragile like kite paper balancing on their rickety pillars as broomsticks on the edge of a juggler's nose" (*The Dragon Can't Dance*).

The late 1950s saw the appearance of Trinidad's most internationally acclaimed novelist, V.S. Naipaul. The son of a journalist, Naipaul grew up in Chaguanas and Port of Spain, winning a scholarship in 1950 to study English at Oxford University. He wrote his first book, *The Mystic Masseur* (1957), at the age of 23 while working for the BBC Caribbean Service in London. It was his fourth, *A House for Mr Biswas*, that made his name in 1961. Drawing on the experiences of his father, the novel explores the frustration and claustrophobia of an ambitious intellectual in a colonial society. Naipaul's ironic treatment of the snobbery, corruption and small-mindedness of Trinidadian life has earned him an ambivalent reputation in his homeland. His brother **Shiva Naipaul** also garnered substantial literary acclaim with books such as *Fireflies* (1970) and *Beyond the Dragon's Mouth* (1984), before his sudden death of a heart attack at the age of forty in 1985.

Trinidad's best known poet, the Nobel prizewinner **Derek Walcott**, was actually born in St Lucia, but lived in Port of Spain for decades, establishing the Trinidad Theatre Workshop (see p.81) there. An accomplished and prolific lyric poet, Walcott draws on the Elizabethan tradition, using both traditional rhyme and metre and free verse to explore issues of exile and identity and evoke the rich, heady atmosphere of the Caribbean.

Among **T&T poets** to look out for are Cecil Herbert, Errol Hill, Barnabos Romon-Fortune, E.M. Roach, H.M. Telemaque, Leroy Clarke, Krishna Samaroo, Wayne Brown and Kevin Baldeosingh. **Women poets** are numerous but hard to find published; perhaps the best anthology is *Washer Woman Hangs Her Poems in the Sun*, which touch on subjects ranging from the mundane to the supernatural, providing endless insights into the Trinbago mentality.

Shiva Naipaul *Beyond the Dragon's Mouth* (Hamish Hamilton, UK) blends journalistic and fictional anecdotes of the author's travels from Port of Spain to London, Liverpool, Hull, Iran and Surinam. *The Chip-Chip Gatherers* (Hamish Hamilton, UK) is a darkly funny tale of the machinations of the one rich man in a poor rural community. His novel *Fireflies* (Hamish Hamilton, UK) chronicles with empathy and ironic humour the moral, financial and spiritual decline of a rich and influential Indo-Trinidadian family.

V.S. Naipaul *A House for Mr Biswas* (Penguin, US/UK). Mr Biswas – a newspaper journalist trapped by poverty into living with his domineering in-laws – struggles to establish his own identity. *In a Free State* (Penguin), a collection of five tales that won the Booker Prize in 1971, explores people's changing roles and attitudes when transplanted from their homelands, while the stories in *Miguel Street* (Andre Deutsch, UK Penguin) paint a picture of community life in Trinidad seen through the eyes of a small boy. *The Middle Passage* (Penguin) – the first of the travel books that have dominated Naipaul's later output – looks at the effects of colonialism on five societies in the Caribbean and South America.

Marion Patrick-Jones *J'Ouvert Morning* (Columbus Publishers, T&T). A novel spanning three generations of ordinary Trinidadians, detailing their lives and tribulations from the melodramatic to the mundane.

Lawrence Scott *Ballad for the New World and Other Stories* (Heinemann, UK). A clever collection of short stories evoking pre-Independence Trinidad and the experiences of a white boy growing up in the colony, with ironic humour and sensitivity.

Samuel Selvon *A Brighter Sun* (Longman Drumbeat, UK). An evocative and amusing story of an Indo-Trinidadian young man learning the responsibilities of adult life during the upheavals of World War II. *The Lonely Londoners* (Longman, UK) is a witty account of a group of West Indian immigrants adjusting to the cold climate, racism and big-city life of 1950s London. Its sequel, *Moses Ascending* (Heinemann, UK), is an ironic tale of an apathetic Trinidadian's experience of the Black Power movement and race relations in 1970s London.

Derek Walcott *Omeros* (Farrar, Straus, Giroux/Faber). An extraordinary tour de force that draws on Homer's *Odyssey* to produce a vast Caribbean epic of the dispossessed. Many of the works in Walcott's *Collected Poems 1948–1984* (Farrar, Straus, Giroux/Faber) evoke the sights and sounds of Trinidad, including the famous "Laventille", dedicated to V.S. Naipaul.

Margaret Watts (ed), *Washer Woman Hangs Her Poems in the Sun* (Ferguson, T&T). An anthology of modern women poets from Trinidad and Tobago, full of marvellous poems tackling everything from Carnival to Caribbean men.

History and current affairs

Michael Anthony *First in Trinidad* (Paria, T&T) An over-detailed account of the first appearances in Trinidad of everything from the postal service to Carnival; his *The Making of Port of Spain* (Caribbean Publications, T&T) and *Towns and Villages* (Circle Press, T&T) will tell you everything you could ever want to know about the capital and many of the the villages.

B. Bereton *A History of Modern Trinidad 1783–1962* (Heinemann, US/UK) The most comprehensive book on the island's history.

James Ferguson *Eastern Caribbean in Focus* (Latin America Bureau, UK). Overview of the history, culture, economics and societies of the eastern Caribbean.

P.E.T. O'Connor *Some Trinidad Yesterdays* (Inprint, T&T). Dry personal reminiscences of the son of a plantation owner and director of Texaco in Trinidad.

C.R. Ottley *Spanish Trinidad* (Longman, UK). An exhaustive account of Trinidad's history from 1498 to 1797. *The Story of Tobago* (Longman, UK) is an engaging account of Tobago's history from the Caribs to Hurricane Flora in 1965.

M.S. Ramesar *Survivors of Another Crossing* (University of the West Indies Press, T&T). An excellent, informative book with photographs recording the experiences of the indentured Indians from 1845 to the 1930s.

Selwyn Ryan *Revolution and Reaction, The Disillusioned Electorate* and *The Muslimeen Grab for Power* (all University of the West Indies Press, T&T). Three excellent accounts of recent T&T history: the first covers the Black Power years, the slump of the 1970s and the subsequent oil boom; the second deals with the economic downturn of the late 1980s, the disintegration of the PNM and the rise and rapid fall of the NAR; while the third analyses the causes and impact of the 1990 coup attempt.

E. Williams *History of the Peoples of Trinidad and Tobago* (A&B Distributors, US). Before becoming T&T's first prime minister, Williams was a respected academic and expert on Caribbean history; his book gives an excellent background to the development of the islands.

Trini life and culture

Gerard A. Besson (ed.) *Trinidad Carnival* (Paria, T&T). Reproduction of Caribbean Quarterly's 1956 Carnival edition, this collection of pieces from eminent Trinidadian academics and musicologists is sometimes a little heavy, but has fascinating accounts of the development of Carnival from the nineteenth century to the 1950s.

Adrian Bird *Trinidad Sweet* (Inprint, T&T). If you ignore the occasional sexist comment this book provides an excellent and detailed insight into Trinidadian culture, mentality and the island. Full of anecdotes, humorous observations and fascinating titbits.

Hunter Davies *A Walk around the West Indies* (Trafalgar Square, US/Orion, UK). Personal travelogue of luxury holidays in the islands, with an interesting chapter on Tobago, but more useful for the perspective it puts on T&T in comparison to the rest of the region (though Trinidad is ignored and branded somewhat dangerous).

Dave DeWitt and Mary Jane Willan *Callaloo, Calypso and Carnival* (Crossing Press, US). Lively and informative cookbook-cum-travel guide, with accounts of T&T, calypso, Carnival, culinary and wider history, and including all the classic recipes, from pelau to black cake.

Patrick Leigh Fermor *The Traveller's Tree* (Penguin, UK). Written in the late 1940s, this classic account of a Caribbean tour has an interesting section on Trinidad, describing Port of Spain with an eagle eye and analysing the island's history, as well as its music and the "saga boy" fashions of the time.

Martin Haynes *Trinidad and Tobago Dialect* (Plus) (self-published, T&T). Hard to get hold of out of Trinidad but well worth it; Trini patois divided up into themes; "jorts" (food) "t'reads" (clothes) and "fete-in" (partying) as well as some beautiful sayings, old wives' tales and proverbs.

C.L.R. James *Beyond a Boundary* (Duke University Press/Random House). Autobiographical book on cricket and life in Trinidad in the 1920s.

Amryl Johnson *Sequins for a Ragged Hem* (Virago, UK). Intense and personal portrayal of Trinidad, Tobago and other Caribbean islands as seen by a woman born in Trinidad but living in Britain.

Paul Keens-Douglas *Lal Shop* (Keensdee, T&T). A collection of anecdotes written for the author's *Sunday Express* column "Is Town Say So". Each piece is a random reproduction of classic "ol' talk", with titles such as "Yu ever stop to wonder how calypsonians get dey name?" or "Dat boil corn sufferin' from real malnutrition". Difficult to get hold of out of T&T, this engaging slice of rum shop banter written in patois gives a good picture of local sensibilities.

Luise Kimme *Chachalaca* (self-published, T&T). Evocative, intense snippets of Tobago life lovingly – and idiosyncratically – described in German and English by emigrant sculptor Kimme. Available from her studio in Tobago (see p.281).

Peter van Koningsbruggen *Trinidad Carnival: Quest for a National Identity* (Macmillan, UK). An excellent examination of attitudes surrounding Carnival and its socio-economic impact on Trinidad.

John Newel Lewis *Ajoupa* (self-published, T&T, o/p). A marvellously idiosyncratic and enthusiastic account of the unique architecture of Trinidad and Tobago, illustrated by the author's superb line drawings.

Zenga Longmore *Tap-Taps to Trinidad* (Hodder & Stoughton, UK). Caribbean travelogue with an excellent T&T account, during which the author is at the mercy of her tyrannical Trini aunt.

Peter Manuel *Caribbean Currents* (Latin America Bureau, UK). Excellent, well-researched account of the Caribbean music scene with a strong T&T section that details the development of soca and calypso as well as Indian music and culture.

Peter Mason *Bacchanal! Carnival, Calypso and the Popular Culture of Trinidad* (Temple University Press/Latin America Bureau). Packed with interviews with calypsonians and costume designers, this is the most up-to-date and informative book on Trinidad's Carnival.

Olga Mavrogordato *Voices in the Street* (Inprint, T&T). Detailing the history of some of the many old buildings around Port of Spain.

John Mendes *Cote Ce, Cote La* (self-published, T&T). The original dictionary of Trinbagonian words, with sections on Carnival and proverbs and drawings by Carnival designer Wayne Berkley. Widely available on the islands.

Raymond Quevedo *Atilla's Kaiso* (University of the West Indies Press, T&T). Written by veteran kaisonian Atilla the Hun shortly before his death, this provides a true insider's view of the development of calypso as well as the lyrics of some of his best compositions.

Lystra St John *Remedies and Recipes of my Ancestry* (self-published, T&T). A materia medica of Trinbago bush medicine with sections on supernatural illness, remedy and ailment lists, botanical and local names for herbs and a selection of African and Trinbagonian recipes.

Keith Warner *The Trinidad Calypso* (Heinemann, UK). Excellent history of calypso.

Steve Vertovec *Hindu Trinidad* (Macmillan, UK). Concise academic review of Hindu religion and culture in Trinidad, with an excess of facts and figures.

Natural history

Richard Ffrench *A Guide to the Birds of Trinidad and Tobago* (Macmillan, UK). Definitive guide to T&T's bird life with entries on all the species that include information on habitat, habits, appearance and calls as well as a description of the islands' natural history and environment. The pocket-sized version with pictures and descriptions of 83 common species is handy for travellers.

Julian Kenny *Native Orchids of the Eastern Caribbean* (Macmillan, UK). Beautifully illustrated orchid guide with special emphasis on Trinidad's orchids, written by a professor at the University of the West Indies.

G.W. Lennox & S.A. Seddon *Flowers of the Caribbean; Fruits and Vegetables of the Caribbean; Trees of the Caribbean* (all Macmillan, UK). Slim and handy reference volumes with glossy, sharp colour pictures and concise accounts.

Guidebooks

Comeau, Guy, Hesterman and Hill *T&T Field Naturalists' Club Trail Guide* (T&T Field Naturalists' Club, T&T). Definitive guide to hiking trails in Trinidad and Tobago with detailed descriptions, lengths and sketch maps. Useful sections on local geology and preparing for a hike but difficult to get hold of, though a new edition is in production.

Richard Ffrench and Peter Bacon *Nature Trails of Trinidad* (S.M Publications, T&T). Easy to use, up-to-date guide to hikes in Trinidad.

Kathleen O'Donnell and Harry Pefkaros *Adventure Guide to Trinidad and Tobago* (Hunter, US). Not very adventurous, and the hand-drawn maps are terrible, but the highly personal style makes for some interesting observations.

Elizabeth Saft (ed) *Insight Guide to Trinidad and Tobago* (APA, UK). Lavishly illustrated and full of good contextual information written by local experts, if a little thin on practicalities.

Index

Will you have enough stories to tell your grandchildren?

Yahoo! Travel

Do You YAHOO!?

The ideas expressed in this code were developed by and for independent travellers.

Learn About The Country You're Visiting
Start enjoying your travels before you leave by tapping into as many sources of information as you can.

The Cost Of Your Holiday
Think about where your money goes - be fair and realistic about how cheaply you travel. Try and put money into local peoples' hands; drink local beer or fruit juice rather than imported brands and stay in locally owned accommodation. Haggle with humour and not aggressively. Pay what something is worth to you and remember how wealthy you are compared to local people.

Embrace The Local Culture
Open your mind to new cultures and traditions. Think carefully about what's appropriate in terms of your clothes and the way you behave. You'll earn respect and be more readily welcomed by local people. Respect local laws and attitudes towards drugs and alcohol that vary in different countries and communities. Think about the impact you could have on them.

Exploring The World – The Travellers' Code
Being sensitive to these ideas means getting more out of your travels - and giving more back to the people you meet and the places you visit.

Minimise Your Environmental Impact
Think about what happens to your rubbish - take biodegradable products and a water filter bottle. Be sensitive to limited resources like water, fuel and electricity. Help preserve local wildlife and habitats by respecting rules and regulations, such as sticking to footpaths and not standing on coral.

Don't Rely On Guidebooks
Use your guidebook as a starting point, not the only source of information. Talk to locals, then discover your own adventure!

Be Discreet With Photography
Don't treat people as part of the landscape, they may not want their picture taken. Ask first and respect their wishes.

Tourism Concern works with people the world over to promote tourism that benefits their communities, but we can only carry on our work with the support of people like you. For membership details or to find out how to make your travels work for local people and the environment, visit our website

Tourism Concern
Campaigning for Ethical and Fairly Traded Tourism

www.tourismconcern.org.uk